BEIJING'S GLOBAL MEDIA OFFENSIVE

A Council on Foreign Relations Book
Oxford University Press

The Council on Foreign Relations (CFR) is an independent, nonpartisan membership organization, think tank, and publisher dedicated to being a resource for its members, government officials, business executives, journalists, educators and students, civic and religious leaders, and other interested citizens in order to help them better understand the world and the foreign policy choices facing the United States and other countries. Founded in 1921, the CFR carries out its mission by maintaining a diverse membership, with special programs to promote interest and develop expertise in the next generation of foreign policy leaders; convening meetings at its headquarters in New York and in Washington, DC, and other cities where senior government officials, members of Congress, global leaders, and prominent thinkers come together with CFR members to discuss and debate major international issues; supporting a Studies Program that fosters independent research, enabling CFR scholars to produce articles, reports, and books and hold roundtables that analyze foreign policy issues and make concrete policy recommendations; publishing *Foreign Affairs*, the preeminent journal on international affairs and U.S. foreign policy; sponsoring Independent Task Forces that produce reports with both findings and policy prescriptions on the most important foreign policy topics; and providing up-to-date information and analysis about world events and American foreign policy on its website, www.cfr.org.

The Council on Foreign Relations takes no institutional positions on policy issues and has no affiliation with the U.S. government. All views expressed in its publications and on its website are the sole responsibility of the author or authors.

BEIJING'S GLOBAL MEDIA OFFENSIVE

CHINA'S UNEVEN CAMPAIGN TO INFLUENCE ASIA AND THE WORLD

JOSHUA KURLANTZICK

OXFORD
UNIVERSITY PRESS

OXFORD
UNIVERSITY PRESS

Oxford University Press is a department of the University of Oxford. It furthers
the University's objective of excellence in research, scholarship, and education
by publishing worldwide. Oxford is a registered trade mark of Oxford University
Press in the UK and certain other countries.

Published in the United States of America by Oxford University Press
198 Madison Avenue, New York, NY 10016, United States of America.

CIP data is on file at the Library of Congress

ISBN 978–0–19–751576–1

DOI: 10.1093/oso/9780197515761.001.0001

9 8 7 6 5 4 3 2 1

Printed by Lakeside Book Company, United States of America

For Caleb and Jonah

Contents

Acknowledgments

This book could not have been written without the generous assistance and wise advice of many people.

At the Council on Foreign Relations (CFR), Richard N. Haass, James M. Lindsay, and Shannon K. O'Neil read drafts of the work and offered critical and insightful comments. Also at the CFR, Elizabeth Economy, Yanzhong Huang, Ian Johnson, Manjari Chatterjee Miller, Mira Rapp-Hooper, David Sacks, Adam Segal, Sheila Smith, Paul Stares, Jacob Ware, and James West contributed important research and analysis and editorial advice. The CFR library offered essential abilities to find nearly anything, and Patricia Dorff and the CFR publications staff worked to bring it to publication. Amy Baker, Janine Hill, Jean-Michel Oriol, Shira Schwartz, and Dominic Bocci helped me in every possible way to raise the funds necessary to research and write this book. Again, Elizabeth Economy offered essential guidance and mentorship.

Outside of the CFR, I am grateful to many people for reading the whole book or portions of it, for sharing and discussing ideas, and for sharing some of their own work on the subject. Among the many who assisted included Geoffrey Cain, Pavin Chachavalpongpun, Sarah Cook, Samantha Custer, Joshua Eisenman, Bay Fang, Richard Heydarian, Van Jackson, Shanthi Kalathil, Bilahari Kausikan, Nadia Madjid, Hunter Marston, Jamie Morgan, Shawn Powers, Mihir Prakash, Maria Repnikova, Sarah Repucci, Sophie Richardson, David Schulman, John Sifton, Michael Sobolik, Devin Stewart, Yun Sun, and multiple other readers and people who provided advice who prefer not to be named.

The Sarah Scaife Foundation and Smith Richardson Foundation's generous grants allowed me to do the research and writing of the book, and the Henry Luce Foundation's and Ford Foundation and Charles Koch Foundation's grants for other work helped inform the project; without their help, it would not have happened. At Smith Richardson, I am specifically grateful to Allan Song, while at Luce, I am grateful to Helena Kolenda and Li Ling. At Scaife, I am thankful to Montgomery Brown; at Ford, I am thankful to Elizabeth Knup; and at Koch, I am thankful to Hugo Kirk.

At Oxford University Press, I am grateful to editor David McBride for his guidance and thoughts in shaping the book and to Emily Benitez as well. I am also grateful to fact checker Ben Kalin for his diligent work on the manuscript. I am especially grateful to Helen Nicholson for shepherding a book that was being updated at the last minutes.

Shira provided not only counsel and advice throughout but also love. Throughout it all, Caleb and Jonah remained the joy in my life. I also want to acknowledge that in the course of writing the book I, and the foreign policy community, lost a brilliant, warm, and beloved figure in Devin T. Stewart. He was my longtime friend and regular collaborator on a wide range of projects and he is sorely missed—by me, and by many others. May his memory be a blessing.

Author's Note

This book went to press as the war in Ukraine erupted and then as the China-Taiwan crisis erupted, and although the book tried to incorporate changes sparked by the Ukraine war and the China-Taiwan crisis, it is impossible to be completely up to date due to the publication process.

Chapter 1

Building a Giant—or a Giant Failure?

In the span of just a few months in 2018, national elections roiled Malaysia and brought what seemed like landmark change to the Southeast Asian state. The country had been a longtime autocracy: Malaysia had been run by essentially the same coalition since it gained independence in 1957, and that coalition had used extensive gerrymandering, handouts of state funds, control of most broadcast and print media, and other tactics to ensure its continuing hold on politics.

Yet in Malaysia, despite gerrymandering and a crackdown on opposition politicians and civil society before the May 2018 elections—as well as a re-election war chest reportedly amassed through a web of flamboyantly shady deals that spanned continents—Prime Minister Najib tun Razak and his coalition seemed at risk.

Najib, though, was not only getting help from his massive war chest, from gerrymandering, and from other dirty tactics. He and his party also had seemingly benefited, in the run-up to the May 2018 elections, from Chinese government attempts to influence the Malaysian vote. Beijing has strong economic and strategic interests in Malaysia and reasons for supporting Najib and his party. China is Malaysia's biggest trading partner, and several Malaysian tycoons have been major investors in China, dating back decades.[1] The Najib government had enjoyed warm ties to Beijing, and Malaysia's dominant political coalition had never lost a national election, providing the kind of stability attractive to China. Najib took a low-profile approach to disputes in the South China Sea and was an early and vocal backer of China's Belt and Road Initiative (BRI), the massive project to aid and finance physical and digital infrastructure in countries around the world. The BRI, launched in 2013, is now one of the largest aid and financing vehicles in the world, with the Organisation for Economic Cooperation and Development (OECD) estimating that it will "add over USD 1 trillion of outward funding for foreign infrastructure over the 10-year period from 2017."[2] A multiethnic country, Malaysia also has a sizable ethnic Chinese population, making up about 23 percent of the total population. Beijing attempts to use such ethnic Chinese populations in other countries to project power, and they often are heavily targeted by China's expanding global media and information efforts. China also cultivates close ties to Southeast Asian states like Malaysia since they are members of the leading regional organization, the Association of Southeast Asian Nations (ASEAN). Because the ASEAN operates by consensus, if Beijing can build close ties with ASEAN members, it can use them to neuter ASEAN-wide efforts to block China's growing assertiveness in regional waters like the South China Sea and other actions Beijing takes in Southeast Asia.[3]

Since the end of the Mao era, Chinese leaders had proclaimed that Beijing did not interfere in other states' affairs, even if the reality did not always reflect this assertion. In the 2018 Malaysian elections, however, there was none of this supposed restraint.

China was seemingly in a strong position to affect the Malaysian election. It is not only the country's major trading partner, but also polls in the 2010s had consistently shown warm views of China among Malaysians.[4] So, Beijing attempted to influence the election both through more open soft power, playing on this seeming warmth among the Malaysian public, and through covert and possibly corrupt means, also known as sharp power. Beijing particularly cultivated Chinese Malaysians, wooing them with an array of soft power. Many Chinese Malaysians get their news through a Chinese-language press in Malaysia that had become increasingly pro-Beijing in the 2000s and 2010s. Leading up to the election, the ethnic Chinese party in Najib's coalition, the Malaysian Chinese Association (MCA), noted that it helped facilitate Chinese investment in Malaysia. Party literature claimed that "voting [for Najib's coalition] equals supporting China," and the Chinese-language media in Malaysia regularly highlight pro-China views and silence opponents of Beijing.[5]

These efforts were, at least, somewhat open. But China also may have used clandestine and more coercive means to bolster Najib, in addition to more open and transparent soft power tools. According to the *Wall Street Journal*, which saw minutes from previously undisclosed meetings, as Malaysia's election loomed, Chinese officials told Najib that Beijing would pressure foreign countries to back off investigations into the allegedly graft-ridden, tanking 1Malaysia Development Berhad (1MDB) state fund, which was hemorrhaging money, and would even bail it out if the administration gave China stakes in Malaysian pipeline and rail projects.[6] Beijing also offered to bug the homes and offices of the *Wall Street Journal* reporters investigating 1MDB.[7]

Beijing did not stop there. Top Chinese diplomats seemed to attend primarily campaign events to support Najib's coalition.[8] As the journalist Teck Chi Wong noted, MCA billboards prominently featured MCA members with Chinese leader Xi Jinping.[9]

China completely failed. In fact, Beijing's efforts backfired. With frustration at 1MDB and other alleged corruption scandals spiking, the opposition put together a broad coalition, led by former prime minister Mahathir Mohamad. Public anger grew over Beijing's efforts to intervene in Malaysian politics and over the unequal terms of some deals signed between the two countries. Never one to avoid pressing a hot poker into a wound, Mahathir stoked anti-China sentiment on the campaign trail, accusing Najib of essentially auctioning off Malaysian sovereignty.[10]

On Election Day, Mahathir's coalition stunned Najib and his coalition to sweep into power.[11] Strikingly, China failed to help win over ethnic Chinese Malaysian voters. While many Chinese Malaysians

have considerable pride in their heritage, Beijing, which often assumes ethnic Chinese automatically have an affinity for China, may
have underestimated their desire to not be seen as loyal to China
above Malaysia.[12] Chinese Malaysians, like many other Malaysians,
were angered at Najib's coalition, which, even as it courted investment and aid from China itself, increasingly demonized Chinese
Malaysians while advocating for the rights of the Muslim Malay
majority.[13] Chinese Malaysians overwhelmingly backed Mahathir's
coalition in the elections.[14] And after Election Day, Mahathir was
still going, making China's loss in Malaysia worse. In August 2018,
he visited China, where in front of top Chinese leaders he warned
Beijing against a "new kind of colonialism," and he pushed China to
redo many of its bilateral deals with Malaysia.[15] He then suspended for
eleven months the construction of the China-backed East Coast Rail
Link, a prestige project for Beijing in Malaysia.[16]

The defeat of Najib and his coalition in 2018 paved the way for the
first transfer of power in the country's independent history, opening
the door to real democracy—although by 2021 that democracy still remained on shaky ground, though stronger than it had been before 2018.
Najib had spent his years as prime minister jetting around the world
and allegedly had used state funds, from entities like 1MDB, to buy
luxuries for his wife, Rosmah Mansor, including a twenty-two-carat
diamond pendant and a massive trove of handbags.[17] Within months
of the election, he was facing bribery and money-laundering charges.
His home had been raided, Malaysian authorities later confiscated over
$270 million in luxury goods from the couple, and the prospect of real
jail time for both Najib and Rosmah loomed.[18] In fact, in July 2020,
Najib was found guilty and sentenced to up to twelve years in jail.[19]

China's Motivations

Malaysia is hardly unique as a place where Beijing has invested heavily
in influence efforts but has had relatively little to show for it. China

long has tried to influence other countries. But in recent decades, as Beijing has become more powerful internationally, as other major powers including the United States have declined in global influence, and as China's increasingly authoritarian domestic politics have led it to become more assertive globally, attempting to displace the United States in many parts of the globe, it has dramatically increased its efforts to wield power within other countries.[20]

To wield this influence, China often is using media and information tools: its expanding state media outlets including the newswire Xinhua, its social media platforms, its deals with local media in many countries, its training programs for foreign journalists, and many other tools.

Beijing's current approach reflects shifts in the mindset of the Chinese leadership as well. While becoming more autocratic at home, it is much more willing to throw its weight around globally and increasingly try to displace the United States regionally, in Asia, and globally as well. As the scholar Rush Doshi notes in his book *The Long Game: China's Grand Strategy to Displace American Order*, in the Xi era, Beijing has expanded from trying to gain regional hegemony to a new "strategy of displacement, one that expands its blunting and building efforts worldwide to displace the United States as the global leader."[21] Beijing's campaigns today reflect a departure from the more limited and defensive Chinese foreign policy of the late Cold War and early post–Cold War eras. To be sure, Beijing today still hopes to shift perceptions among publics, some policymakers, and a range of civil society elites in other countries, sometimes presenting an image of China as a benign actor on a number of issues like climate change, trade, and other areas.

This is a strategy, of presenting China as benign and not interfering in other states, it long has utilized. If it can succeed in this portrayal, it will make it easier for Beijing to gain advantages in its bilateral relations with countries in Southeast Asia and other regions. It also wants to use its influence efforts to get publics and opinion leaders, in other states, to have warmer views of China's global leadership, which would smooth the way to China exerting more power at the United Nations, UN agencies, trade bodies, and many other institutions—power it can use both to undermine the United States and other democracies in these institutions and to grow China's own power at them.[22]

But as China aims to gain regional hegemony and potentially supplant the United States on the world stage, the influence offensive today goes far beyond that long-standing, established effort to present China in a benign light. Instead, it fits into a more assertive Chinese foreign policy overall—one that, under Xi, reflects a combination of three ideas. The first is the perception, among the Chinese leadership and an increasingly authoritarian and nationalistic elite, of being imperiled and surrounded by hostile powers in Asia.[23] The second is the notion that Beijing's time has come—that China has emerged onto the world stage and should reclaim its status as a great power, one that is capable of blunting U.S. power in Asia in many other areas, and, as Doshi has noted, one that puts China in position to "catch and surpass the United States in a competition for global leadership."[24] The third is that China should take a more ideological approach to foreign policy than at any time since the era of Mao Zedong—indeed, that it can and should promote a model of development; spread its model of technology-enabled authoritarianism completed by Chinese tech companies increasingly controlled by Beijing and that are replacing foreign tech companies in China; stoke divisions among leading democracies; increasingly collaborate with Russia, as shown during the Ukraine war; and tarnish the image of democracy itself.

China increasingly and openly wants to reshape the world in its image and is using its influence and information efforts to promote this brand of technology-enabled authoritarianism, a strategy Russia is clearly now copying in the wake of the Ukraine war. It tries to export China's authoritarian approach to speech, politics, and societal control, and uses the influence of globalization—which has linked China to the world and made companies and other countries dependent on China's market and China's policies—to facilitate these exports. Ultimately, if China meets this goal, rather than globalization and economic interchange making Beijing freer, Xi's China would lead companies and political leaders in other states to adopt China's repressive approaches.[25]

Xi has explicitly encouraged Chinese policymakers to hold up China as a model for other states, telling delegates to the 2017 Nineteenth Congress of the Chinese Communist Party, "The China model for a better social governance system offers a new option for other countries and nations . . . who want to speed up their development while preserving their independence."[26] As my colleague Elizabeth Economy has noted, in speech after speech following the 2017 Congress, Xi continued to reference and advocate for China to export its model, which has become defined as technology-enabled authoritarianism.[27] Xi has offered the most explicit endorsement of an exportable Chinese model of development of any leader in China's post-Mao era.

Xi has returned regularly to the idea of China as a model of state capitalism, high growth, and technology-enabled social control, and to the idea that Beijing should export its model.[28] As Human Rights Watch's Maya Wang notes, in an analysis of how China is creating a model, Xi is harnessing "the vast surveillance power amassed by Beijing to the larger ideological project of the state, which combines authoritarianism with practical efficiency to meet the needs of the country's vast populace."[29] China is "selling its blueprint, including the software and hardware it uses in its surveillance regime," as a complete package and parts of a model, according to a study of its surveillance exports by Scott N. Romaniuk and Tobias Burgers, experts on asymmetric warfare.[30]

China's training sessions for foreign officials, its work at global internet conferences aiding other states to implement similar types of surveillance and internet monitoring, and its teaching of other countries how to use laws to foster state capitalism, suppress dissent, and control the internet all show how Beijing is increasingly focused on exporting this model. Economy adds that since Xi's Nineteenth Party

Congress speech in October 2017, China has become increasingly comfortable, both in rhetoric and tactics, in its efforts to export its statist political and economic model around the globe.[31]

Beijing has, she notes, increasingly exported elements of its political and economic model, through a wide range of tools. These include capacity-building programs for developing countries, bilateral training and education programs for other states, multilateral forums at the United Nations and other similar bodies, and other such opportunities to share and impart information with other governments on how to control civil society, foster statist politics and economics, and suppress opposition movements.[32]

As Beijing steps up efforts to export its political and economic model and more countries copy China's model, Economy notes, then more countries that share Beijing's values and norms will likely translate to more support for Beijing and its foreign policies.[33] We will see, throughout the book, many other examples of China attempting to export elements of its model to neighbors and to countries across the globe.

In addition, compared to earlier eras, as China becomes more powerful, it is attempting to use its influence efforts to shape policymakers' and publics' views, in other countries, of their own political systems and leaders—not just of China but of politics in these other countries.

In the 1990s and 2000s, Beijing mostly focused in other countries on boosting perceptions of China. But the Xi-era influence efforts intend to shape narratives, within other states, about those other countries' politics as well—and shaping them in ways that ultimately might benefit Chinese foreign policy. Beijing attempts to reach right into some other political systems and societies, like Australia, Singapore, Taiwan, or Thailand, to influence who gets selected as political leaders, what topics are discussed in those states' domestic politics, how their universities approach issues related to China, and how their local media operates and covers many topics relating to Beijing. In so doing, it wants to get other states to select

leaders who will accede to assertive Chinese behavior on everything from trade to hard security issues, and media outlets that
will do little to question and/or expose Beijing's assertive behavior.
Ultimately, via influence efforts and other tools of traditional hard
power like economic coercion, the Chinese government also wants
to get companies in other countries to echo how Beijing talks
about Chinese politics, the Chinese Communist Party (CCP), and
Chinese foreign policy and thus to amplify China's own positions—
"making the foreign serve China," as the scholar Anne-Marie Brady
has documented.[34] Beijing wants to get foreign companies to self-
censor critiques of China; to accept Chinese demands, for instance,
that foreign firms parrot China's insistence that Taiwan is a part of
China; and to defend China's foreign and domestic politics in their
home countries.[35]

It also wants to use its influence efforts to play more aggressive
defense at home. China using its foreign policy tools to defend the
CCP is not new, but in Xi's era the defensive goals have mutated and
expanded. In every era since the CCP came to power in 1949, an
important driver of Chinese foreign policy has been defending the
CCP's power and dominance at home.[36] As Peter Mattis, formerly
of the U.S. Congressional-Executive Commission on China, noted,
even as China's global interests expand, preventing any actors that
could "undermine or topple the party-state" remains of the highest
concern to Beijing[37]—thus, for instance, the blackout on news about
the Ukraine war in China, since such information might show the
weakness of the authoritarian Russian government and undermine
the Chinese party-state.

But as with the offensive goals, Xi's defensive goals are broader
too than in the recent past. They include, of course, preserving and
defending the CCP using any means necessary, and defending whatever repressive means Beijing uses to maintain that control at home.[38]
But Xi's goals also include shaping images of China abroad, to convince foreign populations that the CCP is the best, and truly only,
organization that could govern China, and to convince the world

that the actions China deems necessary to protect the regime—both at home and abroad—are justified and even admirable. And since in the Xi era the state has become more repressive and the rights abuses greater than in the period under Xi's recent predecessors, while the top leadership has become even more paranoid about external threats to the CCP's dominance, Xi's administration tries to far more assertively penetrate other countries' societies, media environments, and political systems to shore up the CCP's image and power.

Failures

Despite Beijing pouring money, resources, and time into its media and information efforts, and into other types of influence—and despite extensive global news coverage of China's influence strategies— for now its efforts to intervene in other societies have often played out like the experience in Malaysia, where Beijing mostly failed.

So far, indeed, many of China's influence and information tactics have not worked. Doomsayers suggesting that Beijing's influence is, right now, exceptionally skillful and effective are wrong. China has built a giant influence and information apparatus but currently wields it clumsily and often poorly.

Though it has made some inroads, many of China's efforts have stumbled. In some cases, Beijing has had success taking over and controlling the Chinese-language media in states but has had much less success influencing local-language or English-language media in those countries, which are the primary sources of information. In other cases, like Australia and Taiwan, Beijing's influence efforts became so obvious and unwelcome that they sparked an intense blowback, leading to souring public opinion toward Beijing and, in Australia, tough new legislative measures designed to curtail foreign influence efforts—legislation that other democracies are looking at as a possible model.[39]

Overall, despite huge outlays of funds on soft power around the world, including COVID-19 supplies and a Chinese vaccine, all touted incessantly by Chinese diplomats and media, by 2020, 2021, and 2022 China faced historically high unpopularity in many countries.[40] Many states remained angry that the Chinese government had covered up the initial COVID-19 outbreak, a lack of transparency that also highlighted a downside of China's authoritarian model of development; they also were angry at China's rising authoritarianism and militancy, reflected in Xinjiang, Hong Kong, the China-Taiwan crisis, and China's support for Russia in the Ukraine war. In part because of this broader unpopularity, and in part because Beijing has not figured out a way to make its biggest state media outlets—except Xinhua—attractive to a broader audience, China has spent considerable sums expanding outlets like China Global Television Network (CGTN) in Africa, Latin America, and Southeast Asia yet has attracted relatively few viewers in many of these regions.[41]

By 2021 and 2022, Beijing had battered other countries with aggressive diplomacy, continued its Hong Kong crackdown, spread the possibility that COVID-19 originated from a lab leak became more plausible, and defended Russia's war in Ukraine, continuing to back it even as Moscow committed clear crimes against humanity and the Russian offensive faltered. As a result, China had become intensely unpopular not only in places, like Japan, that had long historical tensions with China and where China had already been unpopular for extended periods of time but also in countries like Australia and Spain, which had no historical grievances with China, and where China had enjoyed high popularity for much of the 2010s.[42] Indeed, the Pew Research Center, which conducted the study, found that a majority of people in each of the fourteen surveyed countries had an unfavorable opinion of China.[43] China also likely has become much more unpopular in countries such as those in Eastern and Central Europe—which once viewed Beijing favorably—because of China's support for the Kremlin's war.

Chinese disinformation efforts also have, to now, remained relatively unsophisticated and easy to expose, especially compared to the more nuanced and effective Russian efforts, although the two have started to work more closely together, especially during the Ukraine war. To be sure, China sometimes shies away from Russia's efforts to use disinformation to stoke chaos; Beijing favors shaping long-term narratives about how people in other states view China, China's domestic policies, and China's foreign policy. But when it does wield disinformation, as in Taiwan during the 2019–20 Taiwanese presidential elections, Beijing often puts out clunky, unnuanced false media reports, many of which are easily traced back to China and, when exposed, wind up alienating the citizens of the place Beijing was trying to influence.

China's influence and information campaigns, despite their size and financial resources, also face other hurdles to success that may only loom larger in the future. The more powerful China becomes, the more difficult it may be to wield soft power, since that approach still rests in part on the idea that Beijing is different from the United States—that it is more respectful of other countries' sovereignty and domestic politics. While it still may pay some lip service to noninterference, China's public actions, and its increasingly ham-fisted, nationalistic, and belligerent diplomacy, which helped anger many countries in 2020, 2021, and 2022, belie those claims of noninterference and undermine China's increasingly well-resourced soft power strategies.[44] For instance, Beijing's increasingly aggressive behavior in the Taiwan Strait, in the South China Sea, and in damming the Mekong River, actions that have continued during the global coronavirus pandemic, have undermined the idea of Beijing being committed to noninterference and angered many Southeast Asian states and other countries around the world. And, after all, it is difficult to convince other states of your good intentions when they also catch you meddling in their politics, spreading disinformation throughout their media, making aggressive military moves, or overseeing covert actions to influence their universities.[45]

Future Success

So, China's efforts often have not been as successful as policymakers in some countries, including the United States, have suggested. Yet what skeptics of China's influence and information strategies miss is that Beijing will surely improve—a great deal, and rapidly. Indeed, while I will show some of China's failures throughout this book, failure now does not mean failure forever. The book will suggest ways in which China may gain greater successes in the future, in part by using case studies from some of the first places where China has deployed intensive media, information, and influence strategies—places like Australia, Hong Kong, New Zealand, Southeast Asia, and Taiwan. These case studies offer insight into China's first strategies, their effects, and Beijing's adaptability, and I then go on to examine how China is now using these strategies all over the world—in the United States, Europe, Latin America, Northeast Asia, and many other regions.

Within the next decade, countries might not be so fortunate—and skilled at combating Chinese information and influence—as Malaysia. Indeed, Beijing is learning from its influence failures, and in the next decade it has a high chance of becoming more proficient in wielding soft and sharp power, in ways that will be dangerous to many states, including many U.S. partners, and worrisome for the free flow of information.

There are multiple reasons China will become more effective. Even amidst its failures, Beijing already has developed some successful tools, including the newswire Xinhua and some foreign media outlets where Beijing has used pro-China owners to control these newspapers or online publications in other countries, including in wealthy democracies in Europe and North America.[46] China almost surely will become even more aggressive in its influence efforts in the coming years, focusing even more on coercive, sharp, hidden types of media and information power than more open, soft power and public diplomacy efforts that are easier for journalists, researchers, and governments to expose. China's politicians, though authoritarian, have shown they are capable of learning from failures and adapting, as they already have done with some aspects of China's signature BRI; it is wrong to think that Beijing cannot learn from its influence and information mistakes. With the BRI, Chinese leaders have responded to some complaints, by foreign leaders and other policymakers, that the BRI leads some recipient countries into massive debt by rescheduling loans, curtailing risky lending, and emphasizing to other states that China will be a responsible lender.[47]

It is indeed reasonable to conclude that Beijing's leaders are deft enough to learn from their information and influence mistakes and discard ones that are counterproductive or simply not producing many results. Then, they can focus on strategies that are working and that could work in the future.

And the world is tilting in ways that will benefit China's information and influence efforts. The world is becoming more authoritarian: Freedom House, the monitoring organization, has recorded fifteen straight years of democratic rollback.[48] The global news environment is becoming saturated with disinformation, most news outlets are becoming less trusted, and Beijing is partnering with other major autocrats like Russia to improve its information and influence tactics. In the Ukraine war, according to the *New York Times*, Chinese state media have spread false Russian statements and Chinese diplomats and state media's social media networks have amplified wild Russian disinformation statements, including that the United States was supporting biological weapons laboratories inside Ukraine.[49] Democracies have struggled with internal gridlock, inequality, the COVID-19 pandemic, and increasing popular disillusionment, and they have offered China a greater chance to assume global leadership and advocate for a Chinese model of government and development. If leading democracies do not solve their severe domestic challenges, they will offer even more space for Beijing to advocate for its authoritarian model of development. Distracted, weaker democracies also are easier targets for China's influence efforts.[50]

All of these international developments will make it easier for Beijing to effectively wield information and influence in the future, as soon as later this decade—and to expand its efforts most rapidly in Europe and North America, as it increasingly targets wealthy democracies.

As China learns and launches even more complex and successful influence activities, often relying on more coercive media and information strategies, its efforts could have dangerous implications for other countries' sovereignty, for the free flow of accurate information, for rights and democracy globally, and for the interests of the United States and its partners. China has not yet mastered its strategies, many of which were initially developed in its near neighborhood, but the United States and other democracies should certainly be prepared, well in advance, for the next generation of smarter, better Chinese influence and information techniques.

China Is Expanding Information and Influence Efforts

Beijing clearly is expanding its efforts. Since the late 2000s, and especially since Xi Jinping became president in 2013, the Chinese campaign to wield influence within countries in Southeast Asia, its near neighborhood, Taiwan, and Australia has accelerated rapidly—and we now see that this campaign is accelerating in Africa, Europe, Latin America, and North America. Beijing has built this influence apparatus, often centered on media and information efforts, in an era when Xi is gaining far more control of China's politics at home. It also has built this apparatus at a time when the United States and other leading democracies, focused on their own internal dysfunction and on Russia, the more flamboyant and chaotic authoritarian power, initially paid little attention to China's actions within other countries.

China's leaders make their commitment to this expanding effort clear, and a vast range of data show how Beijing is expanding this campaign. In speeches and important documents, Beijing's top leaders have announced that they intend to wage massive information campaigns in many parts of the world.[51] Over the past fifteen years, top Chinese leaders have repeatedly stated their conviction that Beijing needs to use information to more effectively tell China's story to the world, to bolster what they call China's "discourse power."[52] They further have declared that they view information, including information on the internet, as a "battleground."[53] Indeed, they have explicitly demanded that Beijing improve its global information efforts.[54] "The competition for news and public opinion is . . . a contest over 'discourse power,'" according to documents from the Communist Party's Propaganda Department.[55] Xi has publicly declared, "Wherever the readers are, wherever the viewers are, that is where propaganda reports must extend their tentacles."[56] The Xi administration further has, in documents and speeches, made improving China's media directed toward the world, including Europe and the United States, a high priority and tightened CCP, rather than bureaucratic, control over many outlets that produce media for foreign audiences.[57]

Information indeed has been at the core of China's influence efforts, and throughout our story I will primarily focus on media and information, while also touching more briefly on other tools of influence. Beijing uses a wide range of information strategies and has developed plans to wield influence over all aspects of the global information supply chain.[58] This information offensive, in fact, will be central to China's growing ability to learn from its initial failure and wield influence within societies around the world.

China is concentrating its influence and information efforts on several groups in other countries: top policymakers, lower-level state or local policymakers, civil society leaders, business leaders, university leaders and students, ethnic Chinese populations in other states, and, in many countries, the general public. Beijing is trying to influence these populations to achieve several outcomes desired by the Chinese government, many of which overlap with each other.

Because China has much greater interests globally today, it has expanded its influence campaign, which had already started in places like Taiwan and Southeast Asia and other neighbors of China. Indeed, this current campaign increasingly includes targeting not just developing nations, in Beijing's near neighborhoods like Southeast Asia, but also wealthy democracies like the United States, Australia, Canada, Germany, New Zealand, and the United Kingdom.[59]

More Tools at Xi's Command

Xi has more ability to push an aggressive foreign policy than his immediate predecessors, who governed by elite consensus; by contrast, Xi has centralized power around himself. Although Xi was initially (and wrongly) praised by many domestic and foreign China experts as a potential reformer, he has launched what my colleague Elizabeth Economy has called "a third revolution" in Chinese domestic politics.[60] This "third revolution"—following Mao's communist revolution and Deng Xiaoping's period of reform and opening—includes a centralization of power in Xi's hands, a stifling of discussion about politics, a pervasive effort to assert party control over Chinese society and all layers of government, a construction of (online) walls and other methods of control to keep foreign ideas out of China, the use of the most modern surveillance and artificial intelligence technology to monitor and pacify the population, and the end of term limits on Xi.[61] Xi further has increased state control of the economy, favoring giant state enterprises and ensuring that even large private Chinese companies ultimately answer to the CCP—that they learn to use their corporate power to promote CCP priorities.[62]

Bestriding China as the most powerful leader since Mao, Xi's administration can attempt to project power globally in ways not seen since the height of the Cold War, and Xi simply has more tools of global power than any Chinese leader in modern history. While some of China's efforts to wield influence in other states, often through media and information, draw on strategies Beijing already used for decades in a few places like Hong Kong and Taiwan, they are now backed by more money, more coordination, and more high-level sanction from China's increasingly assertive and authoritarian top leaders. They are also being deployed at the direction of what is now the world's biggest economy (measured by purchasing power parity), the fastest-rising military power, and a diplomatic giant—a much more powerful position than China was in even twenty years ago.

China also, at least initially, took advantage of democracies' focus on other states' influence efforts. Among policymakers and the media in Europe and North America, Russia's efforts to wield influence in other countries, in the mid- to late 2010s, initially received much more attention than China's actions. This focus on Russia, while often warranted, distracted policymakers in many democracies, including the United States, from how China was expanding its own efforts to wield power within other countries. Policymakers' and media outlets' focus on Russia is clearly beginning to change. The Donald Trump administration, for example, accused China of meddling directly in U.S. politics and took some tough actions to check China's influence in the United States; the Joe Biden administration is continuing these tough moves against many Chinese and Russian state media outlets and other types of media and information tools.[63] U.S. media outlets, and media organizations from many other countries, have begun covering Chinese influence activities, including its expanding state media, its Confucius Institute programs, its efforts to wield influence in politics in other countries, and other strategies. And yet much of China's influence activities still receive less attention than those of Russia.

Soft and Sharp Power

In this growing toolbox, China's expanding influence and information efforts include both soft and sharp types of power—and often both at the same time, in the same country.

Soft Power

China has been devoting more resources to soft power for at least three decades, but the pace of this soft power expansion has stepped up in the past decade. I define "soft power" as any effort involving tools of influence other than those of strategic, political, informational, and economic coercion or distortion—coercive, covert, disinforming means of influencing other states would not be included as soft power.[64] (This is a broader definition than the definition of soft power originally conceived by Joseph Nye, but it is one generally used by Chinese officials and academics.) Soft power, however, is relatively transparent and not coercive; it attempts to openly build positive foreign views of a country; it is a power of attraction and of relatively open persuasion. For example, expanding scholarship programs for foreign students or government officials to come study in China would be a type of soft power, as would Chinese state media outlets buying advertising inserts into newspapers and news sites around the world. These efforts are done primarily out in the open and try to foster positive views of China. Some other examples of soft power tools would be cultural diplomacy, foreign aid, the expansion of state media outlets (provided these outlets are offering information, and not disinformation or attempts to limit free expression or distort news), and efforts to encourage people-to-people contacts with other countries via tourism and exchange programs, among others.

If successful, soft power tools—like expanded state media outlets, exchange programs, or cultural diplomacy—wielded by a state can force a shift in the targeted country toward more favorable public and elite views of the targeting country, as well as of its culture, economy, and politics. This kind of state-directed soft power, like expanding state media outlets or creating state programs to train foreign officials, is known as "active" soft power. But soft power tools also can have an effect without a government actively wielding them, through what is called "passive" soft power.[65] Popular culture, via books, news coverage, and other information, can transmit positive messages about a country's people, government, economy, society, and values and founding ideas. More favorable views of a country's culture, people, values, and even government positions on various issues then make it easier for the country wielding soft power to shape narratives and shift views in the recipient country, and potentially achieve its policy objectives.

It is impossible, when discussing soft power, to say that inputs—efforts to build positive public opinion in other states, to boost a country's brand with other states, to create favorable narratives about a country—absolutely lead to results, like recipient states making policy decisions on specific issues.[66] Working on both elites and broader publics, soft power can help grease two states' relations, but no receiving country (a state taking in soft power efforts from another) makes policy decisions due to receiving soft power alone. Likewise, no sending state (a country wielding soft power) deploys soft power believing that it will definitively prompt a certain policy choice in the receiving state.

It is also difficult, as I will show later on, to link shifts in public opinion, or in areas like media viewership or readership, to whether these changes mean China (or any country) necessarily is gaining more influence in another country. It is of course possible that publics could have warm impressions of a country and yet still reject many of its bilateral policy initiatives or its global leadership. And, since much of China's soft power efforts rely on media and information, it is important to note that people in recipient states could consume growing amounts of Chinese media and not be influenced by it—or actually be turned off by it and form more negative opinions of China.

Yet if it is successful, soft power, including more people in a country consuming media and information from the sending country, can foster an overall climate between two countries and overall views of the sending country. A warmer bilateral climate, and more positive views of the sending country, could have an effect on policy choices.

China Builds Up Its Soft Power

In the late 1990s and early 2000s, as a foreign correspondent based in Bangkok, I got a close look as China launched what I called, at the time, a "charm offensive"—a quiet effort to build soft power in Southeast Asia and other developing regions, at a time when the Asian financial crisis and the Iraq War that began in 2003 damaged the image of the United States. (Throughout this book, I call any state "developing" if it is not listed on the World Bank's annual list of "high-income economies." I consider states that are on the World Bank's list to be "developed." Regions such as sub-Saharan Africa that contain primarily developing nations are also classified as developing.[67]) I chronicled that campaign in a 2007 book, *Charm Offensive: How China's Soft Power Is Transforming the World*, and then moved on to other topics. After that time, however, I began to see that China was increasingly applying those tactics to Africa, Australia, Europe, New Zealand, and North America.

Beginning in the 2000s, Beijing's soft power strategies combined media and information efforts with other public diplomacy tools and suggested that the country offered a different kind of developmental model than that of free market democracies. This nascent model was a kind of authoritarian state capitalism, in which private companies had substantial freedoms but the state still dominated much of the economy, and where one party remained firmly in charge yet retained popular support, largely through the cultivation of nationalism among the populace.[68] As the Chinese economy defied many analysts' predictions of a dramatic slowdown or collapse (at least during the 2000s), the model seemed even more attractive abroad. The global financial crisis of 2008–09, which began in the West and would pour fuel on a global democratic regression that had already begun, bolstered Beijing's case for an alternative model of development.[69]

By the 2010s, China had developed world-class technology in many areas related to media and information, such as social media platforms, surveillance tools, telecommunications infrastructure, digital satellite television, Internet of Things technology, and others. So, the Chinese model has come to mean not only authoritarian state capitalism but also, increasingly, the use of this cutting-edge technology designed to control the flow of information online and to surveil populations in a multitude of ways.

Over the past decade, Beijing has upgraded many of its tools of soft power. It has rapidly expanded China's global state media outlets, including CGTN, China Radio International (CRI), Xinhua, and the English-language *China Daily* newspaper, while also using its cash, according to interviews I conducted, to convince some radio stations and cable providers in Southeast Asia and other regions to drop other content and carry CRI and other Chinese state broadcasters.[70]

Since 2009, in fact, when the Chinese government announced a $6.6 billion expansion of its international state media, CGTN and Xinhua have expanded bureaus in Africa, Europe, Latin America, North America, and Southeast Asia. In recent years, sensitive to perceptions of Chinese state outlets as hackish propaganda, these channels have been filling the new and expanded bureaus with respected journalists who have come from CNN, Al Jazeera, the BBC, and many other well-regarded local outlets.[71] *China Daily* also now has deals with at least thirty major news outlets with international reach to publish gauzy and regular inserts in their print newspapers. These inserts, which often effectively blend into the newspapers' normal content, focus on positive news about China's domestic politics and its global role, putting *China Daily* before the eyeballs of readers of the most powerful news sites and newspapers in the world.[72]

Chinese state media outlets also have signed a massive range of content-sharing deals with other outlets around the world, including those in Chinese, English, and many other languages; these deals help state media outlets spread their content into many other countries.[73] As long as that content is truthful information, even if it is spun in ways that make China look good and omits negative coverage of China, it still should be characterized as soft power. Even if it is misleading and/or manipulated disinformation, these deals remain soft power tools. But as I will show, they can quickly cross the line into putting out highly censored, concealed, false, distorted, and disinforming sharp power.

Meanwhile, CGTN and other Chinese state outlets have become more skilled at using social media to promote stories and gain new followers on platforms like Facebook, Twitter, and YouTube. CGTN has more Facebook followers than any English-language news outlet in the world except the BBC. As a result, Chinese outlets have a growing bullhorn to blast out news on issues Beijing cares about.

Beijing also has leveraged the power of prominent private Chinese media companies with close ties to the state, as these private firms have expanded into Africa, Southeast Asia, and other regions. These private companies, including satellite operators, social media firms, and chat platforms, often carry Chinese state media or otherwise serve as vehicles for disseminating pro-China information. Indeed, in part by building up telecommunications infrastructure around the world, Beijing is attempting to control the "pipes" of media and information today—the physical and online infrastructure through which information flows. These pipes include satellite and digital cable companies; social media platforms; messaging apps; companies making telecommunications, surveillance, and Internet of Things infrastructure; and even the basic norms, technical standards, and rules guiding the global internet and internets within various countries.

If China uses these pipes simply to carry information in a neutral way, they would remain tools of soft power, possibly burnishing Beijing's image in developing countries that need this infrastructure. But evidence suggests China will not use the pipes just to carry information in a neutral manner—and so these pipes may not only be tools of Chinese soft power.

Sharp Power

Besides its growing commitment to soft power, China has rapidly expanded its sharp power efforts. Even in the 1990s and 2000s,

Beijing did not use just soft power. It also engaged, at times, in what Christopher Walker and Jessica Ludwig of the National Endowment for Democracy have referred to as "sharp power." China already had used sharp power-type tactics to covertly influence opinion leaders in its near neighborhood, such as in Taiwan and ethnic Chinese communities in Southeast Asia.[74] But its sharp power efforts remained more focused on targets within the Chinese diaspora—like dissidents and Falun Gong practitioners—and on the country's closest neighbors in Asia.

China's sharp power use has grown substantially in the past decade and expanded well beyond these traditional targets to include targets all over Africa, Australia, Europe, Latin America, and North America, as we will see.[75] China has come to rely more on sharp power than on soft power, and it is likely Beijing will lean even harder on sharp power in the 2020s as it improves its information and influence campaigns.

As compared to soft power, sharp power involves efforts, according to Walker and Ludwig's definition, designed to pierce, manipulate, and distract other countries.[76] While soft power tools are generally used out in the open and are designed to boost the attractiveness of the country wielding them, sharp power tools are usually used in covert, opaque ways and are often used to sow negative impressions of the sending state's opponents. Actors engaged in sharp power try to conceal it from public view, or arrange the actions through proxies, to have an element of surprise and also to create plausible deniability for the actor utilizing sharp power.[77] Sharp power is not designed to bolster the wielding state's attractiveness or to openly prod shifts of views toward the wielding country's politics, foreign policy, culture, economy, and other components. Sharp power tools further are designed to confuse, to offer disinformation to people in other countries, whereas soft power efforts usually are not. (For the purposes of the book, I define "disinformation" as deliberately created false information, often designed to cause harm in some way, as compared to "misinformation," which is false information that may be shared widely, such as on social media platforms, but was not necessarily deliberately created to cause some kind of harm.)

Operating covertly is essential to using sharp power for political influence. For example, political leaders sometimes express open support for politicians and political parties in other countries. Former U.S. president Barack Obama essentially endorsed Canadian Prime Minister Justin Trudeau for re-election in 2019, for instance.[78] But these ties were open, and Obama made a public endorsement; publics in the recipient states, like Canada, were aware of what Obama had said and could evaluate it. By contrast, sharp power political influence is usually done in clandestine and opaque ways; most citizens in a targeted country do not understand them.

With sharp power tools, authoritarian states try to undermine or co-opt political leaders in other nations, sow chaos within democracies' political systems, stifle certain types of debate in free societies, and deploy misinformation about issues of importance to autocrats. Sharp power is often more targeted and concentrating than soft power, a broader-brush tool, in trying to influence political, media, educational, and civil society opinion leaders in other countries, both those of Chinese descent and those not of Chinese descent.

In some countries, like Cambodia, Beijing's sharp power efforts aim to help authoritarians close to China achieve their domestic policy objectives. Beijing also uses the sharp power efforts to help lead other countries to adopt repressive, controlling forms of governance similar to China's style of governance—that is, the China model. China also uses its sharp power efforts to coerce opinion leaders from politics, civil society, the media, and academia to advertise China's own talking points about Chinese domestic and foreign policies to audiences in their countries—and to shut down criticism of Chinese policies even in open societies.

China may enjoy an advantage over most freer states in spreading sharp power. While China's domestic media outlets are mostly servile, media organizations in freer states tend to aggressively investigate their governments' foreign policies. So, Beijing can wield sharp power abroad with little fear that mainland Chinese news organizations will examine its actions. Yet democratic governments often have their influence activities exposed by outlets from their own countries, like the *Intercept, ProPublica,* and the *New York Times* in the United States.

Let's use some examples to see the difference between soft and sharp power. China's expanding state media outlets like CGTN and Xinhua around the world, hiring more and better journalists and producing a wider range of programming, are examples of soft power. The outlets expand openly and hire relatively openly, and their programming is accessible openly. But when Chinese state firms, or private Chinese companies or individuals with close links to the CCP, buy up media outlets in other countries and then, with no public notice, prod these outlets to censor their reporting on China or push certain narratives about Beijing and their host countries, they are engaging in sharp power. If China openly launches public relations campaigns in other countries, whether through advertisements placed in local media or even through lobbyists who register in public registries and follow the law, this would be soft power. If Beijing delivers payments or other incentives to foreign politicians, foreign journalists, foreign academic and think tank researchers, and other opinion leaders to promote China's image, push specific Chinese policies, or simply support leaders preferred by China and keep them in office, this would be sharp power. If Beijing openly and publicly offers support for Chinese nationals studying in other countries, such as by having its embassies and consulates provide funding and organization for Chinese student associations abroad, this could be considered soft power. But if those same Chinese embassies and consulates use that funding coercively, to punish students who criticize China or to create "Astroturf" (i.e., essentially false) local grassroots organizations that support China, that would come into the category of sharp power.

Sharp power is not traditional hard power, which is usually displayed openly. China regularly threatens economic and strategic payback for countries that undertake policies that anger Beijing, such as South Korea agreeing to deploy the U.S.-made Terminal High Altitude Area Defense (THAAD) antiballistic missile system in the late 2010s.[79] China openly warned South Korea of economic payback and then Beijing delivered with boycotts of South Korean stores in China.[80] However, China's open threats, while certainly coercive, are a more old-fashioned type of hard power: the use of clear, open economic or military coercion.

As Beijing has expanded its sights, increased its sharp power efforts, and devoted significant resources to improving how it uses sharp power, it has tried to wield sharp power globally. Top leaders in Beijing have been relatively forthright about this shift. Under Xi Jinping, China's United Front Work Department (UFWD), an organization of the CCP historically used for political influence campaigns inside China, has been expanded. Xi has given the UFWD a bigger role globally in its covert and coercive efforts to influence opinion leaders in foreign countries, Chinese students in foreign countries including the United States, and many other people.[81] The Xi administration has centralized and reorganized top-level control of the UFWD, while publicly celebrating its importance in Chinese foreign policy.[82]

Using Both Types of Power Together

The distinction between the two types of power is not exact. Some Chinese tools can be both soft and sharp, and Beijing often uses soft and sharp power in concert in foreign countries. As Nye has noted, China's Confucius Institutes, programs funded by Beijing to promote Chinese-language study at schools in other countries, could be viewed as a soft power tool—open, relatively transparent efforts to bolster China's attractiveness, similar in many respects to older soft power tools like France's Alliance Française programs in other countries.[83] But Nye also says that if "a Confucius Institute . . . tries to infringe on academic freedom—as has occurred in some instances—should it be treated as sharp power intrusion and be closed."[84] This infringement would be coercive and often done opaquely, putting it into the realm of sharp power. Similarly, an expanded state media outlet, like CGTN or Xinhua, would be a soft power tool—unless it is clearly being used, in certain countries, to propagate outright disinformation, in which it crosses the line into being used as a sharp power tool.

How can the two types of power be deployed together? To take one example, Beijing wants to cultivate important journalism voices within other states to bolster its ties with those countries, while simultaneously using sharper power to silence journalists in those same countries that might criticize China's foreign and/or domestic policies. So, Beijing uses soft power (exchange programs, training programs, and other efforts) to woo some journalists and demonstrate China's attractiveness while using sharp power (having pro-China local magnates buy up media outlets critical of Beijing and, with little public notice, coerce them to change their coverage) at the same time and in the same country.

The Threats

The Threat to Information

As China becomes more successful in its influence and information efforts, it poses multiple threats. One of the biggest dangers is that if China learns from its failures, and if its influence efforts become more successful, they could impede the free flow of information, possibly in coordination with Russia, at a time when factual discourse is under threat in many ways. China and Russia already have engaged in the clear cooperation of spreading disinformation related to the Ukraine war with China spreading the Kremlin's disinformation through Chinese channels.

The battle for truthful information is critical to the future of democracy both in existing democracies and in countries struggling to attain self-governance, and crucial to war as well, as has been shown by the information battle surrounding the Ukraine war. Factual information is under siege from all sides—from populist leaders of democracies that lie willfully, from the collapse of traditional media gatekeepers, and from the spread of rumors and lies on social media. A more skillful China, able to quietly coerce media in many countries to avoid scrutiny of Chinese policies, or able to more effectively spread disinformation, will add to the assault on truth.

Overall, China's information efforts, if they extend beyond influence over Chinese-language media and into other languages, could give Beijing more influence over the information that publics in many states consume—on the internet, through social media, on television, and on the radio. Material from China's media outlets could include stories on other countries' political figures and social and economic problems, a broad range of domestic and foreign policies, and many other topics. With this strategy, China could obtain significant leverage in other countries' domestic politics, including the United States. At the same time, China could increasingly control the pipes—telecommunications networks, social media platforms, and other pipes—that deliver information to a wide range of consumers.

China's information strategy also could reshape international news coverage of the country and its foreign, domestic, and economic policies in many media markets. This is especially true in markets where Chinese state media—in Chinese, English, and local languages—have already built something of a foothold, and where Beijing has gained extensive influence over the Chinese-language media and even some portions of the local-language outlets.

And even China's more open and transparent state media outlets are not truly free media—they do not have the editorial independence and freedom of the Associated Press, Reuters, or even Al Jazeera. As the Chinese state media outlets become bigger sources of information for foreign readers, they do present skewed perspectives on China and on many other countries; sometimes their coverage descends into outright disinformation and crosses the line into sharp power.

The Chinese newswire Xinhua in particular is poised, above all other Chinese state media outlets, to become an influential global news brand. Local news outlets worldwide are facing financial ruin, Xinhua offers its wire services cheaper (and sometimes free) than competitors like Bloomberg or Reuters, and a growing number of outlets, on many continents, are increasingly relying on Xinhua news stories.[85] As they do so, Xinhua will increasingly define many outlets' news agendas; newswire stories often establish initial details about a story and frame the coverage of it.

And Beijing could do worse than simply help its biggest outlets, like Xinhua, gain more readers, listeners, and viewers around the world. By having Chinese companies buy up local media outlets in other states or use content-sharing deals to silence media outlets in other countries, Beijing could wield dangerous sharp power. Indeed, it could muzzle independent coverage of China's actions in other countries beyond these regions, while swamping other states with pro-China media.

At the same time, Beijing is cracking down on foreign and Chinese reporters covering sensitive subjects inside the country, even tossing journalists from U.S.-based outlets like *BuzzFeed News*, the *New York Times*, and the *Wall Street Journal* out of the country.[86] A combination of the silencing of independent news coverage of Beijing's actions in other states and the increasingly tough environment for foreign journalists within China will further deprive the world of truthful information about the world's second most powerful state. In an era of increasing tensions between China and many other countries, would opinion leaders in these states be making decisions with accurate information about China and Chinese policies? Would the public understand the stakes involved in a conflict with Beijing?

Though China has proven fairly inept, compared to Russia, in disinformation, as shown during the Ukraine war and Taiwan crisis, it is a fast learner. China could eventually build a larger disinformation apparatus than Russia, and Beijing is now working closely with Moscow on disinformation and learning directly from Russia's strategies, as well as amplifying Moscow's false claims.[87] Indeed, the two countries' relations now are closer than they have been at any time since the early Cold War, and they signed a pact in February 2022 that, although it is not a formal treaty, comes very close to it and vows to together fight liberal democracy worldwide.[88] China could use that apparatus in collaboration with Russia, not just to sow discord and affect one election or one political protest, but to dramatically remake how entire societies think about Chinese domestic and foreign policies, or about their own political systems and societies.

The Threat to Democracy

A second major danger is that Beijing could use its soft and sharp power efforts to shore up pro-China leaders, who often tend to be autocratic rulers. These leaders, like Cambodia's dictator Hun Sen, often also have poor relations with the United States. China's ability to solidify their hold on power binds them to Beijing and potentially gives Beijing more partners in an increasingly tense global contest for power with the United States. In addition, China's soft and sharp power efforts could degrade U.S. partners' views of the United States and bolster their views of China.

Indeed, as China's influence efforts become more effective, they could serve to keep closed, authoritarian societies in place and to promote China's authoritarian model across the world. Much of the analysis of China's sharp power focuses on affecting open societies like Australia or the United States, taking advantage of them, and influencing them in various ways. But China's efforts also could have an effect on closed, more authoritarian societies, such as Cambodia and Uganda, where Beijing's influence could help keep them relatively closed, or could spread China's model to states today somewhere between democracy and authoritarianism.

Bolstering the CCP at Home

A third major danger is that China's expanding soft and sharp power efforts abroad could help reinforce the CCP's hold at home. Even under Xi, the strongest Chinese leader since Mao, and even in a world where China is becoming increasingly powerful, Beijing also seeks to play defense in both domestic and foreign policy. To some extent, even China's biggest global programs, like the BRI, are simultaneously designed to project Chinese power and to protect the party from threats to its survival.

A Brief Road Map

It is critical for policymakers in the United States and other democracies to soberly assess China's influence efforts and to understand which aspects of the country's apparatus already have worked, which have failed, and where China is learning and adapting and likely to improve dramatically in the next decade. It is also essential to determine whether certain Chinese actions are problematic just because China is doing them or whether these actions are inherently bad.

Policymakers and other opinion leaders also should understand that when China's efforts do yield results, foreign governments are not merely passive recipients. In Cambodia, for instance, China can sell Hun Sen's autocratic government on a model of state-dominated capitalism and technology-enabled social control in part because of Hun Sen's authoritarianism and in part because of efforts to woo the Cambodian population.[89] Indeed, in many states, including fragile democracies in Africa, Latin America, and parts of Asia, Beijing pushes its authoritarian model but also takes advantage of the desires of local leaders and the weaknesses of fragile and autocratic states.[90] Or, China may succeed in part because of historical factors inherent in the recipient states. In Thailand, China often can effectively woo the Thai public in part because Thais historically had generally warm feelings toward Beijing, which makes it easier for Beijing to use soft power tools in the kingdom.

To obtain a comprehensive view of China's growing approach to soft and sharp power, I will examine six themes in the coming chapters: **history, motives, opportunities, means, successes and failures**, and **effects**. Finally, I will offer **recommendations** on how to respond to China's soft and sharp power efforts today and in the future, particularly those revolving around information and media. But these recommendations should be nuanced. It is critical to understand which aspects of China's soft and sharp power, wielded through media and information, should not be of concern to foreign governments right now—and possibly might not be threatening in the future. Overreacting to less dangerous aspects could actually risk undermining governments' responses by distracting from the real and growing dangers of Chinese influence, and possibly lead to the stigmatization of people of Chinese descent around the world.

Because media and information are critical to China's soft and sharp power today—and because this book simply cannot cover every type of Chinese influence, or it would weigh more than a David Foster Wallace novel—I will only offer a less detailed examination of tools of soft and sharp power that are based less on media and information. These "old-fashioned," other tools include opportunities for university students in China, the use of the UFWD in other states, and many other tools, though I will have plenty to say about Confucius Institutes, Beijing's more traditional forms of diplomacy, and China's efforts to influence students and universities and research institutes abroad. (I will not focus in depth on the BRI, although it will come up occasionally; the subject has already been well covered in many massive volumes.) I will briefly talk about how China used some of these tools in the 1990s and 2000s, and I will offer a limited discussion of them today, since these types of influence efforts reinforce media and information efforts—and vice versa. But this is not a book about those other types of influence, and I will not explore these other influence efforts in detail: it is a book primarily about China's use of information and media to shape, or fail to shape, other countries. I also will not examine China's military power, except to note the ways in which

China's growing military power affects its ability to project soft and sharp power, and I will not focus our attention on outright espionage.

This book was completed in the middle of 2022; the subject is so intense and fluid that by the time this volume reaches your hands it is possible that Beijing will have altered some of the tactics discussed here, and foreign states will have altered their responses as well. China's relations with the United States, its neighbors, Europe, and so many other parts of the world are, right now, simply so unpredictable.

Some of my investigation here will focus on Australia, Hong Kong, New Zealand, Southeast Asia, and Taiwan. (For the purposes of this book, I define Southeast Asia as the ten countries in the ASEAN—Brunei, Cambodia, Indonesia, Laos, Malaysia, Myanmar, the Philippines, Singapore, Thailand, and Vietnam—plus Timor-Leste.) Yet at the same time, the book will explore China's media and information and influence efforts globally—in Africa, Europe, Russia, Latin America, and North America as well.

China wields sizable influence in Southeast Asia, Taiwan, and Australia and New Zealand—more influence than probably in any other part of the world. It is the region's dominant trading partner and is assertive there militarily, particularly in the South China Sea. In general, China experimented with soft and sharp power with these near neighbors before expanding to other parts of the world.

So, throughout the book I often use Southeast Asian states, Australia, Hong Kong, New Zealand, and Taiwan as important early indicators of Chinese strategy. In other words, they are case studies, because they have been Beijing's initial laboratory. But then I go beyond these initial case studies. I examine how China is expanding its soft and sharp power strategies to many other parts of the world, the effects of that expansion, and what lessons can be drawn from some of these earlier examples—Southeast Asia, Taiwan, and others—for places like Europe, Latin America, and North America, where China's media and information and influence tactics are now growing in ways familiar to Australians, Taiwanese, or Southeast Asians.

Chapter 2

A Short Modern History of China's Soft and Sharp Power Approaches

When the Confucius Institute and the Sirindhorn Chinese Language and Culture Center opened at Mae Fah Luang University in the northern city of Chiang Rai, Thailand, it was inaugurated with the kingdom's highest level of fanfare, with Thai Princess Maha Chakri Sirindhorn having overseen the beginning of construction. China could not have gotten a better ambassador for its new institute: Sirindhorn, daughter of the revered King Bhumibol Adulyadej, was likely the most beloved royal in a kingdom where the monarchy had become almost a personality cult.[1] The princess also had studied at Beijing University and had a close interest in Chinese-language history and culture and language.[2]

China saw that it had gold in the princess. In addition to the ceremony in Chiang Rai, she was designated by the Chinese government as a "people's friendship ambassador" for her efforts to boost exchanges between China and Thailand.[3] She appeared at the launch of Confucius Institutes as far afield as Kyrgyzstan, while making time to serve as an advisor to the program's international magazine.[4]

A Brief Overview

The Confucius Institute at Mae Fah Luang was part of the initial wave of the Confucius project, and Thailand's universities were eager to open many more. The undertaking, in which the Chinese Ministry of Education provides funding for language and cultural programs at partner universities, was spreading quickly in Southeast Asia in the 2000s, but Thailand's involvement was notable for its size. By the latter half of the 2010s, Thailand had twenty-three Confucius Institutes and Confucius Classrooms, Chinese learning programs for schools below university level.[5] By contrast, in the Philippines, a country with some thirty million more people than Thailand, there are five Confucius Institutes.[6]

The Confucius Institute project was launched in 2004; by the late 2010s, 512 institutes and 1,074 classrooms had opened at universities and schools around the world, including many at leading universities in wealthy democracies in Australia, Europe, Northeast Asia, and North America—places known for their academic freedom and quality. This was only one indicator of China's embrace of soft power during that period.[7] Beyond the Confucius Institutes and Confucius Classrooms, in the era of the 1990s and 2000s Beijing would upgrade many other soft power tools. It would begin modernizing its international state media, increasing its overseas aid programs, upgrading its diplomatic corps, devoting larger sums to promoting Chinese culture abroad, improving its elite diplomacy, launching training programs and exchanges for foreigners, and initiating many other soft power efforts.

China was able to launch its charm offensive because it was re-emerging fully in the world—most notably in developing regions like Africa, Central Asia, Latin America, and Southeast Asia but also in Australia, Northeast Asia, and to some extent Europe and North America. It ended its diplomatic pariah status in Southeast Asia, normalizing relations with its neighbors. It joined the World Trade Organization (WTO) in 2001 and began playing a bigger role in other international institutions, such as the International Monetary Fund, which had been dominated by rich democracies.

Its biggest companies began to invest overseas in significant numbers, China began signing free trade deals with neighbors, and by 2009, the country was the biggest trading partner of the Association of Southeast Asian Nations, the ten major states in Southeast Asia, and also was becoming the dominant trading partner of other regions like Australia, Central Asia, Africa, and parts of Latin America.[8]

China also was entering a (mildly) liberal phase politically and economically, which likely improved its global image and smoothed its soft power efforts. Higher-quality, freer journalism and civil society at home—though still heavily constrained compared to countries with truly free presses—allowed Chinese leaders to defend themselves abroad against complaints about their human rights record, and also improved the quality of state media outlets. This space for journalism and civil society was, perhaps, narrower than it had been in the 1980s, but there was far greater freedom in the 1990s and 2000s than there would in the 2010s and 2020s. Investigative Chinese media outlets like the Guangdong-based *Southern Weekend* and the Beijing-based financial publication *Caixin* dug into issues like graft and environmental catastrophes and even some senior members of the Chinese Communist Party (CCP); rights lawyers and other activists kept alive hopes for a more open civil society. Meanwhile, the country wooed foreign businesses aggressively after the 1989 crackdown in Tiananmen Square and other parts of China, which had led to several years of diplomatic isolation and a retrenchment in foreign investment. Tough-talking, forthright Premier Zhu Rongji, who came to office in 1998, promised a more liberal economic environment. Zhu did indeed slash and even bankrupt some state enterprises, while taking some important steps to empower the Chinese private sector.[9]

Broad Goals of the Earlier Soft Power Offensive

During the 1990s and 2000s, China's soft power efforts had several goals, but these goals were generally narrower than those of China's massive soft and sharp power campaigns today. In the earlier era, Beijing hoped to present a more positive face to the world, to shape global narratives about China, and to shift negative perceptions of its domestic politics and foreign policy, particularly among its neighbors. Beijing hoped that boosting images of the country, its leadership, and its people and culture would have an effect on how leaders and policymakers in other states interpreted Chinese foreign policies, and that shifts in interpretation would make it easier to achieve Beijing's strategic goals in Southeast Asia and other regions.[10]

Beijing also was anxious, as always, to protect the rule of the CCP at home. Yang Jiechi, who was China's ambassador to the United States between 2001 and 2005 and foreign minister, said that with public diplomacy, the "highest priority goes to safeguarding and promoting China's national interests."[11]

China consistently portrayed itself as a different type of power from the United States and other leading democracies. In theory, it would be a power that understood developing states' needs, was sensitive to other countries' political and cultural norms, and valued their sovereignty. China's power was growing, but Beijing claimed that it would seek win–win solutions that worked for all nations, and would work to maintain the international system that had developed since the end of World War II.[12]

Of course, China, like all states, had its interests central to its foreign policy, but the country's leaders insisted that they were relatively narrow, particularly compared with the interests of a giant like the United States. As late as 2009, State Councilor Dai Bingguo, one of the most prominent foreign policy figures in Hu Jintao's administration, claimed that China's core interests were just "fundamental system and state security [in China] . . . state sovereignty and territorial integrity . . . and the continued stable development of the economy and society," according to one analysis of Dai's speeches.[13] These interests were, at least according to Dai, mostly domestic (although Beijing considers Taiwan to be a "domestic" interest).

This message was, in many ways, untrue. China repeatedly violated and threatened other nations' sovereignty at the time, from its aggressive moves in the 1990s in the South China Sea to the lobbing of missiles into the Taiwan Strait in early 1996, before Taiwan's national elections. And China's expanding influence would not necessarily produce win-win solutions. In Thailand, for instance, China effectively wooed the population and elites, fostering warm feelings toward Beijing across Thai society.[14] But China's multiple dams on the Mekong River, an invaluable natural resource shared by China and the downstream states of Myanmar, Laos, Thailand, Cambodia, and Vietnam, would cause havoc for Thai fishermen and farmers, depleting water levels and decimating livelihoods.[15]

Still, Chinese leaders conveyed the message that their country would be a different type of power, one that wielded its influence carefully and peacefully, listening to weaker states.[16] This message was reinforced, in many ways, by the approach of leading democracies toward Beijing at the time.

Many top U.S. leaders accepted that China remained an authoritarian state, but they publicly contended that China was making progress toward reform, and that continued interactions between China and the outside world would make Beijing more likely to work with existing international institutions and become a responsible global leader. (The fact that China was increasingly crucial to U.S. businesses' supply chains, and as a market for multinationals, surely played an important role in how American political and corporate leaders assessed China's future prospects.) In 2000, President Bill Clinton, in a speech laying out his argument for admitting China to the WTO, acknowledged that the admittance would not "create a free society in China overnight or guarantee that China will play by global rules."[17] Eventually, though, Clinton argued, "it will move China faster and further in the right direction."[18] This view of China was bipartisan: In 2005, Deputy Secretary of State Robert Zoellick, who served under President George W. Bush, publicly urged China to become a "responsible stakeholder" in the international system, arguing that it was time for Beijing to work to strengthen the system that had "enabled its success."[19]

Why China Launched the 1990s and 2000s Soft Power Campaign

In the 1990s and 2000s, many top Chinese leaders believed that, even as Beijing was re-emerging on the world stage, it was failing, in a world dominated by Western private media outlets and Western governments' state media outlets, to get its preferred narratives across—narratives about China's domestic affairs, foreign policy, economy, human rights practices, and many other issues. The 1989 Tiananmen crackdown, which badly stained Beijing's global image, and China's failure to get the 2000 Olympics, due in large part to other countries' objections about Beijing's horrendous rights record, helped convince Chinese leaders that they needed better ways to shape narratives about China in many other states. China also was launching a "Go Out" economic policy that would lead to a huge spike in Chinese outbound investment. Beijing further joined the WTO in 2001 and, also in 2001, won the bid to host the Olympic Games in Beijing in 2008. These three events further convinced Chinese leaders they had to bolster China's ability to shape foreign narratives—in Southeast Asia, in other developing regions, and in developed democracies as well.[20] (Ultimately, Beijing could not stop human rights protests from erupting before the 2008 Olympic Games.[21])

Chinese leaders, policymakers, and even academics I met at the time were almost uniformly convinced that Beijing was misunderstood or simply demonized in international media outlets. A comprehensive study of Chinese leaders' public statements, in fact, concludes that they saw China as poorly understood in the world, and misrepresented in a largely hostile international media.[22] Confronting this environment, China had to get its own message out and convince the world of its benign intentions, in large part through improved media and information efforts, including by ensuring that Chinese media outlets bolstered their presence in languages other than Chinese and also improving their presence online and, later, on social media.[23] These efforts to get China's message out to the world would grow "in scale and sophistication" while the CCP tightened control over most Chinese media outlets, after Xi Jinping ascended to Chinese leadership in 2012, noted an analysis of China's information strategy by CNA.[24]

China also was looking for ways to smooth the inevitable friction that its growing strategic and economic influence would cause in Southeast Asia and in other developing regions. China's rise already had sparked tensions with several Southeast Asian states. Beijing spent portions of the 1990s squabbling with other claimants of the South China Sea like Vietnam and the Philippines.[25] It still had border disputes with some Asian countries like India. Beijing's neighbors were beginning to accuse China of unfair trade practices, stealing technology, and making it unnecessarily difficult for foreign investors to invest in many sectors in China. An effective soft power campaign could potentially convince elites and publics in Asia and possibly other regions that, even if Beijing became the dominant regional power, there would be little to fear.

By this point, China also simply had greater resources to devote to soft power than it would have in the early post-Mao era. The Chinese economy was back on track after the Tiananmen crackdown; in 2007, the economy expanded by a sizzling 14.2 percent.[26] China's budget was expanding for overseas aid, and older members of the diplomatic corps were retiring and being replaced with younger and better-educated officials.

Meanwhile, throughout Southeast Asia in the 1990s and 2000s, and in some other developing regions, the shifting political environment led to greater political and social freedoms in most states and allowed citizens of Chinese descent to once again celebrate their heritage. This revival in Chinese identity further facilitated Beijing's soft power campaign.

China's emergence on the world stage also made it easier to wield soft power in more passive ways that were not fully controlled by the state. In the 1990s and 2000s, more affluent Chinese began to travel abroad for holidays and make outbound investments, both in Southeast Asia and particularly in Europe and North America, and a growing number of Chinese companies invested overseas. Chinese pop musicians began to sell albums and perform in other parts of Asia, and China began to sell more soap operas across Asia; several would become regular viewing in parts of Southeast Asia.[27]

Historical Roots

China did not invent this first soft power campaign out of nowhere. As Merriden Varrall of the Lowy Institute notes, "The notion of 'using virtue' to attract others to the Chinese cause goes back hundreds, if not thousands, of years."[28] In the imperial era, China exerted enormous cultural influence on neighboring states, although this was not necessarily done in a centralized manner. Later, during the Maoist revolutionary period, China launched a broad range of aid programs across Asia and Africa: technical assistance programs for countries like Ghana and Mali; infrastructure aid for projects like the TAZARA Railway, which links Tanzania and Zambia; and more direct budgetary assistance to countries like Pakistan.[29]

China also wielded sharp power in the Cold War era. It attempted to infiltrate ethnic Chinese associations in Southeast Asia and push them to favor China over Taiwan; it relied on the United Front Work Department (UFWD), and other state-linked organizations, to influence civil society organizations in Southeast Asia and prod them to embrace Maoism; and it backed armed, communist revolutionary groups in many Southeast Asian states, as well as in parts of Africa.[30]

But in the post–Cold War era, as China's economy boomed and its influence tool kit expanded, it could wield much more influence than during the Cold War, though it focused much of its influence on Southeast Asia, Africa, and other developing regions—and not on Europe or the United States. Beijing's active soft power efforts in the 1990s and 2000s were better funded and more clearly thought out than those of Mao's time, when decisions often revolved around the whims of one man and support for insurgents across Africa and Asia alienated many developing countries. Compared to Mao's era, China was run by a series of relatively stolid leaders, seemingly committed to a kind of stable (if repressive) authoritarianism at home and swearing off revolution abroad. In the 1990s, leaders like President Jiang Zemin and Premier Zhu Rongji even offered some promise of a freer, more open future for China.[31] The country sought to present itself to the world as a benign, flexible, increasingly vibrant power that could (supposedly) work well with a broad range of states.

In the charm offensive era, Beijing did not jettison sharp power. It began rebuilding the bureaucratic structures it would later use for coercive, corrupt, disinforming efforts inside other countries, the vital component of sharp power, including the UFWD.[32] It worked to silence Tibetan and Uighur exiles, jailing relatives of prominent Tibetans and Uighurs who had fled the country.[33] It injected false information about Falun Gong into the news environment of countries in Southeast Asia and other regions, and leveraged that false information to convince some leaders in Southeast Asia to crack down on Falun Gong practitioners outside China, claiming that it was a terrorist organization.[34]

But in this earlier era, China had less ability to wield sharp power globally than it does today. It did not have the amount of extensive resources, connections, diplomatic leverage, and technology it does now—the tools needed to pierce and manipulate open societies.

Additionally, China's own internet was nascent and social media did not exist, so it lacked two significant tools of the disinformation aspect of modern sharp power. In this earlier period, Beijing also did not have a clear model of an autocratic power using information to interfere sharply in other states' politics, sow chaos, and/or support specific politicians. Vladimir Putin came to power in Russia on New Year's Eve in 1999. It would be years before Russia effectively demonstrated a model of using disinformation sharp power to pierce and manipulate open societies.

A Well-Timed Charm Offensive

China's soft power campaign proved well timed in the 1990s and 2000s. Other major regional powers, including the United States, were retreating from their own soft power efforts. At the height of the Cold War, the United States had invested heavily in soft power, and Washington and other democratic capitals aggressively battled Maoist China's overtures to many developing states.[35] By the post–Cold War period, soft power often had become an afterthought in U.S. policymaking. Japan too, which had for decades been a dominant power in Southeast Asia, was retreating, as its economy staggered and its government slashed foreign aid.[36]

When President Bill Clinton entered office, the Cold War had ended and the United States seemed to have no real rivals. The new president was focused intensely on the economy.[37] His administration slashed the size of the American diplomatic corps, and the budget for foreign affairs was half the size of what it had been during Ronald Reagan's presidency.[38] Clinton also allowed important components of U.S. public diplomacy—Voice of America, the United States Information Agency, and many academic and other exchange programs—to wither.[39]

Many Asians also believed that the Clinton administration, as well as leading global financial institutions like the International Monetary

Fund (IMF), mishandled the Asian financial crisis of 1997–98. At first, the Clinton administration and global financial institutions seemed deaf to concern throughout Southeast Asia and Northeast Asia during the crisis, reacting slowly and then offering bailouts in countries like Thailand, South Korea, and Indonesia that people in many Asian countries believed came with too-onerous demands for reform.[40] At the height of the crisis, in which economies like Indonesia and Thailand were decimated, news outlets around the world ran front-page photos of IMF head Michel Camdessus, arms crossed sternly, watching as Indonesian President Suharto signed a bailout deal that demanded brutal domestic budget cuts. Suharto was a vicious dictator, but the pictures created an image of Western institutions as uncaring and even neocolonial.[41]

President George W. Bush apparently intended to take a tougher approach toward China than his predecessor had, and also pay more attention to China's neighbors.[42] But after 9/11, the Bush administration instead focused on the Middle East, Afghanistan, and Pakistan and demonstrated little interest in Asia's economic integration and mushrooming trade agreements. Officials from Singapore, probably the closest U.S. partner in Southeast Asia, with whom I spoke, privately pleaded with the White House to send more top U.S. officials to the region. But the White House often sent lower-level officials instead. And in 2007, Bush canceled what would have been the first-ever summit between a U.S. president and leaders of the ten countries in the Association of Southeast Asian Nations.[43]

The Bush administration placed a relatively low priority on many other developing regions too, including Latin America. Meanwhile, the Iraq War badly damaged U.S. soft power. Around the world, public opinion of the United States soured, leaving space for another giant power to play a bigger international role.[44] A 2007 Pew poll revealed that, in twenty-seven of the forty-seven countries surveyed, public opinion viewed China decidedly favorably. Only five of the forty-seven states had decidedly negative views of China.[45]

Taking office in 2009, President Barack Obama's administration vowed to shift foreign policy in multiple ways, some of which helped rebuild the United States' image. By 2012, global public opinion of the United States had mostly rebounded from Bush-era depths.[46] In 2011, and even more so in Obama's second term, the president and his Asia team pushed an ambitious plan to rebuild U.S. links to Southeast Asia and the broader region.[47] The plan, eventually known as "Rebalance to Asia and the Pacific," stepped up security ties with Asian states, tried to put the United States in the middle of Asia's growing economic integration by pushing forward the Trans-Pacific Partnership trade deal, and attempted to bolster U.S. public diplomacy.[48] But this shift enjoyed only mixed success. Even by the end of Obama's second term, the United States' domestic political dysfunction was undermining U.S. soft power and again providing an opportunity for China to look competent in comparison.

China's charm offensive was well timed for other reasons too. Both free market capitalism and democracy began to grow less attractive around the world in the 2000s, a trend that has accelerated in recent years. By the middle of that decade, the monitoring organization Freedom House was recording that democracy was stagnating, and it would regress significantly in the 2010s and early 2020s.[49] After many developing Asian states suffered through the financial crisis of the 1990s, and pro-market policies failed to spark high growth in countries in Africa and Latin America in the early post–Cold War era, there was a ready audience for a different developmental model as well.

Chinese leaders could not have predicted that democracy and free market capitalism would face massive hurdles; almost no one in leading democracies foresaw these problems. Yet these problems turned out to help Beijing.

Leaders of major democracies also made mistakes that undercut democracy's global appeal. The Bush administration linked the calamitous Iraq War to promoting democracy in the Middle East, tarnishing the image of democracy promotion.[50] Democratic leaders also regularly suggested that advances in political freedom would bring economic development and possibly less inequality. Democracy and free market capitalism are not necessarily linked, and links between democracy and higher economic growth are unclear. Hong Kong, for instance, has been regularly ranked the freest economy in the world, without ever sustaining real democratic governance.[51] (To be sure, as Thomas Bollyky of the Council on Foreign Relations and five colleagues have shown, there is evidence linking democracy to an overall better standard of living, such as improvements in public health.[52]) But because many prominent democratic leaders in the 1990s and 2000s, from Bill Clinton to Nelson Mandela, had suggested some essential link between democracy and higher growth, publics believed the rhetoric.[53] When developing economies failed to post strong growth rates, their economic weakness tarnished popular views of democracy as well.[54]

Meanwhile, in the early and mid-2000s, voters in developing countries like Russia, Thailand, Turkey, and Venezuela were choosing leaders who would become essentially elected autocrats: Vladimir Putin of Russia, Thaksin Shinawatra of Thailand, Hugo Chávez of Venezuela, and many others. These elected autocrats were initially chosen in relatively free elections. (Putin's election in 2000 was not entirely fair, but it was far freer than Russian elections today.) They then proceeded to destroy democratic norms and institutions—attacking the free press, undermining the independence of the judiciary and the bureaucracy, and weaponizing the security services against opponents. They further tarnished the image of democracy, and in the following years several developed states, including the United States, began to undergo democratic regression as well, hurting democracy's global image.

The Charm Offensive: Tools

With excellent timing, then, Beijing launched its multifaceted soft power campaign in the 1990s and 2000s. The effort was reflected in statements by senior leaders, in major government documents, and in

China's specific actions. The political report of the Sixteenth National Congress of the Chinese Communist Party, in 2002, refers to the need for the country to build "comprehensive national power," a reference to expanding China's power to include soft power.[55] In 2004, Chinese leaders announced that Beijing was inaugurating a "new Chinese public diplomacy strategy," although the soft power expansion in many respects predated that declaration.[56] In a speech to the Seventeenth National Congress in 2007, Chinese President Hu Jintao declared that the country should "enhance culture as part of the soft power of our country."[57] Chinese academics, who often reflect the emerging thinking of the senior political leadership, also increasingly argued that soft power was essential to China's rise and offered recommendations for bolstering the country's global soft power. Mingyu Lee of the Seoul Institute and Yufan Hao of the University of Macau collected data on the growing discussion of soft power in elite circles in China in the 2000s. As Lee and Hao found, from 2001 to 2014 Chinese scholars published more than five hundred articles and essays focusing on soft power and public diplomacy, a sizable number per year.[58]

China began expanding its information tools and tailoring them to local markets during the charm offensive period. The China Global Television Network (CGTN) went through a broad restructuring in the 2000s, and in 2000 Beijing launched a global channel broadcasting in English.[59] Global Times, a leading, hawkish Chinese newspaper known for its tough commentary on Chinese foreign policy, launched an English-language version in 2009. Throughout the 2000s, Beijing upgraded the quality of China Daily, the major English-language print news outlet, and broadened its global distribution.[60]

These state media outlets could draw on a generation of young Chinese interested in journalism, in part because of the emergence of more aggressive, investigative, semi-independent domestic media during the Jiang Zemin and Hu Jintao eras. This improving pool of talent fed the growth of Xinhua and other global state media outlets, and also improved the quality of reporting at some state media bureaus. As the anthropologist Pál Nyíri writes in *Reporting for China: How Chinese Correspondents Work with the World*, an in-depth study of Chinese journalists globally, prior to the mid-2000s most of the state media's overseas bureaus were "manned by senior journalists, generally men....These posts were often seen as a reward for years of work in China. . . . [The] main job was rewriting stories published in the local news."[61] But by the 2000s, the foreign bureaus of Xinhua, the *People's Daily*, and many other major state media outlets began to expand, in nearly every part of the world including developed democracies in Europe and North America. State media filled open jobs with younger, often female reporters, many of whom had come of age in an era of more liberal press freedoms in China, filed multiple stories a day, and did their best to investigate local events.[62]

Still, even as it built up its staff and began to portray itself as similar to news agencies like the Associated Press, Xinhua hardly gained real independence. It remained both a soft and sharp power agency. It did not, for example, jettison its traditional function of intelligence gathering, a clandestine and coercive sharp power tool.

Beijing also increased training programs for foreign officials, most of whom came from developing regions. The programs often focused on judicial officials, police, military, and economic and agricultural specialists. Although not necessarily advertised as promoting China's economic successes, they implicitly delivered that message on many fronts, according to participants I interviewed and other studies.[63] Programs on development focused on everything from combating poverty to attracting investment to improving agricultural yields, and regularly featured China's successes in these areas. On these less political topics, according to officials I interviewed from Southeast Asia, China attracted officials from a broad range of developing countries, including democracies and authoritarian states—a contrast from training programs for police or judicial officials, which tended to receive participants from neighboring authoritarian states.

The central government in Beijing, as well as provincial governments, also provided new streams of scholarship funding to boost the number of foreign students coming to study at Chinese universities.[64] Most came from developing countries, including those in Southeast Asia; studying in China was cheap or free. In the mid-2000s, three Southeast Asian states were among the top ten countries sending the most students to China.[65] The total population of foreign students in China would roughly quadruple between 2002 and 2016, to 442,000 in 2016.[66] More than 40 percent of these students hailed from neighboring states in Asia and the Pacific.[67]

At the same time, China also was boosting its outbound student population, to Southeast Asian states like Singapore, and also to other regional countries like Australia and New Zealand and to the United States.[68] Foreign students who attended university in China became important conduits of favorable views of China. They brought these positive views back to their countries of origin and sometimes helped recruit more students to attend university in China.[69]

At educational levels below university, Chinese-language classes boomed throughout Southeast Asia in the charm offensive period. Language schools popped up on big highways and tiny streets in Bangkok, Jakarta, Phnom Penh, and other cities and towns. The schools increasingly catered not only to people of Chinese descent (clearly still a sizable market for the language schools) but also to Southeast Asians of other ethnic backgrounds. To some extent, this boom was driven by active promotion from Beijing, including government funding of Chinese-language teachers for Southeast Asian schools.[70] But the growth in Chinese-language learning also had more organic roots, with schools being started by Southeast Asians anticipating local demand.

When China launched the Confucius Institute project in 2004, it established many of the first institutes in developing countries, where universities were happy to find a foreign partner with cash to spread around, and where there were few early concerns about Beijing's largesse affecting academic freedoms. For wealthier universities in developed states, the money offered by the Confucius Institute Headquarters, or Hanban, was not as significant in the context of their overall budgets as that in developing countries. (In July 2020, amidst a slew of negative publicity about Confucius Institutes and their effect on academic freedoms, the Hanban announced that it would be rebranding itself as the Ministry of Education Center for Language Education and Cooperation.[71]) But opening one's doors to a Confucius Institute was an important signal of warmth toward China that administrators and some professors believed could lead to other benefits, and rich universities in rich countries welcomed Confucius Institutes. China was a growing source of foreign students at universities in the United States and other wealthy countries like Australia, Britain, Canada, and New Zealand, and these foreign students paid full tuition.

In the 2004–05 academic year, when the first Confucius Institute opened in the United States, roughly 62,500 Chinese students came to study, 11 percent of the total number of international students in the country.[72] By 2010, there were more than 157,000 Chinese nationals at U.S. universities.[73]

Beijing also expanded elite-to-elite diplomacy, particularly in Asia but also in Africa and Latin America, at a time of growing U.S. unpopularity in all of these regions. Beijing stepped up visits of senior leaders and other top officials to many neighboring states and other developing countries, and welcomed more visits by officials from those states to China.[74] Prashanth Parameswaran of the Wilson Center found that the number of visits by top Chinese leaders to Southeast Asian states, and vice versa, roughly tripled between 1990 and 2007.[75]

Sparked by increasing Chinese affluence, foreign campaigns to woo Chinese tourists, and planning by Beijing to encourage outbound tourism to countries with close diplomatic ties to China, Chinese outbound tourism expanded rapidly in the 1990s and 2000s. This boosted people-to-people contacts between Chinese citizens and citizens in many Southeast Asian states.[76] More than five million Chinese traveled abroad in 1995. By 2018, the number of Chinese traveling abroad (excluding Hong Kong, Taiwan, and Macau) jumped to more than seventy-one million, with seven of the top ten destinations for Chinese tourists being countries in Southeast Asia.[77] Chinese also flocked to European capitals, and by the 2010s China was the fastest-growing market for visitors to Europe.[78] In Thailand, Chinese tourists packed shopping areas, traditional tourist areas, and worship sites. Increasing people-to-people contacts via tourism could be a doubled-edged sword, but generally it fostered increased knowledge of Chinese beliefs, culture, and history, as well as of Chinese views of the region and the world.

During the charm offensive era, Beijing also expanded foreign aid to Africa, Latin America, Southeast Asia, and other regions.[79] Figures on Chinese aid are often hard to calculate, since China does not participate in the Development Assistance Committee group of major donors or adhere to its guidelines when labeling assistance as aid. (Beijing's aid usually comprises a combination of official development assistance with concessional terms, other types of announced aid that do not meet the definition of concessional assistance, and other types of official finance that do not fit into either category.[80]) Still, from 2000 to 2012 China committed more than $52 billion in aid to Africa alone.[81] Chinese aid grew globally by about 22 percent a year in the second half of the 2000s.[82]

The aid totals, in the era before the Belt and Road Initiative (BRI), remained small by comparison to longtime major donors like Japan, the United States, and some European countries. In 2013, Beijing's total contribution to international assistance was about one-quarter the size of total U.S. funding.[83] Yet even before the BRI supersized Chinese aid, Beijing was willing to fund infrastructure and other areas in developing countries that traditional donors had increasingly ignored. And this aid had an effect. In a comprehensive study of 138 countries where China provided aid between 2000 and 2014, AidData found that Chinese aid boosted economic growth in recipient countries by about 0.7 percent on average, two years after the aid project was committed.[84] By contrast, the study found no robust evidence that World Bank aid promoted growth at all.[85] Beijing also used state media, appearances by ambassadors, visits by top Chinese leaders, and other tools to effectively promote its financial diplomacy, including aid programs and promises of new investment.

Chinese leaders, and China's improved diplomatic corps, sold aid and other soft power efforts hard. They used regular appearances at regional summits to announce new aid plans, and often received favorable local media coverage. In part, this was because China was a relatively new major aid donor and diplomatic player. But Beijing also marketed its aid programs effectively.

The 2004 Indian Ocean earthquake and tsunami offered an example of how China benefited in terms of perception from being relatively new to aspects of soft power like major disaster assistance, but also how Chinese officials sold China's actions relatively well. After the tsunami affected much of Southeast Asia, China offered $63 million in aid to Indonesia, mostly to the province of Aceh, which had been utterly devastated, with the capital leveled.[86] Beijing also used both government and private donations to tsunami relief to fund a China-Indonesia "friendship village" in Aceh, where displaced people could move into new homes, with the village signs prominently mentioning Beijing's generosity. Chinese diplomats and state media repeatedly touted the aid, even though the assistance—though generous compared to its previous disaster relief—paled in comparison to Australia, which offered $810 million, and the United States, which sent $350 million and an aircraft carrier group to help with relief efforts.[87]

Promoting a Model?

In this post–Cold War era of expanding Chinese soft power, senior leaders and officials refused to publicly state that Beijing offered a political or economic model for other states. At least in public, they stuck to a basic script, which held that all countries had to follow their own path of development. At a major speech at the United Nations in 2005, for example, Chinese President Hu Jintao reminded attendees that all states should have "respect for countries' right to independently choose their own social systems and paths of development."[88]

By the latter half of the 2000s, Chinese scholars, and even some Chinese diplomats in other countries, quietly changed course. In public, Chinese leaders kept up the same mantra. Yet Chinese officials and scholars, in interviews and with the media, slowly began to suggest that China's development did offer political and economic lessons for other states. Among Chinese officials and scholars, the concept generated significant discussion, in particular during the 2007–08 financial crisis and the continued weakness of developed economies that followed.

Figures show how the concept circulated among Chinese opinion leaders. Pan Wei of the University of Nottingham studied discussions of the China model in articles within China and found that references to the "China model" in headlines of Chinese-language articles grew from around five hundred in 2007 to roughly three thousand in 2008.[89] Indeed, while officials and scholars I dealt with in the mid-2000s stuck to the party line when asked about the idea of a China model—saying, for instance, that every country should follow its own path—by the end of the decade more nationalistic Chinese elites were having robust arguments with me. They talked about the failures of Western models and claimed that China did indeed offer lessons for other states.

Chapter 3

The First Charm Offensive
Sets the Stage for Today

This first Chinese charm offensive, in the 1990s and 2000s, was not so different from soft power efforts pursued for decades by many other countries, including the United States, France, Japan, and the United Kingdom. Certainly, some of China's aid efforts were less transparent than U.S., European, or Japanese aid programs. China's training programs often were conducted with much greater secrecy than other countries' efforts, like the U.S. State Department's International Visitor Leadership Program, which brings foreign opinion leaders from many professional fields to the United States for short-term visits.[1] But overall, in this earlier era China's soft power efforts could be tracked fairly easily and were designed to openly bolster public images of China in other countries. They were combined with some limited covert and coercive sharppower campaigns, but these remained much smaller than today, and focused on Hong Kong, Taiwan, and a few countries in Southeast Asia.

The earlier charm offensive delivered some successes for China, like growing trade links with Southeast Asian states and warmer relations with many Southeast Asian states, but as Beijing became more powerful internationally, more authoritarian at home, and more aggressive globally, these successes would not be enough to ensure positive narratives about China within other states, to facilitate many

Chinese foreign policy objectives, or to halt criticism of China's repressive domestic politics in other states.

Still, this era provided a blueprint for Chinese soft power that Beijing would build on in the next decade and combine with sharp power, increasingly using the two in concert. It set the stage for China's influence and information efforts today. In the 1990s and 2000s, China's soft power helped mitigate regional concerns, within Southeast Asia and in other regions like Africa, the Asia-Pacific, and even Europe and North America to some extent, about Beijing's growing economic and strategic clout. The charm offensive did not extinguish these worries—no public diplomacy could have achieved this in a region like Southeast Asia, which had a long and contentious history of Chinese dominance. But Chinese soft power did help to reduce worries, even as Beijing was emerging as a regional and, to some extent, global giant.

China certainly could have terrified its neighbors. Even in the charm offensive period, it was not difficult to find evidence that Beijing's ultimate goal was to become the regional hegemon in Southeast Asia. China pursued aggressive policies in the South China Sea, and some Chinese scholars, who often serve to enunciate the thoughts of top government officials, admitted that Beijing strove to eventually dominate Asia.[2] Robert Sutter, a former national intelligence officer for East Asia, published a study of China's rise in Asia in 2006, a period when Chinese leaders were still publicly saying that Beijing would stick to a limited and humble foreign policy.[3] In his study—one of many suggesting that Beijing intended to be a dominant power—Chinese policy specialists told him that the party's internal documentation called for China to assume leadership in Asia.[4]

China's neighbors had long memories. Southeast Asian countries like modern-day Vietnam had been tributary states during parts of China's imperial era. Some had fought centuries of wars against the Chinese empire—in the case of Vietnam, against the People's Republic in 1979 as well. Many Southeast Asian countries had battled

Maoist China–backed communist insurgencies within their borders during the Cold War.[5]

Yet in much of Southeast Asia, and in some other parts of the world, China's economic and diplomatic rise in the 1990s and 2000s, though not universally welcomed, did not initially produce the kind of backlash one might have expected. Even in Cambodia, where a generation of Cambodians detested China for backing the murderous Khmer Rouge, views of China shifted between the 1980s, after the end of the Khmer Rouge era, and the mid-2000s. Chinese aid and investment was pouring in, and Phnom Penh was changing from a low-rise, sleepy city ravaged by wars into a mini boomtown dotted with cranes and clusters of construction workers. Chinese-language schools opened in Phnom Penh, and Cambodian workers lined up at building sites funded by Chinese investors.[6] (They would eventually find that Chinese firms were not especially eager to hire them, instead attempting to bring in Chinese workers.[7]) Cambodian Prime Minister Hun Sen harbored deep distrust of Beijing dating from the Khmer Rouge era and Cambodia's long civil war, but ultimately, he changed his tune. In 1988, he had written that "China is the root of all that is evil in Cambodia."[8] By the mid-2010s, he was welcoming a regular stream of Chinese leaders, businesspeople, and officials, grinning broadly as they cut ribbons at new construction and infrastructure projects in the capital city.[9]

Hun Sen's approach served his own authoritarian interests: Chinese aid and investment reduced the leverage over him from rich democracies like the European Union and the United States that gave aid to Cambodia, making it easier for the strongman to ignore pressure on human rights issues. Yet there also was renewed warmth toward China across the popular spectrum inside Cambodia. And China proved popular in many other Southeast Asian states as well. A comprehensive 2005 poll, conducted by GlobeScan and the Program on International Policy Attitudes at the University of Maryland, showed that majorities in several Southeast Asian countries—including regional giants Indonesia and the Philippines—viewed China's influence as positive.[10]

Data from the Asian Barometer, the most comprehensive project to measure public opinion across the region, offered some similar findings. In Cambodia, the third wave of surveys completed by the Asian Barometer showed that as late as the early 2010s, nearly 77 percent of Cambodians thought that China "does more good than harm to the region."[11]

Views of China were relatively favorable in other developing regions too. The Afrobarometer project, an undertaking similar to the Asian Barometer, found that in the mid-2000s more than 60 percent of people in Africa thought that China helped their country.[12] In Latin America, surveys throughout the 2000s by the analogous Latinobarómetro survey series revealed that a majority of people in Latin America had a "good" or "very good" opinion of China.[13]

Even in developed democracies where the national media regularly covered Chinese rights abuses even in this era—crackdowns on Falun Gong practitioners and religious minorities, abuses of Tibetans and other ethnic minorities, persecution of some prominent dissidents— Beijing's public image was much better than today, and better than it had been in the late 1980s and early 1990s. A study by the *Economist* of views of China in 123 countries in the 2000s and 2010s found that 2007 marked the high point of approval of China's leadership.[14] That year, Chinese leaders had an average net approval rating of +11, and this was in a study that included many developed democracies where Beijing's rights abuses were well known and where they, by the early 2020s, would have sharply negative views of Beijing.[15] Indeed, this approval rating would fall dramatically within the next decade.

China was not only winning over publics. In interviews with Southeast Asian opinion leaders in the 2000s—politicians, civil society leaders, journalists, and religious leaders—I found surprising optimism about China's emerging regional and global role, even in countries where anti-China sentiment runs deep, like Vietnam. Many Southeast Asian politicians were convinced that China would eventually surpass the United States in setting the trade agenda across Asia. This was a reasonable projection—Beijing's economy was becoming intertwined with those of its neighbors, and after 2016, the Trump administration basically abdicated global trade leadership, including in Asia. (By 2020, it had fully become true, as a China-led multilateral trade deal, the Regional Comprehensive Economic Partnership, joined together a network of Asian states.) And they expressed more optimism than I had expected that Beijing could transform into a relatively responsible leader on some of the most important regional issues, like public health, regional security, and even the environment—shocking views, given that China at the time was choking many of its own cities with pollution.[16]

China's Charm Offensive Was Not Novel

China was not, of course, the first country to attempt to influence Southeast Asia; it copied some of the soft power tactics used by the United States for decades. In the decades after World War II, as Thailand became strategically vital to U.S. interests, the Thai public was inundated by U.S. soft power. The deluge ranged from official U.S. government programs to bring artists or musicians to other countries on programs like the Jazz Ambassadors or the Rhythm Road, similar if larger than China's cultural programming in the region in the 1990s and 2000s; to the massive amount of U.S. popular culture that started filtering into Thailand; to efforts by the U.S. government to boost tourism to U.S. partners in Asia, another strategy China would employ.[17] (Matthew Phillips, a historian of Thailand during the Cold War, notes that "tourism had thus emerged as a supremely ideological activity," pushed in part by the U.S. government to show off American wealth and success.[18]) Like some of the Thais who would later take part in visitor programs and trainings in China, Thai elites who studied in the United States often returned home with positive impressions and far greater knowledge of American culture and of government values and norms. Back in the kingdom, these Thai elites ascended to positions of business and political leadership.[19]

Phillips notes that even many Thais who had concerns about how U.S. influence might eventually affect Thailand's politics often marveled at the United States and expressed a desire to be accepted as a U.S. partner. Senior U.S. diplomats and leaders released a steady stream of government information programs in the kingdom that played on these already-emerging ideas of the United States as modern and prosperous. They also rolled out red-carpet treatment to the Thai king and queen, the ultimate symbol of the country, during the glamorous young royals' 1960 trip to the United States.[20]

Warmer public opinion, particularly notable among the increasingly Americanized Thai elite, made it easier for Cold War Thai leaders to align with the United States on important policy decisions, just as warm Thai public opinion toward China made it easier, decades later, for Thai leaders to shift closer to Beijing. Thailand's pro-U.S. Cold War–era decisions included participating in the Southeast Asia Treaty Organization—a collective regional defense pact that also included the United States—and eventually sending Thai troops to fight alongside U.S. and South Vietnamese forces in the Vietnam War.

To be sure, the United States was not universally beloved in the kingdom during the Cold War, and Thai leaders made decisions for many reasons, including hard strategic ones. Cold War–era Thai rulers—almost always military men aligned with the royal palace—made the calculation that security ties with Washington would protect the kingdom from a communist threat, and would deliver economic rewards as well.[21] Thailand received more than $2 billion in U.S. assistance between 1950 and 1975.[22] Some Thais recognized that Washington's backing helped keep Thai military leaders in power, dictatorships resented by segments of the Thai population. Anti-Americanism grew among segments of the Thai populace in the 1960s. But even at the height of the Vietnam conflict, Thai governments remained supportive of the war, in part because of the enduring appeal of the United States among the Thai population.[23]

The Specifics of How China's First Charm Offensive Worked (to a Point)

Though not nearly as potent as U.S. soft power in the Cold War, China's charm offensive proceeded in a similar manner. Some of the methods of promoting people-to-people ties were similar: bringing foreign students to Chinese universities, establishing Confucius Institutes (instead of U.S. Cold War–era international educational programs established in a broad range of countries), promoting Chinese schools at lower educational levels via Confucius Classrooms targeting primary and secondary schools, and sending more Chinese students and Chinese teachers abroad (instead of projects like the Peace Corps.).[24] Through elite-to-elite public diplomacy and support for cultural programming, among other efforts, Beijing further helped bolster a renaissance in ethnic Chinese celebration of their heritage in Southeast Asia in the 1990s and 2000s.

In the decades of the Cold War, ethnic Chinese citizens of Southeast Asian countries had often been forced to repress their heritage, but by the 1990s and early 2000s, Southeast Asian Chinese again were celebrating their backgrounds. Of course, Beijing's soft power efforts were not the only reason for a resurgence in heritage celebrations, or for Southeast Asian Chinese's growing willingness to run for higher political office. Shifting domestic politics in Southeast Asia, including the freer political environment in countries like Indonesia, Malaysia, and Thailand, facilitated growing acceptance of Southeast Asian Chinese.

Yet China's efforts to promote itself as a constructive, helpful actor and to support ethnic Chinese cultural programming made it safer for Southeast Asian Chinese to display their heritage. Beijing's funding and public support for language and culture programs, done out in the open as clear soft power efforts, helped normalize these celebrations of heritage regionally.[25] In Thailand, where in the late 1940s and early 1950s governments had severely curtailed education in Chinese and raided the offices of many Chinese publications and community groups, Chinese New Year again became a major holiday.[26] In the 2000s, ethnic Chinese community organizations and other associations openly flourished throughout the kingdom.[27]

In Indonesia during the Suharto era, Indonesian Chinese had been harshly stigmatized and forced to assimilate and hide their heritage. During the 1965–66 massacres and Suharto's rise to power, the Indonesian military and vigilante groups targeted Indonesian Chinese mercilessly. Rioters targeted Indonesian Chinese again as recently as 1998, during the Asian financial crisis and Indonesia's economic and political meltdown.[28] But by the 2000s, Indonesian Chinese had relaunched Chinese New Year celebrations and packed Chinese-language schools. In interviews I conducted at the time with Indonesians of Chinese descent, many touted the regional normalization of China, China's cultural influence, and the growing popularity of China's government and Chinese trade ties as reasons that it had become easier for them to display their ethnic heritage openly again.

Indonesian Chinese now even ran for important offices, and many of them spoke openly about their background.[29] By 2009, Basuki Tjahaja Purnama, a charismatic Indonesian Chinese politician known by his nickname, Ahok, had won a parliamentary seat, which he then used to propel himself to higher office. He won the deputy governorship of Jakarta in 2012, teaming up with his ally, then-governor Joko Widodo, known as Jokowi. Ahok became the governor of Jakarta in 2014 when Jokowi was elected president of Indonesia.[30] Ahok's meteoric rise was curtailed in 2017 when he lost a hotly contested Jakarta gubernatorial election in which he fought smears related to his Chinese and Christian identity.[31] After the election, he was jailed on dubious blasphemy charges.[32] The steep downfall was a result of both the economic downturn and a rise in anti-Indonesian Chinese sentiment, prompted in part by intolerant, increasingly populist politicians and religious leaders, who rallied the support of more conservative, hardline Indonesian Muslim sentiment against Ahok.[33]

Making Public Opinion Work for China

This increased interest, and growing people-to-people interactions, helped foster warmer public views of China in many developing regions and even in richer democracies. In Thailand, China's growing appeal to the public was increasingly obvious and shown in part by the warm reception for Chinese investment, Confucius Institutes and Confucius Classrooms, and rapidly increasing Chinese tourism.[34] By 2010, there were 615,270 students studying Chinese in Thailand, in a country that had banned Chinese education during the Cold War. According to the Thai scholar Kornphanat Tungkeunkunt, in 2010 Thai higher education authorities reported that there was a rapidly "increasing demand for Chinese language learning among Thai students."[35]

This warmth was reflected in polling as well. Even as late as 2014, amid more openly stated Chinese ambitions to regional dominance that worried some Thai security experts and policymakers, Thais still had positive views of China. In 2014, a Pew Global Research study of public opinion of China found that 72 percent of Thais viewed China favorably, one of the most positive figures of any country surveyed.[36]

Beijing encouraged Thais to advertise to their leaders this warmth toward China. Beijing focused on Thais of Chinese descent, who make up a substantial portion of the Thai population, but it tried to encourage many other Thais as well. The Chinese embassy in Bangkok sponsored Chinese New Year celebrations. Beijing established the first Chinese cultural center in Southeast Asia in Bangkok, near the Chinese embassy, and diplomats encouraged Thai Chinese and others to frequent it for exhibitions, films, singing contests, and many other events.[37] Kornphanat notes that events at the cultural center "clearly show[ed] that Beijing perceives the ethnic Chinese worldwide as cultural agents, whose cultural practices can be used to push China's soft power."[38] China's state media, which was openly expanding in Thailand, regularly focused on Thailand-China links. The

People's Daily established its first Southeast Asian edition in Thailand in 2012. Xinhua and other state media companies also expanded the amount of their coverage of Thailand in the 2000s and then launched social media outreach in Thai.[39] Beijing relaunched a Thai-language radio station that had broadcast pro-communist messages during the Cold War.[40] In addition, diplomats and visiting Chinese leaders often spoke of the close, friendly links between the two states.[41]

Thai politicians, who also were being aggressively wooed by Chinese leaders and diplomats, responded to public opinion. The charismatic populist Thaksin Shinawatra, who served as prime minister from 2001 to 2006, held splashy public events in regions of China from which his family originally hailed. Accompanied by reporters, lion dancers, and photographers, he visited the house where his mother had lived in Guangdong.[42] He then used coverage of that visit to portray himself as skilled at building China-Thailand links.[43] The closer ties with China were not merely symbolic. Benjamin Zawacki, Asia Foundation program specialist, who specializes in Chinese-Thai relations, notes that, as China's image improved in the kingdom during Thaksin's time in office, which was in part due to Beijing's soft power efforts, the two countries signed a free trade agreement, held a broad range of joint military drills, and inked major strategic agreements that promised even closer military cooperation and increased trade in the future.[44]

Of course, just as with Thailand's Cold War relationship with the United States, Thai politicians had reasons for cultivating links with China besides public opinion. Thaksin and many other Thai elites believed that China served Thailand's strategic interests. They wanted to use China to reduce Thailand's extreme dependence on the United States, in an era in which the George W. Bush administration had become decidedly unpopular in Thailand.[45] Thaksin may have had personal reasons for boosting ties to China as well. A billionaire telecommunications tycoon before he became prime minister, he had courted investment from China for his satellite telecom business. Eventually, he succeeded in getting a deal that allowed his broadband satellite company to operate in China.[46] Many other Thai elites, including politicians, were doing extensive business with China by the 2000s.[47] Still, it is hard to imagine the Thai government shifting so heavily toward a cozy relationship with China if it had not had so much support from its citizens.

During this same period, pro-Chinese sentiment was growing in Malaysia. The country had been the first member of the Association of Southeast Asian Nations (ASEAN) to establish formal diplomatic ties with China, in 1974, but by the 1990s and 2000s the relationship was positively booming.[48] In 2007, Pew found that 83 percent of Malaysians had a positive view of China, the highest figure of any state (other than China) surveyed in Asia.[49] In a survey taken in the mid-2010s, the Asian Barometer found that 75 percent of Malaysians thought that China had a positive effect on the region.[50]

China facilitated positive Malaysian views through several soft power efforts. Between 2000 and 2016, Malaysia received more Chinese aid than any other state in East Asia and the Pacific, even though it is one of the wealthier countries in the region.[51] As in Thailand, Beijing bolstered cultural diplomacy in Malaysia and expanded its scholarships for students to study in China and for officials to come to China for training courses.

Chinese officials and leaders constantly touted Malaysian opinions of China in visits and private meetings with Malaysian politicians and other elites. This smoothed the way for a succession of Malaysian governments, in the 2000s and early 2010s, to form a comprehensive strategic partnership with China, to downplay Malaysian concerns about China's assertive behavior in the South China Sea, and to aggressively woo more Chinese direct investment, among other measures.[52] The long-governing Barisan Nasional coalition, which cared little about the autocratic nature of the Chinese government, responded to China's efforts. "China's popularity within the government extends beyond [then–prime minister] Najib," noted an AidData analysis of Malaysian views of Beijing and the effect of these views on policymaking.[53]

As in Thailand, Malaysian leaders made policy choices not just because of Chinese soft power and Malaysian public opinion. The ruling coalition and even the opposition wanted to promote Malaysian investment in China and facilitate Chinese investment in Malaysia, which was booming. They also wanted to play China off the United States, especially as the image of Washington during the Iraq War became toxic in Muslim-majority states. But China's broad popularity in Malaysia helped create the environment for the tighter bilateral relationship. As Malaysian politicians even admitted in conversations, China's broad popularity in Malaysia made it easier, at least for a time, for Malaysian officials and leaders to openly welcome Chinese investment, even though some civil society groups in other parts of Asia had begun to raise questions about whether such investment would harm labor rights, the environment, local workforces, and corruption. China's popularity in the country also made it easier for Malaysian leaders to accommodate Chinese influence within the ASEAN, China's growing militarization of the South China Sea, and other Chinese policy priorities, especially compared to leaders from some other Southeast Asian states, like Singapore and Vietnam, where views of China were more mixed or negative.

The Limits of Soft Power?

By the middle of the 2000s and the early 2010s, some Southeast Asian states often were consulting quietly with Chinese leaders before making decisions at major ASEAN meetings, although China is not a member of the ASEAN.[54] This was a victory for Beijing, which now had sizable influence over the most influential regional organization in Asia. Southeast Asian states and China were not making joint decisions at ASEAN meetings, but China seemed, to most observers, to be gaining significant input into ASEAN decisions and positions before they were finalized, and some ASEAN countries were tilting the organization to favor China's aims.[55] In other parts of the world, China had become increasingly influential in regional institutions in Africa, Latin America, and Central Asia, in part because of warmer public and elite-level views of China.

Were leaders in these regions consulting with China because Chinese soft power had boosted public and elite opinions of Beijing in Southeast Asia, eventually filtering up to leaders, and how they acted at meetings? Were Southeast Asian leaders consulting with Chinese officials because of fear that, if the ASEAN did not at least take Beijing's views into consideration at meetings, China would only take a tougher approach to regional challenges like contested territorial waters? Were they doing so to ensure that the ASEAN better balanced its ties between China and the United States, the dominant regional power? Were these leaders making sure to solicit Chinese officials' input because these consultations might help facilitate much-needed Chinese investment, especially in some smaller ASEAN states like Cambodia? Beijing's munificence almost surely came linked with pressure for Cambodian officials to consult with China about ASEAN decision-making, and push other ASEAN states as well, before the ASEAN released major statements or took actions.

Southeast Asian leaders were making decisions because of all of these factors. But warmer public views of China in Southeast Asian states, created in part by China's soft power efforts at the time, played some role in the decision-making, since they allowed some Southeast Asian leaders to work more closely with Beijing, convinced that their decisions enjoyed public support at home.

There is also the possibility that China's soft power was most effective in helping produce policy wins in states, like Thailand, where Beijing already had relatively strong bilateral relationships before the 1990s. In other words, Beijing might have been concentrating its soft power efforts in places that Chinese leaders thought were the most open to Beijing's influence.[56] China's soft power might simply have worked better in Southeast Asian states where public opinion of China was already relatively warm due to historical factors.

However, there is some evidence that, during this period (and, as we will see, these days), Beijing did not concentrate its soft power efforts in states that already had significant bilateral ties to Beijing, warm public and elite views of China, and/or a history of aligning with Beijing on foreign policy. The Philippines, a U.S. treaty ally and long one of the most pro-U.S. countries in Asia, and a place with negative popular views of China in the 1990s, was a major target of Chinese soft power in the charm offensive era.[57] Australia, a country with deep economic links with China but also a population that historically held negative, sometimes racist views of China, also was a central target of Chinese soft power in this era. In both of these states, soft power played a role in producing relatively warm views of China, and those warmer views helped generate Chinese policy victories, at least for a time.[58]

Polling by the Lowy Institute, the Australian think tank, found that in 2006, as China targeted Australia with soft power efforts and as trade ties blossomed, Australians had a strongly net positive view of China, though by the late 2010s that view would turn more negative than positive.[59] Pew Research Center polling found that 63 percent of people in the Philippines, even more a target of Chinese soft power efforts like media expansion, training programs, and cultural diplomacy, had a favorable view of China in 2002; that number would drop sharply to 38 percent in 2014, as the Philippine public grew angry after Beijing claimed the disputed Scarborough Shoal in the South China Sea, belying claims of noninterference.[60] In places where China was building up soft power, Chinese officials and other pro-China figures, like Chinese businesspeople making investments in Australia or the Philippines, conveyed their opinions to the local media and to political leaders.[61]

Warm public views of China conveyed to leaders had an effect. In the Philippines, they made it easier for Philippine leaders, including then-president Gloria Macapagal Arroyo, to welcome promised major new Chinese investments in the Philippines' rail system in the 2000s, in a country where major inbound Chinese investment had aroused fears in the past.[62]

The Failures—and Motivations—for China's Efforts Today

Even during this period, however, optimism about China becoming a positive force in its nearest neighborhood was not universal. Singapore and Vietnam, for example, remained more skeptical of China as a regional leader than Indonesia, Malaysia, the Philippines, Thailand, and Timor-Leste. But by the mid- and late 2010s, China's favorability ratings in many other Asian states had fallen, and a backlash began to build against Chinese influence. This backlash would motivate Beijing to increase its soft power strategies but also to invest much more heavily in sharp power, which it could deploy to wield influence even as it was becoming more unpopular in other states.

Chapter 4

Motivations for China's Modern Influence Campaign

At the height of China's initial charm offensive, South Korea seemed to be cautiously buying what Beijing was selling. South Korea was a major target of China's cultural diplomacy in the 2000s. Beijing opened more Confucius Institutes in South Korea than in any country besides the United States and the United Kingdom.[1] By 2014, South Koreans also made up around 16 percent of all international students in China, the biggest group of students from any one country.[2] And their pop cultures began to overlap: South Korea's powerful culture industry, including its soapy television dramas and K-pop (Korean pop) bands, became enormously popular in China.[3]

The combination of China's soft power offensive, the pop culture links between the two states, booming bilateral trade, and a desire among some South Korean policymakers to diversify away from a reliance on the United States did prompt relatively warm views of Beijing during the first charm offensive period. According to the South Korean and Chinese scholars Min-gyu Lee and Yufan Hao, South Korean views of China became steadily more positive between 1988 and 2000.[4]

But Chinese soft power, its focus in the charm offensive era, faced major hurdles in South Korea as the 2010s wore on, and by the time of Xi Jinping's first term (2013–17), South Korean public opinion was hardening against China. It was not totally negative, when compared to countries even more skeptical of China's rise, like Japan or Vietnam. But the mood in South Korea was souring. Beijing's behavior made it much harder for it to woo South Korea with soft power efforts—China's increasing willingness to throw its weight around geopolitically, clearly abandoning its stated concept of noninterference, alienated South Koreans and undermined much of the goodwill created in the previous decades. For instance, after Seoul and Washington decided to deploy the U.S.-made Terminal High Altitude Area Defense (THAAD) anti-missile system in South Korea in 2016, Beijing hit back hard—with coercive hard power. It forced retail stores from Lotte, one of South Korea's biggest companies, to close up shop in China.[5] Beijing banned K-pop bands from performing in China, cutting them off from an important market.[6] There were also campaigns in the Chinese state media to boycott South Korean products and restrict travel, and Beijing temporarily halted group tours to the country. The tourism boycott alone reportedly cost South Korea some $6.8 billion in 2017, destroyed travel agencies, and infuriated South Koreans.[7] (South Korea–China relations warmed slightly in the late 2010s, but there remained a significant backlash against China in South Korea; a 2019 poll by the Asan Institute for Policy Studies showed that China was viewed unfavorably by South Koreans.[8])

Besides rising anger at Chinese actions perceived as bullying, South Korea, one of the freest countries in Asia, was not particularly interested in Beijing's authoritarian politics. The China model's appeal in South Korea faltered even more as Xi moved his government away from the relatively stable, collective authoritarianism that had prevailed since Mao's time and toward one-man rule.

South Korea's growing disdain for the China model was not unique. Asians from the region's freest countries, like South Korea, perhaps reflecting on the freedoms gained since the fall of their own dictatorships, increasingly saw China's type of government as unstable and unappealing, and China's regional behavior caused blowback among its neighbors. In other democracies around the world, including in developing regions, China's public image began to take hits as well. And Chinese state media, operating fairly openly but less effective as a soft power tool in a free country like South Korea than in an authoritarian state like Cambodia with few independent media outlets, could have only a minimal effect on South Korean views of China's political system.[9] In an analysis released in 2018 and based on a region-wide survey of young men and women, Yida Zhai of Shanghai Jiao Tong University found that, while only 44 percent of young Chinese thought China was politically unstable, more than 70 percent of young South Koreans believed that China's political instability was rising.[10] Zhai further found that not only South Koreans but also high percentages of young people in free states like Japan and Taiwan saw Xi's China as increasingly unstable and were convinced that "the rise of China has been threatening the global order."[11]

As the studies of elite Southeast Asian opinion released by the Institute of Southeast Asian Studies (ISEAS)–Yusof Ishak Institute in Singapore in 2019 and 2020 showed, most Asians, publics and elites, see China as a rising power, probably destined to be the dominant regional power; many see Beijing as already the dominant regional actor.[12] They are not wrong: China has become the leading actor in intra-Asian trade and a vital donor and investor; has embarked on highly aggressive regional diplomacy, punishing countries that block its diplomatic aims; and has been aggressively building up its military installations in the South China Sea and other regional waters. Indeed, the survey data from both Asian Barometer and the ISEAS–Yusof Ishak Institute revealed that publics and elites in even U.S. allies and staunch partners like Japan and Singapore already believe China is the most influential state in Asia. In Asian Barometer's fourth wave of surveys, which relied on data from the early to mid-2010s, 61 percent of Japanese people believed that China had the most influence regionally, while only 29 percent believed that the United States had the most influence.[13]

China's hard power, like its military buildup, and its increasingly central role in Asian trade, substantiated these views. But by the mid- and late 2010s, many Asians—not only in Southeast Asia but also in regions like Northeast Asia and South Asia, and in Australia and New Zealand—also were pessimistic about how China would wield its growing power in Asia, as Beijing undercut its own long-standing narrative that its rise would be peaceful, and as its soft power efforts increasingly failed.

That pessimism reigned despite sizable Chinese investments in soft power. Indeed, China's earlier "charm offensive" soft power approach was failing. In a 2013 study of several Asian states' efforts to wield soft power, Ian Hall of Griffith University in Australia and Frank Smith of the University of Sydney found that China was allocating more money for soft power than any other Asian country.[14] (Indeed, George Washington University's David Shambaugh estimated that, by 2015, the Chinese state was spending a staggering $10 billion on soft power promotion annually.[15]) Yet Hall and Smith noted that, by the early 2010s, there was only a minimal correlation, if at all, between China's investments in soft power and how citizens of other states across Asia viewed the People's Republic.[16]

In his analysis released in 2018, Yida Zhai found that, while South Koreans—and most of the young people surveyed from other Asian states—believed that China was now a powerful actor in Asia, a majority of the young South Koreans agreed with the proposition that "the rise of China has been threatening the global order."[17] Other studies confirmed these fears, revealing increasingly negative views of China across Asia. A 2019 survey of Southeast Asians by the ISEAS–Yusof Ishak Institute found that while a majority of respondents already believed that China has the most economic and political influence in the region, nearly half of respondents said that "China will become a revisionist power with an intent to turn Southeast Asia into its sphere of influence."[18] It also found that, as in many other Asian countries and increasingly in developed democracies, a majority of respondents had either little or no confidence that "China will 'do the right thing' in contributing to global peace, security, prosperity, and governance."[19]

Motivations for China's Current Influence Campaign

China's current influence and information campaign stems from several factors. The failures of the charm offensive, heavily reliant on soft power, were a driving force behind China's new and (somewhat) different global influence campaign. This failing charm offensive was a major reason Beijing now has redoubled its influence efforts, by trying to increase its soft power campaign after earlier failures—and by pouring much more resources into sharp power, to which it had paid less attention earlier and now saw could reap greater benefits. In addition, the modern-day influence campaign was motivated by China's growing global power and its view that Beijing had not been able to get its voice across in global media and information—in its near neighborhood and particularly in the media markets of rich, powerful countries like the United States, Britain, France, Japan, Australia, and Germany. Shifts in Chinese domestic politics and the weaknesses of many democracies to influence efforts also were factors behind Beijing's expanded influence campaigns.

Soft power is inherently tricky to measure, but there are some ways to anecdotally assess its effectiveness or lack thereof. In the 1990s and 2000s, public polling in Asia and other parts of the world, as I have shown, revealed relatively positive views of China. Although all of this public warmth toward China cannot directly be attributed to Beijing's soft power efforts, its new aid programs, enhanced cultural and public diplomacy, efforts to woo foreign students and bolster training programs, and other soft power strategies played a role in boosting public opinion of China, as many Southeast Asian policymakers and civil society activists admitted at the time to me. And as I just showed, successful soft power campaigns, like China's efforts in Southeast Asia in the 1990s, 2000s, and early 2010s, can make it easier for leaders to adopt policy positions favorable to China, because they have less fear of a public backlash—in this case, a backlash against favoring Beijing.

It is even more challenging to quantify the effects of soft power. The organization AidData, at William & Mary University, has tried to quantify the effect of five aspects of China's soft power in the Asia-Pacific region: cultural efforts, exchange programs, financial efforts, elite-to-elite diplomacy, and informational efforts, including Chinese state media. They found that, at least until the mid-2010s, public diplomacy overtures appeared to be paying off for Beijing in terms of more favorable public perceptions of China.[20] AidData's study found that China's public diplomacy, or soft power, was associated with people from East Asia and the Pacific "viewing China as having a positive influence and a development model to which their countries should aspire."[21] Their study further showed that this effective soft power strategy created a "good neighbor dividend" in much of East Asia and the Pacific that made it easier for China to open market opportunities in neighboring states, and that the soft power offensive was correlated with East Asian and Pacific states voting more regularly with China at the UN General Assembly.[22] Voting patterns at the UN General Assembly are often used as a tool quantify states' alignment with each other on policy choices.[23] (Indeed, thirty-five years before the AidData study, the U.S. Congress mandated that the U.S. State Department provide an annual report examining foreign states' voting behaviors at the United Nations—including how often they voted with the United States—as a means in part of assessing the effectiveness of U.S. diplomacy and soft power.[24])

Yet at least since the mid-2010s, views of China have gone downhill in Southeast Asia and other regions such as Europe, Latin America, and North America, as China's soft power effort has stumbled, and then has been torpedoed by China's handling of COVID-19. Instead of China's soft power smoothing the way for other countries to believe it would do the right thing, and for politicians in other countries to work with China without fears of a public backlash, China has in recent years become more unpopular. And strikingly, despite the George W. Bush administration mostly ignoring Southeast Asia and the Barack Obama administration paying only intermittent attention, the United States still remained relatively popular with Southeast Asians, a legacy in part of U.S. soft power reserves, and highly popular in Northeast Asia, much of Europe, and Australia and New Zealand. Though Southeast Asians increasingly doubted whether the United States could contest China as the region's dominant economic actor and even the region's preeminent military power, in an Asian Barometer study of Southeast Asian views, over 70 percent of Burmese, Cambodians, Filipinos, Singaporeans, Thais, and Vietnamese had "strongly positive views" of the United States.[25]

What went wrong with the earlier soft power effort? The charm offensive stumbled for several reasons. As China's outbound investment and foreign aid continued to expand, it was no longer a new source of cash in many developing states. The public relations boost Beijing had gotten simply from becoming a large investor and donor began to fade. Meanwhile, by the mid- and late 2010s, media outlets in freer states in Asia, Africa, Latin America, and other parts of the world were scrutinizing the downsides of China's investments— environmental problems, labor rights issues, lack of transparency—and other problematic aspects of China's regional behavior, significantly complicating Beijing's soft power efforts. Even in less-free states, like Cambodia or Vietnam, it was still possible for citizens to share information on social media, including about China-backed projects in their countries. Cambodians and Vietnamese regularly shared stories on social media outlets about problems with Chinese-funded projects, and Cambodians and Vietnamese staged protests, like blocking roads, to protest against China-backed projects' environmental damage and other problems.[26]

Given the lack of transparency in many Chinese aid projects, the potential for aid and investment to foster corruption, the environmental damage caused by projects skirting local environmental laws, and the displacement of locals, public concerns about Chinese funds increased in states from Colombia to Kenya to Zambia—and attracted the attention of politicians and civil society leaders in many regions of the world beyond Southeast Asia. A study by the RWR Advisory

Group found that about 14 percent of China-funded infrastructure projects between 2013 and 2018 had run into major problems, including public opposition over issues related to labor, transparency, and other concerns.[27] Meanwhile, angry protests about Chinese projects mushroomed in Africa, parts of Latin America, and Europe, among other regions.

Myanmar and Cambodia show in some detail how the charm offensive faded, in many developing regions, as initial exuberance about China's trade and aid in Southeast Asia dimmed and concerns spread about the downsides of Chinese aid and investment. By the middle of the 2010s, China was by far the most important external diplomatic actor and donor in these two states. Chinese officials played a central role in rocky peace negotiations between the Myanmar government and an array of insurgent groups; China poured investment into Yangon, Myanmar's biggest city; and Chinese leaders built close links with army generals and civilian leaders like Aung San Suu Kyi, the state counselor and de facto president.[28]

But Myanmar society opened up after the onset of civilian rule in 2010–11 and the formal end of junta dominance, and before the 2021 coup imposed military rule again. Myanmar reporters and activists exposed the dangers of some China-backed projects, and these reports spread easily in the country, where the cost of mobile phones was dropping and every bus driver, farmer, and monk seemed to be on Facebook.[29] With these reports came angry protests. Thousands of citizens, including farmers and monks, demonstrated for months in 2012 against a planned large copper mine in central Myanmar called Letpadaung, run by a Chinese company in partnership with the Myanmar military. Protestors claimed that thousands of people were being forced off their land and that the mine would be an environmental disaster.[30] The authorities responded with brutality, firing water cannons and even highly dangerous white phosphorous at demonstrators who were sitting in and blocking some parts of the facility.[31] It was reported that fifty people were injured; it was likely many more. The brutality, which many protestors linked to

Myanmar's need to protect Chinese investments, further diminished Beijing's reputation in the country, as did a leak of waste in 2015 from the mine.[32] Chinese soft power efforts—cultural events, trainings for local Myanmar officials, the expanding presence of Chinese state media in Myanmar—were not enough to counteract this growing anger from some Myanmar citizens, and Beijing often lacked the adaptability to use its soft power tools, like its training programs or expanding state media, to show contrition for some of the problems in Myanmar and make credible vows to improve the standard of Chinese investments. It also still seemed unwilling to alter the same behavior—problematic investments, increasingly aggressive diplomacy, military buildups—that had caused a blowback in regional public opinion of Beijing.

In Cambodia too, public anger flashed at China, despite Cambodia's authoritarian political climate and China's extensive soft power efforts in Cambodia, including expanding state media, huge aid outlays, and scholarships for Cambodian students and officials to study in China, among other efforts. Big Chinese investments in Cambodia increasingly displaced local residents, who received little or no compensation amidst a flurry of land grabbing abetted by Cambodia's own authoritarian and corrupt political climate.[33] Cambodians chafed at how places like Sihanoukville, once a quiet seaside town, had been completely transformed by investment. Developers pushed out small Cambodian merchants in the Sihanoukville area as resorts, condos, and flashy gambling palaces shot up to cater to Chinese tourists.[34] Cambodians also complained that many Chinese megaprojects and Chinese-owned factories imported Chinese labor, and Chinese project managers were uninterested in hiring Cambodians, especially for positions in which it was possible to advance.[35] A study of Chinese firms and migrants in Cambodia by Pál Nyíri of Vrije University in Amsterdam found that in garment making, Cambodia's biggest manufacturing industry, "most factories employ scores, and the largest ones hundreds, of skilled transferees or new recruits from [China]."[36] Again, as Cambodian public sentiment soured on China, China's state media outlets, diplomats, and officials seemed at a loss regarding how to respond to this criticism and control it.

China's Passive Soft Power Faced Limits

The charm offensive also faltered because Beijing's ability to employ soft power was hampered by the way in which it exported its culture. China focused on using the government to promote its culture directly, and these active, government-dominated tools could be effective. By the mid-2000s Beijing was overseeing some 1,300 cultural exchanges annually with other countries and international cultural organizations, roughly 500 percent more than in the 1990s.[37] Beijing sponsored a "Year of Chinese Culture" in 2006, which included supporting Chinese New Year celebrations in capitals like Bangkok, London, and Paris, and the events in Bangkok drew sizable crowds.[38] It backed a major international Buddhism forum, held in Hangzhou in 2006, seeking to link China's history of Buddhism to Chinese soft power.[39] It held the 2010 World Expo in Shanghai, a kind of modern-day World's Fair, to showcase Shanghai, China's increasing modernization, its high-tech industry, and aspects of traditional Chinese culture.

But China lagged badly when it came to passive soft power cultural exports like music, film, literature, and art that function best without government control.[40] China had modest passive exports in its near neighborhood but failed almost completely to export music, film, literature, and art to Europe, North America, Latin America, and other regions beyond its near neighborhood.

Traditionally, these passive exports can be far more influential in shaping foreigners' perceptions of a country's people, values, and culture than government-backed soft power. Although some Chinese pop artists broke into the K-pop scene, they still mostly performed in China itself and did not become global phenomena like South

Korea's Psy (of "Gangnam Style" fame) or, later, the K-pop international megastars BTS. There was no Chinese Beatles, who burst onto U.S. television in the 1960s and became global icons, in the process helping redefine the international image of the United Kingdom as the hip, cool place of "Swinging London," rather than a country of post–World War II austerity, ancient prime ministers, and dour people choking in smoggy, sooty air.

To be sure, China was developing one of the biggest domestic film industries in the world, and it boasted some popular athletes, artists, actors, and filmmakers. The NBA star Yao Ming, the women's tennis star Li Na, the director Zhang Yimou, the actor Jackie Chan (originally from Hong Kong), and others enjoyed international popularity, which reflected well on China. (Many of these stars did have warm relations with the Chinese government, but other than Zhang Yimou, state support was not the core factor behind their international popularity.) Yet for all the size of China's film industry, the blockbusters it produced, like *Wolf Warrior 2*, an action movie released in 2017 that told a story of a former Chinese special forces soldier who saves workers at a factory in Africa (and confronts a dastardly American villain), targeted a domestic audience and had little global appeal—whether in other Asian countries or in Europe, North America, and Latin America.[41]

The hardening environment for political freedom within China further hindered the global appeal of the country's pop culture. Artistic repression, which increased in the Hu Jintao era and became far more brutal under Xi, made it harder for Chinese artists, musicians, writers, and filmmakers to produce the kind of quality and independent work that has worldwide appeal. This type of independent, universally resonant work historically had bolstered the soft power of countries like the United States, France, or the United Kingdom—and in the 2010s and 2020s boosted the soft power of South Korea. And independent Chinese artists and filmmakers had made modest soft power inroads into Europe, other parts of Asia, and North America.

Take Chinese artist Ai Weiwei, whose works have appeared in prestigious galleries all over the world, and whom the Chinese government commissioned to design the "Bird's Nest" stadium for the 2008 Beijing Summer Olympics. He became renowned in Europe and North America and was feted as one of the world's leading modern artists. He could have potentially helped Beijing spread its charm offensive into Europe and North America, regions where his art was wildly popular and valuable. Yet as Ai Weiwei became openly political, he fell out of favor with the government. In 2011, Chinese authorities tossed him in jail for eighty-one days, and in 2016, his lawyer, Xia Lin, was sentenced to twelve years in jail on dubious fraud charges.[42]

The lack of passive soft power had a clear effect. In a comprehensive comparison of countries' soft power, produced by the consulting firm Portland and released in 2019, China ranked twenty-seventh of thirty states studied.[43] China ranked behind not only pop culture giants like France, South Korea, the United Kingdom, or the United States but also the Czech Republic and Portugal, which probably last counted as a soft power giant and international power around the time the printing press was a hot new technology.[44] In Portland's analysis, China performed poorly in areas of passive appeal, like the appeal of its political system and values—values that looked even worse to many outsiders as the People's Republic was becoming more authoritarian.[45] It performed poorly not only among neighboring states but also in many other regions of the world, including Europe and North America, where China now wields almost no soft power and where publics have some of the most negative views of China among any countries in the world.[46]

Beijing's active soft power efforts, including its large aid programs and its touting of the Belt and Road Initiative (BRI) as a cultural and historical link to other countries, also seemed to have done little to convince other states they shared values with China.[47] It also performed poorly in the culture rating, an area where passive soft power would show up.[48]

Chinese State Media Often Remained Unconvincing

Meanwhile, although Beijing poured money into its state media in the 1990s and 2000s, Xinhua, China Global Television Network (CGTN), and other outlets, soft power tools for the most part, still were perceived abroad as boring and propagandistic.[49] State media journalists struggled to appeal to foreign audiences while not running into trouble with censors in their own government. In most countries, global outlets like the BBC and domestic news organizations offered intense competition for CGTN and Xinhua in English and local languages. The BBC's global reach, and highly regarded independent reporting, rubbed off on views of the United Kingdom. Indeed, the BBC's impressive brand helped make the United Kingdom the leader in Portland's global soft power index in 2018 and second in the report in 2019.[50]

James Palmer, a longtime China writer and deputy editor at *Foreign Policy* who once worked for Chinese state media in Beijing, captured the problem facing China's state outlets and why they were not boosting Beijing's soft power. CGTN, he wrote, was

> stuck with a fundamental problem. For the channel to be successful as propaganda, it has to appeal to a foreign audience. But the elements that would be persuasive to foreigners, whether informed reporting . . . or political extremism, are anathema to the people the station answers to back home. Actually growing the station's audience is far, far less important to the midlevel party apparatchiks who ultimately control it than making sure they avoid political errors.[51]

The same problems Palmer outlined about CGTN existed for Xinhua, China Radio International, and other state media outlets, particularly in the charm offensive era. Within Xinhua and CGTN, many reporters understood that, even though the outlets were expanding in budget and head counts, the cautious, controlling nature of their work environment was creating bland, uninteresting products that could not boost China's soft power the way Beijing hoped. Mark Bourrie, a Canadian journalist and academic who worked for Xinhua's Ottawa bureau in the early 2010s, told me that while Xinhua at first seemed superficially open to independent reporting, it soon became clear that managers would ensure that controversial topics were avoided, and the bureau's leadership had little idea of how Canadian politics and news worked. The most important job for Xinhua in Ottawa was to produce stories that would please senior leaders in Beijing, which often meant avoiding the hottest and most interesting stories—the same stories that might attract readers and possibly make Xinhua more popular.[52]

At that time, Chinese state media outlets hired only a handful of foreign journalists who understood freer media environments, and it was not enough to create a critical mass within bureaus to make them capable of producing appealing enough reporting that they would capture local media consumers' interest, particularly in states in Europe, North America, Latin America, Africa, and Asia with high levels of press freedom where China's media still came across as intensely propagandistic. Nyíri produced a thorough study of Chinese correspondents working abroad in the early 2010s and heard similar stories. In his research, he found that at state media, news stories "printed, broadcast, or posted online [in Chinese media] rarely reflect reporters' views alone. . . . They are refracted through the preferences of editors and *lingdao*," or managers who constrain the reporting.[53]

Ultimately, China began to recognize the flaws in its approach. From the late 2010s through today, it has launched an effort to make Chinese state media more attractive and provocative, to build the kind of outlet that could bolster China's soft power. It has started promoting outlets intensely on social media, hiring experienced foreign journalists, and using partnerships, journalism training programs, and content-sharing deals with prestigious international media outlets to broaden China's international reach.

Palmer, however, believed that China's state media could never become attractive to news consumers. He wrote:

There were two possible models for a station like CGTN, flush with the cash of an autocratic state that wanted a global voice: Al Jazeera and Russia Today. Qatar's Al Jazeera offered the ideal of being a serious news station that presented an alternative perspective on the world. Russia Today, now known as RT, was in contrast a genuinely effective and disruptive propaganda outlet that spread fear, uncertainty, and doubt to Moscow's advantage.[54]

China, he argued, would not be able to follow Al Jazeera's model of producing quality content on many issues, other than news topics that were related to Qatar. Qatar is a small country, and few people have interest in its domestic politics. Reporters at Al Jazeera thus are able to cover a broad range of regional and international topics without straying into something that might be sensitive to Qatari leaders, who seem willing to allow a high degree of excellent reporting on a wide range of issues. (There are certainly areas, like Israel or Saudi Arabia, in which Al Jazeera's coverage is not free, and in the case of Israel has included some open anti-Semitism.[55]) They can produce what Palmer (among many others) called "a serious news station that presented an alternative perspective on the world" despite Qatar's authoritarian politics.[56] And Al Jazeera has become a major soft power tool for Qatar. "The establishment of the Aljazeera media empire by the Qatari government in 1996 has given the country unprecedented exposure in the world," notes one study of Al Jazeera's soft power effects by Osman Antwi-Boateng, a professor in the United Arab Emirates.[57] Al Jazeera has become a major force in influencing attitudes and minds in the Middle East, promoting Qatar's image, he notes.[58] But for a global giant like China, unlike tiny Qatar, almost any international news topic could have an angle that relates to the Chinese government, and many people across the world take an interest in China's domestic politics and economy.

China's media could instead try to copy RT, Palmer noted—a disruptive, hypercontrarian, controversial television channel that, for all its fearmongering, disinformation, and soft-pedaling of Kremlin abuses, was often exciting and alternative enough to attract international viewers. Chinese state media, Palmer argued, could never be as challenging as RT, since China, unlike Russia, was not interested in simply sparking chaos and being provocative.[59]

And yet, by the end of the 2010s and early 2020s, Beijing would be attempting in some respects to copy both Al Jazeera and RT and would work more closely with RT and other Russian state outlets to disseminate conspiracy theories. It would work to make Xinhua, CGTN, and other state media look more like independent, Al Jazeera–style outlets, boosting the presence of these media giants on social media globally, hiring quality local journalists in multiple countries, and taking other steps to improve their prestige. At the same time, some Chinese state outlets were engaging in the provocative, trolling, contrarian style common to Russian media, and sometimes, as the Ukraine war raged, working with Russian media on these efforts.

The International Environment Changes— and Other Countries Rebel Against Chinese Behavior

But the fact that China's earlier, soft power-centered charm offensive faltered was not the only reason Beijing has tried to build an even bigger influence apparatus and has shifted to focus more on sharp power. The international environment was shifting too in the latter half of the 2010s, creating motivations and opportunities for China to redouble its influence efforts. This continues today. As democratic powers in Europe, North America, and Northeast Asia have had to deal with their own increasingly dysfunctional domestic politics and staggering economies, it became easier for China to promote its ideological model and, increasingly, to gain control of the actual infrastructure through which information travels—communications hardware, social media platforms, apps, and other infrastructure, as Sarah Cook of Freedom House has noted.[60] Together, all of these trends have motivated Beijing to refine its soft power strategies, like its state media outlets and its training and exchange programs for students and officials, and to massively upgrade its ability to penetrate other states with sharp power, like the coercion of other countries' media, politicians, and universities.

China has become a more powerful international actor—within international institutions like the World Bank and the United Nations, in projecting military power, and in taking leadership on major issues like climate change, public health, and trade as other powers like the United States, Canada, Japan, and the European Union shrank from leadership. As Yanzhong Huang of the Council on Foreign Relations has noted, in an article with this author, China has become a central actor in UN agencies, with its citizens heading four of the fifteen UN specialized agencies.[61] China increasingly has dominated UN bodies like the UN Human Rights Council and would play a central role in negotiating the 2015 Paris climate agreement.[62] And under Hu Jintao and then Xi Jinping, China has not only become more powerful but also openly assertive about its foreign policies and its growing global footprint.

China's growing global assertiveness has led to a backlash, in some countries, against China's diplomatic style and its actual foreign policy behavior, making it much tougher for Beijing to convince other countries that it would be some benign actor on the global stage— and convincing Chinese officials they needed both a better soft power strategy and a more comprehensive sharp power strategy. Since the death of Mao, Chinese leaders' portrayal of China as a realist, modest actor in global affairs had been central to Beijing's foreign policy brand. Did this idea of Chinese humility convince everyone in other countries? Of course not. But it became even harder by the middle of the 2010s. When Xi Jinping came to power in 2013, he vowed to restore China's international power while also centralizing control over domestic politics.

Xi did not demonstrate humility. In documents and speeches, Xi promised that he would make China strong again.[63] He has vowed to deliver a great rejuvenation of the Chinese nation and to take a bigger role in global leadership, and signed the aforementioned pact with Russia to combat liberal democracy worldwide.[64] Unlike previous Chinese leaders who had shied away from touting China as a model, Xi held up China as a model for other societies. He openly flexed the country's military muscles, speeding up the pace of militarization in the South China Sea, launching aggressive moves in other territorial waters like the East China Sea, setting up China's first overseas base in Africa, making forays to claim disputed territory along the Indian border, and other efforts.[65] The Xi administration took advantage, in 2020, of some Southeast Asian states like the Philippines being over-whelmed with COVID-19—at one point a host of top Philippine military commanders were sick or in isolation from the virus—to push forward with China's aggressive behavior in the South China Sea, at a time when rivals were weakened.[66] Xi also increased the pace of China's military modernization, attempting to make the People's Liberation Army a "military and naval power commensurate with that of a great power," according to a 2019 analysis of China's military and security developments by the U.S. Department of Defense.[67] Xi's administration took a harder line on land border disputes as well. In 2017, in a portion of the tiny South Asian state of Bhutan called Doklam, which was of strategic importance to India, China began to build a road, likely the first step to solidifying control of the area. (A few months later, under pressure from Indian forces, China halted the road construction.[68]) Then, in 2020, China and India had a major skirmish along their high-altitude Himalayan border, and China then claimed part of Bhutan as its own territory; a report in *Foreign Policy* then showed that China had actually been building settlements inside Bhutan.[69]

At regional meetings in Asia, the Pacific, and sometimes Africa and Latin America, where, in the 1990s and 2000s Chinese leaders and diplomats had cooed to Asian counterparts that Beijing would be a solid but not overbearing ally, by the 2010s Beijing's tone had changed; that tone was beginning to harden even further with counterparts in Europe and North America. Even before Xi Jinping became president,

Chinese Foreign Minister Yang Jiechi had unleashed a diatribe at Southeast Asian leaders at an Association of Southeast Asian Nations (ASEAN) summit in Hanoi in 2010.[70] "China is a big country and other countries are small countries, and that is just a fact," Yang said, after ASEAN leaders complained bitterly about Beijing's policies in the South China Sea.[71]

Other ministers and ambassadors, inculcated in China's increasingly nationalistic domestic politics and education system, began regularly venting prickly, nationalist, bombastic rhetoric at foreign states, including increasingly in Europe.[72] In 2018, China's ambassador to Sweden blasted Swedish police for removing Chinese tourists trespassing in a hostel, demanding an investigation and claiming that getting thrown out of a hostel was a "serious violation of the life safety and basic human rights of Chinese citizens."[73] Some of the most aggressive, nationalistic diplomats moved up quickly through the foreign ministry.

In 2019, Beijing promoted Zhao Lijian from the second-ranking diplomat in the Chinese mission in Islamabad, a relatively obscure job, to a high post in the foreign ministry's information department.[74] In Pakistan, Zhao had become known for tweeting so often he would put Donald Trump's Twitter habits to shame—51,000 tweets in four years.[75] Rather than affecting humility, as many Chinese diplomats had in the 1990s and early 2000s, Zhao used Twitter to hit hard at critics of China. He told other countries that "Xinjiang is none of your business" and claimed that many British citizens were "descendants of war criminals" after the UK government called on Hong Kong authorities to treat protestors there with restraint.[76]

This growing assertiveness, both in diplomatic rhetoric and in actual foreign policy behavior, as well as China's subsequent isolation from the world in 2021 and 2022 as it stuck to its zero-COVID policy even as the rest of the world abandoned this strategy, clearly sparked a backlash. In states close to China like India, Japan, and Vietnam, where anti-China sentiment already was close to the surface and Beijing had significant territorial disputes, angry, even violent anti-China protests erupted regularly, and politicians slammed China routinely.[77]

In Europe and North America, this growing assertiveness, which cul-
minated also in Beijing supporting Russia's invasion of Ukraine and
seeming to draw a line between autocracies and democracies, sparked
a backlash as well, amidst concerns about what kind of power China
was becoming. But even in places where there was less history of tensions with Beijing, China's increasingly nationalistic rhetoric and more
aggressive behavior, as well as, in 2021 and 2022, its growing isolation
from the world due to its COVID policies, sparked fear and resentment
in places like Africa, Australia, Latin America, and the Pacific Islands.[78]

So, with more wide-ranging regional and global interests, bigger
ambitions on the world stage, fewer restraints in boasting about
its power and future ambitions, and yet countries rebelling against
Beijing's more aggressive rhetoric and behavior, China needed a
bigger soft and sharp power apparatus to defuse the tensions its activities were raising. Was Beijing ready to fully displace the United States,
in every region of the globe? Certainly not. But Beijing had clear ambitions to dominate Asia and at least to make major inroads into U.S.
dominance elsewhere on earth.[79]

Domestic Chinese Politics

As China's initial charm offensive of the 1990s, 2000s, and early 2010s
faced cracks, the domestic environment within China was changing
rapidly too. Xi came to power, centralized his rule, and adopted a far
more assertive view of China's role in the world. His administration
looked to build a revamped soft power apparatus and a more aggressive sharp power strategy to implement Xi's much bolder, more nationalistic vision of China's place in the world and also to deal with
the blowback against China's broader, more assertive foreign policies
and its enhanced repression at home. The most powerful and autocratic Chinese leader since Mao, Xi also needed a bolder influence
campaign to protect the ways he was remaking Chinese foreign policy
and domestic politics.[80]

Remember that since taking over the Chinese leadership in 2013, Xi has launched what the Council on Foreign Relations' Elizabeth Economy has called "a third revolution" in Chinese domestic politics, seeking a "great rejuvenation of the Chinese nation."[81] (The first revolution was Mao's communist revolution and the second was Deng Xiaoping's period of reform and opening.) Xi's revolution involves several components, but overall, he has sought to increase the power of the Chinese Communist Party (CCP) in all realms of Chinese life, including private companies, the government bureaucracy, the arts, people's private lives and communications, and once-autonomous regions of China like Hong Kong.[82] Abroad, he is building a more muscular China in almost every area of foreign relations, with China no longer seeking just regional dominance but, increasingly, global dominance.[83]

To achieve the goals at home, Xi has concentrated political control in his hands; silenced voices throughout Chinese society who are even mildly critical of the CCP and his leadership; harshly repressed some of the more restive, ethnic minority–dominated regions of China; and fostered a Mao-esque personality cult around himself. Under Xi, China has eliminated term limits for presidents, almost ensuring that he will get a third term in office and creating the possibility that he could become a Putinesque leader for life—which might make it easier for Xi to oversee a long-running influence campaign. He also has made good on his ambitions to re-establish tighter CCP control of the economy—even of some of the most successful private companies, like Jack Ma's Alibaba and the Ant Group fintech company.[84] Richard McGregor, a longtime China analyst now affiliated with the Lowy Institute in Sydney, notes that Xi codified his ambitions, making them crystal clear, as he renewed his oath of office at the Party Congress in 2017. In that speech, Xi declared, "Government, military, society, and schools, north, south, east, and west—the party is the leader of all."[85] Abandoning the collective leadership style of predecessors Hu Jintao and Jiang Zemin, the charismatic Xi has surrounded himself with a notably weak State Council of other top leaders.[86] To bolster the personality cult, Xi's face decorates public locales and private spaces all over China, another method of linking him visually to Mao, and the CCP has fetishized its top leader's ideas, known as "Xi Jinping Thought," to an absurd extent.[87] (Under Xi, in 2018, Beijing placed Xi Jinping Thought into China's constitution.[88]) This personality cult, however, has had major downsides as well. Xi's administration committed China to a zero-COVID strategy of eradicating the virus any time it appeared in the country, even as other states abandoned this approach in 2021 and 2022. As Xi stuck to this approach—to shift from it would mean admitting the greater leader, Xi, was wrong—he cratered China's economy, sealed off whole cities with massive lockdowns, sparked some popular dissent, damaged global supply chains, and drove away foreign businesses, among other effects.

Xi's administration also has both played on and continued to foster an increasingly sour, assertive Chinese nationalism, and this growing nationalism and Xi's assertiveness have pushed China toward a much more aggressive attempt at global influence. In the 1990s, after the chaos of the Tiananmen Square crackdown and the collapse of the Soviet Union, CCP leaders instituted a "patriotic education" campaign to teach Chinese students about the importance of the party and to help shore up the party's legitimacy.[89] Beijing also would place nationalism, along with economic growth, at the core of the party's appeal to the public. The curriculum that Beijing promoted in schools helped cultivate an increasingly nationalist mentality among younger Chinese, now a generation in its twenties, thirties, and forties.[90] Decades of education, mass media, and statements by top Chinese leaders promoting Chinese nationalism and portraying China as a victim of foreign states, combined with a lack of accurate sources of information entering China, have succeeded in fostering a prickly, intense nationalism, at least among Han Chinese.[91] The state has particularly succeeded in inculcating this sour nationalism among younger Chinese, who now tend to be more nationalist than older generations.[92]

Indeed, Xi has aimed for centralization of political and economic power and ensuring party dominance of all aspects of society. On his watch, Beijing has increased CCP control of private business and shifted more economic power to state companies and also made it harder for foreign firms to operate inside China. Xi has championed China's giant state enterprises while throttling the dynamic private sector, even though it contributes about two-thirds of the country's annual growth.[93] Xi has placed state enterprises at the center of an industrial plan, called "Made in China 2025," designed to upgrade a broad range of Chinese industries, making them world leaders.[94] In response, even the richest, most internationally famous Chinese tycoons and entertainers, and the biggest private Chinese firms, have taken steps to ingratiate themselves with Xi and the top leadership—and to signal that, if needed, their companies could be utilized internationally as tools of the CCP, giving China's global influence campaign the potential weight of the Chinese private sector as well. A 2020 study by the *Economist* found that while private Chinese companies used to downplay their links to the CCP, they have increasingly highlighted their fealty to Xi and the CCP. The study noted that "references by both state-owned firms and their private-sector peers to Mr. Xi's guidance have increased more than twenty-fold since 2017."[95]

Some Xi-era repression entails newer forms of brutality, and the Xi administration needs its global influence campaigns in part to protect China from criticism of this repression, and also potentially to export these ultramodern repressive tactics. Xi's administration has expanded the use of surveillance tools and other technology to monitor and control the population—a kind of cyber-authoritarianism, which China is perfecting, that could be a model for other autocrats and aspiring autocrats. Across Xi's China, the authorities are stepping up the use of facial recognition tools and imposing new barriers on the internet and social media—almost total barriers to any outside information during the period of the Ukraine war.[96] Increasingly, China's high-tech, effective social control makes the type of technology-assisted autocracy once imagined in dystopian science fiction such as *Minority Report* look like a gauzy Disney fantasy.

Xi is assertive on his own accord, but he also seems more paranoid than his recent predecessors about a global environment that is threatening to China's future, even in an era of broader U.S. retreat from international institutions and global leadership.[97] Such paranoia adds to the perceived need for a more aggressive global influence campaign, in a world in which the Xi administration sees China as surrounded by enemies. Xi traces this threatening global environment back to 1989. Like Deng (and, to a lesser degree, Jiang and Hu), Xi seems to view the demise of the Soviet Union—and the Color Revolutions of the 2000s—as instructive. A few months after becoming president, he reportedly told a closed-door meeting of senior CCP leaders that the party should learn from the "deeply profound" lessons of the former Soviet Union.[98] Xi reportedly asked the leaders, "Why did the Soviet Union disintegrate? Why did the Soviet Communist Party collapse? An important reason was that their ideals and convictions wavered."[99]

That global strategic environment, in the view of the Chinese leadership, continues to threaten the CCP's existence. Even more than his previous two predecessors, Xi seems convinced that China cannot shift the global strategic environment through internal reform and co-operation with other major powers. He seems to believe that, even if modest U.S.-China cooperation can be found, smoothing over some trade disputes, Beijing and Washington are destined for a modern-day version of the Cold War, which should also entail an influence campaign. In September 2019, at a peak of U.S.-China tensions over issues ranging from trade to protests in Hong Kong, Xi delivered a blistering speech to CCP colleagues.[100]

In it, he reminded them—about sixty times—that China must "struggle" to become more powerful, and he made clear that threats like the United States would not stop his administration or his goal to make China the leading power regionally and eventually globally.[101] He said: "For those risks or challenges that jeopardize the leadership of the Communist Party and China's socialist system; for those that endanger China's sovereignty, security and development interests; for those that undermine China's core interests and major principles; and for those that deter China's realization of a great national rejuvenation, we will wage a determined struggle against them as long as they are there. And we must win the struggle."[102]

China's soft and sharp power campaigns are central to winning this struggle, as is exporting the country's model of development. Xi has offered the most explicit endorsement of an exportable Chinese model of development of any leader in China's post-Mao era. Xi declared China's ambitions at the Party Congress in 2017, saying that the Chinese system offers "a new option for other countries and nations who want to speed up their development while preserving their independence."[103] In a speech to foreign leaders a few months later, he tempered his words somewhat, saying that China will not "export a China model." Yet at other times he has returned to the idea of China as a model of state capitalism, high growth, and technology-enabled social control, and his growing relationship with Russia, cemented by the Ukraine war, has suggested the two authoritarian powers would promote their alternative models to liberal democracy.[104]

Moscow's Sharp Power Efforts—and What They Showed China

Another factor was that, unlike in the charm offensive era, when China had no other model for sharp power, by the mid-2010s Russia's sharp power efforts demonstrated—to China and the world—how effective a sharp power campaign could be. And China has begun to learn from Russia's effort—sometimes directly, through meetings with Russian officials and other interactions with Russian sharp power specialists, and sometimes simply by watching Russian actions from afar.

Moscow has always relied on sharp power far more than Beijing. It cannot boast the ability to wield much soft power: there are no

globally famous Russian companies like Tencent or Alibaba, no internationally known brands like TikTok or Huawei or WeChat, no massive state outlay for cultural diplomacy or attracting foreign students
to Russian universities or promoting Russian-language studies abroad,
and certainly no successful model of development. Vladimir Putin's
social conservatism and illiberalism do enjoy some global appeal, particularly among more traditional conservatives in the United States,
Europe, and parts of Africa—though they have become less willing
to announce any affinity with the Kremlin since the Ukraine war.[105]
But the Kremlin's message remains out of touch with trends toward
greater social liberalism in much of the developed world. It has little
ability to wield soft power, which persuades and attracts other states,
and it has squandered much of what soft power it had, even among
countries and groups that were once sympathetic, with its invasion of
Ukraine.

Given these soft power limitations, the Kremlin focuses on coercive, manipulating, and covert sharp power, as well as, obviously,
outright military force: spreading disinformation, cultivating political
leaders in other states through secret deals, hacking and leaking information to embarrass democratic leaders, and many other destabilizing
efforts. These techniques can be traced back at least to the war between Russia and Georgia in 2008.[106] Moscow used an extensive disinformation campaign to claim that Georgia was committing major
human rights violations against Russian speakers inside Georgia.[107] At
that time, many leading democracies barely understood Moscow's use
of sharp power and were unprepared to respond. Russia then used this
disinformation campaign, to which Georgia (and also these external
actors) responded slowly, as justification for an invasion of the country,
and then an occupation of South Ossetia and Abkhazia, which broke
away from Georgia.[108]

Over the next decade, Russia made information warfare a cen-
terpiece of its overall strategic approach to both hot wars (like the
Ukraine conflict, where it has, however, been less successful in its disinformation efforts) and many so-called "gray-zone conflicts, while

increasingly shutting down all outlets, online or otherwise, that delivered factual information inside Russia." Gray-zone conflicts exist below the level of actual violence but are ways for states to use tactics like information warfare (as well as other strategies like espionage and forced technology transfers) to gain advantages against democratic powers.[109] And the Kremlin's sharp power tools became far more sophisticated. In elections in Europe and North America, Moscow used disinformation, a central sharp power tool, amplified on social media platforms through bots and other deceptive tools, to foment discord and foster hyperpartisanship. Sometimes, it used information warfare on social media platforms to support preferred candidates, while concealing that the campaigns originated in Russia. In other cases, the Kremlin covertly spread damaging information about candidates who were hostile to Moscow's aims.[110] Moscow even expanded its sharp power tactics in regions like Africa and Latin America, where Russia had been a minor player before the late 2010s and beyond.[111] Most infamously, the Kremlin oversaw a successful campaign to hack the Democratic National Committee during the 2016 U.S. presidential campaign.[112]

Even outside of election season, Russia has wielded sharp power in Africa, Europe, North America, and other regions. Yet it has clearly struggled with the information battle over Ukraine, in part because the U.S. administration smartly "pre-butted" Putin's disinformation efforts, which were further spread by Chinese media and other Chinese sources, by calling them out before Putin could spread his theories, and also because some of the disinformation efforts were shut down by major social media platforms—or just seemed so impossible given Russia's losses in the conflict.

But still, Russia has become particularly skilled in using sharp power to covertly influence elections. In an analysis of Russian interference efforts, Lucan Ahmad Way and Adam Casey of the University of Toronto found that Russia tried to influence the results in sixteen elections in Europe and North America between 2015 and 2018. They concluded that, in nine of these elections, the candidate that Russia preferred won, although it can be difficult to conclusively prove that Russia's meddling made the difference.[113]

Chinese officials and leaders clearly have taken notice of Russia's triumphs. To be sure, China had been utilizing coercive and covert sharp power in Taiwan and parts of Southeast Asia for decades. But Russia's striking victories in Europe and North America showed to Chinese leaders and officials how poorly prepared democracies were to address sharp power tactics. Overall, as we have seen, the two authoritarian giants are now closer, strategically, than at any point in decades. The partnership between Russia and China includes military cooperation, advanced arms sales, allying to combat liberal democracy and the West, and allying to support organizations to rival the Bretton Woods institutions.[114] An extensive analysis of Russia's behavior, prepared by the U.S. Department of Defense in an unclassified version and released before the Ukraine war, concluded that "Russia has entered into a strong alliance with China, one that is mutually beneficial."[115]

As part of this closer partnership, Beijing apparently has studied and learned from Moscow's use of disinformation and other means to covertly and coercively interfere in other states' politics and societies. In 2018, 2019, and 2020, for instance, China utilized disinformation campaigns in Hong Kong clearly modeled on Russian tactics, though they were not nearly as sophisticated.[116] Chinese officials also have said that Moscow's successes in altering elections in Europe and the United States made them think about how Beijing could replicate such victories and which Kremlin tools China should copy. The Lowy Institute's McGregor, in a *Washington Post* article on China's increasingly aggressive foreign policy posture, said that "one Chinese official told me in a moment of candor that Russia's success prompted them to take a fresh look at what tools they could use to infiltrate politics in places like the Philippines and Taiwan, either to tip the scale in favor of a preferred candidate or to undermine and discredit the democratic process."[117]

Some Southeast Asian and Taiwanese officials, observing China's growing range of influence tactics and how similar some of them are to the Kremlin's methods, are increasingly convinced that China is learning sharp power tactics directly from Moscow and are then applying them in China's neighborhood. Taiwan, the place most clearly affected by Chinese influence operations in the past, now faces an onslaught of disinformation. The V-Dem Institute, an organization based at the University of Gothenburg in Sweden that researches democracy and threats to democracy, has concluded that Taiwan is subjected to more disinformation from a foreign state than any other place in the world.[118] Many of China's specific disinformation strategies toward the island seem to be copied from Russian efforts and designed to promote specific pro-China candidates and tear down their rivals, while China also has begun to use its outlets to promote Russian disinformation in parts of the globe, especially about the Ukraine war, NATO, and the growing conflict between autocracies and democracies.[119] As it ramps up its efforts, China can call on a massive army of trolls and other contacts to promote disinformation. The cybersecurity firm Recorded Future, in a study comparing Russian and Chinese disinformation and other online influence strategies, found that China has a vast number of trolls at its disposal.[120]

Opportunity

There is another reason too that China is building a bigger and revamped soft power apparatus and a much bolder sharp power effort today: opportunity. Two major openings have presented themselves to Beijing. The first stems from the potential meltdown of some of the world's biggest democracies and the general political chaos across the globe.[121] The second is that China now has a chance to wield sharp power because most countries have been, at least until recently, unprepared to recognize it and combat it.

Chapter 5
Opportunities

Some of the motivations for China's expanded soft and sharp power campaigns today were the limits of its earlier charm offensive, the seismic changes in Chinese domestic politics during the era of Xi Jinping, the growing appeal of China's developmental model amidst democracies' domestic problems, and the simple fact that China is becoming a major global power—economically, strategically, and diplomatically. As a more dominant power, Beijing needs a bigger set of tools to protect and expand its strategic and economic reach, across a far broader array of regions, and to mitigate the growing anger in some countries over China's more assertive diplomacy and foreign policy choices.

But there is a fourth motivating factor behind this expanded campaign as well: opportunity—particularly, opportunity to wield sharp power. Many democracies seemed quite vulnerable to sharp power. And by the 2010s, China had greater resources to deploy on sharp power tactics that already had begun to show promise, and was learning from Russia's sharp power examples.

Having gained some experience with sharp power influence historically in places like Hong Kong, Taiwan, and Southeast Asian states like Singapore and Thailand, Beijing began to adopt these strategies more assertively, in a more widespread manner. Taiwan and Southeast Asian states like Singapore had long experience with Chinese sharp power efforts like covert strategies to infiltrate and influence local business associations, and had built up some government resources to assess and combat this sharp power influence. But by the 2010s, Beijing began to revamp its soft power strategies and aggressively deploy its sharp power in developed democracies. Many of these states, including leading democracies like the United States, Germany, Australia, New Zealand, and Canada, were unprepared for China's sharp power efforts. They were, essentially, soft targets. They may have had defenses against outright espionage and some cybersecurity defenses, but they had open, free political systems, media systems, and university systems, with few controls on foreign interference. And unlike Singapore or Taiwan, they had little historical memory of Chinese influence efforts and few people—at least at first—trained to combat them.

Russia Attracts the Attention

Russia's growing use of sharp power seems to have influenced Beijing in several ways. It offered a model for using sharp power to manipulate and influence developed states, and Beijing began to learn some of Moscow's specific strategies in areas like disinformation.

Russian activities may have had an additional benefit for China's buildup of sharp power: distracting the media and policymakers, at least in Europe and North America where Russia concentrated its efforts, from China's own increasing use of sharp power efforts. The Kremlin was not exactly shy about its activities (although they would sometimes issue pro forma denials), with Russian embassies trolling the 2016 Hillary Clinton campaign during the rollout of information that had been reportedly hacked by Russia, and it combined information warfare with brutal, James Bond–esque assassinations in foreign countries, like the United Kingdom, that were guaranteed to get massive press coverage. Moscow's use of sharp power drew widespread attention from democratic governments and international news outlets.[1] Throughout 2017 and much of 2018, the U.S. Special Counsel investigation into the 2016 election, as well as revelations of attempted Russian meddling in European elections, only added to the intensive media coverage of Russian sharp power. In conversations with congressional staffs, I found that until mid-2019, the group of people on Capitol Hill focused on Chinese soft and sharp power remained relatively small, and they were struggling to get up to speed on Beijing's strategies.

By 2020, 2021, and 2022, the pendulum had swung somewhat. The U.S. media, and many U.S. policymakers, had begun moving the other way, still paying attention to Russian activities but also increasingly highlighting China's influence activities, and particularly its sharp power efforts in areas like U.S. universities, some U.S. local and state politicians, and the U.S. Chinese-language and English-language media.[2] The Ukraine war further focused democratic policymakers' attention, drawing together democracies in Europe and North America, who imposed tough crackdowns, often bans, on Russian state media and also, much more aggressively scrutinized Chinese and Russian influence and information activities. Yet even as the Ukraine war raged, and even while U.S. opinion leaders, and increasingly their peers in the United Kingdom and some European states, began to pay more attention to Beijing's actions, they often failed to distinguish which Chinese actions were truly dangerous and which were not.

Even without the example of Russian sharp power, China's leaders could not have missed how unprepared the United States and many other countries were to address Chinese information and influence efforts for much of the 2010s. Some states were unprepared for Chinese efforts in part because Beijing until recently shied away from the obvious, often traceable and conspiratorial kinds of interventions Moscow has favored, like hacking emails and leaking them through famous proxies such as WikiLeaks.[3] China had not adopted these tactics because Beijing still, despite Xi's railing against the West, wants to be seen internationally as a responsible global leader—while, of course, engaging in sharp power efforts behind the scenes. If China pursued Moscow's flamethrower approach, Beijing would undermine its own efforts to look responsible, though China began to turn on the flamethrower in recent years. And unlike Russia, where oil and gas made up about 50 percent of all exports, at least before the Ukraine war and a ramp-up of measures against Russia's oil industry by the United States and some of its partners. Beijing is not usually interested in doing catastrophic damage to the economies of major democracies, just to weaken those states, though it does increasingly try to portray democracies as failing to provide public goods, in contrast to China's system—even as Beijing itself has undermined some of its own prosperity and innovation through its stifling authoritarianism, cult of personality rule, and zero-COVID strategy.[4] For instance, while Russia used a wide range of influence tactics to push Brexit, China never would have pushed for Brexit, or for economic meltdowns in other European states. (In 2015, Xi Jinping reportedly told British Prime Minister David Cameron, in private, that Beijing preferred that the United Kingdom remain in the European Union.[5]) Beijing wants to maintain these other large economies as major markets for Chinese goods and sources of technology transfer.[6]

China's sharp power approach is subtler, geared toward using covert, coercive, and manipulating actions without advertising them.[7] This subtler, often more pervasive approach is harder to detect than Russia's style, and frequently harder to combat.

Take, for instance, how Chinese officials increasingly cultivated state and local officials in the United States and other countries, with little monitoring or pushback until at least the early 2020s. (In this section, the term "state" refers to a subnational unit, such as a U.S. state, Canadian province, or Thai province.) As a report on Chinese influence efforts by Stanford's Hoover Institution concluded, "Most PRC attempts to influence American opinion and practices occur at the local level," where many officials know little about the ways in which Chinese sharp power may work and often do not think about the geostrategic consequences of decisions related to China.[8] A similar lack of preparation was visible among regional and local officials in Canada, the United Kingdom, and most of Europe as well. Few mayors, state legislators, state senators, or even governors in the United States and many other democratic countries employ staff members with the background and time to investigate Chinese influence operations, or to develop expertise about China at all, other than perhaps learning about how to promote trade with China. (There are, of course, exceptions. The mayors of cities like Los Angeles, New York, and Tokyo have large staffs, including many people working for them with experience in foreign policy.[9]) Even when national-level governments pay closer attention to Chinese influence activities, as began to happen in the United States and other democracies in 2019 and 2020, this attention rarely filters down to scrutiny of local and state-level politicians. Chinese officials have cultivated local and state leaders—not only in the United States but also in many other countries—in part because there are fewer safeguards on foreign influence efforts with cities or states.[10]

In one such alleged operation, eventually revealed by the news outlet *Axios*, a Chinese operative developed extensive ties to local politicians in the U.S. Bay Area and other parts of California, coming into contact with many of the biggest players in Northern California while also attending major conferences for U.S. mayors, and launching romantic relationships with at least two midwestern U.S. mayors as well.[11]

Other important institutions in developed democracies, from universities to companies to major media outlets to national governments, also seemed unprepared to deal with Chinese sharp power until recently, a vulnerability noticed by Chinese officials. A detailed report by the U.S. Senate Permanent Subcommittee on Investigations found that many U.S. universities had allowed Confucius Institutes to be set up on their campuses with minimal oversight and little knowledge of the Chinese governance of the Confucius Institute program, even though the institutes can come with strings that compromise academic freedom—and even though many researchers believe the United Front Work Department (UFWD) ultimately oversees or heavily influences Confucius Institutes.[12] It further found that from 2004 to 2019, the U.S. Department of Education offered no guidance to universities on how to handle foreign funding and did not conduct regular oversight to see how these foreign dona-tions were being used.[13] (The Department of Education began to more closely scrutinize foreign funding of universities in 2019, but it remains unclear how thoroughly they will do this.[14]) Even as Washington began to more closely watch U.S. universities for how they raise foreign money and the Department of Justice began an ini-tiative that scrutinized potential Chinese espionage in areas of tech-nology and other types of intellectual property, this scrutiny mainly focused on federally sponsored science and math programs, though it began to have an effect on Confucius Institutes by 2021 and 2022, as they started to close in the United States and some other democracies. (The China Initiative was ended by the Biden administration, in part because many of the cases it tried to make failed, and in part because it was perceived by some researchers as unfairly targeting Chinese-Americans and Chinese permanent residents.)[15]

The quality of compliance at U.S., Canadian, and European uni-versities and some think tanks also varies widely.[16] Compliance cen-ters at some universities and think tanks analyze potential gifts from national and foreign donors and ensure that these gifts do not com-promise academic freedoms and are given in a manner consistent with national laws. But at some universities, particularly those with weak central administration and strong peer pressure to attract donors, top university leaders may not even know what deals some parts of their schools are making with foreign donors.[17]

For their part, U.S. public universities (with some exceptions) tend to at least consider how accepting funds from China or other au-thoritarian donors might affect academic discourse and the univer-sities' reputation. In 2017–18, the University of Texas at Austin's new China policy center planned to accept a donation from the China–United States Exchange Foundation (CUSEF), which is headed by the former Hong Kong chief executive Tung Chee-hwa. CUSEF has tight links to the Chinese Communist Party (CCP) and is extensively reported to be a part of China's UFWD influence efforts.[18] (The University of Texas already had a Confucius Institute on campus, but the new center was supposed to focus on policy issues, not language studies.) Tung was vice chair of the Chinese People's Political Consultative Conference, which is supposed to be an advisory body for the Chinese government but is essentially the national-level institution of the UFWD.[19] Bethany Allen-Ebrahimian, one of the most experienced reporters covering Chinese influence, noted that CUSEF is "a registered foreign agent [i.e., registered by the U.S. Department of Justice] bankrolled by a high-ranking Chinese government official with close ties to a sprawling Chinese Communist Party apparatus that handles influence operations abroad."[20] Eventually, under pressure from within the ranks of professors and also from Texas Senator Ted Cruz, the China center rejected the donation.[21]

Overall, U.S. public universities seem to have a higher degree of skepticism toward foreign donations than many private universities and other research organizations, like many think tanks. At private universities, which are not subject to freedom-of-information requirements of the type that the University of Texas faces, there is often far less transparency. While the University of Texas at Austin rejected the CUSEF funding, private universities like Johns Hopkins University and American University, among others, have accepted it, as have prominent think tanks including the Center for American Progress, the Atlantic Council, and the Center for Strategic and International Studies, among others.[22]

In Europe and other democratic regions, universities and think tanks also have struggled to come up with clear guidance for how to deal with donors linked to Beijing, although some democracies have begun to institute new legislation scrutinizing foreign donations to universities, foreign investment in media, and foreign investment in information technology. (Some more authoritarian European states, like Hungary, even are encouraging Chinese universities to set up campuses in their countries, which raises the prospect of these universities being used as propaganda tools.[23]) In Britain, media outlets and investigative researchers have revealed that few British universities and research institutions have clear policies about how to comprehend, monitor, and potentially stop funding from China or research cooperation with China that might be linked to the CCP or potentially have worrisome national security implications.[24] These universities may now begin to develop such policies, in part because Britain, with a new Economic Crime Bill, is coming to terms with how much Russian money has flowed into the country, including to universities, but the United Kingdom has not yet developed clear policies on Chinese funding for universities and research institutions.[25]

Meanwhile, within the U.S. government, in Canada, and in most of Europe, even as some politicians began to pay more attention to China's influence tactics, top leaders often acted slowly. In 2016, Congress allocated additional funding under the 2017 National Defense Authorization Act to expand the State Department's Global Engagement Center (GEC), which is supposed to identify and counter propaganda, primarily from Russia but also from China and other actors.[26] However, the State Department initially did not request the money or make an effort to spend it, nor did it make an effort to hire and expand the office's ability to counter propaganda, undermining the initial efforts to staff up and combat Chinese sharp power strategies.[27] Finally, well into the Trump presidency, the GEC began to expand, bolstering its efforts to monitor and combat Chinese and Russian propaganda, hiring more staff, and beginning to develop an effective response.[28]

Until recently, European and UK politicians also mostly remained focused on Russian influence, not Chinese activities, and they have stepped up that focus on Russian influence in 2022 as the Ukraine war has revealed the extent of Russian investment in the United Kingdom and some European countries.[29] In collaboration with the Global Public Policy Institute, the Mercator Institute, a leading German think tank, noted that "Beijing's efforts have received much less scrutiny than the efforts of Putin's Russia," that "Europe's gates are wide open" to Chinese influence, and that Europe has a wide range of business and political enablers of Chinese sharp power tactics.[30] By 2019, when the European Commission declared China a "systemic rival" to Europe, European officials were just beginning to investigate Chinese courting of European right-wing populists, who have ascended into leadership positions across a range of Central and Eastern European states.[31] More broadly, most politicians at the European Parliament, and in the United Kingdom and member-states of the European Union, still had little understanding of how Beijing tries to wield information and more traditional influence tactics. In 2020, recognizing this lack of knowledge, a group of Conservative members of the British Parliament formed a group to research and understand Chinese activities, and some politicians in continental states took similar measures, but by then they were already playing catch-up.[32]

China Notices Other Democracies' Blind Spots

With a few exceptions, countries in developing regions were even less prepared than wealthy democracies to combat Chinese influence. Few African, Eastern European, Latin American, or South Asian states have laws circumscribing foreign interference (including foreign money) in politics, like the U.S. federal law banning political contributions from foreign nationals or the new Australian laws limiting foreign involvement in politics.[33] Many are weak democracies with few checks on corruption of any kind, politicians who have no interest in investigating any dirty dealing, and anticorruption authorities who have their hands full dealing with domestic graft unrelated to China. Even in the Czech Republic, one of the most prosperous countries in its region, President Miloš Zeman built ties to Beijing in ways that potentially opened his government up to influence in its internal affairs; only in recent years has the Czech Republic begun to push back against Chinese influence.[34] Zeman allowed the head of CEFC China Energy, a Chinese company with close links to the Chinese government, to be his close advisor; this is as if the prime minister of the United Kingdom picked a Russian oil oligarch to advise 10 Downing Street.[35] Meanwhile, a prominent Czech university established a Czech-Chinese center for research that wound up closely collaborating with the Chinese embassy in Prague, until it was exposed by the media.[36] Slovak universities also had few safeguards on cooperation with Chinese partners that could be problematic for national security reasons or were closely linked to the CCP.[37]

And these countries are all democracies, or quasi-democracies, with relatively strong democratic institutions and some degree of the rule of law. In less democratic states—weak democracies like Serbia, hybrid political regimes like Tanzania and Zambia or Hungary under Viktor Orban, or autocracies like Cambodia and Myanmar—China's sharp power doesn't come up against many safeguards at all. Indeed, it is even welcomed by politicians, like Cambodia's Hun Sen, who want to copy Chinese methods and utilize Chinese political links and technology to maintain dominance of their own political systems.[38]

Struggling Democracies

If the increasingly obvious vulnerability of other states offered a first major opportunity for China to wield sharp power, the growing unpopularity of democracy and free market capitalism in some areas of the world provided a second one. If democracy struggled in the 2000s, by the 2010s it had hit the canvas, gasping and clutching its bruises.

The 2008–09 global economic crisis erupted outward from the overleveraged and often rotten U.S. financial system, and even citizens in many developed countries began questioning capitalism's core tenets. In the years after the crisis, many young Americans embraced aspects of socialism, and populist leaders rose to power in Europe, the United States, and parts of Asia.[39] The populists rose while demonizing elites, including financial elites.[40] In 2019, one Gallup study showed that four in ten Americans would rather live in a socialist country than a capitalist one.[41] This was a striking finding given that socialism had long been a loaded word in U.S. politics, linked to

U.S.-Soviet Cold War competition, tarred by its associations with the twentieth century's brutal communist leaders, and regularly used as an epithet by U.S. conservatives.[42] A similar skepticism about free market capitalism spread in other nations as well.[43]

Meanwhile, in the 2010s more states regressed from democracy; in its 2021 Freedom in the World index, Freedom House noted that global democracy had declined for fifteen years in a row.[44] By 2014, Thailand was run by a junta that created the most repressive Thai military regime in decades.[45] In Myanmar, just three years after the party of the Nobel laureate Aung San Suu Kyi took over the government, the country witnessed a crackdown on free speech and press freedom and a genocidal campaign against the Rohingya, a religious and ethnic minority; Suu Kyi was then removed in a 2021 military coup that led to further repression and an outright failed state.[46] In Brazil, Hungary, India, Mexico, the Philippines, Poland, Serbia, Sri Lanka, and Turkey, among other countries, illiberal populists won free and fair elections and then began decimating democratic norms and institutions—a process made easier by the novel coronavirus, which often allowed illiberal leaders to grab more power during states of emergency. In other countries, from Benin to Bolivia to El Salvador to Tanzania to Zambia, leaders who were democratically elected—and not populists—used various tactics to stifle opposition, sometimes with the help of the military.[47] Overall, for the first time in decades, public opinion data by the mid-2010s suggested that authoritarianism was becoming an attractive global alternative to democracy, including in nations that had been democratic for decades (or centuries). Research by the political scientists Yascha Mounk and Roberto Foa in 2016, for instance, revealed that a plummeting percentage of young people around the world believed that it was important for a country to be governed democratically.[48] During the 2010s, the United States, meanwhile, fell from being ranked as a full democracy to being ranked as a flawed democracy in the Economist Intelligence Unit's annual Democracy Index, a U.S. democratic regression found in studies by other organizations like Freedom House.[49] The United States' score in Freedom House's index fell even further in 2021 and 2022, amidst a highly partisan environment surrounding the 2020 presidential election, the outgoing president's claim that he had actually won the election, and worrying signs of collapsing public faith in the U.S. electoral system.[50] Other prominent democracies too, like India, Indonesia, and Brazil, fell in Freedom House's annual index as well, signifying their democratic backsliding.

The coronavirus pandemic exacerbated this democratic backsliding, as some illiberal leaders grabbed more power under the guise of public health emergencies, and even some of the most developed democracies initially imposed new restrictions on civil society and other freedoms, although most eased these restrictions within a year or two into the pandemic, while China and some other authoritarian states did not.[51] Research by Freedom House documented that democracy had weakened in eighty countries since the onset of the novel coronavirus, in part because of these initial restrictions, though in some countries those temporary restrictions were eventually removed.[52]

The abdication of international leadership by democratic powers came from heads of government and increasingly nationalistic parties in democracies, and the pandemic exacerbated trends of looking inward in many countries—especially in China but also in many leading democracies, at least until the Ukraine war snapped some prominent democracies out of their foreign policy isolation. In Europe, support for nationalist political parties grew throughout the 2010s, leading to issues like Brexit and the dominance of Italian politics by nationalist, populist parties; the coronavirus pandemic sparked new rises of nationalism across the continent. Though nationalist and populist parties were unsuccessful in gaining some of their biggest goals, like winning the presidency of France, even when they did not achieve these results, their presence shifted national debates toward their populist, often isolationist, views—though these were undermined somewhat as much of Europe united against Russia.

In the Donald J. Trump administration, the White House not only embraced some isolationist foreign policies but also demonstrated a lack of interest in soft power, a major part of an active foreign policy. In March 2017, Office of Management and Budget Director Mick Mulvaney released the Trump White House's first budget. Although Congress allocates funds, the White House budget serves to broadly showcase a president's policy priorities. The document proposed a 28 percent reduction in the State Department budget, including deep cuts to foreign aid. "It is not a soft power budget," Mulvaney told reporters. "This is a hard-power budget, and that was done intentionally. The president clearly wants to send a message to our allies and to our potential adversaries that this is a strong-power administration."[53] Congress eventually resisted most of these cuts, but the White House tried to slash aid and other soft power tools again. In 2019, it even attempted an unusual end-around to bypass Congress's power of the purse, ordering a review of foreign aid that Congress had already allocated and attempting to freeze the funds at the same time.[54] (Under congressional pressure, the White House killed the plan.[55]) The White House also fired many of the top diplomats in the State Department and then left their positions unfilled, sinking morale at Foggy Bottom.[56]

The White House took a similarly dim view of U.S. state-sponsored soft power tools besides the diplomatic corps and foreign aid. In a speech in 2019, Trump talked about several leading U.S.-sponsored state broadcasters, like Radio Free Europe and Voice of America, as if they no longer existed and suggested that the United States needed a new state broadcaster.[57] His choice to lead the parent organization for the U.S.-sponsored state broadcasters, Michael Pack, would in 2020 attempt to undermine the editorial freedom of outlets like Voice of America and to simply gut some of these state broadcasters, firing their news chiefs in a purge in June 2020.[58]

Given these developments, including democratic regression in the United States, it was probably not surprising that measures of U.S. soft power showed a decline. In the comprehensive 2019 Soft Power index, cowritten by the Portland consultancy group and the University of Southern California Center on Public Diplomacy, the United States fell to fifth place.[59] (At the time this book was written, the 2019 index was the most recent one that had been released.) In 2016, the United States had ranked at the top of the list.[60]

The breakdowns in democracies, powerful states' disinterest in wielding their own soft power, and the absence of clear global leadership all offered chances for China to wield both soft and sharp power. As democracies struggled, a vacuum emerged for Beijing to restore its image, to sell itself as a responsible leader, and to tout its model of development to populations around the world—particularly in the early period of the COVID-19 pandemic, as Beijing got its epidemic under control at home and the virus wreaked havoc on Europe and the United States. (Later, Beijing's disastrous zero-COVID strategy undermined its global influence, isolated itself from the world, hindered its economy, and generally proved disastrous.) Beijing could again present itself as the adult in the room on important international issues, such as public health and climate change, at a time when few other countries seemed up to, or interested in, the challenge of leadership.

There is a link too between these two opportunities presented to China. Democratic powers' internal political divisions and deteriorating political systems have made it harder for them to develop coherent responses to foreign influence—or, really, to push through important legislation on most issues, especially in the United States, where partisan polarization is at highs not seen since the nineteenth century. With a few exceptions, like Australia, Singapore, and Taiwan, democracies had not until recent years developed extensive responses to foreign influence that enjoy the support of all political parties. In the highly partisan environments consuming many democracies, even issues related to national security, once a preserve of cross-party cooperation, have become highly polarized. The United States and the European Union have begun to develop such a response, but their efforts to respond to Chinese influence and information tactics are still plagued with challenges—and until the late 2010s and early 2020s, these responses barely existed at all. In other words, opportunity two, democracies' political dysfunction, made it easier, for a time, for China to exploit opportunity one, democracies' lack of readiness to combat foreign influence.

China—and Russia—prefer it this way, of course. The autocratic powers woo and potentially co-opt parties within democratic political systems—the Alternative for Germany (AfD), the KMT in Taiwan, the Lega Nord in Italy, Fidesz in Hungary, and others—so that democracies' consensus toward China or Russia splinters, although in the wake of the Ukraine war some of those parties are shedding their links to the Kremlin and desperately scrambling to whitewash their past praise of Vladimir Putin, though not necessarily to China.[61] (Some are not even going that far; Fidesz continues to harbor clear sympathies for Russia and its leadership, despite Hungary's position within the European Union.) Or they aggressively court one or two powerful political leaders—like former Philippine president Rodrigo Duterte and current Philippine president Ferdinand Marcos Jr and Czech Republic president Miloš Zeman—who, by themselves, can prevent any consensus from emerging on how to address foreign meddling. What's more, in too many democracies, leaders who may have benefited from foreign influence, or who simply are unsure how to respond, stoke partisanship to conceal their weak responses or how they actually sought foreign help for political gain.

Australia and New Zealand: Canaries

Two of the biggest opportunities for expanded influence efforts were Australia and New Zealand. There were places where China modified its soft power efforts and drastically increased its sharp power strategies in the 2010s. Indeed, as the 2010s went on, China relied even more on sharp power generally and demonstrated an ability to learn from its sharp power efforts and improve them over time. Beijing bolstered its sharp power strategies in Australia and New Zealand even as Canberra and Wellington struggled at first to focus on Chinese

influence efforts and remained distracted in part by their own domestic politics, which included in Australia constant in-fighting
within ruling parties, as prime ministers launched internal coups and
toppled each other. Yet China's influence efforts in Australia and New
Zealand, as we will see, eventually came to light and backfired in
some ways against Beijing; the two countries adopted tougher measures against foreign interference, and their experiences helped wake
up other states to how quickly Beijing was building its influence
apparatus and particularly its sharp power.[62]

Australia and New Zealand long have represented prosperity, progressive government, and strong democracies; they are usually ranked
as far stronger democracies than the United States and most countries in Western Europe—not to mention other states in Southeast
Asia or Eastern Europe, like the Czech Republic, where Beijing also
was building up influence efforts. In analyses like the Economist
Intelligence Unit's annual Democracy Index, for instance, Australia
and New Zealand regularly rank as two of the freest democracies in
the world.[63] Indeed, Australia and New Zealand leaders pride themselves on standing up for rights, democracy, and discretion in intelligence affairs. The countries are members of the Five Eyes group,
one of the closest intelligence-sharing networks in the world, linking
Australia and New Zealand with Canada, the United Kingdom, and
the United States.[64] The two countries also have demonstrated highly
effective political leadership on some issues in recent years, even as
they failed, for a time, to implement thorough, all-of-government
measures to block Chinese influence. When the novel coronavirus
began to spread globally in early 2020, Australia and New Zealand
imposed some of the toughest lockdowns in the world—and got
strong buy-in from the population in each country for their measures, which worked at least for a time, although both states eventually
relaxed their measures.

Yet Australia and New Zealand still had major blind spots to
Chinese influence tactics, at least in the mid-2010s. Australia had
six prime ministers between 2010 and 2020, as Australian politicians

knifed each other in the (figurative) back within their own political coalitions, causing administrations to rise and fall. Although most of the Australian transfers of power in this decade took place within the same parliamentary political coalitions, the in-fighting undermined foreign policy continuity and focus, including on issues related to China, now Australia's dominant trading partner.[65] In New Zealand, meanwhile, political in-fighting was not necessarily an impediment to tougher scrutiny and action against Chinese influence efforts. Instead, New Zealand's political establishment—wary of alienating the biggest trading partner of a small country almost totally reliant on trade and potentially distracted by the sinecures many top New Zealand politicians were receiving at Chinese companies—remained in willful denial about China's ability to covertly and coercively use sharp power in New Zealand.[66]

New Zealand

With the two democracies distracted or essentially in denial about growing Chinese influence efforts, Beijing used sharp power to penetrate Australian and New Zealand politics, academia, and society. As Anne-Marie Brady of the University of Canterbury in Christchurch noted in an extensive analysis of Chinese penetration of New Zealand, the government in Wellington for years in the 2010s allowed Beijing to steadily gain power to shape New Zealand policymaking, largely through sharp power influence, taking virtually no actions in response.[67] Indeed, Brady showed that the CCP has, through the use of informants, financial support, and other types of supervision, thoroughly and mostly covertly penetrated New Zealand ethnic Chinese organizations and created pro-Beijing ethnic Chinese organizations to counterbalance those ethnic Chinese groups that remain less pro-Beijing.[68] The pro-Beijing groups, she notes, usually affiliate with the UFWD; they increasingly dominate discourse in the country's ethnic Chinese community.[69] According to Brady, Beijing also has gained de facto control of most Chinese-language news outlets in the country, and Beijing's representatives in New Zealand use local Chinese student associations to try to shape pro-Beijing opinion and shut down critical discussions about China on New Zealand campuses. She shows that Chinese groups also have funneled money into New Zealand politics, and the Chinese government has built multiple links to top New Zealand politicians and business leaders, in part by orchestrating cushy postretirement sinecures for some of them at Chinese state firms.[70] In addition, Beijing has stepped up people-to-people links between Chinese enterprises, many of them state owned or with state connections, and New Zealand companies.

Beijing has used these links in several ways. Beijing's growing influence over Chinese-language outlets, Chinese community associations, and Chinese university groups in New Zealand has allowed the Chinese government to utilize these actors as, essentially, agents of China's foreign policy. Community leaders sympathetic to Beijing organize large numbers of pro-China events, particularly in Auckland, that attract the attention of politicians and counterprotest against New Zealand organizations that hold demonstrations when Chinese top officials visit the country.[71] The Xi administration further has pushed for ethnic Chinese in other countries sympathetic to Beijing to become highly involved in local politics, running for office and becoming significant donors.[72] While the ethnic Chinese community makes up a minority of New Zealand citizens, discourse within the community has broader effects on New Zealand policy—community leaders play a vital role in informing New Zealand politicians and shape broader New Zealand public opinion. Ethnic Chinese businesspeople and community leaders, including some Chinese nationals (not New Zealand citizens), and China-based companies have in the past decade become some of the most important sources of donations to and organizing efforts for both of New Zealand's major political parties. (They seemed to favor the National Party for much of the 2010s, perhaps because it was the party in power at that time, but give to both parties.[73]) Politicians take note. As prominent politicians from the National Party, one of the country's two leading parties, increasingly echoed Beijing's policy positions in the 2010s, and some National Party leaders apparently accepted questionable donations Chinese businesspeople, the National Party boosted its share of ethnic Chinese voters in New Zealand, taking 75 percent of the ethnic Chinese vote in New Zealand's 2014 national elections.[74] This boost in votes provided important margins in some parliamentary seats.

Meanwhile, New Zealand politicians with growing links to Chinese donors and Chinese firms have parroted China's view of its domestic and foreign policies, both to the New Zealand media and to media in other countries. Some New Zealand companies with close commercial ties to Chinese firms, and New Zealand business leaders who have taken jobs at prominent Chinese companies, also increasingly have served as mouthpieces for Beijing's policy perspectives, echoing China's views on Xinjiang, Hong Kong, Beijing's assertive approach to regional waters, and many other issues.[75] (Indeed, as Brady notes, Beijing often utilizes local business leaders, employed at Chinese firms or China-backed entities like research organizations, to promote Beijing's policy positions.[76]) This is a boon for China; prominent politicians and business leaders from New Zealand were delivering China's preferred messages, and New Zealand citizens were much more likely to give these messages a sympathetic listening coming from a New Zealand political leader than coming from Xi Jinping or another top Chinese official.

The ethnic Chinese community in New Zealand increasingly provides candidates for higher office as well. One prominent New Zealand member of parliament, Yang Jian, worked in Chinese military intelligence for some fifteen years before immigrating to New Zealand and becoming a citizen in 2004, giving him obvious potential links to the CCP; he also taught in China at a prominent school known for preparing Chinese intelligence members.[77] Yang at one point said he had been a member of the CCP in the past but was not a member any longer. (Yang had hidden these details from any public profile in English.[78]) Yang was a member of the National Party, which was in power between 2008 and 2017; he was, as Anne-Marie Brady has noted, picked to run for office in part so that the National Party could continue wooing the important ethnic Chinese vote.[79]

Between 2014 and 2016, Yang sat on the Parliamentary Select Committee for Foreign Affairs, Defense and Trade, which played a major role in New Zealand's China policy.[80] As a member of parliament, he did not need security clearance to view sensitive and classified information, including information related to China. With his background, if he had applied for a job in the New Zealand government instead of running for parliament, he almost surely would have been denied a security clearance. Yet Yang seemingly played a major role in shaping New Zealand's China policy when the National Party was in power, as Wellington became increasingly unwilling to challenge China on issues ranging from rights abuses to its tough approach to the South China Sea. He also personally accompanied National Party prime ministers in meetings with senior Chinese leaders and served as a substantial fundraiser and organizer for the National Party within the New Zealand ethnic Chinese community.[81]

Yang also seemed to involve other top New Zealand politicians in questionable meetings with Chinese officials, where they too parroted China's views on a wide range of issues. Yang organized a 2019 trip to China by National Party leader Simon Bridges, apparently with little consultation with New Zealand officials focused on China; Bridges also built links with a number of Chinese donors.[82] On the trip, Bridges met with China's former domestic public security chief (in other words, meeting the head of the secret police), lavished somewhat sycophantic praise on the CCP during an interview in China with China Global Television Network (CGTN), and also essentially avoided offering even the mildest questions about Beijing's crackdown in Hong Kong, departing from the New Zealand government position of expressing concerns about increasing rights abuses in the Special Administrative Region.[83] With these comments, Bridges simply joined other top New Zealand politicians and business leaders in echoing Beijing's language on issues of importance to China.

Another National Party member of parliament, Todd McClay, received $100,000 in donations from one such Chinese-owned company.[84] He then publicly echoed Beijing's rhetoric on issues like Xinjiang, downplaying rights abuses against Uighurs and claiming that prison camps in Xinjiang were "vocational training centers," the same rhetoric used by the Chinese government.[85]

New Zealand offered up little defense at first to China's influence operations in the 2010s. Beyond Brady's academic exposure of Chinese sharp power in New Zealand, foreign intelligence officials warned Wellington as well. In 2018, as Brady noted, Canada's national intelligence service produced a lengthy report on the implications of China's global rise and influence activities.[86] The document cited New Zealand as a textbook example of China's aggressive influence strategies, declaring that China saw the country "as a soft underbelly through which to access Five Eyes intelligence."[87] Perhaps most alarmingly, the Canadians concluded that "the PRC has not had to pressure New Zealand. . . . Successive New Zealand governments have actively courted it."[88] Peter Mattis, a former Central Intelligence Agency analyst specializing in China issues, told a congressional committee that New Zealand's membership in Five Eyes should be reconsidered, given what he believed was China's apparent penetration of the country.[89] Mattis's comments sparked a furious response in New Zealand—the president of the ruling Labor Party claimed that he had no idea what Mattis was talking about when he discussed Chinese influence in New Zealand.

Yet Wellington's guard remained down for a long time, which Chinese officials could not help but recognize. After Anne-Marie Brady and some New Zealand investigative reporters exposed the extent of Chinese influence in the country's media and information market and politics, the revelations detonated like a bomb among a small circle of political and defense elites. In conversations with New Zealand opinion leaders after Brady's revelations, I found that they

regularly discussed Brady's work and its charges. Some clearly believed that Brady's detailed accusations, and concerns raised by other
countries about penetration of New Zealand, were accurate. But for
years, senior politicians from both major parties in Wellington seemed
uninterested in self-scrutiny, determined not to dig too deeply into
stories of Chinese influence.

For most of the 2010s, and even after the National Party lost to the
Labor Party in 2017, top New Zealand politicians avoided looking too
hard at Beijing's influence activities or talking about them in public.
When New Zealand Prime Minister and Labor Party leader Jacinda
Ardern, first elected in 2017, faced questions about the challenge of
Chinese influence, she for years remained uncharacteristically dismis-
sive and bland for a leader known for bold stances on many other
issues, like confronting online extremism; promoting a progressive ap-
proach to family leave; and, later on, addressing COVID-19.[90] The
New Zealand parliamentary committee tasked with investigating
foreign influence initially refused to meet with Brady, the country's
leading expert on China's sharp power tactics.[91] When asked by the
Washington Post about China interfering in New Zealand politics,
Ardern seemed reluctant to even venture a substantive comment. "We
are aware of issues of foreign interference," she told the *Washington
Post.* "We've got good infrastructure, but we just need to make sure it's
keeping pace."[92] According to Brady, Wellington also looked the other
way as China acquired from New Zealand "military technology and
knowhow, which appear to be in breach of New Zealand's laws [and]
international obligations."[93] Meanwhile, National Party leader Bridges
initially defended his controversial 2019 trip to China and Yang Jian
emailed National Party members to tell them he was "pleased" with
Bridges's itinerary in China.[94]

Finally, near the end of 2019, amidst substantial pressure from
allies and some New Zealanders concerned about Wellington's vulnerability, and amidst obvious, growing authoritarianism in China,
Wellington applied increasing scrutiny to China's activities within
New Zealand. Rebecca Kitteridge, director of the New Zealand

Security Intelligence Service, the main national intelligence agency, told a parliamentary inquiry into foreign influence activities that the intelligence agency had "seen activities by state actors that concern us" and that "motivated state actors are adept at finding weaknesses or grey areas to help them to covertly build and project influence."[95] In a confidential cable written from the British High Commission in Canberra (and colorfully named "Australia and New Zealand Approaches to China: Same Meat, Different Gravy"), diplomats in the United Kingdom's embassy in Australia noted that there was a growing "sense of vulnerability to [Chinese] sharp power" both in Australia and in New Zealand.[96]

The Ardern administration took an even tougher line toward China over the following three years. It banned large foreign donations in its political system. Although Wellington clearly stated that this ban was done after thorough analysis and singled out no country in particular, China was the most obvious major foreign donor. New Zealand also began to scrutinize other Chinese influence tactics more closely and to investigate the details of many political donations, although again New Zealand leaders and officials were careful to note that these investigations of political donations strictly followed New Zealand law and did not target any one country.[97] The country's Serious Fraud Office reportedly began to investigate donations to both the National Party and the Labor Party following allegations of improper donations to the National Party from a Chinese businessman, Zhang Yikun, whom Brady, among others, has said was part of UFWD operations.[98] In early 2020, the Serious Fraud Office charged Zhang Yikun with corruption.[99] (The office also charged three other people with corruption at the same time, although it did not file any charges against Bridges.) New Zealand's Security Intelligence Service reportedly began analyzing Yang Jian, and he eventually decided not to stand for re-election in national elections held in 2020 and dominated by Ardern's party.[100] Leaders of all of New Zealand's political parties also began to step up pressure on members to assess links to China. Still, even with these reforms, the foreign influence law contained loopholes, like allowing foreign-owned companies registered in New Zealand to make political donations.[101]

As more revelations of China's influence activities in New Zealand came to light and Beijing's regional diplomacy became more belligerent in 2020, 2021, and 2022, New Zealand lawmakers also subtly began to shift Wellington's approach to China beyond applying stricter scrutiny of influence activities. Beyond stepping up scrutiny of foreign interference in New Zealand politics, the Ardern administration gradually became more critical of China's rights abuses, including in places like Hong Kong and Xinjiang, and suspended its extradition treaty with Beijing because of the implementation of the new Hong Kong national security law.[102] The Ardern government, with some support from the opposition as well, also has initiated a de facto ban of Chinese telecommunications giant Huawei from New Zealand's 5G buildout. Wellington also has become more openly critical, in defense papers and other public statements, of China's buildup in regional waters and other assertive regional military decisions.[103] Wellington further supported Australia's renewed efforts to provide a counterweight to China's increasingly dominant diplomatic presence in many South Pacific states, although it did not join the new United States–Australia–United Kingdom trilateral security partnership, which will provide Australia with nuclear-powered submarines and which is seen as a direct move by Australia (and the United States and the United Kingdom) to confront China; New Zealand has not allowed nuclear-powered submarines in its waters for decades.

The Ardern government also has begun to consider limits on foreign influence over the local media. It did so after Anne-Marie Brady's research into Chinese influence activities and extensive other revelations of Beijing trying to use its control of local Chinese-language media.[104]

Australia

Beijing's influence tactics have been equally extensive in Australia and also relied largely on covert and often coercive sharp power. Most of

China's Australia activities, in fact, were "designed to remain hidden from public view, often arranged indirectly through proxies, in order to create a layer of plausible deniability," noted one extensive investigation into influence activities in Australia by the Center for Strategic and International Studies.[105] As in New Zealand, the Chinese government has essentially gained control of most Chinese-language media in Australia. In some cases, Beijing has achieved this control because advertisers apply pressure on any Chinese-language outlets critical of Chinese government policies. In other cases, pro-Beijing businesspeople like Chau Chak Wing, a billionaire real estate magnate who emigrated from China to Australia decades ago, have in recent years established Australian Chinese-language media outlets sympathetic to Beijing or bought up existing, respected outlets and altered their coverage. In 2004, for instance, Chau funded the creation of the *Australia New Express Daily*, a New South Wales–based Chinese-language publication that published clearly pro-Beijing content. In 2009, he told the *Age*, a Melbourne-based publication, that Beijing "found this newspaper [the *Australia New Express Daily*] very commendable because we never have any negative reporting [about China]."[106]

Australian news outlets that criticize China are punished harshly. After one Australian-Chinese newspaper published a story about organ harvesting in China, for example, one of the French accommodations giant Sofitel's Sydney hotels canceled a promotional deal with the Chinese paper.[107] "Our newspaper was invited by the Sofitel marketing team to be in their lobby as reading material for Chinese travelers," the newspaper said in a statement. "However, after a few weeks, Sofitel received a call from the Chinese Consulate asking them to remove our newspaper or face financial consequences. Sofitel does a lot of business with China."[108]

Australian investigative journalists from the *Sydney Morning Herald* further reported that the Chinese government applied pressure on Chinese companies to place advertisements in Australian Chinese-language outlets perceived to be sympathetic to Beijing or to pull ads from outlets that displeased the Chinese government.[109] Memos from the Sydney local council, for example, revealed that Sydney officials received intense pressure from Chinese officials to ban *Vision China Times*, a paper that continues to publish coverage critical of Beijing. (A report by the International Federation of Journalists further noted that Chinese state security officers camped out at the Beijing offices of one advertiser for Vision Times Media to intimidate him into pulling advertising from *Vision China Times*.[110]) "This morning I had a call from [a Chinese consulate employee] to remind us that he would like to keep a friendly relationship between China and [the province of] New South Wales," one memo said. "He wanted to make sure that there were no embarrassing situations this year and re-iterate their position involving anti-China groups."[111] The council complied with Chinese officials' wishes.

Beijing's influence has drastically transformed the Australian and New Zealand Chinese-language media environment, curtailing negative coverage of China in much of the local Chinese-language media and stripping out any independent reporting. In so doing, China is narrowing the information about Beijing available for Chinese-language speakers in Australia and New Zealand, major political constituencies and influences on China policy, and priming them to support China's foreign and domestic policies. As Reporters Without Borders notes in an analysis of China's global media footprint, Chinese-language "newspapers such as New Zealand's *Chinese Herald* and Australia's *Pacific Times*, which used to be independent and critical of the Chinese regime, are now its propaganda mouthpieces."[112]

One editor at a leading Chinese-language publication in Australia was even more damning. Reflecting on the influence of advertising from firms based in China, the purchases of media outlets by pro-Beijing interests, and direct pressure on local outlets from Chinese diplomats in Australia, he told reporters from the *Sydney Morning Herald* that "nearly 95 percent of the Australian Chinese newspapers have been brought in by the Chinese government to some degree."[113]

In Australia, the Chinese embassy and consulates also have become closely involved in funding and overseeing many Chinese student groups at universities in the country, including the Chinese Students and Scholars Association (CSSA), the leading Chinese students' organization. (An investigation by the Australian Broadcasting Corporation's *Four Corners* show found that the CSSA in the Australian Capital Territory, home to the Australian National University, was incorporated with documents filed in 2012 that claim the CSSA's job is to "facilitate the connection between the embassy and the Chinese students and scholars."[114]) Beijing has utilized this influence over students in Australia to limit discourse about China in multiple ways, yet Australian universities are heavily dependent on revenues from Chinese national students and are unwilling to push back against Beijing's growing influence over student organizations.

The Chinese-reading and Chinese-speaking community in Australia, as in New Zealand, is a minority of the total population, but it wields significant influence in politics and in China policy, because of its growing size and extensive political donations. The population of Australian voters of ethnic Chinese descent—many of whom do read or speak Chinese—nearly doubled between 2006 and 2016, and seems likely to continue growing at a rapid pace.[115] All major Australian parties now look at Chinese-Australians, who are not necessarily loyal to any one party, as a critical bloc that can swing local and national elections. And Beijing hoped, by using control of the media, Chinese associations, and Chinese student groups, to present the Chinese-Australian community as united in its warm views toward China—a point that is disputable, since opinion on many aspects of China is split within the Australian-Chinese community. Indeed, beyond student events, the Chinese embassy and consulates in Australia have often engaged in what one investigation by the Center for Strategic and International Studies of their efforts called "'political astroturfing' events to make it seem as if there is overwhelming grassroots support in the ethnic Chinese community for Beijing and its policies [like Beijing's South China Sea policies] while also drowning out critics."[116]

Were the Chinese-Australian community united in this way, it would be a potential threat to any Australian politicians who criticized Beijing or went against China's major policy preferences.[117] Politicians being politicians and wanting to get elected, Australian politicians, in theory, would then be reticent to cross a powerful constituency that supposedly was united in pushing for China's policy preferences, though the supposed unanimity of the Chinese-Australian community was far from the truth.

Beyond trying to sway the Australian-Chinese community and present it as a pro-China bloc to Australian politicians, China tried to influence Australia through quiet and often coercive funding of universities, research institutions, and politicians and parties. This type of sharp power did not rely on rallying the whole Chinese-Australian community but rather on covert well-placed injections of funds to institutions and policymakers who could shape Australia's China policy. Australians of Chinese descent and Chinese nationals who reside in Australia have become major contributors to Australian university departments, think tanks, and other research institutions focused on China policy. Most notably, a wealthy businessman and big political donor named Huang Xiangmo provided essential start-up funding for the Sydney-based Australia-China Relations Institute (ACRI). Chinese state firms like the Bank of China and the China Construction Bank also provided funding for the ACRI.[118]

Yet the ACRI was hardly alone among Australian institutions bringing in funding from Chinese national donors with close ties to the Chinese government or Australian-Chinese with pro-Beijing views. (The ACRI was later completely altered and became detached from Huang and also much less clearly pro-China in its viewpoints.) Huang himself funded other institutions like the Australia-China Institute for Arts and Culture, at a different university in Sydney, and spread his money generously around the Liberal, National, and Labor Parties. Multiple other donors with close links to the CCP, or Chinese companies with state links, also poured funds into Australian institutions.[119]

The ACRI, at least initially, fit the bill of an organization that received this funding and then generally advocated close ties between Canberra and Beijing. The ACRI's own initial stated purpose was promoting "a positive and optimistic view of Australia-China relations," and critics said that it played down any tough analysis of China's increasingly assertive regional foreign policy and crackdown at home and essentially was promoting China's interests exclusively in Australia.[120] (The ACRI later revised its mission to "inform[ing] Australia's engagement with China through research, analysis, and dialogue grounded in scholarly rigor," and hired a respected former intelligence chief to run the operation.[121])

Before the shift, however, the ACRI also helped arrange lavish trips to China for Australian journalists, who were often accompanied on the visits by then-ACRI head Bob Carr, a former Australian foreign minister known as one of the prominent Australian opinion leaders most solicitous of China. On the trips, they toured Chinese infrastructure projects and met CCP officials but did little in the way of serious journalism; information about the exact details of the trips was often omitted.[122] Returning from one such visit, the Australian journalists organized by the ACRI "collectively published 15 articles upon their return, objectively conveying China's voice and detailing how Australia could benefit from China's economic growth," according to reports in the Australian press.[123] The ACRI itself published reports like a supposed analysis of Australian views on China's approach to regional waters like the East China Sea, which claimed that Australians do not want to be involved in an East China Sea dispute between Tokyo and Beijing but with little evidence to back up this argument, which certainly would be one welcomed by China.[124] The ACRI also held meetings with top CCP officials too, according to Australian reporting.[125]

As in New Zealand, Beijing also has wielded extensive power within Australian politics by cultivating politicians from all leading parties and then attempting to use this cultivation to push the politicians to support Beijing's approach to the South China Sea, to alter

Australia's trade and defense policies toward China, and to avoid criticism of China's rights abuses and model of development. Huang Xiangmo was one prominent donor cultivating Australian politicians and pushing them toward views sympathetic to Beijing, though he was hardly alone; Chau Chak Wing also gave lavishly to both the Liberal and Australian Labor Parties, as did other Chinese nationals living in Australia and Australians of Chinese descent with pro-Beijing views.[126] For his efforts, Chau Chak Wing, who belonged to a leading UFWD organization, built relationships with a range of top Australian politicians, including former prime ministers John Howard and Bob Hawke, and also took over a major newspaper, as mentioned earlier; he also began brokering major China–Australia business deals.[127]

Huang, who also had close links to the UFWD, was particularly generous. He and his close business associates donated millions to Australian politicians in the mid-2010s, spreading the money among the major parties with no sunlight about how they were handing out funds.[128] This spending came at the same time as Huang was distributing money to the ACRI and other think tanks and research organizations focused on China policy.

Like Chau's giving, Huang's donations, which supposedly also included a gift to prominent New South Wales politician Jamie Clements of a box of wines with cash in it worth US$27,000, funding for Clements's legal fees in a sexual harassment investigation, and funding for Australian Labor Party Senator Sam Dastyari's legal fees, clearly came with political strings.[129] In 2016, Huang reportedly canceled a new donation of some US$290,000 to the Australian Labor Party, shortly before federal elections, when Labor's defense spokesperson slammed Beijing's approach to the South China Sea.[130] That same year, Dastyari held a press conference, before elections, which was organized by Huang—essentially a media get-together organized by a donor. At the press conference, and even though the Australian Labor Party had stepped up criticism of Beijing's South China Sea policy, Dastyari announced that "the South China Sea is China's own affair" and added that a Labor Party, if in power, would certainly know that it was not its place to be involved in South China Sea policy.[131] Essentially, at the press conference Dastyari just echoed Beijing's view of the South China Sea and suggested that, if elected, Labor would follow Beijing's view. As Prime Minister Malcolm Turnbull, of the Liberal–National Coalition, later said, Dastyari essentially took Huang's money and then "delivered essentially Chinese policy statements" in return.[132] Australian news outlets later revealed that Dastyari had tried to help Huang with Australia's immigration office in Huang's efforts to get citizenship.

Dastyari took other questionable measures as Australian intelligence officials and the media began to sniff around regarding Huang's donations. Dastyari reportedly told Labor's New South Wales party leader, Kaila Murnain, who was concerned about Huang's donations, to "cover your arse" about the source of funding; Murnain did not tell investigators at first about suspect donations from Huang.[133] (Dastyari, according to a *Sydney Morning Herald* investigation, later told an investigative commission that Murnain was "shitting herself" at the time about the funding, that he now believed Huang was an agent of Chinese influence, and that Dastyari should have been more skeptical of donations coming from Huang and other donors.[134]) As Australian authorities began investigating donors and some politicians receiving funds from foreign sources, Dastyari even cautioned Huang that Australian intelligence had tapped Huang's mobile phone, after Australia's intelligence agency had briefed politicians about their investigations into Huang and his potential links to the CCP. (Dastyari further told Huang that if they met in the future, they should not bring their mobile phones with them and they should meet outside, probably to make surveillance harder.[135]) So, Dastyari potentially revealed sensitive information that had been briefed to politicians.[136]

As in New Zealand, Beijing also courted Australian political elites by offering sinecures to former politicians who still wield significant power within their parties. Again, this financial support came with little public transparency. For instance, former prime minister Paul Keating became the head of the International Advisory Council of the state-owned China Development Bank. Keating also became one of the sharpest Australian critics of any efforts by Canberra to push back against China's influence efforts, South China Sea policy, or human rights abuses.[137] Beyond Keating, former prime minister Bob Hawke has become a major facilitator for mergers and deals with Chinese companies, while former foreign minister Alexander Downer and former Victoria premier John Brumby served on the board of Chinese telecommunications giant Huawei.[138] Even more egregiously, notes an extensive investigation into Chinese influence in Australia by the Center for Strategic and International Studies, former trade minister Andrew Robb "was given a lucrative consulting contract the day he left office by Landbridge Group, the Chinese company that won a 99-year lease to operate the Port of Darwin. Robb's deal was essentially a part-time job paying [roughly] US$630,000 a year."[139]

Backlash

Media revelations of Chinese influence activities, including the high-profile story of Dastyari and his eventual exile from politics, as well as pressure on the Australian government from policymakers critical of China's activities, led to growing public distrust of Beijing in Australia and tougher restrictions on foreign interference Down Under. Public views of China chilled in Australia, and policymakers realized, as one investigation into China's influence tactics by the Center for Strategic and International Studies noted, "perhaps no country has been as roiled politically by China's growing influence and political ambitions as Australia has."[140] China's growing use of economic coercion against Australia, its bullying diplomacy, and, ultimately, its support for the Ukraine war further cooled Australian public opinion on Beijing.

Australian intelligence agencies began to significantly increase their focus on Chinese influence activities. As early as 2015, Australia's national intelligence agency had begun warning politicians of the problems of Chinese national money sloshing in Australia's political system.[141] The next year, the Australian government, under Prime Minister Malcom Turnbull, launched an extensive intelligence investigation into China's influence activities Down Under.[142] But as in New Zealand, Canberra in the late 2010s quickly expanded intelligence efforts to identify people in Australia who might be linked to Chinese influence efforts toward Australian academia, media, and government, and Australian authorities have arrested at least one suspect so far, a man who had been closely involved in a range of Chinese-Australian groups.[143] Many prominent donors and political figures came under scrutiny without yet being arrested. Huang Xiangmo, under investigation for his ties to the CCP, was denied a bid for Australian citizenship in 2019 and then barred from entry into Australia on national security grounds and had his assets frozen in Australia as well; he stepped down from the ACRI board also.[144] Dastyari stepped down from parliament in late 2017, in a cloud of disgrace due to his links to Huang and other Chinese donors, and his political efforts on their behalf, were revealed; he eventually cooperated with an extensive investigation into his actions and broader Chinese influence efforts.[145] In 2019, former foreign minister Carr ended his time at the ACRI, and Australian politicians began railing against universities and other research institutes taking money from foreign sources—usually meant to mean China. As the *Guardian* noted, the Australian Senate in August 2020 announced the beginning of an investigation into "national security risks affecting the Australian higher-education and research sector" and that Australian Member of Parliament Bob Katter said that Australian universities had their "snouts . . . well and truly in the trough" of foreign money.[146]

Beyond the closer scrutiny from intelligence agencies, Australia responded to China's influence efforts with one of the world's most robust set of safeguards against foreign influence in politics, investigations into foreign influence activities in politics and media, and open dialogue about investigations into foreign influence activities in academia and civil society. Stories about Dastyari and other politicians linked to Chinese donations resonated with policymakers and the public, and Canberra's pushback against foreign influence moved far beyond the realm of intelligence agencies. (In 2020, Australian public sentiment toward China would sour further, as the two countries squabbled over foreign influence efforts, trade battles, increasingly hostile rhetoric toward Australia by Chinese diplomats, and revelations that the Chinese app WeChat had censored a post by Australian Prime Minister Scott Morrison, infuriating Canberra.[147]) With both Labor and Liberal-National leaders openly angered by China's influence activities in Australia, in 2018 Canberra passed a wave of bipartisan legislation banning foreign interference in Australian politics. Canberra banned political donations from foreigners, forced lobbyists for foreign governments to identify themselves in a public register, and implemented other sunlight measures—and also revamped its espionage statutes.[148] Beijing issued rhetorical threats warning Australia about implementing these new laws and imposed new customs rules on some Australian products, but Canberra went through with the new rules limiting foreign interference. This new Australian legislation was not explicitly written to target China, but Beijing obviously was the primary concern.

Beyond legislation, Canberra also has launched a committee that seems further designed to limit China's efforts to use its content-sharing deals and other leverage over the Australian media, and Australian parliamentary committees in 2020 also began a robust investigation into Chinese influence activities on university campuses in Australia.[149] Canberra also drew up an explicit set of guidelines for research universities to follow in dealing with foreign collaborators, to prevent espionage and dangerous foreign influence efforts.[150] (Australian researchers author more papers with Chinese coauthors than with coauthors from any other country.[151]) The guidelines are detailed regarding how research universities should deal with foreign collaborators and any possible influence efforts. Many Australian universities already have revised their collaboration practices because of these new guidelines.[152] To further assist Australian universities, Canberra has launched a new integrity unit to help universities assess and respond to emerging foreign threats to higher education.[153] And the Australian Strategic Policy Institute, partly funded by Australia's defense department, has created a report and database called the China Defense Universities Tracker, with the goal to "help universities, companies and policy-makers navigate engagement with research institutions in China." The tracker "sorts Chinese institutions into categories of very high risk, high risk, medium risk, or low risk" for their links to the Chinese military and security establishment.[154]

The Australian government also began to more aggressively monitor some of China's activities at global agencies like the World Health Organization, to criticize Beijing for its authoritarian and opaque governance, and to put limits on Chinese inbound invest-ment into Australia. In 2020, as the novel coronavirus spread around the world, Australia led calls for an independent investigation into the origins of the virus and its spread, which infuriated Beijing, fur-ther souring bilateral tensions.[155] The Australian government began taking tougher actions against Chinese companies' potential involve-ment in sensitive sectors as well, banning Huawei from Australia's 5G network and applying stricter scrutiny of other Chinese investments in the country.[156]

Angered by Australia's hardening approach on multiple fronts, including the call for a real investigation into the origins of COVID-19, the Chinese government hit back with tariffs on Australian barley and beef and, later in 2020, banning Australian coal exports to China as well, a potentially huge blow to the Australian economy.[157] Yet Australia held firm, refusing in 2021 and 2022 to jettison its new scru-tiny of China's influence activities in politics, Chinese inbound in-vestments, and China's power over Australian media, universities, and civil society. It has, indeed, both shown how China's influence activ-ities can rebound against Beijing and provided some clear defensive strategies for other countries to consider.

Chapter 6

The Soft Power Toolkit

Media and Information Coming Through the Front Door

W hile Beijing rapidly expanded its influence efforts in Australia and New Zealand, it was pursuing a similar expansion of influence tactics in Africa, Latin America, North America, and Southeast Asia. In many of these regions, like Africa and Southeast Asia, Beijing has placed a greater priority on cultivating soft power than in a place like Australia, where China has never had as warm relations with the public as with a country like Kenya, South Africa, Malaysia, or Thailand. (Still, China is also leaning more and more on sharp power even in places like Southeast Asia where it has an opportunity to build soft power.) The China Global Television Network (CGTN) and Xinhua have been at the center of that effort to rebuild China's soft power, to modernize it, and to learn from the failures of soft power in the charm offensive era.

Indeed, CGTN tried to build itself a presence that could rival other global broadcasters like Al Jazeera, RT, the Turkish global broadcaster TRT World, and, the Chinese government hopes, giants like CNN and the BBC. During the past three years, while working on this book, I have appeared several times on CGTN, via Skype, to discuss current events in Southeast Asia.[1] Before the interviews, the booking process moved as professionally as any I have encountered with other outlets, including National Public Radio, the Australian Broadcasting Corporation, and the BBC. The bookers for China's state television channel, most of whom previously worked for outlets other than CGTN, did not warn me about topics to avoid or offer points to emphasize. The anchors, usually operating from the CGTN Washington bureau, handled the interviews smoothly and fluently. (Before starting this book, I had never appeared on Chinese state media, but I thought it would be valuable to do it to get a sense of how state media bureaus treat guests in democracies. I did not accept any money for my appearances.[2])

The CGTN shows seemed similar in style and tone to guest appearances I had done on other international outlets, like the BBC or the Australian Broadcasting Corporation, which are more muted than U.S. cable channels, with none of the four-people-shouting-at-once melees one might see on CNN or MSNBC at night. To be fair, my appearances did not touch on the most sensitive issues to the Chinese government, like Hong Kong, Taiwan, or Xinjiang—but China's relations with Southeast Asian countries are not wholly uncontroversial, and no one guided my interviews.

The Big State Media (Mostly) Come in the Front Door: CGTN, Xinhua, China Radio International, and Media Soft Power

The CGTN shows I appeared on were easily viewable, online or on many major U.S. cable networks—they were in many ways the opposite of covert sharp power. Indeed, Chinese state media, including CGTN, Xinhua, China Radio International (CRI), and other major outlets, tend to come in through what one might call the "front door," using soft power more than sharp. (I'll look at "back door" approaches in the next chapter.) When a viewer turns on CGTN, they know they are watching CGTN, whose logo appears regularly on the screen.

They do not have to search hard to comprehend that CGTN is a channel controlled by the Chinese state and that they are watching content produced by a Chinese state channel. A simple Google search of CGTN turns up these facts. Of course, most news consumers do not reflexively Google the outlets they are reading or viewing; the point is, CGTN and CRI's background can be readily understood by news consumers in many states, including in less developed countries. In Cambodia, for instance, people surveyed by organizations like Gallup seem to understand that CRI is a Chinese state media product.[3] Studies of African news consumers reach similar conclusions.[4] To be sure, the big state media are primarily used as tools of soft power, but they also can be used as sharp power weapons, which I will examine in the next chapter.

But compared to many of China's other media and information tools—like Beijing gaining power over Chinese-language outlets abroad through covert measures, engaging in outright disinformation on social media, concealing state media content through content-sharing deals, or using cash payouts to coerce politicians in other countries—China's biggest state media outlets more often enter countries through the front door. The biggest outlets are usually those easiest for media consumers to identify as controlled by Beijing. And CGTN, Xinhua, and CRI's more public, open profiles make it easier to assess whether the big state media are succeeding in winning new audiences. Because the content comes in through the front door, it is possible to assess whether these outlets are gaining popularity with viewers, readers, and listeners in other countries, though it is certainly harder to analyze how that popularity might affect China achieving its foreign policy goals in various countries. This is much harder to do for Chinese media and information tools coming in through the back door. Indeed, because the state media outlets are more transparent than many other Chinese influence tools, I can show how, other than the increasingly potent Xinhua, many of these state outlets have been failures to date.

An Environment Ripe for
Authoritarian Media

Xi's administration is boosting its focus on media and information at the perfect time for authoritarian countries to offer alternatives to major international media companies and to prominent local outlets in many countries. Today, media outlets around the world face massive financial and political strains. Hemorrhaging advertising revenue, they are downsizing or shutting down entirely, leaving some newsrooms looking more like vacant lots than vibrant news-gathering enterprises; the global pandemic has only further added to the news industry's shedding of jobs.[5] This is not a new trend—it dates to the early dot-com era—but it has sped up in recent years. Between 2001 and 2016, newspaper publishing in the United States lost more than half the jobs in the industry—a higher rate of job loss than was sustained in coal mining, which is not exactly an industry of the future.[6] This enormous attrition rate means that smaller news outlets are shutting their doors. Between 2003 and 2018, according to a study by UNC Center for Innovation and Sustainability in Local Media, more than one in five newspapers in the United States closed, leaving half of the counties in the country with only one newspaper; some sizable cities in the United States will be left with no daily newspapers at all.[7] Once-famed outlets like the *Daily News* in New York are shutting their newsrooms entirely.[8] And, with a few rare exceptions like the *New York Times* and the *Washington Post*, which have continued to grow (in part, on the *Post*'s part, because of the personal wealth of the *Washington Post*'s owner, Jeff Bezos), most of the biggest international outlets have less money to dig into important stories, especially in places like sub-Saharan Africa, Southeast Asia, and Latin America, which are usually lower priorities at Western outlets than Europe, North America, the Middle East, and China.[9] CGTN and Xinhua and other Chinese state outlets often have focused their expansions on these ignored areas.

Meanwhile, the expansion of social media and the sped-up pace of news gathering and reporting have deluged news consumers with information, often with the effect of leaving readers, listeners, and viewers feeling like they are standing under a Niagara Falls of content. There is so much information gushing onto their phones, tablets, televisions, computers, and other devices, from genuine news outlets, aggregators, social media commentators, questionable opinion publications, YouTube videos, and many other sources. With this much information, it becomes harder for all but the savviest news consumers to know which stories they should read, and which contain wholly factual content.

Many financially struggling media outlets in democratic countries are simultaneously under pressure from their own elected leaders. These leaders hail from both the right and the left of the political spectrum, but many of them are populists who seek to discredit the media, demonize reporters as purveyors of "fake news," and attempt to convince populations that news outlets cannot be trusted and even potentially should be targets of violence.[10] They also regularly promote conspiracy theories, fringe news outlets that have minimal standards for factual reporting and analysis, and content on social media that seeks to delegitimize major media outlets and create an environment in which citizens are so overwhelmed with false information they no longer know what to believe.[11] And mainstream media outlets often hurt themselves too with major recent mistakes like U.S. outlets' coverage of the run-up to the 2003 Iraq War and the mainstream U.S. media's general inability to believe that Donald Trump could win the 2016 presidential election.

This combination of factors is destroying trust in the media—in North America and Europe, but also in many developing regions as well. A 2019 study by the Columbia Journalism Review, Ipsos, and Reuters found that Americans had less trust in the media than in any other institution besides Congress, which is generally hated.[12] Polling shows a similar trend of public distrust toward the media in the Philippines, where both former president Rodrigo Duterte and current president Ferdinand Marcos Jr endlessly batter the media in both public speeches and informal settings.[13] In his usual hyperbolic style, Duterte did not just tweet about so-called fake news or lead rally chants criticizing reporters. He also warned Philippine journalists, "Just because you're a journalist you are not exempted from assassination, if you're a son of a bitch"; shut down ABS-CBN, one of the country's largest broadcasters; and oversaw multiple criminal cases against Nobel Prize laureate Maria Ressa, probably the country's most famous investigative journalist, after the website she founded, *Rappler*, exposed abuses in Duterte's brutal drug war.[14] She was convicted in October 2021, the same month she won the Nobel Peace Prize, along with Russian journalist Dmitry Muratov, for defending press freedom.[15]

This story is playing out not only in the United States but also in nearly every region in the world. In India, Indonesia, Thailand, Brazil, Turkey, Hungary, Mexico, and many other states leaders routinely attack the media as liars, partisans, and disloyal citizens—and many also have used the coronavirus pandemic to step up assaults on the press.[16] The monitoring organization Freedom House noted in its *Freedom of the Press* report that, overall, "freedom of the media has been deteriorating around the world over the past decade. . . . [A]n independent press is under attack."[17] In a report, Freedom House further found that since the onset of the novel coronavirus pandemic, democracy and rights, including press freedom, have regressed in some eighty countries around the world.[18]

An environment in which resources for quality media are decreasing, leaders are demonizing media outlets, and publics' trust in journalism is falling potentially makes it easier for both Chinese state media and Chinese-controlled and Chinese-linked media (those not officially owned by the state but controlled by pro-China individuals or companies) to gain readers, viewers, and listeners. (Of course, it opens the door for other state media as well.) If all reporting is untrustworthy, readers and viewers might think, is CGTN or CRI or Xinhua necessarily any worse? Could these channels be alternative sources of information in an environment where most of the biggest media name brands are suffering? What's more, if global media companies like the BBC, with business facing various cost challenges and to some extent declining revenues, have fewer resources to cover places like Southeast Asia, Africa, Latin America, or even once-premier postings like the Middle East and Europe, perhaps people in those regions should instead tune into Chinese state media, which is expanding its coverage and has extensive resources to cover local stories, at least in theory.

Russian state media outlets certainly benefited from decreasing public trust in the media, at least until the Ukraine war, when Russian state outlets' access to many foreign markets in leading democracies was cut off, though they continued to provide alternative sources of news in some countries. For years, the Russian state channels won viewers in many countries with their alternative perspectives to the mainstream media. The television network RT and the global Russian news agency Sputnik position themselves as alternative sources of information to the mainstream media in many countries and regularly highlight that mainstream media are biased, partisan, and untrustworthy—a claim that only, at least until the Ukraine conflict, led to the shutting of these outlets by technology companies and television providers in some countries and turned them into pariahs in others. This made it easier for the Russian outlets to attract readers, viewers, and listeners. The Russian state outlets suggest that they are providing valuable, controversial news and opinion supposedly absent (or concealed on purpose from readers by shadowy forces) from the mainstream media in places like the United States, Central and Eastern Europe, and Western Europe, among other regions. To hammer home this point, RT ran a high-profile advertising campaign, called "Question More," which presents the Russian channel as delivering truths that cannot be found on major Western networks and online news outlets. "We want to complete the picture rather than add to the echo chamber of mainstream news; that's how we find an audience," Anna Belkina, the RT head of communications, told the *New York Times*.[19]

Indeed, on many occasions, RT's stories also aim to show that the reporting of outlets ranging from the *New York Times* and the *Washington Post* to major European news outlets is misleading at best and badly biased at worst. This is a tactic to further damage foreign publics' trust in their domestic media outlets and also to promote RT's own coverage. RT, which aggressively targeted YouTube as a venue for its stories, became the most widely viewed global news network channel on the platform, where its often-provocative content has proved popular on a site where edgy and even conspiratorial content plays well with viewers.[20] (YouTube has vowed to label videos on its site from state-backed broadcasters but has been inconsistent in following through; as of this writing, YouTube also is the last remaining global media platform that Vladimir Putin allows in Russia, even though, after the Ukraine invasion, YouTube promised to ban access outside Russia to Russian state media channels, though it remains unclear whether it has done so in many countries.[21]) Up until the Ukraine conflict, the Russian channels also had proven willing to have outspoken commentators, from both the left and the right of the political spectrum in North America and Europe, on Russian shows, even if those figures cannot be controlled so easily. The acclaimed, Pulitzer-winning journalist and author Chris Hedges hosted a show on RT America, and Pulitzer-winning journalist Glenn Greenwald has often appeared on the network. To be sure, RT seems to prefer hosts and guests who are critical of their own countries' domestic politics and foreign policies, as Greenwald and Hedges are, but simply having them on the air meant RT is taking some degree of risk in its programming.[22]

Money, Money, Money

China is pouring money into state media outlets to make them appear more professional and help them have a bigger international effect. Beijing is dumping cash into state outlets even though some evidence suggests that sharper tactics, like Beijing quietly gaining control of most Chinese-language outlets in a country, are more effective at influencing populations in other countries than the softer strategy of expanding big state media outlets. Still, at least one major state media outlet, Xinhua, has become a powerful Chinese tool, and could become far more powerful in the future.

The Chinese government's funding for state media dwarfs that of any other country's state media funding, including the United States.[23] As part of China's expansion of its international state media in the past decade, CGTN, CRI, and Xinhua have opened and expanded bureaus in the United States, Africa, Europe, Latin America, and Southeast Asia.[24] In 2018, CGTN reportedly spent around $500 million to promote the network in Australia alone and has also engaged in extensive promotion in Europe and North America.[25] Still, Beijing does not provide the only source of funds for state media. According to Si Si, who was a visiting fellow at the Reuters Institute for the Study of Journalism at the University of Oxford, CGTN's advertising revenues have boomed since the mid-1990s, and the channel "now has sufficient revenue to finance its overseas operations from advertising."[26] (Other analyses challenge this view, but the point is that CGTN gets state infusions and also raises considerable funds from advertising.)

CGTN now says that it is broadcasting to 1.2 billion people across the world, in Chinese, English, and other languages, including French and Russian.[27] *China Daily*, Beijing's most prominent global English-language newspaper, asserts in various briefings and media kits for advertisers that it has an international print circulation of eight hundred thousand to nine hundred thousand, with online readership much higher.[28] Theoretically, that reach would make CGTN the world's biggest television network, but those figures just include the number of people who have *access* to its broadcast—people for whom the channel is available on their television sets or other devices.[29] In reality, the figures for how many people are actually watching CGTN are much lower—lower even in the United States than for other, more obscure

Chinese-language channels—and far lower than the figures for giants like the BBC and CNN.[30] While CGTN claims that it can be viewed in 170 countries, a 2019 analysis by Reporters Without Borders found that it broadcasts in 140.[31] CGTN reaches thirty million households in the United States—though as we will see, its actual viewership in the United States and other parts of North America is much lower.[32]

With a boost in funding for the newswire itself and for advertising its coverage, Xinhua has continued to expand with a goal of having two hundred foreign bureaus, hiring between six thousand and ten thousand new journalists to fill those bureaus, even as other global newswires like Reuters and the Associated Press have laid off thousands of staff.[33] CRI is growing as well. Sarah Cook of Freedom House has found that the number of radio stations carrying CRI increased from thirty-three stations in fourteen countries in 2015 to fifty-eight stations in thirty-five countries in 2018.[34] (These figures do not include stations that CRI partners with, which run a modest amount of CRI content.) CRI now broadcasts in over sixty languages and is available on more short-wave frequencies than the once-giant Voice of America, which has cut much of its short-wave services.[35] CRI also has become the second-biggest radio broadcaster in the world, behind only the BBC—at least in terms of the potential audience falling within its airwaves, if not in terms of actual listeners.[36]

Other Chinese state media outlets, including those from provincial capitals, also are expanding internationally. The *People's Daily*, the official newspaper of the Chinese Communist Party (CCP), launched an English-language app in 2017 and has increasingly expanded its English offerings.[37] Provincial TV stations like Hunan TV, Guangdong TV, Beijing TV, and Jiangsu TV, among others, have signed deals with satellite providers to carry their programs in many other countries.[38]

Meanwhile, Hunan TV, aka Hunan Satellite TV, the most popular provincial station within China, with the second-largest audience across China (behind CCTV-1, domestically), is increasingly available in Japan, North America, Southeast Asia, and other regions, where it operates as Hunan STV World; it also is spreading its streaming video outlet, Mango TV.[39] Of all the provincial stations, Hunan has been the savviest in its entertainment offerings, like reality shows about the children of celebrities, Thai costume dramas, and Korea-inspired singing shows. Mango TV offers a range of reality shows and also picks up some international reality shows and competitions, copying some aspects of reality shows from other parts of Asia as well as aspects of Netflix; it has created a popular YouTube channel.[40] William Yuen Yee of the Jamestown Foundation notes that Mango TV has become one of the most popular channels in neighboring Vietnam.[41] Mango TV, and Hunan TV in general, has been so savvy, in fact, that it has been slammed by the CCP for focusing too much on entertainment and not enough on party ideology—and even for becoming too popular.[42] In one notice sent to Hunan TV, the CCP warned that the station was swinging between social benefits and economic benefits, failing to fulfill the mission of being a mouthpiece of the ruling party.[43] Yet the entertainment quality that gets Hunan TV in trouble with the CCP also makes it desirable to some Chinese-speaking foreign audiences, and Hunan's international arm has expanded into Southeast Asian markets.

Yet although these Chinese channels are available in an increasing number of states in Southeast Asia and around the world, many have gained little audience share. In some cases, the networks do not release information about their overseas users, or they release information about the number of households they are in but no information about how many people are actually watching their offerings. Mango TV International, for instance, claims to reach some twenty-two million users of streaming video around the world, but this figure says little about whether it is just people who downloaded Mango TV International's app or whether it is people who actually streamed a Mango TV International show.[44]

And yet using the Freedom of Information Act, I obtained over twenty studies, produced by Gallup as a contractor for the U.S. government, of viewing habits in countries in Africa, Southeast Asia, and parts of South and Central Asia, among other regions. They focus on

Chinese broadcast and radio outlets and generally show that, even though these Chinese broadcast outlets are now widely available in many countries, they often attract low viewership numbers. In Laos, for instance, a country on China's borders with extensive penetration of Chinese provincial and national channels and a growing population of Chinese speakers, one Gallup study of viewership in Laos found only 1.2 percent of the country's population regularly watched Chinese broadcasting, a much lower figure than those who watched Voice of America or Radio Free Asia or Thai channels.[45] (Thai channels have an obvious advantage in Laos in that most Laotians can understand Thai, as the two languages are similar.) Other studies of the penetration of Chinese state media, such as those done by Freedom House, suggest that Chinese state media have not been successful in establishing themselves as sources of information for many people in many Southeast Asian states.

While pouring money into outlets like Xinhua, CGTN, and CRI, Beijing also has tasked its growing pool of diplomats with helping get state media more exposure around the world, in part by publishing in these state media outlets and convincing local opinion leaders to publish in these outlets or appear on the outlets. Some Chinese officials, according to former staff at the U.S. Agency for Global Media, also have tried to convince foreign radio and television stations to drop their current broadcasting formats and run CGTN or CRI. Staff at the U.S. Agency for Global Media, which oversees American broadcasters like Radio Free Asia, have reported that Chinese officials have in recent years stepped up their approaches to local stations.[46] The Chinese representatives try to convince local radio stations that run Radio Free Asia, Voice of America, and other U.S.-funded media outlets to drop those broadcasts and switch to running Chinese state programming instead. They often dangle considerable bonuses to stations willing to switch programming. And they try to get stations to switch when they perceive U.S. weakness. In Indonesia, for instance, according to a former representative from U.S. state media outlets, representatives for CRI approached Indonesian stations that carried

Voice of America, particularly at times, like in 2014, when it appeared that the United States was going to slash Voice of America broadcasting in Indonesia.[47]

A station changing formats for financial reasons is standard in the radio industry. In my hometown of Hartford, Connecticut, radio stations switched formats all the time; one station popular in my household, FM 102.9, went from top forty to album rock to oldies to classic rock.[48] But having official government representatives twist arms to get stations to switch formats is not routine, and U.S. diplomats with whom I spoke could not remember any instance in which they played such a role in pushing local stations to use Voice of America or Radio Free Asia coverage.

Journalists

As I earlier noted, Beijing was, at least before the Ukraine war undermined RT's global brand, trying to copy *both* Al Jazeera and RT in its global media and information push. Beijing tries to present Chinese state media as trustworthy, giving quality reports from experienced correspondents, like Al Jazeera does. It also sometimes, but less often, copies RT's approach of providing controversial, conspiratorial, supposedly alternative options to democracies' mainstream media.[49]

Many CGTN employees, however, say Chinese leaders see Al Jazeera as the main model—a state media outlet that has built international credibility through its reporting on its region and also on many other parts of the world yet also effectively tells the "story" about the Middle East that Qatar wants out in the world. And Beijing is trying to pull off the trick of expanding and professionalizing its international state media while at the same time destroying independent journalism within China, and (sometimes) increasing censorship of Chinese correspondents filing for state media from abroad.[50] This is, to say the least, a tricky balancing act to pull off.

Beyond the big state media outlets, Beijing appears to be trying to create some niche outlets that could be modeled after Al Jazeera's reporting—at least, they could be given a façade that makes them seem independent, able to produce innovative and somewhat independent journalism. For example, in 2016 a state company, Shanghai United Media Group, launched the English-language *Sixth Tone*, an online news publication. Although it is a domestic Chinese outlet, and thus subject to all state censorship regulations, *Sixth Tone*, and its related Chinese publication, *The Paper*, produces slick, fun, fascinating content, with skillful use of graphics and video storytelling that appear focused on readers in North America and other English-speaking readers interested in China—making it what the China reporter Bethany Allen-Ebrahimian likened to the *Vox* of Chinese media.[51]

Sixth Tone focuses on well-reported human-interest features, including ones that delve into some topics that present China negatively, and has a relatively flat hierarchical structure. Its reporters are given significant leeway to operate, as long as they do not cross certain lines prohibited by the CCP.[52] As Merriden Varrall of the Lowy Institute writes in a report surveying Chinese state media, "The example of *Sixth Tone* shows that state media in China can create credible and appealing news"—contrary to assertions that Chinese state media, unlike Al Jazeera, should always be bland. Varrall argues that "*Sixth Tone* has an entirely different look and feel to CGTN, and indeed, some savvy China-watchers are not even aware that *Sixth Tone* is Chinese government media."[53] If Beijing can keep its hands off *Sixth Tone* and adopt many of the ways the outlet operates for other state media—admittedly a gargantuan task—it could make CGTN and other state media more formidable media organizations globally.

Beijing has dedicated extensive resources to making the bigger state outlets appear capable of producing quality journalism, going on a multiyear hiring binge and aggressively recruiting foreign journalists from international news organizations as well as from high-quality local outlets in countries ranging from Nigeria to the United Kingdom.[54]

CGTN in particular has wooed foreign journalists, as several journalists told the author, from other global outlets and from prominent local television outlets in certain countries, with the promise of financially stable careers and the chance to cover prestigious beats— the White House, major trade deals, prominent capitals in Africa and Europe, and other areas. It has particularly tried to woo reporters in places like Europe, North America, and Asia with such opportunities, since in all of these places many local outlets are downsizing. And it often takes years of scrambling up the corporate ladder for a reporter to land at a station like CNN or the BBC or a newspaper or online news outlet like the *New York Times*. As a result, CGTN, and to a lesser extent other state media, had, at least until the United States and some European countries began to scrutinize CGTN more closely in 2020 and 2021, been able to attract talented foreign reporters, editors, producers, and bookers in media capitals like Washington and in regions where CGTN is expanding, like Africa and Southeast Asia.[55]

CGTN has made a concentrated effort to recruit high-level talent to produce its stories and shows. Among many other hires, it brought aboard Jim Laurie, a veteran Asia correspondent, as a consultant, and Edwin Maher, a twenty-five-year veteran of the Australian Broadcasting Corporation, to anchor a show from Beijing.[56] It hired Mike Walter, a five-time Emmy Award winner; Phillip TK Yin, who formerly worked for CNBC and Bloomberg Television; and the Peabody Award winner Jim Spellman, a former CNN reporter, to work out of CGTN's Washington bureau.[57] In the Philippines, CGTN hired Barnaby Lo, a highly respected local journalist who previously worked for ABC News, CBS News, and prominent local programming.[58]

In some countries, CGTN and Xinhua managers even are willing to hire local journalists who have built reputations for tough reporting on issues related to China, like Chinese companies' labor and environmental policies. Dayo Aiyetan, a highly respected investigative journalist in Nigeria, said in an interview with the author that CGTN representatives attempted to hire him in 2012. He had gained local fame for digging into issues ranging from graft to environmental damage, and had already written stories on Chinese businesspeople exploiting corruption in Nigeria to illegally log local forests.[59] CGTN's representatives were well aware of his tough reporting when they tried to hire him, and seemed to think that his reputation would help burnish the credentials of their Nigeria bureau.[60] Dayo turned them down, but other acclaimed journalists in Africa have since moved over to CGTN and Xinhua bureaus in Africa.[61] Hiring these reporters could give CGTN credibility with local audiences for producing independent journalism.

Although Chinese outlets are snapping up foreign reporters and trying to show themselves capable of producing quality reporting, the strangulation of Chinese domestic media in the late 2000s and 2010s has made it harder for state media giants to attract the best Chinese talent. Early in the Hu Jintao era, when the domestic media outlets were still freer, ambitious Chinese reporters seeking to do independent work could, with at least some plausibility, see themselves working at CGTN, whose leaders declared that the channel wanted to challenge CNN's type of reporting.[62] But since then, Beijing has closed many groundbreaking domestic media outlets and silenced other liberal and critical voices in Chinese society, like the Beijing-based think tank the Unirule Institute of Economics.[63] By the end of the 2010s, according to the Committee to Protect Journalists, China was holding more reporters in jail than any other country in the world.[64] Writers have been forced to make televised "confessions" for simply reporting basic news stories, like the ups and downs of the Chinese stock markets.[65] The outlets that have stayed open have had to conform to a bevy of new restrictions, such as no longer being able to even choose their own headlines, which are often dictated by Beijing.[66] Independent investigative reporters who still try to publish critical work find that they cannot find an outlet to publish them and are harassed and jailed.[67] Indeed, Chinese news outlets have stopped, for the most part, covering breaking news stories that could be in any way sensitive to the government.[68]

With this crackdown, Hu and Xi's administrations forced out of journalism many talented and independent young Chinese reporters.[69] The reduced quality of China's domestic media not only made finding the best Chinese journalists a tougher task for state media but also at least marginally damaged the international appeal of Chinese state outlets. Some opinion leaders in foreign states do understand how press freedom has been destroyed in China—and this destruction makes it harder for Beijing to sell Xinhua, CGTN, or other outlets to foreign opinion leaders as trustworthy and independent. Jian Wang, an expert on Chinese public diplomacy at the University of Southern California, asks this critical question in a study of Beijing's media strategy: "Skeptics . . . point out that China's domestic media and communication enjoys little credibility, so how is it then possible for the country to gain the trust of international audiences?"[70]

Yet state media firms still do not lack for Chinese applicants. They can find significant numbers of young Chinese journalists to work abroad for outlets like Xinhua or CGTN. In his study of Chinese foreign correspondents, the anthropologist Pál Nyíri notes that Chinese state media still attract some skilled young Chinese journalists to work overseas. These journalists claim that, once posted overseas, they enjoy a fair amount of editorial freedom.[71] In a survey of Chinese state media journalists in Africa by Vivien Marsh of the University of Westminster in London, CGTN reporters claimed to have written multiple stories that reflected poorly on African governments without being censored by Beijing or local managers. These journalists claimed that their work was similar to Al Jazeera or BBC coverage of Africa.[72]

Some foreign employees of CGTN and Xinhua argue that, within bureaus in Australia, North America, Southeast Asia, and other regions, these news outlets operate much like CNN, Al Jazeera, or other news organizations for which they previously worked. This is especially true for foreign reporters operating in these bureaus, who have less interaction with censors and the Central Propaganda Department. A CGTN reporter argued to me that the network's Washington bureau staff was similar to a BBC or MSNBC bureau.[73]

Other non-Chinese journalists working for CGTN and Xinhua in bureaus in Australia, Europe, North America, and Southeast Asia made similar claims. A producer who came to CGTN's Washington bureau from highly respected international outlets said to me she received little direct interference in most stories. No one she knew at CGTN's operations in the United States thought of themselves as propagandists. She added that, on many topics, panels on CGTN talk shows could be quite ideologically diverse and even hosted guests who were generally critical of China, for instance, when producing shows on the deteriorating U.S.-China relationship. She admitted that there were issue areas that CGTN producers would not touch, although she claimed that the number of untouchable topics was small—Taiwan, Xinjiang, and a small handful of other areas. Another noted to me that CGTN had rapidly expanded its digital output, including videos made just to put online, explainer videos, and other content, and that oversight of these digital operations resembled the oversight he had witnessed at major U.S.-based news organizations, including script approval and fact-checking. He did note, however, that when scripts were checked before production, script editors, often foreigners, went through the write-ups, but at least one more senior Chinese national manager at a bureau had to approve the script too before it could be produced.

A review of CGTN's regular offerings in the United States confirms this. Panels do circle around and avoid the topics most sensitive to China—Tibet, ethnic minorities in China, Hong Kong, Taiwan— and it is hard to imagine the most hawkish U.S.-based China commentators appearing on the channel. But on topics like trade, broader U.S.-China relations, China's relations with other states in Asia, and issues even less sensitive to Beijing, panelists do participate in debate, and stories sometimes offer relatively nuanced context.

Beyond talk show panels, CGTN's U.S.-based journalists have produced some serious news features and film-length feature stories on
topics that do not directly touch on the Chinese government but
certainly are worth in-depth treatment, like the opioid crisis in the
United States and the global increase in migration (which was obviously stalled by COVID-19). CGTN's U.S. arm has received a significant number of awards in recent years. It won twenty-seven from the
White House News Photographers Association in 2019 for various
aspects of its photographic coverage, including its news special reports, magazine features, and news series.[74] CGTN's U.S. wing won an
Emmy in 2016 for a newsmagazine feature on a successful American
female gymnast who was born with no legs.[75] CGTN's U.S. operations have won numerous other awards from other New York–based
critics' associations and international television critics' associations.[76]

CGTN has not just produced serious work in the United States. In
interviews, Southeast Asian academics, politicians, and businesspeople
noted the growing professionalization of Chinese state media—even
though CGTN has not made major inroads in audience share in the
region.

Self-Censorship Among Journalists

Within state media, overt censorship has become somewhat less pre-
dictable in recent years, at least on issues other than those most sensitive to Beijing. It has at times become harder to anticipate how
Central Propaganda Department officials in China will respond to
stories in foreign bureaus, as Xi Jinping has made China increasingly
authoritarian, especially in the COVID era. In his survey of Chinese
correspondents working overseas, Pál Nyíri notes that one reporter
produced an interview with Myanmar's then de facto head of government, Aung San Suu Kyi. (Suu Kyi was jailed after the February 2021
coup in Myanmar put the military formally in charge of the country
again.) Yet Chinese censors cut portions of the interview in which

Suu Kyi offered some criticisms of China, even though the journalist thought his editors would protect him from censorship.[77]

Of course, on issues of sensitivity, Beijing enforces strict censorship of Chinese state media, and of private media outlets based in China. Reporters Without Borders notes that, in 2016, the leak of documents known as the Panama Papers highlighted that close relatives of Xi Jinping and Li Peng, the powerful former prime minister, apparently had used shell companies in Panama to hide their wealth. International news outlets aggressively covered the revelations, but China's censors quickly ensured that all Chinese media would not touch the topic.[78] As Reporters Without Borders notes, "The Party sent this notice to Chinese media on 4 April 2016: 'Find and delete reprinted reports on the Panama Papers. Do not follow up on related content, no exceptions. If material from foreign media attacking China is found on any website, it will be dealt with severely.'"[79]

More often than outright censorship, which is still present on many issues, state media editors and reporters undertake anticipatory self-censorship, refusing to cover stories that could present Beijing in a negative light, even without bosses telling them not to report on such areas. Anticipatory self-censorship has become common in realms far beyond Chinese state media. It has become prevalent in many areas where Beijing wields power: the global film industry; the international publishing industry; Chinese-language media outlets based in many countries around the world; the multinational business world, including giants from Apple to Marriott to the National Basketball Association; and many other areas of business, the arts, culture, and academia.[80] I will discuss this increasingly pervasive self-censorship, in which these foreign companies or prominent individuals quash any critiques of China before they even could emerge within their firms and organizations, in the next few chapters, where we examine the cumulative effects of China's soft and sharp influence strategies today.

But if self-censorship about China has filtered into so many areas of global business, arts, and academia, then self-censorship is even more commonplace at Chinese state media outlets, despite the assertions of foreign journalists at state media that oversight processes are similar to those at CNN or the BBC. One former producer at CGTN's Washington bureau said to me that even if overt censorship was uncommon other than on issues of highest importance to Beijing, the bureau's employees imbibed an atmosphere of caution and quiet self-censorship. Some China critics would come on air, but bookers often screened potential interviewees. She said that if bookers were looking for guests to appear on an interview show, they would watch prospective guests' previous interviews or search through their writings to discern their views on China. Self-censorship carried over onto the air too. The booker said that many guests seemingly understood that to come on CGTN means anticipatory self-censorship. They usually avoided overt criticism of China during their appearances on the network—even while the same guests criticized Chinese policies in other forums.

Even Yang Rui, the outspoken host of *Dialogue*, a prominent CGTN English-language talk show, and one of CGTN's most famous personalities, cops to self-censorship. In an interview with the academic Ying Zhu, Yang admitted that, while he has aspirations to copy tough shows like the BBC's *HARDtalk*, in Chinese media "you can't maneuver freely, asking whatever questions you like. You've got to be restricted."[81] Ultimately, this self-censorship—and the prospect that higher-ups in Beijing could always kill stories on major topics, via gag orders from the Central Propaganda Department—takes a toll on a news outlet's workforce and undermines its credibility.

Sometimes, the self-censorship emerges because journalists at the state outlets come to understand the limits that have been put in place all around them. Many African journalists who work for Chinese state media say there are clear limits to how much independence they are granted. In a study of African journalists working for Chinese outlets, Emeka Umejei of the American University of Nigeria found that Chinese editors at African outlets still exercise gatekeeping of stories. One top African editor told Umejei, in a comment echoed by other editors who had worked at *China Daily*, Xinhua, and CGTN in Africa:

> There is the African level of gatekeeping [to prevent stories that are too critical of China or possibly of local governments], which is the second level of gatekeeping, and the final level of gatekeeping is the Chinese. There is freedom to suggest stories and how they should be done but again, there is a final gatekeeping which is the Chinese that will decide on which stories are going to be handled and how.[82]

To ensure positive coverage of China, another former CGTN booker said, the channel would pack shows held in front of live audiences—even when such shows were held on U.S. college campuses, supposedly bastions of free discussion and inquiry. In December 2018, CGTN held a town hall at an auditorium on the campus of the elite George Washington University (GW) in Washington, DC. The town hall explored forty years of China's economic reforms and the effects of the Chinese boom on the world. It featured several prominent and respected China experts, including Yukon Huang of the Carnegie Endowment for International Peace, Martin Jacques of Cambridge University, and Robert Hormats of Kissinger Associates.[83] Probably to capitalize on the host university's prestige, CGTN featured GW in its coverage; it did a separate small segment called "Making of a Town Hall" that slickly showed the event being set up at GW.[84]

The booker noted that, while the concept of a town hall is one in which audiences freely question the speakers, in advance of the event CGTN closely scrutinized audience attendees and tried to investigate their backgrounds. CGTN's Washington bureau managers, the booker said, then attempted to block any potential town hall attendees who might have been critical of China in the forum.[85] This scrutiny of attendees and outright blocking of potential attendees who might have been critical of China in the forums should have raised red flags for a preeminent academic institution that values its independence, but it either went unnoticed by GW management or was simply tolerated. And the strategy seemed to work—the town hall presented a relentlessly optimistic view of China's past reforms and future potential,

ignoring China's increasingly authoritarian state and also mostly elid-
ing China's major long-term economic challenges.

Of course, all networks and news outlets have some degree of bias
and even possible censorship, and subtle pressure on journalists exists
everywhere—and sometimes not so subtle. Democratic countries are
full of partisan outlets where management shapes news stories. In
2016, for instance, according to an investigation by Jane Mayer of the
New Yorker, FoxNews.com allegedly buried a story by one of its own
online reporters about then-candidate Donald Trump's relationship
with the porn actress who goes by the name Stormy Daniels.[86] In
democracies, stories can be shaped for nonideological reasons that
still impede independent journalism. But the pressures that exist at
CGTN and other Chinese state media outlets are stronger and clearer,
and they affect a broader range of topics than those at Fox News or
NBC News.

Copying RT and Sputnik's Styles

While CGTN and Xinhua have expanded, become more professional,
attempted to lure better journalists, and mostly shied away from completely conspiratorial reporting, at least before the Ukraine war, a few
Chinese state media outlets already increasingly resembled Russian
state media's more no-holds-barred approach.

The ultranationalist, rabble-rousing *Global Times* has taken approaches like the provocative, argumentative, and conspiracy-minded
Russian outlets, mixing nationalism with efforts to mock the United
States and other countries—a strategy increasingly employed by
Chinese diplomats on Twitter as well, inspired by Xi Jinping's exhort-
ations about a more assertive foreign policy, and following the lead of
Chinese uber-nationalist, "wolf warrior" prototype, and increasingly
influential, foreign ministry spokesperson Zhao Lijian.[87] Controlled
by the *People's Daily*, *Global Times* often reports or editorializes on sensitive topics the *People's Daily* usually doesn't touch, like the dissident

Chinese artist Ai Weiwei or the 1989 Tiananmen crackdown—but always strongly backing the Chinese authorities.[88] Among Chinese academics and journalists, *Global Times* has a reputation for shoddy reporting and editorials, but it still has about ten million daily readers inside China.[89]

Outside China, *Global Times* has used its uber-hawkish editorials and its top editor's skill at sparking controversies to make it relevant on social media internationally, in part because its content elicits responses from foreign officials and opinion leaders. These responses can keep *Global Times* content alive internationally for several news cycles on platforms like Twitter, as foreign opinion leaders tweet about it or write about it on other social media platforms and the newspaper's editor and other journalists sometimes parry back. (Unsurprisingly, Twitter, like Facebook, is banned in China, but Chinese state media outlets have built massive global followings on these platforms, and *Global Times* is highly active on them.[90]) *Global Times* also has signed a deal to exchange personnel with Sputnik, presumably so the two can learn more from each other.[91]

Global Times's leaders, like those of successful provocateurs such as *Breitbart* in the United States, seem to care little whether readers like or hate *Global Times*'s stories, as long as the pieces draw interest. The publication also sometimes appears to be used by China's government to send out trial balloons for potential foreign policy moves and a reflection of some hardline top Chinese officials' thinking, at least according to the controversial former top editor, Hu Xijin, who announced his retirement as editor in late 2021 but will continue to be a commentator.[92] Beijing then gauges foreign reaction to what appears in *Global Times*. *Global Times*, for instance, has repeatedly threatened Australia over getting involved in South China Sea territorial disputes in what seems like potential shots from Beijing over Canberra's bow—warning, for example, that if Australia became involved in the South China Sea, "it would be a shame if one day a plane fell from the sky and it happened to be Australian."[93]

Peter Cai of the Lowy Institute's *Interpreter* spoke with a number of *Global Times* reporters in part about how the paper assesses its effect internationally.[94] He was told that management believed that one of the main performance indicators for *Global Times* "is how many times it gets cited in foreign press, so editors often use colorful and outrageous language to attract foreign media's attention."[95] Indeed, editorials in *Global Times* often appear to be written specifically with attracting foreign media attention and coverage in mind, thus amplifying the message. These range from overtly nationalistic messages, like arguing for a Chinese nuclear arms buildup or the need to reunify Taiwan with the Chinese mainland by force, to needling foreign audiences by calling the U.S. Congress "rascally varmints" and saying the British people have a "losing mind-set."[96] In all of these instances, portions of these provocative editorials were also featured in the social media accounts of Chinese diplomats known for their aggressive online rhetoric and also were picked up by Western media outlets and commentators, giving them a longer life in the media ecosystem.

To further spread its message in the United States, *Global Times* in 2013 launched a U.S. edition in English and Chinese. It also launched a European edition in 2016 and used its European debut to mock the United Kingdom, writing articles with titles mocking Britain's exit from Europe and essentially saying China would take its place in trading with the continent.[97] Its U.S. and European editions do not have broad readership—*Global Times* claims a print circulation of two hundred thousand for its English edition, a figure that includes print readership in many countries—but through these editions *Global Times* attracts more notice from U.S. and European policymakers and other opinion leaders.[98] (*Global Times* allegedly has a daily print circulation of some 2.6 million in Chinese, in addition to its larger overall readership in Chinese online.[99]) And when these opinion leaders respond to *Global Times* articles, either on social media platforms or by citing them in their own op-eds and columns, they only draw more eyeballs to the outlet.

Increasingly, other Chinese state media outlets are circulating conspiracy theories like *Global Times* or promoting fiery commentary, particularly about the Ukraine war. Chinese state media have, during the Ukraine war, increasingly spread Russian-style ultranationalist and conspiratorial content, even as hawkish Chinese diplomats have parroted disinformation about the Ukraine conflict as well, in press briefings and on their official accounts on major social media platforms.[100] Even as many Russian state media have been limited or removed from major social media platforms like Twitter and Facebook, Chinese state media have pushed Russian narratives and even bought ads promoting Russian narratives on Facebook and other sites, allowing the Kremlin to continue to spread its message even when it cannot do so directly.[101]

A Consistent Message by State Journalists

Could self-censorship, though bad for the cause of truthful reporting, be a boon for the effectiveness of Chinese state media? The ability to unify around Beijing's preferred message could, in theory, give Chinese state media and state-linked media an advantage in influencing foreign populations. In a study of the coordination of Chinese state media and Chinese-language media that are not technically state media but have close links to Beijing, like Chinese-language outlets abroad owned by tycoons close to Beijing, the research organization AidData suggests that the lack of freedom within China's media is indeed an advantage in trying to influence foreign states. AidData notes that "low levels of media freedom at home enable Beijing to deploy a formidable set of trusted mouthpieces as an extension of the state in promoting its preferred narrative."[102]

In other words, Chinese state media, and private media controlled by owners and editors with strong pro-Beijing leanings, can coordinate messages with effectiveness because these outlets often are delivering the same stories and opinions to audiences overseas.

China's lack of media freedoms does help Beijing promote co-operation among many outlets and coordinate messaging. China's state-controlled and state-influenced media outlets also add their messages to those delivered by Chinese officials, ambassadors, and senior leaders, who publish op-eds in other outlets.[103] But even some outlets with links to Beijing resist such coordination. The growing influence of Beijing in the Hong Kong media has had a significant effect—in Reporters Without Borders' World Press Freedom Index, Hong Kong has dropped from being ranked as one of the freest media environments in the world two decades ago to ranking somewhere in the middle of all places surveyed, a massive drop as China has imposed severe restrictions on the free press, including essentially shutting down the fiercely independent *Apple Daily*, neutering the trusted Hong Kong city radio and television broadcaster, and closing most remaining free outlets.[104]

Consistent messaging can backfire. Bureau chiefs and top editors for Chinese state media still rarely get promoted for producing independent, quality content, no matter how often top CGTN leaders say they want to be in the league of CNN and BBC or how many skilled foreign reporters state outlets hire. Bureau chiefs and managers, as the author heard from former state media employees, get promoted for satisfying top management, who rarely welcome edgier, quality reporting. Many Xinhua articles, CGTN pieces, and CRI radio pieces may be consistent, but they hammer home biased and simply untrue "reporting" on the most sensitive topics to Beijing, like Taiwan, Xinjiang, global tensions over China's technology companies, and other issues, so the stories will prove acceptable to the top leadership in Beijing rather than news consumers in foreign countries. This is "domestic signaling," as the *Guardian* called it in an exposé of China's soft and sharp power efforts—"telegraphing messages [via reporting in state media] that demonstrate loyalty to the party line in order to curry favor with senior officials."[105] In the most extreme circumstances, state media outlets, including Xinhua, revert to reporting on sensitive issues that sounds like older Chinese propaganda from the 1960s or 1970s—tinny and clearly false—in a way that they now sound when talking about China-Russia relations or about the Ukraine war.[106]

Such domestic signaling does not plague every state media story; in the most effective outlets, like *Sixth Tone*, it is concealed amidst a story that looks virtually the same as an article from a leading outlet based in a democracy. And in fact, some *Sixth Tone* stories, about social and economic issues that do not directly imply criticism of the government, do read similarly as a piece from the *New York Times* or the *Guardian*.[107] *Sixth Tone* even sometimes reports on issues that could portray provincial or city governments, or the central government itself, in a negative light—new outbreaks of COVID-19 in China, chemical pollution in China's waterways, slow economic recovery from the effects of the pandemic in some parts of the country.[108] But the persistence of domestic signaling certainly undermines the brand of many state media outlets, preventing them from being taken seriously enough as credible news outlets.

Consistent Messaging Does Not Always Work

Consistent messaging also can lead state media outlets to become so presumptuous that they simply cannot believe emerging news stories that do not conform to the predictions and messages provided by Beijing. *Foreign Policy*'s James Palmer offers one notable example of how state media groupthink can backfire, exposing state outlets as slow and unprepared to respond to real news events that Beijing did not anticipate. Before Hong Kong's November 2019 district council elections, Palmer reported, top editors and other managers in Chinese state media genuinely believed that pro-Beijing candidates would perform well.[109] This presumption defied reality—Hong Kongers had been protesting for months and were enraged at pro-Beijing Hong Kong politicians. But, as Palmer notes, the state media leadership was so delusional—receiving coordinated but totally incorrect messages from Beijing and the CCP's Hong Kong–based intelligence organization about the vote—that some state media outlets were told to file dispatches the night before the elections.[110] These dispatches assumed that the pro-Beijing candidates in Hong Kong would perform well, and even would increase their majorities in the district councils.[111] State media managers then apparently were shocked when pro-democracy candidates thrashed pro-Beijing types in the elections, winning three times as many district council seats as before, amid the highest turnout ever for local contests.[112]

In fact, despite these supposed advantages at coordination, within relatively free and East Asian and Pacific states, China's state media have struggled in fostering broadly positive images of China. Research by AidData, the same organization that theorized about the effect of Chinese media coordination, also found that journalists in freer states in the East Asia and Pacific region overall have been the "most vocal" about concerns regarding Chinese state media and other Chinese information efforts.[113]

Training Programs

China's training and exchange programs for journalists began to expand in the 2000s, and their scale has grown exponentially in the Xi era, at least before China largely closed its borders due to its zero-COVID policy. These programs have become another way for Beijing to promote its state media to other countries and also, potentially, to get journalists from other countries to return home and write positively about China. The introduction to a 2019 Reporters Without Borders study of China's state media noted that "the [Chinese] regime has managed to convince tens of thousands of journalists in emerging countries [and, I would note, some wealthy states] to go on all-expense-paid trips to Beijing."[114] The trips range from four or five days, in which journalists visit Chinese media outlets, meet with officials, and sometimes take a short vacation, to ten-month training programs. The longer programs involve taking classes on Chinese politics, the Chinese economic system, the Chinese media, Chinese foreign policy, and other topics, as well as interviewing Chinese officials and entrepreneurs and doing internships at Chinese media outlets.[115]

These trips are covered by Xinhua's lavish subsidies or are paid for with other Chinese government funds.[116] They mostly bring journalists from developing countries, although they have included reporters and editors from middle-income states, like Argentina.[117]

Since 2016, Beijing has been bringing about one hundred journalists annually from Africa, South Asia, and Southeast Asia to China for extended fellowships, which also include comfortable accommodations in luxury apartments in Beijing and a monthly stipend, as well as trips around China.[118] In 2019, China formally opened the China-Africa and China-Asia Pacific press centers in Beijing, which coordinate many of these fellowships.[119] China also now has a press center running training programs for visiting journalists from Latin America and the Caribbean, and has expanded the training programs in China to include many Latin American, South Asian, European, and Central Asian journalists as well.[120] By 2019, the study by Reporters Without Borders had found that roughly 3,400 journalists from at least 146 countries had come to China for some sort of training and/ or exchange program, including the ten-month stints.[121] That figure may actually be low, especially if one takes into account the number of journalists who come on shorter visit and training programs. Beijing has signaled that it plans to continue expanding the programs, so it is likely the number of journalists being brought to Beijing for training will grow annually in the coming decade, provided that China ends its isolationist zero-COVID policy and begins to once again open its borders and end its harsh lockdowns and attempts to eradicate the virus. The Forum on China-Africa Cooperation has called for China to train one thousand African media professionals each year, and indeed research by Maria Repnikova of the Wilson Center suggests China is already training some one thousand African journalists annually.[122]

The ten-month programs provide journalists with a relatively deep immersion in the country. Some participants in the longer programs suggested that they did involve aspects of journalism training, but others have said that they were basically extended propaganda trips designed to simply sell China to foreign journalists. "In China, media trainings are in actuality free public relations trips to China that follow a conveniently pro-government agenda," Juan Pablo Cardenal, a leading Spanish journalist focusing on China, wrote in an assessment of Chinese influence on Latin American journalists and other opinion leaders.[123] Still, prominent and respected outlets in Africa, Latin America, South Asia, and Southeast Asia—the *Indian Express*, for instance, and Kenya's *Business Daily*, part of the biggest media group in East Africa—now take part in China's programs.[124]

In some respects, China's training and exchange programs resemble long-standing efforts by the United States and other countries to bring foreign journalists for visits and training programs. Other major powers, like the United States, also bring in foreign journalists to study the domestic media climate. But these programs, like the U.S. State Department's Edward R. Murrow Program, usually last only a few weeks.[125] (Private organizations in the United States, like Harvard University, have programs, like the Nieman Fellowship, that allow journalists to come from all over the world, but these often mix classes and support for the journalists' own research.[126])

And unlike U.S. visitor programs for foreign journalists, which clearly are tools of soft power, China's training programs can be both soft and sharp. Beijing's journalist programs are, on their face, essentially soft power tools. China does not force anyone to go on the trips; the trips are advertised in recipient countries; and participants openly receive funding for travel, living expenses, and basic essentials. The payments are not done opaquely. The trips advertise China in ways that echo how U.S. visitor programs advertise the United States and potentially bolster U.S. soft power.

However, the effect of these trips could be coercive—the trips could in theory corrode independent coverage of China in other countries, since they could encourage self-censorship about China among reporters who have completed the trips. While some trips to China allow accurate messages about China, the CCP, and Chinese foreign policy to seep in through diffusion, many former participants report, in oral histories of the programs and from an investigation of it, that they got clear instructions about how they should report on China both during the program and when they returned home. According to Ananth Krishnan, a former visiting fellow at Brookings India who studied the longer training programs, one Southeast Asian journalist who went said that participants were told "explicitly" to only parrot Chinese foreign ministry lines in reporting on issues related to the South China Sea and should churn out positive stories about China.[127] Krishnan also noted that, during the fellowships, the reporters "cannot undertake individual reporting trips unaccompanied by government minders as they are not independently accredited— and are hence hamstrung from reporting on issues seen as 'sensitive,' from human rights to Tibet and Xinjiang."[128] What's more, visiting journalists are regularly fed misinformation or denied unrestricted access to places they want to report on, especially when they seek to visit areas sensitive to the Chinese government like Xinjiang or Tibet. The introduction to the Reporters Without Borders study of these training programs notes that the programs are designed for foreign journalists "to 'train their critical mind' in exchange for favorable press coverage" when they return home.

Yet the reality is that many, and probably most, of these trips have little effect on foreign journalists' coverage of China, and China has had to pull back on these trips and visits by foreign officials in the years in which, starting in 2020, it pursued a zero-COVID strategy and essentially isolated itself from the world. Certainly, the programs seem popular—and why not, since they are often relatively lavish? A 2020 study by the International Federation of Journalists (IFJ), of the media in fifty-eight countries and territories (including both developed and developing states), found that a majority of respondents who had participated in the training programs thought they were a positive experience overall.[129]

Some of the programs may have an effect, although China's self-isolation means that the programs will essentially have to be restarted anew once Beijing drops its zero-COVID approach. One diplomat who closely follows Chinese influence offered a specific illustration from his own country, one of the Southeast Asian states known for its skepticism about China's growing power. Editors from his country who travel to China on the training programs, he claimed, often come home and become more likely to rely on Chinese state media for information and for reprinting articles. They even, he said, are more likely to parrot Chinese state media's views on major domestic and foreign policy issues once they return home. He also noted that, after a trip for journalists from his country to China's Xinjiang province, where human rights groups accuse Beijing of imprisoning as many as one million Muslim Uighurs in detention camps, some reporters who had joined the trip returned home and downplayed abuses in Xinjiang, echoing Beijing's line.

Indeed, wined and dined, some visiting journalists may wind up being more sympathetic to Beijing, as appeared to have occurred with journalists after trips to Xinjiang. China has utilized these trips, with a great deal of efficacy, to soften and silence criticism of abuses against the Uighurs among journalists in developing countries, according to several studies. The 2020 IFJ report notes:

> [Many journalists surveyed had] remarked on a recent Chinese interest in Muslim journalists. In some countries, the Chinese embassy has sought out journalists working for Islamic media, organizing special media trips to showcase Xinjiang as a travel destination and an economic success story. One clear focus from the articles produced by journalists on these trips is to accuse the Western media of propagating "fake stories" about Xinjiang. These trips are designed to redirect attention from Western media reports of up to 1 million Uighurs being held in political indoctrination camps in the province. Entrepreneurs with large business interests in China have also acted as proxies by inviting

senior journalists on trips to Xinjiang and introducing them to provincial leaders.[130]

But overall, training programs so far do not dramatically sway media coverage of China in recipient countries at this point or prompt broad censorship about China in local media in other states. While journalists on many of the training programs may come from states poorer than China—Kenya, Liberia, Malawi, the Philippines, and others—their home countries almost always have more robust press freedoms than China, one of the most repressive media environments in the world.[131] And many participants in journalism training programs are appalled by the state of press freedoms in China, and by other rights abuses, which they can see despite government officials' efforts to stop them. Maria Repnikova, of Georgia State University, has intensively studied training programs for Africans in China, including journalists from Ethiopia. (Ethiopia certainly would not be considered a place known for media freedom, but it is freer than China.) She found that the training programs in China had little effect on how Ethiopians viewed China, noting in an interview with the *Washington Post*, "On the one hand, participants noted feeling inspired by the scale and speed of China's development. At the same time, thus far, these programs appear to incite limited emulation."[132] Similarly, the *Columbia Journalism Review* has collected an oral history of journalists who traveled to China for foreign press training programs and exchanges.[133] Some participants interviewed in the *Columbia Journalism Review*'s oral history expressed positive opinions of the training program. But others simply got a close-up, nasty look at a highly authoritarian media environment. Bonface Otieno, a reporter for the *Business Standard* in Kenya, took part in a press training program in 2017. She said:

> They took us to museums, markets, social joints, all kinds of places, to show us how they do their stuff. The problem with these guys, though, was that the moment you ask them hard questions they feel offended. We wanted to understand why the media in China does not ever criticize the government. . . . But I felt their answers were not here and

not there, they were not satisfactory. . . . If the Chinese brought me to Beijing to influence my journalism, they failed.[134]

Narratives

Chinese state media outlets also try to portray themselves, in developing regions, as more sympathetic to developing countries—in places like Africa, Latin America, or Eastern Europe, for instance—than major Western outlets. In several studies of Chinese state media's approach to Africa, Iginio Gagliardone, of the Oxford Internet Institute, found that state media "emphasized [their] ability to offer comprehensive reporting on Africa (largely because of the vast resources [CGTN] is able to mobilize, to cover the continent) and its commitment to tell a different African story"—a positive story that positions Chinese media as allied with Africans against a Western media that has long focused on the negative about the continent.[135] Chinese state media also focuses on the negative consequences of Western interventions in places like Africa, Central Asia, the Middle East, and Southeast Asia, and in particular the supposed negative consequences of U.S. actions in Africa, according to a study of stories that appeared in Xinhua and *China Daily* by researchers at South African and British universities.[136] Gagliardone also finds that China often has tried to use its influence to fit into information and media projects already being developed by African states.

In one notable example, Chinese state media has attempted to make inroads in Kenya, the leading economy in East Africa and historically the major regional hub for media companies. CGTN appears on the national Kenyan broadcaster each night. It also made Nairobi its first broadcast hub outside of China, which, when it was built, was the biggest non-African broadcasting hub on the African continent.[137] CRI opened an AM channel that could be accessed across the country, as well as three FM channels dedicated to its programming, with the FM station broadcasting in English, Swahili, and Chinese.[138] As a result,

Chinese media outlets, which increasingly try to feature African hosts on radio and television, are becoming recognizable to Kenyans. A survey of young African students who closely follow international media in Africa found that many Kenyan students perceived CGTN as "a reputable international media organization" and that major media figures from CGTN were widely known in Kenya.[139] One of the students in the survey told the interviewers, "The stories there [on CGTN], I can resonate with them."[140]

It is possible that providing a "different story" can win over more readers, viewers, and listeners in Africa, Southeast Asia, and other developing regions. A study by Catie Snow Bailard of GW used Pew Global Attitudes polling and analyzed the effect of Chinese media expansion in Africa on public opinion on the continent. It found some correlation between the size of a Chinese media presence in an African state and more favorable popular opinions of China on a range of topics in Ghana, Kenya, Nigeria, Senegal, South Africa, and Uganda.[141] (Overall, in research done by organizations like the Pew Research Center, African states tend to view China more favorably than countries from most other regions of the world anyway.[142])

China's Other State Media Outlets Still Struggle

Yet China's biggest state media outlets, other than Xinhua, still struggle to find audiences, despite their expansion and modernization. As these state media outlets expand, and if Chinese state media can become more trusted by consumers, they could become bigger weapons for Beijing. If Beijing created globally respected state media outlets, it could disseminate pro-China content openly through them. This would be a double bonus for China, since positive views of Chinese state media would reflect well on China itself, much as Voice of America proudly advertises its links to the U.S. government in its bid to win over listeners. But it remains a big question whether China's state media outlets can win news consumers' trust.

I have already mentioned the challenges Chinese provincial outlets have faced expanding into Southeast Asia. In Africa, CGTN and other outlets have made some of their biggest investments and gained some credibility among local audiences. But this effect is limited—Chinese media outlets' audience shares and perceived credibility still lag behind local news sources and the BBC and other Western broadcasters, and their credibility is hardly going to be helped by parroting Russian disinformation and spreading clearly false stories about the Ukraine conflict. Overall, studies by Herman Wasserman and Dani Madrid-Morales show that China's state media outlets in Africa are far from approaching the reach of the major Western channels.[143] In the Ivory Coast, for instance, CRI has made efforts to expand its programming and reach a broader audience, but a Gallup media survey that I uncovered shows that it had been almost completely unsuccessful. Gallup revealed that CRI reached less than 1 percent of Ivorians weekly, the second-worst figure of any of the twenty-three radio networks analyzed in the survey.[144] By contrast, the BBC reached 13.7 percent of Ivorians weekly, and Voice of America reached about 5 percent.[145] In Nigeria, a much bigger target for China's soft and sharp power campaigns than the Ivory Coast, both CGTN and CRI performed miserably in a similar Gallup study. In Nigeria, CGTN had 3.7 percent of the total audience reach of international TV networks in the country, about one-quarter the audience of the BBC; CRI was listened to by less than 1 percent of Nigerians tuning in to international broadcasting.[146]

Many Africans still see Chinese outlets as propaganda.[147] For instance, Vivien Marsh of the University of Westminster notes that Chinese state media's lack of coverage of Pope Francis's visit to Africa in 2015, a story of clear local interest, shows how censorship impedes hyperlocalization.[148] (China does not have diplomatic relations with the Vatican, although the two sides have become closer in recent years.)

Even in Kenya, the hub of Chinese state media expansion in West Africa, Chinese outlets have fared relatively poorly. Polling, such as a study done by Abdirizak Garo Guyo and Hong Yu, suggests that most Kenyans who consume news do not even utilize Chinese state media or barely use it at all.[149]

These figures are consistent with the still-low audience share of CGTN, CRI, and state media outlets, save Xinhua, in many other regions of the world. In Asia, Chinese broadcast and radio state media outlets have not reached a large audience. A Gallup study of the weekly reach of television stations in Vietnam found that CGTN was only watched by 0.7 percent of Vietnamese adults, far less than the BBC, CNN, France's TV5 Monde Asie, and South Korea's Arirang TV— a low figure I did not find surprising, given that most Vietnamese opinion leaders I know never tune in to Chinese state media.[150] Two-thirds of Vietnamese who watched the BBC said they trusted that outlet a great deal, but only about 7 percent who watched CGTN said the same. In Cambodia, even though China has heavily promoted its state media outlets, another study I obtained through the Freedom of Information Act process found that CRI lagged nearly every other international and local radio broadcaster in the country in terms of weekly listeners.[151]

In leading democracies too, in Europe and North America, CGTN has largely fizzled, though their content does spread to some extent among local Chinese-speaking communities when it is shared on WeChat and other social media platforms; China's links to the Ukraine war are going to hurt CGTN and other state media even more. In the United Kingdom, which has a sizable audience of people who are fluent in Chinese, a study found that CGTN was being watched by a minimal number of Britons—even before the British government kicked CGTN off the air in 2021 because it did not have autonomy from the Chinese state.[152] And while CGTN has a wide reach in the United States and Canada in terms of households in which it is available, this reach does not mean people are tuning in to the network. Sarah Cook of Freedom House, who has closely studied Chinese media in the United States, believes that CGTN's actual viewership numbers in the United States lag even those of New Tang Dynasty TV, a station available in far fewer U.S. households.[153] Similarly, though CGTN launched a CGTN Europe subsidiary in 2019 via its London hub, it has made little inroads into the continental European market, where there are many countries with dominant state broadcasters, as well as extensive satellite offerings, and European governments that are now increasingly watchful and critical of CGTN and other Chinese state media's offerings.[154]

Similarly, throughout Latin America, including in several large democracies, CGTN's Spanish-language channel has significantly expanded the number of households in which it is available over the past decade but has not proved popular.[155] As multiple experts on China's relations with Latin America have told me, Chinese news content is not widely viewed in Chile, Argentina, and Brazil, among other Latin American states.[156] A comprehensive study of CGTN-Espanol, CGTN's Spanish-language channel, by Peilei Ye and Luis A. Albornoz indeed suggests that the network's "audience and visibility was still low" and that the Chinese government usually releases information only about the size of the audience CGTN potentially reaches—the number of households it is available in—and not the actual audience, probably because the actual audience size is embarrassingly low.[157]

The continuing climate of self-censorship at CGTN, which has only gotten worse as Beijing has pursued a zero-COVID policy unpopular with the Chinese public and as the Ukraine war has polarized the world and seemed to make the Chinese leadership more paranoid, always threatens to undermine whatever gains in credibility it has made from hiring established reporters from independent global media organizations and from well-respected local outlets. In a study of CGTN, Merriden Varrall of the Lowy Institute finds that the organization remains "closed, competitive, and characterized by a lack of trust among employees. . . . Due to the lack of trust, there is an almost total lack of incentive to push boundaries, including in topics and stories being covered, and how particular topics were addressed."[158]

Chinese State Media on Social Media:
Giants or Minnows?

Meanwhile, CGTN and other Chinese state media may be using social media platforms to appear like giants, but they are not at this point getting much real appeal on these platforms. (Chinese social media and messaging platforms like WeChat, which still remain increasingly powerful tools, are a different story.)

Beijing's deep pockets also may be helping it gain followers for its state media outlets on global social media platforms, another tactic to bolster the prestige and credibility of outlets like CGTN and Xinhua. China's major outlets have some of the highest numbers of Facebook followers of any media company on earth. By the end of 2019, they accounted for five of the six media outlets with the most followers on Facebook.[159] Chinese state media achieved this dominance even though the government blocks Facebook inside the country, meaning that few if any of the followers of CGTN, Xinhua, or other state media outlets come from China itself.[160] CGTN's English-language page now has more than 117 million Facebook followers globally, the most of any media company in the world.[161] CGTN was adding followers on Facebook in 2019 and 2020 forty times as fast as CNN, a better-known global media brand—a staggering disparity.[162] *China Daily, People's Daily*, and Xinhua are just behind CGTN, and their numbers dwarf the numbers for major Western news outlets like the BBC, CNN, and the *New York Times*.[163]

Even *Global Times*, the hawkish, ultranationalist state media newspaper and online news outlet, which is more of a niche publication than Xinhua, has over sixty-five million followers on Facebook, more than the *New York Times*.[164] Yet the *New York Times*, a global news giant with bureaus all over the world, gets roughly 240 million visits per month to its website, while *Global Times*, a minnow in terms of bureaus and total staff, gets about 30 million.[165]

Within Southeast Asia too, my own research and research by other analysts, like the Center for Naval Analyses, shows that Chinese state media outlets are racking up large numbers of Facebook followers in some countries, although the amount of real, authentic engagement seems low.[166] In the Philippines, the biggest Chinese state media companies, like CGTN and Xinhua, average more than 900,000 followers for their Facebook pages, in Thailand CRI's Facebook page has 2.5 million followers, and in Indonesia the biggest Chinese state media companies average roughly 650,000 followers.[167] (To be fair, these figures pale in comparison to the number of followers for the Facebook pages of the biggest Philippine and Indonesian media companies, like Kompas.com, but most of these outlets operate in local languages, giving them larger potential audiences.[168]) In addition, Chinese state media outlets enjoy massive penetration of their stories on WeChat, the messaging, social media, and payment platform widely used in China, and increasingly used across North America and Southeast Asia as well, although Washington moved to crack down on the ability to use WeChat within the United States.

Chinese state media outlets also are boosting their followings on Twitter. Twitter, like Facebook, is banned in China, and the Xi administration has made it extremely difficult for Chinese citizens to access both platforms via virtual private networks. Yet by the end of 2021, CGTN's official Twitter page, @CGTNOfficial, had over thirteen million Twitter followers.[169] While this was less than CNN, CGTN was gaining followers at twice CNN's daily rate.[170] CGTN also boasted nearly twice as many followers on Twitter as Al Jazeera English, which may be better known internationally.

The sizable figures can have an effect on the international image of CGTN, Xinhua, and other state outlets. By suggesting that these outlets are enormously popular on social media, the high numbers of followers may make them seem more prestigious, and thus more attractive to readers and viewers.

Inorganic

Despite Chinese state media outlets' enormous number of followers, much of their Facebook and Twitter content generates few comments in response, raising suspicions about how many real followers they have, and on Twitter Beijing uses fake followers to retweet Chinese diplomats, according to the Associated Press.[171] CGTN America, despite its hires of prominent journalists and production of some genuinely high-quality videos and shorter pieces, still struggles to attract a more than ten thousand or twenty thousand viewers for its offerings on YouTube.[172] By contrast, videos from CNN often attract hundreds of thousands or even millions of viewers on YouTube.

As I have found by studying who interacts with China's biggest state media outlets on social media platforms, photos, not articles, are the content on CGTN's Facebook page that generate the most interaction with other Facebook users. That photos dominate CGTN's share of interactions suggests but does not prove that CGTN's stories do not spread widely on Facebook, despite CGTN's staggering number of supposed Facebook followers. In addition, a sizable amount of CGTN's share interactions come from promoted, or paid for, content.[173]

Perhaps unsurprisingly, then, a study by Joyce Nip and Chao Sun of the University of Sydney and comparing the influence of Chinese and U.S. news sources on social media platforms found that China's big outlets, with so many dubious followers and fans, did not have the effect one might think given their massive Facebook and Twitter numbers. Instead, they discovered that "US sources are more influential [than Chinese ones] as a whole in setting the news agenda and amplifying certain news events" on social media platforms.[174]

Indeed, Chinese state outlets' presence on social media may be inorganic. While Facebook and Twitter claim they are cracking down on manipulation of their platforms to reduce purchased fake "likes" and fake followers, cybersecurity companies have demonstrated that it remains possible to buy large numbers of followers and likes on social media platforms.[175] Despite Chinese state media outlets' enormous number of followers, most of their Facebook and Twitter content indeed generates few comments in response, raising suspicions about how many legitimate followers they have.[176] In an investigation, the business publication *Quartz* found that few of Chinese state media's followers came from the world's biggest English-speaking countries, which would be the most natural audiences for English-language Facebook pages.[177] Instead, the investigation showed, most Facebook followers of these sites come from countries known for "running 'click farms' where companies can buy" Facebook likes, reposts, and followers.[178]

Indeed, CGTN and other state outlets may be using social media platforms to appear like giants, but they are not yet getting much genuine traction with users on these international platforms. CGTN's generally boring, staid offerings on YouTube generate minimal actual interactions from viewers and few of the comments common on most popular YouTube channels.[179] And outside the United States, a sizable percentage of CGTN and Xinhua's YouTube content still seems clumsy and even occasionally anachronistic and racist. In 2017, according to the Australian Broadcasting Corporation, Xinhua produced a video for its YouTube channel, amid tensions between Delhi and Beijing over border issues, that contained racist portrayals of Indians and of India more broadly.[180]

In addition, a sizable amount of CGTN's share of interactions came from paid-for content—basically, posts that CGTN pays to be pushed into users' Facebook news feeds, where it appears as sponsored content.[181] (In 2020, Facebook banned ads on the platform from state-controlled media companies.[182]) Twenty-two percent of all of CGTN's Facebook posts were promoted content, as Hunter Marston showed. Many major news organizations, in contrast, shy away from using promoted content as much.[183] They may do so because their own, organically created content is interesting enough for users to share, even without the news organizations paying to push these stories into users' Facebook news feeds. For instance, on the Facebook pages of the BBC, CNN, and Al Jazeera, the vast majority of the content is organic.[184]

Chapter 7

Xinhua and Content-Sharing Deals

A Success Story

Among all the Chinese state media outlets, Xinhua stands as the most internationally influential today, and the one with the most potential to affect the global news industry in the future and thus bolster China's soft power worldwide. Beijing has placed a high premium on modernizing Xinhua and getting foreign news outlets to use Xinhua stories, in the process legitimizing Xinhua to some editors and readers. Beijing also has aggressively signed content-sharing deals between Xinhua and foreign outlets, to help get Xinhua before the eyes of more readers and to bring more prestige onto the Chinese newswire. Beyond Xinhua, China has used content-sharing deals for other state media outlets, like *China Daily*, for similar effects.

Like other Chinese state outlets, Xinhua is expanding. A study by the Pentagon released in late 2018 found that Xinhua had 162 foreign bureaus in 2017 and was rapidly expanding, with a goal of around 200 bureaus.[1] By early 2021, Xinhua had a reported 181 bureaus globally, and that number seemed to be growing in 2022.[2] This would give Xinhua a reach close to that of the Associated Press, which has around 250 bureaus worldwide, or the BBC, which is a giant in Africa, Asia, and other regions.[3]

Meanwhile, the Chinese newswire has a massive advantage over most of its competitors, in that it does not have to make a profit.[4] It can afford to give some of its content away to news outlets in relatively poor countries, and sometimes to news outlets in wealthier states with warm relations with China.[5] (The Associated Press is a nonprofit, but it can't afford to lose money the way Xinhua can.) This financial advantage is allowing Xinhua to become increasingly accessible to many developing-world newsrooms that cannot afford other wire services.[6]

In some poorer states, local outlets increasingly depend on Xinhua as a primary source of international wire copy. Similarly, in many states the China Global Television Network (CGTN) partners with local state broadcasters, like the Kenyan national broadcaster KBC, which run CGTN content, including news and TV dramas.[7] National broadcasters like KBC have been hit hard by the internet and the expansion of satellite media; they need content, and Chinese state media outlets are happy to oblige. Xinhua has targeted Africa in particular for expansion. Xinhua now has about twenty bureaus on the continent, and CGTN operates in six languages across Africa.[8]

Covering Undercovered Stories

Xinhua also is attempting to boost its credibility in other ways in Southeast Asia and other areas closest physically to China or where populations have relatively positive images of China. In Southeast Asia and Africa, where Xinhua has poured resources into expansion, the Chinese state newswire can cover stories that may not get mentioned by other media organizations such as Reuters, the Associated Press, Agence France-Presse, or large international newspapers with foreign staffs. (CGTN also has begun adopting a strategy of trying to cover many stories ignored by big broadcasters like the BBC and CNN, particularly in regions like Southeast Asia, like the details of Southeast Asian summits.) One former U.S. official analyzing China's expanding state media called this a "hyperlocal approach," a strategy focused on offering detailed stories in regions that Chinese editors may believe are not getting this type of detailed coverage from many other international outlets.[9]

Xinhua journalists, for instance, usually (before COVID-19) pack regional summits in Southeast Asia, where the Association of Southeast Asian Nations (ASEAN) and its various suborganizations seem to hold talk shops nearly every day of the year.[10] (They surely will pack summits again after the pandemic.) Most other newswires and global outlets have few or no reporters at these meetings, unless they are major summits involving top Southeast Asian leaders. But Xinhua covers nearly every detail of them. Prashanth Parameswaran, a scholar who once worked for the prominent Asian affairs website the *Diplomat*, did sometimes cover the smaller ASEAN gatherings. He would often find himself the only non-Xinhua reporter at such affairs.[11] With so much reporting at these events, Xinhua is able to provide more copy about the summits for news outlets in Southeast Asia than competitors like the Associated Press.

Partnerships

Xinhua and other Chinese state media also are borrowing credibility through partnerships with other outlets, particularly respected local media outlets known for their independent reporting in developed democracies and other places with high levels of media freedom. State media firms often attempt to launch high-profile partnerships, focused on joint events or other types of public cooperation, with major global media outlets. These deals, however, are not usually covert, sharp power strategies. They usually are not efforts to smuggle Xinhua or CGTN content into other, more prestigious news outlets, where readers or viewers will consume that content without knowing its original provenance. Instead, these partnerships are designed to put Xinhua, and to some extent other state outlets, on the radar of editors and publishers at news outlets globally, making them more likely to use Xinhua stories in the future.

Sometimes, the partnerships literally involve positioning, like holding summits where the logos of Chinese state media are plastered on the same stages as the logos for leading international media companies from democratic states. For instance, in 2018 Xinhua and the Associated Press together announced that they were cooperating in areas including new media.[12] If the 175-year-old Associated Press—winner of fifty-six Pulitzer Prizes and starchy defender of press standards—is willing to partner with Xinhua, then the latter should be respectable, right? (Under fire from the U.S. Congress, the Associated Press defended the linkage, noting that the "business relationship with Xinhua is completely separate and firewalled from its journalistic coverage of China."[13]) Xinhua also has built cooperation agreements with other major global and regional newswires, including Agence France-Presse.[14]

Beijing supplements the partnerships with media summits held in China, often with Xinhua as a central sponsor. China has halted these for now, as it has virtually isolated itself from the world with its zero-COVID strategy, but once that strategy ends it will surely go back to all of these gatherings, invites to journalists and officials, and all other types of events and efforts at wooing foreign opinion leaders. The gatherings—the World Media Summit, the BRICS Media Summit (for journalists from developing states), and others—also serve to portray Xinhua and other state media outlets as major, legitimate news organizations. On some occasions, China has held these meetings with major international partners from Europe and North America, including Reuters, the Associated Press, and News Corporation, and their involvement adds to the image of Xinhua as a legitimate news source.[15]

Other, regional summits feature Xinhua and other state media brands alongside prominent outlets that cover countries in one region, like Latin America and Eastern Europe. For instance, in 2018, Xinhua, in partnership with Argentina's state media, organized a summit in

Buenos Aires that brought together thirteen Chinese media outlets and some one hundred news agencies from Latin America and the Caribbean to discuss possible areas of cooperation.[16]

Content-Sharing Deals

These partnerships also often include content-sharing deals with foreign media outlets, in which they agree to use Xinhua copy for some stories. Content-sharing deals are not necessarily sharp power. When these deals are signed and the stories from Chinese state media outlets like Xinhua are openly marked as coming from Xinhua, the deals should be considered soft power tools—where the stories come from is not concealed. However, if these content-sharing deals potentially wind up with news copy being printed or shown in foreign outlets without any labeling about where it comes from, as already seems to be occurring, these deals should be considered sharp power—they are concealed, leaving news-consuming publics in the dark about where information comes from.[17]

Xinhua has signed content-sharing deals with outlets on every continent. Indeed, even in Europe, where most countries have relatively free media environments, outlets in at least six countries have signed content-sharing agreements with China's state media, including Xinhua. Xinhua also is inking memoranda of understanding (MOU) with journalists' unions in many countries, including in both developed and developing states.[18] The 2020 report by the International Federation of Journalists found that 36 percent of journalism unions that responded to the survey, which covered fifty-eight countries and territories including many developed states, "had been approached by a Chinese entity to sign an MOU, and 14 percent of respondents having signed an agreement."[19] Some of these MOUs were signed with China's state-run journalists' "union," but some were signed with Xinhua to bolster content-sharing deals between specific outlets and the Chinese newswire.[20] Xinhua has inked content-sharing deals with some of the biggest news organizations in developing countries, like Kenya's National Media Group.[21]

By the late 2010s, Chinese state media had signed content-sharing deals with Chinese-language outlets in Australia, Brazil, Canada, France, Germany, Hungary, Indonesia, Ireland, Italy, Japan, Malaysia, Mexico, Myanmar, the Netherlands, New Zealand, the Philippines, Portugal, South Africa, Spain, Sweden, the United Kingdom, the United States, and at least ten other countries.[22] These countries may rethink such deals as China supports the war in Ukraine and Chinese state media spread Russian disinformation, but so far they have not done so. Indeed, a significant percentage of these content-sharing deals were in countries, in Europe, Northeast Asia, and North America, with some of the freest media markets in the world.

The *Financial Times* dug into these deals, establishing a database of the partnerships. The database reveals that by the late 2010s, more than two hundred local news outlets in other countries—outlets supposedly independent of Beijing—had signed content-sharing deals with Chinese state media.[23] By comparison, in the late 2000s fewer than fifty outlets around the world had such deals.[24]

The content-sharing deals span a staggering array of countries. Research by AidData suggests that in the Asia-Pacific, China seems to prioritize signing content-sharing deals with countries with the largest populations, with its neighbors in Asia, and with the most developed states.[25] China Radio International (CRI) subsidiary Global CAMG Media Group, for instance, now comanages one of the biggest stations in Manila, a prominent station broadcasting to Jakarta and its suburbs, a leading station in Yangon, and a station in Phnom Penh, and has a cooperation deal with one of the top music and news channels in Bangkok.[26] But outside of Asia, these deals—examined by the *Financial Times* and my own research—do not seem to fit a particular pattern, other than that Chinese outlets sign as many as they can.

Many, though far from all, of these deals were with Xinhua. And just as Chinese state media are rapidly ramping up collaboration with Chinese-language outlets around the world, they are expanding their content-sharing deals with English-language outlets, as well as those in other local languages, including outlets in Argentina, Australia, Bangladesh, Belarus, Germany, India, Kenya, Laos, Morocco, Myanmar, Nigeria, Thailand, and the United States, among many others.[27] With these deals, content originating with China's state outlets, including primarily Xinhua, is potentially delivered to hundreds of millions of news consumers globally.[28]

Xinhua woos some of its partners by noting that the Chinese agency will allow them to become less dependent on Western newswires— a selling point, I have found, in states like Cambodia and Thailand where governments and some media executives believe that Western news agencies ignore their country or view it through a negative lens. Xinhua also, to be sure, tells many potential partners that it will offer them its service at rates far cheaper than competitors like the Associated Press or Reuters—or for free.[29] Xinhua also tells potential partners that it is branching into new areas of journalism and technology, like artificial intelligence, and may have an advantage in these realms over other newswires.[30] Since most news outlets are looking for the latest technology to cut costs and speed up the production of stories, Xinhua's foray into artificial intelligence, though still nascent, may help it sign up even more foreign partners.[31]

Many of these companies signing content-sharing deals with Chinese state media outlets like Xinhua are in states that have free or relatively free media climates, and yet even in these states some news outlets, albeit not the highest-profile global outlets like the *New York Times* or the BBC, are publishing Chinese state media content. Even in a country like Singapore, where the government is highly suspicious of Beijing's influence operations and takes aggressive measures to stop them, Chinese-language news outlets increasingly rely on Xinhua for international news stories.[32]

Xinhua even has signed content-sharing agreements with some highly respected news agencies and national broadcasters in Asia and Europe—although for now primarily to provide them with financial stories about business, finance, and economics in China. In 2017,

a Xinhua financial coverage subsidiary signed deals to share business stories with Germany's Deutsche Presse-Agentur and Poland's
Polish News Agency, as well as with Class Editori in Italy, Le Soir in
Belgium, and Athens News Agency in Greece, among others.[33] In
2019, Xinhua signed deals with RAI, Italy's public broadcaster, and
with ANSA, Italy's leading wire service, to work together to launch a
Xinhua Italian Service, and ANSA since has been running about fifty
stories per day on its site.[34] In the years between 2018 and 2021 alone,
Xinhua signed content-sharing agreements with newspapers, online
news sites, and other news outlets in Italy, Nigeria, Oman, Rwanda,
Senegal, Thailand, Laos, Belarus, and Vietnam, among other states.[35]
Xinhua also has inked content-sharing deals with news services in
Australia, even as the Australian Broadcasting Corporation, one of
the most respected television and radio companies in the world, also
launched partnerships with *China Daily* and other Chinese state
media companies.[36] Again, these outlets may rethink all their partnerships with state media because of the Ukraine war, but they have not
yet done so with Chinese media, simply only cutting off Russian state
media's access to many democratic markets.

Unlike with many other types of Chinese state media, Xinhua
readers usually do not have to actively choose to read the Chinese
state newswire. In fact, as several scholars who analyzed Xinhua's
content-sharing deals have noted, they often go largely unreported
outside of China, and most readers, even in places with freer presses,
are unlikely to notice Xinhua showing up in bylines.[37] News consumers read their favorite newspapers or magazines or scroll to their
favorite news sites—and wind up on Xinhua wire stories, increasingly carried by leading outlets. Most news consumers do not check
the bylines of news articles they are reading or which news agency
produced an article; if it is in their favored news outlet and it is on a
topic of interest, they read it. By comparison, CGTN and CRI have
to be actively tuned into, often on satellite TV, in other countries, and
so viewers or listeners have to actively decide to watch or listen to
these outlets, instead of being passively directed to Xinhua stories, as

often happens with people reading news online and finding stories, passively, from any newswire.

Xinhua's Potential Effect

A powerful, expanded Xinhua, more than other Chinese state media, could have a transformative effect on the news industry. With the potential to be first to breaking news stories as it expands its network of bureaus and reporters, Xinhua could cause reverberations through the global news business, transforming how some of the most important topics are covered.

Newswires are not sexy, especially to casual readers. They produce copy that is simple, short, and usually lacking in the kind of storytelling common in longer newspaper, website, or magazine features. When I worked for Agence France-Presse, one of the major global newswires, in the early 2000s, we usually followed a clear and defined style in our pieces, which rarely ran more than six hundred words. We also often produced ten or more stories a day—on slow days. Due to wire reporters' anonymity and wire stories' ubiquity in news outlets, the newswires' role in global media coverage is not well understood by many media consumers. Few readers know the names of newswire reporters.

And yet newswires often are the first to report on major stories, and their simple, easy-to-understand copy regularly acts as the real first draft of history. Those stories often then get "picked up," or run by other major news outlets, and with a first-mover advantage the newswires play a central role in establishing the core of a story and the tone of the coverage. And some major news outlets are already used to using Xinhua stories about economic and political issues in China, since Xinhua often provides the first reporting of statements from political conferences inside China or from appearances by Chinese leaders. If Xinhua, inking more and more content-sharing deals, is able to write that first draft about stories outside of China and set the tone and parameters for international coverage by other outlets, it can have a huge effect on how the global public understands the news.[38] As the Associated Press and Reuters have done for years, Xinhua would be able to initially define news stories for outlets from a broad range of countries—television stations, newspapers, online outlets, and others.

Many Xinhua stories look, in their style and format, little different from wire pieces one might see from Agence France-Presse, the Associated Press, Bloomberg, or Reuters. The Xinhua stories are usually brief, spare, and seemingly just the facts, like any other newswire. This resemblance to the classical newswire style makes it harder for time-strapped editors at many publications, especially younger and inexperienced editors, to tell if there is anything different between Xinhua stories and those of its competitors. And the content of Xinhua articles about events having little or nothing to do with China—stories about events in Africa, Europe, North America, or Latin America that do not touch on China, or major financial stories that do not closely involve China, to give some examples—is often indistinguishable from the content of articles produced by other major newswires. Even stories that might affect China or might portray Chinese competitors in a negative light, like political turmoil in the United States, are usually covered in Xinhua in a relatively straightforward way, though a close reading often shows how Xinhua shades these types of news articles in ways that portray Chinese competitors negatively and reflect well on China's leadership. Yet this relatively straightforward nature of many Xinhua stories makes it easier for editors at news outlets to justify using Xinhua copy, in addition to the financial reasons for using Xinhua.[39]

To be sure, Xinhua shies away from coverage of topics that could potentially portray China in an extremely negative light, and its coverage of issues that portray China positively is not unbiased and independent. And Xinhua has a history of serving not only as a newswire but also as some functions of an intelligence agency. Today, Xinhua bureaus continue to provide, according to Reporters Without Borders, in addition to its news stories, secret intelligence briefings that it delivers to top Chinese Communist Party (CCP) leaders, classified as "internal reference" reports.[40]

Editors at the most prestigious, independent global news outlets know that Xinhua stories related to China often are biased and have the resources to use many other news agencies; they are wary of using Xinhua copy other than when it is absolutely essential, like when Xinhua is the only agency with a story on a Chinese government data release or a speech by a Chinese leader. But many other news outlets, particularly those with fewer resources and/or less knowledge of the biased nature of Xinhua's reporting, are using its copy—and will use it even more in the future as Xinhua expands, as the whole news industry continues suffering financial difficulties, and if Xinhua signs further content-sharing deals with outlets in places with high levels of press freedom, like Australia or Italy. Moves like these could signify to editors in these states that it is acceptable to use Xinhua, especially when the other newswires cost more.[41] Already, as Sarah Cook of Freedom House has noted, there are signs of such acceptance; she writes, "Much of the China-related news coverage offered by one of Italy's major news agencies is [already] drawn from Xinhua."[42]

"Borrowing the Boat" and "China Watch"

Content-sharing agreements are classic strategies designed to potentially conceal Beijing's hand—to get people in foreign countries to imbibe Chinese ideas. With content-sharing deals, an outlet like Xinhua is "borrowing the boat to go out to sea," a phrase initially used by Wang Gengnian, the head of CRI.[43] Miguel Martin, a journalist who studies Chinese influence efforts and goes by the penname Jichang Lulu, notes that "borrowing the boat" entails "presenting the views of the Chinese government to a worldwide audience . . . while crafting a delivery [system]" of media platforms "where the connection to a Chinese state entity" is at least somewhat hidden.[44] It potentially allows China to take advantage of media outlets in other countries that have reputations as trustworthy news sources and often have sizable audiences of viewers, readers, and listeners.[45]

And borrowing the boat is consistent with a classic, long-standing Beijing strategy of "making the foreign serve China"—getting foreigners to push the Chinese government's ideas, policies, and values, so that the pressure does not seem to come from Beijing. In this case, foreign media outlets, rather than foreign celebrities like LeBron James, foreign politicians, or foreign multinationals, serve China.

The strategy works only if the content is appealing enough to recipient audiences to get Beijing's message across and if China finds partners who do not ask too many questions about airing state media stories. As Wang said, Chinese state media should match "what we would like to broadcast" with "what overseas audiences care about."[46] This means picking foreign outlets willing to cooperate with CRI, CGTN, Xinhua, and others and providing them with stories tailored but subtle enough to inject Beijing's biased point of view about various issues.

Beijing uses an insert drawn from the English-language *China Daily* for another borrowed-boat tactic—one in which China pays to publish this insert in many of the world's most prestigious print and online outlets. Most of these outlets are based in countries that rank among the highest in the world on the Reporters Without Borders annual Press Freedom Index.[47] Yet Beijing has utilized a strategy of paying the most prestigious print and online news outlets in the world to place its state media inserts in the middle of their newspapers, prominently on their websites, or both. The inserts, usually drawn from *China Daily*, are slickly produced and called "China Watch." State propaganda regularly appears, for instance, in a professional-looking and stylishly laid-out eight-page "China Watch" section tucked into the print version of major outlets. The articles look like real news stories, though they do often have disclaimers noting that they are advertorials. Since these disclaimers are often small and somewhat hard to find, "China Watch" straddles the line between open, or soft power, and a sharper form of influence.

The "China Watch" inserts offer puff pieces drawn mostly from *China Daily*. To take one such example, in March 2019 a "China Watch" in the *Washington Post* featured a column about the "festive atmosphere" in Tibet, a region where, in fact, Tibetans have little to celebrate; Human Rights Watch reports that political prisoners in Tibet, including many monks, are serving long sentences with no information about their whereabouts, or even whether they are alive.[48] (The *Washington Post* has stopped running the "China Watch" inserts.[49])

Running the section makes financial sense for many news outlets whose budgets are increasingly precarious. *China Daily* spent more than $15 million in the United States to influence opinion in the United States in 2017 and 2018, according to a study by Freedom House.[50] Since it does not employ many editorial staff in the United States, most of that money went to American outlets (including outlets like the *Washington Post* and the *New York Times*) to pay them to run "China Watch."[51] According to the Foreign Agents Registration Act (FARA) reports filed with the U.S. Justice Department, *China Daily* spends more money annually on influence in the United States than many entire governments spend on U.S. influence activities.[52] Overall, between 2016 and 2020, *China Daily* paid almost $19 million to U.S. news organizations, according to the reports filed with the U.S. Justice Department.[53]

China Daily says it has deals with forty media organizations around the world, although growing scrutiny of Chinese state media in developed democracies has led some prominent news outlets, like the *New York Times*, Britain's *Daily Telegraph*, and Australia's *Sydney Morning Herald* and *Australian Financial Review* to stop running "China Watch" and similar inserts.[54] Beijing claims a circulation for "China Watch" of four million—four million that would presumably include a large pool of opinion leaders in major world capitals, since most of the inserts are placed in outlets in big cities.[55]

And even with some news outlets in developed democracies ending their relationships with *China Daily*, others continue to run the advertorials, presumably since they need the money. "China Watch" reaches the Japanese newspaper *Mainichi Shimbun*'s print subscribers, for instance.[56] In June 2020, the *Los Angeles Times*, which had implemented cuts in pay and furloughs as the coronavirus pandemic decimated advertising, ran an eight-page advertising insert of "China Watch" in its Sunday edition, a signal that more publications may take Beijing's money as the outlets become desperate.[57] Filings from the U.S. Justice Department released in 2021 and reported on by investigative journalist Chuck Ross found that not only the *Los Angeles Times* but also *Time* magazine, the *Chicago Tribune*, the *Houston Chronicle*, and the *Financial Times*, among other outlets, continued to take money from *China Daily* and run its sections.[58] Britain's *Daily Mail*, whose online site has the biggest audience of any English-language news outlet in the world, created a separate content-sharing deal with the *People's Daily*, another big state media outlet.[59]

Some publications do note in a disclaimer that the content is produced and published by *China Daily* and that *China Daily* is linked to the government of the People's Republic of China, but again the disclaimer is easily missed. And while a disclaimer is also included for the *Daily Mail*'s "Mail Online" site that content is provided by the *People's Daily*, that disclaimer is even less clear about the *People's Daily*'s links to the Chinese government.[60]

How Xinhua Has an Effect

In Thailand, a country ruled for much of the past decade by a repressive military junta, and where information about powerful actors like the army and monarchy can be dangerous to dig up, *Khaosod* has built a reputation as one of the most respected news outlets. In fact, although *Khaosod* is a mass market daily with a broad readership, it is known for aggressive reporting on taboo subjects in Thailand, including the monarchy and government repression. It has hired famed reporters like Pravit Rojanaphruk, one of the kingdom's most fearless journalists. Pravit resigned in 2015 from his former employer, the *Nation*, after being detained by the Thai army for an "attitude adjustment session" in a cell with no ventilation, for the "offense" of writing critically about the junta.[61] (He also claimed in a tweet that he had been essentially fired; he said that management had asked him to resign to spare the *Nation* from more military pressure.[62]) *Khaosod* still hired him. Pravit received an International Press Freedom Award in 2017 from the Committee to Protect Journalists. He still regularly faces harassment and intimidation.[63]

Khaosod maintains a large reader base. Its Thai edition boasts approximately nine hundred thousand daily subscribers, in a country of roughly seventy million.[64] *Khaosod* also produces an English-language website that publishes tough investigative reporting. The publication is part of the bigger Matichon Group, also known for its quality, independent journalism. Heavy on politics, Matichon's weekly magazine is as much an essential read for Thai politicians and other Bangkok influencers as *Politico*'s top stories are in Washington.[65]

This reputation for quality, independent journalism did not stop *Khaosod* and the Matichon Group from partnering with state media from a country with one of the most repressive press environments in the world. In 2019, *Khaosod* and the Matichon Group announced a content-sharing deal with Xinhua, and *Khaosod* began running Xinhua articles, for free.[66] The fact that Xinhua was free mattered, even to a prominent and powerful organization like Matichon Group. As in other parts of the world, Thai media outlets face mounting financial pressures, and a wire service that offers thousands of stories per day without cost was a hard deal to turn down.[67] However, *Khaosod* at least identified the articles as coming from Xinhua, so that readers could know where the pieces originated. In some other cases, Chinese state media slip their copy into local media outlets without any attribution at all, or it can be difficult to tell that the articles come from Chinese state media when a reader scrolls through many stories in a row.

Among the first Xinhua pieces *Khaosod* ran were articles on the 2019 Hong Kong protests that portrayed the protestors as tools of

Western agitators and China's Xinjiang province as a place where "equality, solidarity and harmony among ethnic groups and religions have prevailed, and people are enjoying peace and stability."[68] Neither of these claims is true. (Rights advocates claim that the Chinese authorities have detained as many as a million Uighurs in Xinjiang and have perpetrated widespread sexual violence against Uighur women, among other massive abuses; the U.S. government has labeled Beijing's repression of Uighurs a "genocide."[69])

Xinhua also provides *Khaosod* with a steady stream of soft, cuddly features about China. Sometimes these articles are about things that are *literally* cuddly, like stories about panda twins born in the wild in Sichuan province.[70]

When the respected Matichon Group inked a content-sharing deal with Xinhua, other Thai news outlets followed suit, and Xinhua gained a large audience among Thai opinion leaders and the public. (Xinhua produces stories in Chinese, English, and Thai.) Many did not have Matichon's financial resources, so the prospect of a massive newswire providing them content for free or at a significant discount was appealing. (Xinhua provides content in many languages, including English, but also translates up to a hundred stories per day into Thai for Thai media outlets.)[71] The outlets working with Xinhua included a broad range of publications, from starchy state broadcasters to online publications targeted at younger Thais. Among these were the Thai state broadcaster NBT, which has a national reach; the publication *Manager Online*, a mass market outlet with a smaller following than *Khaosod*; and Voice Online, the website of possibly the most progressive television station in Thailand.[72]

The *Nation*, which despite its challenges with Pravit remains a prestigious English-language news site in Thailand, had signed its own content-sharing deal with Chinese state media. It participates in the Asia News Network (ANN), a media colloquium in which more than twenty news outlets from across the region reprint stories from each other—including *China Daily*.[73] Many ANN outlets are established and respected brand names, not just the *Nation* but also the

Jakarta Post, the *Philippine Daily Inquirer*, and other high-profile media properties.[74] Yet they all regularly pick up content from *China Daily*, even though it is a state outlet with none of the editorial independence enjoyed by most other ANN members.

In total, by the end of 2019, twelve Thai outlets had signed content-sharing deals with Chinese state media.[75] Some of them touted the deals with Xinhua proudly and displayed Xinhua content openly, making them essentially soft power efforts—even though, because of the slanted nature of Xinhua's content, these Thai outlets were still offering newswire stories through a Chinese prism. Other Thai outlets, like Matichon, seemed more reluctant to publicize the agreements. "Thai media [will] receive news directly from a Chinese news agency, instead of a second-hand information from Western media only," Chaiwat Wanichwattana, a journalist who worked at the business outlet *Than Sethakit* and heads the Thai-Chinese Journalists Association, said at a discussion timed to some of the signings. "This kind of cooperation [between Xinhua and Thai media outlets] is most welcome."[76] The other Thai media executives who attended the discussion, according to the outlet Khao Sod, also seemed happy about how well Chinese state media stories performed for them, saying that since they started using Xinhua stories, Thai readers had displayed a growing interest in stories about China's domestic affairs. Bhuvadej Chirabandhu, from the Thai news site *Sanook*, another outlet that had begun working with Xinhua, reported that at least 1.4 million of *Sanook*'s readers had read Xinhua content posted on its site.[77]

Teeranai Charuvastra, a journalist at *Khaosod*, noted that China has long attempted to influence the Thai media, and indeed most of the Chinese-language media in Thailand now take pro-Beijing stances or are neutral toward China.[78] "But what's changed in 2019," he wrote, "is their aggressive outreach to mainstream Thai-language media, with a goal of having pro-China content routinely reproduced on those platforms under the model of Western wire services."[79] While it is impossible to definitively prove that people who read certain news stories make decisions because of those news stories, especially since there is a sea of news outlets in Thailand, Teeranai and other observers note that the encroachment of Chinese state media has had an effect. Utilizing these content-sharing deals and other links to Thai media, Teeranai noted, the Chinese embassy in Bangkok has successfully gotten even Thai outlets known for their independence to publish op-eds basically echoing Chinese government positions on various issues—editorials in the most prominent Thai outlets, read by Thai policymakers.[80] And, Teeranai noted, Chinese diplomats were not shy about contacting Thai reporters, often through messaging apps, and asking them to publish a certain story recommended by the Chinese embassy.[81]

Within a few months, it became clear to the public and Thailand experts that the deals were helping to shape Thailand's media environment, particularly with respect to a critical issue for Beijing. In January and February 2020, as the coronavirus that originated in Wuhan spread to Southeast Asia and around the world, Thai outlets' links to Chinese state media appeared to influence how Thai organizations portrayed the outbreak. Thailand's Channel 3, one of the country's most-watched broadcast channels, even announced a deal in the early days of the outbreak to carry Xinhua's reporting on the virus.[82]

Xinhua's coverage, though sometimes factual and on the face of it little different in style from other newswires, often downplayed the threat of the virus within China and to other countries. As the *Thai Enquirer* reporter Jasmine Chia noted, by partnering with Xinhua and often using Xinhua stories, many Thai outlets "outsourced" coverage of the pandemic, with such coverage often echoing Chinese government views; the Thai outlets gave the Thai public and opinion leaders coverage that conditioned them to see news through Chinese narratives and perspectives.[83] This "outsourced" coverage often highlighted the (genuinely) heroic efforts of doctors and ordinary citizens in combating the virus—stories then carried by Channel 3 on its social media platforms and disseminated to large numbers of Thais.[84] This coverage also regularly highlighted the Chinese government's desire for other states not to bar Chinese citizens. The coverage by Xinhua, unlike coverage in outlets like Reuters and the Associated Press, ignored the ways in which Beijing initially had covered up signs of an outbreak, including by silencing an early whistleblowing doctor who later died, as well as the growing anger among the Chinese populace at the government's response.

Emboldened, by March and April of 2020, as the virus raged in Europe and the United States, the Chinese government began touting itself as newly able to lead on global public health—and possibly many other issues as well—given how China had acted and the United States had fumbled.[85] Chinese state media, including those reprinted in Thailand, enthusiastically embraced this narrative, suggesting that the coronavirus would be the first major global crisis where China would take the lead internationally while the United States did little and flailed with its domestic response.[86] Even as some world leaders simmered at how China's initial lack of transparency hindered global control of the pandemic—a simmering that would turn into a dramatic downturn in global opinion of China and eventually a Chinese lockdown that lasted so long it began to anger Chinese citizens—media like Xinhua trumpeted the gratitude of other world leaders, like Serbian President Aleksandar Vučić, who, while declaring a state of emergency, announced, "European solidarity does not exist, that was a fairy tale on paper. I believe in my brother and friend Xi Jinping, and I believe in Chinese help."[87]

The Back Door

But China does not just attempt to get its state media in through the front door, putting Xinhua, CGTN, and other outlets in front of international media consumers in a relatively open manner. It also works through the back door, in sharper and more opaque ways.

Chapter 8

The Sharp Power Toolkit

Media and Information Slipping Through the Back Door

As in Australia and New Zealand, China is expanding its sharp power efforts globally—and often with more success than its soft power strategies. Unlike the more transparent soft power efforts, China's back-door, sharper strategies are often designed to conceal Beijing's hand—to get people in foreign countries to consume Chinese media and imbibe Chinese ideas, without understanding what they are taking in.

China wields a vast array of back-door, sharp power media and information strategies, so in this chapter we will outline Beijing's sharp efforts that directly relate to media outlets: how China is trying to smuggle information into foreign viewers' screens, tablets, phones, and other places by taking de facto control of much of the Chinese-language media abroad and sometimes by inking content-sharing deals that do not show where the articles hail from; how China is trying to silence many leading Chinese-language media outlets, and outlets in other languages, that provide critical, independent coverage of the country; and how Beijing is helping other states set up their own domestic media outlets modeled on China's highly controlled media.

We will wait until the next chapter, however, to examine means of sharp power that are one step—or at least a half step—removed from actual media outlets. These one-step-removed tools include potential weapons that are not based directly on media outlets, like Confucius Institutes at university campuses or Chinese businesspeople or other opinion leaders funneling money to politicians and political parties in other states. They include sharp power tools centered on controlling the rules of information globally and the "pipes" through which information flows, like telecommunications networks, social media platforms, search engines, and web browsers. These pipes then can be utilized to spread Chinese state media or private Chinese media with pro-Beijing affinities. Or these tools use the gains made by China in its sharp media strategies to achieve specific, highly directed goals—to spread certain types of disinformation, or to promote or punish businesses and political leaders in other countries.

The Back Door

Certainly, state media outlets' stories can come in the back door, as can other media companies controlled or influenced by the Chinese government. When content comes in through the back door, without a clear message of the origin of the information or how it was produced, consumers may not understand that they are reading, listening, or watching media influenced or controlled by Beijing.

The big state media, then, are often used as tools of soft power, but they also engage in sharp practices, far more so than in the charm offensive era of the 1990s and early 2000s, when the big state media had less ability to utilize sharp power. Sometimes, the big state media outlets spread false information around the world, facilitate censorship, and engage in practices that are far from transparent. These practices would not be acceptable at leading private media outlets from democratic states, or even at state-backed broadcasters from democracies, like Voice of America.

Beijing slips pro-China media through the back door in multiple ways that barely existed in the charm offensive era. When Beijing inks deals with foreign media outlets in which Chinese media content is reprinted without any clear attribution, it is coming in through the back door, in a covert manner.

The tailored content offered through borrowed boats often contains false information and outright propaganda, in addition to not always being labeled as originating from state media. Consumers may be unable to spot the false reporting, since the content comes to them via a trusted local news brand—and especially when that news article is not labeled as hailing from Chinese state media. They may be particularly unable to spot the falsehoods and propaganda coming in on borrowed boats in places where citizens already have weak media literacy, since their own domestic media is not particularly free.

In addition to the content-sharing deals, Beijing is making shorter-term agreements with media outlets in other countries to have the local companies coproduce stories with Chinese state media—and these often do not reveal the Chinese part of the partnership. In Argentina, for instance, the China Global Television Network (CGTN) and the Argentinian network Grupo America, the second-biggest media conglomerate in the country, together produced a series of documentaries about the history of Argentina-China diplomatic ties.[1] While Argentina ranks only in the middle tier of countries in the Reporters Without Borders annual ranking of press freedom, CGTN also has coproduced programming with stations in Germany, a country ranked by Reporters Without Borders as one of the freest media environments in the world.[2] In the Philippines, which has one of the least free media environments, the government-run radio broadcaster signed a deal with China Radio International (CRI) to coproduce a radio show, which was blasted by some Philippine social media users for relentlessly promoting Chinese propaganda, although research by Freedom House has suggested that this inundation of social media and some Chinese state media has had little penetration into the Philippine public discourse, amidst a high degree of public skepticism about China.[3]

Phoenix Television and the Hong Kong Media: Owning the Outlets

Sometimes Beijing does not need partnership agreements that conceal that content is coming from Chinese state media; it can take a more direct route by simply owning seemingly local and global media organizations, ones that purport to be more independent than state media but still deliver heavily pro-Beijing messages. Or it can utilize financial incentives to gain de facto control of news outlets.

This ownership has become a major tool in spreading pro-China content in Hong Kong—and increasingly in Australia, North America, Southeast Asia, and other regions.[4] In Hong Kong, Beijing essentially owns the newspapers *Ta Kung Pao* and *Wen Wei Po*, via the liaison office of the Chinese government in Hong Kong, and it maintains extensive control over Phoenix TV, a channel headquartered in Hong Kong as well as in Shenzhen. It now exerts even more control over the media in Hong Kong via the new national security law, which has facilitated the crushing of nearly every truly independent media outlet in Hong Kong and has driven many foreign correspondents and entire foreign bureaus out of Hong Kong.[5] The law will likely eventually crush all independent media in Hong Kong, essentially making its media coverage like that of any other Chinese city.

Phoenix TV not only reaches populations in Hong Kong and China but also has separate, successful channels catering to Chinese-language viewers in Europe and North America, among other regions.[6] As Reporters Without Borders notes in an analysis of China's growing global media footprint, "Certain Chinese-language media outlets in Hong Kong under Beijing's partial or full control, such as *Ta Kung Pao*, *Wen Wei Po* and Phoenix TV, play an important role in disseminating Chinese propaganda in overseas Chinese communities."[7] Phoenix TV has gained a broad audience among Chinese-speaking Americans and Canadians, giving it considerable influence and reach in North America.[8] Across its international channels, which

include Phoenix TV in North America and a channel that broadcasts in Europe, among others, it claims to have a global audience
of roughly 360 million viewers, although it has not produced hard
viewership statistics to back up that claim.[9] It produces a quality mix
of miniseries, movies, talk shows, and business and political news, and
its production values are generally high, which makes it attractive to
audiences. It is not officially Chinese state media, which may add to
its foreign appeal. On some occasions, it also has featured stories that
clearly would never appear on state media, like running a newscast in
2005 about the death of Zhao Zhiyang, the former Chinese premier
and general secretary of the Chinese Communist Party (CCP), whose
name was basically banned from state media after the Tiananmen
Square massacre and the purge of Zhao.[10]

This thin veneer of past rebelliousness may make Phoenix TV more
attractive globally, and its attractiveness makes it useful for spreading pro-Beijing content. Phoenix TV's founder Liu Changle served
as a Chinese military officer during the Cultural Revolution and
the more progressive period afterward, producing propaganda as a
military journalist, despite sometimes straining at the constraints of
China's censors in the 1980s.[11] He continues to hold clearly pro-
Beijing views. A state-owned Chinese company, the telecommunications giant China Mobile, holds a significant percentage of Phoenix
TV shares, as does a company owned by another large state firm, the
Bank of China. Phoenix TV broadcasts in China, which gives Beijing
vast leverage over the channel. Phoenix TV has amassed a large audience there, in part because of its production values and its history of
being a half step removed from state media, and its programming in
China has become critically important to Phoenix TV's revenues. And
even Liu apparently was not pro-Beijing enough for the Communist
Party; perhaps his few minor attempts in the past to produce independent news doomed him.

In April 2021, Beijing imposed even tighter control over Phoenix
TV, as Liu sold his whole controlling stake in Phoenix's parent company to two shareholders. One new shareholder is run by a leading

former CCP official and is, according to the investigative outlet Asia Sentinel, a media company administered by the central government in Beijing.[12] The other new shareholder is controlled by Pansy Ho, a major pro-Beijing tycoon.[13] Pansy Ho has no other media companies and no experience in media, so, Asia Sentinel reported, it is highly likely that her firm bought a share of Phoenix media at "the wishes of Chinese leaders."[14]

Whatever its past (occasional) willingness to practice independent journalism, especially in the freer Jiang Zemin and early Hu Jintao periods, in the Xi era Phoenix TV has become even more servile, as the media environment inside China itself has become the most constrained and repressive in decades. Since the mid-2010s, for instance, Phoenix TV has aired a series of stark, almost surely coerced confessions from critics of China who were detained in brutal ways, like several Hong Kong–based booksellers who were kidnapped and brought to mainland China.[15] Despite Phoenix TV's flashy and modern production values, the "stories" of confessions would not have been out of place on the most propagandistic outlets in China.

CRI, meanwhile, has been making quiet investments in other stations around the world and then getting pro-China content on the air on these stations.[16] An investigation by Reuters found that CRI had quietly used its investment to take over at least thirty-three stations around the world, including in the United States, and have them air pro-China content, usually in local languages and not in Chinese— so that they can reach a wide audience.[17] This content is broadcast without listeners knowing that the stations receive CRI investment, a use of opaque, sharp power.

Beijing further has taken de facto control of many Chinese-language outlets around the world, in ways that lack transparency and are essentially covert. He Qinglian, one of the most famous scholars of Chinese-language media, has done an extensive survey of the issue in a wide range of countries. The Chinese-language media landscape outside of China is vast: there are some sixty million people of Chinese descent worldwide who do not live in mainland China.[18] According to the acclaimed author He Qinglian, who studies Chinese language media around the world, while a decade ago most Chinese-language outlets outside mainland China were relatively independent, today the majority have become what she calls "red" or "pink"—clearly pro-China in their coverage ("red") or at least relatively pro-China in their coverage ("pink").[19] In other words, Beijing has largely succeeded in the aim of controlling Chinese-language media in most other countries.[20]

For many Chinese leaders and officials, the fact that so many Chinese-language news outlets around the world have adopted pro-Beijing editorial tilts is just natural, since Beijing views ethnic Chinese anywhere as naturally loyal to China. Beijing has achieved this control of Chinese-language media around the world in several ways. In some cases, Beijing quietly provides financial incentives for Chinese-language outlets that develop a pro-Beijing tilt. In other cases, Beijing gains influence over Chinese-language media via "negative" influence efforts—for example, by punishing Chinese-language media outlets, and individual reporters and editors, that dare criticize Beijing.

In many countries, companies sympathetic to Beijing—either Chinese companies or local companies whose management is pro-Beijing because it makes business sense to be, or for other reasons—utilize advertising to influence coverage of Beijing in the local Chinese-language press. In Thailand, for instance, Chinese-language news outlets have learned over the past twenty years that if they run generally pro-Beijing coverage, they will attract advertising from Thai firms who have extensive business links in China or who rely on Chinese consumers and investors. China has become Thailand's biggest bilateral trading partner, its largest source of inbound tourism, and one of the most important investors in Thai companies, real estate, and infrastructure; the number of Thai businesses reliant on China in some way has mushroomed.[21] And while Thai-language outlets are the most widely read in the country (though, we have seen, they too are influenced by Beijing via new content-sharing deals), there remains a Chinese-speaking and -reading community in Thailand, wielding considerable power among senior politicians and business leaders, and many Thais are increasingly studying Chinese, adding to its readership in the kingdom.[22]

Companies with owners favorable to Beijing challenge independent coverage outside of Southeast Asia as well; this is becoming a growing phenomenon. Australian Chinese-language outlets, of instance, face the same challenge, as do Chinese-language outlets in Canada. Outlets that publish news articles and opinion pieces, as journalist John Garnaut has found, favorable to Beijing are rewarded with advertising from local firms sympathetic to China or from mainland Chinese companies. The few Australian Chinese-language outlets that remain critical of Beijing find advertising pulled both by local companies run by ethnic Chinese and by many multinational firms—even as, overall, the Australian government's position toward Beijing has hardened, under both Liberal-National and Australian Labor governments, and even as Australian public opinion has turned strongly against China.[23] Most of these local outlets cannot survive without advertising. And yet, while the Australian Chinese community does read non-Chinese outlets, the Chinese-language outlets play a major role in swaying opinion among the ethnic Chinese community— which, as we have seen, itself plays an increasingly important role in Australian politics as a kind of swing vote, as well as in business and academia.

In other cases, individual pro-Beijing businesspeople in other countries buy up local Chinese-language outlets and transform their coverage. Some of these businesspeople view China warmly due to business ties or familial and historical links to the country. Others have ideological sympathies with China—not necessarily for China's professed communist ideology but rather an affinity for the China model of autocratic, statist capitalism. Still other businesspeople who buy up news outlets may have United Front Work Department (UFWD) links, while also obtaining logistical and financial support from the UFWD in buying up and running news outlets.

In Malaysia, for instance, the ethnic Chinese tycoon Tiong Hiew King made his money in timber, historically a corrupt and dirty business in the country, with billions allegedly siphoned from the state purse and staggering amounts of kickbacks given to government ministers.[24] Over decades, Tiong became known not only for his strong support for the long-ruling, authoritarian Malaysian government but also for views generally sympathetic to China's foreign policy and style of government, and he regularly met with top CCP leaders.[25] In 2016, for instance, during a speech at a media summit in Hong Kong, Tiong sharply rebuked Hong Kong residents who might consider themselves independent of China and warned them that any discussion of Hong Kong independence must die down.[26]

In the past two decades, Tiong has bought up much of the Chinese-language media in Malaysia, where the ethnic Chinese make up the second-largest ethnic group in the country, and several Chinese outlets are among the most influential in Malaysia. Over that period, this media has shifted from holding a diverse range of viewpoints to generally fostering pro-Beijing views, and Tiong has been a primary factor in this change, though not the only one: Chinese-language television in Malaysia has become dominated by channels that are either Chinese state channels or, like the private channels CTiAsia and Phoenix TV, known for relatively pro-Beijing coverage.[27] Still, his outlets comprise about 70 percent of the print media market, including the newspaper *Sin Chew Daily*, the most prominent Chinese-language print news outlet in Malaysia.[28]

Tiong's Malaysian outlets, and his media companies in other parts of the region, print heavily pro-Beijing coverage of events in China, much of which is indistinguishable from China's state media material. Murray Hiebert, a Southeast Asia expert at the Center for Strategic and International Studies, reports that an editor who worked on Tiong's outlets said he wanted to turn its flagship paper, *Ming Pao* in Hong Kong, into a "pro-mainland paper."[29] His outlets' coverage has a follow-on effect on other Chinese media in Malaysia as well, according to many Malaysian journalists. Since Tiong's outlets have a big share of the market, and *Sin Chew Daily* in particular is the biggest Chinese-language outlet in the country, when Tiong's companies publish stories about Malaysia-China relations or other topics regarding China, other Malaysian news outlets often feel pressure to write about the same topics.[30] They frequently do so, even though the original articles they are seeking to match, like those in *Sin Chew Daily*, avoid any criticism of China.

In recent years, as Tiong has aged and reportedly developed health challenges, he has tried to sell some of his media holdings.[31] He looked for a buyer in 2016 for a portion of his empire, One Media Group, which produces several magazines in Hong Kong. He then sold most of One Media to a Chinese state firm.[32] Given that sale, it is easy to imagine that Tiong's media company ultimately will dispose of its other properties to a mainland Chinese state or private firm.

Malaysia is but one example of a larger trend. In Taiwan, Beijing has achieved some control of the domestic media, mostly in a sharp power manner—even though the Taiwanese government does not allow Chinese entities to directly own media outlets on the island.[33] Since in Taiwan Chinese is the primary language, control of the Chinese-language media means one can reach nearly all Taiwanese—though Taiwan has also developed a high degree of resiliency to media influenced by China, in part because it has faced such an onslaught from China and in part because its government has taken tough measures in response.

In one of the most notable examples of China essentially buying up outlets, in 2008 Want Want China Holdings, a food and beverage company led by one of Taiwan's richest people, Tsai Eng-meng, bought the *China Times* media group.[34] The company made most of its money in China, and Tsai was known for extreme obsequiousness to Beijing; in 2012, he told the *Washington Post* that the 1989 Tiananmen Square massacre had not happened.[35] The circumstances of Tsai's purchase were unusual. Want Want bid twice as much as the next bidder, and many Taiwanese media experts speculate that the Chinese government financially assisted the acquisition.[36] The Taiwan media specialist

Chien-Jung Hsu suggests, in an extensively documented analysis, that the publicity department of the Central Committee of the CCP and the CCP's Taiwan affairs office became involved and aided in the purchase.[37] Another prominent, independent Taiwanese news outlet, *Apple Daily*, part of a bigger Hong Kong–based media group, reported in 2019 that Want Want's parent company receives the equivalent of hundreds of millions of U.S. dollars in subsidies from the Chinese government, although it did not claim that these subsidies were a direct quid pro quo for certain media coverage.[38]

Instead of relying on businesspeople in other countries sympathetic to Beijing, on other occasions Chinese state companies and private firms themselves invest in Chinese-language publications and broadcast outlets abroad. Phoenix Media's (parent of Phoenix TV) shares, for instance, are partially owned by a company administered by Beijing.[39] Private Chinese firms have become increasingly subservient to Beijing in the Xi era, so the difference between a state-owned and private Chinese company investing in Chinese-language media abroad has narrowed. In Hong Kong, even though a small handful of news outlets continued to publish independent reporting until 2021 and even, modestly, into 2022 (though they have little future), a 2019 analysis by the Committee to Protect Journalists and the Hong Kong Journalists Association found that "mainland Chinese authorities or corporations led by Communist Party members control nine of twenty-six mainstream media outlets including the dominant TV broadcaster . . . and the [then] dominant English newspaper, the South China Morning Post, in the special administrative region."[40] Matthew Schrader, in a report for the Alliance for Securing Democracy and the German Marshall Fund of the United States, noted that "a majority of the individuals who own Hong Kong media outlets sit on [the party's] Chinese People's Political Consultative Congress or National People's Congress."[41] And all this came before Beijing tightened the screws substantially on Hong Kong in 2020, with the new national security law, and then forced the closure of most remaining truly independent media outlets in Hong Kong.

Or take the case of Thailand, which, as we saw, has one of the largest diaspora ethnic Chinese populations in the world. *Sing Sian Yer Pao*, a Thai Chinese-language news outlet, had built a reputation over decades for fair, critical reporting on China. But it has now sold 20 percent of its shares to the Chinese media conglomerate Nanfang Media Group, whose parent owner is the government of Guangdong province.[42] Nanfang Media once was known for relatively groundbreaking, independent coverage within China.[43] But in recent years, as Xi has become more powerful, Nanfang reportedly has adopted a range of internal measures designed to reduce "negative" coverage in its outlets—presumably coverage that reflects poorly on Beijing or on provincial leaders. It has vowed to ensure that its publications' editors hew closely to the party's line.[44]

Since the sale to Nanfang, *Sing Sian Yer Pao*'s coverage of China issues has become much more sycophantic.[45] Meanwhile, new Chinese-language outlets have launched in Thailand in recent years too. According to the study by Reporters Without Borders, new outlets like *ThaiCN*, *ASEAN Commerce*, and *ASEAN Econ* "all appear to be discreetly linked with each other and with Chinese state media."[46]

A similar metamorphosis has occurred with SkyLink television, a Chinese-language broadcaster available via satellite in the United States, where new owners of some Chinese-language outlets have dramatically altered the way that they cover Beijing. According to an investigation of SkyLink by the journalist John Pomfret, in 2009 a private Chinese firm bought SkyLink from its original Taiwanese owners.[47] Three years later, he notes, that firm sold SkyLink to a Chinese state-owned media company. SkyLink now broadcasts coverage into the United States that is virtually indistinguishable from that of CGTN, whereas in the past it had broadcast more independent coverage of China. Similarly, according to Pomfret's investigation, *World Journal*, a prominent and long-respected Chinese-language newspaper in the Bay Area and read by Chinese speakers across the United States, for years produced independent coverage of both China and a wide range of other news. In recent years, however, *World Journal* has toned down any coverage of events that could portray Beijing in a bad light and has started to take more pro-Beijing stances on issues like claims in the South China Sea.[48] A Hoover Institution investigation, led by Pomfret, into *World Journal* and other Chinese-language media in the United States further suggests that the owners of the news outlet may have pushed for this shift, as they want to protect their business interests in China; it also suggests that they have come under pressure from Chinese consulates and embassies in the United States.[49] Online Chinese-language outlets with reach in North America, like *Duowei*, also have toned down any critical coverage of China, as they have been bought by owners who have aired strongly pro-Beijing views and have extensive business interests in China. Indeed, that same Hoover Institution study of Chinese-language media in the United States claims that "China has all but eliminated the independent Chinese-language media outlets that once served communities in the United States, through a mix of co-option and aggressive expansion of its own competitors."[50]

Sometimes, the Chinese government gains de facto control of Chinese-language news organizations not because owners sympathetic to Beijing take over outlets or Chinese entities buy up the media companies, but as prominent pro-China local organizations, some with UFWD links, build up a web of ties to senior editors at the local news outlets. Such groups use their stature in the local community and their members' ability to direct advertising to publications that offer favorable coverage of China. In the Philippines, according to a report by the Center for Strategic and International Studies, local pro-China associations have built close ties to the *World News*, a Philippine Chinese-language newspaper, helping shape *World News* coverage.[51] In Australia, representatives of Chinese groups, including Australian branches of the Chinese Students and Scholars Association (CSSA), a global organization for Chinese nationals studying in other countries, meet with management at leading Chinese-language newspapers and help influence their coverage. Although the CSSAs do plenty of benign work, such as helping Chinese students abroad with issues like finding housing, they also, according to Alexander Bowe, formerly of the U.S.-China Economic and Security Review Commission, typically have close links to Chinese embassies and consulates. In fact, the CSSAs play a central role in the UFWD's efforts to influence Chinese communities, Chinese-language media, and other actors in foreign states.[52]

Launching China-Style Outlets

Not content to control such a large share of the global Chinese-language media market, Beijing also appears to be trying to help other countries set up domestic news outlets modeled on Chinese state media. In Cambodia, Beijing has helped back a Khmer-language channel called Nice TV, which launched in 2017 and puts out pro-China content and a broad range of other material.[53] Beijing also has strongly backed another news outlet in Cambodia called Fresh News, which now closely resembles Chinese state media and has proved to be a force in shaping Cambodian news discourse. Fresh News, which operates primarily in Khmer, has become probably the most powerful media outlet in Cambodia (far more influential than Nice TV), close to the prime minister and often vilifying the opposition.[54] Unlike Chinese state media, which reports from Gallup show draw a minimal audience in Cambodia, Fresh News is popular with Cambodians.[55] It deluges the population with pro–Hun Sen stories and wild conspiracy theories about the opposition, but its wild, confrontational style has given it popularity.[56] Indeed, it has become one of the top fifty most popular websites in Cambodia, trailing mostly giant global sites like Facebook and Google and an array of webcam and pornography sites.[57]

In Laos, meanwhile, Beijing also has funded a new television station, Lao Army Television Channel 7.[58] Lao Defense Minister Chansamone Chanyalath called the station China's "special gift for the Lao Army, government, and the Lao people," according to Radio Free Asia.[59]

Fresh News's owner has based its approach on domestic Chinese media outlets, with their professional look and mix of soft feature stories, pro-government news, and conspiratorial nationalism that sees Western democracies as meddling in China's domestic affairs. Its coverage is punchy—and, well, fresh—but never strays into critical reporting on Hun Sen and his party. The outlet also lavishly praises China in many articles, offering a range of stories that portray China's aid, diplomacy, and investments in Cambodia in a positive light.[60] The owner has sent his staff on trips to China paid for by the Chinese government, and Fresh News uses Xinhua for much of its coverage of international affairs.[61] In 2018, it launched a Chinese-language version of its site to serve the growing Chinese diaspora in Cambodia. The Cambodian government, which in the past five years has forced many independent media outlets like *Cambodia Daily* and independent radio stations to close, clearly sees Fresh News as an example for the rest of the Cambodian media.[62] The government also ordered the expulsion of civil society organization National Democratic Institute, among other increasingly harsh measures.[63]

Beijing is bolstering its efforts to create more of these kinds of outlets in other countries, advising state broadcasters on how to create seemingly professional and relatively entertaining—but ultimately biased—news. Though China has paused some of these efforts while it confronts its problems at home due to its disastrous COVID strategy and the ensuing anger from the population, it likely will resume these endeavors to create China-style media in other countries in the near future.

Negative Measures

While Beijing gains de facto ownership of many Chinese-language media outlets, it is simultaneously working to suppress negative coverage of China at publications it does not yet control, a clear example of sharp power. It has had success with negative measures in the past but may struggle more now because of the war in Ukraine; China's more obvious ties to Russia; the possibility, though not likely, that China will supply Russia with weapons that could be used in Ukraine; and Beijing's regular, intensive rhetorical backing of Moscow. (To be sure, China has kept some of its options open; its big banks are unlikely to evade global sanctions against Russia, because China does not want to be cut off from the global financial system.) As in Australia, companies based in China may pull ads from news outlets critical of the Chinese government or reward outlets that avoid such criticism. And in recent years Beijing also has made life much harder for foreign reporters working in China. Foreign journalists are denied visas or forced out of the country, authorities harass Chinese nationals who work as translators and fixers with major international news outlets, state security has stepped up surveillance of foreign news reporters in China, and the national government has made areas of the country like Tibet and Xinjiang virtually off-limits for reporters. When the Chinese authorities discover local reporters who have been working with foreign reporters from major news outlets, helping provide information for their stories, they often detain these local reporters.[64]

Beijing also has punished major global outlets, like the *New York Times*, the Australian Broadcasting Corporation, and the *Guardian*, for critical reporting by blocking their sites from being accessed inside China, and indeed censoring virtually all outside information in 2022, a censorship that became even more intense because of the Ukraine war and also because of growing unrest within China against Beijing's unpopular lockdowns and general COVID policies. (The website of the think tank where I work, the Council on Foreign Relations, is now blocked in China, as are the websites of many other foreign think tanks and research institutes.[65]) Increasingly, reporters themselves are being blocked. Beijing expelled Megha Rajagopalan, the longtime China bureau chief for *BuzzFeed News*, in 2018, after she published extensive reporting on abuses in Xinjiang.[66] Then, in 2020, China expelled multiple reporters from the *New York Times*, the *Wall Street Journal*, and the *Washington Post*; due to the crackdown, by the end of

September 2020, the *Washington Post* did not have a correspondent based in China anymore, for the first time in forty years, although it eventually placed another reporter in China, but then seemed to move that reporter's home base to Taiwan.[67] In August 2020, the last two journalists representing Australian media had to be evacuated from China by the Australian government following a five-day diplomatic standoff, after being questioned by Chinese authorities in relation to the detention of an Australian news anchor working for CGTN.[68] Beijing also expelled the *Economist*'s Hong Kong reporter in 2021.[69] And yet, in taking these harsh actions against journalists, China often angered many of the countries whose nationals were forced out as Beijing banned reporters, and actually stained Beijing's global image.

In recent years, Beijing also has stepped up efforts to silence and punish exile news outlets that report on abuses toward China's ethnic and religious minorities. These outlets, like the U.S.-based Radio Free Asia, which produces detailed coverage of events in places like Xinjiang that are inaccessible to most foreign reporters, feature the reporting of Tibetans, Uighurs, and other minorities who have fled China. Despite living in exile, the reporters rely on networks of sources still inside the country. Most of these exiles still have not only sources but also family members back in China, and the Xi administration has ferociously pursued relatives as punishment for the reporting—and probably to try to shut up Radio Free Asia and its peers. Chinese hackers apparently have launched cyberattacks at exile media outlets. (Hackers linked to China also apparently have tried to paralyze major global outlets like the *New York Times* and the *Wall Street Journal* with cyberattacks.[70]) The Chinese authorities reportedly have placed some family members of exiled reporters in shorter-term detention centers, but other relatives seemingly were handed longer jail terms.[71] Several Radio Free Asia reporters have noticed that relatives living in China simply have seemingly disappeared, their whereabouts unknown.[72]

Overall, as Freedom House's Sarah Cook notes, Beijing utilizes a range of tools "to induce self-censorship among media owners and their outlets headquartered outside mainland China."[73] Individual journalists are incentivized toward self-censorship, she says, through Beijing's increasing use of only short-term visas for foreign journalists, refusals to renew visas, and strict limitations on the numbers of correspondents most major global media outlets can employ in their bureaus in China.[74] In addition, she notes, "Chinese diplomats, local officials, security forces, and regulators both inside and outside China . . . obstruct newsgathering, prevent the publication of undesirable content, and punish overseas media outlets that fail to heed restrictions [with] economic 'carrots' and 'sticks' to induce self-censorship among media owners and their outlets headquartered outside mainland China. [This includes] indirect pressure applied via proxies— including advertisers, satellite firms, and foreign governments—who take action to prevent or punish the publication of content critical of Beijing."[75]

Beijing regularly bans Chinese-language publications that try to cover China critically from operating in China at all, or even from accessing Chinese diplomats and officials in other countries. In 2017, New Tang Dynasty TV, a relatively independent Chinese-language television channel based in New York, said that one of its senior reporters was refused accreditation to the UN General Assembly due to pressure from Beijing.[76]

Chinese officials also increasingly apply pressure on outlets outside of China to punish journalists who write critically about Chinese leaders or policies. Sometimes, the pressure comes as "just" intensive and scary rhetorical attacks on the journalists or surveillance, without some clear attempt to physically harm them or get them fired. In early 2019, a *Star Vancouver* reporter, Joanna Chiu, published a scoop that Canada's ambassador to China said it "would be great for Canada" if the U.S. government ended its request to extradite the senior Huawei executive Meng Wanzhou. Meng had been arrested in Canada and faced charges in the United States of bank fraud and wire fraud and theft of trade secrets, and the Canadian ambassador was quickly fired.[77] After Chiu's story, state media outlets like *Global Times* used their massive social media platforms to assail Chiu, and she wrote that she felt unsafe even though she remained in Canada.[78] At roughly the same time, the *Wall Street Journal* revealed that the Chinese security forces had offered a neighboring government, Malaysia, to surveil *Wall Street Journal* reporters in Hong Kong, including physically surveilling them and tapping their devices.[79]

On other occasions, Chinese officials, pro-China citizens, or businesses dependent on Chinese capital in other countries appear to have pushed directly for reporters to be fired. In 2015, the editor-in-chief of a Chinese-language newspaper in Canada known for being sympathetic to Beijing, the *Chinese Canadian Post*, was fired after she published a column that could have been interpreted as critiquing the Chinese government and its alleged links to a prominent Canadian politician.[80] In 2016 and 2017, two different reporters were fired from the *Global Chinese Press*, also in Canada, for what they claimed was content seen as critical of or potentially "displeasing" to Beijing.[81] In 2018, Azad Essa, a South African journalist, abruptly had his column in the *IOL* newspaper canceled by Independent Media, the owner of the news outlet and one of the biggest media companies in South Africa.[82] Reporters Without Borders ranks South Africa as having one of the freest media environments in Africa and notes that press freedom is better in South Africa than in the United States.[83] But Essa's column had criticized Beijing's treatment of Uighurs, and he almost immediately got his column nixed.

Essa later wrote that he was not particularly surprised that his column was pulled. A Chinese state entity owns 20 percent of Independent Media, and Chinese firms have become major investors and players throughout the media landscape in South Africa and other parts of sub-Saharan Africa.[84] He had seen, before writing the column, that Independent Media's outlets had lavished praise on China's approach to South Africa and the continent generally. They continued to do so after the column was canceled.

Sometimes journalists even face threats of violence, although it can be hard to connect the attacks to the Chinese government. Chinese security forces have confronted BBC reporters trying to interview protestors in China and regularly have harassed reporters from the BBC, the *New York Times*, and many other outlets.[85] In January 2014 Kevin Lau, the former hard-driving editor of the Hong Kong newspaper *Ming Pao*, was attacked in Hong Kong by two men with a cleaver and badly injured. This kind of violence has become common against journalists working in Hong Kong's Chinese-language outlets. The Committee to Protect Journalists notes that, in just one year (2013),

> two men wielding batons attacked Chen Ping, publisher of the weekly *iSun Affairs*, on the streets of Chai Wan [a Hong Kong neighborhood]. In June that year, someone in a stolen car rammed through the gate at the home of [publisher of an independent newspaper] Jimmy Lai, leaving an axe and machete at the scene. Days later, a *Sharp Daily* reporter was attacked and injured. Shortly after that, three masked men wielding knives threatened distribution workers and burned 26,000 copies of Next Media's flagship *Apple Daily*. The Hong Kong Journalists Association cited 18 cases of assault or harassment in 2013.[86]

Lai's house was firebombed in 2019, one of many such attacks against Chinese-language reporters in Hong Kong that year. In 2020, he was arrested by the Hong Kong authorities for allegedly being involved in an "illegal assembly" during the 2019 protests.[87] Later that year, he was arrested again, under the harsh new national security law enacted by Beijing, and police raided the newsroom of *Apple Daily* and the publication was ultimately shuttered.[88] Nearly every other independent outlet in Hong Kong closed down, and Lai was sentenced to thirteen months in prison for participating in a pro-democracy assembly.

Over a period of three months at the end of 2015, five people connected to Hong Kong's Mighty Current Media and its bookstore, which publishes books about China's top leadership, disappeared, reportedly abducted by Chinese security services.[89] The Hong Kong bookseller Gui Minhai was sentenced to ten years in prison for "illegally providing intelligence overseas."[90] In January 2019, Chinese authorities detained Yang Hengjun, an Australian citizen of Chinese descent, while he was traveling to China and charged him with espionage.[91] While in detention, Yang reportedly went without seeing any family members or lawyers, was routinely shackled in chains and subjected to daily interrogations, and was only allowed to shower once a week.[92] The following year, the Chinese authorities detained an Australian-Chinese journalist for CGTN based in Beijing, Cheng Lei, alleging that she was suspected of crimes that somehow endangered China's national security.[93]

In some cases, Beijing has enlisted governments with which it has close ties to apply pressure on journalists critical of China. In Turkey, where the government has waged a war against independent media over the past decade, and where ties with Beijing are warming, officials have openly said that they will "eliminate any media reports targeting China."[94] In 2019, Nepal's state news agency launched an investigation into three of its own journalists, apparently after pressure from the Chinese embassy, when they translated and then published a news article about the Dalai Lama.[95] The same year, authorities in Thailand arrested a Taiwanese man for broadcasting independent news stories into China.[96]

Overall, an International Republican Institute study of China's growing effect on democracies and hybrid regimes found that a number of countries are increasingly working to foster fawning coverage of China in their local press.[97] In Ecuador, for instance, the administration of President Rafael Correa exercised enough control of the media and civil society to prevent extensive negative coverage of a wide range of economic and security agreements signed with Beijing.[98] In Zambia, the state broadcaster ZNBC partnered with the Chinese firm StarTimes and received loans to upgrade the state broadcasting system.[99] The joint venture granted StarTimes a majority stake—60 percent—effectively ceding control of the system to China and ensuring only positive coverage for Beijing and its influence in Zambia. The government of President Edgar Lungu has also worked to censor and discourage any criticism of China in media outlets it does not directly control.[100]

Conversely, as multiple Southeast Asian journalists have noted in conversations, news outlets that consistently produce coverage sympathetic to China find a world opened up to them. It becomes relatively easy for their reporters and editors to get visas to China. They can obtain interviews with Chinese officials and diplomats in Southeast Asia—and the same holds true for outlets sympathetic to China in Australia, Latin America, New Zealand, and North America.

After failing to silence some outlets, however, Beijing has tried to control the flow of information in a different way—by dominating the actual networks that carry vital news around the globe.

Chapter 9

Controlling the Pipes

Even as China attempts to use the control over media and information it has amassed, it is also working to dominate the "pipes" through which information moves and to wield influence in "old-fashioned" ways like controlling student groups, politicians, think tanks, and other organizations in foreign countries. I use the term "pipes" to mean the broad underpinnings of global information networks, including the actual physical infrastructure and the rules and norms that govern how information flows. More specifically, these pipes include the physical telecommunications networks for wireless and wired data; mobile phones and other devices that display information; tools that create the Internet of Things; tools that allow for surveillance; leading search engines, web browsers, and social media platforms; and the standards that govern the internet. (The "Internet of Things," or IoT, refers to internet-connected devices, the connections between devices, and the services and networks that support these connections.)

With greater influence in these areas, China would not have to rely as much on other countries to disseminate Xinhua, China Global Television Network (CGTN), and China Radio International (CRI), or on media coverage from local Chinese-language outlets controlled by Beijing. Instead, it could use its own pipes to more aggressively, and mostly covertly, spread state media coverage onto internet networks, social media platforms, mobile phones and other devices, browsers, and television conglomerates controlled by or closely linked to the

Chinese government, which would deprive news consumers in many countries of independent coverage about China—and also in some cases about their own governments, in places where Chinese state media report little about the repressiveness of other countries. If Beijing had more control of the pipes of information, it also could, within foreign countries, more easily censor negative stories and social media conversations and spread stories, rumors, opinions, accusations, blandishments, and other types of disinformation, obviously types of sharp power.[1] Ultimately, it could use the pipes to help foreign countries copy China's surveillance strategies and to export China's model for a closed and controlled domestic internet, part of Beijing's overall model of technology-enabled authoritarianism.

Chinese state companies are laying down many of the new physical or virtual pipes for global information flows. The state-controlled China Telecom, for instance, has rolled out the third-biggest mobile phone network in the Philippines, despite concerns raised by security experts and some lawmakers about Beijing dominating a portion of the country's mobile infrastructure.[2] China Telecom partnered with Chelsea Logistics as well as the tycoon Dennis Uy, a close ally of former Philippine president Rodrigo Duterte, in obtaining and rolling out its mobile network.[3] This is a strategy Chinese state firms have used in many countries. By partnering with local tycoons currently in favor with government leaders, Chinese firms often are able to land contracts to build mobile and fixed internet infrastructure, sometimes without any transparent bidding processes. In Africa, Beijing has become by far the dominant builder of new physical infrastructure to transmit information. China Telecom and ZTE, whose biggest shareholder is a state-owned enterprise, are building the core of new mobile and fiber-optic networks across Africa, competing largely with Huawei, which is a private Chinese company but has historic links to the People's Liberation Army.[4]

Although some of these Chinese companies are not state firms, they rely on funding from Chinese state banks and China's sovereign wealth fund, have boards packed with top Chinese Communist Party

(CCP) officials, and have extensive other connections to senior CCP leaders. They ultimately must operate under rules set by the Chinese central government.[5]

In return, they get help. Under China's Digital Silk Road (DSR) initiative, part of the Belt and Road Initiative (BRI), many Chinese companies that build telecommunications infrastructure in Africa and other regions get loans from Chinese banks on extremely generous terms.[6] Non-Chinese competitors face huge hurdles in corralling the same level of diplomatic support from their own governments or getting anything like the cheap financing, usually from Chinese state banks, that Chinese companies enjoy. By 2020, China had already signed agreements on DSR cooperation with, or provided DSR-related investment to, at least sixteen countries.[7] But the true number of agreements and investments is likely much larger, because many of these go unreported: memoranda of understanding between China and other countries do not necessarily show whether China and another country have embarked upon close cooperation in the digital sphere. Some estimates suggest that one-third of the countries participating in the BRI—139 in 2021, according to an accounting by a Council on Foreign Relations task force—are cooperating on DSR projects, although as the coronavirus pandemic hit, many countries could not pay back BRI loans, and Beijing's BRI diplomacy withered somewhat as China focused on its own domestic problems.[8]

By 2020, Huawei had signed more than fifty commercial contracts around the world to build next-generation 5G networks, though it began to lag in developed markets—and was banned in much of Europe, in Australia, in the United States, and in some other leading democracies—and is likely to face much higher obstacles to many markets in the wake of the Ukraine war, which has led democracies to have greater suspicion of all firms from both China and Russia.[9] Still, it is poised to be the dominant 5G provider in sub-Saharan Africa (where there is less condemnation of Russia's actions and a physical remove from the Ukraine war), with competitors lagging behind. In Southeast Asia, meanwhile, Huawei already has built many of the shorter undersea cables linking the region's telecommunications networks, and the company has inked deals to develop 5G networks in Cambodia, the Philippines, and Thailand—and possibly with Indonesia as well, countries that seem unconcerned about security issues with Huawei and also have minimal interest in the Ukraine war.[10] And in the Pacific Islands—where Beijing has in recent years exerted increasing influence strategically, trying to sign a deal with Pacific states that would drastically increase Beijing's presence in the region—Huawei and other Chinese tech giants have competed aggressively with Australian and other Western companies to make new deals in places like Fiji. Around the world, Huawei is completing thousands of miles of undersea cable, through which most telecommunications traffic travels.[11] In Central Asia, meanwhile, Huawei has already become the dominant provider of new 5G technology, including in the region's most populous state, Uzbekistan, and its freest, Kyrgyzstan.[12]

Even in some democracies where leaders have significant concerns about allowing Chinese companies to build telecommunications infrastructure, Huawei has made inroads, although some of its efforts will now stall in richer and democratic countries worried about the downsides of being reliant on Huawei and other Chinese tech firms. Yet Huawei's low costs and high levels of experience with technology often give them a leg up in getting contracts to build infrastructure, particularly in developing countries. Huawei also has become increasingly innovative, becoming one of the biggest investors in research and development of any tech company in the world.[13]

Chinese firms are winning IoT contracts as well. Beijing has placed a particular priority on this sector since at least the late 2000s, when then-premier Wen Jiabao declared it a national priority.[14] Emily de La Bruyère and Nathan Picarsic, formerly of the consulting firm Long Term Strategy Group, have written that Chinese companies have built "a network of sensors [in China]—including but not limited to surveillance cameras, car navigation systems, and smart electricity monitors." Any information that is gathered is passed along to the China Academy of Sciences (CAS), a leading Chinese research institution.[15]

According to de La Bruyère and Picarsic, "CAS explains that the system is a 'test zone for a global network.'"

Most notoriously, within China the state's massive use of the IoT has helped create a developing "social credit system," which, as it advances, could give the ruling party enough information to create a social credit score for each Chinese citizen. The project remains under development, with pilot portions being created, but in some places, like the western province of Xinjiang, Beijing already has implemented far-reaching technological authoritarianism to control the minority Uighur population.[16] Nationally, if other parts of China become like Xinjiang, the potential consequences of this Big Brother technological authoritarianism are immense. As de La Bruyère and Picarsic note:

> Bad driving might mean demerits. So might playing too many video games or taking too much toilet paper from a public restroom—or speaking ill of the government. Poor scores bear consequences. The Party can use them to limit travel, job eligibility, internet speeds, and even animal ownership.[17]

The social credit system has some less dystopian uses. It has been utilized, to this point, primarily by the government to help streamline the business environment and enforce judgments against abusive businesses. But its potential to turn into a much larger, Orwellian program is dangerous, even though the program remains relatively limited for now.[18] Now, large Chinese companies are building on their domestic experience, including using information for surveillance and intense social monitoring, to win big contracts and joint contracts for IoT projects around the world—even in Europe, where governments are often most protective of privacy.[19] In 2018, the European Union passed extensive online privacy legislation that gave EU internet users more control over their personal data, among other changes.[20] But many EU states still trusted Chinese firms to build their information infrastructure, including infrastructure for the IoT—a contract some may now retract in the Ukraine war environment, but which some will not.[21] Poland and other European states have given IoT contracts to Chinese companies, like the surveillance camera giant Hikvision, which is part of a massive state enterprise.[22] Chinese-built surveillance camera systems even have been used in official buildings in Europe and North America, including departments of the UK government and U.S. military bases.[23] In 2019, the U.S. government added Hikvision and several other Chinese firms to an economic blacklist, in part due to their involvement in abuses in Xinjiang.[24] (The Hikvision cameras were being used on U.S. bases right up to the ban.[25]) But even these U.S. actions did not appear to stop the firms' global expansion.

Social Media Platforms and Mobile Phones

Social media platforms are another kind of information pipe. A decade ago, Chinese companies had virtually no presence on social media. Since then, Chinese firms like WeChat, Weibo, and TikTok have expanded quickly, both at home and abroad.

TikTok, the short-video app, now rivals longer-established social media networks like Twitter and Instagram in terms of new users and is gaining massive cultural influence among preteens, teens, and young adults around the world. In 2021, the latest full year for which this book had data, it had the most downloads of any app, even though it was only launched globally in 2017.[26] (For those readers unfamiliar with the stratospherically popular app among younger people, TikTok features videos of up to three minutes, usually set to music and featuring a variety of dances, memes, and challenges, as well as the ability to "duet," a way to interact with and create new content by adding your own video to that of another person.) The app has become omnipresent on the phones of high school and college students, with an estimated 40 percent of its users between the ages of sixteen and twenty-four.[27] It has spawned a new generation of social media influencer around the world, with some young people moving into content houses across cities like Los Angeles to collaborate on making videos together and celebrities making their names first through their TikTok videos.[28]

TikTok's parent company, the Beijing-based ByteDance Limited, presents itself as a global firm and TikTok as no different from platforms run by U.S.-based companies like Facebook or Twitter. ByteDance even says Beijing does not have jurisdiction over content on TikTok at all.[29] But as we will see, these claims ring hollow.

The China-based app WeChat and the social media platform Weibo also have begun to spread outside China. WeChat, owned by the Chinese conglomerate Tencent, combines messaging, social media, ride hailing, online shopping, and payment tools, among other features. Within China, it has become a ubiquitous tool: many middle-class Chinese have come to rely on it for much of their family, social, and work lives. (Other leading global messaging sites, like WhatsApp, Facebook Messenger, and Line, are banned in China, which has helped WeChat corner the market.) Li Yuan, a Hong Kong–based technology columnist for the *New York Times*, notes that one-third of WeChat users within China spend four hours or more a day using the app.[30] She also notes it has replaced business cards for many Chinese—people just add each other as WeChat contacts—and has helped make mobile payment common even in rural China.[31] Together, nearly forty-five billion messages are sent on WeChat each day.[32]

Usage of WeChat is spreading among Chinese speakers in every corner of the world—it has 1.24 billion users and has expanded across Southeast Asia and South Asia.[33] The United States, meanwhile, is believed to be the second-largest source of WeChat users, behind China.[34] WeChat also has exploded in usage in North America: The Trump administration tried to crack down on it and its parent company with an executive order—but WeChat is still accessible in the United States, since the Biden administration rescinded plans to ban its service in the United States.[35]

WeChat is popular in other countries as well. In Thailand, nearly 20 percent of the population uses the app.[36] In Malaysia, a country of around thirty-two million people, there are reportedly twenty million WeChat accounts.[37] (One user can have multiple accounts, however.) The app's group chats, which can include up to five hundred people, are channels for the spread of information sympathetic to the CCP, while people who offer critical commentary in the chat are censored.[38] (While WeChat is not known primarily as a news app, its content often contains news stories, links to stories, and discussions about stories, making it a major disseminator of information about Chinese domestic and foreign policies.) In northeast Asia, WeChat has become the second most popular messaging app in Mongolia and has become widely used in Japan and South Korea.[39]

Of course, Tencent and some other Chinese companies like ByteDance are technically private firms. Still, even private Chinese companies like these two giants ultimately answer to Beijing's rules and regulations—all the more so as Xi Jinping has made clear that private companies must be totally subservient to the increasingly authoritarian state. (The Chinese government also directly owns a portion of a firm that oversees ByteDance inside China.) Top executives meet with Chinese leaders and have no choice but to follow Chinese regulations on content, as long as they are Chinese firms based in China. No matter how much ByteDance might claim it is private and just the parent company of TikTok, it ultimately, via TikTok, has access to users' information from countries around the world, and former TikTok employees say that ByteDance exerted tight control over TikTok operations in the United States, among other countries.[40]

While Chinese social media platforms are spreading, Chinese mobile phone makers also are enjoying success, particularly in developing regions like Africa, South Asia, and Southeast Asia. In these places, inexpensive Chinese phones have gained huge market shares, competing with more expensive rivals like Samsung and Apple.[41] Many Chinese mobile phone makers honed their skills in the hyper-competitive domestic Chinese market, where battles between firms, over intellectual property and marketing and other areas, are so brutal they make scrums between U.S. tech giants look like a tea party. And because China was an early adapter in many new smartphone-related features like having one super app like WeChat, Chinese firms actually have surpassed non-Chinese rivals in developing many apps beloved by consumers, as well as developing specific innovations for markets in Africa and other developing regions.[42] WeChat's cashless payment feature, for instance, is sophisticated and easy to use.[43]

The numbers do not lie. Today, China-based mobile phone companies make more than half of the phones purchased annually in Africa, including both smartphones and budget phones.[44] In Southeast Asia, they are becoming increasingly popular, after garnering two-thirds of the market in India, a major geopolitical rival, and much of the market in China.[45] Chinese mobile phones, according to data from Hong Kong–based market research firm Counterpoint Research, make up four of the five most popular brands in India—their price and relative quality have made them irresistible.[46]

Many Chinese-made phones come loaded with the apps of the biggest Chinese social media platforms and web browsers, giving them an instant entrée to users in Africa, Southeast Asia, South Asia, and other regions, although they also have been accused of coming preloaded with spyware.[47] The Indian government, which has become increasingly hawkish toward China under Prime Minister Narendra Modi, has become so concerned about the prevalence and popularity of Chinese mobile apps that the Modi administration in 2020 banned TikTok and WeChat and many other China-based apps from India, a move echoing the Trump administration's 2020 pressure on TikTok and WeChat.[48] (We will examine the measures taken by the United States against TikTok and WeChat in more detail in the following chapters.) But these measures against Chinese apps remain scattershot or nonexistent in other parts of South Asia, and Chinese phones continue to sell well across the subcontinent.

Satellite and Cable Networks

Chinese companies also are gaining ground in the global digital television market. They are no longer just copying foreign technologies but have become innovative and competitive. The Chinese pay television company StarTimes, for example, has become one of Africa's leading digital television operators.[49] With its cheap TV packages and easy-to-install hardware, it can reach formerly unserved populations from Kenya to Nigeria to Rwanda.[50] "The pay TV company [i.e., StarTimes] is leading the continent's transition from analog to digital television with some of the world's most affordable cable/satellite TV packages priced as low as $4 per month. In the burgeoning Digital TV sector, StarTimes is far and away the market leader. The company's reach covers 90 percent of the continent's population," wrote Eric Olander of the South Africa–based China Africa Project.[51] It currently has around ten million subscribers on the continent, but this is expected to grow to over sixteen million in the next four to five years, according to research by Digital TV Research.[52] StarTimes already has the most pay television subscribers in East Africa, and is becoming a major player in southern Africa and West Africa as well.[53] The company has announced nascent plans to expand its inexpensive services into Latin America as well.[54]

Other large Chinese companies are entering the digital and satellite television markets in Africa, South Asia, and Southeast Asia.[55] ZTE has launched digital television services in Pakistan and is exploring other markets, while Chinese provincial and national state television networks are expanding into neighboring Southeast Asian cable markets like Laos, Timor-Leste, and Vietnam.[56]

Using the Pipes, Part 1: Suppression, Surveillance, and the China Model

By controlling pipes for information, Beijing can exert influence through omission. In other words, what does not appear about China in the media in other states can be as important as what does appear. As Chris Walker and Shanthi Kalathil of the National Endowment for Democracy have noted to me on several occasions, in a view shared by other analysts, one of the best—if trickiest—ways to understand if China's influence campaigns are having an effect is to assess what discussions about China no longer happen among business, political, media, and civil society opinion leaders in other states.[57]

Beijing wants to silence conversations about many topics—Xinjiang, Tibet, the South China Sea, China's ties to Russia, China's disastrous management of COVID in 2021 and 2022, and so on. It wants to make these tough topics disappear—poof. And if they disappear for an extended period of time from media coverage and public conversations in other countries, that disappearance feeds on itself, creating a greater boon for China. Publics and opinion leaders do not learn about these issues sensitive to China; over time, publics and opinion leaders become less informed about these issues; with less information, they naturally speak and write about the topics less and less.

It is next to impossible for China to get positive coverage about these topics if they are covered openly and fairly. China could achieve this outcome, of course, through clear and open threats to punish other countries with economic measures, diplomatic measures, or other sanctions, for instance. But the bullying approach, though it certainly has worked with foreign companies and some foreign states fearful of being excluded from China's market or facing other sanctions from Beijing, has major downsides as well. Few people like being threatened, and the natural human response is to fight back. Such bullying makes China seem menacing and often prods opinion leaders in democracies to respond angrily. Open bullying tends to attract the attention of top politicians and other opinion leaders in foreign states, putting them in a position in which they feel they have to respond for fear of looking weak.

More often than bullying, Beijing encourages self-censorship through a combination of incentives and unpredictable and often vague threats. The incentives are obvious: the vast China market for companies; training programs and lucrative visits for officials and some journalists; the possibility of access to the country for academics focusing on China; Chinese diplomatic support and aid for some political leaders abroad; Chinese young men and women studying abroad, which are often the biggest source of foreign students in leading democracies and thus important sources of income for universities; Chinese financing for foreign companies; and other types of incentives. The threats, however, are often purposely left vague. Beijing may declare that certain countries, companies, or individuals are offending the entire Chinese nation simply for noting Taiwan on a map, highlighting abuses in Xinjiang, or taking other such actions. At other times, the Chinese government may say nothing at all. At still other times, Beijing cracks down hard for perceived offenses—banning foreign individuals with platforms like movie stars, suddenly severing important economic ties, ending companies' access to the Chinese market, and other measures.[58] It's hard to predict which infraction will trigger the government's ire.

A combination of incentives and erratic, sometimes harsh, punishments can be highly effective at fostering self-censorship. "A vague accusation pressures an individual to curtail a wider range of activity," the China expert Perry Link, professor emeritus at Princeton and chancellorial chair at the University of California at Riverside, wrote in a famous essay on how the Chinese state constricts speech and other freedoms. "If I don't know exactly why I was 'wrong,' I am induced to pay more attention to the state's strictures in every respect."[59]

That fear need not be created by a power that constantly snarls and punishes, Link noted, but instead the fear is created by the state lying in wait, occasionally acting, and inducing self-censorship. "In sum, [the] Chinese government's censorial authority in recent times has resembled not so much a man-eating tiger or fire-snorting dragon as a giant anaconda coiled in an overhead chandelier."[60] Most of the time, he explained, the snake coiled overhead doesn't move: "It doesn't have to. It feels no need to be clear about its prohibitions. Its constant silent message is 'You yourself decide,' after which, more often than not, everyone in its shadow makes his or her large and small adjustments— all quite 'naturally.'"[61]

WeChat provides another opportunity for Beijing to help contain what appears in the news about China in other countries. As users outside China have gravitated to the app, including its popular messaging service, WeChat has become a central source of news for many Chinese-language speakers beyond the mainland. Wanning Sun, of the University of Technology Sydney, has found that while most Mandarin speakers in Australia do not get much of their news directly from Chinese state media, a majority of them do access WeChat and obtain news from it, such as from news shared in groups and messages.[62] In fact, Sun found that about 60 percent of Mandarin speakers in Australia used WeChat as their primary source of news and information.[63]

Yet much of the news shared on WeChat stems from Xinhua, *Global Times*, CGTN, and other state media outlets, which are controlled by Beijing and uncritical of the Chinese government. Case studies of Mandarin speakers in Australia and their use of WeChat found that, during some periods of time, most channels they accessed had no stories about Chinese politics.[64] Mandarin-speaking Australians who relied on WeChat for news often were getting no news about Chinese politics at all.[65]

Monitoring and Censoring on Social Media

The Chinese government, however, is getting plenty of news about what users of WeChat, and several other social media platforms, are interested in. WeChat offers no privacy protections like end-to-end encryption, and the Chinese government extensively monitors and censors content on the platform.[66] As Bradley Thayer of the University of Texas at San Antonio and Lianchao Han, a longtime China activist, note, all information on WeChat is "monitored, collected, stored, analyzed, censored and accessed by Chinese authorities."[67] Indeed, WeChat (and other Chinese social media platforms) readily shares information with Beijing. The app reportedly surveys millions of messages every day, flags some for sensitive content, and stores their information; all messages sent via WeChat travel to Tencent servers in

China and are vulnerable to being accessed, monitored, and censored by the Chinese authorities.[68] In assessing the encryption protections of the biggest messaging apps in the world, Amnesty International gave WeChat's parent company a grade of 0 out of 100, by far the lowest score of any of the eleven messaging app parent companies studied.[69] (Facebook received a score of 73 and Apple got a score of 67.[70]) The company appears to be constantly upgrading its ability to monitor and censor content, improving significantly in these "skills" each year. In fact, cybersecurity researchers have noted that WeChat appears to have developed one of the most sophisticated and constantly evolving protocols for censorship of any platform or messaging service, and these can be applied for messaging originating outside of China.[71]

Within China, where surveillance cameras are nearly everywhere, the population has lived under an authoritarian regime for decades. As internet freedoms have been eroded in recent years and were decimated in 2022 in part via a state crackdown on many large information technology (IT) firms, many citizens have resigned themselves to the fact that WeChat's messages, group chats, and other services simply are not private. (This decimation, along with China's repressive zero-COVID policies and anemic economy, incidentally, is costing China in driving away some of its best talent in IT fields, as their companies are increasingly dominated by the state, social controls are increasing, they feel that innovation is not rewarded, and they fear launching start-ups.[72]) Li Yuan of the *New York Times* says that Chinese citizens "often feel powerless and fatalistic when it comes to censorship and surveillance" on WeChat.[73] In addition, Li Yuan notes that young Chinese feel very disillusioned with the current government, especially younger Chinese who would be critical to the IT industry.[74]

Consumers outside China, however, while certainly wary of big Western tech companies mishandling their data, have not become accustomed to social media and search platforms surveilling them as extensively as WeChat or censoring what they write online. When stories break about data breaches on major U.S.-based platforms like WhatsApp, which had a flaw in 2019 that could have allowed people to install spyware on it, they spark significant public anger and a response from big Western tech firms.[75]

There is evidence that WeChat is applying tactics outside China that it uses inside the country, thus potentially curtailing critical discussions about Beijing in developed democracies like the United States, Australia, and European countries. Sarah Cook of Freedom House shows that WeChat is "systematically monitoring conversations of users outside China and flagging politically sensitive content for some form of scrutiny," including messages in both English and Chinese, as well as other languages.[76] In the mid-2010s, WeChat informed users that messages they were sending were being blocked—probably because they contained keywords like "Xi" or "CCP" or a host of other words related to Chinese politics, social issues, human rights, or foreign policy. Now the app does not even take this step. Instead, it simply filters and halts messages, including some from outside China, without users even knowing they have been censored.[77] A study of WeChat by Citizen Lab at the University of Toronto found that "WeChat communications conducted entirely among non-China-registered accounts are subject to pervasive content surveillance that was previously thought to be exclusively reserved for China-registered accounts."[78] While many WeChat users in China may know about this surveillance, users outside China are often not so prepared—and in any event WeChat is so dominant in the market for Chinese-language platforms that people still use it.

Weibo, a microblogging site similar to Twitter, has come under even closer scrutiny and control from Beijing than WeChat, likely because it had become the premier site for discussions in China on current events. In the early 2010s, according to a study in the *Atlantic,* Chinese users often used Weibo to condemn local governments and even the national regime.[79] But by the late 2010s, Beijing had neutered discussion on Weibo and was much more closely monitoring users both inside and outside of the country. Over four weeks in the fall of 2018 alone, the state closed about ten thousand accounts on major Chinese social media platforms and then warned Weibo and WeChat that their "irresponsibility and lax management" was allowing the platforms to continue "growing wild and creating chaos."[80] A Chinese official told the *South China Morning Post* that the crackdown was just the beginning of "new measures to manage a new industry." The official suggested that this type of repression, which would include serious punishment for some people using these platforms for criticism, now would become the norm.[81] The following year, Beijing shuttered the Weibo account of Yu Jianrong, a prominent intellectual and researcher at the Chinese Academy of Social Sciences, along with many other users who had avoided the 2018 dragnet. Yu had amassed more than seven million followers and become a prominent influencer, partly because in the past he had posted calls for political reform.[82] While he stopped posting about politics and instead stuck to posts about art and other apolitical topics, he was still shut down.[83]

Modeling a Closed Internet

China also offers other countries a tested model of how to control a domestic internet, by blocking content and monitoring and punishing internet users. Beijing promotes its model of a closed, monitored, filtered internet in several ways. It trains foreign officials and holds high-level meetings with national and local leaders from Russia to Africa to Southeast Asia, where Chinese officials and corporate executives promote internet control technologies. The number of these trainings in information management has increased since the mid-2010s, and trainings often focus on how China has blocked certain social media platforms, forced domestic social media platforms to submit to state guidelines, and used a range of filtering methods to scrub social media and messaging sites.[84] According to an estimate by Freedom House, China has held trainings and seminars on information management with officials from thirty-six countries.[85] The true number of countries that have sent representatives to China to study information management is probably much higher, since Freedom

House only analyzed officials from sixty-five countries. (There are 193 member states in the United Nations.)

Many of these training programs do not explicitly focus on information management and control. But people who have attended trainings on issues not explicitly labeled as information management say that even events focused on areas like policing, the judiciary, and the internet more generally often include discussions of China's model of governance, and even how Beijing manages the Chinese internet. This assistance includes hiring advisors who understand China's model of the internet and soliciting investments from a broad range of Chinese technology firms. Beijing supplements these efforts by teaching lower-ranking foreign officials about China's internet strategies.[86] For instance, China is establishing training centers within China for officials from other regions, primarily those of developing countries.[87] (Some training centers piggyback on existing programs for Chinese officials from various provinces.) These training centers do not just specialize in the internet; they also include courses and discussions on public opinion management and information management, and some have instructed officials from countries like Vietnam in how to control the internet and social media.[88]

Freedom House's study of these trainings showed that many countries often follow up on trainings, like the ones that were done for Southeast Asian states, by importing specific types of Chinese assistance and introducing cybersecurity laws that constrain the internet in similar ways to China's controls.[89] Russia, in the wake of the Ukraine war and Russia's isolation from much of the world, now has almost fully shuttered its internet from outside sites, including social media giants like Facebook, Twitter, and Instagram, so that it resembles the Chinese internet model in many respects, with the state in near-total control.

And in recent years Southeast Asian states like Vietnam, Cambodia, and Thailand appear to have modeled their increasingly tough cybersecurity laws, which include clauses allowing for widespread blocking of information, massive government monitoring of domestic internets, and provisions to force companies to keep data locally, on China's own efforts to control its domestic internet, or to have sent officials to China to study cybersecurity practices and then brought those practices back home.[90] After the Myanmar military took control of that country in a coup in February 2021, it also quickly moved to implement a broad cybersecurity law, similar in many respects to Chinese laws, that will force internet service providers to store consumer data in a way that will allow for monitoring and surveillance, and that will allow the government to conduct widespread surveillance of the domestic internet for a variety of other reasons as well.[91] At nearly the same time that Myanmar was cracking down on its domestic internet, Cambodia passed a tough new law aimed at controlling its internet, and similar to Chinese controls of its domestic internet.[92]

Using the Pipes, Part 2: Disinformation

With growing influence over search engines, social media platforms, and web browsers, Beijing has in the past few years increased its use of disinformation, a tactic it historically avoided outside its own borders and a few nearby places like Taiwan. Overall, until quite recently Beijing had amassed little experience pushing false stories to create societal divisions in other states, manipulating results on search engines, or creating false personas online to meddle in politics in other countries. Beijing's lesser interest in using disinformation abroad stemmed in part from China's desire to be perceived as a responsible, stable global power; so much of China's information efforts are designed to advertise Beijing's positive influence on the world that being caught going full crazy, Kremlin style, could undermine this positive messaging as well.[93] Just as importantly, Beijing remained more focused on suppressing or preempting content online than in injecting outright false information than Moscow—at least before the Ukraine war. "The Russians have been the most creative and persistent at using social media to manipulate public opinion, but they've been targeting many countries over many years," Philip Howard, director of the Oxford Internet Institute research organization, told a reporter.[94] To be sure, though Russia has had continued success manipulating foreign public opinion in some countries during the Ukraine war, its success rate has dwindled due to the omnipresent coverage of destruction in Ukraine.

Yet at least since 2018, and certainly since 2019, Beijing has become more willing, both in its neighborhood and, to some extent, in other regions, to meddle on global platforms like Facebook, Twitter, and YouTube and to utilize the more divisive, hyperpolarizing tactics embraced by Moscow—and now to share Moscow's disinformation about Ukraine and other topics.[95] Beijing appears to be learning about disinformation strategies and state media from Moscow and may be impressed by the success the Kremlin has had in disrupting elections across the West and fomenting disinformation in places as far-flung as Africa and Latin America. The two autocratic giants also seem more united than in the past in trying to specifically undermine democratic societies from within, to attack U.S. global influence, to sow division within other important democratic actors like the European Union, and to jointly promote disinformation.[96] A 2020 study by the Center for a New American Security think tank found that "China appears to be gleaning best practices from Moscow and has begun to adopt some of the Kremlin's tactics," like inundating social media platforms with coordinated, disruptive, and fake narratives, which is Moscow's forte, instead of trying to use social media platforms in more limited ways such as to censor information Beijing does not want out.[97]

The two autocrats also seem to be starting to use disinformation to amplify each other's narratives on certain issues, as has clearly been shown during the Ukraine conflict, though China has not yet leapfrogged Russia in the skill of many disinformation efforts. Russian disinformation that portrays the United States and other democracies poorly seems to lay the groundwork for Chinese information efforts that portray Beijing's model of governance as superior to that of democracies.[98]

China also, notably, has begun using both information and disinformation strategies not only to meddle in politics in other countries but also against major corporations that take actions that displease Beijing. In 2021, for instance, after the global fashion giant H&M, Nike, and some other apparel retailers publicly raised concerns about the use of forced labor to produce cotton in Xinjiang that is then utilized in these giants' products, Beijing undertook an information and disinformation campaign against the Sweden-based H&M.[99] The strategy proved effective, as H&M quickly backpedaled. Announcing its quarterly results in March 2021, the company noted that "its commitment to China remained strong and it was dedicated to regaining the trust and confidence of customers, colleagues and business partners there," according to a press release from H&M.[100]

Another strategy Beijing is increasingly using is Facebook content farms, with postings that seem to originate from one or two sources but are deceptively tailored to look like a large number of unique postings. In Malaysia, several groups have in recent years created fake accounts, pages, and groups—a tactic common in Russian efforts—and then used them to promote disinformation about U.S. politicians and U.S. politics, and about democratic political systems in general. Some of these inauthentic Facebook pages seemed to have originated in China, and they blended fairly sophisticated commentary on Malaysian life and politics with pro-China messaging and disinformation about the United States and democratic countries.[101] In addition, an investigation by the respected Malaysian media organization Malaysiakini found that major Chinese-language media in Malaysia were prominent importers of false information, probably originating in Chinese state media, about Hong Kong, Hong Kong protestors, and other aspects about Hong Kong.[102]

As China and Russia increase their cooperation in disinformation and other information tools—they are sharing knowledge at joint forums, at summits, and in many other ways—their coordination almost surely will increase. The two autocrats may be working with other authoritarian states on disinformation as well. A study originally uncovered by *Politico* and produced by the U.S. State Department's Global Engagement Center, which tracks disinformation and propaganda, found that China, Iran, and Russia were increasingly converging on disinformation narratives about the United States, and particularly about the U.S. response to the novel coronavirus.[103] The same report suggested that Beijing was allowing Moscow access to China's domestic internet to spread more disinformation to the Chinese populace about Beijing and Washington's responses to COVID-19.[104] Their converging messaging on COVID-19 suggested that autocratic states had managed the outbreak well (in reality, Iran had mismanaged it horrendously), and that the U.S. response to the crisis had been disastrous.[105] (China's response in 2021 and 2022 to the crisis also was disastrous.)

China certainly has experience with disinformation at home. A report by researchers at Harvard University concludes that Beijing has for years overseen a massive domestic disinformation campaign. King and his coauthors note that "the Chinese government fabricates [often fake] posts ... 448 million social media comments a year," which are packed with disinformation "to distract the [domestic Chinese] public and change the subject" from sensitive issues.[106]

Now, the global appeal of platforms like WeChat, combined with the fact that people engaging in disinformation constantly search for new platforms, makes it possible that the app will become a vector for deliberate falsehoods in the future, if it is not one already. WeChat could be used by Beijing, or by pro-China individuals not directly controlled by the government, to spread disinformation. Again, WeChat has become a massive vector for spreading falsehoods within China, though it is often unclear whether these falsehoods are being perpetuated just by individual users with no links to Beijing or are organized by the state.[107] Although WeChat claims that it is fighting disinformation, including by employing its own fact checkers, its platform clearly is open to manipulation by Beijing. It is also almost impossible to comprehensively study how the platform combats false information, since WeChat's management is so opaque. The app regularly lists the most popular recent rumors being spread on the messaging service, allegedly as a way to fight so-called fake news.[108] But as multiple cybersecurity experts have noted, given Beijing's sway over WeChat, this strategy could allow the Chinese government to portray true stories, about Chinese policy or politics or other sensitive issues, as rumors on WeChat—and then have these "rumors" debunked.[109]

In Taiwan, the place most clearly affected by disinformation, primarily from state actors and nonstate actors linked to China, officials have confronted Beijing covertly funding local politicians, influencing or controlling Taiwanese media stations, and other types of meddling for decades. But in recent years, Taiwan has faced a growing onslaught of disinformation from China. This campaign has become more sophisticated and increasingly resembles Russian tactics—manipulation of search results, injection of false stories into Taiwanese social media platforms, and the distribution of memes through bots. Of all the places in the world, Taiwan is probably the one where China's disinformation tactics have become the most sophisticated.

Some of China's specific disinformation strategies toward the island seem designed to promote specific pro-China candidates and to divide society against itself. "China is following the steps from Russia," Yi-suo Tzeng, head of cyberwarfare at the Institute for National Defense and Security Research in Taiwan, told reporters, a view echoed by other Taiwanese researchers and intelligence officials.[110]

In one notable example of the increasing deployment of false stories in Taiwan, a China-based content farm published an article in 2018 purportedly about stranded Taiwanese who were trapped at the airport in Osaka, Japan, during a major typhoon.[111] The story, later shown to be fake and created by someone with a mainland Chinese Internet Protocol (IP) address, suggested that the Chinese mission in Osaka had sent buses to rescue Chinese nationals trapped at the airport, but the Taipei Economic and Cultural Representative Office in Osaka, the de facto Taiwanese mission in that Japanese city, had not.[112] *Global Times* and the site Guancha.cn—which have become

main actors in laundering fake content into the world of more respectable media outlets—ran the story, and it was distributed widely,
including in respectable media outlets.[113] But the story was not true:
The Chinese mission had not sent any buses, and all evacuation buses
were actually arranged by Osaka's Kansai airport.[114] However, filled
with shame over the suggestions in the story that Taiwan's mission
in Osaka had abandoned Taiwanese, Taiwan's representative in Osaka
committed suicide.[115]

Increasingly too, some of the disinformation tactics originally tried
in Taiwan are then replicated in parts of Southeast Asia and sometimes
globally, according to a study by Doublethink Lab, a research organization based in Taiwan.[116] Sometimes, the organization has found,
the disinformation spreads via the social media accounts of Southeast
Asian Chinese migrants in Taiwan, who wittingly or unwittingly
spread this disinformation initially spread on the island.[117]

Since the coronavirus emerged from China and spread around the
world, Beijing seems again to be adopting a more global, Russian-
style disinformation campaign, one focused on sharing rumors, outright fabrications, and conspiracy theories to confuse foreign publics,
conceal Beijing's guilt over letting the virus initially emerge, sow
distrust, and smear the United States, Europe, Australia, Taiwan, and
other leading democracies—and more broadly suggest that democracy itself is failing at times of citizens' critical needs. This disinformation strategy has been repeated during the Ukraine war. (In the
past few years, China and Russia have publicly stated that their state
media will work together as partners to "tell each other's stories well";
they are clearly taking this step already.[118]) For instance, state media
outlets like the *People's Daily*, Chinese public statements, and Chinese
campaigns—often masked—on social media platforms abroad and at
home have promoted disinformation suggesting that the U.S. government was hiding the extent of the (admittedly bad) COVID-
19 outbreak within the United States, that the United States might
even have caused the spread of the pandemic, and that the origins
of the virus will never be known.[119] Chinese information operations

amplified the poor initial responses to the pandemic by the United States and many major European countries while largely ignoring the effective early responses by Taiwan, Japan, South Korea, Australia, and New Zealand—and injecting massive amounts of disinformation into Taiwan to suggest that "democracy is a failure" even though Taipei had managed one of the best initial COVID-19 strategies.[120]

A study of China's disinformation tactics since the pandemic began, by the Washington-based CNA research group, showed that Beijing's "disinformation campaign" around COVID-19 was "unprecedented" in scope and scale—reminiscent of Moscow's massive disinformation campaigns, and globally widespread.[121] Similarly, an analysis by the National Endowment for Democracy of the convergence between Chinese and Russian disinformation tactics, related to coronavirus, amidst a broader trend in information collaboration between the two authoritarian giants, revealed that each country's state media, officials, and online campaigns on global social media platforms—some done via bots and seemingly fake personas—amplified each other's false, toxic messaging about the pandemic, including falsehoods about how it originated and falsehoods about how democracies are responding.[122]

Whether Beijing continues down this road may depend on how successful its coronavirus information campaign becomes—so far, it has not been that successful, especially because of Beijing's own problems handling the pandemic at home. In other words, if China's embrace of Kremlin tactics in the current situation proves successful, Beijing could well be tempted to repeat these strategies more in the future.

Chapter 10

Old-Fashioned Influence

As I noted back in Chapter 1, this book is not primarily about "old-fashioned" types of influence, the types that mostly involve actual personal contact: cultural and educational diplomacy, funding political parties in other states, gaining control of student groups in other countries, using allies among other states' business and political elites to sway policy, utilizing the United Front Work Department (UFWD), and other tactics. (Of course, China has modernized many of these types of influence; I use the term "old-fashioned" as a simple way to distinguish them from information and media tools.)

Some old-fashioned tools are softer, like cultural and educational diplomacy. Meanwhile, others, as I discussed regarding Australia and New Zealand, are clearly sharper, like wielding the UFWD among communities of ethnic Chinese in other countries or directly interfering in other states' politics through donations to politicians. I have, at times, discussed these old-fashioned types of influence in order to reveal how China's charm offensive emerged in the 1990s, to understand why that offensive failed, and to round out the picture of how China blends old-fashioned influence and information control today in countries like New Zealand. And it is important to remind ourselves of how China has bolstered these tools, and how they potentially reinforce Beijing's information strategies—even though China's old-fashioned influence tactics fail as often as its information strategies.

Continuity

For one, there is continuity between China's information efforts today and its old-fashioned influence attempts. Compared to the 1990s and 2000s, when Beijing utilized a limited amount of sharp power, in part because it lacked the capacity for global, broad-reaching sharp power, today China tries to wield sharp, old-fashioned influence around the world—as widely as it tries to extend its control over information. For instance, in the Xi era Beijing has boosted the size and power of the UFWD and given it far more latitude to wield political influence in other countries—and particularly among ethnic Chinese, university groups, political parties, and student organizations in other countries.[1] The UFWD uses operations, mostly covert and often manipulative, to influence ethnic Chinese communities in other states, foreign governments, and foreign civil societies, and to wield power in communities beyond ethnic Chinese, to "take actions or adopt positions supportive of Beijing's preferred policies," as Alexander Bowe, a former analyst for one prominent U.S. congressionally appointed committee, noted in a report on the UFWD.[2]

Overall, under Xi, the UFWD has increased in size and bolstered its attempts to penetrate and manipulate ethnic Chinese associations, political parties, and other organizations outside China, and particularly in Southeast Asia and other parts of the Asia-Pacific.[3] Beijing has always viewed ethnic Chinese in other countries as naturally inclined to support China, essentially destined to support the Chinese Communist Party (CCP)—though this is far from true. Still, Beijing considers them ripe targets for *qiaowu*, which the New Zealand–based political scientist James Jiann Hua To has defined as efforts to "rally support for Beijing amongst ethnic Chinese outside of China through various propaganda and thought-management techniques" as well as to monitor ethnic Chinese populations abroad.[4] UFWD-linked organizations have used their influence to sway voting among ethnic Chinese in other countries and even potentially insert people with links to the department and affiliated groups into electoral politics in other countries like New Zealand, as we have seen.[5] UFWD-linked figures have played sizable roles as donors and organizers in these countries' politics, and they increasingly have brought their influence tactics into state and local politics, as well as races for individual legislative districts in other countries. As a report on UFWD influence in Australia noted, "Both major party candidates for a seat in parliament during the 2019 Australian federal election had reportedly either been members of united front groups or had travelled on united-front-sponsored trips to China."[6] (Australia has since severely tightened its laws on foreign interference in politics, surely with China in mind.) UFWD-linked organizations also have penetrated many ethnic Chinese civic and business organizations in Southeast Asia.[7] Chinese operatives have penetrated local, state, and to some extent national politics in the United States as well.[8]

In education too, the softer strategies of the charm offensive era have given way to a combination of soft and sharp influence. As discussed earlier, China has, in recent years, expanded its efforts to woo foreign students, and also to send more Chinese students abroad, soft power efforts that can yield significant results in boosting future opinion leaders' views of China. Over 50 percent of the students coming to China now hail from neighboring states in Asia, but sizable numbers are arriving from Africa and Europe as well, including Russia.[9] Some students from developing countries surely came because of scholarships and other forms of aid, which Beijing has expanded dramatically in the past decade.[10] They also may have come because of new institutional partnerships between Asian schools and Chinese universities and the growth of Chinese-language schools throughout Asia and other regions.[11]

At these schools, administrators often promote the idea that students could go on to attend university in China, and Beijing also regularly hosts principals and other administrators from such schools in Southeast Asia and other regions.[12] The administrators' visits to China do not focus solely on the appeal of sending secondary students to

Chinese universities, but they do serve as an important promotional tool for Chinese universities. Educators often go home, to Southeast Asia and other regions, and publicize to students the possibility of attending university in China.[13]

In a post–COVID-19 world, the numbers of foreign students in China may grow, since Chinese universities are pushing to attract students from regions outside Asia, including Africa and Latin America, and the allure of making connections in China and learning Chinese remains strong for students from many developing nations. However, China's zero-COVID policies and isolation from the world in 2021 and 2022 could slow this effort. Particularly among neighboring states in South Asia and Southeast Asia, China was perceived as an increasingly attractive place to study, at least before China's zero-COVID strategy and isolation from the world in 2021 and 2022; it may well become perceived as attractive once again. After it deals with its COVID strategy, China may become an even more attractive destination for higher education as the United States increasingly makes it harder for foreign students to attend university there.[14] Australia, Canada, and New Zealand certainly may get many of the foreign students who would have otherwise gone to the United States, but China likely will attract some as well.[15]

China has expanded its soft power efforts designed to woo local and provincial opinion leaders in other countries as well. Beijing has expanded its "sister cities" project, launching so many—they now have over 2,500 sister cities and provinces in other countries.[16] In this program the cities usually send students on exchanges, offer exchanges of opinion leaders, and promote business ties with each other. They often prove a valuable way of making contacts between local politicians in China and other countries. China has been particularly aggressive in establishing sister cities with countries in East Asia and the Pacific region.[17]

At the same time, it has bolstered official visits and exchanges of political delegations with countries in Africa and Latin America as well, with many of these exchanges taking place among local and provincial-level politicians. Joshua Eisenman of Notre Dame University found that the number of these exchanges between China and African states grew from twenty-six in 2006 to forty-one two years later; by the late 2010s, he notes, in forthcoming research, the number of exchanges had expanded to more than sixty annually.[18]

Yet these tools are sometimes utilized in a sharp way, with Chinese officials monitoring politicians or students who attend exchanges and then putting pressure on them, through Chinese embassies or consulates back in their home countries, to censor local media reporting on China and shut down local civil society events or exhibits that might be critical of China.[19]

This type of soft power is having an effect. A study by AidData found that these efforts to promote study in China, at least before the pandemic, had a significant effect—over a third of international students who studied in China said they learned about the scholarship from a public announcement, often at their schools, while roughly another third said they heard about it from personal contacts, which would include administrators at their schools.[20] Together, the men and women who have studied in China, and the Chinese who have studied abroad, have become a kind of Chinese brand ambassadors, as AidData has found, with positive views of China that they have brought home.[21] In a separate, recent study of foreign students coming to China for university on Chinese government scholarships, researchers Myungsik Ham and Elaine Tolentino found that these foreign students generally returned home with more positive views of China than when they had left.[22]

Students, Universities, and Sharp Power

Yet students, and particularly Chinese national students who study abroad, also have increasingly been used as tools of sharp power. China's government, through the UFWD and linked organizations and through embassies and consulates abroad, has increased monitoring of Chinese studying abroad and increasingly used student groups to establish CCP cells on campuses in the United States and many other countries and to intimidate critics of China on university campuses.[23]

An investigation by *Foreign Policy* found that Chinese student associations in the United States—like counterparts in places such as Australia—"regularly accept funds from their local [Chinese] consulates and many officially describe themselves as under the 'guidance' or 'leadership' of the embassy."[24] These organizations in the United States routinely use their influence to censor criticism of Beijing, control student events related to China, and put pressure on Chinese national students who openly express criticism of China's foreign policies or domestic policies.[25] In addition, as another study by the Center for Strategic and International Studies showed, some student groups and ethnic Chinese community organizations are utilized by the UFWD in Australia to help people with sympathetic views of China's foreign policies to "rise to local prominence" and wield influence within universities and local communities.[26] (Australian universities are highly dependent on income from foreign students, especially Chinese students, and have seemed reluctant to investigate and crack down on student groups that could be linked to the UFWD, though that is beginning to change as public opinion hardens against Beijing in Australia, and as universities recognize the dangers to academic freedom caused by some of these student groups.)

These student groups and community organizations—in the United States, Australia, Europe, and other regions—use their events to promote Beijing's narratives about its foreign and domestic policies and also use contacts within universities and Australian-Chinese communities to silence critical views of Beijing and even try to shut down critical events before they occur, in Australia, the United States, and many other places.[27] Indeed, Beijing has increasingly used Chinese student groups on foreign college campuses, including some affiliated with the UFWD and funded by the Chinese government, to control discussion about China on campus, censor students and professors critical of Beijing, and lead protests on campus against invited speakers with links to Tibet, Taiwan, or organizations critical of the Chinese government or even posters on campus that highlight China's rights abuses in places like Xinjiang and Hong Kong.[28] (Xi Jinping himself noted that such students should be a priority of UFWD work, during a speech in 2015, and the Chinese government has publicly stated that the main type of Chinese students associations overseas should be directly guided by Beijing and its embassies.[29]) A study by the Australian Strategic Policy Institute found that, in Australia and other countries, these students associations have surveilled Chinese nationals studying abroad, organized "rallies and promotional events in coordination with the Chinese government," and pressured Chinese national students studying abroad, and sometimes other students as well, not to discuss topics sensitive to Beijing.[30] Similarly, a study by the Washington-based Wilson Center of Chinese government influence at U.S. universities found that groups of Chinese national students, and some Chinese diplomats in the United States, had monitored other Chinese nationals studying in the United States, influenced them to censor comments about China, and tried to retaliate against them financially for being critical of Beijing.[31]

A wide range of reporting has found that Chinese diplomats stationed in the United States and students have retaliated against U.S. universities who invited speakers on topics sensitive to Beijing, pushed faculty to remove research and teaching materials on sensitive subjects, and harassed, intimidated, and abused Chinese national students who were critical of Beijing or spoke out about sensitive subjects.[32] This activity has had a chilling effect: Chinese students and non-Chinese nationals at many universities increasingly censoring themselves in speaking about topics related to China in classrooms; fewer and fewer universities inviting speakers who comment on sensitive topics like Taiwan, Tibet, or Xinjiang; and even leading academics becoming more cautious about any open criticism of the Chinese government, according to researcher Isaac Stone Fish in a study of

Chinese influence efforts' effects on U.S. universities—a finding consistent with much of the anecdotal evidence I have amassed.[33]

As Stone Fish noted, some of this effect is obvious, like when schools such as North Carolina State and Columbia University cancel visits by the Dalai Lama or talks about topics sensitive to Beijing under pressure from Chinese influence. But often it happens in less well-covered ways, with Chinese national students being harassed and bullied on social media to censor themselves, or with professors self-censoring for fear of pressure from Chinese diplomats, officials, and student groups.[34]

A lengthy Human Rights Watch study of China's effect on academic freedom abroad went even further, finding in detail that Chinese government pressure, via Confucius Institutes, Chinese diplomats, Chinese student groups, and other sources, was constraining academic freedom in many countries, including the United States, Australia, and other states.[35] Indeed, Human Rights Watch documented that Chinese officials threatened scholars outside China, warning them not to criticize the Chinese government in classrooms, and also prodded academics to self-censor due to fear for their Chinese national students and their families back home, if the academics or those students had expressed sentiments critical of Beijing.[36] They also showed that Chinese students abroad were probably monitoring other Chinese national students at their universities.[37] Particularly, students who are critical of Beijing are tracked and then might be reported to Chinese student associations with connections to Chinese diplomats and the UFWD, who might then apply pressure on the critical students and their families.

Human Rights Watch's investigators also found that several universities, in the job hiring process, questioned candidates about their views on Confucius Institutes, probably to ensure that the candidates would approve of the institutes, while at other U.S. universities, senior administrators discouraged professors from teaching about subjects that might anger Beijing and "cancelled appearances by speakers they believed the Chinese government would deem 'sensitive,' and in one of those cases, the dean explained to a faculty member that the school did not want to lose its growing number of students from China."[38]

Confucius Institutes

In some cases, Confucius Institutes, the Chinese language and culture centers seeded by Beijing on foreign college campuses, have contributed to silencing critical campus commentary about China, as has Beijing's willingness to offer visas to foreign researchers who avoid criticism of Chinese policies but withhold visas from scholars most critical of Beijing.[39] Indeed, a U.S. Government Accountability Office study of Confucius Institutes found that a broad range of school officials, researchers, and other staff from schools that hosted the institutes expressed concerns that they could be narrowing dialogue on campus about China and limiting academic freedom on topics considered sensitive by Beijing.[40]

More damningly, a Senate Homeland Security subcommittee report, which studied the effect of Confucius Institutes on schools and universities in the United States, found that the Confucius Institutes at some one hundred U.S. universities were threatening academic freedom by shutting down discussion at them and on campus more broadly about sensitive topics related to China and establishing a culture of self-censorship.[41] And Human Rights Watch's investigation found that many academics were uncomfortable with having Confucius Institutes on campus and believed that some Confucius Institutes were trying to silence criticism—like when Victoria University in Australia canceled an on-campus showing of a film critical of China and Confucius Institutes, in part because of pressure from Chinese diplomats, and probably also because Victoria feared losing its Confucius Institute.[42] Indeed, a follow-up 2021 study about Beijing's influence on education in Australia released by Human Rights Watch found that, among the roughly 160,000 Chinese national students enrolled in Australian universities, there was a persistent climate of

fear of criticizing Beijing, China's foreign policies, or Chinese domestic policy.[43] This fear, and an emerging culture of self-censorship
about Beijing, the report found, stemmed from Chinese government
monitoring of students in Australian universities, pressure from diplomats on students to report on their peers, and embassy and consulate
dominance of student groups on campus—but also from the effect of
partnerships like Confucius Institutes.[44]

A similar, thorough report on the effect of Confucius Institutes on
campuses in the United States, done by the National Association of
Scholars, found that directors of Confucius Institutes in the United
States were creating taboos on discussion of topics censored in China,
like the massacre at Tiananmen Square in 1989 and other topics.[45] It
also showed that institutes appeared to be providing their teachers with
stock answers to questions about sensitive topics on China (like saying
that Tiananmen has historic architecture when asked about events at
Tiananmen Square) and facilitated a climate of self-censorship among
professors on campuses, even among those working on China issues
but not directly linked to Confucius Institutes.[46]

Following these reports, the tide began to turn against Confucius
Institutes in many countries, and China's use of the institutes as a soft
power tool has become increasingly endangered, except perhaps in
parts of Asia where publics still have fairly warm views of Beijing. In
2020, a letter from the U.S. State Department to the boards of U.S.
institutions of higher education noted that the U.S. government had
designated Confucius Institutes' U.S. hub a mission of a foreign government, in part because the Confucius Institutes served as an "arm
of the Chinese state and are allowed to ignore academic freedom."[47]
This designation allows the U.S. government to require much greater
information about the workings of the headquarters, forcing the
Confucius Institute's U.S. headquarters, and probably U.S. campuses,
to report more regularly on the Confucius Institutes' activities in the
United States.[48]

With growing controversy swirling around the Confucius Institutes,
some universities in the United States and several other democracies

clearly started to feel that the Confucius Institute programs were not worth whatever they brought in funding and connections that could help these universities with programs in China.[49]

At least forty Confucius Institutes closed in the United States in 2018, 2019, and 2020 alone, and overall, at least one hundred of the U.S.-based Confucius Institutes had closed by early 2022.[50] More U.S. colleges and universities suggested that they will close their Confucius Institutes in the coming years. It is entirely plausible that by the middle of the 2020s, there will be no Confucius Institutes left in the United States, signaling a major soft power defeat for China, and also to some extent a blow to China's sharp power efforts, since there was some evidence that Confucius Institutes had been used in the United States to covertly undermine academic freedoms. The first U.S. university to open a Confucius Institute, the University of Maryland, shut down its Confucius Institute in 2020.[51] To be sure, some universities that are closing Confucius Institutes are still partnering with the Chinese government on other education programs, or possibly accepting money from Chinese state-linked organizations, but those that are doing so are under intense scrutiny from the U.S. Congress, activist groups, and researchers focused on Confucius Institutes and Chinese influence on U.S. campuses. Thus, it will be difficult for U.S. universities to replace Confucius Institutes with similarly large-scale programming that partners with Beijing or Chinese government-linked actors.[52]

In other parts of the world, pressure has built on Confucius Institutes to close as well. As the Australian government closely scrutinizes foreign funding of Chinese government propaganda efforts in Australia and Chinese government funding for a wide range of activities in Australia, all of the Confucius Institutes set up at Australian universities are likely to close.[53]

European countries are shutting down Confucius Institutes too, despite the risk that doing so might infuriate Beijing, a diplomatic power and major trading partner. Sweden, which opened the first Confucius Institute in Europe, already has closed all its Confucius Institutes.[54] Multiple major German universities are closing their

Confucius Institutes, as are Norwegian, French, and Canadian universities, among schools located in leading democracies.[55] With growing government and activist pressure on universities in the United Kingdom to terminate Confucius Institute agreements, most UK schools likely will follow suit, and pressure is mounting on the Japanese and South Korean governments to close Confucius Institutes as well. China is likely to be left with Confucius Institutes only in developing countries, many of them authoritarian, a situation likely to limit China's ability to wield global influence, and reflecting China's failures in both soft and sharp power.

Chapter 11

China's Mixed Effectiveness

In the two years before Taiwan's 2020 presidential election, Beijing seemed to be wielding an increasing amount of power over the island, particularly through media and information. Since Taiwan's domestic media is almost exclusively in Chinese, the island offers one of the best opportunities for Beijing to influence local media and utilize that influence to intervene in politics.

Beijing, in fact, appeared to be working to put its own man into Taiwan's presidency. Two years earlier, in 2018, Chinese-controlled media outlets had played a significant role in helping Han Kuo-yu, a relatively obscure politician from the Kuomintang (KMT) party, win the mayor's race in Kaohsiung, a major southern city.[1] Han appeared to support closer links with China, a typical KMT position. He traveled to the mainland to meet with top Chinese officials, and accepted that China and Taiwan were essentially part of the same country, a formulation that the rival Democratic Progressive Party (DPP), which held the presidency, rejects.[2] Han also had sustained a middling career in the KMT. He had served as an undistinguished member of parliament between 1993 and 2002, worked at an agricultural corporation, and then lost a race for the KMT leadership in 2017. His political career appeared over.

Given that his career was treading water at best, and that the DPP had controlled Kaohsiung for twenty years, Han hardly seemed like a solid bet to win the 2018 mayor's race. But he triumphed, backed by Taiwanese media favorable to Beijing. (To be fair, Han's blunt, off-the-cuff speaking style, similar in some ways to the style of populists like the Philippines' Rodrigo Duterte, won him media coverage in the 2018 mayoral race and boosted his campaign.[3]) He also appeared to benefit from an enormous campaign, orchestrated from China, on social media, to back his candidacy.[4] Han also somehow managed to raise the most money of any mayoral candidate, even though he got little support from his own KMT party coffers.[5] A *South China Morning Post* article on Han's rise noted that "he received neither money nor resources [from his party]—Han was seen as little more than electoral cannon fodder in the [mayoral] race for a seat his party had no expectation of winning."[6] In 2019, an alleged Chinese spy who defected to Australia claimed that he had helped funnel some $3 million in funds to Han's mayoral campaign from mainland Chinese sources.[7] Han denied that he had received such funds.

China's efforts to tilt the playing field for Han continued the next year, as the revived politician ran for president against the DPP incumbent Tsai Ing-wen. Beijing openly loathed Tsai and generally hated the DPP. After all, Tsai lacerated China's approach to Hong Kong and pushed to preserve Taiwan's freedoms by building closer ties to other countries in the region.[8]

Bolstered by the seemingly out-of-nowhere Kaohsiung win, Han took the KMT nomination for president. With the race for the presidency heating up, Taiwan's National Security Bureau divulged in 2019 that several Taiwanese media outlets were collaborating with Beijing. Taiwanese media outlets, including the powerful Want Want China Holdings (remember—the owner of *China Times* and other outlets), which backed Han, were receiving instructions directly from the Chinese government's Taiwan Affairs Office, according to the *Financial Times*.[9] Want Want was something between a borrowed boat and a bought boat—it was not directly owned by a Chinese firm, but its owner was clearly pro-Beijing and might have received funds from Beijing. Allegedly, Want Want China Holdings reporters said that they got calls every day from the Chinese government's Taiwan Affairs

Office, which told them how to shape their articles about the presidential race.[10] (The company denies this occurred.)

Other Taiwanese websites appeared to just publish Chinese propaganda directly about Han and Tsai, which China mixed into an election cocktail with other disinformation tactics.[11] In the months before the January 2020 election, sketchy YouTube videos that appeared to come from China spread false information about the election, while fake Facebook posts circulated rumors and falsehoods.[12] Some disinformation efforts seemed designed to produce voter apathy; some appeared specifically designed to promote Han.

Yet Han's campaign ultimately failed—miserably. Chinese officials did not seem to understand that, as they increased sharp power efforts in Taiwan, these efforts could be exposed and ultimately rebound against Beijing as the Taiwanese public learned about Chinese meddling. That is indeed what happened. As local and foreign media outlets exposed the scale of China's influence over the Taiwanese media, popular anger crested, right in time for the presidential election. (China's own state media even foolhardily reported on Beijing's efforts to wield information and traditional influence in Taiwan and other places.[13]) During the campaign, thousands of Taiwanese voters took to the streets to protest against what they called the "red media," local outlets apparently taking orders from Beijing.[14] These protests further helped spark growing resiliency in Taiwan against Chinese disinformation, with citizens becoming much more aware of Beijing's efforts and the Taiwanese government taking a wide range of measures to educate their citizens about digital literacy.

Often, it was tiny, start-up Taiwanese media companies that exposed China's efforts to dominate the local media and other sectors. This has become a theme: China faces persistent threats from scrappy, new media outlets in Taiwan and other countries. In Taiwan, for instance, new outlets have emerged in recent years to fill the void in quality reporting left by existing publications abandoning critical coverage of China. These new media companies, like Taiwan's NewTalk, are often nonprofits and lack owners who can be influenced by Beijing.[15]

As Taiwanese and foreign outlets shed light on China meddling in the Taiwanese media and in other areas of Taiwan, popular anger bubbled up, and Tsai slammed China's interference.[16] She repeatedly highlighted Chinese meddling in Hong Kong and Taiwan in the days before the presidential vote, telling attendees at her final rally, "Young people in Hong Kong have used their lives and blood and tears to show us that 'one country, two systems' is not feasible."[17]

This message resonated with the Taiwanese public. In January 2020, Tsai won a landslide re-election, taking 57 percent, and winning more raw votes than any candidate since Taiwan introduced direct presidential elections in 1996.[18] Her party maintained its majority in Taiwan's legislature as well. Observers of the election noted that China's influence efforts, combined with the crackdown in Hong Kong at the time, backfired and drove voter turnout to historic highs, leading to a Tsai landslide.[19] By the end of 2020, Han had even been driven from his mayoralty; he was removed as Kaohsiung mayor by a recall election, with even city residents angry at him.[20] Beijing did not initially reflect on Tsai's re-election, at least in public. But at least some Chinese officials may recognize that wielding sharp power on the island can backfire, or at least fail to move the situation in Beijing's favor, even as Beijing continues to step up military pressure on Taiwan.

As Tsai's re-election ultimately showed, and as we have already seen in some of our previous chapters, Beijing's efforts to use influence over media and information for political gains has not always proven a stirring success. Yes, China has its fingers in many Taiwanese media outlets and can unleash disinformation on the island. It can elevate a relatively obscure figure like Han. But China's attempts to use its state media, and its sharp control of media outlets, for tangible gains have run into major roadblocks—in Taiwan and in other places as well.

Overall, indeed China's media and information campaign has enjoyed only mixed success—for now, in Taiwan and elsewhere; in Taiwan it has largely failed, with the island developing significant resiliency to Chinese information and disinformation, and actually serving as an example for other places.

As this book went to press, China took further, aggressive military steps which further alienated the Taiwan people and forever severed any possibility that Taiwan would reunite peacefully with the mainland, or that any Taiwanese parties, like the KMT, which were even modestly pro-China, would not survive while remaining supportive of Beijing. (The book will almost surely be written, with edits closed, while this China-Taiwan crisis is still going on, but it is important to include just a taste of how China's military approach to Taiwan added to all the other factors that have soured the globe on Beijing and made its diplomacy, media, information, and old-fashioned influence tactics harder to accomplish.)

Following a visit to Taiwan by U.S. Speaker of the House Nancy Pelosi, the highest ranking congressional official to visit Taiwan in twenty-five years, China responded harshly.[21] It launched missiles in areas around Taiwan, including areas claimed by Japan—which surely further soured Japanese public opinion about China and stiffened Japan's resolve to defend Taiwan—and held military exercises very close to Taiwan.[22] China also used its exercises in an attempt to show it could close the Taiwan Strait, and banned Taiwanese exports of some agricultural products and other items, which made up little of Taiwan's economy.

In fact, the bans only made the Taiwanese government work harder to speed up their plan to find alternative markets to China for Taiwanese products, and to encourage other countries in the region to do so as well, knowing that if China took more severe military action in Taiwan it would threaten their exports to China too.[23] (China could not really crack down hard on the most valuable Taiwanese exports, semiconductors, since China needs them badly and is unable to produce semiconductors of similar quality.[24]) China, meanwhile, has completely destroyed any hope it had of ever convincing the Taiwanese, via soft power, that they should want to reunite with China. Even back in 2015, 90 percent of younger Taiwanese saw themselves as Taiwanese, not Chinese.[25] Now, with the increasing economic and military coercion applied by Beijing, it is likely nearly the entire Taiwanese population feels that way, and has no desire to ever becoming part of the People's Republic.

In many cases, indeed, China's efforts have failed outright. Indeed, Xi Jinping's bold goal to wield media and information power globally, a priority noted in the Chinese Communist Party's (CCP's) Five-Year Plan (which specifically calls on China to build flagship media outlets abroad and wield more international communications power), has not worked to great effect.[26]

China's soft power, for instance, has not prevented publics in many countries from souring on Beijing's increasingly assertive "wolf warrior" global diplomacy and use of economic coercion, being angry at how China hid the initial origins of the COVID-19 pandemic and now is imposing self-isolation and zero-COVID policies that are harming the world economy, becoming shocked at China's crushing of freedom in Hong Kong, fuming at how China sometimes seemed to be taking advantage of other countries' COVID-19–related weaknesses to push Beijing's regional and global ambitions, or becoming angry and scared by how China is menacing Taiwan—the type of menacing it could easily apply to other countries in its region with which it has disputes, like the Philippines, Japan, Vietnam, and others.

In fact, in public opinion studies released in recent years, such as those conducted by Pew, opinions of China have turned sharply negative in countries from Australia to Germany to South Korea to Sweden to many other states.[27] Australia, Japan, and South Korea, among other states, slammed China's aggressive military maneuvers around Taiwan after Pelosi's visit.[28]

And while some Southeast Asian states, in the immediate aftermath of China's actions toward Taiwan, seemed unsure how to respond and did not want to openly come out and say they would cut economic ties with Beijing if it invaded Taiwan—China is their biggest market—there was intense fear in Vietnam, Indonesia, the Philippines, and other Southeast Asian states with disputes with China. New Philippine president Ferdinand Marcos Jr, who had come into office with warm views of China, seemed to signal in a meeting with U.S.

Secretary of State Anthony Blinken that he would be moving closer to Washington, a treaty ally; Marcos seemed thrown off by Beijing's actions toward Taiwan.[29] Indonesia, meanwhile, held massive joint military exercises with the United States (and other regional powers like Japan, Australia, and Singapore for the first time) while China was menacing Taiwan, a set of exercises that, while planned in advance, also sent a signal to Beijing.[30]

In Pew's research, negative views of China reached historic highs in many of these states—the most negative views since Pew started asking foreign publics about China over ten years ago.[31] The following year, Pew Research's study of views of China showed similarly negative views of Beijing across most of the countries studied.[32] China's rhetorical support for Russia, promoting of Russian views via disinformation and official statements, and overall support for Moscow, as well as its menacing of Taiwan, which worries not only China's neighbors but resonates with small states in many parts of the world—even if Beijing chooses not to directly backfill Russian arms or to offer Moscow a major economic lifeline—are only going to worsen views of China in democracies in Europe and probably many other parts of the world. In the 2021 Pew study, even countries like the United Kingdom and Spain that had had positive views of Beijing only a few years prior now had sharply unfavorable views of China.

Similarly, the 2021 survey of Southeast Asia, conducted by the Singapore-based think tank Institute of Southeast Asian Studies (ISEAS)–Yusof Ishak Institute, found that people surveyed in most Southeast Asian states were developing increasing concerns about China and its regional influence—even though most Southeast Asians agreed that China had been the most helpful major power in dealing with COVID-19.[33] The 2022 survey showed similar results—high levels of concern throughout Southeast Asia about China's regional influence.[34] Although most Southeast Asian states had not developed more confidence in the United States during the Donald Trump administration, in the 2021 ISEAS–Yusof Ishak Institute study of the regions, the percentage of Southeast Asians who would choose the

United States over China, if forced to side with one of the two major regional powers, rose by nearly 10 percent.[35]

Nearly half the respondents in the ISEAS–Yusof Ishak study agreed with the statement that "China is a revisionist power and intends to draw Southeast Asia into its sphere of influence," and very few, even in countries where Beijing has expended considerable soft power, agreed either that "China is a benign and benevolent power" or that "China is a status quo power and will continue to support the existing regional order."[36] Similar results appeared in the 2022 study. What's more, it is almost certain that, after China's aggressive maneuvers around Taiwan, there will be an even lower number of respondents who believe China is a benign and benevolent power. Meanwhile, it is further almost certain that many countries in Southeast Asia, already a center of the global arms trade, will be furiously upgrading their militaries, with Taiwan doing so as well.

Beijing also is still far from achieving comprehensive content suppression in most parts of the world, in making critical discussions of Beijing disappear from local media in many countries, and in shaping daily conversations about China's domestic and foreign policies among opinion leaders and publics. It is not easy to judge when conversations are no longer happening or to understand what topics no longer get discussed; overall it can be difficult to see the direct effects of Beijing's media and information efforts. There is no real poll that can measure what people are not saying, and it is far simpler to report what people are discussing.

Still, what we have seen already and what we see here is that for now, Beijing has had a decidedly mixed record, at best, in its media and information battle. Its borrowed and bought boats—local outlets that run Chinese state media content, have signed deals to share stories, or have simply been sold to Chinese firms and pro-Beijing owners—have burrowed into local media environments and dominated them in some countries. But these borrowed and bought boats also are sparking a backlash against Beijing's tactics, though bought boats remain more effective in shaping narratives about Beijing and reducing critical local coverage of China.

Meanwhile, China's biggest state media outlets, other than Xinhua, which is becoming a significant weapon, have not gained noticeable increases in audience share in most countries; their audiences are still miniscule in most places, even in parts of Southeast Asia like the Philippines and Thailand. Meanwhile, a growing backlash against Russian state media in much of Europe, North America, and other parts of the world could have follow-on effects of how people view Chinese state media. China's training programs for journalists, while expanding rapidly into both developing and developed states, have not necessarily created a dramatic shift in how foreign reporters view or write about China. China's self-isolation from the world in recent years, the result of its zero-COVID policy, has curtailed these trips and led many longtime foreign reporters who'd been based in Beijing to leave, a move that only led to them shifting operations for covering China to places like Taiwan, which cannot be what China wanted— reporters based in Taipei covering China, and those reporters now seeing firsthand, from Taipei, China's menacing of the island. And until recently, Beijing's approach to disinformation has often been clumsy, and it has been clumsy around its Taiwan actions—often resorting to propaganda and angry diplomatic rants that seem stale. However, China is rapidly gaining sophistication and becoming much more dangerous, particularly as its cooperation with Russia grows so rapidly because of the Ukraine war and the increasing ties between top officials from both states.

Finally, China's growing control of information pipes—buying the boats, controlling the ways information travels, dominating the governance institutions related to information—has proven highly effective in helping Beijing control how people access news around the world. Indeed, through control of information pipes and export of China's ideas of how to monitor and censor information and surveil citizens, Beijing can offer other countries a whole model of how to control a population, and its authoritarian model is being adopted in Southeast Asian states like Cambodia, Myanmar, Thailand, and Vietnam; African states like Ethiopia and Rwanda and others; and Middle Eastern countries like Egypt, among others. Most notably, China's intensive control methods, particularly its use of internet content suppression and filtering, have been rapidly adopted by Russia in 2021 and, even more quickly, by Russia in 2022.

The Backlash Against Borrowed Boats

Taiwan is not unique in how Beijing has used its influence over local media outlets to gain control of some of the local Chinese-language media and other tools like portions of the business community—and then tried to use that power to support favored opinion leaders and tear down opponents of China. To be sure, as AidData has suggested, borrowed boats like content-sharing deals could theoretically be a boon for China, since they allow Chinese media companies to essentially borrow the credibility of local media outlets.[37] Yet Taiwan also is not unique in showing that the more heavy-handed the methods Beijing uses are—and they really do not get more heavy-handed than China's approach to Taiwan in the summer and fall of 2022—the more it risks a local backlash and a government commitment to fight back—and that it is often easier for governments to uncover information about China's content-sharing deals and other borrowed boats than it is to learn about instances in which clearly pro-China owners have actually taken ownership of media outlets.

Beyond Australia and Taiwan, which I already discussed, a backlash is brewing against China's use of borrowed boats to control parts of local media, and Taiwan's example of uncovering borrowed boats is being studied by countries in Europe, parts of Southeast Asia, and many other parts of the world. Southeast Asian states, like Singapore, have begun to consider tougher measures to scrutinize China's information activities. Singaporean officials, for instance, have expressed concerns to many local publishers about the growing use of Xinhua and other Chinese state media in the Chinese-language press in Singapore—essentially borrowed boats. At the same time, Singapore has stepped up scrutiny of China's traditional influence activities on the island and toward the island—most recently in 2020, when a Singaporean national was arrested in the United States on charges of spying for China and admitted to the charges.[38] He had previously been a student at a leading Singaporean university, where he was recruited by China to spy.[39]

China's attempts to influence media, information, and other tools have fostered backlashes outside its near neighborhood as well. In the United States, Beijing's de facto control of most Chinese-language media, in part through borrowed boats, can only give Beijing so much influence, since the Chinese-language press remains a tiny slice of the overall U.S. media market. And, it would have little impact since public opinion has turned so intensely negative among the U.S. population toward China that even if the Chinese language market was bigger, it would have a modest effect on the overall United States, with U.S. public opinion so sour on Beijing. Even so, Congress and the executive branch have begun scrutinizing China's content-sharing deals and other types of borrowed boats, building firewalls against the potential effects of China's state media inside the United States, and taking a broad range of other actions against both Chinese soft and sharp power in the country.

Close U.S. allies like Canada and the United Kingdom have followed suit, with the United Kingdom revoking the license for the China Global Television Network (CGTN) to operate in Britain.[40] Following a lengthy investigation into CGTN and its operations in the United Kingdom, in 2021 the UK government said that television stations in Britain must have editorial oversight over their programming to receive a license and they also must not be controlled by political organizations—CGTN's license holder in the United Kingdom did not have editorial oversight, and the channel had a close affiliation with the CCP, though CGTN still was able to broadcast in

Britain, just barely, through obscure entry points into TV and mobile devices in the United Kingdom.[41]

The crackdown in the United States has vastly increased in scope in the years since 2019. The FBI created a task force to investigate Chinese influence in U.S. domestic politics and has ramped up its investigations into Chinese espionage, and the Pentagon has outlined an approach that would require a whole-of-government response to Beijing's growing global influence.[42] However, at times these investigations seemed to have veered into fishing expeditions focusing on Chinese researchers, leading to the Biden administration's closure of Justice's China Initiative. Yet, Justice and the FBI continue to make Chinese espionage and influence activities one of their highest priorities.

Prominent U.S. congresspeople and senators have echoed this growing scrutiny, and as we saw in the prior chapter, Congress has launched intensive oversight of Confucius Institutes, China's other types of funding for education in the United States, and other aspects of Chinese influence on university campuses. Indeed, the Confucius Institute project has come under intense scrutiny not only in the United States but also in Australia, Europe, Japan, and many other democracies, and is largely failing to extend China's influence in leading democracies as Confucius Institutes shut down.

The U.S. government also has forced Chinese state media outlets to begin registering as foreign agents of influence. The U.S. State Department declared that nine Chinese state media organizations would now be considered foreign missions in the United States.[43] This designation subjects outlets like Xinhua and CGTN to even greater scrutiny from the U.S. government, beyond the (modest) scrutiny of filing Foreign Agent Registration Act forms with the Justice Department. It essentially declares that they are no longer considered journalism organizations, but rather appendages of the Chinese state. They are forced to provide the U.S. government the names and personal information of people working for these outlets in the United States.[44] And in the summer of 2020, the

Trump administration issued executive orders targeting two massive Chinese social media players, WeChat and TikTok. One executive order, issued for claimed reasons of national security against companies owned by Chinese giant Tencent, essentially banned WeChat from being updated via an app store in the United States.[45] The order related to TikTok, combined with administration pressure on TikTok's parent company, eventually led to the Trump administration ordering ByteDance to divest TikTok on national security grounds, possibly by selling TikTok's U.S. assets to American companies.[46] However, those executive orders were stalled by court challenges, and the Biden administration revoked the executive orders related to TikTok and WeChat, though as of the writing of this book the Biden administration was considering tough action limiting TikTok.[47]

These actions were part of a broadly tough approach by the Trump White House, amidst deteriorating bilateral tensions, and a tough approach that clearly continued into the Biden administration, which started off matching many of the Trump administration's tough China rhetoric and actions. Congress, both Republicans and Democrats, has strongly supported this tough approach as well. The Trump White House closed the Chinese consulate in Houston, alleging that it had been a center for espionage; in retaliation, Beijing closed the U.S. consulate in Chengdu.[48] As China harshly repressed rights, detained protestors, and stifled media freedoms in Hong Kong, the U.S. government imposed sanctions on eleven top officials in Hong Kong and mainland China, including the chief executive of Hong Kong.[49] The Biden administration further sanctioned Chinese surveillance and biotechnology firms that it says are involved in massive abuses in Xinjiang.[50] Meanwhile, the U.S. Congress later passed a massive spending bill designed to boost production of semiconductors in the United States and bolster supply chain security, reducing potential U.S. reliance on China.[51]

Beijing wasted no time in hitting back, imposing sanctions on multiple U.S. officials and foreign policy specialists, including the heads of

U.S.-based democracy promotion organizations and several senators and congresspeople known for hawkish views on China.[52]

Then, as China stood by Russia during the Ukraine war (and also reportedly did nothing to try to stop Putin from going to war, months before the Ukraine invasion, after being warned of the possibility by U.S. officials), the Biden administration offered even starker warnings. The president himself warned Beijing that, at this epochal moment transforming the global geopolitical landscape, it should back away from Russia. Biden reportedly personally spoke with Xi and told him that the U.S.-China relationship, and Beijing itself, would face severe consequences if China firmly backed Russia against the allied response to Moscow, such as by having Chinese financial firms continue to work with Moscow despite sanctions; if major Chinese corporations defied sanctions; or if China provided significant economic or military backing for Russia.[53] (Many big Chinese banks and corporations likely will follow the sanctions, since Russia is a small market for them.) During the Taiwan crisis, Biden further held long calls with Xi and publicly made clear that the United States would come to Taiwan's defenses if Taiwan were attacked, even though China has made major gains, from a decade ago, in a potential battle over Taiwan.[54]

Even beyond close U.S. allies like the United Kingdom, other democracies also have begun to respond with concern and tougher actions toward China's sharp power, as they have seen how Beijing has tried to utilize borrowed boats, and other tools, to shape news coverage and sometimes boost specific politicians and undermine other political leaders. To take just a few examples, as we discussed, India banned TikTok, WeChat, and, in total, nearly sixty Chinese apps; European Commission head Ursula von der Leyen used a virtual European Union–China summit to denounce China's repression in Hong Kong and its influence activities; and German politicians pushed both thenchancellor Angela Merkel and current chancellor Olaf Scholz, known for relatively accommodating views toward China, to take a much harsher approach toward China's control of information.[55]

Indeed, beyond the United States, leading democracies like Germany, France, Australia, Canada, and the entire European Union, which once were reluctant to take as tough measures toward Beijing, are also hardening their bilateral relations.

In Europe, where many governments were slower to understand China's information and influence activities than the United States or Britain, countries also are taking much tougher actions against China's efforts—a process turbocharged as European states suddenly have woken up to the threats of autocratic states making major investments in local media markets or spreading state media in local media markets. European states are assessing ways to better monitor or prevent Chinese state investment into media and information sectors, as European capitals increasingly understand the strategic value of these sectors.[56] (Ten European Union members still have not created effective mechanisms to screen foreign investments however, which has brought them intense criticism from other EU members.[57]) China's increasingly aggressive diplomacy, menacing of Taiwan, cover-up of the early period of the novel coronavirus, and the possibility that the cover-up might have involved covering up a leak from a Chinese lab further embittered EU states. As public opinion toward China has soured across Western, Central, and Eastern Europe, some of which are small states that not only resent China's support for Russia but also sympathize with Taiwan, leaders throughout the region have more openly criticized Chinese diplomacy and called for greater safeguards not only on Chinese investment in certain sectors but also on a range of Chinese influence activities.

In undemocratic states rife with corruption, it is easier for China to gain control of media landscapes, and other valuable levers in society, just by cultivating a small circle of top leaders. But even in some democracies with relatively weak safeguards on influence and corruption, policymakers have begun to respond more assertively to China's media and information tools as they have been exposed and proven unpopular with general publics. In the Czech Republic, we have seen how China attempted to wield influence among top political leaders. But despite Beijing wielding significant influence over many Czech leaders and trying to wield power over the Czech media, a backlash built, and Czech civil society and Czech leaders have become so embittered that they have scrutinized and taken steps to uncover and end Chinese information and influence operations. The Czech media served as "a skeptical antidote to the promotion of closer Czech-Chinese relations" even as pro-China attitudes expanded among leading politicians, according to a study by researchers at AMO, a Prague-based research institution, in collaboration with the U.S.-based National Endowment for Democracy as well as the Central and Eastern European Center for Asian Studies and the Institute of Asian Studies.[58] In fact, they found, even as Beijing was cultivating Czech politicians and using its influence in the local press to further China's interests, the Czech media took "a largely concerned and often openly critical perspective of China."[59]

As in places like Taiwan and Hong Kong, newer Czech media outlets, some of which were less partisan, less constrained by top executives willing to bend to China, and less dependent on advertising, often proved highly critical of Chinese influence activities. Overall, AMO's research showed, only 14 percent of Czech media outlets portrayed China positively.[60] This figure came out before the Ukraine war, and in all likelihood China's portrayal in the Czech media is now even worse.

This tough media scrutiny created linkages, in many Czechs' minds, between China's influence and Czech corruption, and China's image in the country began to plummet by 2019. (It did not help Beijing's case that it failed to deliver on promises of massive new investment in the country.[61]) A Czech party called the Czech Pirate Party, which had lambasted China's influence efforts, scored well in European parliamentary elections in 2019.[62]

Broader Soft Power Failures

The failures of these big state outlets, which are largely vehicles of soft power; the overall turn in public opinion against China in many democracies; the hardening approach toward China in Europe and Northeast Asia and even parts of Southeast Asia; the closures of Confucius Institutes—all of these failures are reflected in how poorly China fares in studies of soft power in Asia and around the world, such as Pew polling of various countries' views of China. It does not help, either, that China's private sector cultural exports, such as movies, art, music, literature, video games, and other culture products, which also can bolster soft power, are hampered by China's crackdown on rights and freedoms.

Beijing still has significant private sector soft power cultural exports, or at least the potential to wield private sector soft power cultural exports. Although the most recent Portland consultancy Soft Power Index ranks China twenty-seventh out of thirty countries studied, it ranks China eighth in the subindex related to culture, noting that China boasts the world's most UN Educational, Scientific and Cultural Organization (UNESCO) World Heritage Sites, continues to attract a significant amount of tourism, performs exceptionally well in the Summer Olympic Games, and attracts sizable numbers of foreign students—or at least, it will probably continue to attract tourists and students once China opens its borders again.[63] But in some realms, the tightening constraints on speech and art inside China have undermined Chinese private sector cultural exports.

To take one example, the appeal of Chinese TV show exports globally. South Korea, a far smaller country, regularly outpaces the value of China's TV show exports. Indeed, the country has become a global cultural juggernaut. It has exported an increasingly successful Korean film and scripted shows industry, which includes *Parasite*, winner of Best Picture at the 2020 Academy Awards; the Netflix hit *Squid Game* and many other Korean shows that have become huge hits on Netflix; and K-pop megastars like BTS.

Although China ranked second in the Lowy Institute's most recent Asia Power Index—the United States ranked first—Beijing's high numbers come mostly from its ranking as first in economic capability, military capability, and future resources.[64] The Asia Power

Index's measures of China's influence over Asia's information land-scape, including its influence stemming from Chinese state media, show far less impressive results. The Lowy Institute study uses influ-ence maps, based upon internet search trends, to assess Asians' interest in regional media outlets, according to a summary of the study by Bonnie Bley, one of its primary researchers.[65] The influence maps show that CGTN is only the tenth most popular broadcaster in the Asia-Pacific region, and CGTN's regional appeal remains a fraction of that of CNN. As Bley notes, the maps show that CGTN's "reach is inconsequential when compared to the United States' CNN, which exceeds China's CGTN by a staggering 78 points."[66] Other Chinese outlets except Xinhua also fare badly on these influence maps, and are likely to fall further as a result of regional distrust of China following the China-Taiwan crisis.

China Handles Media Failures Poorly

At times when China's efforts to use media and other influence strat-egies for tangible gains fail or when influence activities like Confucius Institutes falter, Beijing often resorts to bluster and heavy-handed pressure.

As we have seen, just as Xi has increased the CCP's control over all aspects of policymaking within China, he also has placed the CCP, and specifically top CCP officials, in even more control of foreign influence activities, including media and information tac-tics. Centralizing power helps Xi build his cult of personality, but it also inhibits diplomats' and intelligence operatives' ability to op-erate in the other countries and to do the kind of work that could help China gain an extensive understanding of other societies—and to respond skillfully when its media and information activities are exposed. Though China is opening new embassies and consulates at breakneck speed, fear of Beijing pervades these outposts. And fear makes diplomats and other officials dumb—they wall themselves off from most local opinion leaders, they avoid local reporters other than in formal settings, and they forego efforts at real conversation with locals. By contrast, Russian intelligence and diplomats seem to have gained a granular understanding of societies, from North America to Africa.[67] Such knowledge has proven an asset for Russian state media outlets and for Russian disinformation strategies, as even during the Ukraine war Russian state media outlets and other Russian disseminators of disinformation have managed to get their messages into major social media platforms through a range of intermediaries, despite these platforms' bans on Russian state media outlets.

China responds bluntly when its media, information, or other influence efforts are exposed—a response that then undermines Beijing's desire to look like a responsible, stable partner for other states and often only feeds a local backlash against China. To be sure, China has become so economically powerful in some states that when its influence operations are exposed, it can simply use its economic might to batter foreign leaders into saying little about Beijing's actions.

But even with greater economic power, China does not always get its way. It has, in fact, routinely failed to utilize its economic power to cow not only Taiwan, which was mostly unaffected by China's bans on various exports, but also larger European countries like France. It has even failed to intimidate smaller European states like Lithuania, to which it applied massive economic coercion, and the Czech Republic, and coercion will become even tougher as these small states see how Beijing treats Taiwan. Faced with tough scrutiny in the Czech Republic, Beijing canceled a Prague Philharmonic Orchestra tour to China and started openly threatening Prague city leaders.[68] But outright bullying only further alienated Czechs, as one might imagine. The Prague Philharmonic Orchestra musicians declared they would rather abandon the (lucrative) Chinese tour than submit to political pressure calling on the musicians to reject the actions of the mayor of Prague.[69] Ordinary Czechs and some top officials publicly protested Chinese influence.

Indeed, a study by the Pew Research Center found that Czechs now had a more negative view of China than people in any other country polled in Europe other than Sweden—where a backlash against Beijing also was in full force.[70] In Sweden, the government summoned the Chinese ambassador to Stockholm for a dressing down after he tried to publicly intimidate Swedish media outlets and other Chinese influence efforts were revealed, and the ambassador also blasted the Swedish government for giving a human rights award to Gui Minhai, a Swedish publisher detained in China.[71] Sounding more like Michael Corleone at Lake Tahoe than a credentialed and veteran diplomat, the ambassador, Gui Congyou, had announced on Swedish public radio, "We [China] treat our friends with fine wine, but for our enemies we have shotguns."[72] Yet such aggressive diplomacy only further turned Swedish public opinion against China.

What Works? On Disinformation, China Is Learning Fast, Though Still a Laggard

But China's offensive is not failing everywhere—and China is learning from its mistakes and will become far more effective over the next decade. From a clumsy start, disinformation has begun to be a powerful weapon for China. Beijing clearly has stepped up its use of disinformation in Taiwan, Hong Kong, parts of Southeast Asia—and now globally.

Beijing has not enjoyed disinformation triumphs comparable to Russia's. In the 2020 Taiwanese presidential elections, China's combination of media influence and disinformation did not help Han. Instead, clumsy Chinese disinformation was widely noticed by average Taiwanese and sparked popular protests.[73] The Taiwanese government imposed tougher new laws designed to curb disinformation and built a partnership with Facebook to crack down on false posts.[74] These measures have helped protect Taiwan from disinformation in the most recent crisis with China.

Similarly, in Hong Kong in 2019, 2020, and 2021, China engaged in a major disinformation campaign targeting protestors and the general public, with apparently fake accounts linked to China spreading disinformation about Hong Kong protests on Facebook, Twitter, YouTube, and other platforms.[75] The accounts tried to portray all protestors as violent radicals with no clear aims other than seeking independence from the mainland.[76] Yet in reality most protestors were nonviolent and did not advocate independence.

But China's attempts at disinformation in Hong Kong, a place where netizens have extensive knowledge of China and Chinese tactics, remained unsophisticated. In part, this may be because, at home, Beijing is used to having control of Chinese social media platforms, which makes it far easier for the government or individuals to launch campaigns.[77] China's initial forays into disinformation and influence campaigns abroad resembled copies of domestic campaigns to shape public opinion, which take place in a censored internet environment where there is only one narrative: the CCP's. But abroad, these campaigns run into competing narratives online that Beijing has not yet learned to effectively navigate—spamming posts on social media is not as effective in shaping or influencing opinion when there are other narratives out there on Facebook, Twitter, and other platforms, at least not before Beijing cracked down so hard in Hong Kong that alternative narratives virtually vanished.[78]

An Australian Strategic Policy Institute (ASPI) analysis of Beijing's disinformation strategies offered scathing conclusions of Beijing's tradecraft and of how China's efforts failed in Hong Kong, probably leading Beijing to impose harsh and essentially direct rule in the city. Sure, China blanketed social media platforms with disinformation about the protests, but Beijing's efforts lacked coherence and skill. "This was a blunt-force influence operation, using spam accounts to disseminate messaging, leveraging an influence for hire network," the ASPI report noted.[79] The messaging was not coordinated, the report concluded, and appeared to have little understanding of how to target communities in Hong Kong and elsewhere—how to win allies and divide enemies online, as Russian social media warriors do.[80] Some of the accounts used to spread disinformation in Hong Kong appeared to have been purchased on the black market from Facebook and Twitter users, which made them more likely to seem fake to people who saw them on these social media platforms.

By comparison, Russian disinformation specialists often create their own fake accounts on Twitter and other platforms from scratch, which allows them to build the accounts into real-seeming profiles. This process makes these accounts seem realer to other people on the social media platforms. The Hong Kong "operation [was] in stark contrast to the efforts of Russia's Internet Research Agency (IRA) to target U.S. political discourse, particularly through 2015–2017," the ASPI report noted.[81] "The Russian effort displayed well-planned coordination"; was picked up widely in the U.S. media; understood the local audience, including U.S. colloquial language; and was highly effective at sparking divisions within segments of the U.S. population. In part, it found, the Russians were successful because they created their accounts from scratch, learning about U.S. society and politics and formulating fake profiles that seemed highly real and believable—and had real effects, reaching large target audiences.[82] Russia also has been successful, at least before the Ukraine war soured its image, because its disinformation efforts have focused on highlighting negative developments and critical opinions of the West and generally fomenting chaos while mostly avoiding talking about Russia, a strategy Beijing avoided until recently.[83]

Another study comparing Russian and Chinese disinformation efforts, by the Hoover Institution, came to similar conclusions. It found that "Russia's covert information operations on social media often involve sophisticated personas, developed over a period of years. They do ethnographic research (IRA operatives toured the United States) and ingratiate themselves into the communities, like Black Lives Matter communities, they are pretending to be members of. . . . They put in effort to build relationships with influencers, to ensure that authentic influential voices amplify their [Russian] content such as by mentioning and replying to high-profile accounts in hopes of getting retweeted"[84] But they conclude: "None of this is true of China's attempts [at disinformation]. . . . Its accounts acquire few, if any, real followers, have minimal amplification from authentic influencers. . . . Chinese operators do not appear to have done the psychological or ethnographic research required to create convincing accounts on Western platforms."[85]

Because China's disinformation was clumsy in Hong Kong, it quickly caught the attention of security at many social media platforms and search engines. Facebook, Google, and Twitter removed many pages and accounts that seemed to be Beijing-backed disinformation efforts related to Hong Kong protests.[86]

Beijing recently has begun to shift its strategy, particularly during the COVID-19 pandemic and now during the Ukraine war, as it has started to copy Russia's offensive techniques, developed more skill in spreading chaotic disinformation, and proved more willing to directly attack other countries' politics and leaders. Given China's ability to adapt, it is reasonable to assume that Beijing's disinformation will become more skillful and more effective—though it has not been so in the current Taiwan crisis.

At first, like its failures to use disinformation during the Taiwanese presidential campaign, China's clumsy COVID-19–related disinformation initially was quickly exposed and only angered other countries. China's efforts still remained clumsier than Russia's—Twitter suspended many Chinese accounts in 2020 that it claimed were part of a disinformation campaign related to COVID-19, and many such accounts were easy to trace, since they were unsophisticated, with the Twitter personas seemingly having no real persona, which signifies their inauthenticity.[87] According to a study by researchers at Stanford University, China began circulating disinformation abroad about the virus as early as January 2020, but it stepped up its disinformation campaign in February and March, as China began to contain its domestic outbreak, the United States struggled with its outbreak, and Beijing shifted to using COVID-19 to bolster its global power.[88]

China repeatedly denied concealing the initial outbreak of the virus and underestimated the total number of Chinese deaths and infections.[89] Beijing tried to sow doubt about the fact that the virus originated in Wuhan. Anonymous commentators in the *People's Daily* claimed that COVID-19 "did not necessarily originate in China," while CGTN reporters also suggested the virus might have come from somewhere else, and many Chinese commentators argued that China's tough response (once it had admitted it had an outbreak) bought time for the world.[90] Many of these conspiracy theories are almost certainly untrue.[91]

But Beijing has marshaled more resources as the COVID-19 crisis has gone on and, for a time, shown increasing skill in its information and disinformation operations around the pandemic. Despite takedowns by Twitter and other social media platforms of false Chinese accounts spreading conspiracy theories, China has regrouped, made its efforts more nuanced, and become better able at concealing false social media accounts used to spread disinformation. (Beijing was behind at least ten thousand suspected fake Twitter accounts spreading disinformation about Hong Kong and later about COVID-19, according to research by ProPublica.[92] In June 2020, Twitter took down roughly 170,000 fake accounts that appeared to be linked to an online influence campaign stemming from China targeting perceptions about COVID-19, Hong Kong protests, and other issues.[93])

At times, Beijing has made nuanced and country-specific adjustments to its campaigns.[94] Matt Schrader, formerly of the Alliance for Securing Democracy, notes that "the CCP has also demonstrated its ability to tailor its message to the concerns of its audience. [For instance,] top tweets from Beijing's mission to the EU have targeted European anxieties over a perceived American withdrawal from important global institutions [during the COVID-19 crisis] by emphasizing China's willingness to cooperate internationally," such as on global public health challenges.[95]

This perception of what the United States might do was not unfounded and of the United States' problems was not without evidence—the Trump administration did withdraw the United

States from the World Health Organization during the COVID-19 pandemic, refused to cooperate in a global effort to develop a vaccine, and had the highest death toll from the virus of any country in the world.[96] But China's information strategies, which sometimes accurately portrayed the chaotic U.S. response, often verged into disinformation when suggesting the United States had been involved in creating the virus as a bioweapon and using a range of Chinese social media platforms, bots, and other tools to spread that false claim.[97] These Chinese outlets tried to spread this disinformation at the same time that global public opinion was hardening against Beijing for its initial handling of the novel coronavirus and then its "wolf warrior" diplomacy and actions toward Taiwan.

Although Chinese media outlets and diplomats had not previously had much success turning their large numbers of followers on platforms like Facebook and Twitter into actual interactions, turning to conspiracy theories likely will, in the future, help them attract much more attention among foreign users, even if it did not help China much during the pandemic. As Laura Rosenberger, formerly of the German Marshall Fund, notes, conspiracy theories help build an audience for messaging, Chinese or otherwise, on virtually any social media platform, and Beijing has become increasingly willing to promote conspiracies, alone or with Moscow. After all, Facebook and other platforms feed off extreme, conspiratorial theories—their algorithms often wind up promoting some of the wildest, most aggressive conspiratorial statements and commentators.[98]

And in the long term, Beijing may not have to rely so much on building up its effectiveness on platforms like Facebook and Twitter, which are banned in China, and with which many Chinese operatives may have less experience. If social media platforms based in China, like TikTok, gain broader global popularity (Remember, TikTok is already the most popular website in the world, and has become the most visited social media platform in the world.), Beijing may be able to use those platforms for widespread disinformation, and potentially for data harvesting about populations in other countries as well.[99]

China seems to be working more with other actors to improve the quality of its fakes, and Chinese diplomats have become more active on social media platforms. An assessment by the Alliance for Securing Democracy shows that, between 2019 and 2020, there was a 300 percent increase in Chinese officials' use of Twitter; the quality of fakes appears to be improving.[100]

U.S. intelligence sources also have noted that Chinese intelligence agents, or people linked to them, seemed to be using text messaging and secure messaging apps to sow panic in the United States about COVID-19, highlight fissures in U.S. society, and spread a narrative about the failure of U.S. government responses to COVID-19.[101] U.S. officials had not previously noticed Chinese intelligence agents trying to spread disinformation into U.S. citizens' cell phones via text messaging, a further sign that Beijing was attempting more aggressive, granular, Russia-style disinformation tactics.[102]

This aggressive nature characterized much of China's COVID-19 messaging. A study from the Alliance for Securing Democracy of China's disinformation related to COVID-19 suggested that Beijing soon moved away from early messaging about the crisis, which featured China's domestic response and its efforts at international cooperation, and shifted toward a "more confrontational posture on COVID-19 [that] represents a clear departure from its past behavior and signals a move toward a style of information manipulation more like Russia's," which included the global spreading of the conspiracy theory that the United States created the virus as a bioweapon.[103] Meanwhile, Beijing increasingly used its information campaigns to highlight systemic challenges within the United States that—unlike COVID-19—had nothing to do with China at all, like U.S. problems with racial justice.

Aggressive but Alienating: "Wolf Warriors" and a Wuhan Leak?

Still, the COVID-19–related information and disinformation strategies, combined with China's initial cover-up of the virus, infuriated many other states. Within the United States anger was hardly limited to the Trump White House. U.S. Democratic Party leaders blasted China, and while on the campaign trail in 2020 Democratic nominee, and eventual presidential victor, Joe Biden ran an ad blaming President Trump for being too soft on China.[104] Polling of the U.S. public in 2020 and 2021 showed both Democrats and Republicans were developing intensely negative views of China, a trend that surely continued into 2022.[105]

Leaders and publics from Europe, Australia, and parts of Asia also grew increasingly frustrated with Beijing's attempts to spin the COVID-19 crisis—while Beijing also was stepping up its more assertive diplomacy and military actions, including continuing efforts to dominate the South China Sea and saber-rattling with India and aggressive, often vitriolic diplomacy.[106] As French President Emmanuel Macron said in an interview with the *Financial Times*, "Let's not be so naive as to say [China has] been much better at handling this. There are clearly things that have happened that we don't know about."[107] The leader of Italy's Lega Nord party, Matteo Salvini, told the Italian parliament that China's initial COVID-19 response could qualify as "a crime against humanity."[108]

Indeed, the pandemic crisis—and subsequent criticism of China's initial handling of the outbreak—brought a fierce reaction from Chinese diplomats and state media. This growing so-called "wolf warrior" diplomacy (named after the Chinese action movies *Wolf Warrior* and *Wolf Warrior 2*), which began before COVID-19 but ramped up as the virus spread, has seen Chinese diplomats move to attack other countries in aggressive and often insulting language on social media and in official statements, and even to use large gatherings and private meetings with other diplomats to insult peers and try to bully them.[109] Foreign governments noted, for instance, that Zhao Lijian, the Chinese diplomat who regularly promoted wild, angry, conspiratorial views when he was an official in Pakistan, was not disciplined but instead was promoted to that top position at the foreign ministry and apparently was received with a celebration in Beijing by young diplomats.[110] They noticed too that Hua Chunying, another intense practitioner of wolf warrior diplomacy, was elevated to the top of the foreign ministry's information department; that other top diplomats who blasted foreign countries, like Lu Shaye, who had been ambassador to Canada, also were promoted; and that increasing numbers of Chinese diplomats were opening Twitter accounts and using them to spread conspiracies, bash foreign countries, and swaggeringly boast about China.[111] (Indeed, the author Peter Martin notes, in a recent book on modern Chinese diplomacy, that in 2019 Xi Jinping had encouraged such efforts, sending a note to Chinese diplomats telling them to demonstrate "fighting spirit."[112]) They witnessed Chinese diplomats, in person, becoming increasingly vehement, even angry, at public events: At a forum of Pacific Island countries in September 2018, China's representative to the meeting kept trying to interrupt everyone.[113] In private, one-on-one meetings, foreign diplomats, who in the Hu era were able to speak relatively openly with some Chinese peers, noticed that their Chinese compatriots now simply clammed up, berated foreign diplomats in private, handed out copies of books fulsomely praising Xi Jinping, or gushed about Xi.[114] As Martin notes, the Xi administration understands that Beijing needs extensive diplomatic efforts; China now has more consulates and embassies around the world than the United States, and the Xi administration has repeatedly increased the budget for diplomacy.[115] Yet the aggressive behavior, sycophantic praise for Xi, and inability to engage in any kind of real dialogue, even in private, with peers undermined China's image with other countries and also hindered its diplomats' actual ability to work with other countries and within global institutions.

And they, of course, noticed even more public versions of wolf warrior diplomacy, which seemed to become more intense after the early months of COVID-19. When Australia, for instance, called for an independent probe of the coronavirus pandemic, the Chinese embassy in Canberra slammed the call as "pitiful" and the Chinese foreign ministry accused the Australian government of "ideological bias and political games," dismissing the call for a probe as "political maneuvering."[116] China further retaliated by banning beef from several major slaughterhouses in Australia and slapping tariffs on barley imports, and Australian public opinion of China plumbed new lows.[117]

By 2021, as the possibility that the virus had not spread by skipping from animals to people at a market in China but actually had leaked from a lab in Wuhan became more widely discussed, populations and leaders in a range of countries became even angrier at Beijing. As the Council on Foreign Relations' Yanzhong Huang noted in the *Washington Post*:

> Should proof emerge that the virus came from a research lab, and not (for example) a meat-and-fish market, the discovery would make headlines globally. It might also precipitate a free fall in China's relationship with the outside world—even if nations simply come to believe that the balance of the evidence suggests that China is covering up a lapse at one of its labs (since a smoking gun may never be forthcoming). Such a shift in views about the origins of the virus would deal a severe blow to China's soft power.[118]

That soft power was already damaged enough when other countries believed Beijing helped spread the virus by covering up its initial transmission from animals to humans. Even before the idea of a lab leak became taken more seriously by epidemiologists, world leaders, and other opinion leaders, polling data showing collapsing global opinions of China was driven in large part by publics' anger at how Beijing had initially concealed what was believed to be a virus that came from animals. Polls released by Pew Research in late 2020 and again in 2021 showed large majorities of people in countries including the United Kingdom, the Netherlands, Germany, France, and Canada having sharply negative views of China—much more negative than they were in the 2010s—and that these negative views were driven in some part by how Beijing had handled the pandemic.[119] In fact, a Pew Research study of fourteen advanced economies found that publics in all fourteen states had negative views of China, and in the United States, a regular poll by the Chicago Council on Global

Affairs, released in 2020, showed that Americans had their most negative views of China of any time since the council's polling began, in
1978.[120]

Public opinion of China probably dropped further, in 2022,
as Beijing reported, in the second quarter of 2022, virtually zero
growth.[121] Since China's developmental model is premised in part on
the idea that Beijing can consistently deliver high growth, this collapse in growth, brought on by Xi's misguided zero-COVID strategy,
which decimated the Chinese economy, also probably hurt Chinese
soft power. Then, the Taiwan crisis further turned people in many
countries against Beijing, which looked like a bully.

An even more recent study conducted by a consortium of think
tanks (the European Think-Tank Network on China), of seventeen
European countries and EU institutions including both some of
the richest European states and some of the poorer ones, concluded
that "Chinese soft power in Europe—defined as the ability to influence preferences through attraction or persuasion—has fallen on
hard times."[122] It concluded that 2020 had been an "*annus horribilis* for
China's image in Europe" and noted that another poll, by Sinophone
Borderlands, of people in thirteen European countries—and including many Eastern European states—found that people in ten of the
thirteen countries now had much more negative views of China
than positive views.[123] That report by the Sinophone Borderlands
project, which surveyed 19,673 Europeans in thirteen countries on
their opinions of the People's Republic of China (PRC), found that
the only places where respondents had more positive views of China
than negative were Russia, Serbia, and Latvia.[124] In 2021, Pew followed
up with another study of global public opinion of China. In the study,
most of the people surveyed had little confidence in Xi Jinping to "do
the right thing in world affairs" and had extremely negative views of
the Chinese leader himself.[125]

A leak from a Chinese lab, covered up by Beijing, as Yanzhong
Huang notes, would be perceived globally as far worse than animal-
to-human transmission initially covered up by China; a lab leak and

cover-up would more directly implicate the Chinese government and seem akin to Chernobyl—a devastating cover-up on that scale that could decimate Beijing's global credibility. (In addition, if credible reports eventually entered Chinese cyberspace that the virus leaked from a Wuhan lab and was covered up, it could foster much higher levels of domestic mistrust of Beijing, further hampering China's global ambitions.[126]) And although at the beginning of the pandemic most researchers believed that the virus had spread from animals to humans, by the middle of 2021 intelligence agencies, news agencies, and epidemiologists were considering more seriously the possibility that the virus leaked from a Wuhan lab, though the majority of researchers still believe the virus was transmitted from animals to humans in a market or in some other fashion.[127]

Meanwhile, China's export of vaccines, sometimes at discounted rates or given freely to developing countries, was not exactly bolstering its global image either, even though, by 2022, China had exported many vaccines.[128] China did not allow its vaccines' efficacy trials to be released with full transparency, and as countries began to import and use Chinese vaccines, they often found the jabs worked poorly compared to those manufactured by Pfizer-BioNTech and Moderna.[129] The vaccine made by Sinovac was shown, in trial data, to have an efficacy rate of around 51 percent, and trial data showed the Sinopharm vaccine to have an efficacy rate of around 79 percent.[130] (Trial data showed that Pfizer-BioNTech's vaccine was 95 percent effective.[131]) China's own top disease control official said in April 2021 that Chinese-made vaccines did not have high effectiveness against COVID-19 and that Chinese officials were considering mixing some of the vaccines to improve their effectiveness, comments that did not exactly reassure Chinese citizens or people in countries reliant on Chinese-made vaccines, which were not mRNA vaccines like those made by Pfizer and Moderna.[132] Reports of significant new outbreaks in countries like Chile reliant on Chinese vaccines did not provide comfort.[133] Nor did the fact that officials in countries like the United Arab Emirates, which had made Chinese vaccines central to their vaccination strategy, were encouraging some of their citizens to get extra doses of their Chinese vaccines—in effect, booster shots—only a few months after getting the first jabs,[134] or that countries like Malaysia, which initially used Chinese vaccines, later decided to switch primarily to Pfizer and other mRNA vaccines.

According to diplomats from a range of Southeast Asian countries, Beijing's gloves-off approach, even as COVID-19 raged, only made Southeast Asian officials and leaders more suspicious of China. More suspicious officials are likely to heighten their defenses, to the extent that they can, against everything from China's military assertiveness to Chinese sharp power to Beijing's state media outlets.

The annual surveys of Southeast Asian opinion leaders by the ISEAS–Yusof Ishak think tank in Singapore find that Southeast Asian respondents view China (along with India) as the least trusted partner in the region of any major power, trailing the United States, Europe, and Japan.[135] The study revealed that distrust of China had grown significantly, throughout Southeast Asia, since the late 2010s—probably in part, as with developed countries, because of how Beijing initially handled COVID-19. That distrust grew in 2022 and was exacerbated by the Taiwan crisis.

China's aggressive diplomacy backfired so badly that Xi Jinping seemed to realize it was actually hurting Beijing's efforts to wield regional and global power. In a speech to Chinese officials at a Politburo meeting in June 2021, a speech that was highlighted by Xinhua, Xi declared that Beijing needed to work to create a "trustworthy, lovable and respectable" image and must expand China's "circle of friends." China, he said, should be "open and confident" but also "modest and humble." The speech appeared to be a clear signal from Xi for Chinese diplomats to tone down their aggressive behavior, at least in public, though not necessarily China's more aggressive disinformation operations and more covert influence campaigns. Whether even Xi will be able to shift China's diplomacy remains an open question—and one to which we will soon return. And Xi himself somewhat undercut that message of humility by his assertive actions toward Taiwan, by not demoting his most aggressive diplomats, and by using the occasion of the one hundredth anniversary of the Communist Party to give a bellicose speech blasting unnamed "foreign forces" and promising that anyone trying to "bully" China would "have their heads bashed bloody against a Great Wall of steel forged by over 1.4 billion Chinese people."[136]

China's Disinformation Dilemma

Beijing also still confronts a major dilemma as it moves closer to a Russian model of disinformation and as it collaborates with other autocrats. The more China's disinformation style resembles Russia's bomb-throwing, manipulative approach—and the more that other countries expose Chinese disinformation that resembles Russia's—Beijing's approach is bound to clash with its overall goals, even in the era of "wolf warrior" diplomacy, of promoting China as a global leader and an alternative to the United States and other leading democracies. We have seen that Beijing's messaging, on state media and other information tools, historically has focused more on promoting China's domestic and international leadership than on tearing down other states. The Alliance for Securing Democracy study showed:

> To date, just over 50 percent of CGTN and CCTV video content has focused on China. By comparison, only four percent of RT America and RT UK's video content has focused on Russia, with little to no coverage of Russian domestic issues, culture, or politics.[137]

It may be challenging, though not impossible, for Beijing to balance Russian-style disinformation strategies, which often are exposed and prove highly alienating to other states, with continued efforts to promote Chinese regional and global leadership—especially at a time when global public opinion of China is already falling off a cliff.

What Works: Bought Boats and Threats

Beijing is enjoying greater successes in other areas. Buying its own boats, meanwhile, has proven more effective for Beijing than borrowed-boat tactics; often, Chinese ownership of local outlets is harder for governments to trace and police than borrowed-boat tactics. China's threats against major global media companies also have become increasingly effective. To be sure, some borrowed boats have helped spread Chinese state media into local outlets and seem to be shifting some discourse about China. A study by the research organization AidData, previously mentioned in this book, found that, at least in East Asian and Pacific countries, Chinese media's content-sharing partnerships with local outlets were correlated with greater approval of the Chinese leadership, an important tool for prodding East Asian leaders, and particularly Southeast Asian leaders, to at least accept China's growing control over regional organizations, to partner with China on trade deals, and to accede to other Chinese goals.[138]

But bought boats have proven even more valuable for China, since they are far easier than borrowed boats for Beijing to use as bullhorns and cudgels to shape public opinion. Unlike content-sharing deals with borrowed boats, which may use some Chinese content while also producing other reporting, bought boats often wholly import pro-China coverage.

The result of Beijing's bought-boats expansion extends far beyond Asia. The expansion of bought boats has created a situation in which, today, even in places with generally free presses like Australia, Canada, New Zealand, the United Kingdom, the United States, and (to some extent) Malaysia and Thailand, few Chinese-language outlets scrutinize Beijing's domestic and foreign policies. As we have seen, while the Chinese-reading population in these places, like Australia, New Zealand, Malaysia, and Thailand, remains a fragment of the overall adult population, Chinese readers wield extensive influence in politics, business, and other elite circles. As their media diet becomes increasingly pro-Beijing and China uses other tools to influence them, these populations also are gaining influence in local politics.

In countries where Chinese-language readers and speakers are a much smaller fragment of the population and so their influence is more diluted, China's growing control over the Chinese-language press may have less effect, overall, in national and local politics. Most of the outlets based in the United States, for instance, are now controlled by individual owners or companies strongly sympathetic to Beijing, are owned by Chinese state firms, or are discreetly controlled directly by the Chinese government itself.[139] And while the biggest state media outlets, like CGTN, may not have large audiences in the United States, other Chinese-language bought boats certainly do. If Chinese-language news consumers in the United States want independent coverage of China and the world from an outlet based in North America, they basically have just New York–based New Tang Dynasty Television (NTDTV) and the *Epoch Times*, a streaming TV station, newspaper, and website backed by Falun Gong. Unfortunately, although *Epoch Times* produces some quality investigative reporting on China, in recent years, it has embarked on a metamorphosis that has done significant damage to its credibility.[140] While still offering plenty of China coverage, according to investigations by the *New York Times*, the *New Republic*, and other outlets, it also has ramped up its coverage and sharing, on its site and on Facebook, of Info Wars–esque conspiracy theories about the United States, Europe, and elsewhere, building a sizable audience in North America and Europe but also becoming a leading source in amplifying all manner of conspiracy theories. Many of the conspiracy theories produced by publications linked to *Epoch Times* have nothing to do with China at all but rather with QAnon, fake claims of voter fraud in the United States, and other issues.[141]

Despite their flaws, NTDTV and the *Epoch Times* at least provide some independent coverage of China. Yet few U.S. cable systems carry NTDTV, compared to the number of cable systems that carry CGTN and Phoenix TV, a bought boat that enjoys broad popularity in the

United States and around the Chinese-speaking world. Sarah Cook of Freedom House estimates that Phoenix TV reaches nearly eighty million U.S. households.[142] By comparison, NTDTV reaches only about six million U.S. households.

Chinese consular officials in the United States apply direct and indirect pressure on U.S. cable companies not to carry critical channels like NTDTV—and this pressure has been, up to now, extremely successful. Cook notes that NTDTV representatives have said that several U.S. cable companies will not even meet with them, probably due to pressure from Chinese officials. When one cable company, RCN, considered carrying the channel, Chinese diplomats threatened an RCN executive and RCN backed off.[143]

This pressure, combined with Beijing's control of bought and borrowed boats as pro-China owners buy up outlets in the United States and Beijing inks content-sharing deals, serves to limit how many Chinese speakers and readers in the United States have access to independent coverage of China. Overall, notes a Hoover Institution comprehensive study of the Chinese-language media market in the United States, "Beijing seems to be winning the battle against Chinese-language outlets expressing dissenting views," including Chinese-language online and social media–only outlets operating in the United States; it is using its leverage to enforce ideological discipline, in terms of news and opinion coverage, among a range of Chinese outlets in the United States.[144] The space for truly independent Chinese-language outlets in the United States, the Hoover Institution's analysis notes, has shrunk to just a few media companies.[145] And while changing the media diet of Chinese readers and speakers in the United States might not have the same decisive effect on national politics that bought and borrowed boats are having in Australia, Malaysia, New Zealand, Singapore, or Thailand, the shifting media diet in the United States does affect a sizable chunk of people—though that influence, right now, would be hard to break through the overall severely negative U.S. views of China. Roughly three million people in the United States speak Chinese at home, and many of these speakers have significant influence in local, state, and congressional politics in states such as California, New York, Texas, and other major states.[146]

In Europe and other parts of the world, Beijing also increasingly controls the Chinese-language press via its bought boats. We have seen how Beijing has gained control over much of the Chinese-language press in Australia and New Zealand. Beijing also now controls the existing Chinese-language print media in France, and Chinese state broadcast outlets and Phoenix TV, a quasi-state outlet, are the Chinese-language broadcast stations available to Chinese-language viewers in France.[147] In Canada, the print Chinese-language media is dominated by Canadian-produced versions of *Sing Tao*, a news outlet based in Hong Kong that is considered strongly supportive of Beijing, and which is owned by the daughter of the head of a major Chinese property company.[148] A former journalist from *Sing Tao*'s Canadian editions, Victor Ho (who is not related to owner Charles Ho), has said that although the Canadian Chinese publications did produce relatively straightforward news about Canada, it took its copy about China straight from coverage produced by *Sing Tao* in Hong Kong and mainland China—coverage that was highly pro-Beijing.[149]

Beijing also has gained growing control over the Chinese-language media landscape in the United Kingdom, although the UK government has begun to push back. According to the *Financial Times*, China appears to have gained significant influence over the *UK-Chinese Times*, one of the main Chinese-language publications in Britain, which has a content-sharing agreement with the *People's Daily* and picks up dozens of identical stories about China from that state outlet.[150]

China's growing navy of bought boats is helping limit discourse about Beijing in many parts of the world. Particularly in Southeast Asia and Africa, but also to some extent in Latin America and Eastern Europe, critical discussions of China seem to be muted more and more. Influenced by bought and borrowed boats and by traditional influence efforts, Thai opinion leaders have become much more reluctant to discuss China's growing power in the kingdom anymore or other issues that reflect negatively on Beijing, all of which were common topics of conversations with Thai opinion leaders ten years ago. Some Thai leaders surely still have concerns about Thailand becoming too economically and strategically dependent on China, about Beijing's dams on the upper Mekong River and their effect on the kingdom, or about specific Chinese projects like a Belt and Road Initiative (BRI)-linked plan to build a high-speed rail from China into Laos and then Thailand. Some Thai military officers in particular still clearly worry about becoming too dependent on Chinese assistance and Chinese gear. And some younger progressive Thai activists have openly broadcast their support for Hong Kong protestors against the Chinese government, part of what is becoming known as the "Milk Tea Alliance," a solidarity movement of pro-democracy activists from around the region. And yet there is far less negative coverage of China in the Thai media sphere these days, and less discussion among opinion leaders of concerns about Chinese policies.

Overall, not only is China portrayed more positively in the Thai media than in the past, according to many Thai journalists, but also serious critiques of China are vanishing from many Thai outlets. Among some activists on social media in the kingdom, it is a different story, as we have seen—social media denizens invested in the Milk Tea Alliance regularly criticize aspects of Chinese foreign policy, China's infrastructure projects, and other issues.[151] But in the broader Thai media, biting critiques and tough investigative pieces on China largely have vanished. This shift is not due to only one factor. Thai voices have become muted in part because of China's growing economic and strategic power in the kingdom, in part because of the overall decline in press freedom in the kingdom, and in part because of Beijing's growing, direct control of sectors of the Thai media.

Beijing has achieved some similar successes in Indonesia. There, some issues most sensitive to the CCP—most notably, the genocide of Uighur Muslims in Xinjiang, which would be a natural topic of discussion in Indonesia, the country with the most Muslims in the world—are becoming less visible in the Indonesian media, and also vanishing from conversations among Indonesian opinion leaders. They have become less visible as Beijing has aggressively lobbied Indonesian leaders of Muslim organizations to stay quiet about abuses in Xinjiang and also lobbied prominent Indonesian journalists. Chinese officials have organized strictly guided tours of Xinjiang for Muslim leaders, politicians, journalists, and academics to show the conditions in what Beijing says are re-education camps where Muslims are taught new skills.[152] China has brought in journalists and social media influencers from Indonesia for tours of other areas of China, encouraging them to push a positive narrative of the country overall.[153] The combined effects of this campaign to influence opinion and control local narratives—both on the treatment of Uighurs and on China more broadly—has produced results, with Indonesian media generally reporting positively on China and the leadership of some of Indonesia's largest Muslim organizations and news outlets often echoing Beijing's line on the need to address a supposed extremism problem in Xinjiang through re-education—re-education programs that are actually concentration camps.[154] Often, Indonesian media commentary and elite opinion leaders just shy away entirely from discussing the abuses in Xinjiang.[155] Notably, according to Southeast Asia scholar Murray Hiebert, Indonesian opinion leaders have not been reluctant to criticize the Myanmar government's massive abuses of the Rohingya or the Myanmar military's coup—Myanmar has little soft or sharp power in Indonesia—yet these same Indonesian opinion leaders whitewash China's treatment of the Uighurs.[156]

Thailand and Indonesia may be part of a regional trend of negative coverage about China disappearing from Southeast Asian media, and from media across Asia more broadly—in part because of China's increasing use of bought boats, though some of these Chinese gains in how Beijing is portrayed were rolled back during the Taiwan crisis. In its 2019 study of China's relations with East Asian and Pacific states, AidData found that, even though most East Asian and Pacific news outlets today report more on human rights generally than they did in the mid-2000s, they do not report any more regularly on human rights in China than they did fifteen years ago.[157] In other words, these outlets devote more space to human rights coverage than before. But they do not seem to have used that increase to cover Beijing's abuses, even though China has become far more repressive domestically, and more assertive in fostering rights abuses abroad, since the mid-2000s.

Similarly, even as public opinion of China plummeted in 2020, 2021, and 2022 in many parts of Asia, Europe, Australia and New Zealand, and North America, China continued to garner positive media coverage in some developing regions—though its relationship with Russia hurt it in developing regions like Eastern Europe. A survey released in 2021 by the International Federation of Journalists (IFJ), a federation of journalists' trade unions, found that reporters in more than half the countries surveyed said they believed "that coverage of China in their national media was more positive since the start of the pandemic."[158] In a handful of the countries, local journalists even reported that Beijing was "seen as the purveyor of the most accurate information about the new coronavirus, showing its growing influence over global narratives."[159] Yet many of the respondents in the IFJ study were from developing countries, probably places where China's vaccine diplomacy has had a greater effect, where there has been less negative coverage of Beijing's initial pandemic cover-up—and where Beijing has had some success in using bought boats, Xinhua, and other tools to shape local media environments and views of China.

Threats

China's blunt threats against global news organizations also have been effective tools. A comprehensive report by PEN America, an organization dedicated to protecting media freedoms, found that some of the biggest global media companies, like Bloomberg News and Reuters, appeared to be self-censoring content on their Chinese-language sites, likely to please Beijing.[160] The report also found that the prestigious Australian Broadcasting Corporation has been accused of censoring coverage of potentially sensitive political issues for Beijing in order to maintain market access in China.[161] Elsewhere, the Chinese-language version of the *New Zealand Herald,* the New Zealand publication with the largest readership, had edited translated articles or omitted articles entirely that depicted the Chinese government in a negative way—in one case replacing a story with a version provided by an unspecified Chinese wire service.[162]

Bloomberg News has knuckled under in other obvious ways as well. After Bloomberg's newswire did a major 2012 story about the wealth of some of Xi's relatives, the company faced intense pressure from the Chinese government. Beijing ordered Chinese state firms not to buy new leases for the Bloomberg terminals central to the company's business model. *Bloomberg News* then killed a big follow-up investigation about ties between Xi, his family, and Wang Jianlin, one of China's wealthiest tycoons.[163] "It [the story about Xi's family wealth] is for sure going to, you know, invite the Communist Party to, you know, completely shut us down and kick us out of the country," *Bloomberg News*'s then-editor-in-chief Matthew Winkler said, according to audio obtained by National Public Radio.[164] "So, I just don't see that as a story that is justified." After killing the story, according to National Public Radio (NPR), Bloomberg allegedly went to great lengths to silence the reporters who did the investigation, and even to silence one of their spouses, the well-known China scholar Leta Hong Fincher.[165] *Bloomberg News* denied pressuring anyone to sign nondisclosure agreements, but documents reviewed by NPR contradict that claim.

There are exceptions. The *New York Times* has not given in to Chinese pressure tactics, like having its website being blocked in China for years, its reporters' visa applications to work in China slow-walked or denied, and its correspondents being tossed out of the country.[166] The *New York Times* continues to aggressively cover sensitive topics like abuses in Xinjiang; it published a long article in 2019, using leaked Chinese documents, that revealed how China was systematically organizing mass detentions of Uighurs.[167] The *New*

York Times also published the story about Xi's family links to Wang Jianlin by the reporter who had done the killed story for *Bloomberg News* and then basically re-reported it for the *New York Times*.[168] Despite similar pressure, including having some of their reporters expelled from China, the *Wall Street Journal* and the *Washington Post* also have continued to publish tough, detailed investigative reports on topics like China's surveillance technology and rights abuses. The *Wall Street Journal* was a finalist for the 2021 Pulitzer Prize for international reporting for its coverage of China and Xi Jinping, even though Beijing had tossed multiple *Wall Street Journal* reporters from the country.[169] Beijing also has not been able to silence coverage of China's abuses by Uighur or Tibetan journalists at Radio Free Asia and similar outlets staffed by exiles even as it has punished and detained relatives of these exiles.[170]

Although I do not delve deeply into Hollywood in this book—there are excellent books devoted just to China's effects on the U.S. film industry—Hollywood reveals an obvious example of Beijing applying a combination of the anaconda in the chandelier described by Perry Link, bountiful incentives, and getting its way.[171] With Hollywood, Beijing has used harsh but often vague and inconsistent threats— the anaconda in the chandelier—and incentives to ensure fear among pretty much everyone who creates, finances, and distributes films. Two decades ago, when the Chinese film market was much smaller, Beijing was weaker diplomatically, and China was not investing in Hollywood coproductions, Hollywood still produced films on issues related to Chinese human rights abuses, Tibet, and other topics highly sensitive to Beijing. Martin Scorsese made the film *Kundun* about the fourteenth Dalai Lama, a movie that portrayed China's invasion of Tibet, and Mao Zedong himself, in a negative light. Disney released *Kundun* over Beijing's objections in 1997.[172] That same year, an already famous Brad Pitt starred in *Seven Years in Tibet* as an Austrian mountaineer who witnessed the 1950 Chinese invasion of that country.[173]

But times have changed. Rarely do most major Hollywood films touch on Taiwan, Tibet, Xinjiang, the Chinese government's human rights record, the famine and abuses of the Mao era, and many other subjects, although some streaming services have bucked the trend, and it is notable that musicians often buck the trend. When the Marvel Cinematic Universe superhero movie *Doctor Strange* was being developed more recently, writers changed a central character, the Ancient One, from being Tibetan, as the character was in the original comic books, to being Celtic. (A white woman, Tilda Swinton, played the character.[174]) One of the screenwriters admitted that the studio erased any Tibetan references from the film for fear of Beijing's response.[175] Similarly, the 2012 remake of *Red Dawn*, a (pretty bad) Cold War–era movie about a U.S.-Soviet conflict, initially cast Chinese villains. Though *Red Dawn*'s remake was almost guaranteed to be schlocky, casting Chinese adversaries made some sense if the remake was going to portray the United States and its major superpower competitor, as the original had done. But after the film was finished, distributors suddenly decided to digitally alter the villains to make them North Korean to avoid angering Beijing and possibly losing business in China.[176] And when Tom Cruise and Paramount Pictures made a much-anticipated sequel to *Top Gun*, the 1980s Cruise megahit, they dressed the seemingly ageless actor in the same bomber jacket he wore in the original. Yet that classic jacket had some minor changes— it no longer featured the Taiwanese flag on a patch, as it had in the original, probably because Chinese tech giant Tencent, an investor in the film, objected.[177]

Even potential scenes that do not explicitly portray China in negative ways can get short-circuited. Emails leaked by North Korean hackers showed that Sony Pictures executives prevented the makers of the film *Pixels*—a ludicrous Adam Sandler comedy named by the Golden Raspberry Awards as one of the worst movies of 2015—from creating a pointedly stupid scene in which aliens blew up part of the Great Wall of China.[178] Peter Shiao, the founder of a film studio that does Hollywood-Chinese coproductions, told Reuters, "I think the studios have grown pretty savvy. For a type of movie, particularly the global blockbusters, they are not going to go and make something that the Chinese would reject for social or political reasons. That is already a truism."[179]

Chinese leaders did not call the *Doctor Strange* screenwriters and tell them to change the character, and they did not tell the producers of *Red Dawn* to change the identities of the film's villains. As veteran Hollywood writers and directors admit, the anaconda is certainly present: Brad Pitt apparently was barred from China after *Seven Years in Tibet* for around two decades, the production that made the film was banned for five years, and some Hollywood blockbusters are banned from being shown in China, not always for clear reasons.[180] And massive incentives like Chinese co-investment in films and access to China's massive film market mean that self-censorship has become the norm in Tinseltown, especially as the film industry struggles mightily to rebound from the global pandemic and the paradigm shift caused by the rise of streaming giants like Netflix.[181] Chinese firms have been co-investors in some of the biggest Hollywood blockbusters, dating back to the mid-2010s. Indeed, forty-one of the one hundred highest-grossing Hollywood films released between 2014 and 2018 had Chinese investors.[182]

The self-censorship is particularly noticeable too because Hollywood often touts itself as committed to free speech and long has been considered a major tool of U.S. soft power. But Hollywood writers and producers say that anticipatory self-censorship has become so common that ideas that in any way negatively reflected on Beijing would not even get beyond initial writers' meetings.[183] Knowing that studios and producers would shut down such negative portrayals, writers self-censor early about China in the filmmaking process. "Hollywood decision-makers and other filmmaking professionals are increasingly making decisions about their films—the content, casting, plot, dialogue, and settings—based on an effort to avoid antagonizing Chinese officials who control whether their films gain access to the booming Chinese market," notes a comprehensive report on Beijing's influence in Hollywood by PEN America, an organization that defends free expression.[184]

Some films have gone so far as to insert pro-China concepts and statements. The 2019 animated movie *Abominable*, a joint production between DreamWorks, which is partly owned by the multimedia giant NBCUniversal/Comcast, and China's Pearl Studio, showed a map that displayed China's version of territorial claims in the South China Sea, claims hotly disputed by other regional states.[185] The map was featured in the movie even though the film has nothing to do with the South China Sea—it is about plucky teenagers trying to save a yeti.

The COVID-19 pandemic, while souring global opinion on China, only made Hollywood more dependent on the Chinese market. With theaters in many developed countries closed, China remained one of the few big markets in 2020 and 2021 where people continued to watch movies at actual movie theaters, allowing Hollywood studios to release their films in theaters rather than having to delay them, sell them to streaming services, or stream them on their own services. China passed the United States in 2020 as the biggest market for movie ticket sales, partly because so many Chinese movie theaters remained open for much of 2020.[186] With the possibility that the pandemic, a massive boon for streaming, permanently shifted many film fans away from ever setting foot in theaters in many countries, China seemed poised to become an even more central source of revenue for U.S.-based global film giants.

The fact that Chinese-made films are, simultaneously, becoming more popular among Chinese filmgoers only seems to have made Hollywood more desperate to hang on to the giant Chinese market.[187] As Aynne Kokas of the University of Virginia, author of the acclaimed book *Hollywood Made in China*, noted to CNN Business, "If China doesn't need US movies, Hollywood studios will have to dramatically reduce their spending on big budget blockbusters. The current budgets are unsustainable without access to the China market. That could fundamentally change the model of the US film industry."[188] Similarly, the gaming industry, which grew enormously during the pandemic as people were stuck at home and which, like Hollywood, often presents itself as an avatar of free speech, also has given in to pressure from China, now the most lucrative gaming market in the world.[189] Riot Games, a U.S.-based gaming company, censored its online forums in 2019, blocking terms like "Uyghur" that the Chinese government wanted them to censor.[190]

What Works: Controlling the Information Pipes and Internet Governance

By controlling information pipes, Beijing also is becoming more effective in ensuring that discussions about certain issues stop taking place in other countries. Even when cable and satellite companies are not explicitly increasing the reach of Chinese state media, for instance, they can alter narratives and images of China by deciding what channels they *do not* feature. In this manner, Chinese satellite and cable companies can eliminate content potentially critical of Beijing.

StarTimes, the Chinese satellite company that has expanded across Africa, demonstrates this pattern, as the company is helping to ensure that some topics about China vanish from African televisions. Certainly, StarTimes's inexpensive television is desired by many people in Africa, for reasons having nothing to do with Beijing. The company provides quality and cheap programming that people want. On a soccer-mad continent, StarTimes shows the English FA Cup, Italy's Serie A, the World Cup, Champions Cup, Germany's Bundesliga, and France's Ligue 1.[191] Yet the company also makes it harder for Africans to access channels like the BBC, which offer critical and independent coverage of China, by making StarTimes packages that include the BBC and other international options more expensive than packages that include Chinese state media outlets and local outlets.[192]

The less often critical reportage about China appears, as one might see on the BBC, the more likely people in other countries do not get the full picture of China's domestic and foreign policies. And in places where StarTimes is potentially gaining greater control over national broadcasters, like in Zambia, local media watchdog groups have warned that it appears to be giving even greater priority to channels focused on fluffing Beijing's image.[193] Zambia's media watchdog claimed that StarTimes's joint venture there was using new bandwidth allocated in part for the national broadcaster to broadcast Chinese channels rather than local ones.[194] StarTimes appears to be becoming a model as well, as Chinese firms link up with other national television broadcasters in countries like Cambodia, Laos, Timor-Leste, and other states. As in Zambia these national broadcasters, linked with Chinese firms, will likely push critical content off the most widely watched networks in these countries.

China's exports of surveillance technology and other types of pipes also have helped Beijing export its model of information. In Zimbabwe, for instance, the repressive government has not only imported Chinese surveillance technology but also sent many officials to China to learn about information management.[195]

In some other cases, countries do not appear to be directly bringing in Chinese expertise but still have adopted internet control measures that seem modeled on China, bolstering Beijing's goal of spreading the idea of a closed and sovereign internet. In other words, China's internet governance diffuses to other authoritarian states or hybrid regimes, even if Beijing does not directly instruct them. As we have seen, Thailand, for instance, passed a new cybersecurity law in 2019 similar to China's internet laws, although it remains unclear whether Thai leaders explicitly asked Chinese officials to advise them.[196] In Vietnam, whose government maintains prickly relations with Beijing, the administration has in recent years implemented new cyberspace legislation, similar to the Chinese model, which makes it far easier for the state to filter and monitor online content.[197] In Myanmar, the junta government, which seized power in February 2021, quickly tried to implement new cyberspace laws and regulations similar to China's internet laws.[198] In Cambodia, the government has created a new set of rules governing its domestic internet that essentially copying the Chinese model.[199]

China's influence on domestic internets extends well beyond Asia. Overall, a study by the think tank New America found that a growing number of states "have begun to exert tighter control over the internet within their borders," often due to the influence of China, the biggest advocate for closed domestic internets in the world.[200] In essence, these states are copying China's model of a closed internet in which the national government has the power to dictate internet traffic domestically and also censor traffic and surveil citizens.[201]

Zimbabwe is copying Beijing's model of a closed and filtered internet, pushing through legislation that will give the Zimbabwean government extensive powers to monitor internet users and possibly censor or arrest them.[202] Similarly, in Ethiopia the government has not only imported Chinese surveillance technology and sent officials to study in China but also increasingly modeled its domestic internet on China's example. Chinese giant ZTE helped Ethiopia's state internet provider build out newer-generation networks, and in the past five years Addis Ababa has repeatedly monitored and censored social media.[203] Uganda has taken similar measures as well, apparently relying on Chinese advisors to help the government determine how to more effectively control social media use and the domestic internet in general.[204]

Meanwhile, Turkey has taken steps to put into place a system of internet controls similar to those in China.[205] Egypt, which has built increasingly close links to Beijing in recent years, also has taken steps to put into place a China-style system of internet controls, while multiple other Middle Eastern states have sent officials to Chinese seminars on cybersecurity and China's attempts to control the internet.[206] In Central Asia, according to Reporters Without Borders, Tajikistan has adopted a Chinese-style system of internet control, and it is likely that other Central Asian states, all of which are already highly authoritarian (except Kyrgyzstan), will follow suit.[207]

Russia, as we have seen, is copying China's internet model. Even before the Ukraine war led to a dramatic clampdown on the domestic Russian internet, the Kremlin appeared to be seeking Beijing's help in shutting down and monitoring the Russian internet. For years, despite Vladimir Putin's tight grip on politics, the Russian internet remained freer than its Chinese counterpart and featured open criticism of the government and even Putin himself.[208] But by 2019, Russia had enacted new measures designed to create what the Kremlin called a "sovereign internet," wording similar to how Beijing describes its model of a national, closed internet.[209] The legislation allows Russia to create a national domestic internet that could be cut off from the world and to allow the Kremlin to more easily monitor online discourse and censor users.[210] Prior to the enactment of the law, delegations from the Cyberspace Administration of China had met with Russian officials to discuss national internet strategies and cooperation on global internet issues.[211] The Chinese delegations also met with leaders from several of the largest Russian internet companies.[212] Then, in 2022 Putin imposed draconian restrictions on the domestic internet and blocks on many external platforms, preventing them from operating in Russia.

Working with Moscow, Beijing also increasingly uses international forums about cyberspace to promote China's model of a closed, controlled internet, one run by governments rather than determined by the interplay of private companies, civil society, and (to a limited extent) governments. Other authoritarian states, like Iran and Saudi Arabia, also support this concept of closed, nationally controlled internets rather than an essentially open, global internet.[213] But China and Russia are by far the major actors promoting a closed model.[214]

Beijing has become increasingly assertive about exporting its models of government and development, through speeches by top leaders, information sessions for foreign officials, training sessions about China's internet models, and many other tactics. It did so even though that more assertive diplomacy eventually ran into challenges due to growing global mistrust of China because of its lack of transparency about the initial beginnings of COVID-19, its links to Russia, the Taiwan crisis, and to some extent because of the overly pugnacious approach of some Chinese diplomats.[215]

The spreading model offers a win-win-win proposition for Beijing. If autocrats apply China's model and are able to anticipate and suppress dissent, other autocrats likely will look to Beijing for guidance as well. Their governments will turn to Chinese technology, and some Chinese firms will make money in what are fast-growing economic sectors—sectors in which Beijing believes Chinese firms should be global competitors and is using massive state capital to support their rise as global competitors, even as the Xi administration reins in some of the political activities and speech of leading Chinese companies and entrepreneurs. And the more governments buy from Chinese companies, the more experience these firms get in multiple business environments, the more they refine their products, and the more effective the technologies they produce.

Experience gained by Chinese firms abroad also potentially helps them refine their technology at home—refinements that could bolster the control the CCP has over its population, a level of social control that has already been tightened significantly because of Beijing's zero-COVID strategy. In addition, the security flaws found in Chinese surveillance technology, and the state links of many Chinese surveillance firms, raise the real possibility that Beijing could benefit by gaining surreptitious access to information about other countries' citizens. Beijing could gain access to critical data about corporate leaders, political leaders, civil society leaders, and anyone else watched and monitored by equipment a country buys from a Chinese surveillance company. This would be a potentially grave national security risk for other states, not to mention simply a massive invasion of people's privacy.

This blueprint is also helping prop up repressive regimes, from Africa to Latin America to the Middle East to Southeast Asia—and propping up authoritarian regimes could be a boon to Beijing. Beijing has built solid relations with some democratic countries. But overall, the majority of China's closest partners are autocratic governments and hybrid regimes: Cambodia, Ethiopia, Myanmar, Pakistan, Russia, Thailand, and many others. If this blueprint assists other autocratic governments in maintaining control of their populaces, they become even easier for Beijing to work with—not only on economic or strategic issues but also on allowing Beijing to dominate their information pipes. Many of these autocratic or hybrid regimes, where civil society and independent journalism remain weak, are more likely than democracies to sign cooperation deals with Beijing to allow Chinese firms to build parts of their satellite or cable networks, develop large portions of their telecommunications infrastructure, and control their information pipes in other ways. So, Beijing is afforded greater opportunities to build out their information pipes. And greater control of information pipes facilitates the further spread of Chinese state media, like StarTimes favoring Chinese state media channels.

In addition, if more autocratic governments remain in power, and if more hybrid states like Ecuador or Zambia slip toward authoritarianism, these developments undermine democracy's spread worldwide. The more democracy falters or never truly develops in other countries, the easier it becomes for Beijing to claim that democratic governance is a failing model. To be sure, democracy's success or failure has much to do with domestic factors in most countries. But if Beijing's blueprint for high-tech authoritarianism undermines democracies, it adds fuel to today's global democratic recession.

Of course, states can come up with ideas for suppression on their own. And many Africans, and people in other regions like Latin America and Southeast Asia, welcome China's investment in mobile and fixed internet and the Internet of Things, even as they worry about the possibility that Beijing will use the infrastructure to spy on other countries, censor local media, promote false information, and export China's own repressive approach to the internet and surveillance.

In his study of China-Africa relations and the future of the internet in Africa, Iginio Gagliardone of the Oxford Internet Institute notes that repressive African governments do not necessarily need China's prompting to think about enacting technology-enabled authoritarianism to crack down on information and close their internets. (His argument holds true for repressive states outside of Africa as well.)

Many autocratic or hybrid African states, he notes, have been trying to repress information for years; the idea is not exactly new to places like Chad, Eritrea, Ethiopia, Mali, Sudan, Tanzania, or Zimbabwe, some of which are among the more repressive states in the world. Quite a few of these authoritarian regimes utilized the U.S.-led war on terrorism as rationales for repressive domestic measures, even before China began modernizing their information pipes and offering advice.[216] Still, China's technology and ideas, and Beijing's successes at home, bolster these states' abilities to dominate information. Beijing's efforts at controlling the internet far surpass anything most other authoritarian states had accomplished, and Chinese technology boosts the ability of repressive regimes to keep domestic internets censored.

Internet Governance

Beyond the physical pipes, Beijing (and Moscow) have won victories for themselves by building up their strength in global forums on the internet, but they also have become more influential as democracies have become less assertive in these arenas. Back in 2012, during a session of the International Telecommunication Union (ITU), the UN agency that handles global information issues, China, Russia, and several other states attempted to pass a resolution that would have supported the idea of cybersovereignty—of closed and national internets.[217] The resolution failed, as leading democracies together blocked it.

But Moscow and Beijing did not give up. China increased its attempts to use bilateral meetings with other countries to promote a closed, sovereign internet model.[218] The two authoritarian powers also agreed, during a major internet governance conference that Beijing holds each year in the eastern Chinese town of Wuzhen, to cooperate in battle against what they label "illegal online content."[219] What the two authoritarian powers decide is illegal remains somewhat unclear, but it obviously could include all sorts of online speech. Together, the two powers now use the annual meeting in Wuzhen, which has become a massive event, to lobby officials from other states to support closed, heavily controlled internets.[220] Xi himself has appeared at the summit, where he has called on attendees to support "the transformation of the global system of internet governance."[221]

The two powers also have bolstered their influence at the ITU, which has been headed since 2014 by Houlin Zhou, a Chinese citizen who worked for the Chinese government before moving to the ITU.[222] In recent years, the two authoritarian giants have gained an increasing number of supporters at the ITU for proposals favoring the idea of cybersovereignty. These proposals also usually call for the ITU and the United Nations to play a bigger role in setting global internet rules and norms.[223] Beijing has enjoyed success lobbying within the ITU because it has paid close attention to the organization and to other bodies that set standards for communications, as well as to UN technical agencies in general. (Chinese nationals now run four of the United Nations' fifteen specialized agencies, in part because Beijing sends senior officials to push for Chinese goals.[224]) Adam Segal of the Council on Foreign Relations notes that "over the last decade, Beijing has increased the skill, sophistication, and size of the delegations it sends to [internet and mobile network] standards organizations" and now often sends the biggest delegations of any participating country.[225] "Chinese policymakers," he notes, "believe they would have a larger say in regulating information technology and defining the global rules for cyberspace if the UN played a larger role in Internet governance."[226]

This belief makes sense. At least before the Ukraine war, China and Russia had gained a significant number of allies at the ITU, especially among developing countries, and many developing countries seem disinterested in the Ukraine conflict and willing to continue their support for Russia and China. It is easier for Beijing and Moscow to lobby governments at the ITU than it is for them to sway the diverse array of private companies, technical bodies, civil society groups, and some governments, who together historically have determined internet governance in a bottom-up manner.

If the ITU and thus the United Nations become more powerful in internet governance, Beijing will wield more influence—and its model could become ascendant.[227] Beijing is already using these governance structures to help divide the world into states with open internets and those with closed ones, and to win more converts to China's internet model. In early 2020, as the world was distracted by the novel coronavirus, China (allied with Russia and Saudi Arabia) quietly began using the ITU to push a major reordering of the global internet. Huawei, China's Ministry of Industry and Information Technology, and several major Chinese state tech companies together proposed, at the ITU, a new standard for internet network technology.[228] The changes proposed by the Chinese agencies and Chinese companies would potentially split apart the global internet and give more state internet service providers—and thus states themselves—far more control over how people use the internet, and over their data.[229]

What Works: Xinhua

We have discussed Xinhua's reach and potential power at length already. Xinhua, alone among China's biggest state media outlets, has expanded dramatically while also boosting its global audience and gaining significant credibility. It has inked many content-sharing deals, including for stories in languages other than Chinese. It is likely that, in the next decade, with the COVID-19 pandemic forcing some news outlets to cut staff, and with media outlets suffering financially from eviscerated advertising revenues, the appeal of signing deals with Xinhua, a cheap or free newswire, will only increase.[230] Indeed, Xinhua could become China's most powerful information weapon.

By 2022, Xinhua had not yet forged enough connections with editors at the most prestigious international publications to consistently write the first draft of global news stories. Since many major global outlets like the BBC and the *New York Times* do not regularly use Xinhua stories, distrusting the newswire's independence and accuracy, these Xinhua stories do not circulate in international news coverage as widely as those of the Associated Press or Reuters. But that may be changing rapidly, as Xinhua expands. On some occasions, in places where it has a massive manpower advantage, like Southeast Asia and, of course, China itself, Xinhua is beating competitors to stories or is covering stories that competitors do not have the resources to cover. As Xinhua grows and other newswires struggle financially, the Chinese newswire likely will get to more stories first—and may earn editors' and publishers' trust.

Eventually, if governments and news organizations do not put roadblocks in its place, Xinhua copy will appear in more and more news outlets, shaping public and elite opinion in countries, as it already does in places like Thailand. A range of evidence shows Xinhua's growth in size and influence. The Lowy Institute's maps of digital influence in Asia show that Xinhua is making inroads across the region. Indeed, the maps show that Xinhua has become the second most influential news agency regionally, behind only the Associated Press, and that Xinhua is making significant gains in influence in the media environment of several Northeast Asian and Southeast Asian states.[231]

Notably, media outlets have been signing deals to carry Xinhua even in countries where the U.S. government and private nonprofits hailing from democratic states have invested heavily in promoting the creation of a vibrant local media. In Afghanistan, for instance, where donors including the United States have plowed money into the local media, an IFJ report shows that Xinhua has inked contracts with twenty-five to thirty Afghan media outlets. These deals include ones with some of the biggest television stations and websites in the country.[232]

The IFJ report notes that China's content-sharing deals have helped reshape journalists' messaging about Beijing in multiple countries, including those known for robust local journalism. Its survey of Philippine journalists found that China's increasingly close links with the Philippines' state television, the Philippine News Agency, and the Philippine Information Agency, built through content-sharing and training programs, are having an effect on Philippine news outlets' coverage of China, even though the Philippine population remains highly distrustful of Beijing and the country still has a relatively robust domestic media.[233]

Indeed, China's closer links to Philippine media, and the spreading use of Xinhua in the Philippines, are depriving Philippine news consumers of independent reporting on Beijing. These shifts are depriving Filipinos of independent coverage *even as* Beijing squeezes the Philippines in the South China Sea, and even though the population as a whole in the Philippines has not become markedly more pro-China. "The way they write their stories now, they reflect the way how Xinhua or how the state media in China is writing their stories," one [Philippine] journalist told IFJ. "It's normally propaganda."[234] Another told IFJ, "Instead of getting insights on journalism from free countries like the United States, United Kingdom, Western Europe and even Japan, they [journalists in the Philippines] are learning state control."[235]

Xinhua is gaining readership in many states through such content-sharing deals, or simply because more news outlets are choosing to use Xinhua stories. And as Xinhua buys access and gets into more websites, newspapers, and magazines, its stories will become as ubiquitous as those of the Associated Press. Then Xinhua will be able to shape even more of the world's news coverage.

Chapter 12

A Path Forward

Pushing Back Against China's Information and Influence Activities

A Shifting Task

When I started researching this book in 2017, China's information and influence efforts were receiving little media coverage and only a modest amount of interest from policymakers. The tectonic shifts in global politics sparked by Brexit, the election of Donald Trump, shifts in the U.S. posture toward many traditional allies, and the resurgence of Russia and Russian influence activities were front and center in news reports and in policymakers' minds.

But in the past five years, countries from the United States to Australia to Germany to Singapore to Taiwan have become increasingly concerned about the threat of Chinese media and information strategies. They also have become much more worried about China's traditional influence efforts: the United Front Work Department (UFWD) courting ethnic Chinese; Beijing paying politicians in foreign states or otherwise influencing them to act on China's behalf; China's growing relationship with Russia and use of Russian tactics; China's growing assertiveness toward Taiwan; and China shaping discourse on China within university campuses, in Hollywood, among major multinational corporations, and among leading multilateral organizations, in part through massively increased spending.[1] According to a report by the Center for Responsive Politics, which was able to draw on heightened U.S. transparency about foreign influence spending, Chinese spending on foreign agents in the United States—state media and other information, lobbyists, and other types of foreign agents— grew from around $10 million in 2016 to around $64 million in 2020, making China the biggest spender of any country on foreign influence operations inside the United States.[2]

By 2022, at the time of writing, the U.S. Congress had passed a bill, signed by the president, designed to support the U.S. semiconductor industry and thus potentially reduce Beijing's control of information pipes.[3]

As we have seen, several European governments, meanwhile, are beefing up their knowledge of China's information and influence activities by tasking their intelligence agencies to investigate Chinese information and influence activities. In March 2021, the largest grouping in the European Parliament, the center-right Group of the European People's Party, released a strategy paper on Europe's relations with China that highlighted, among other things, the need to confront Chinese influence operations in Europe, the need for a more effective means of screening foreign investment into Europe including Chinese investment in European media firms, and the need for "an EU-wide regulatory system to prevent media companies either funded or controlled by governments to acquire European media companies."[4] The strategy paper also suggested multiple other ways to counter Chinese disinformation, provide greater transparency to Chinese borrowed and bought boats, and combat Chinese influence efforts.[5] Some European states already have adopted these recommendations.

Europe also put on hold a major investment deal with China, due to concerns about China's increasingly aggressive diplomacy, its behavior toward Taiwan, the need to screen investments into Europe, and Beijing's rights abuses in places like Hong Kong and Xinjiang. China further began to lose the support of traditional allies in Europe, like trade groups in Germany and other countries. Some European states, along with the United States and Taiwan, began working to limit China's access to certain types of semiconductors—a move that gained particular speed after the China-Taiwan crisis in the summer and fall of 2022.

The COVID-19 crisis provided Beijing an opportunity to demonstrate global leadership—but also has increased many foreign leaders' suspicions of how China uses information in dangerous ways.[6] Indeed, Chinese leaders seemed to see the COVID-19 crisis, the bungling of the response in the United States, and the subsequent unrest over systemic racism in the United States as a turning point in global affairs, one that could leave the door ajar for another country to take the place of the United States and cement China's rise to global leadership. But we have seen that China's own actions during COVID-19—spreading disinformation, covering up the initial outbreak, using "wolf warrior" diplomacy to lash out at other states and then add economic coercion, revelations of major problems and inequalities in Belt and Road Initiative (BRI) deals that countries now struggled to repay, and then China's disastrous zero-COVID strategy in 2021 and 2022—badly damaged its global reputation. The Ukraine war, and China's role in it, and then the Taiwan crisis, has further soured many states on Beijing.

By 2022, when I was completing this book, many states, shocked at the penetration of Chinese influence efforts, were recognizing that Beijing was investing heavily in both soft and sharp power tools and that China's public messaging had become more sophisticated than it was in the 1990s or 2000s. As we have seen in previous chapters, many countries have begun to respond assertively to China's actions.

So, the task in assessing China's information and influence activities has changed in part from what it was in 2016 or 2017. Policymakers in many regions are beginning to recognize the threat of Beijing's expanding media, information, and traditional influence actions. They are starting to take some actions against China's efforts, such as the United Kingdom and some other European countries taking outlets like the China Global Television Network (CGTN) off the air, Australia heightening scrutiny of China's investment in media and information in the country, the United States forcing Chinese state outlets to register as foreign agents, or the leading group in the European Parliament calling for much tougher measures against Chinese influence and information activities.[7]

Yet many of these countries still have only a rough grasp on the extent of China's information tools and a limited idea of how well Beijing is using its information and influence toolkit. Even more important, they often actually overestimate Beijing's successes so far and yet remain at the same time unprepared for China to adapt and improve in the future. This book, by looking in part at China's information and influence efforts in its initial targets in Asia, and also in part at how Beijing is expanding those efforts globally, helps provide guideposts for how political leaders and civil society leaders should respond to China's information and influence tactics.

Foreign states for one need to *build a broader, deeper base* of knowledge of China's information, media, and influence campaigns. But they also should improve at *assessing which of Beijing's tools right now are ineffective and which are effective* and then try to *predict* ways in which China will have success in the future. As we have seen, China has often failed in many, though not all, of its current media and information efforts and created a blowback against it. Yet in some states policymakers do not seem to grasp how China has failed in many of its information and influence efforts. No country can combat all of China's tools, and it makes little sense to spend extensive resources battling Chinese tools that are currently ineffective.

Policymakers and other opinion leaders thus should improve at analyzing which Chinese information strategies work and do not work today and communicating China's real failures on many fronts. They also *should improve at "pre-butting" disinformation* spread by China, in the way that the Biden administration successfully predicted and pre-butted disinformation it believed the Kremlin was about to release justifying an invasion of Ukraine. At the same time, policymakers and other opinion leaders should learn how Beijing is adapting, why China will become more proficient in using its information and influence tools in the future, and *how to prepare* for China to become more successful. Countries should *bolster their defenses* against greater Chinese information and influence success in the future, while also *going on the offensive* with their own soft—and sometimes sharp—power efforts now, while China is still often struggling with its media and information efforts.

From the United States to the European Union to Japan to the Philippines, this offensive may require reinvesting in tools like state-sponsored media, diplomatic corps, exchange programs for foreign opinion leaders, and other areas whose budgets have been gutted in recent years. Finally, countries pushing back against China's information and influence efforts should *contrast* their own strengths with Beijing's continuing weaknesses.

Build a Better Knowledge Base

Political and business leaders throughout the world still need to know more about Beijing's media, information, and traditional influence efforts. In particular, in all responses to China's information and influence efforts, politicians and civil society leaders from democracies need to collaborate with their counterparts in other democracies, sharing research, analysis, and responses to China's actions. Since many of China's sharp power efforts increasingly resemble Russian efforts to promote divisions between democracies and disunity within democracies (and have become even closer to Russian responses in the wake of the Ukraine war), responses to Chinese information and influence efforts should ideally come from democracies working together. This type of collaboration will strengthen democracies' resilience to sharp power efforts and build better collaborative comprehension of soft and sharp power tactics and effects.[8]

For one, countries should develop a better understanding of how the big state media outlets are run, both from Beijing and in foreign bureaus—and particularly how they use content-sharing deals with local outlets to get Xinhua, CGTN, and China Radio International (CRI) stories into the local Chinese-language and vernacular press. Xinhua should be the focus, most of all, as it has the most potential for success. They also should conduct more regular, thorough assessments of the reach and popularity of China's biggest global state media outlets. These assessments should be made public. In the United States, these assessments could be released as part of the annual reports of the U.S.-China Economic and Security Review Commission or as annual reports released by the U.S. Agency for Global Media (USAGM). As of this writing, the U.S. Congress bill designed to confront China contained within it a fund for countering Chinese influence efforts, but it remained unclear—if the money for this fund even was appropriated—how the fund would be utilized.[9] In some drafts of the bill, Congress proposed establishing a Social Media Data and Threat Analysis Center, within the Office of the Director of National Intelligence, to detect and study Chinese information and influence operations in state media and social media, and also supported other U.S. government agencies conducting further research into Beijing's state media and social media activities globally.[10] One effective use of such a threat analysis center, and such research, would be to use its research to release an annual report on the reach and popularity—or, often, unpopularity—of China's biggest global state media outlets. These studies could be shared with democratic partners, and other leading democracies could conduct their own assessments of the reach and popularity of China's major state media outlets. Together, this research, developed to include a comprehensive set of variables that would analyze the extent of China's media activities and assess the ways in which they have (or have not) transformed local media environments and affected politics and civil society in other countries, could produce a more complete picture of how Chinese state media operate and whether they are gaining traction globally.[11]

Such studies—which would show the reality of how much audience share Chinese state outlets are actually obtaining in various countries—will be critical for understanding whether Beijing's soft power efforts are gaining interest in various regions; so far, as we have seen, many of the state media outlets besides Xinhua are not gaining much traction, and China's COVID-19 response globally and its failures with its domestic COVID strategy, its aggressive diplomacy, its support for Russia, and its behavior toward Taiwan have only further undermined Beijing's soft power, even in regions like Southeast Asia where many people have had favorable views of Beijing in the past.[12] The studies, which should be shared widely among democracies, also should assess the extent to which the big state media outlets are benefiting from having their stories circulate on WeChat and other Chinese social media platforms and the extent to which internet searches for Chinese state media stories suggest interest in their coverage in various countries.

Right now, opinion leaders in many countries anxiously talk about the spread of Chinese state media, based on media reporting and a few academic studies. But they usually have no real, concrete studies of state media's audience share or how little audiences in various countries often trust CGTN, CRI, or other Chinese outlets. Funds from the U.S. Congress, the Japanese parliament, the European Union, individual European states, the Canadian government, and other democratic actors to conduct such in-depth research will be critical to understanding China's state media, as well as how Beijing uses social media to spread state media stories. These funds could be utilized to support government research into Chinese state media, and they also could flow to civil society organizations that have already done some of the most comprehensive state media research.

Recognize Ineffectiveness

What we have seen, however, and what greater research would probably show at this point is that other than Xinhua, most of the Chinese state media outlets have gained little traction in most parts of the world and that China's soft power, and some of its sharp power, has to date often been ineffective. To be sure, China has become a growing presence in most media markets, and this expansion has sped up in 2020, 2021, and 2022. A 2021 study by the International Federation of Journalists of journalism unions from around the globe found that "the percentage of nations reporting China to have a visible presence in their media ecosystems was up from 64 percent to 76 percent" between 2019 and 2020, though many of these media ecosystems were in countries with less free media environments.[13] To be sure, this ineffectiveness does not mean countries should avoid plowing money into studying Chinese state media and other information operations; by contrast, they should invest heavily in this research.

Still, as we have seen through the studies by Gallup and other analysts discussed here, while Chinese state media outlets have had a more visible presence in many media markets, they are not attracting many eyeballs or listeners. CGTN and CRI have barely made a dent in many markets, and further research would almost surely confirm this point. The experiences thus far of CGTN and CRI suggest that foreign countries need to be less worried about these outlets and their potential effectiveness and danger to accurate reporting and coverage in other countries—even a decade from now.

Even with massive resources, CGTN and CRI have had trouble reaching sizable audiences in most foreign countries, even developing countries, and their large followings on social media platforms like Facebook do not seem organic. For instance, a study of major Chinese state media Facebook pages, by Stanford's Cyber Policy center and using the tool Crowd tangle, found that CGTN and other Chinese state media outlets together had a staggering number of page likes on their Facebook pages—nearly one hundred million total among the outlets, in the period between December 31, 2019, and March 16, 2020.[14] But despite these supposed page likes, Chinese state media outlets paid for many ads that helped create impressions and likes on Facebook, casting into doubt these outlets' level of genuine interaction with real social media users.[15] (The same study found that most mainstream U.S. media outlets have far smaller numbers of page likes than Chinese state media outlets, and seemingly smaller audiences on Facebook, but the research I have presented previously in this book shows that these mainstream media outlets generally have a much higher percentage of actual audience interaction rates.[16]) Even populations in authoritarian developing countries have proven themselves mostly uninterested in CGTN and CRI; these outlets could adapt and gain wider audiences, but as we have seen they appear less well positioned to do so than Xinhua, even over the next decade, and thus likely will remain the weakest tools in China's media and information toolkit.

Some Chinese scholars and even officials seem to recognize that Beijing has not yet reached a significant audience with its attempts at building discourse power: An article written by Ministry of Foreign Affairs spokesperson Hua Chunying in the *Study Times*, the Chinese Communist Party (CCP) Central Party School's official paper, noted that China's "speaking power" globally remained weak and overmatched.[17] Hua's paper predated Xi's conciliatory speech in June 2021, suggesting that Beijing was actually gaining little discourse power and possibly alienating foreign audiences with its increasingly strident approach to information and diplomacy, though China's diplomacy afterward actually got more aggressive in dealing with democracies, and Xi seemed to approve of that wolf warrior continued style—which only ramped up during the Taiwan crisis.

Sure, CGTN, CRI, and *China Daily* are state media outlets, much of their content is propaganda-esque, and it is reasonable to have them register under laws like the U.S. Foreign Agents Registration Act or similar acts in other countries. It also is reasonable to continue to assess their reach to check whether their actual audience share is improving—but countries' resources would be better marshaled against other Chinese tools that have more proven effectiveness today and are likely to be effective in the future.

In addition, much—though not all—of these big state media out-lets' activities are overt and more transparent than those of the bought and borrowed boats, or of Chinese disinformation efforts. The big state media outlets' ratings can be measured and their audience share assessed; some of their budgets are accessible; their programming can be labeled clearly as state-linked media content.

With further reliable, regular information about how many viewers or listeners actually pay attention to the Chinese state media out-lets that have so far proven unable to gain much traction with for-eign audiences, the United States and other countries could more credibly assess whether CGTN and CRI are having any real effect in shaping public opinion abroad. The reports on CGTN, CRI, and *China Daily* should be made public. By making reports publicly ac-cessible, the United States or other leading democracies investing in such research, such as Canada, Australia, or European states, would be helping countries that wanted to analyze the real reach, or lack thereof, of CGTN or CRI or other Chinese state media but did not have the resources—or the political will—to do so.

So, if such research confirmed the current ineffectiveness of CGTN or CRI, policymakers' time would be better spent focusing on areas where Beijing is having success already: Xinhua, Xinhua's content-sharing deals, Beijing's de facto control of local Chinese-language outlets, and other Chinese tools like Beijing's attempts to control information pipes and, along with Russia, model a closed internet and a broader model of technology-enabled authoritarianism via international meetings, standards on internet governance, and other methods.

Focus on Effective Tools: Predict and Prepare

Countries desperately need to expand their knowledge of Chinese tools that are already working, to combat those that are working, and to prepare for them to be more effective in the future. Chinese leaders are authoritarian, but they are not completely isolated from feedback. China's ability to adapt its landmark BRI suggests that, in fact, Beijing is sometimes capable of responding to policy failures and external criticism and then shifting its policy tools.[18] Beijing has shifted its messaging around the BRI to attempt to downplay its global ambitions, working to highlight local benefits BRI projects bring to recipient countries, especially as some studies, like one released by AidData, showed that many of China's BRI contracts contained troubling clauses.[19] According to AidData, China's contracts "contain unusual confidentiality clauses that bar borrowers from revealing the terms or even the existence of the debt. Second, Chinese lenders seek advantage over other creditors, using collateral arrangements such as lender-controlled revenue accounts and promises to keep the debt out of collective restructuring ('no Paris Club' clauses). Third, cancellation, acceleration, and stabilization clauses in Chinese contracts potentially allow the lenders to influence debtors' domestic and foreign policies."[20]

Some BRI projects and programs themselves have shifted as well, from the initial emphasis on massive infrastructure projects to a newer focus on health aid (clearly a result in part of the COVID-19 pandemic), education including vocational training, technology as part of the Digital Silk Road, and other areas beyond hard infrastructure.[21]

And the BRI is hardly the only example of Chinese adaptation; Beijing has a history of adaptation. As China's soft power charm offensive faltered in the 2010s, Beijing changed tack and placed more emphasis on sharp power. Indeed, as we discussed throughout this story, by the end of this decade Beijing is likely to be much more successful in its influence and information efforts in Southeast Asia, and in many other parts of the world as well.

So, as Chinese leaders recognize which media and information tools are most effective, and as some foreign states begin to respond, China is likely to adapt its information strategies, focusing on those that are most effective and jettisoning those that are failing and are alienating other countries.

To be sure, at least in the early 2020s a process of rapid adaptation that restores China's soft power, boosts its global image, gains interest in its state media beyond Xinhua, and upgrades its information operations is a high bar for Beijing to clear. As Xi essentially admitted in his June 2021 speech, China's global image has plummeted: Its mismanagement of COVID-19, its wolf warrior diplomacy including hyperaggressive Foreign Ministry spokesman Zhao Lijian, its military adventurism near Taiwan and in the South China Sea, and its too-blunt information and disinformation campaigns have soured many countries on Beijing, at least for now. As we have seen, this has led to real ramifications beyond declining global opinion of Beijing, including Chinese companies' loss of major contracts abroad, the suspension of the China-Australia Strategic Economic Dialogue, the holdup of Chinese trade deals with Europe and other entities, a military buildup by countries in Southeast Asia and a shift by some of them toward Washington, and many other consequences.

Indeed, it is an open question whether Chinese diplomats, Chinese information warriors, and Chinese state media will adapt and made inroads at boosting China's global image once again. Xi has continued to issue tough speeches and has made an arrangement with Russia just short of an alliance, while China has essentially isolated itself from the world via its zero-COVID strategy. And as multiple analysts have noted, the wolf warrior diplomacy is highly popular among the Chinese public and in some ways may be an outgrowth of a more assertive, even hyperaggressive strain of Chinese nationalism; reining it in would mean taking apart an approach that enjoys wide public support in China.[22] In addition, the wolf warrior style, as well as the often overly blunt information and disinformation campaigns, has spread throughout China's diplomatic corps, information warriors, and other officials, also making it harder for Xi to rapidly roll back. As researchers Yaoyao Dai and Luwei Rose Luqiu showed, the percentage of "combative" Chinese foreign ministry speeches more than doubled between 2012 and the late 2010s.[23] This ethos has become engrained in Chinese diplomats—and they lambasted the new senior Biden administration officials in the first major U.S.-China bilateral meeting in Alaska in early 2021; they have come to understand that this type of diplomacy is viewed favorably by the top Chinese leadership.[24]

After all, any large bureaucracy—in China, or in a democratic country—is by nature hard to change. And in an authoritarian system in which policy can change rapidly for lower-ranking officials without them being consulted in any serious manner, many officials will be reluctant to change course, even though top leader Xi has spoken, until they feel fully comfortable that the wind might not blow back the other way. After all, in post-1949 China policy has changed, and then changed back again, many times, with those that adhered to the first policy shift brutally punished, such as during the punishments meted out to officials who spoke openly during the Hundred Flowers Campaign.

But over the next decade, China might be able to adapt, especially if the pandemic is eventually controlled around the world, memories of China's initial role in it fade somewhat, the Xi administration invests more in subtler types of disinformation and information, and Beijing pulls back some of its most aggressive diplomats and comes out of the Ukraine war without its reputation completely tarnished. As we discussed earlier, despite Xi's centralization of control, which does indeed hinder Chinese diplomacy and media and information efforts, it has shown adaptability in other policy areas. Beijing is likely to invest significantly more time and money in improving its information and influence efforts, probably with Russia's help, and Beijing's growing economic might will put it in a position to build—and control—more of the information pipes around the world.

In addition, the global shift away from democracy and toward authoritarianism, and major democracies' focus on their own domestic challenges, likely will make it easier for Beijing to bolster its information and influence campaigns between now and 2030—and to promote its model of technology-enabled authoritarianism. Beijing also will continue to learn from Russia, which is teaching China about more sophisticated disinformation strategies. (Democracies' unity in the Ukraine conflict does not, alas, conceal major problems domestically in democracies like the United States, France, South Korea, and the United Kingdom, among others.) And the continuing financial distress of most media outlets worldwide, in developed and developing countries—unless, of course, they are supported by significant new cash infusions from U.S., European, or other funds to support independent media, or figure out other ways to make revenues—could provide further opportunities for Beijing to convince editors and publishers to use free or discounted Chinese content from Xinhua. The financial distress also could provide significant opportunities for companies or individuals with CCP ties to purchase financially insolvent local media outlets and alter their coverage.

Bought Boats and Training Programs

States and independent researchers should focus on studying bought boats—of who actually owns their biggest domestic media outlets, including those in local languages and those in foreign languages—and on devising ways to prevent China from gaining more bought boats. Countries with sizable Chinese-speaking populations—Australia and New Zealand, Europe and North America, and Southeast Asia—also should analyze how China will adapt and expand its control over local Chinese-language media via bought boats, and how much better Beijing may become at dominating the messaging and reporting of local Chinese-language media in many parts of the world.

Such scrutiny could not be applied only to ownership of Chinese-language outlets. Such a decision would potentially be perceived as racist, and also would exclude important information, since countries should want to know who owns any major media outlets, and companies with Chinese state links, or individuals with close ties to the CCP, increasingly are investing in media in languages other than Chinese.

In most countries today, if policymakers want to understand who owns domestic media outlets, they have to rely on a patchwork of business licensing agreements, corporate and regulatory filings, research by academics and think tank experts, and news outlets' own reporting on media ownership. Yet these bought boats, in particular, have allowed Beijing to dominate the Chinese-language media market in many states, and to make inroads into local-language and English-language markets as well. In Australia, for instance, the fact that major domestic Chinese-language outlets have been purchased by individuals in partnership with Chinese state firms, or have developed sourcing agreements with Chinese state media, was revealed by investigative reporting by Australian media companies.[25] Even in places with extensive knowledge of China, like Taiwan, it is usually researchers, like media specialist He Qinglian, who have dug the deepest into Chinese ownership of local media outlets.[26]

To better understand who now owns major domestic media outlets, governments should expend more resources studying the ownership structure of the one hundred biggest outlets in their country, calculated by revenues, including certainly those in Chinese. This could be done by contracting out studies to some of the same researchers who have been doing work on these issues independently, to tap their knowledge and also ensure that governments were not seen as snooping on domestic journalism companies. The United States and other large democracies also could task at least one diplomat in each U.S. embassy to focus primarily on Chinese information and influence efforts, and also should become more willing to share such reporting on China's efforts with diplomats from other leading democracies.

In short, governments should treat the media and information sector as one of critical national security importance and apply to it the same scrutiny they apply to ownership of companies in areas like aviation and defense. Greater scrutiny would make it easier for national communications agencies, if allowed by law, to demand that media companies be forthcoming about foreign ownership stakes.[27] After all, as we have seen, in places like Australia, Hong Kong, Taiwan, Thailand, or the United States, Chinese state companies do not necessarily invest in local media outlets, though this does sometimes happen; they often exert de facto control of local Chinese-language media outlets because individuals with links to the CCP sit on boards or in high positions of editorial management. And even if governments ultimately do not impose new limitations on foreign investment in media and information sectors, this research could at least foster transparency and greater awareness about who actually controls Chinese-language media outlets and other media companies. Most democracies could not stop such outlets from covering China favorably or writing pro-Beijing editorials any more than they could stop them from writing editorials critical or favorable toward any country.[28] But at least sunlight would be shed on who really owns these media companies.

How to create greater transparency and awareness? Governments that already have commissions designed to assess foreign investments in their countries—like the Committee on Foreign Investment in the United States or Australia's Foreign Investment Review Board—should task those commissions with closely scrutinizing new investments in media and information.[29] If such commissions do not already include strict scrutiny of foreign ownership and investment in media and information, they should include this scrutiny in the future. Countries that do not have such commissions should create them—not only for media and information but also for other sectors of importance to national security. It is certainly possible that the Ukraine war, and the recognition by many countries of the massive reach of Russian state media and other information operations, and China's actions toward Taiwan, may lead countries to create such commissions for all types of sectors critical to national security.

Beyond the United States, Australia, and a few other countries, some democracies seem to be realizing that they need to consider media and information a critical sector and apply strict scrutiny to foreign investment. Indeed, many European politicians have stated that the European Union and individual European states should adopt such measures; a group of EU lawmakers in 2021 produced a report encouraging the European Union to "develop an EU-wide regulatory system to prevent media companies either funded or controlled by governments to acquire European media companies."[30]

But in many cases, media outlets and information companies already have foreign owners, or simply have local owners with strong sympathies toward the Chinese government. This is not illegal anywhere, but it can become problematic in terms of coverage of Beijing. So, it falls to civil society—other news outlets, media watchdogs, individual politicians, and academics—to scrutinize how local publications, in Chinese and local languages, cover Beijing, and whether this coverage shifts over time, and why. Policymakers can help promote this scrutiny by funding research—via universities or other institutions—into how the local media, including the Chinese-language media, cover Chinese foreign and domestic policy. And leading democracies can support civil society and research organizations in other countries that monitor local media, and independent media outlets that cover local news, including China's local influence.

New Media and Asymmetric Media Responses

Policymakers also should support new media outlets that target China's borrowed and bought boats—both by providing independent news coverage of China and sometimes by exposing how Beijing has come to control outlets in various countries. Democracies, like Australia, Singapore, Taiwan, or the United States, could offer broadcasting—independent Chinese-language programming available in other countries—to serve as an alternative to Beijing's state media and to local Chinese-language outlets that have been taken over or co-opted by Beijing.

This creation of independent Chinese-language outlets would be an asymmetric way to take on China's borrowed and bought boats, a way not just to protect countries from China taking over Chinese-language media but to offer specific and proactive alternatives to Beijing's dominance of such media. In addition, the United States and other countries could create funds to support investigative journalism and independent media in general, such as digital start-ups that examine Chinese influence activities, in countries in Asia and other regions where Beijing is wielding more influence.[31]

One idea, in the U.S. context, would be for the U.S. Agency for International Development (USAID) to create a major global fund to support independent media, which would focus on developing country-independent media outlets.[32] USAID and other donors also could boost support for media literacy campaigns in foreign countries, which will help media consumers understand better where they get their news from.[33] European states also should heavily support such a fund. Indeed, as some European politicians have suggested, the European Union should create a European Democratic Media Fund designed to support independent journalists around the world, including those investigating Chinese rights abuses, influence activities, and information activities.[34]

As we have seen, just a few such independent outlets in places like Taiwan already have proven important voices for factual, tough reporting on China, which has proven critical for Taiwan in 2022.[35] Offering sizable new U.S., European, or other sources of funds from leading democracies to independent media, even if these outlets do not specifically scrutinize China, simply reduces the financial burden on media companies and makes them potentially less likely to have to turn to using Xinhua or other Chinese content.[36] Indeed, other major donors like Japan and Australia should back a global fund to support independent media in developing countries.

Research into content-sharing deals could be accompanied by a more thorough study of China's journalism training programs, which have been modestly effective thus far. These could include efforts to quantify the number of foreign journalists being trained in China and to obtain detailed information on the actual programming and coursework of these trainings. A more thorough analysis, supported by democratic governments and conducted by civil society organizations, would help policymakers assess whether they are really steering foreign reporters and editors toward more favorable coverage of China and having any effect on press freedom within other countries. Reports from attendees of these training programs, and initial research on these training programs, by Maria Repnikova of Georgia State University and reported in the *Washington Post*, suggest that China's trainings have had little effect on journalists returning to their home countries, but more study of the expanding training programs, once they get started again in China after China reopens to the world, is necessary, as some reports suggest that programs for Indonesian journalists are having an effect in prompting journalists to adopt more pro-China viewpoints.[37]

Xinhua

States also need to expand their knowledge of the ways in which Xinhua has gained audiences in other countries by signing content-sharing deals. As we have seen, Xinhua has already become quite effective. It has been more effective at reaching a broad audience than any other major Chinese state media outlet, and foreign policymakers should learn much more detailed information about Xinhua's global expansion.

Xinhua will almost certainly become even more powerful over the next decade as well. In my projection, of the big Chinese state media outlets, foreign states are most vulnerable to Xinhua, which could be an increasingly influential newswire, with content increasingly available in many local news outlets, a growing staff, and an increasing number of content-sharing deals with high-quality local outlets in other countries.

Developing states, and particularly those in Africa, Southeast Asia, and parts of Eastern Europe, are some of the most vulnerable to the growing influence of Xinhua, since they have few restrictions on content-sharing deals, and since editors and publishers in these regions seem most willing to sign content-sharing deals with Xinhua. Xinhua may well become a central plank of news stories in countries in these regions, as more and more news outlets rely on Xinhua—which is hardly independent from Beijing—for articles on a wide range of topics. Governments in these countries, local journalism organizations, and editors and publishers need to apply much stricter scrutiny to content-sharing deals with Xinhua and think twice about whether they want to have local news outlets increasingly rely on Xinhua articles.

States thus should try to prevent Xinhua from gaining ground on other newswires and from being legitimized as a news source with credibility comparable to other newswires with real editorial independence. Countries should take every measure possible to limit Xinhua's expansion, its content-sharing deals, and its legitimization as a quality news source. Policymakers, of course, cannot stop news organizations from subscribing to Xinhua, especially in developing countries where news outlets have few resources and Xinhua may be offered for free. But they can try to delegitimize Xinhua—to remind the world that Xinhua is not an independent source of news coverage. Foreign officials and diplomats should highlight Xinhua's state background and how it serves a dual function as a CCP intelligence agency.

Experts on China and on media freedom also should commit to this battle. Media watchdog groups, from Germany to Thailand to the United States, should highlight Xinhua's background and expose news organizations that sign content-sharing deals with Xinhua. Further, they should pressure such outlets to drop these deals and prod editors not to hire journalists who previously worked at Xinhua.

Highlighting Xinhua's state background can help prevent the newswire from hiring quality local journalists and might dissuade editors from using its stories. In an analysis of the CCP's increasing international media presence, Sarah Cook of Freedom House notes that "professional journalists and informed audiences in many countries" are not necessarily attracted to Chinese state outlets when their official origins are exposed.[38] She notes, "In Peru, Xinhua failed to market its services to the country's main privately owned outlets, reportedly because they felt uneasy accepting content, even free of charge, from a foreign state-run news agency."[39] Similarly, in some of the freest Southeast Asian states, like Indonesia, news outlets also are reluctant to use Xinhua content because editors distrust Xinhua's origins. Meanwhile, leading independent newswires, like the Associated Press, should refuse to cooperate with Xinhua, other than on the most essential issues.

Information Pipes and Governance

China already has had some success using its growing control of information pipes and influence at international internet meetings to control the flow of information, and the narratives about China, in some states. As Beijing potentially builds out more of the world's information pipes, its power to use these pipes to shape discourse will grow, and policymakers need to prepare to combat China's control of information pipes.

Countries should take several steps to reduce China's potential control over the pipes that carry information, including wireless networks, satellite television networks, social media platforms, and internet bodies. To be fair, many governments have taken more steps against Chinese control of information pipes than they have against other aspects of China's information apparatus. The United States and some other countries skeptical of Huawei's growing global influence have devoted significant intelligence and judicial resources to studying the company.[40] The Federal Bureau of Investigation (FBI) and other law enforcement agencies have focused on China as what FBI Director Christopher Wray has called a "whole-of-state" threat, including China's potential control of information pipes; even with the ending of the FBI's China Initiative, it will continue this intense focus on China.[41] In addition, many governments have begun closely monitoring China's surveillance technology exports. The United States also has passed legislation that restricts technology purchases from Huawei and other Chinese companies and moved to restrict sales by U.S. companies of technology and equipment to companies that do business with Huawei and to stop federal agencies from buying from any company that uses Huawei and several other Chinese companies' equipment.[42] The congressional bill also supports helping U.S. firms split from their reliance on any Chinese technology by providing significant amounts of government support for semiconductor research and development and production, as well as research into other new technologies where China is gaining edges.

The U.S. government has also led a campaign to persuade many allies to bar Huawei components from 5G networks. While this has yielded mixed results as of the writing of this book, at least globally, it has had significant effects in Europe and parts of Asia and among many other democracies around the world, severely crimping Huawei's business in many important markets. The United Kingdom has banned purchases of new Huawei equipment for 5G networks.[43] The European Union has heightened scrutiny of Huawei, and multiple European countries already have banned Huawei from their networks or are considering banning Huawei from their 5G networks. (Huawei has been more successful at continuing to win contracts in Africa and some other developing regions, though it also has lost contracts in key states in Southeast Asia in 2021 and 2022.) These measures, though tough, are reasonable, as allowing Huawei to build telecommunications networks raises vast potential security problems. Indeed, one analysis suggests that Huawei has in recent years lost most of the new 5G contracts up for bid in Europe to Ericsson—and is losing significant market share globally both as a telecommunications equipment maker and as a smartphone maker.[44] Its chip developer is also struggling, since it lost some access to supplier Taiwan Semiconductor Manufacturing Company because of U.S. export controls, and as the United States has prodded the Dutch company that makes the machines that produce the most complex semiconductors not to sell these machines to China.[45] Perhaps recognizing these barriers, Huawei has sold its budget cell phone line to another Chinese company, is trying to beef up its own domestic chip-making abilities, and is focusing on other areas of development in Europe.[46] Still, this decline in Huawei's networking equipment contracts shows heightened scrutiny is already having a significant effect.

Meanwhile, the Trump White House took actions to neuter WeChat and TikTok within the United States. And even though the Biden administration revoked the WeChat and TikTok executive orders, which had already been delayed by court challenges, the Biden White House issued an order requiring the Commerce Department to launch a wide-ranging investigation into "apps with ties to foreign adversaries that may pose a risk to American data privacy or national security," according to tech publication the *Verge*. One U.S. official told the *Verge* that this investigation obviously would focus in some part on China, saying, "The challenge that we're addressing with this Executive Order is that certain countries, including China, do not share these commitments or values and are instead working to leverage digital technologies and American data in ways that present unacceptable national security risks."[47]

Thus, WeChat and TikTok still could be banned or, in the case of TikTok, forced to be divested from Chinese parent ByteDance; the Biden administration seems increasingly suspicious that TikTok is truly free of Chinese government influence. The Trump administration also launched the Clean Network Program to prevent any Chinese technology from being used within the U.S. telecommunications system.[48] In defending its actions, the Trump White House argued that TikTok or WeChat could amass personal data about Americans and send it to the Chinese government. The Trump administration also noted it was concerned that these apps could be used to spread disinformation within the United States. As we have seen, other democracies concerned about the influence of Chinese social media platforms, like India, have banned TikTok and WeChat.[49]

Despite this pressure and serious inroads against Huawei in providing 5G technology, in many cases leading democracies still struggle to convince developing states, and even some other developed countries, to take tough measures against China's control of information pipes—but not because little is known about Beijing's actions, though more certainly could be known. They have struggled in developing countries in particular because the technologies China provides—in 5G, in surveillance technology, and in other realms—are cheap and effective, and countries like the United States have squandered diplomatic capital in other ways unrelated to China. Huawei operates in over 170 countries today and is reportedly making more research and development investments than any other company in the world.[50] Despite the pressure on it from Washington, London, and some other capitals, Huawei continues to sign new deals to build countries' 5G infrastructure, though it has been weakened in some of the biggest markets in the world.[51]

Still, policymakers should not stop scrutinizing and trying to regulate Chinese satellite networks, wireless networks, and social media platforms, especially as China becomes more powerful in its control of information pipes over the next decade, and also developing industrial policies to help support production of new technologies essential to 5G and other high-tech areas. U.S. policymakers should continue trying to limit Huawei's ability to expand its 5G networks, such as by cutting off Huawei's access to global chip manufacturers, banning other Chinese technologies from military use in the United States, and pressuring foreign militaries not to use Chinese surveillance technology or install apps for Chinese social media platforms on any military communications technology.

Policymakers also should focus on how China, often working with Russia, uses international internet conferences and the United Nations to promote its agenda of a closed and filtered internet. Chinese and Russian collaboration in these forums is almost surely going to expand in the next decade, as the two authoritarian powers have increasingly converged in their approach to the internet in the wake of the Ukraine war, and also worked more closely together on disinformation efforts; we have seen China aggressively sharing Russian disinformation about Ukraine.[52] As a National Endowment for Democracy study of Chinese and Russian approaches to the internet notes, the two countries have concentrated their cooperation at the United Nations and UN-related organizations, where they are promoting their norms on closed internets and cybersovereignty, and the two powers likely will increase this cooperation.[53]

In response, democracies need to step up their game at major internet forums, and at other UN forums as well. Democracies too often have ignored bodies like the International Telecommunication Union (ITU), allowing autocrats like China and Russia to use these organizations to promote their views of closed, sovereign internets. Washington often has failed to offer the developing countries that make up much of the ITU a clear vision for future internet governance. To compete at the ITU and other forums, leading democracies will have to work together, pay much closer attention to the decisions being made at these bodies, and develop common goals, like ensuring that resolutions do not pass advocating for sovereign internets. They also should make protecting a free and open internet a central goal of their foreign policies and of their rights advocacy.

At the same time, leading democracies can model free and open internets at home, combating disinformation while maintaining free discourse. In so doing, they can show countries around the world that could be swayed by China or Russia why a free and open internet is best for commerce, culture, and business. A free and open internet helps promote innovation and connect businesses to peers in other countries, and generally provides predictability in the business environment.[54]

Democracies thus should stop undercutting their efforts to promote internet freedom. They are undercutting themselves in several ways. Prominent democratic leaders like French President Emmanuel Macron have called for controls on the internet to battle extremism— Macron used a global forum on the internet to issue what seemed to be a call for greater policing of the web.[55] Bangladesh, India, Indonesia, Singapore, and developing democracies have shut down the internet in portions of their country for periods of time or imposed new restrictions on internet content—restrictions that have only gotten tougher as democracies battle the novel coronavirus pandemic. As democracies themselves become more skeptical of internet freedom, they hinder their ability to lobby, globally, for a free and open internet; instead, they should collaborate to support a globally free and open internet.

In the United States too, Washington is undercutting its promotion of global internet freedom by presiding over declining online openness at home. According to Freedom House, online freedom in the United States declined for three straight years between 2016 and 2019.[56] It notes that this decline occurred because of growing online surveillance of the public by law enforcement agencies and the increasing spread of disinformation on U.S. social media not only by foreign actors but also by domestic ones.[57] Again, democracies' own self-inflicted wounds are making it easier for China (and Russia) to promote closed internet models and wield sharp power via the internet and social media.

Disinformation

States should prepare for Beijing to move more thoroughly toward Russian-style disinformation tactics, which China already has previewed during the pandemic, the Ukraine war, and the Taiwan crisis, and generally to utilize less clumsy, more organic, and more skillful types of disinformation over the next decade. Right now, intelligence sharing on China's disinformation efforts remains scattershot, especially among countries in Asia most affected by such tactics. (Singapore and Taiwan are notable exceptions.) Most countries have done minimal analysis of disinformation on WeChat and TikTok. The United States and other countries also have only begun to examine the ways in which Chinese and Russian disinformation efforts may be building upon each other and coordinating with each other, though this analysis has stepped up since the Ukraine conflict.

The United States could lead an effort to promote intelligence sharing on China's disinformation efforts, but such an effort will require significant (if quiet) cooperation from Australia, India, Indonesia, Japan, Malaysia, Singapore, South Korea, and Taiwan, among others. These other countries are just as, if not more, exposed to Chinese disinformation efforts than the United States. Several, including Singapore and Taiwan, already have built up significant intelligence-gathering methods about Chinese disinformation efforts, so their input would be vital, as they have learned a great deal about China's efforts that could be shared with Taiwan and Singapore's partners.[58]

States also should aggressively combat China's increasingly wide-spread use of disinformation. Responding to Beijing's growing use of aggressive disinformation, governments should put more pressure on social media platforms to research the activities of state-backed disinformation agents and publicly release information about these disinformation activities. Facebook, Twitter, and other major social media platforms have increased their staffing for studying disinformation and banned some state actors like some coming from Russia, but it is far from enough to deter the disinformation efforts of major state-backed actors, especially those from China. Governments cannot compel private companies to hire people, but if the major social media platforms do not devote more thorough efforts to researching state-backed disinformation, releasing reporting about state-backed disinformation operatives, and aggressively banning such operatives, governments could use public hearings and legislation to shame social media companies to take such steps.[59] Despite their massive capitalization, enormous reach, and significant lobbying operations, the social media platforms are clearly worried about expanded government regulation, and so might respond to more aggressive public hearings.

Twitter and Facebook both already have taken some important steps toward self-regulation. Twitter has banned state-owned media from paying to promote tweets or offering other ads on the platform, and both have taken dramatic actions against Russian state media.[60] Twitter has also moved to ban all paid political advertising globally on the site, citing specifically manipulated media and viral misinformation, and has increasingly tried to label false or disputed information on Twitter coming from politicians.[61] In August 2020, Twitter began marking tweets and profiles from state-owned media accounts as "state-affiliated media."[62] Facebook also has banned advertising, within the United States, from state-owned media outlets.[63] Facebook also has declared it would label content from state-controlled media outlets as "state-backed" to provide more transparency about these outlets' posts.[64] Still, Facebook should work closely with media experts to ensure that it limits truly state-controlled outlets like CGTN under the editorial control of a foreign government, while excluding outlets from this policy, like Voice of America or Agence France-Presse, that may receive state funds but enjoy editorial independence.

It seems that Facebook will still allow state-owned media outlets (other than Russian ones) to buy advertising on the platform to promote their content to people outside of the United States. This dichotomy—banned in the United States but allowed elsewhere—makes little sense and could easily allow state-owned media to promote content in developing democracies where outlets like CGTN and Xinhua are actually gaining more viewers and readers than in the United States.

Democracies also should support research into boosting the digital literacy of their citizens so that they become more skilled at noticing disinformation. Finland and Taiwan, for instance, already have developed model programs to improve citizens' digital literacy. Finland launched such efforts back in 2014, when few countries were paying attention to online disinformation.[65] Finland's efforts have been shown in studies to have significantly improved citizens' ability to spot fake news.[66] Other democracies should model digital literacy efforts on programs from Finland and Taiwan: Democracies' education departments should create digital citizenship courses for schools, universities, and the broader public. In Taiwan, the government drives trucks to rural parts of the island so that officials can reach everyone with programming on how to identify fake news.[67] Leading democracies also should support civil society organizations, particularly in Asia, that promote digital literacy. And they should learn about how Taiwan's government has fought disinformation by effectively timing news cycles to release correct information, ensuring, as Aaron Huang of the U.S. Foreign Service notes, "that clarifications spread faster and further than false news—so that facts dominate the information space before falsehoods do."[68]

Governments beyond the United States and India should warn China-based social media platforms, like TikTok, that if they want to continue to have access to consumers in other countries, they should aggressively increase their staffing for addressing state-backed information and publish their internal investigations into state-backed disinformation operations. These apps surely could bolster Beijing's global disinformation efforts, since they may provide vehicles for China to penetrate other societies, collect data on people in other states, and spread disinformation. TikTok, which is much more reliant on the global market than WeChat, at least appears open to dialogue about disinformation and to becoming a global media company that can be genuinely scrutinized by lawmakers from other countries. For example, in July 2020 TikTok signed on to the European Union's Code of Practice on Disinformation, pledging to do more to fight disinformation on the platform.[69]

Policymakers in many countries could attempt to put pressure on WeChat as well. But there is little evidence so far that the company would be responsive, as its business model is still heavily dependent on business inside China.

So, should other countries follow the path of the United States and ban TikTok, WeChat, and other Chinese apps, a move that was made without a broader plan to protect digital privacy within the United States and broader oversight of social media firms and their apps? Certainly, democracies should maintain the highest possible level of scrutiny of TikTok, WeChat, and other Chinese social media apps;

they clearly can be used for disinformation, censorship, and the exfiltration of data. TikTok, for instance, which harvests vast amounts of users' data, claims that it has not given any users' information to Beijing, but the U.S. government is investigating whether the company has exfiltrated a range of data back to China.[70] (Another app owned by ByteDance, Douyin, which is essentially the Chinese version of TikTok, clearly employs censorship and monitoring of users.[71])

But there are reasons not to ban all of China's apps. For one, tools like WeChat are essential for people outside China to communicate with relatives, friends, and other acquaintances inside the country, and banning the app potentially severs that important line of people-to-people contact. It also remains unclear whether it is even possible to enforce such bans, unless democracies want to create their own versions of China's Great Firewall, anathema to the idea of internet freedom; otherwise, people in democracies will likely still be able to access such apps through remote servers and other tools.[72]

There are two more important reasons not to ban such apps without a more thought-through plan. Banning TikTok, WeChat, and potentially multiple other apps could speed up a global divide between countries with open and closed internets and could make it seem like democracies are adding to this division. Of course, by trying to export its model of a closed and monitored internet and by banning many apps at home, China is playing the biggest role in fostering this divide. But if democracies impose harsh bans, they further move the world toward a "digital Berlin Wall" situation, a prospect that will undermine any hope for global internet freedom.[73]

Most important, as Aynne Kokas of the University of Virginia has noted, even if countries ban TikTok and WeChat, there are so many other ways that Chinese firms can exfiltrate data from the United States or other countries. Any company that has operations in China—Chinese firms like e-commerce giant Alibaba or foreign firms like Zoom, for instance—could potentially be forced to harvest information on users around the world, pursuant to Chinese law,[74] not to mention that apps based in democracies, from companies like

Facebook, also harvest huge amounts of users' data, though they argue that they use the data for targeted advertisements and tailored services, and not to give to an authoritarian government.[75] On apps and platforms based in democracies, like Facebook, disinformation coming from people living in democracies is rife as well—in some ways the biggest problem on Facebook, Twitter, and other U.S. platforms today is actually disinformation originating from domestic sources.

Digital Privacy as an Asymmetric Response

As a result, the best response to the global spread of China's apps and social media platforms would be for countries to develop rigorous regimes to protect consumers' data. In a sense, this would be an asymmetric response to China's efforts. Rather than simply specifically pushing back at the threat of disinformation by calling out China's disinformation and putting pressure on social media companies to stop it, by developing rigorous privacy regimes, democracies together would create a system that provided much greater transparency about online data and stricter safeguards against all types of disinformation. Such a strategy, aspects of which already are in place in the European Union, would involve a comprehensive program to safeguard users' data without targeting companies from one country, and regulation that would force all companies, including Chinese firms, to be transparent about what they do with users' data. Then, if a company exfiltrates users' data to China (or another authoritarian state that could weaponize the data), democracies could ban that firm.

Traditional Influence Efforts and Asymmetric Responses

Countries also should focus intensely on Beijing's traditional influence efforts in the realms of education, politics, and ethnic Chinese organizations. These have already enjoyed some success and are likely to become more effective in the next decade. Australia's new legislation on foreign influence efforts, passed in 2018, offers a model for raising awareness of foreign influence in politics and combating it.[76] Under a series of new laws passed, Australia banned foreign political donations, introduced a registration scheme similar to the Foreign Agents Registration Act in the United States, and made it illegal for any person to knowingly interfere in or attempt to influence "Australian politics on behalf of a foreign principal."[77] The legislation is intentionally broad, and, in addition to expanding a list of national security offenses, it makes it a crime to "engage in any covert activity on behalf of a foreign government that aims to influence the process of Australian politics" and includes penalties of up to twenty years in prison.[78]

While the legislation has faced some criticism, including concerns of being too far-reaching and possibly encroaching on legitimate political expression, it should serve as a model for how other democracies can begin to address foreign influence and interference, especially for states in Western and Central Europe that still lag far behind Australia in understanding and addressing foreign influence activities. Indeed, political leaders and civil society leaders from wealthy democracies should work together, both informally and at formal meetings like the Group of Seven, to develop similar, comprehensive legislation designed to prevent their political systems from foreign influence. By collaborating and developing similar standards, democracies would show their resilience and also make it harder for China to cherry-pick democracies with weaker safeguards on influence activities.[79]

Countries also should require national judicial agencies to develop task forces specifically focused on United Front Work Department (UFWD) operations and designed to foster transparency and broader public knowledge about these operations—particularly in ethnic Chinese communities that are often targets and among universities and other research institutions that are targets. In the United States, Australia, and many European countries, academic institutions for years welcomed Confucius Institutes or welcomed partnerships with Chinese counterparts without really digging deeply into their partners' governance or how the partnership or Confucius Institute would operate. In other words, they did not perform enough due diligence.[80] These institutions have begun to undertake more due diligence but could still improve, and these task forces necessarily should be in close contact with the types of institutions the UFWD targets. Once these task forces do serious digging, they should share their information on UFWD activities with state and local law enforcement; the UFWD often works on local and state (or provincial) levels. As noted in excellent work by Larry Diamond and Orville Schell on how to respond to Chinese influence efforts, task forces should work closely with ethnic Chinese communities and universities to ensure also that these efforts are not seen as witch hunts focused on ethnic Chinese including Chinese national students, and to ensure that the rights of the ethnic Chinese citizens of these countries are fully protected.[81] But the United States and other countries should also take the offensive against the UFWD, using intelligence and diplomatic resources to hunt down UFWD funding for organizations around the globe, and begin pushing private institutions to cease receiving funding from UFWD-linked groups.

More broadly, democracies need to bolster the resources of their intelligence agencies, law enforcement agencies, foreign ministries, and research organizations to expose UFWD actions so that these groups can recognize early signs of UFWD activities on university campuses, with policymakers, and with other groups. Democracies should consider applying sanctions on top UFWD leaders within China as well, although this should not be a first step in the checklist of measures against UFWD activities.[82]

Countries also need to much more carefully scrutinize foreign sources of funding for educational institutions, making transparency about funding paramount. Governments and civil society leaders should require universities to offer full disclosure about their agreements regarding Confucius Institutes, and about all other sources of foreign funding above $50,000 or the equivalent in other currencies; the current threshold for reporting is gifts of $250,000. Political leaders and civil society leaders should pressure book publishers, especially in academic publishing, to disclose such sources of funding as well. China has increasingly applied pressure on the publishing industry to self-censor regarding topics considered sensitive by Beijing, and several academic publishers have shamefully complied, according to the PEN American Center.[83]

Governments should not specifically ban certain sources of foreign funding or force Confucius Institutes and Confucius Classrooms to close. After all, some research conducted by Naima Green-Riley of Harvard University suggests that "Confucius Classrooms," designed for K–12 schools, and probably Confucius Institutes are not that effective at influencing the views of, at least, American students who attend them; her study found "that American students—even young high-schoolers—are discerning and able to process conflicting signals in the learning environment [of Confucius Classrooms]."[84] But governments can pass legislation that ensures that Confucius Institutes on campuses operate under domestic laws and are completely managed by the host institutions, and also are transparent about their governance in Beijing and whether they are linked to the UFWD, as the Australian Strategic Policy Institute and others have alleged.[85] If Confucius Institutes cannot operate with significant transparency about their agreements and comply with rigorous faculty oversight, they should be shuttered. It is likely that, in most leading democracies, Confucius Institutes will not be able to operate with such transparency and to accept such management by host institutions, and thus in democracies most of these institutes likely will be shuttered.

Other countries also could emulate the U.S. Congress's approach, which includes aggressive scrutiny by lawmakers of Confucius Institutes in their home districts and increasing pressure on Confucius Institutes to operate under the management of host institutions, comply fully with local laws, show they are independent from the UFWD, and do nothing to harm academic freedom.[86] They further should consider copying the U.S. government's strategy of making Confucius Institute headquarters in various states register as foreign missions, in order to force them to be more transparent about their activities.[87] Indeed, some other democracies are already taking these steps, which in part is why many Confucius Institutes are closing, but they should be widely adopted by democracies in Asia, Europe, Latin America, and other parts of the world.

Avoid Overly Broad Responses

Combating Chinese efforts that are working is critical. But for now, with China failing in many of its information and influence activities, it is important for foreign states to understand Beijing's failures and successes, not to overhype China's current effectiveness, and to promote how poorly Beijing has done in many of its strategies.

States should, as we just discussed, pay close attention to tools like Xinhua that are already having success. But they should not take an overly broad response to China's information and influence activities—especially against those that are not currently working. An overly broad response could in fact undermine democracies' own strengths—openness, free media environments, transparency, and in many cases multicultural societies in which ethnic Chinese are equal citizens.

Take the decisions by the U.S. government, in 2020, to expel many employees of Chinese state media outlets, cutting the number of Chinese nationals who could work for state outlets in the United States, and then sharply curtailing work visas for any Chinese national reporters working in the United States, even if they were not working for Beijing's state media.[88] These actions came after making the Chinese state media outlets register as foreign agents—a reasonable decision—and as foreign missions. As we have seen, while Chinese state media outlets indeed sometimes serve as intelligence-gathering operations, outside Xinhua they have not actually won many viewers or listeners in many countries, and their influence in the United States remains relatively limited. Take also the failures of the FBI's China Initiative, which often seemed to target Chinese-Americans or permanent residents with cases that were not espionage and perhaps nothing more than regular scientific research.

The decision to force these Chinese state media outlets to essentially cull employees could have made Washington look, to many other countries, like it was cracking down on the press and engaging in tit-for-tat press bans with one of the most restrictive governments in the world; the decision to limit the work visas of Chinese national reporters even if they were not working for state media only reinforced a perceived racial component of the U.S. action. Washington's decision also was porous, since Chinese state media outlets could potentially replace the Chinese nationals by hiring people who are residents or citizens of the United States but still might have pro-Beijing views and/or the willingness to adopt such views once hired by a state media outlet. And the failures of the China Initiative made the United States, to some eyes, look racist, providing an obvious talking point for Chinese diplomats and state media.

Washington's approach to state media also provided an opportunity for Beijing to retaliate. China quickly did, expelling reporters from the *New York Times*, the *Washington Post*, the *Wall Street Journal*, and other outlets whom it had long had its sights on, and requiring these outlets (and CNN and Voice of America) to fire Chinese nationals.[89] Beijing then failed to renew the work visas of most American reporters in China.[90] The expulsions and other Chinese actions deprived global news consumers, and leaders, of important conduits of information about China and stories about Beijing's response to COVID-19, amidst a pandemic that originated within China.[91] Even some journalists harshly critical of Beijing—and even some who themselves had once been banned from China for reporting on particularly sensitive issues—said that the U.S. decision was wrong. "Given the fact that it's vital to have good information out of China right now because of coronavirus, the U.S. decision was pretty disastrous timing," Megha Rajagopalan, a correspondent for *BuzzFeed News* who was essentially tossed out of China in 2018 after reporting on abuses in Xinjiang, told the *New York Times*.[92]

Perhaps, as the journalist and author John Pomfret has suggested, the United States should offer a clear cap on Chinese state media's head counts in the United States and ask Beijing to agree to a similar cap on U.S. reporters in China. The United States would then allow Beijing to send whomever they want to work for state media and agree to let U.S. media companies send any reporters to China they pick.[93] (The Biden administration and China negotiated the return of some foreign reporters to China, but the intensely authoritarian atmosphere in China has led to foreign journalists decamping for Taiwan or Singapore anyway, to report on China from those places.)

Emphasize Chinese Failures and Failures of the China Model

To undermine China's information and influence efforts, leading democracies also should take tough steps to expose China's media failures and Beijing's political, diplomatic, and economic weaknesses to the world.

Indeed, by highlighting China's failures and contrasting them with democracies' abilities to continue to deliver important global leadership and public goods at home, leading democracies could help puncture China's formal diplomacy and public diplomacy, showing Beijing's weaknesses in various ways. For one, although some countries have indeed embraced aspects of the Chinese technology-enabled authoritarian model, many elements of the China model remain highly unpopular among publics in most countries. As projects associated with the BRI come under increased scrutiny—like piling debts on tiny Laos and causing a debt crisis there, or pouring debts into Sri Lanka, whose government collapsed—and Chinese diplomats and state media have taken a more aggressive public stance toward other states, and as China's initial cover-up of COVID-19 soured foreign publics, global public opinion of China has fallen, as we have discussed in detail.[94]

The China model also depends on Beijing maintaining relatively high economic growth rates—as it had for decades, until 2020. The COVID-19 pandemic hit China's economy hard in 2020, with the economy contracting in the first quarter for the first time in decades.[95] Though China rebounded faster than most other countries in the world, it has now entered significant and sustained economic stagnation due to its zero-COVID approach. Stagnation or decline in China's growth will badly undermine its developmental model and its ability to promote that model abroad.[96] The fact that China seems to have turned inward during the pandemic, as the last country to pursue a zero-COVID approach and making it nearly impossible for foreigners to visit while also strictly limiting outbound tourism, will also potentially hinder China's ability to sell its model to the world.

Even before the outbreak of COVID-19, China's economy was grappling with major, structural issues that likely will undermine growth for years and also make it harder for Beijing to promote its model abroad. Leading democracies should use public diplomacy and formal diplomacy to highlight China's increasingly inward-looking style of politics, China's long-term economic and political problems, and the endemic corruption within the CCP. As we have seen, these structural issues inhibiting the Chinese economy include the Xi administration's prioritization of state enterprises over private firms, the real engines of China's growth, a massive debt load as compared to gross domestic product, the aging and shrinking of the population, productivity slowdowns throughout the Chinese economy along with rising wages, the spread of large-scale corruption in government and big business, the crushing of innovative firms, the increasing isolation from the world, the persistence of high levels of inequality, the continued supply chain problems, and some multinationals' decoupling from China as trade tensions increase between Beijing and Washington.[97]

With less emphasis on high growth as a source of legitimacy, Beijing will instead continue ramping up nationalism as seen in the intensely nationalistic propaganda coming out of Beijing during the

Taiwan crisis, and propagating the cult of personality around Xi to unify the population. These decisions could further dent the appeal of China's model to people in other countries, and democracies should take every opportunity to highlight China's nationalistic, bullying wolf warrior diplomacy; intense control of private companies by the CCP; rights abuses; support for Russia in the Ukraine war; menacing of small countries; and lack of gender equity in business and politics.[98] Indeed, angry, xenophobic nationalism, stoked by Beijing, undermines China's ability to advertise its model and present itself as a global leader.

Xi's extremely authoritarian grip on power, undermining collective decision-making in China and sidelining experts in areas ranging from public health to economics, may further threaten Beijing's long-term prosperity. His cult of personality hinders rational decision-making at all levels of Chinese government and leads to Chinese policymakers simply becoming paralyzed, unable to do rational analysis because so much decision-making is consolidated at the top.[99] He also has complicated any future succession planning, which Beijing had handled smoothly in the transition from Jiang Zemin to Hu Jintao, leaving the country in potential crisis if Xi were to die or suddenly get sick—a crisis that could in some ways mirror the era after Mao's death.[100]

In addition, as Xi assumes even more control over economic policymaking, he runs the risk of ignoring expertise, and thereby further denting the growth critical to China's model of development, as Elizabeth Economy and other scholars have noted. And his increasing insertion of the CCP into private enterprise could choke off innovation in China, hurt the private sector that provides the majority of new jobs, and drive creative Chinese entrepreneurs out of the country.[101] The CCP, and many top Chinese companies and institutions, also continues to discriminate heavily against ethnic minorities and women, leading to rampant gender imbalances at top levels of the CCP, a waste of talented people who could otherwise be powering the economy, and the creation of an increasingly angry feminist movement in China.[102]

Rivals of China like the United States and Japan should use every diplomatic tool to highlight China's brittle diplomacy and other flaws, and to highlight how China's state media often is propagandistic and ineffective in drawing actual audiences. Policymakers should publicize to the world, using data like that collected here, how few people currently watch or trust the content of CGTN or CRI and many other Chinese state media outlets, and they should take every opportunity to highlight and broadcast Beijing's continuing outbursts of angry, wolf warrior diplomacy.

The United States and its allies should support countries, such as Australia, Taiwan, and Lithuania, that face economic coercion and diplomatic bullying—let alone the threat of outright military conflict. U.S. officials and leaders from other democracies should rhetorically condemn those behaviors and use summits and other meetings, as well as social media, to highlight China's growing economic and diplomatic bullying of countries. The United States and its partners also should take steps to open their markets to products from countries, like Taiwan and Australia, that China is blocking in various ways. In less wealthy states facing Chinese coercion, the United States and its partners should be prepared to offer limited grants and loans, as the European Union has offered to Lithuania.[103]

In addition, they should emphasize areas where leading democracies have outshone China in supporting global governance and providing global public goods, demonstrating the gaps in China's global leadership ability and the continued ability of democracies to lead. For instance, the United States and European countries should not try to directly challenge China's ability to back infrastructure—a losing proposition, given the size of the BRI—but instead take a page from Japan's approach to the BRI. Japan, perhaps the developed democracy with the most extensive background in combating China strategically, is challenging China's infrastructure push but is not trying to match the BRI in total size. Japan instead has focused on supporting decarbonization and other greener infrastructure efforts in Southeast Asia, committing billions to promoting clean energy in a region where

China continues to back dirty coal plans that are unpopular among many local citizens and civil society groups.[104] Should this effort be welcomed by Southeast Asian states, it is likely Japan will expand this focus to other parts of the world. Japan's decarbonization effort not only highlights leading Japanese technology and shows states that Japan is serious about climate change, a critical issue, but also leads to extensive discussion of how China continues to support often-unpopular dirty coal projects. Other democracies should join Japan in supporting this approach to infrastructure, and indeed the Biden administration seems poised to at least make this approach central to its relations with developing countries.[105]

Leading democracies also should point out the failures of Chinese vaccines to provide enough immunity to COVID-19 and should donate generously to global programs to get much-needed vaccines to poorer countries around the world, for free or for cheap prices.[106] Developed states have started in this direction, with the G-7 pledging to donate one billion COVID-19 vaccines to poorer states; around half of those doses will come from the United States.[107] But the vaccine donations should have come quicker than the G-7 pledged.[108] The United States and other democracies could build on this global vaccine effort to focus more extensively on global public health issues affecting poorer countries, another area where many democracies can outcompete China. And leading democracies should keep their own universities open to foreign students—top foreign students still generally prefer universities in wealthy democracies to studying in China, even if China is gaining—thereby focusing on a major strength that, unlike infrastructure, Beijing cannot yet come close to matching.[109]

In speeches by leaders from major democracies, in commentary by ambassadors and officials from major democracies, and in other types of information outreach, democracies also should aggressively highlight potential weaknesses in the China model and China's intense unpopularity in many countries. They should emphasize the ways in which China's surveillance exports could create Xinjiang-like surveillance states in foreign countries buying up Chinese technology. They should emphasize how poorly Beijing responded at first to the COVID-19 outbreak and how this response shows the inherent failures of the opaque, unfree China model and is alienating many Chinese citizens and driving them abroad just as it is hurting the Chinese economy. They should highlight the fragility of China's long-term economic model, with its growing party dominance of the private sector and its one-man rule that looks more like Mao's era now than the technocratic era of Hu Jintao or Jiang Zemin; showcase Beijing's brittle and furious and bullying diplomacy; discuss China's lack of gender equity; and highlight the resiliency and vibrancy of democracies' political and economic systems.[110]

The United States and its partners should also take advantage of Beijing's current unpopularity, information failures, and policy missteps to build new partnerships and deepen existing ones—especially at this critical time of the Taiwan crisis. These should include making the Quadrilateral Strategic Dialogue, an organization including the United States, India, Japan, and Australia, into a more robust defense partnership and potentially adding new members to it in the future. Taking advantage of China's policy missteps also should certainly include rebuilding troubled defense and strategic relationships with U.S. treaty allies in Southeast Asia, Thailand, and the Philippines, despite Thailand's semi-autocratic government and the Philippines' election of Ferdinand Marcos Jr as its new president.

On the economic side, it should include turning the nascent Indo-Pacific Economic Framework for Prosperity into something beyond a talk shop—an agreement that ultimately provides U.S. market access to countries that sign up to get them to agree to regional standards on digital trade, supply chains, and other issues. Providing U.S. market access would help bring more countries firmly into the agreement and would strengthen this partnership as a bulwark against China.[111]

Focus on Xi

Too often, leaders in the United States and many other countries have used broad invectives to condemn China, making it seem like their problem is with Xi, the CCP, and the general Chinese public.[112] But bundling all three together is counterproductive. Even if the Chinese public itself is becoming more nationalistic, other democracies should maintain the focus on the CCP and on Xi himself. Such an approach helps prevent the stigmatization of the Chinese people, inside China or in countries around the world.[113] It also makes it easier for the continuation of a broad range of people-to-people contacts with China, which can be important tools for building ties even when high-level geopolitical relations turn cold.

And, when Chinese aid to other countries seems designed primarily to support only Chinese firms—or Chinese firms and a few local leaders in other states—democracies should point out these flaws and help other countries renegotiate deals. The Trump administration offered a model of how to do so, sending U.S. experts to Myanmar and helping Myanmar renegotiate the size and scope of a series of controversial Chinese-funded projects including a deep-water port and industrial zone.[114]

Get Your Own Houses in Order

While countries are assessing which of China's strategies to worry less about and predicting and preparing for China's future moves and future strengths, they also should bolster their own soft—and sharp—power resources. To more effectively draw distinctions between democracies and China and use asymmetric measures, democracies need to rebuild their own political systems and soft power toolkits. States can more clearly offer contrasts to China's media and information tools if they rebuild their own soft power toolkits.

Strengthen Democracies' Media Outlets

The United States' big government-controlled outlets, like Radio Free Asia, Radio Free Europe/Radio Free Liberty, and Voice of America, provide essential reporting, in many languages, to a wide range of countries, including many authoritarian states where these outlets offer some of the only independent coverage. Radio Free Asia, Voice of America, and other U.S. government–backed outlets remain far more popular, in most countries, than China's international state media, and far more trusted as well. Through their work, they convey U.S. values of press freedom and accountability.

The Trump administration, unfortunately, denigrated Voice of America and the body overseeing these outlets, the USAGM. The Trump White House repeatedly pushed to cut funding for the USAGM, although its efforts to do so were generally rebuffed by Congress.[115] Trump (wrongly) accused Voice of America of promoting Chinese propaganda, simply for reporting that the city of Wuhan, the initial epicenter of the COVID-19 pandemic, reopened after the Chinese government curtailed domestic transmission of the virus.[116] In a statement posted on the White House site in May 2020, the Trump administration claimed, "VOA too often speaks for America's adversaries—not its citizens."[117] The then-head of Voice of America, Amanda Bennett, responded by noting that the channel reports accurately and had widely covered aspects of the COVID-19 pandemic that portrayed China in a negative light, including running stories on Beijing's disinformation efforts and many pieces on Beijing's lack of transparency in the early days of the virus's spread within China.[118]

Meanwhile, the head of the USAGM, a documentary filmmaker named Michael Pack, seemed to be seeking to push USAGM broadcasters closer to propaganda entities, rather than independent news organizations. Shortly after his Senate confirmation in June 2020, Pack sacked the senior executives and boards of the major federally funded broadcasters, like Radio Free Asia, Radio Free Europe/Radio Liberty, and several others.[119] (According to a whistleblower complaint, he also apparently spent $2 million in taxpayer money to create dossiers of information designed to be used in the firings.[120]) He replaced the boards, which had been staffed with regional and broadcasting experts, with people known for loyalty to the Trump administration but with little experience in broadcasting.[121] Several of the people fired filed suit, claiming that Pack had destroyed federal guarantees of the broadcasters' independence, allowed for political interference into these outlets' newsrooms, and was essentially turning them into propaganda outlets.[122] They later wrote a joint warning letter saying that Pack was a "long-term threat to the credibility and professionalism" of the U.S. state broadcasters.[123] Pack then fired several more USAGM executives, who claimed they had been removed for speaking up about mismanagement and about violations of the firewall that is supposed to protect these outlets' editorial independence, and apparently approved an investigation into one of Voice of America's best-known reporters, White House reporter Steve Herman, for supposed bias against the Trump administration.[124] As National Public Radio reported, Pack also had "withheld visa extension for journalists [working for these U.S. state outlets] who are foreign citizens, requiring their return to their home countries."[125]

Then, late in Pack's tenure, more scandals erupted. The attorney general of the District of Columbia sued Pack, claiming that he had illegally taken some $4 million from a nonprofit and funneled it to his documentary company.[126]

Pack's decisions had some support among experts on the USAGM and information warfare, but they also came in for bipartisan criticism on Capitol Hill and among policymakers outside of Congress.[127] Ilan Berman, an expert on information warfare at the American Foreign Policy Council, argues that the White House needs to make outlets like Voice of America more clearly accountable to U.S. government messaging, since "the past few years have seen the advent of a new phenomenon which could be called 'authoritarian media,' entailing the weaponization of news, both real and fabricated, by hostile actors in order to advance a concrete set of foreign policy and national security objectives."[128] Pack has said that some U.S. state outlets were seeking to purposely sabotage the Trump administration and he was purportedly trying to make them more like government propaganda.[129]

The White House and State Department should take the opposite approach toward the USAGM, a vital tool of soft power. (Indeed, shortly after Joe Biden was sworn in as president on January 20, 2021, Pack resigned at Biden's request, and the Biden administration restored the positions of some of the fired heads of the USAGM news services, like Radio Free Asia.[130]) They should highlight the fair and unbiased reporting of outlets like Voice of America, Radio Free Asia, and others—even if that reporting sometimes contains stories that portray U.S. politics in a harsh light—as a sharp contrast from China's propagandistic state media. Rather than cutting budgets or trying to make Voice of America and Radio Free Asia more clearly and vocally pro-American, Washington should boost funding for them and should make sure to keep on the foreign nationals working for these outlets whom Pack tried to remove, many of whom are the best communicators to places like Cambodia, Laos, Vietnam, Tibet, or Xinjiang that are still run by highly authoritarian regimes.[131] Other countries with major government-backed state media outlets that have a wide global reach, like France, also should recognize the value of investing in these media companies while maintaining their independence.

Undercutting the independence of these U.S. government–funded outlets would only hurt their credibility abroad, and thus that of the United States. Such changes would make these U.S. outlets seem more like the "authoritarian media" in other countries that Berman rightly describes.[132] (Pack's decisions also seemed to temporarily paralyze a part of the USAGM, the Open Technology Fund, which helps support anti-censorship and anti-surveillance tools in other countries and regions, including embattled Hong Kong; the effect on the Open Technology Fund drew harsh bipartisan criticism.[133]) And citizens in other countries do not always clearly distinguish between reporting coming from U.S. government–backed outlets like Voice of America and reporting from non-government-backed outlets like the *New York Times*. So, if U.S. state media outlets are presenting pro-U.S. propaganda, this could lead foreign citizens to think private outlets like the *New York Times* are doing the same.

Stand Up for a Free Press

At the same time, officials from democracies with strong traditions of a free press should refrain from attacking journalists. While rhetorically attacking journalists has unfortunately become a common part of U.S. domestic politics—and politics in some other democracies—such vitriol only undermines the idea that these states enjoy free, unbiased presses. These attacks make it harder for leaders and diplomats to differentiate democratic governments' approaches to media from that of China, and they undercut efforts to stand up for press freedoms in other countries.

Instead, U.S. officials should rhetorically back a free press not just when it is politically convenient—like in criticizing the lack of press freedom in countries such as Cuba, Iran, or Venezuela—but at all times. Such a strategy, again, would help draw sharp contrasts from China's censorious and sometimes brutal approach to media and information.

Meanwhile, the United States and other countries should demand reciprocity in areas where China has gained influence. For instance, countries should continue allowing Confucius Institutes, provided they follow basic guidelines for academic freedom and faculty governance, but in return should insist that China not put limitations on branches of foreign universities operating in the People's Republic or on other types of public diplomacy. (The same study by the U.S. Senate's permanent subcommittee on investigations that examined Confucius Institutes also found that China had interfered with U.S. public diplomacy projects in China over eighty times in recent years.[134])

Restore Other Types of Soft Power

Beyond boosting the resources of Voice of America and Radio Free Asia, the U.S. government should take other measures to restore active U.S. soft power; other democracies should rebuild their active soft power as well, since democracies should collaborate, whenever possible, in responding to China's actions. Remember, active soft power stems from government actions, while passive soft power stems from private companies operating overseas, cultural exports, global perceptions of a country's values, and other activities not controlled by a government.

Given the tumult in the United States, U.S. passive soft power still remains stronger than one might imagine, though clearly damaged by international concerns about eroding U.S. commitments to rights and about U.S. domestic turmoil. Yet U.S. passive soft power is not fully drained. Outside of Europe, where overall approval of the United States has taken the worst hit, favorable views of the United States remain relatively high. A Pew poll in 2017 found that 49 percent of those surveyed had favorable views of the United States.[135] That favorable opinion rose to 50 percent in 2018, a 2020 update showed that favorable views of the United States had risen to 54 percent, and in 2021 U.S. favorability across multiple foreign countries rose to 62 percent.[136]

U.S. cultural and commercial exports still dominate the world, and the country remains the center of global news coverage; when someone was needed to lead the Ukraine response, it had to be the United States. If the United States can address the domestic economic, social, and political flaws now visible to the world, it still has reservoirs of passive soft power to draw upon. And the fact that U.S. news retains this centrality allows the United States to rebuild its image (if it can) in plain view of the globe. The 2020 U.S. Black Lives Matter (BLM) street protests sparked similar events from Berlin, Germany, to Perth, Australia, probably the farthest city in the world from the U.S. capital. In so doing, they showed that events in the United States still resonate globally.[137]

Washington can restore its active soft power as well. Boosting funding for active soft power now may seem like a luxury, given that U.S. government resources are strained by the COVID-19 crisis. But bolstering soft power comes at a bargain cost, compared to the overall scope of the U.S. budget and the budgets of other leading democracies. Unfortunately, in 2020, the United States abruptly ended the Peace Corps' and Fulbright's longstanding exchange programming in China.[138] Even in an era in which China is becoming more authoritarian, these institutions still provide opportunities for locals to interact with Americans in a nonpolitical way and to see some of the values of U.S. society. The Trump administration worked to try and undermine other sources of U.S. soft power as well, including repeatedly attempting to slash the State Department and foreign aid overall budgets and blocking the USAID from dispersing foreign aid abroad.[139] While most of these budget cuts were blocked by Congress, they signaled a disdain for soft power.

The Trump administration was not the first, however, to undervalue active soft power; many successive White Houses have ignored this tool. A 2019 report by the congressionally mandated U.S. Advisory Commission on Public Diplomacy noted that the U.S. government's funding for public diplomacy, active soft power efforts, has barely risen since the 1980s, even though the world's population is much larger now and the scope of information tools is much broader.[140] Overall, U.S. public diplomacy spending accounts for less than one-fifth of a percent of all discretionary spending by the U.S. federal government, even though active soft power and passive soft power have been central to U.S. influence in the world for decades.[141]

The United States and other democracies can rebuild active soft power in several other ways, beyond improving U.S. government–sponsored broadcasting like Voice of America and Radio Free Asia. A modest increase in funding could help Washington build on the model started by Fulbright University Vietnam, a university launched in Vietnam and partly funded by the U.S. government. The university has proven popular with the Vietnamese public. Congress could help fund similar Fulbright universities in other parts of the world.[142] Such an expansion of Fulbright universities would be particularly valuable at a time when Beijing is supporting its own, China-backed university campuses and research centers in Southeast Asia.[143] The U.S. government also should increase funding for journalism exchange programs, rethink cuts to the Peace Corps, and consider creating a new program within the State Department that would bring more foreign diplomats to the United States for training programs and to attend U.S. graduate schools.[144] More broadly, democracies should expand visitor exchange programs, which bring a broad range of professionals—doctors, teachers, and many others—to countries for short educational courses and other types of people-to-people exchanges.[145] It could model some of these programs on the Young Southeast Asian Leaders Initiative, a U.S. program launched in 2013 that has brought a broad range of Southeast Asian opinion leaders to the United States for professional and academic exchanges and other types of networking.[146]

To maintain comparative advantage in higher education, leading democracies also should reconsider their increasingly stringent immigration rules, which discourage many foreign students.[147] Foreign students often become effective ambassadors of democracies' soft power.[148] Yet in recent years, the United States and several other democracies have stepped up measures designed to limit foreign student populations.[149] Some limits may make sense. In the most sensitive areas of the hard sciences—areas with direct implications for military and security technology—stricter controls on foreign students are warranted. And of course, foreign students, including Chinese nationals, can come to the United States and other democracies and return home just as nationalistic as before—or more so. Many Chinese men and women, as Elizabeth Economy has noted, have attended university in the United States or Australia and, back in China, remain supportive of authoritarian rule and antagonistic toward leading democracies.[150]

But extending limits beyond a small category of foreign students working in sensitive areas or who have clear military backgrounds will backfire on democracies. Issuing blanket bans on foreign students or blanket revocations of visas, and especially Chinese students, only has the effect of making that democracy look racist and disdainful of intellectual exchange, thereby undermining its soft power.[151] And while some students from China and other authoritarian states come to school in democracies and find their social and political views completely unchanged, others do find their worldviews transformed by studying abroad. In addition, many students from authoritarian states, including China, wind up staying in the United States after graduation and becoming highly productive members of U.S. society.

Bolster Democracy Itself

Ultimately, improved soft power measures should be combined with some rethinking of democracies' foreign policies and major changes designed to improve democracies' own societies. If civil society weakens in leading democracies, if political leaders in prominent democracies do not appear committed to democracy itself, and if media organizations in democracies stray from providing objective reporting, democracy will suffer within individual countries. At the same time, these states—including the United States—will become more vulnerable to external sharp and soft power.[152]

The United States, and other leading countries, should reassure the world that they are recommitted to the institutions and norms of global governance, to strengthening democracy at home, and to showing that democratic states can deliver global public goods. Successfully rebuilding democracy at home is the most important step to rebuilding the global image of democracies as worthy of admiration. The Biden administration seems to understand this challenge; Biden has repeatedly spoken about restoring U.S. democracy and also about needing to show the world that democracy "works" in providing freedoms but also in overseeing stable societies and promoting growth.[153] Whether the United States and other major democracies are up to either task remains to be seen.

China's model today, which it is increasingly trying to export, appears attractive to some other states in part because so many large democracies today are struggling—with economic meltdowns, poor national leadership, hyperpartisanship, weakening civil societies and shrinking media sectors, economic inequality, and a loss of trust in political systems.[154] These problems may be worse in some democracies, like Brazil, France, Indonesia, the United Kingdom, and the United States, than in others. But overall, democracy has been badly tarnished in recent years. The United States itself has fallen over the past four years in Freedom House's annual Freedom in the World reports, which measure the strength of democracies on a range from zero to one hundred. The United States dropped from a score of eighty-nine out of one hundred in 2017 to a score of eighty-three out of one hundred in 2021, which ranked the United States behind Mongolia, Croatia, Argentina, Sao Tome and Principe, and other countries one does not necessarily associate with robust democracy.[155] The Economist Intelligence Unit, in its annual Democracy Index rankings, no longer lists the United States as a full democracy. Instead, the United States has slipped into the category of "flawed democracy," putting it in the same category as Albania, Panama, and Moldova, among others.[156] In a 2021 Pew study, publics in countries like Germany, New Zealand, and other democracies no longer saw U.S. democracy as an example for other states, and indeed expressed grave concerns about U.S. democracy.[157]

And just as the Soviet Union highlighted racism in the United States during the Cold War to dent U.S. soft power, the Chinese government uses formal diplomacy and its information and media tools to broadcast democracy's failures. As the United States descended into street protests, some violent, in June 2020, Chinese officials and state media frequently highlighted police crackdowns on protestors. They used the response to protests to troll American counterparts, as an excuse to highlight the supposed benefits of China's authoritarian regime and U.S. decline, and accused the United States of hypocrisy, citing criticisms of China's crackdown on pro-democracy protests in Hong Kong.[158]

It is beyond the scope of this book to offer detailed recommendations about how democracies can restore their norms and institutions; forests have been felled in recent years to produce a raft of books on rebuilding democracy and addressing many democratic societies' deep ills. But leading democracies certainly need to address their many problems, not only to fix their societies and politics, but also to remain compelling alternative models to China. Ultimately, if leading democracies cannot right themselves, China will have far greater room to deploy its soft and sharp power tools—and much greater success as well.

Notes

I have indicated throughout the extensive notations where any parts of the book were based on my prior published research, but minor portions of the book also are based on a yet-unpublished CFR Discussion Paper.

CHAPTER 1

1. Lidiana Rosli, "China Remains Malaysia's Largest Trading Partner, 10 Years Running," *New Straits Times*, January 30, 2019, https://www.nst. com.my/business/2019/01/455955/china-remains-malaysias-largest-trading-partner-10-years-running. For a major example of Malaysian tycoons' long history in China see Wei Gu and Wayne Ma, "Kuok Cools on China as Tycoon Exits Hong Kong Media," *Wall Street Journal*, December 15, 2015, https://www.wsj.com/articles/kuok-cools-on-china-as-tycoon-exits-hong-kong-media-1450179228.
2. OECD, *China's Belt and Road Initiative in the Global Trade, Investment, and Finance Landscape* (Paris: OECD Publishing, 2018), https://www.oecd. org/finance/Chinas-Belt-and-Road-Initiative-in-the-global-trade-inv estment-and-finance-landscape.pdf.
3. Mary Kozlovski, "Sea Dispute Lingers at ASEAN Summit," *Deutsche Welle*, November 22, 2012, https://www.dw.com/en/sea-dispute-ling ers-at-asean-summit/a-16397985; Manuel Mogato, Michael Martina, and Ben Blanchard, "ASEAN Deadlocked on South China Sea, Cambodia Blocks Statement," *Reuters*, July 25, 2016, https://www.reut ers.com/article/us-southchinasea-ruling-asean/asean-deadlocked-on-south-china-sea-cambodia-blocks-statement-idUSKCN1050F6.
4. "Opinion of China," Global Indicators Database, *Pew Research Center*, last modified March 2020, https://www.pewresearch.org/global/datab ase/indicator/24/.
5. Teck Chi Wong, "Playing the China Card Is Unlikely to Save the MCA," *New Mandala*, May 8, 2018, https://www.newmandala.org/

mca-china-card. Also, "Chinese Propagandists Court the Southeast Asian Diaspora," *Economist*, November 20, 2021, https://www.econom ist.com/asia/2021/11/20/chinese-propagandists-court-south-east-asias-chinese-diaspora.

6. Tom Wright and Bradley Hope, "WSJ Investigation: China Offered to Bail Out Troubled Malaysian Fund in Return for Deals," *Wall Street Journal*, January 7, 2019, https://www.wsj.com/articles/how-china-fle xes-its-political-muscle-to-expand-power-overseas-11546890449/.

7. Wright and Hope, "China Offered to Bail Out Troubled Malaysian Fund in Return for Deals."

8. Teck Chi Wong, "Playing the China Card Is Unlikely to Save the MCA." Also, Murray Hiebert, *Under Beijing's Shadow: Southeast Asia's China Challenge* (Lanham, MD: Rowman and Littlefield, 2020), 366–67.

9. Wong, "Playing the China Card Is Unlikely to Save the MCA."

10. Richard Javad Heydarian, "Malaysia's New Government Is Pushing Back Against China," *Al Jazeera*, September 4, 2018, https://www. aljazeera.com/indepth/opinion/malaysia-government-pushing-china-180903094313472.html. Also, Liz Lee, "Selling the Country to China? Debate Spills into Malaysian Election," *Reuters*, April 26, 2018, https:// www.reuters.com/article/us-malaysia-election-china/selling-the-coun try-to-china-debate-spills-into-malaysias-election-idUSKBN1HY076.

11. They did not just stun Najib; many foreign observers, including myself, believed Najib was too entrenched to lose.

12. Peter T. C. Chang, "Ethnic Chinese in Malaysia Are Celebrating China's Rise—but as Multicultural Malaysians, Not Chinese," *South China Morning Post*, May 11, 2018, https://www.scmp.com/comment/insight-opinion/article/2145521/ethnic-chinese-malaysia-are-celebrating-chi nas-rise.

13. Praveen Menon, "Attack on Chinese Billionaire Exposes Growing Racial Divide in Malaysia," *Reuters*, March 9, 2018, https://www.reut ers.com/article/us-malaysia-politics-kuok-analysis/attack-on-chin ese-billionaire-exposes-growing-racial-divide-in-malaysia-idUSKC N1GL0OM.

14. James Chin, "The Malaysian Chinese Association, Set Adrift in Need of a Direction," *Channel News Asia*, October 30, 2018, https://www.chan nelnewsasia.com/news/commentary/mca-malaysian-chinese-associat ion-party-election-results-shift-10875556.

15. Lucy Hornby, "Mahathir Mohamad Warns Against 'New Colonialism' During China Visit," *Financial Times*, August 20, 2018, https://www. ft.com/content/7566599e-a443-11e8-8ecf-a7ae1beff35b.

16. Joseph Sipalan, "China, Malaysia Restart Massive 'Belt and Road' Project After Hiccups," *Reuters*, July 25, 2019, https://www.reuters.com/article/us-china-silkroad-malaysia/china-malaysia-restart-massive-belt-and-road-project-after-hiccups-idUSKCN1UK0DG.

17. Trinna Leong, "Malaysian Police Seize 284 Luxury Bags, 72 Bags of Cash and Valuables from Najib-Linked Apartments," *Straits Times*, May 18, 2018, https://www.straitstimes.com/asia/se-asia/dozens-of-hermes-birkin-bags-and-other-items-seized-from-najib-linked-apartment; Tashny Sukumaran, "From Malaysia's 'First Lady' to 'Bag Lady': Why Rosmah Mansor's Vast Collection of Hermes Birkins Caused a Social Media Storm," *South China Morning Post*, May 24, 2018, https://www.scmp.com/week-asia/politics/article/2147614/malaysias-former-first-lady-becomes-bag-lady-why-rosmah-mansors.

18. A. Ananthalakshmi, "Malaysia's First Lady Linked to $30 Million Worth of Jewelry Bought with 1MDB Funds," *Reuters*, June 16, 2017, https://www.reuters.com/article/us-malaysia-scandal-rosmah/malaysias-first-lady-linked-to-30-mln-worth-of-jewelry-bought-with-1mdb-funds-idUSKBN1970YK; Hannah Ellis-Petersen, "Najib Raids: $273 in Goods Seized from Former Malaysian PM's Properties," *Guardian*, June 27, 2018, https://www.theguardian.com/world/2018/jun/27/najib-raids-273m-of-goods-seized-from-former-malaysian-pms-properties.

19. Richard C. Paddock, "Najib Razak, Malaysia's Former Prime Minister, Found Guilty in Graft Trial," *New York Times*, July 28, 2020, https://www.nytimes.com/2020/07/28/world/asia/malaysia-1mdb-najib.html.

20. Elizabeth Economy, "Exporting the China Model," Prepared Statement Before the U.S.-China Economic and Security Review Commission, March 13, 2020, https://www.uscc.gov/sites/default/files/2020-10/March_13_Hearing_and_April_27_Roundtable_Transcript_0.pdf; Rush Doshi, *The Long Game: China's Grand Strategy to Displace American Order* (New York: Oxford University Press, 2021), 4–5.

21. Doshi, *The Long Game*, 4–7.

22. Doshi, *The Long Game*, 104–5.

23. Lyle J. Goldstein, "China's Biggest Fear: U.S.-Indian Encirclement," *National Interest*, February 11, 2015, https://nationalinterest.org/feature/chinas-biggest-fear-us-indian-encirclement-12225; Felix K. Chang, "China's Encirclement Concerns," *Foreign Policy Research Institute*, June 24, 2016, https://www.fpri.org/2016/06/chinas-encirclement-concerns/; Emma V. Broomfield, "Perceptions of Dangers: The China Threat Theory," *Journal of Contemporary China* 12, no. 35 (2003): 265–84; Li Yang, "'China Threat' Theory Is Absurd," *China Daily*, September 2, 2010,

http://www.chinadaily.com.cn/opinion/2010-09/02/content_11245 047.htm; Shannon Tiezzi, "Beijing's 'China Threat' Theory," *Diplomat*, June 3, 2014, https://thediplomat.com/2014/06/beijings-china-threat-theory/.

24. Doshi, *The Long Game*, 264.

25. See, for instance, Matthew Yglesias, "The Raging Controversy over the NBA, China, and the Hong Kong Protests, Explained," *Vox*, October 7, 2019, https://www.vox.com/2019/10/7/20902700/daryl-morey-tweet-china-nba-hong-kong, for an overview of this challenge.

26. Simon Denyer, "Move Over America: China Now Presents Itself as the Model 'Blazing a New Trail' for the World," *Washington Post*, October 19, 2017, https://www.washingtonpost.com/news/worldviews/wp/2017/10/19/move-over-america-china-now-presents-itself-as-the-model-blazing-a-new-trail-for-the-world/.

27. Economy, "Exporting the China Model."

28. See, for example, Jessica Chen Weiss, "No, China and the U.S. Aren't Locked in an Ideological Battle. Not Even Close," *Washington Post*, May 4, 2019, https://www.washingtonpost.com/politics/2019/05/04/no-china-us-arent-locked-an-ideological-battle-not-even-close/?utm_term=.84193cbe600a.

29. Maya Wang, "China's Techno-Authoritarianism Has Gone Global," *Foreign Affairs*, April 8, 2021, https://www.foreignaffairs.com/articles/china/2021-04-08/chinas-techno-authoritarianism-has-gone-global.

30. Scott N. Romaniuk and Tobias Burgers, "How China's AI Technology Exports Are Seeding Surveillance Societies Globally," *Diplomat*, October 18, 2018, https://thediplomat.com/2018/10/how-chinas-ai-technology-exports-are-seeding-surveillance-societies-globally/.

31. Economy, "Exporting the China Model."

32. Ibid.

33. Ibid.

34. Anne-Marie Brady, *Making the Foreign Serve China: Managing Foreigners in the People's Republic* (Lanham, MD: Rowman and Littlefield, 2003).

35. Ibid.

36. See, for example, Peter Mattis, "U.S. Responses to China's Foreign Influence Operations," Testimony Before the House Committee on Foreign Affairs, Subcommittee on Asia and the Pacific, March 21, 2018, https://docs.house.gov/meetings/FA/FA05/20180321/108056/HHRG-115-FA05-Wstate-MattisP-20180321.pdf, for an excellent overview of the CCP's Leninist view of its political power and how that should be defended.

37. Ibid.

38. Wenfang Tang, "The 'Surprise' of Authoritarian Resilience in China," *American Affairs* 2, no. 1 (Spring 2018), https://americanaffairsjournal. org/2018/02/surprise-authoritarian-resilience-china/; Mercy A. Kuo, "China's United Front Work: Propaganda as Policy," *Diplomat*, February 14, 2018, https://thediplomat.com/2018/02/chinas-united-front-work-propaganda-as-policy/; Amy Qin and Javier C. Hernandez, "How China's Rulers Control Society: Opportunity, Nationalism, Fear," *New York Times*, November 25, 2018, https://www.nytimes.com/interactive/ 2018/11/25/world/asia/china-freedoms-control.html.

39. For instance, Australia passed new foreign interference laws in 2018 largely to stop Chinese influence; "Australia Passes Foreign Interference Laws amid China Tension," *BBC*, June 28, 2018, https://www.bbc. com/news/world-australia-44624270; Fabian Hamacher and Yimou Lee, "Taiwan Passes Law to Combat Chinese Influence in Politics," *Reuters*, December 31, 2019, https://www.reuters.com/article/us-tai wan-lawmaking/taiwan-passes-law-to-combat-chinese-influence-on-politics-idUSKBN1YZ0F6.

40. Kat Devlin, Christine Huang, and Laura Silver, "Unfavorable Views of China Reach Historic Highs in Many Countries," *Pew Research Center*, October 6, 2020, https://www.pewresearch.org/global/2020/10/06/ unfavorable-views-of-china-reach-historic-highs-in-many-countries/ . Also, Sarah Cook, "Beijing's Global Megaphone: The Expansion of Chinese Communist Party Media Influence Since 2017," *Freedom House*, January 2020, https://freedomhouse.org/report/special-reports/beijings-global-megaphone-china-communist-party-media-influence-abroad.

41. Reports, produced by Gallup, received March 5, 2019, from the U.S. Agency for Global Media (USAGM) under the Freedom of Information Act (FOIA) process. The reports show minimal interest in Chinese state media and include:

1) Analytical Report for Cambodia Media Use Survey, September 2017

2) Analytical Report for Indonesia Media Use Survey, July 2016

3) Analytical Report for Laos Media Use Survey, January 2017

4) Analytical Report for Media Use Survey of Ivory Coast, June 2017

5) Analytical Report for Media Use Survey of Kenya, June 2017

6) Analytical Report for Media Use Survey of Southern Mali, October 2017

7) Analytical Report for Myanmar Media Use Survey, June 2016

8) Analytical Report for Nigeria Media Use Survey, July 2016

9) Analytical Report for North Korea Traveler/Refugee/Defector Survey, undated

10) Analytical Report for Uzbekistan Media Use Survey, August 2017
11) Analytical Report for Vietnam Media Use Survey, December 2016.

42. Devlin, Huang, and Silver, "Unfavorable Views of China Reach Historic Highs in Many Countries."

43. Ibid.

44. For instance, on the backlash to China's strategies, see Amy Searight, *Countering China's Influence Activities: Lessons from Australia* (Washington, DC: Center for Strategic and International Studies, July 2020), https://www.csis.org/analysis/countering-chinas-influence-activities-lessons-australia.

45. Joseph S. Nye Jr., "Democracy's Dilemma," *Boston Review*, May 16, 2019, http://bostonreview.net/forum/democracys-dilemma/joseph-s-nye-jr-sharp-power-not-soft-power-should-be-target. Also, Salvatore Babones, "It's Time for Western Universities to Cut Their Ties to China," *Foreign Policy,* August 19, 2020, https://foreignpolicy.com/2020/08/19/universities-confucius-institutes-china/.

46. See, for instance, "Media," in *China's Influence & American Interests: Promoting Constructive Vigilance*, ed. Larry Diamond and Orville Schell (Stanford, CA: Hoover Institution Press, 2019), 100–19.

47. James Kynge and Jonathan Wheatley, "China Pulls Back from the World: Rethinking Xi's Project of the Century," *Financial Times*, December 10, 2020, https://www.ft.com/content/d9bd8059-d05c-4e6f-968b-16722 41ec1f6.

48. Freedom House, *Freedom in the World 2021: Democracy Under Siege* (Washington, DC: Freedom House, 2021).

49. Edward Wong, "U.S. Fights Bioweapons Disinformation Pushed by Russia and China," *New York Times*, March 10, 2022, https://www.nytimes.com/2022/03/10/us/politics/russia-ukraine-china-bioweapons.html.

50. Chris Buckley and Steven Lee Myers, "As the West Stumbles, 'Helmsman' Xi Pushes an Ambitious Plan for China," *New York Times*, October 29, 2020, https://www.nytimes.com/2020/10/29/world/asia/china-xi-communist-party-meeting.html.

51. Peter Mattis and Brad Carson, "Peter Mattis on the Intentions of the Chinese Communist Party," *Jaw-Jaw*, podcast audio, War on the Rocks, May 28, 2019, https://warontherocks.com/2019/05/jaw-jaw-peter-mattis-on-the-intentions-of-the-chinese-communist-party/.

52. "Chinese Discourse Power: China's Use of Information Manipulation in Regional and Global Competition," *Atlantic Council*, December

2020, https://www.atlanticcouncil.org/wp-content/uploads/2020/12/China-Discouse-Power-FINAL.pdf.

53. See, for example, "Telling China's Story to the World," *China Daily*, November 7, 2016, http://www.chinadaily.com.cn/opinion/2016-11/07/content_27291258.htm. Also, Shannon Tiezzi, "Chinese Military Declares Internet an Ideological Battleground," *Diplomat*, May 21, 2015, https://thediplomat.com/2015/05/chinese-military-declares-the-internet-an-ideological-battleground/. Also, Rush Doshi, "China Steps Up Its Information War in Taiwan," *Foreign Affairs*, January 9, 2020, https://www.foreignaffairs.com/articles/china/2020-01-09/china-steps-its-information-war-taiwan.

54. Elizabeth Bachman, *Black and White and Red All Over: China's Improving Foreign-Directed Media* (Arlington, VA: CNA, 2020), 1–2.

55. Doshi, "China Steps Up Its Information War in Taiwan."

56. David Bandurski, "How Xi Jinping Views the News," *China Media Project*, March 3, 2016, http://chinamediaproject.org/2016/03/03/39672/.

57. Bachman, *Black and White and Red All Over*, 23.

58. Doshi, "China Steps Up Its Information War in Taiwan."

59. See, for example, Kurt M. Campbell and Ely Ratner, "The China Reckoning: How Beijing Defied American Expectations," *Foreign Affairs* 97, no. 2 (March/April 2018): 60–70.

60. Elizabeth Economy, *The Third Revolution: Xi Jinping and the New Chinese State* (New York: Oxford University Press, 2018).

61. Ibid.

62. Ibid.

63. Joel Gehrke, "State Department Prepares for Clash of Civilizations With China," *Washington Examiner*, April 30, 2019, https://www.washingtonexaminer.com/policy/defense-national-security/state-department-preparing-for-clash-of-civilizations-with-china; Mark Landler, "Trump Accuses China of Interfering in Midterm Elections," *New York Times*, September 26, 2018, https://www.nytimes.com/2018/09/26/world/asia/trump-china-election.html; Jeff Mason and Daphne Psaledakis, "Trump Security Adviser Says China Has Biggest Election-Interference Program," *Reuters*, September 4, 2020, https://www.reuters.com/article/us-usa-election-china/trump-security-adviser-says-china-has-biggest-election-interference-program-idUSKBN25V2NY.

64. For more on these definitions, see Joseph Nye, *Bound to Lead: The Changing Nature of American Power* (New York: Basic Books, 1991); Joseph Nye, *Soft Power: The Means to Success in World Politics* (New York:

Public Affairs, 2004); Joshua Kurlantzick, *Charm Offensive: How China's Soft Power Is Transforming the World* (New Haven, CT: Yale University Press, 2007).

65. Samantha Custer et al., *Ties That Bind: Quantifying China's Public Diplomacy and Its "Good Neighbor" Effect* (Williamsburg, VA: AidData at William & Mary, 2018), https://www.aiddata.org/publications/ties-that-bind.

66. Ian Hall and Frank Smith, "The Struggle for Soft Power in Asia: Public Diplomacy and Regional Competition," *Asian Security* 9, no. 1 (2013): 9.

67. "World Bank Country and Lending Groups," *World Bank 2020 Data*, https://datahelpdesk.worldbank.org/knowledgebase/articles/906519#High_income.

68. Tang, "The 'Surprise' of Authoritarian Resilience in China"; "Xi's Embrace of False History and Fearsome Weapons Is Worrying," *Economist*, October 3, 2019, https://www.economist.com/china/2019/10/03/xis-embrace-of-false-history-and-fearsome-weapons-is-worrying.

69. Joshua Kurlantzick, *State Capitalism: How the Return of Statism Is Transforming the World* (New York: Oxford University Press, 2016), discusses these themes in more detail.

70. Interviews with officials from the USAGM.

71. Louisa Lim and Julia Bergin, "Inside China's Audacious Global Propaganda Campaign," *Guardian*, December 7, 2018, https://www.theguardian.com/news/2018/dec/07/china-plan-for-global-media-dominance-propaganda-xi-jinping.

72. Ibid.

73. Emily Feng, "China and the World: How Beijing Spreads the Message," *Financial Times*, July 12, 2018, https://www.ft.com/content/f5d00a86-3296-11e8-b5bf-23cb17fd1498.

74. Russel Hsiao, "CCP Propaganda Against Taiwan Enters the Social Age," *China Brief* 18, no. 7 (April 2018), https://jamestown.org/program/ccp-propaganda-against-taiwan-enters-the-social-age/.

75. Christopher Walker and Jessica Ludwig, "From 'Soft Power' to 'Sharp Power': Rising Authoritarian Influence in the Democratic World," in *Sharp Power: Rising Authoritarian Influence* (Washington, DC: National Endowment for Democracy, December 2017), https://www.ned.org/wp-content/uploads/2017/12/Sharp-power-Rising-Authoritarian-Influence-Full-Report.pdf.

76. Ibid.

77. Searight, *Countering China's Influence Activities*, 3–4.

78. Rob Gillies, "Obama Endorses Trudeau in Unprecedented Endorsement," *Associated Press*, October 16, 2019, https://apnews.com/article/6d242ba7022a4333ac99a57816f53ce8; Byron Tau, "Telephone Transcripts Show Warm Rapport Between Bill Clinton, Tony Blair," *Wall Street Journal*, January 8, 2016, https://www.wsj.com/articles/BL-WB-60203.

79. Javier C. Hernandez, Owen Guo, and Ryan McMorrow, "South Korean Stores Feel China's Wrath as U.S. Missile System Is Deployed," *New York Times*, March 9, 2017, https://www.nytimes.com/2017/03/09/world/asia/china-lotte-thaad-south-korea.html.

80. Ibid.

81. Alex Joske, "Reorganizing the United Front Work Department: New Structures for a New Era of Diaspora and Religious Affairs Work," *China Brief* 19, no. 9, (May 9, 2019), https://jamestown.org/program/reorganizing-the-united-front-work-department-new-structures-for-a-new-era-of-diaspora-and-religious-affairs-work/.

82. Ibid.

83. Nye, "Democracy's Dilemma."

84. Ibid.

85. Isaac Stone Fish, "Is Xinhua the Future of Journalism?," *Newsweek*, September 3, 2010, https://www.newsweek.com/chinas-xinhua-future-journalism-71961. See also Joshua Darr, "Local News Coverage Is Declining—and That Could Be Bad for American Politics," *FiveThirtyEight*, June 2, 2021, https://fivethirtyeight.com/features/local-news-coverage-is-declining-and-that-could-be-bad-for-american-politics/.

86. Austin Ramzy and Edward Wong, "China Forces Out Buzzfeed Journalist," *New York Times*, August 23, 2018, https://www.nytimes.com/2018/08/23/world/asia/china-buzzfeed-reporter.html; Lara Jakes, Marc Tracy, and Edward Wong, "China Announces That It Will Expel American Journalists," *New York Times*, March 17, 2020, https://www.nytimes.com/2020/03/17/business/media/china-expels-american-journalists.html.

87. Steven Lee Myers and Paul Mozur, "China Is Waging a Disinformation War Against Hong Kong Protestors," *New York Times*, August 13, 2019, https://www.nytimes.com/2019/08/13/world/asia/hong-kong-protests-china.html; Edward White, "Taiwan Warns of 'Rampant' Fake News amid China Interference Fears," *Financial Times*, April 2, 2019, https://www.ft.com/content/0edbf61e-01a6-11e9-99df-6183d3002ee1; Lawrence Chung, "Taiwan Gets Tough over Fake News Blamed

on Beijing 'Disrupting Its Democracy,'" *South China Morning Post*, July 27, 2019, https://www.scmp.com/news/china/politics/article/3020 261/taiwan-gets-tough-over-fake-news-blamed-beijing-disrupting-its; Alexander Gabuev and Leonid Kovachich, "Comrades in Tweets? The Contours and Limits of China-Russia Cooperation on Digital Propaganda," *Carnegie Moscow Center*, June 3, 2021, https://carnegiemos cow.org/2021/06/03/comrades-in-tweets-contours-and-limits-of-china-russia-cooperation-on-digital-propaganda-pub-84673.

88. Robin Wright, "Russia and China Unveil a Pact Against the West," *New Yorker*, February 7, 2022, https://www.newyorker.com/news/daily-comment/russia-and-china-unveil-a-pact-against-america-and-the-west.

89. David Hutt, "China's Largesse Abets Cambodia's Clampdown," *Asia Times*, September 26, 2017, https://asiatimes.com/2017/09/chinas-largesse-abets-cambodias-clampdown/. See Hiebert, *Under Beijing's Shadow*, 141.

90. David Shullman, ed., *Chinese Malign Influence and the Corrosion of Democracy: An Assessment of Chinese Interference in Thirteen Key Countries* (Washington, DC: International Republican Institute, 2019), https://www.iri.org/wp-content/uploads/legacy/iri.org/chinese_malign_i nfluence_report.pdf.

CHAPTER 2

1. Karla Cripps, "Why Thai People Are Wearing Yellow Shirts," *CNN*, May 4, 2019, https://www.cnn.com/asia/live-news/thai-king-coronat ion-live-updates-intl/h_5c6537d5620a21dea0452d7d562ef507; "Public Urged to Wear 'Coronation Yellow,'" *Bangkok Post*, February 26, 2019, https://www.bangkokpost.com/thailand/general/1636254/public-urged-to-wear-coronation-yellow.

2. "Thai Princess Studies in Beijing," *Xinhua*, February 15, 2001, http:// arabic.china.org.cn/english/FR/7670.htm; "Princess Sirindhorn, Champion of Sino-Thai Friendship," *Xinhua*, September 25, 2019, http://www.xinhuanet.com/english/2019-09/25/c_138422043.htm; Non Naprathansuk, "Confucius Institutes in Thailand: Why Thailand Embraces China's Soft Power Initiatives?," Maejo University, Chiang Mai, Thailand, https://www.academia.edu/27918602/Confucius_ Institutes_in_Thailand_Why_Thailand_Embraces_Chinas_Soft_Po wer_Initiatives.

3. Laura Zhou, "Over Decades, Thai Royal Family Has Forged Personal Bonds with China's Leaders," *South China Morning Post*, October 13, 2016, https://www.scmp.com/news/china/diplomacy-defence/arti cle/2027529/sino-thai-friendship-can-weather-royal-succession.

4. Non, "Confucius Institutes in Thailand."

5. Ibid.

6. For example, http://www.ateneoconfucius.com/; https://www.ci.upd. edu.ph/; https://www.addu.edu.ph/blog/2020/01/26/strengthening-ties-and-deepening-knowledge-with-the-addu-confucius-institute/; http://confucius.auf.edu.ph/; https://bulsu.edu.ph/confucius/ home.html.

7. Ibid.; Juan Pablo Cardenal, "China in Latin America: Understanding the Inventory of Influence," in *Sharp Power: Rising Authoritarian Influence* (Washington, DC: National Endowment for Democracy, December 2017), https://www.ned.org/wp-content/uploads/2017/12/Sharp-Power-Rising-Authoritarian-Influence-Full-Report.pdf.

8. Nargiza Salidjanova and Iacob Koch-Weser, "China's Economic Ties with ASEAN: A Country-by-Country Analysis," U.S.-China Economic and Security Review Commission, March 17, 2015, 4–9, https://www. uscc.gov/sites/default/files/Research/China%27s%20Economic%20T ies%20with%20ASEAN.pdf.

9. "What He Did, and Left Undone," *Economist*, March 6, 2003, https:// www.economist.com/asia/2003/03/06/what-he-did-and-left-und one; Fred Hu, "Zhu Rongji's Decade," *Wall Street Journal*, March 10, 2003, https://www.wsj.com/articles/SB104724760137643900; Simon Rabinovitch, "China Reforms Chip Away at Privileges of State-Owned Companies," *Financial Times*, November 19, 2013, https://www.ft.com/ content/42fc92d4-510a-11e3-b499-00144feabdc0; Zhu Rongji, *Zhu Rongji on the Record: The Road to Reform 1991–1997* (Washington, DC: Brookings Institution Press, 2013).

10. In AidData's *Ties That Bind* report, they have constructed a methodology for how Chinese public diplomacy actually affects other states' policy preferences, at least in Asia: Samantha Custer et al., *Ties That Bind: Quantifying China's Public Diplomacy and Its "Good Neighbor" Effect* (Williamsburg, VA: AidData at William & Mary, 2018), https://www. aiddata.org/publications/ties-that-bind. I do not believe soft power can work so clearly as the exact process they lay out, but their methodology is important and helps provide a foundation for thinking about how Chinese soft power, or public diplomacy, can produce policy objectives.

11. Yang Jiechi, "Promoting Public Diplomacy," *China Daily*, September 2, 2011, http://www.china.org.cn/opinion/2011-09/02/content_2 3337863.htm. See also Falk Hartig, "How China Understands Public Diplomacy: The Importance of National Image for National Interests," *International Studies Review* 18, no. 4 (December 2016): 660, for its references to Beijing's views on soft power.

12. See, for example, Behzad Abdollahpour, "China's 'Win-Win' Development Strategy Will Prevail," *Asia Times*, October 2, 2019, https://asiatimes.com/2019/10/chinas-development-policies-in-70-years-perspective/.

13. Xiao Qiang, "Dai Bingguo: The Core Interests of the People's Republic of China," *China Digital Times*, August 7, 2009, https://chinadigitaltimes.net/2009/08/dai-bingguo-%E6%88%B4%E7%A7%89%E5%9B%BD-the-core-interests-of-the-prc/.

14. "Chapter 2: China's Image," in "Global Opposition to U.S. Surveillance and Drones, but Limited Harm to America's Image," *Pew Research Center*, July 14, 2014, https://www.pewresearch.org/global/2014/07/14/chapter-2-chinas-image/.

15. Tom Fawthrop, "Thailand's Energy Review 'Pauses' Mekong Dam," *Mekong Eye*, June 14, 2018, https://www.mekongeye.com/2018/06/14/thailands-energy-review-pauses-mekong-dam/.

16. Wang Yi, "Toward a New Type of International Relations of Win-Win Cooperation," Speech by Foreign Minister Wang Yi at China Development Forum, Ministry of Foreign Affairs of the People's Republic of China, March 23, 2015, https://www.fmprc.gov.cn/mfa_eng/wjb_663304/wjbz_663308/2461_663310/t1248487.shtml; Chen Xulong, "Win-Win Cooperation: Formation, Development, and Characteristics," *China Institute of International Studies*, November 17, 2017, https://www.ciis.org.cn/english/ESEARCHPROJECTS/Articles/202007/t20200715_3604.html; "China President Xi Says Goal of Belt and Road Is Advance 'Win-Win Cooperation,'" *Reuters*, April 25, 2019, https://www.reuters.com/article/us-china-silkroad-xi/china-president-xi-says-goal-of-belt-and-road-is-advance-win-win-cooperation-idUSKCN1S205Z.

17. "Full Text of Clinton's Speech on China Trade Bill," *New York Times*, March 9, 2000, https://archive.nytimes.com/www.nytimes.com/library/world/asia/030900clinton-china-text.html.

18. Ibid.

19. Robert B. Zoellick, "Whither China: From Membership to Responsibility?," Remarks to National Committee on U.S.-China

Relations, September 21, 2005, https://2001-2009.state.gov/s/d/for mer/zoellick/rem/53682.htm.

20. Elizabeth Bachman, *Black and White and Red All Over: China's Improving Foreign-Directed Media* (Arlington, VA: CNA, 2020), 21–22.

21. Bachman, *Black and White and Red All Over*, 1–2.

22. Falk Hartig, "How China Understands Public Diplomacy: The Importance of National Image for National Interests," *International Studies Review* 18 (2016): 655–56.

23. Ibid.; Bachman, *Black and White and Red All Over*, 29–30.

24. Bachman, *Black and White and Red All Over*, 1–2.

25. Philip Shenon, "China Sends Warships to Vietnam Oil Site," *New York Times*, July 21, 1994, https://www.nytimes.com/1994/07/21/world/ china-sends-warships-to-vietnam-oil-site.html; Philip Shenon, "Manila Sees China Threat on Coral Reef," *New York Times*, February 19, 1995, https://www.nytimes.com/1995/02/19/world/manila-sees-china-thr eat-on-coral-reef.html.

26. "China GDP: How It Has Changed Since 1980," *Guardian*, March 23, 2012, https://www.theguardian.com/news/datablog/2012/mar/23/ china-gdp-since-1980.

27. Weida Li, "Chinese Soap Opera My Fair Princess Reruns to Massive Audience," *GB Times*, February 7, 2018, https://gbtimes.com/chinese-soap-opera-my-fair-princess-reruns-to-massive-audience.

28. Merriden Varrall, "The Patchy Results of China's Soft Power Efforts," *Interpreter*, March 16, 2018, https://www.lowyinstitute.org/the-inte rpreter/patchy-results-chinas-soft-power-efforts; Merriden Varrall, "Chinese Diplomacy and the Social Imaginary of Chineseness" (PhD thesis, Free University Amsterdam, June 2013), https://research.vu.nl/ ws/portalfiles/portal/42119557/complete+dissertation.pdf.

29. Patrick Kilby, "China and the United States as Aid Donors: Past and Future Trajectories," *Policy Studies* 77 (2017): 18–20, https://www.eas twestcenter.org/system/tdf/private/ps077.pdf?file=1&type=node&id= 36374; Joel Atkinson, "Aid vs. 'Aid': Foreign Aid in Mao-Era China's Public Diplomacy," *Australian Journal of Politics and History* 65, no. 2 (2019): 196–214.

30. For instance, China provided extensive support for communist armed rebels in what was then Burma.

31. Anne-Marie Brady, "*Plus Ça Change?*: Media Control Under Xi Jinping," *Problems of Post-Communism* 64, no. 3–4 (2017): 128–40.

32. See, for example, June Teufel Dreyer, "A Weapon Without War: China's United Front Strategy," *Foreign Policy Research Institute*, February 6, 2018,

https://www.fpri.org/article/2018/02/weapon-without-war-chinas-united-front-strategy/.

33. "Xinjiang Authorities Jail Family Members of Two Uighurs in Exile for Travel, Overseas Ties," *Radio Free Asia*, August 28, 2020, https://www.rfa.org/english/news/uyghur/overseas-08282020164436.html. Also, Andrew Jacobs, "Two Relatives of a Tibetan Monk Who Died in Prison Have Been Arrested," *New York Times*, July 19, 2015, https://www.nytimes.com/2015/07/19/world/asia/china-2-relatives-of-a-tibetan-monk-who-died-in-prison-have-been-arrested.html.

34. "Dangerous Meditation: China's Campaign Against Falungong," *Human Rights Watch*, January 2002, https://www.hrw.org/reports/2002/china/; Andrew Demaria, "China: Falun Gong a Global Threat," *CNN*, August 6, 2002, http://www.cnn.com/2002/WORLD/asiapcf/east/07/23/china.falungong; Andrew Jacobs, "China Still Presses Crusade Against Falun Gong," *New York Times*, April 27, 2009, www.nytimes.com/2009/04/28/world/asia/28china.html.

35. For more on U.S. use of soft power before and after the Cold War, see Joseph S. Nye, "Soft Power," *Foreign Policy* no. 80, Twentieth Anniversary (Autumn 1990): 153–71.

36. Masahiro Kawai and Shinji Takagi, "Japan's Official Development Assistance: Recent Issues and Future Directions," Policy Research Working Paper 2722, World Bank, November 2001, http://documents.worldbank.org/curated/en/348641468756616047/pdf/multiopage.pdf; Izumi Ohno, "Japan's ODA Policy and Reforms Since the 1990s and Role in the New Era of Development Cooperation," *National Graduate Institute for Policy Studies*, 2014, http://www.grips.ac.jp/forum-e/IzumiOhno_E/lectures/2014_Lecture_texts/03_KOICA_Ohno_1125.pdf.

37. John M. Broder and Jack Nelson, "Clinton's Laser Focus Diffuses on Wide Agenda," *Los Angeles Times*, April 19, 1993, https://www.latimes.com/archives/la-xpm-1993-04-19-mn-24765-story.html.

38. Jeremy Konyndyk, "Clinton and Helms Nearly Ruined State. Tillerson Wants to Finish the Job," *Politico*, May 4, 2017, https://www.politico.com/magazine/story/2017/05/04/tillerson-trump-state-department-budget-cut-215101.

39. Amy Magaro Rubin, "Clinton Agrees to Fold USIA into State Department," *Chronicle of Higher Education*, May 2, 1997, https://www.chronicle.com/article/Clinton-Agrees-to-Fold-USIA/75138.

40. Andrew Pollack, "IMF, with the Help of Asians, Offers Thais $16 Billion Bailout," *New York Times*, August 12, 1997, https://www.nytimes.com/1997/08/12/business/imf-with-the-help-of-asians-offers-thais-16-bill

ion-bailout.html. Also, Frontline, "The Crash: Timeline of the Panic," *PBS*, accessed February 17, 2022, https://www.pbs.org/wgbh/pages/ frontline/shows/crash/etc/cron.html.

41. Seth Mydans, "Crisis Aside, What Pains Indonesia Is the Humiliation," *New York Times*, March 10, 1998, https://www.nytimes.com/1998/03/ 10/world/crisis-aside-what-pains-indonesia-is-the-humiliation.html.

42. See, for instance, John W. Lewis, "The Contradictions of Bush's China Policy," *New York Times*, June 2, 2001, https://www.nytimes.com/2001/ 06/02/opinion/the-contradictions-of-bush-s-china-policy.html.

43. Richard Cronin, "The Second Bush Administration and Southeast Asia," *Stimson Center*, July 17, 2007, https://www.files.ethz.ch/isn/ 45521/Bush-SEA_KF_Cronin_17July2007.pdf.

44. Joshua Kurlantzick, *Charm Offensive: How China's Soft Power Is Transforming the World* (New Haven, CT: Yale University Press, 2007); Andrew Kohut, "How the World Sees China," *Pew Research Center*, December 11, 2007, https://www.pewresearch.org/global/2007/12/ 11/how-the-world-sees-china/.

45. Kohut, "How the World Sees China."

46. "Chapter 1: Views of the U.S. and American Foreign Policy," in "Global Opinion of Obama Slips, International Policies Faulted," *Pew Research Center*, June 13, 2012, https://www.pewresearch.org/global/2012/06/ 13/chapter-1-views-of-the-u-s-and-american-foreign-policy-4/.

47. For Hillary Clinton's original outline of the rebalance, known then as the pivot, see Hillary Clinton, "America's Pacific Century," *Foreign Policy*, October 11, 2011, https://foreignpolicy.com/2011/10/11/ameri cas-pacific-century/.

48. Office of the Press Secretary, "Advancing the Rebalance to Asia and the Pacific," White House, November 16, 2015, https://obamawhitehouse. archives.gov/the-press-office/2015/11/16/fact-sheet-advancing-rebala nce-asia-and-pacific.

49. Freedom House, *Freedom in the World 2007: The Annual Survey of Political Rights and Civil Liberties* (Lanham, MD: Rowman & Littlefield, 2007), https://freedomhouse.org/sites/default/files/2020-02/Freedom_in_t he_World_2007_complete_book.pdf.

50. Thomas Carothers, "Democracy Promotion Under Obama: Finding a Way Forward," Policy Brief 77, *Carnegie Endowment for International Peace*, February 2009, https://carnegieendowment.org/files/democr acy_promotion_obama.pdf.

51. Terry Miller, Anthony B. Kim, and James M. Roberts, *2019 Index of Economic Freedom: 25th Anniversary Edition* (Washington, DC: Heritage

Foundation, 2019), https://www.heritage.org/index/pdf/2019/book/index_2019.pdf.

52. Helen Epstein, "Good News for Democracy," *Lancet* 393, no. 10181 (2019): 1569–668, https://www.thelancet.com/journals/lancet/article/PIIS0140-6736(19)30431-3/fulltext. Also, Thomas Bollyky et al., "The Relationships Between Democratic Experience, Adult Health, and Cause-Specific Mortality in 170 Countries Between 1980 and 2016: An Observational Analysis," *Lancet* 393, no. 10181 (2019): 1628–40, http://dx.doi.org/10.1016/S0140-6736(19)30235-1.

53. I first referred to this effect in my book *Democracy in Retreat: The Revolt of the Middle Class and Worldwide Decline of Representative Government* (New Haven, CT: Yale University Press, 2014), 51, 183–84.

54. Ibid.

55. Li Mingjiang, "Soft Power in Chinese Discourse: Popularity and Prospect," RSIS Working Paper No. 165, Nanyang Technological University, Singapore, January 2008, https://www.researchgate.net/publication/30066572_Soft_Power_in_Chinese_Discourse_Popularity_and_Prospect.

56. Yiwei Wang, "Public Diplomacy and the Rise of Chinese Soft Power," *Annals of the American Academy of Political and Social Sciences* 616 (2008): 263, https://www.jstor.org/stable/25098003.

57. Min-gyu Lee and Yufan Hao, "China's Unsuccessful Charm Offensive: How South Koreans Have Viewed the Rise of China over the Past Decade," *Journal of Contemporary China* 27, no. 114 (2018): 867, https://www.tandfonline.com/doi/abs/10.1080/10670564.2018.1488103.

58. Ibid.

59. Daya Kishan Thussu, Hugo de Burgh, and Anbin Shi, eds., *China's Media Go Global* (New York: Routledge, 2018), 69.

60. Hilton Yip, "China's $6 Billion Propaganda Blitz Is a Snooze," *Foreign Policy*, April 23, 2018, https://foreignpolicy.com/2018/04/23/the-voice-of-china-will-be-a-squeak/.

61. Pál Nyíri, *Reporting for China: How Chinese Correspondents Work with the World* (Seattle: University of Washington Press, 2017), 25–26.

62. Ibid.

63. For instance, Radomir Tylecote and Henri Rossano, "Discussion Paper: China's Military Education and Commonwealth Countries," *Civitas*, November 2021, https://www.civitas.org.uk/publications/discussion-paper-chinas-military-education-and-commonwealth-countries/.

64. "Why China Is Lavishing Money on Foreign Students," *Economist*, January 26, 2019, https://www.economist.com/china/2019/01/26/why-china-is-lavishing-money-on-foreign-students.

65. Prashanth Parameswaran, "Measuring the Dragon's Reach: Quantifying China's Influence in Southeast Asia (1990–2007)," *Monitor: Journal of International Studies* 14, no. 2 (2010): 37–53.

66. Custer et al., *Ties That Bind*, 12.

67. Ibid.

68. "Outbound Mobility: Past Years," *Institute of International Education*, accessed February 17, 2022, https://www.iie.org/Research-and-Insights/Project-Atlas/Explore-Data/China/Outbound-Mobility---Past-Years.

69. Custer et al., *Ties That Bind*.

70. I discuss this boom at length, based on my reporting, in Kurlantzick, *Charm Offensive*.

71. Zhuang Pinghui, "China's Confucius Institutes Rebrand After Overseas Propaganda Rows," *South China Morning Post*, July 4, 2020, https://www.scmp.com/news/china/diplomacy/article/3091837/chinas-confucius-institutes-rebrand-after-overseas-propaganda.

72. Institute of International Education, "Leading Places of Origin of International Students, 2003/04–2004/05," *Open Doors Report on International Education Exchange*, https://www.iie.org/Research-and-Insights/Open-Doors/Data/International-Students/Places-of-Origin/Leading-Places-of-Origin/2004-05.

73. Institute of International Education, "Top 25 Places of Origin of International Students, 2009/10–2010/11," *Open Doors Report on International Education Exchange*, https://opendoorsdata.org/data/international-students/leading-places-of-origin.

74. Custer et al., *Ties That Bind*, 16.

75. Parameswaran, "Measuring the Dragon's Reach."

76. Tony S. M. Tse and J. S. Perry Hobson, "The Forces Shaping China's Outbound Tourism," *Journal of China Tourism Research* 4, no. 2 (2008): 136–55, https://www.tandfonline.com/doi/pdf/10.1080/19388160802279459.

77. Cheng Si, "China Still No. 1 Outbound Tourism Market: Report," *China Daily*, March 13, 2019, http://www.chinadaily.com.cn/a/201903/13/WS5c88f6aca3106c65c34ee74c.html.

78. Claudio Rosmino, "How Is Europe Preparing for the Return of Chinese Tourists," *EuroNews*, December 22, 2020, https://www.euronews.com/next/2020/12/22/how-is-europe-preparing-for-the-return-of-chinese-tourists.

79. Junyi Zhang, "Chinese Foreign Assistance, Explained," *Brookings Institution*, July 19, 2016, https://www.brookings.edu/blog/order-from-chaos/2016/07/19/chinese-foreign-assistance-explained.

80. See Axel Dreher et al., "Aid, China, and Growth: Evidence from a New Global Development Finance Dataset," Working Paper 46, *AidData*, October 2017, https://www.aiddata.org/publications/aid-china-and-growth-evidence-from-a-new-global-development-finance-dataset, for a more complete definition and analysis of China's aid.

81. Robert A. Blair, Robert Marty, and Philip Roessler, "Foreign Aid and Soft Power: Great Power Competition in Africa in the Early 21st Century," Working Paper 86, *AidData*, August 2019, http://docs.aiddata.org/ad4/pdfs/WPS86_Foreign_Aid_and_Soft_Power__Great_Power_Competition_in_Africa_in_the_Early_21st_Century.pdf.

82. Zhang, "Chinese Foreign Assistance, Explained."

83. Ibid.

84. Dreher et al., "Aid, China, and Growth."

85. Ibid.

86. Thomas Lum, Wayne M. Morrison, and Bruce Vaughn, "CRS Report for Congress: China's 'Soft Power' in Southeast Asia," *Congressional Research Service*, January 4, 2008, https://fas.org/sgp/crs/row/RL34310.pdf.

87. Esther Pan, "Tsunami Disaster: Relief Effort," *Council on Foreign Relations*, February 15, 2005, https://www.cfr.org/backgrounder/tsunami-disaster-relief-effort.

88. Hu Jintao, "Build Towards a Harmonious World of Lasting Peace and Common Prosperity," Statement at the United Nations Summit, New York, September 15, 2005, https://www.un.org/webcast/summit2005/statements15/china050915eng.pdf.

89. Wei Pan, "Western System Versus Chinese System," China Policy Institute, Briefing Series Issue 61, University of Nottingham, July 2010, https://www.nottingham.ac.uk/iaps/documents/cpi/briefings/briefing-61-chinese-western-system.pdf.

CHAPTER 3

1. "International Leadership Visitor Program," U.S. Department of State, https://eca.state.gov/ivlp.

2. "Remarks of Chinese Premier Wen Jiabao," *Harvard Gazette*, December 11, 2003, https://news.harvard.edu/gazette/story/2003/12/harvard-gazette-remarks-of-chinese-premier-wen-jiabao/; Zheng Bijian,

"China's 'Peaceful Rise' to Great-Power Status," *Foreign Affairs* 84, no. 5 (September/October 2005), https://www.foreignaffairs.com/articles/asia/2005-09-01/chinas-peaceful-rise-great-power-status; Esther Pan, "The Promise and Pitfalls of China's 'Peaceful Rise,'" *Council on Foreign Relations*, April 14, 2006, https://www.cfr.org/backgrounder/promise-and-pitfalls-chinas-peaceful-rise.

3. Robert G. Sutter, "China's Rise and U.S. Influence in Asia: A Report from the Region," *Atlantic Council*, July 29, 2006, https://www.atlanticcouncil.org/wp-content/uploads/2006/07/060820-China_US_Asia.pdf.

4. Ibid.; Office of the Secretary of Defense, "Annual Report to Congress: Military and Security Developments Involving the People's Republic of China 2019," *U.S. Department of Defense*, May 2019, 5–6, https://media.defense.gov/2019/May/02/2002127082/-1/-1/1/2019_CHINA_MILITARY_POWER_REPORT.pdf.

5. Joshua Kurlantzick and Yanzhong Huang, "China's Approach to Global Governance," *Council on Foreign Relations*, June 2020, https://www.cfr.org/china-global-governance/.

6. I discuss the growth of Chinese-language schools in this era at length in my book Joshua Kurlantzick, *Charm Offensive: How China's Soft Power Is Transforming the World* (New Haven, CT: Yale University Press, 2007). Also, Cindy Co and James Reddick, "In Cambodia's Chinese Language Schools, a Hard Push for Soft Power," *Phnom Penh Post*, December 18, 2017, https://www.phnompenhpost.com/national-post-depth/cambodias-chinese-language-schools-hard-push-soft-power.

7. For instance, Mech Dara, "Hun Sen: Claim That China Is 'Invading' Kingdom Is Crazy," *Phnom Penh Post*, October 25, 2018, https://www.phnompenhpost.com/national/hun-sen-claim-china-invading-kingdom-crazy. There are many similar stories detailing the large numbers of Chinese workers who've come to Cambodia to work on various projects.

8. Alex Willemyns, "Analysis: Time, Cash Heal All Wounds," *Phnom Penh Post*, October 13, 2016, https://www.phnompenhpost.com/national/analysis-time-cash-heal-all-wounds.

9. "Cambodia Opens China-funded Bridge for Traffic," *Xinhua*, January 24, 2011, http://www.chinadaily.com.cn/china/2011-01/24/content_1 1907394.htm; Va Sonyka, "PM Inaugurates Bridge in Takhmau City," *Khmer Times*, August 3, 2015, https://www.khmertimeskh.com/58244/pm-inaugurates-bridge-in-takhmau-city/; Prak Chan Thul, "Chinese President Xi Jinping Visits Loyal Friend Cambodia," *Reuters*, October

13, 2016, https://www.reuters.com/article/us-china-cambodia/chin ese-president-xi-jinping-visits-loyal-friend-cambodia-idUSKCN12D oNV; "Cambodian PM Says Spent $40 Million on Unspecified Arms from China," *Radio Free Asia*, July 29, 2019, https://www.rfa.org/engl ish/news/cambodia/china-weapons-07292019171125.html.

10. "22 Nation Poll Shows China Viewed Positively by Most Countries," *Program on International Policy Attitudes*, March 5, 2005, https://drum.lib. umd.edu/bitstream/handle/1903/10666/China_Mar05_art.pdf;jsessio nid=635510E412FB72A070291CE7FD3D6F46?sequence=2.

11. Liu Kang, Min-Hua Huang, and Lu Jie, "How Do Asians View the Rise of China?," *Asian Barometer Survey Conference*, http://www.asianbarome ter.org/publications/12e5aa4d6c68ee05b5def6e98afc2627.pdf.

12. "Round 4: 2008/2009," Afrobarometer, https://afrobarometer.org.

13. "Opinion of China, 2001–2018," Latinobarómetro, http://www.lati nobarometro.org/latOnline.jsp.

14. "China's $10bn Annual Spending on Soft Power Has Bought Little of It," *Economist*, May 24, 2019, https://www.economist.com/graphic-det ail/2019/05/24/chinas-10bn-annual-spending-on-soft-power-has-bou ght-little-of-it.

15. Ibid.

16. Isaac Stone Fish, "Unlivable Cities," *Foreign Policy*, August 13, 2012, https://foreignpolicy.com/2012/08/13/unlivable-cities/.

17. Matthew Phillips, *Thailand in the Cold War* (New York: Routledge, 2016). Phillips discusses these U.S. programs at length throughout the book. Also, see "Jazz Diplomacy: Then and Now," U.S. State Department Dipnote, April 30, 2021, https://www.state.gov/dipnote-u-s-departm ent-of-state-official-blog/jazz-diplomacy-then-and-now.

18. Phillips, *Thailand in the Cold War*, 151.

19. See, for instance, Benjamin Zawacki, *Thailand: Shifting Ground Between the U.S. and a Rising China* (London: Zed Books, 2017).

20. "Documentary of the First Official Visit to the United States of His Majesty King Bhumibhol Adulyadej in 1960," *U.S. Embassy & Consulate in Thailand*, October 28, 2016, https://th.usembassy.gov/vdo-remember ing-king-bhumibol-adulyadejs-state-visit-u-s-1960/.

21. See, for instance, Daniel Fineman, *A Special Relationship: The United States and Military Government in Thailand, 1947–1958* (Honolulu, Hawaii: University of Hawaii Press, 1997).

22. "Thailand's Strategic Reappraisal," in *Editorial Research Reports 1975*, vol. I, http://library.cqpress.com/cqresearcher/cqresrre1975062700.

23. In one of the most comprehensive articles on the U.S.-Thai security relationship during the Vietnam War, drawing on a range of primary documents, Arne Kislenko notes that "many Thais welcomed an expanded American military role in Vietnam." Arne Kislenko, "A Not So Silent Partner: Thailand's Role in Covert Operations, Counter-Insurgency, and the Wars in Indochina," *Journal of Conflict Studies* 24, no. 1 (2004), https://journals.lib.unb.ca/index.php/JCS/article/view/292.

24. For example, see Ethan Epstein, "How China Infiltrated U.S. Classrooms," *Politico*, January 16, 2018, https://www.politico.com/magazine/story/2018/01/16/how-china-infiltrated-us-classrooms-216327/.

25. Kornphanat Tungkeunkunt, "China's Soft Power in Thailand Culture and Commerce: China's Soft Power in Thailand," *International Journal of China Studies* 7, no. 2 (2017), https://www.researchgate.net/publication/326080395_China's_Soft_Power_in_Thailand_Culture_and_Commerce_China's_Soft_Power_in_Thailand/citation/download.

26. York A. Weise, "The 'Chinese Education Problem' of 1948—Thai Governmental Repression as Perceived by the Thai Chinese Press," Occasional Paper No. 15, Southeast Asian Studies at the University of Freiburg, April 2013, https://www.southeastasianstudies.uni-freiburg.de/Content/files/occasional-paper-series/op15.pdf.

27. Kornphanat, "China's Soft Power in Thailand Culture and Commerce."

28. See, for instance, Geoffrey Robinson, *The Killing Season: A History of the Indonesian Massacres, 1965–66* (Princeton, NJ: Princeton University Press, 2018).

29. Grace Tan-Johannes, "Why More Chinese Indonesians Are Learning Mandarin, and Nurturing Their Children's Sense of Belonging to Chinese Culture," *South China Morning Post*, August 23, 2018, https://www.scmp.com/lifestyle/families/article/2160779/three-reasons-more-chinese-indonesians-are-learning-mandarin-and; Jacqueline Knörr, "'Free the Dragon' Versus 'Becoming Betawi': Chinese Identity in Contemporary Jakarta," *Asian Ethnicity* 10, no. 1 (2009): 71–90, https://www.tandfonline.com/doi/full/10.1080/14631360802628467.

30. Corry Elyda and Fedina S. Sundaryani, "Ahok Becomes Jakarta Governor Today," *Jakarta Post*, November 19, 2014, https://www.thejakartapost.com/news/2014/11/19/ahok-becomes-jakarta-governor-today.html.

31. "How Fake News and Hoaxes Have Tried to Derail Jakarta's Election," *BBC*, April 18, 2017, https://www.bbc.com/news/world-asia-39176350.

32. Carool Kersten, "Jakarta Governor's Blasphemy Conviction Shows Democracy and Tolerance Under Threat in Indonesia," *Newsweek*, May

11, 2017, https://www.newsweek.com/ahok-religious-intolerance-indonesia-607343. Also, "Jakarta's Christian Governor Ahok Sentenced to Two Years in Jail for Blasphemy," *Reuters*, May 9, 2017, https://www.newsweek.com/jakartas-former-governor-ahok-jailed-blasphermy-605618.

33. Tom Allard and Agustinus Beo Da Costa, "Indonesian Islamist Leader Says Ethnic Chinese Wealth Is Next Target," *Reuters*, May 12, 2017, https://www.reuters.com/article/uk-indonesia-politics-cleric-exclusive/exclusive-indonesian-islamist-leader-says-ethnic-chinese-wealth-is-next-target-idUSKBN18817N.

34. Kornphanat, "China's Soft Power in Thailand Culture and Commerce."

35. Ibid.

36. "Chapter 2: China's Image," in "Global Opposition to U.S. Surveillance and Drones, but Limited Harm to America's Image," *Pew Research Center*, July 14, 2014, https://www.pewresearch.org/global/2014/07/14/chapter-2-chinas-image/.

37. Kornphanat, "China's Soft Power in Thailand Culture and Commerce."

38. Ibid.

39. Ibid.; Tyler Roney, "Chinese Propaganda Finds a Thai Audience," *Foreign Policy*, August 28, 2019, https://foreignpolicy.com/2019/08/28/chinese-propaganda-finds-a-thai-audience/.

40. Murray Hiebert, *Under Beijing's Shadow: Southeast Asia's China Challenge* (Lanham, MD: Rowman and Littlefield, 2020), 322.

41. "Vice Foreign Minister Zhang Zhijun Talks About Vice President Xi Jinping's Visits to Vietnam and Thailand," Ministry of Foreign Affairs of the People's Republic of China, December 24, 2011, https://www.mfa.gov.cn/ce/cemn/eng/gnyw/t890786.htm.

42. "Thai PM Seeks Out Roots in Meizhou," *China Daily*, July 4, 2005, http://www.chinadaily.com.cn/english/doc/2005-07/04/content_456688.htm.

43. Ibid.

44. Zawacki, *Thailand*.

45. Ibid.

46. Duncan McCargo and Ukrist Pathmanand, *The Thaksinization of Thailand* (Copenhagen: Nordic Institute of Asian Studies, 2004), 56–58.

47. Blake Schmidt and Natnicha Chuwiruch, "Thailand's Richest Family Is Getting Richer Helping China," *Bloomberg*, April 24, 2019, https://www.bloomberg.com/news/articles/2019-04-23/richest-family-in-thailand-is-getting-richer-by-helping-china.

48. Joseph Lelyveld, "China and Malaysia Establish Relations," *New York Times*, June 1, 1974, https://www.nytimes.com/1974/06/01/archives/china-and-malaysia-establish-relationsl-large-chinese-population.html. Also, Dawn Chan, "PM Outlines Three Areas to Further Boost Malaysia-China Relations," *New Straits Times*, October 14, 2021, https://www.nst.com.my/news/nation/2021/10/736538/pm-outlines-three-areas-further-bolster-malaysia-china-relations.

49. "Chapter 3: Views of China and Its Increasing Influence," in "Global Unease with Major World Powers," *Pew Research Center*, June 27, 2007, https://www.pewresearch.org/global/2007/06/27/chapter-3-views-of-china-and-its-increasing-influence/.

50. Yu-tzung Chang and Yun-han Chu, "Xi's Foreign Policy Turn and Asian Perceptions of a Rising China," *Global Asia* 12, no. 1 (Spring 2017, http://www.asianbarometer.org/publications//38bd8798df38c115ef8a76646fd41fb4.pdf.

51. Samantha Custer et al., *Ties That Bind: Quantifying China's Public Diplomacy and Its "Good Neighbor" Effect* (Williamsburg, VA: AidData at William & Mary, 2018), 15, https://www.aiddata.org/publications/ties-that-bind. AidData calls this aid "Official Finance with Diplomatic Intent"; China does not participate in the Organisation for Economic Cooperation and Development's Development Assistance Committee (DAC) group of donors and its aid is sometimes opaque, but AidData essentially classifies this as aid, since at least 25 percent of this funding is a grant, which conforms to the DAC definition of aid.

52. Yantoultra Ngui, "China Elevates Malaysia Ties, Aims to Triple Trade by 2017," *Reuters*, October 4, 2013, https://www.reuters.com/article/us-malaysia-china/china-elevates-malaysia-ties-aims-to-triple-trade-by-2017-idUSBRE99304020131004.

53. Custer et al., *Ties That Bind*, 30.

54. For instance, Ananth Baliga and Vong Sokheng, "Cambodia Again Blocks ASEAN Statement on the South China Sea," *Agence France Presse*, July 25, 2016, https://www.phnompenhpost.com/national/cambodia-again-blocks-asean-statement-south-china-sea.

55. Ibid.

56. Shannon Tiezzi, "How China Wins Friends and Influences People," *Diplomat*, June 27, 2018, https://thediplomat.com/2018/06/how-china-wins-friends-and-influences-people/.

57. I talk about these efforts at length in Kurlantzick, *Charm Offensive*.

58. "Feelings Toward Other Nations," Lowy Institute Poll 2019, *Lowy Institute*, https://lowyinstitutepoll.lowyinstitute.org/themes/feelings-towards-other-nations/.

59. Ibid.

60. "Opinion of China: 2002," Global Indicators Database, *Pew Research Center*, https://www.pewresearch.org/global/database/indicator/24/. On the seizing of Scarborough Shoal, see Ely Ratner, "Learning the Lessons of Scarborough Reef," *National Interest*, November 21, 2013, https://nationalinterest.org/commentary/learning-the-lessons-scarborough-reef-9442.

61. Custer et al., *Ties That Bind*.

62. Roel Landingin, "Philippines: China-Funded Northrail Project Derailed," *Financial Times*, October 10, 2012, https://www.ft.com/content/7f7f314c-522b-3a68-b6ad-4188ff607f4d.

CHAPTER 4

1. "South Korea 'Suspends Visas' for Chinese Teachers at Confucius Institutes," *Agence France-Presse*, February 1, 2017, https://www.scmp.com/news/asia/east-asia/article/2067162/south-korea-suspends-visas-chinese-teachers-confucius-institutes. Also, "Confucius Institutes Around the World," DigMandarin, https://www.digmandarin.com/confucius-institutes-around-the-world.html.

2. Min-gyu Lee and Yufan Hao, "China's Unsuccessful Charm Offensive: How South Koreans Have Viewed the Rise of China over the Past Decade," *Journal of Contemporary China* 27, no. 115 (2018): 867–86.

3. Ibid.

4. Ibid.

5. Joyce Lee and Adam Jourdan, "South Korea's Lotte Reports Store Closures in China Amid Political Stand-off," *Reuters*, March 5, 2017, https://www.reuters.com/article/us-southkorea-china-lotte/south-koreas-lotte-reports-store-closures-in-china-amid-political-stand-off-idUSKBN16D03U.

6. Lauren Teixeira, "K-Pop's Big China Problem," *Foreign Policy*, July 30, 2019, https://foreignpolicy.com/2019/07/30/k-pops-big-china-problem/.

7. Echo Huang, "China Inflicted a World of Pain on South Korea in 2017," *Quartz*, December 21, 2017, https://qz.com/1149663/china-south-korea-relations-in-2017-thaad-backlash-and-the-effect-on-tourism/.

8. Scott A. Snyder, "South Koreans and Americans Agree on How to Deal with China," *Asia Unbound*, October 21, 2019, https://www.cfr.org/blog/south-koreans-and-americans-agree-how-deal-china.

9. A portion of this section was adapted from Joshua Kurlantzick, "Everyone's Getting Mad at China: A Shift, or Nothing New?," *Asia Unbound*, November 22, 2019, https://www.cfr.org/blog/everyones-getting-mad-china-shift-or-nothing-new.

10. Yida Zhai, "The Gap in Viewing China's Rise Between Chinese Youth and Their Asian Counterparts," *Journal of Contemporary China* 27, no. 114 (2018).

11. Ibid.

12. "The State of Southeast Asia: 2019 Survey Report," *ASEAN Studies Center, ISEAS-Yusof Ishak Institute*, January 29, 2019, https://www.iseas.edu.sg/images/pdf/TheStateofSEASurveyReport_2019.pdf; "The State of Southeast Asia: 2020 Survey Report," *ASEAN Studies Center, ISEAS-Yusof Ishak Institute*, January 16, 2020, https://www.iseas.edu.sg/wp-content/uploads/pdfs/TheStateofSEASurveyReport_2020.pdf.

13. Yun-han Chu, Liu Kang, and Min-hua Huang, "How East Asians View the Rise of China," *Journal of Contemporary China* 24, no. 93 (2015).

14. Ian Hall and Frank Griffith, "The Struggle for Soft Power in East Asia: Public Diplomacy and Regional Competition," *Asian Security* 9, no. 1 (January 2013).

15. David Shambaugh, "China's Soft-Power Push," *Foreign Affairs* 94, no. 4 (July/August 2015), https://www.foreignaffairs.com/articles/china/2015-06-16/china-s-soft-power-push.

16. Hall and Griffith, "The Struggle for Soft Power in East Asia."

17. Zhai, "The Gap in Viewing China's Rise Between Chinese Youth and Their Asian Counterparts."

18. "The State of Southeast Asia: 2019 Survey Report," *ASEAN Studies Center, ISEAS-Yusof Ishak Institute*, January 29, 2019, https://www.iseas.edu.sg/images/pdf/TheStateofSEASurveyReport_2019.pdf.

19. Ibid.

20. Samantha Custer et al., *Ties That Bind: Quantifying China's Public Diplomacy and Its "Good Neighbor" Effect* (Williamsburg, VA: AidData at William & Mary, 2018), 4–5, https://www.aiddata.org/publications/ties-that-bind.

21. Ibid., 45.

22. Ibid., 48–53.

23. For an early analysis of this phenomenon, see Soo Yeon Kim and Bruce Russett, "The New Politics of Voting Alignments in the United Nations

General Assembly," *International Organization* 50, no. 4 (Autumn 1996): 629–52.

24. Margaret Seymour, "Measuring Soft Power," *Foreign Policy Research Institute*, December 14, 2020, https://www.fpri.org/article/2020/12/measuring-soft-power/.

25. Richard C. Bush and Maeve Whelan-Wuest, "How Asians View America (and China)," *Brookings Institution*, January 18, 2017, https://www.brookings.edu/blog/order-from-chaos/2017/01/18/how-asians-view-america-and-china/.

26. See, for example, Tuan Anh Luc, "Demonstrations in Vietnam Should Be a Wake-up Call for China," *East Asia Forum*, July 14, 2018, https://www.eastasiaforum.org/2018/07/14/demonstrations-in-vietnam-should-be-a-wake-up-call-for-china/; "Thousands Protest Against Myanmar Mega-dam," *ASEAN Post*, April 23, 2019, https://theaseanpost.com/article/thousands-protest-against-myanmar-mega-dam; and Gene Ryack, "A Hitch in the Belt and Road in Myanmar," *Diplomat*, December 3, 2020, https://thediplomat.com/2020/12/a-hitch-in-the-belt-and-road-in-myanmar/.

27. James Kynge, "China's Belt and Road Difficulties Are Proliferating Across the World," *Financial Times*, July 9, 2018, https://www.ft.com/content/fa3ca8ce-835c-11e8-a29d-73e3d454535d.

28. "China's Role in Myanmar's Internal Conflicts," USIP Senior Study Group Final Report, *United States Institute of Peace*, September 2018, https://www.usip.org/sites/default/files/2018-09/ssg-report-chinas-role-in-myanmars-internal-conflicts.pdf; Nan Lwin, "China Leads Investment in Yangon," *Irrawaddy*, July 26, 2019, https://www.irrawaddy.com/business/china-leads-investment-yangon.html; "China, Myanmar Vow Closer Ties as Suu Kyi Visits Beijing," *Associated Press*, August 20, 2016, https://apnews.com/8bca717683d74c23926bda4fd95b4f2e; Jane Perlez, "In China, Aung San Suu Kyi Finds a Warm Welcome (and No Talk of Rohingya)," *New York Times*, November 30, 2017, https://www.nytimes.com/2017/11/30/world/asia/china-myanmar-aid-sanctions.html.

29. Aung Zaw, "The Letpadaung Saga and the End of an Era," *Irrawaddy*, March 14, 2013, https://www.irrawaddy.com/opinion/the-letpadaung-saga-and-the-end-of-an-era.html.

30. Jason Burke and Swe Win, "Burma: Riot Police Move in to Break Up Copper Mine Protest," *Guardian*, November 29, 2012, https://www.theguardian.com/world/2012/nov/29/burma-riot-police-mine-protest.

31. Ibid.; Thomas Fuller, "Violent Raid Breaks Up Myanmar Mine Protest," *New York Times*, November 29, 2012, https://www.nytimes.com/2012/11/30/world/asia/myanmar-security-forces-raid-protest-camp.html; Lawi Weng, "Use of Phosphorus in Protest Raid Outrages Activist, Victims," *Irrawaddy*, January 31, 2013, https://www.irrawaddy.com/news/burma/use-of-phosphorus-in-protest-raid-outrages-activist-victims.html.

32. "Myanmar: Suspend Copper Mine Linked to Ongoing Human Rights Abuses," *Amnesty International*, February 10, 2017, https://www.amnesty.org/en/latest/news/2017/02/myanmar-suspend-copper-mine-linked-to-ongoing-human-rights-abuses/.

33. Andrew R. C. Marshall and Prak Chan Thul, "Insight: China Gambles on Cambodia's Shrinking Forests," *Reuters*, March 6, 2012, https://www.reuters.com/article/us-cambodia-forests/insight-china-gambles-on-cambodias-shrinking-forests-idUSTRE82607N20120307; Simon Denyer, "The Push and Pull of China's Orbit," *Washington Post*, September 5, 2015, https://www.washingtonpost.com/sf/world/2015/09/05/the-push-and-pull-of-chinas-orbit/?utm_term=.1518ff271208; Aun Pheap, "Returnees on UDG Site to Be Evicted," *Cambodia Daily*, June 16, 2016, https://english.cambodiadaily.com/news/returnees-on-udg-site-to-be-evicted-114190/; James Kynge, Leila Haddou, and Michael Peel, "FT Investigation: How China Bought Its Way into Cambodia," *Financial Times*, September 8, 2016, https://www.ft.com/content/23968248-43a0-11e6-b22f-79eb4891c97d; Alisa Tang and Prak Chan Thul, "Amid Land Grabs and Evictions, Cambodia Jails Leading Activist," *Reuters*, February 24, 2017, https://www.reuters.com/article/us-cambodia-landactivist/amid-land-grabs-and-evictions-cambodia-jails-leading-activist-idUSKBN164009; Andrew Nachemson, "'This Is My Land': Cambodian Villagers Slam Chinese Mega-Project," *Al Jazeera*, September 20, 2018, https://www.aljazeera.com/indepth/features/land-cambodian-villagers-slam-chinese-mega-project-180920150810557.html.

34. Hannah Ellis-Peterson, "How Chinese Money Is Changing Sihanoukville—'No Cambodia Left,'" *South China Morning Post*, August 7, 2018, https://www.scmp.com/magazines/post-magazine/long-reads/article/2158621/how-chinese-money-changing-sihanoukville-no.

35. Pál Nyíri, "New Chinese Migration and Capital in Cambodia," *Trends in Southeast Asia* 3 (2014): 6–7.

36. Ibid.

37. Hongyi Lai, "China's Cultural Diplomacy: Going for Soft Power," in *China's Soft Power and International Relations*, ed. Hongyi Lai and Yiyi Lu (London: Routledge, 2012), 88–89.

38. Ibid.

39. Ibid.

40. Shambaugh, "China's Soft-Power Push."

41. Chris Buckley, "In China, an Action Hero Beats Box Office Records (and Arrogant Westerners)," *New York Times*, August 16, 2017, https://www.nytimes.com/2017/08/16/world/asia/china-wolf-warrior-2-film.html; Zephing Huang, "China's Answer to Rambo Is About Punishing Those Who Offend China—and It's Killing It in Theaters," *Quartz*, August 8, 2017, https://qz.com/1048667/wolf-warriors-2-chinas-answer-to-rambo-and-about-punishing-those-who-offend-china-is-killing-it-at-the-box-office/.

42. "Chinese Artist Ai Weiwei Describes His 81 Days in Prison—and the Extreme Surveillance, Censorship, and 'Soft Detention' He's Endured Since," *Artspace*, December 20, 2018, https://www.artspace.com/magazine/interviews_features/qa/the-most-shocking-image-i-can-remember-is-seeing-myself-in-the-mirrorchinese-artist-ai-weiwei-55832; "Ai Weiwei Beijing Studio Demolished 'Without Warning,'" *BBC*, August 4, 2018, https://www.bbc.com/news/world-asia-china-45070214; Tom Phillips, "China: Lawyer for Ai Weiwei Jailed for 12 Years in 'Severe Retaliation,'" *Guardian*, September 22, 2016, https://www.theguardian.com/world/2016/sep/22/china-lawyer-for-ai-weiwei-jailed-for-12-years-in-severe-retaliation.

43. Jonathan McClory, ed., "The Soft Power 30: A Global Ranking of Soft Power 2019," *Portland Consulting Group*, https://softpower30.com/wp-content/uploads/2019/10/The-Soft-Power-30-Report-2019-1.pdf.

44. Ibid.

45. Ibid.

46. Laura Silver, Kat Devlin, and Christine Huang, "Unfavorable Views of China Reach Historic Highs in Many Countries," *Pew Research Center*, October 6, 2020, https://www.pewresearch.org/global/2020/10/06/unfavorable-views-of-china-reach-historic-highs-in-many-countries/.

47. James Crabtree, "Making (Limited) Inroads: Why China's Belt and Road Struggles to Deliver Goodwill," in Jonathan McClory, ed., "The Soft Power 30: A Global Ranking of Soft Power 2019," *Portland Consulting Group*, https://softpower30.com/wp-content/uploads/2019/10/The-Soft-Power-30-Report-2019-1.pdf.

48. McClory, ed., "The Soft Power 30: A Global Ranking of Soft Power 2019."

49. Shambaugh, "China's Soft-Power Push."

50. Matt Gillow, "The BBC and Soft Power," *British Foreign Policy Group*, March 13, 2020, https://bfpg.co.uk/2020/03/the-bbc-and-soft-power/ . Also, McClory, ed., "The Soft Power 30: A Global Ranking of Soft Power 2018," *Portland Consulting Group*, https://softpower30.com/ wp-content/uploads/2018/07/The-Soft-Power-30-Report-2018.pdf; McClory, "The Soft Power 30: A Global Ranking of Soft Power 2019."

51. James Palmer, "China's Global Propaganda Is Aimed at Bosses, Not Foreigners," *Foreign Policy*, October 1, 2018, https://foreignpolicy.com/ 2018/10/01/chinas-global-propaganda-is-aimed-at-bosses-not-for eigners/.

52. Ibid. Also, author interview with Mark Bourrie.

53. Pál Nyíri, *Reporting for China: How Chinese Correspondents Work in the World* (Seattle: University of Washington Press, 2017), 55.

54. Palmer, "China's Global Propaganda Is Aimed at Bosses, Not Foreigners."

55. For instance, Sam Kestenbaum, "Al Jazeera Sorry for 'Mistakenly' Tweeting Anti-Semitic Meme," *Forward*, June 1, 2017, https://forward. com/fast-forward/373513/al-jazeera-sorry-for-mistakenly-tweeting-anti-semitic-meme/; "Al Jazeera Suspends Journalist for Holocaust Denial Video," *BBC*, May 20, 2019, https://www.bbc.com/news/ world-middle-east-48335169.

56. Palmer, "China's Global Propaganda Is Aimed at Bosses, Not Foreigners."

57. Osman Antwi-Boateng, "The Rise of Qatar as a Soft Power and the Challenges," *European Scientific Journal* 9, no. 31 (November 2013): 350–68.

58. Ibid.

59. Palmer, "China's Global Propaganda Is Aimed at Bosses, Not Foreigners."

60. Sarah Cook, "Escalating Chinese Government Internet Controls: Risks and Responses," Written Testimony Before the Congressional-Executive Commission on China, April 26, 2018, https://www.cecc.gov/sites/ chinacommission.house.gov/files/documents/Freedom%20Ho use%20-%20CECC%20%20Testimony%20-%20Cook-final.pdf; Sarah Cook, "China's Cyber Superpower Strategy: Implementation, Internet Freedom Implications, and U.S. Responses," Written Testimony Before the House Committee on Oversight and Government Reform, Subcommittee on Information Technology, September 26, 2018, https://freedomhouse.org/article/chinas-cyber-superpower-strategy-implementation-internet-freedom-implications-and-us.

61. Joshua Kurlantzick and Yanzhong Huang, "China's Approach to Global Governance," *Council on Foreign Relations*, June 2020, https://www.cfr.org/china-global-governance/.

62. Shannon Tiezzi, "China Celebrates Paris Climate Change Deal," *Diplomat*, December 15, 2015, https://thediplomat.com/2015/12/china-celebrates-paris-climate-change-deal/; Justin Worland, "It Didn't Take Long for China to Fill America's Shoes on Climate Change," *Time*, June 8, 2017, https://time.com/4810846/china-energy-climate-change-paris-agreement/; Patrick Wintour, "China Starts to Assert Its World View at UN as Influence Grows," *Guardian*, September 24, 2018, https://www.theguardian.com/world/2018/sep/24/china-starts-to-assert-its-world-view-at-un-as-influence-grows; Ted Piccone, "China's Long Game on Human Rights at the United Nations," *Brookings Institution*, September 2018, https://www.brookings.edu/research/chinas-long-game-on-human-rights-at-the-united-nations/; Lindsay Maizland, "Is China Undermining Human Rights at the United Nations?," *Council on Foreign Relations*, July 9, 2019, https://www.cfr.org/in-brief/china-undermining-human-rights-united-nations.

63. Kim Tae-Hwan, "China's Sharp Power and South Korea's Peace Initiative," *Korea Economic Institute*, July 29, 2019, http://keia.org/sites/default/files/publications/kei_jointus-korea_2019_2.2.pdf.

64. Elizabeth Economy, "Excerpt: The Third Revolution," *Council on Foreign Relations*, 2018, https://www.cfr.org/excerpt-third-revolution.

65. Ely Ratner, "Exposing China's Actions in the South China Sea," *Council on Foreign Relations*, April 6, 2018, https://www.cfr.org/report/exposing-chinas-actions-south-china-sea; "China Has Militarized the South China Sea and Got Away with It," *Economist*, June 21, 2018, https://www.economist.com/asia/2018/06/21/china-has-militarised-the-south-china-sea-and-got-away-with-it; Scott N. Romaniuk and Tobias Burgers, "China's Next Phase of Militarization in the South China Sea," *Diplomat*, March 20, 2019, https://thediplomat.com/2019/03/chinas-next-phase-of-militarization-in-the-south-china-sea/; Chris Buckley, "China Claims Air Rights over Disputed Islands," *New York Times*, November 23, 2013, https://www.nytimes.com/2013/11/24/world/asia/china-warns-of-action-against-aircraft-over-disputed-seas.html; "China Says U.S. Should Respect China's Air Defense Zone," *Reuters*, March 23, 2017, https://www.reuters.com/article/us-china-usa-defence-idUSKBN16U0SB; Ronald O'Rourke, "U.S.-China Strategic Competition in South and East China Seas: Background and Issues for

Congress," *Congressional Research Service*, September 24, 2019, https://fas.org/sgp/crs/row/R42784.pdf.

66. Robert A. Manning and Patrick M. Cronin, "Under Cover of Pandemic, China Steps Up Brinkmanship in South China Sea," *Foreign Policy*, May 14, 2020, https://foreignpolicy.com/2020/05/14/south-china-sea-disp ute-accelerated-by-coronavirus/. See also Richard Javad Heydarian, "China Seizes Covid-19 Advantage in South China Sea," *Asia Times*, April 1, 2020, https://asiatimes.com/2020/04/china-seizes-covid-19-advantage-in-south-china-sea/.

67. Office of the Secretary of Defense, "Annual Report to Congress: Military and Security Developments Involving the People's Republic of China 2019," *U.S. Department of Defense*, May 2019, ii, https://media.defense.gov/2019/May/02/2002127082/-1/-1/1/2019_CHINA_MI LITARY_POWER_REPORT.pdf.

68. Steven Lee Myers, "Squeezed by an India-China Standoff, Bhutan Holds Its Breath," *New York Times*, August 15, 2017, https://www.nyti mes.com/2017/08/15/world/asia/squeezed-by-an-india-china-stand off-bhutan-holds-its-breath.html; Simon Denyer and Annie Gowen, "India, China Agree to Pull Back Troops to Resolve Tense Border Dispute," *Washington Post*, August 28, 2017, https://www.washingtonp ost.com/world/india-withdraws-troops-from-disputed-himalayan-region-defusing-tension-with-china/2017/08/28/b92fddb6-8bc7-11e7-a2b0-e68cbfob1f19_story.html; Ankit Panda, "Disengagement at Doklam: Why and How Did the India-China Standoff End?," *Diplomat*, August 29, 2017, https://thediplomat.com/2017/08/disengagement-at-doklam-why-and-how-did-the-india-china-standoff-end/.

69. Jin Wu and Steven Lee Myers, "Battle in the Himalayas," *New York Times*, July 18, 2020, https://www.nytimes.com/interactive/2020/07/18/world/asia/china-india-border-conflict.html; Steven Lee Myers, "Beijing Takes Its South China Sea Strategy to the Himalayas," *New York Times*, November 27, 2020, https://www.nytimes.com/2020/11/27/world/asia/china-bhutan-india-border.html; Robert Barnett, "China Is Building Entire Villages in Another Country's Territory," *Foreign Policy*, May 7, 2021, https://foreignpolicy.com/2021/05/07/china-bhutan-bor der-villages-security-forces/.

70. Ben Lowsen, "China's Diplomacy Has a Monster in Its Closet," *Diplomat*, October 13, 2018, https://thediplomat.com/2018/10/chinas-diplomacy-has-a-monster-in-its-closet/.

71. "The Dragon's New Teeth," *Economist*, April 7, 2012, https://www.economist.com/briefing/2012/04/07/the-dragons-new-teeth.

72. Lowsen, "China's Diplomacy Has a Monster in Its Closet."

73. Ibid.

74. Owen Churchill, "Chinese Diplomat Zhao Lijian, Known for His Twitter Outbursts, Is Given Senior Foreign Ministry Post," *South China Morning Post*, August 24, 2019, https://www.scmp.com/news/china/diplomacy/article/3024180/chinese-diplomat-zhao-lijian-known-his-twitter-outbursts-given.

75. Ibid.

76. Ibid.

77. "Vietnam Anti-China Protest: Factories Burnt," *BBC*, May 14, 2014, https://www.bbc.com/news/world-asia-27403851;   Richard   C. Paddock, "Vietnamese Protest an Opening for Chinese Territorial Interests," *New York Times*, June 11, 2018, https://www.nytimes.com/2018/06/11/world/asia/vietnamese-protest-chinese.html;   Manoj Kumar, "Indian Traders Burn Chinese Goods in Protest over Blacklisting Veto, Trade," *Reuters*, March 19, 2019, https://www.reuters.com/article/us-india-china-trade/indian-traders-burn-chinese-goods-in-protest-over-blacklisting-veto-trade-idUSKCN1R01NU; "Japan Defense Paper Slams China's 'Coercive' Maritime Demands," *Agence France-Presse*, July 21, 2015, https://www.businessinsider.com/afp-japan-defence-paper-slams-chinas-coercive-maritime-demands-2015-7/?IR=T&r=SG; Chieko Tsuneoka, "Japan Slams China Over Sea Strategy," *Wall Street Journal*, August 2, 2016, https://www.wsj.com/articles/japan-slams-china-over-sea-strategy-1470111240.

78. "China," *Gallup*, accessed February 17, 2022, https://news.gallup.com/poll/1627/china.aspx.

79. Hunter Marston, "The U.S.-China Cold War Is a Myth," *Foreign Policy*, September 6, 2019, https://foreignpolicy.com/2019/09/06/the-u-s-china-cold-war-is-a-myth/; Oriana Skylar Mastro, "The Stealth Superpower," *Foreign Affairs* 98, no. 1 (January/February 2019), https://www.foreignaffairs.com/articles/china/china-plan-rule-asia;   Max Fisher and Audrey Carlsen, "How China Is Challenging American Dominance in Asia," *New York Times*, March 9, 2018, https://www.nytimes.com/interactive/2018/03/09/world/asia/china-us-asia-rivalry.html; Dave Lawler, "China's Blueprint for Global Dominance," *Axios*, April 8, 2019, https://www.axios.com/china-plan-global-superpower-xi-jinping-5954481e-02c8-4e19-a50c-cd2a90e4894f.html;   Frederick Kempe, "The World China Wants," *Atlantic Council*, April 14, 2019, https://www.atlanticcouncil.org/content-series/inflection-points/the-world-china-wants/; Ho Kwon Ping, "China Is Replacing the US

in a New Global Order, Whether the World Likes It or Not," *South China Morning Post*, September 19, 2018, https://www.scmp.com/comment/insight-opinion/united-states/article/2164722/china-replacing-us-new-global-order-whether.

80. Sarah Cook, "The Long Shadow of Chinese Censorship: How the Communist Party's Media Restrictions Affect News Outlets Around the World," *Center for International Media Assistance*, October 22, 2013, https://www.cima.ned.org/wp-content/uploads/2015/02/CIMA-China_Sarah%20Cook.pdf; Sarah Cook, "Chinese Government Influence on the U.S. Media Landscape," Written Testimony Before the U.S.-China Economic and Security Review Commission, May 4, 2017, https://www.uscc.gov/sites/default/files/Sarah%20Cook%20May%204th%202017%20USCC%20testimony.pdf; Sarah Cook, "The Globalization of Beijing's Media Controls: Key Trends from 2018," *Freedom House*, December 19, 2018, https://freedomhouse.org/blog/globalization-beijings-media-controls-key-trends-2018.

81. Elizabeth Economy, *The Third Revolution: Xi Jinping and the New Chinese State* (New York: Oxford University Press, 2018).

82. Ibid. See also Chris Buckley, Vivian Wang, and Austin Ramzy, "Crossing the Red Line: Behind China's Takeover of Hong Kong," *New York Times*, June 28, 2021, https://www.nytimes.com/2021/06/28/world/asia/china-hong-kong-security-law.html.

83. Economy, *The Third Revolution*, 11. See also Rush Doshi, *The Long Game: China's Grand Strategy to Displace American Order* (New York: Oxford University Press, 2021).

84. Jing Yang, "Jack Ma's Ant Plans Major Revamp in Response to Chinese Pressure," *Wall Street Journal*, January 27, 2021, https://www.wsj.com/articles/jack-mas-ant-plans-major-revamp-in-response-to-chinese-pressure-11611749842.

85. Richard McGregor, *Xi Jinping: The Backlash* (Melbourne: Penguin Random House, 2019), 3.

86. Bates Gill, "Xi Jinping's Grip on Power Is Absolute, but There Are New Threats to His 'Chinese Dream,'" *Conversation*, June 27, 2019, https://theconversation.com/xi-jinpings-grip-on-power-is-absolute-but-there-are-new-threats-to-his-chinese-dream-118921.

87. Chris Buckley, "Xi Jinping Thought Explained: A New Ideology for a New Era," *New York Times*, February 26, 2018, https://www.nytimes.com/2018/02/26/world/asia/xi-jinping-thought-explained-a-new-ideology-for-a-new-era.html; Matt Ho, "A Simple Guide to Xi Jinping Thought? Here's How China's Official Media Tried to Explain It,"

South China Morning Post, October 18, 2018, https://www.scmp.com/ news/china/politics/article/2169151/simple-guide-xi-jinping-thou ght-heres-how-chinas-official-media.

88. Viola Zhou, "Have X-Ray Vision? You'll Need It to Understand Xi Jinping," *Inkstone*, October 19, 2019, https://www.inkstonenews.com/ politics/peoples-daily-makes-xi-jinping-thought-infographic-annivers ary/article/2169306.

89. Jamil Anderlini, "Patriotic Education Distorts China World View," *Financial Times*, December 23, 2012, https://www.ft.com/content/ 66430e4e-4cb0-11e2-986e-00144feab49a.

90. Ibid.

91. Salvatore Babones, "The Birth of Chinese Nationalism," *Foreign Policy*, May 3, 2019, https://foreignpolicy.com/2019/05/03/the-birth-of-chin ese-nationalism/.

92. Adam Ni, "Assessment of the Effects of Chinese Nationalism on China's Foreign Policy," *Divergent Options*, June 10, 2019, https://www.realc leardefense.com/articles/2019/06/10/assessment_of_the_effects_of_ chinese_nationalism_on_chinas_foreign_policy_114489.html; Vivian Wang and Amy Qin, "As Coronavirus Fades in China, Nationalism and Xenophobia Flare," *New York Times*, April 16, 2020, https://www. nytimes.com/2020/04/16/world/asia/coronavirus-china-nationalism. html; John Mac Ghlionn, "The U.S. Should Take Note of China's New Generation of Nationalists," *Newsweek*, September 13, 2021, https:// www.newsweek.com/us-should-take-note-chinas-new-generation- nationalists-opinion-1627177.

93. Rainer Zitelmann, "State Capitalism? No, the Private Sector Was and Is the Main Driver of China's Economic Growth," *Forbes*, September 30, 2019, https://www.forbes.com/sites/rainerzitelmann/2019/09/30/ state-capitalism-no-the-private-sector-was-and-is-the-main-driver-of- chinas-economic-growth/#77ee09c727cb; Orange Wang and Sidney Leng, "Chinese President Xi Jinping's Show of Support for State- Owned Firms 'No Surprise,' Analysts Say," *South China Morning Post*, September 28, 2018, https://www.scmp.com/economy/china-econ omy/article/2166261/chinese-president-xi-jinpings-show-support- state-owned-firms; Bob Davis, "Trade Talks Spotlight Role of China's State-Owned Firms," *Wall Street Journal*, January 26, 2019, https://www. wsj.com/articles/trade-talks-spotlight-role-of-chinas-state-owned- firms-11548504001.

94. Scott Kennedy, "Made in China 2025," *Center for Strategic and International Studies*, June 1, 2015, https://www.csis.org/analysis/made-china-2025;

Wayne M. Morrison, "The Made in China 2025 Initiative: Economic Implications for the United States," *Congressional Research Service*, April 12, 2019, https://crsreports.congress.gov/product/pdf/IF/IF10964/4; Emily Crawford, "Made in China 2025: The Industrial Plan That China Doesn't Want Anyone Talking About," *PBS*, May 7, 2019, https://www.pbs.org/wgbh/frontline/article/made-in-china-2025-the-industrial-plan-that-china-doesnt-want-anyone-talking-about/.

95. "Xi Jinping Is Trying to Remake the Chinese Economy," *Economist*, August 15, 2020, https://www.economist.com/briefing/2020/08/15/xi-jinping-is-trying-to-remake-the-chinese-economy.

96. Ross Andersen, "The Panopticon Is Already Here," *Atlantic*, September 2020, https://www.theatlantic.com/magazine/archive/2020/09/china-ai-surveillance/614197/.

97. Anna Fifeld, "Paramount and Paranoid: China's Xi Faces a Crisis of Confidence," *Washington Post*, August 3, 2019, https://www.washingtonpost.com/world/asia_pacific/paramount-and-paranoid-chinas-xi-faces-a-crisis-of-confidence/2019/08/02/39f77f2a-aa30-11e9-8733-48c87235f396_story.html.

98. Chris Buckley, "Vows of Change in China Belie Private Warning," *New York Times*, February 14, 2013, https://www.nytimes.com/2013/02/15/world/asia/vowing-reform-chinas-leader-xi-jinping-airs-other-message-in-private.html?hpw.

99. Buckley, "Vows of Change in China Belie Private Warning."

100. Zhou Xin and Sarah Zheng, "Xi Jinping Rallies China for Decades-Long 'Struggle' to Rise in Global Order, amid Escalating US Trade War," *South China Morning Post*, September 5, 2019, https://www.scmp.com/economy/china-economy/article/3025725/xi-jinping-rallies-china-decades-long-struggle-rise-global.

101. Rush Doshi, "The Long Game: China's Grand Strategy to Displace American Order," *Brookings Institution*, August 2, 2021, https://www.brookings.edu/essay/the-long-game-chinas-grand-strategy-to-displace-american-order.

102. Robin Fu, "President Xi's 'Struggle' and the Future of U.S.-China Relations," *U.S.-China Perception Monitor*, September 13, 2019, https://uscnpm.org/2019/09/13/president-xis-struggle-future-u-s-china-relations/.

103. Simon Denyer, "Move Over, America. China Now Presents Itself as the Model 'Blazing a New Trail' for the World." *Washington Post*, October 19, 2017, https://www.washingtonpost.com/news/worldviews/wp/2017/10/19/move-over-america-china-now-presents-its

elf-as-the-model-blazing-a-new-trail-for-the-world/?utm_term= .a2efb346dc8e.

104. See, for example, Jessica Chen Weiss, "No, China and the U.S. Aren't Locked in an Ideological Battle. Not Even Close," *Washington Post*, May 4, 2019, https://www.washingtonpost.com/politics/2019/05/04/no-china-us-arent-locked-an-ideological-battle-not-even-close/?utm_t erm=.84193cbe600a.

105. Alex Altman and Elizabeth Dias, "Moscow Cozies Up to the Right," *Time*, March 9, 2017, https://time.com/4696424/moscow-right-kremlin-republicans/; Rosalind S. Helderman and Tom Hamburger, "Guns and Religion: How American Conservatives Grew Closer to Putin's Russia," *Washington Post*, April 30, 2017, https://www.washingtonpost.com/polit ics/how-the-republican-right-found-allies-in-russia/2017/04/30/e2d83 ff6-29d3-11e7-a616-d7c8a68c1a66_story.html; Matt Bradley, "Europe's Far-Right Enjoys Backing from Russia's Putin," *NBC News*, February 12, 2017, https://www.nbcnews.com/news/world/europe-s-far-right-enj oys-backing-russia-s-putin-n718926; Michael Carpenter, "Russia Is Co-opting Angry Young Men," *Atlantic*, August 29, 2018, https://www.thea tlantic.com/ideas/archive/2018/08/russia-is-co-opting-angry-young-men/568741/; Adrienne Klasa et al., "Russia's Long Arm Reaches to the Right in Europe," *Financial Times*, May 23, 2019, https://www.ft.com/content/48c4bfa6-7ca2-11e9-81d2-f785092ab560.

106. Max de Haldevang, "How Russian Trolls' Support of Third Parties Could Have Cost Hillary Clinton the Election," *Quartz*, February 18, 2018, https://qz.com/1210369/russia-donald-trump-2016-how-russian-tro lls-support-of-us-third-parties-may-have-cost-hillary-clinton-the-elect ion/; Robert Windrem, "Russian's Launched Pro-Jill Stein Social Media Blitz to Help Trump Win Election, Reports Say," *NBC News*, December 22, 2018, https://www.nbcnews.com/politics/national-security/russi ans-launched-pro-jill-stein-social-media-blitz-help-trump-n951166.

107. Gabriella Gricius, "How Russia's Disinformation Campaigns Are Succeeding in Europe," *Global Security Review*, May 11, 2019, https:// globalsecurityreview.com/russia-disinformation-campaigns-succeed ing-europe/.

108. Ibid. See also Todd C. Helmus et al., "Russian Social Media Influence: Understanding Russian Propaganda in Eastern Europe," *RAND Corporation*, 2018, https://www.rand.org/pubs/research_reports/RR2 237.html.

109. The Center for Strategic and International Studies has a concise def-inition of gray-zone conflicts on its website: "Competing in the Gray

Zone," *Center for Strategic and International Studies*, accessed February 17, 2022, https://www.csis.org/features/competing-gray-zone.

110. Naja Bentzen, "Foreign Influence Operations in the EU," *European Parliamentary Research Service*, July 2018, http://www.europarl.europa.eu/RegData/etudes/BRIE/2018/625123/EPRS_BRI(2018)625123 _EN.pdf; Matt Apuzzo, "Europe Built a System to Fight Russian Meddling. It's Struggling," *New York Times*, July 6, 2019, https://www.nytimes.com/2019/07/06/world/europe/europe-russian-disinformation-propaganda-elections.html; Vivienne Walt, "Why France's Marine Le Pen Is Doubling Down on Russia Support," *Time*, January 9, 2017, https://time.com/4627780/russia-national-front-marine-le-pen-putin/; Max Seddon and Michael Stothard, "Putin Awaits Return on Le Pen Investment," *Financial Times*, May 4, 2017, https://www.ft.com/content/010eec62-30b5-11e7-9555-23ef563ecf9a; Jason Horowitz, "Audio Suggests Secret Plan for Russians to Fund Party of Italy's Salvini," *New York Times*, July 10, 2019, https://www.nytimes.com/2019/07/10/world/europe/salvini-russia-audio.html.

111. Jolanta Darczewska, "The Anatomy of Russian Information Warfare: The Crimean Operation, a Case Study," *OSW Point of View* 42 (May 2014), https://www.osw.waw.pl/sites/default/files/the_anatomy_of_russian_info rmation_warfare.pdf; Christopher S. Chivvis, "Understanding Russian 'Hybrid Warfare' and What Can Be Done About It," Testimony Before the House Committee on Armed Services, March 22, 2017, https://www.rand.org/content/dam/rand/pubs/testimonies/CT400/CT468/RAND_CT468.pdf; Sophia Porotsky, "Analyzing Russian Information Warfare and Influence Operations," *Global Security Review*, February 8, 2018, https://globalsecurityreview.com/cold-war-2-0-russian-information-warfare/; Davey Alba and Sheera Frenkel, "Russia Tests New Disinformation Tactics in Africa to Expand Influence," *New York Times*, October 30, 2019, https://www.nytimes.com/2019/10/30/technology/russia-facebook-disinformation-africa.html; Shelby Grossman, "Russia Wants More Influence in Africa. It's Using Disinformation to Get There," *Washington Post*, December 3, 2019, https://www.washingtonpost.com/politics/2019/12/03/russia-wants-more-influence-africa-its-using-disinformation-get-there/.

112. Greg Miller and Adam Entous, "Declassified Report Says Putin 'Ordered' Effort to Undermine Faith in U.S. Election and Help Trump," *Washington Post*, January 6, 2017, https://www.washingtonpost.com/world/national-security/intelligence-chiefs-expected   in-new-york-to-brief-trump-on-russian-hacking/2017/01/06/5f591416-d41a-11e6-9cb0-54ab630851e8_story.html.

113. Lucan Ahmad Way and Adam Casey, "Russia Has Been Meddling in Foreign Elections for Decades. Has it Made a Difference?," *Washington Post,* January 5, 2018, https://www.washingtonpost.com/news/mon key-cage/wp/2018/01/05/russia-has-been-meddling-in-foreign-electi ons-for-decades-has-it-made-a-difference/.

114. Graham Allison, "China and Russia: A Strategic Alliance in the Making," *National Interest,* December 14, 2018, https://nationalinterest.org/feat ure/china-and-russia-strategic-alliance-making-38727

115. "Russian Strategic Intentions," A Strategic Multilayer Assessment White Paper, *NSI,* May 2019, https://nsiteam.com/social/wp-cont ent/uploads/2019/05/SMA-TRADOC-Russian-Strategic-Intenti ons-White- Paper-PDF-1.pdf.

116. Steven Lee Myers and Paul Mozur, "China Is Waging a Disinformation War Against Hong Kong Protesters," *New York Times*, August 13, 2019, https://www.nyti mes.com/2019/08/13/world/asia/hong-kong-protests-china.html; Kate Conger, "Facebook and Twitter Say China Is Spreading Disinformation in Hong Kong," *New York Times*, August 19, 2019, https://www.nyti mes.com/2019/08/19/technology/hong-kong-protests-china-disinformation-facebook-twitter.html.

117. Richard McGregor, "Trump Wants China to Help Him Win. China Wants Nothing to Do with Him," *Washington Post*, October 11, 2019, https://www.washingtonpost.com/outlook/trump-wants-china-to-help-him-win-china-wants-nothing-to-do-with-him/2019/10/10/15fddd9a-eadf-11e9-9c6d-436a0df4f31d_story.html.

118. Anna Lührmann et al., *Democracy Facing Global Challenges: V-Dem Annual Democracy Report 2019* (Gothenburg: V-Dem Institute, May 2019), https://www.v-dem.net/static/website/files/dr/dr_2019.pdf; Joshua Kurlantzick, "How China Is Interfering in Taiwan's Election," *Council on Foreign Relations*, November 7, 2019, https://www.cfr.org/in-brief/how-china-interfering-taiwans-election.

119. Sheridan Prasso and Samson Ellis, "China's Information War on Taiwan Ramps Up as Election Nears," *Bloomberg Businessweek*, October 23, 2019, https://www.bloomberg.com/news/articles/2019-10-23/china-s-information-war-on-taiwan-ramps-up-as-election-nears.

120. Insikt Group, "Beyond Hybrid War: How China Exploits Social Media to Sway American Opinion," *Recorded Future*, March 6, 2019, https://www.recordedfuture.com/china-social-media-operations/.

121. Richard Haass, *A World in Disarray: American Foreign Policy and the Crisis of the Old Order* (New York: Penguin Press, 2017).

CHAPTER 5

1. Luke Harding, "Alexander Litvinenko: The Man Who Solved His Own Murder," *Guardian*, January 19, 2016, https://www.theguardian. com/world/2016/jan/19/alexander-litvinenko-the-man-who-solved-his-own-murder; Elias Groll, "A Brief History of Attempted Russian Assassinations by Poison," *Foreign Policy*, March 9, 2018, https://foreig npolicy.com/2018/03/09/a-brief-history-of-attempted-russian-ass assinations-by-poison/; Luke Harding, "The Skripal Poisonings: The Bungled Assassination with the Kremlin's Fingerprints All Over It," *Guardian*, December 26, 2018, https://www.theguardian.com/news/ 2018/dec/26/skripal-poisonings-bungled-assassination-kremlin-putin-salisbury.

2. See, for instance, the extensive coverage of how a Chinese asset, probably a spy, attempted a broad range of influence efforts in California politics. (Although she was probably a spy, she was conducting influence campaigns as much as she was engaged in intelligence.) Bethany Allen-Ebrahimian and Zach Dorfman, "Suspected Chinese Spy Targeted California Politicians," *Axios,* December 8, 2020, https://www.axios. com/china-spy-california-politicians-9d2dfb99-f839-4e00-8bd8-59dec 0daf589.html.

3. Paul Sonne, "A Russian Bank Gave Marine Le Pen's Party a Loan. Then Weird Things Began Happening," *Washington Post*, December 27, 2018, https://www.washingtonpost.com/world/national-security/a-russian-bank-gave-marine-le-pens-party-a-loan-then-weird-things-began-happening/2018/12/27/960c7906-d320-11e8-a275-81c671a50422_st ory.html.

4. "Russia Exports," *Trading Economics*, accessed February 17, 2022, https:// tradingeconomics.com/russia/exports.

5. Ben Blanchard and Sarah Young, "China Hopes to See a United E.U., Xi Tells Britain on Visit," *Reuters*, October 23, 2015, https://www.reut ers.com/article/uk-china-britain-idUKKCN0SG2WE20151023.

6. For an overview of the differences between Chinese and Russian tactics to European economies, see Thorsten Benner et al., "Authoritarian Advance: Responding to China's Growing Political Influence in Europe," *MERICS*, February 2018, https://merics.org/sites/default/ files/2020-04/GPPi_MERICS_Authoritarian_Advance_2018_1.pdf.

7. For an overview of the comprehensive nature of Chinese sharp power, see, for instance, Christopher Walker, "China's Foreign Influence and Sharp Power Strategy to Shape and Influence Democratic Institutions,"

Testimony Before the U.S. House Permanent Select Committee on Intelligence, May 16, 2019, htttps://www.ned.org/chinas-foreign-influe nce-and-sharp-power-strategyto-shape-and-influence-democratic-institutions/.

8. Larry Diamond and Orville Schell, "Chapter 2: State and Local Governments," in *Chinese Influence and American Interests: Promoting Constructive Vigilance*, Hoover Institution, 2018, https://www.hoover. org/research/chinas-influence-american-interests-state-and-local-gove rnments.

9. Ibid. The mayor of Tokyo is called the governor of Tokyo prefecture, but her position is similar in many respects to that of a mayor of a U.S. city.

10. Ibid.

11. Bethany Allen-Ebrahimian and Zach Dorfman, "Suspected Chinese Spy Targeted California Politicians," *Axios,* December 8, 2020, https:// www.axios.com/china-spy-california-politicians-9d2dfb99-f839-4e00-8bd8-59decodaf589.html.

12. "China's Impact on the U.S. Education System," United States Senate Permanent Subcommittee on Investigations," February 2019, https:// www.hsgac.senate.gov/imo/media/doc/PSI%20Report%20Ch ina's%20Impact%20on%20the%20US%20Education%20System.pdf; Alex Joske, "The Party Speaks for You," *Australian Strategic Policy Institute*, June 9, 2020, https://www.aspi.org.au/report/party-speaks-you.

13. "China's Impact on the U.S. Education System," United States Senate Permanent Subcommittee on Investigations," February 2019.

14. Erica L. Green, "Universities Face Federal Crackdown over Foreign Financial Influence," *New York Times,* August 30, 2019, https://www.nyti mes.com/2019/08/30/us/politics/universities-foreign-donations.html.

15. Ryan Lucas, "The Justice Department Is Ending Its Controversial China Initiative," *National Public Radio*, February 23, 2022, https://www.npr. org/2022/02/23/1082593735/justice-department-china-initiative.

16. The Council on Foreign Relations' (CFR's) site notes: "CFR does not accept funding from foreign governments, nor does it accept grants or membership from entities that are majority-owned or controlled by foreign governments. The organization also does not accept money from the U.S. government except to cover some of the costs of up to six visiting fellows each year who are employees of the U.S. government and spend an academic year at CFR's New York office." See "Funding," *Council on Foreign Relations*, https://www.cfr.org/funding.

17. Green, "Universities Face Federal Crackdown over Foreign Financial Influence."

18. Shannon Najmabadi, "After Cruz Raises Worries About 'Propaganda,' UT Says It Won't Accept Money from Chinese Foundation," *Texas Tribune*, January 15, 2018, https://www.texastribune.org/2018/01/15/ut-wont-accept-funding-chinese-foundation-after-criticism-cruz-profess/; Bethany Allen-Ebrahimian, "This Beijing-Linked Billionaire Is Funding Policy Research at Washington's Most Influential Institutions," *Foreign Policy*, November 28, 2017, https://foreignpolicy.com/2017/11/28/this-beijing-linked-billionaire-is-funding-policy-research-at-washingtons-most-influential-institutions-china-dc/. Also, John Dotson, "The China-U.S. Exchange Foundation and United Front 'Lobbying Laundering' in American Politics," *China Brief*, September 16, 2020, https://jamestown.org/program/the-china-u-s-exchange-foundation-and-united-front-lobbying-laundering-in-american-politics/.

19. Alexander Bowe, "China's Overseas United Front Work: Background and Implications for the United States," *U.S.-China Economic and Security Review Commission*, August 24, 2018, https://www.uscc.gov/sites/default/files/Research/China's%20Overseas%20United%20Front%20Work%20-%20Background%20and%20Implications%20for%20US_final_0.pdf; Najmabadi, "After Cruz Raises Worries About 'Propaganda,' UT Says It Won't Accept Money from Chinese Foundation"; Allen-Ebrahimian, "This Beijing-Linked Billionaire Is Funding Policy Research at Washington's Most Influential Institutions."

20. Ibid.

21. Najmabadi, "After Cruz Raises Worries About 'Propaganda,' UT Says It Won't Accept Money from Chinese Foundation."

22. Allen-Ebrahimian, "This Beijing-Linked Billionaire Is Funding Policy Research at Washington's Most Influential Institutions.". Also, Dotson, "The China-U.S. Exchange Foundation and United Front 'Lobbying Laundering' in American Politics"; "What We Do: Research," China-United States Exchange Foundation, https://www.cusef.org.hk/en/what-we-do/research; "2019 CUSEF Student Trip to China," American University School of Communications, https://www.american.edu/soc/resources/cusef-graduate-trip-to-china.cfm.

23. Henry Ridgwell, "Hungarian Plans for First Chinese University in Europe Prompt Security, Propaganda Fears," *Voice of America*, May 13, 2021, https://www.voanews.com/a/europe_hungarian-plans-first-chinese-university-europe-prompt-security-propaganda-fears/6205780.html.

24. See, for example, Radomir Tylecote and Robert Clark, *Inadvertently Arming China? The Chinese Military Complex and Its Potential Exploitation*

of Scientific Research at UK Universities (London: Civitas: Institute for the Study of Civil Society, 2021). See also Alex Joske, "The China Defence Universities Tracker," *Australian Strategic Policy Institute*, November 25, 2019, https://www.aspi.org.au/report/china-defence-universities-tracker.

25. "Britain Widens Russian 'Dirty Money' Crackdown with New Law," *Reuters*, February 28, 2022, https://www.reuters.com/world/uk/brit ain-widens-russian-dirty-money-crackdown-with-new-law-2022-02-28/.

26. Craig Timberg, "Effort to Combat Foreign Propaganda Advances in Congress," *Washington Post*, November 30, 2016, https://www.washing tonpost.com/business/economy/effort-to-combat-foreign-propaga nda-advances-in-congress/2016/11/30/9147e1ac-e221-47be-ab92-9f2 f7e69d452_story.html; Joshua Fatzick, "US Senate Panel OKs Funds to Fight Online Propaganda," *Voice of America*, December 1, 2016, https://www.voanews.com/a/online-propaganda-congress-national-defense-authorization-act/3619241.html.

27. Patrick Tucker, "Analysts Are Quitting the State Department's Anti-Propaganda Team," *Defense One*, September 12, 2017, https://www.def enseone.com/technology/2017/09/analysts-are-quitting-state-depa rtments-anti-propaganda-team/140936/; Gardiner Harris, "State Dept. Was Granted $120 Million to Fight Russian Meddling. It Has Spent $0," *New York Times*, March 4, 2018, https://www.nytimes.com/2018/ 03/04/world/europe/state-department-russia-global-engagement-cen ter.html; Deirdre Shesgreen, "Trump's State Department Lacks Money, Clear Mandate to Fight Russian Disinformation, 'Fake News,'" *USA Today*, September 21, 2018, https://www.usatoday.com/story/news/ world/2018/09/21/trump-administration-lacks-resources-fight-russ ian-fake-news/1292089002/.

28. Harris, "State Dept. Was Granted $120 Million to Fight Russian Meddling."

29. Emilian Kavalski and Maximilian Mayer, "China Is Now a Power in Europe, but Fears of Interference in the EU Are Simplistic and Misguided," *Conversation*, May 9, 2019, https://theconversation.com/ china-is-now-a-power-in-europe-but-fears-of-interference-in-the-eu-are-simplistic-and-misguided-116193.

30. Benner et al., "Authoritarian Advance."

31. Peter Martin and Alan Crawford, "China's Influence Digs Deep into Europe's Political Landscape," *Bloomberg*, April 3, 2019, https://www.

bloomberg.com/news/articles/2019-04-03/china-s-influence-digs-deep-into-europe-s-political-landscape.

32. See, for example, Thomas des Garets Geddes, "British MP Tom Tugendhat on the New China Research Group: We Need to Understand China Better," *MERICS,* June 4, 2020, https://merics.org/en/podcast/british-mp-tom-tugendhat-new-china-research-group-we-need-understand-china-better.

33. "Who Can and Can't Contribute," *Federal Election Commission,* accessed February 17, 2022, https://www.fec.gov/help-candidates-and-committees/candidate-taking-receipts/who-can-and-cant-contribute/#:~:text=Foreign%20nationals,%E2%80%94%20federal%2C%20state%20or%20local; Christopher Knaus, "Australia's Weak Donation Laws Allowed $1 Billion in Dark Money to go to Political Parties over Two Decades," *Guardian,* January 31, 2021, https://www.theguardian.com/australia-news/2021/jan/31/australias-weak-donation-laws-allowed-1bn-in-dark-money-to-go-to-political-parties-over-two-decades.

34. Rob Schmitz, "Czech-Chinese Ties Strained as Prague Stands Up to Beijing," *National Public Radio,* October 30, 2019, https://www.npr.org/2019/10/30/774054035/czech-chinese-ties-are-affected-as-prague-stands-up-to-beijing.

35. Philip Heijmans, "The U.S.-China Tech War Is Being Fought in Central Europe," *Atlantic,* March 6, 2019, https://www.theatlantic.com/international/archive/2019/03/czech-zeman-babis-huawei-xi-trump/584158/.

36. Alžběta Bajerová, "The Czech-Chinese Centre of Influence: How Chinese Embassy in Prague Secretly Funded Activities at the Top Czech University," *China Observers in Central and Eastern Europe,* November 7, 2019, https://chinaobservers.eu/the-czech-chinese-centre-of-influence-how-chinese-embassy-in-prague-secretly-funded-activities-at-the-top-czech-university/.

37. Matej Šimalčík, "Slovak Universities Have a China Problem . . . and They Don't Even Know It," *China Observers in Central and Eastern Europe,* March 15, 2021, https://chinaobservers.eu/slovak-universities-have-a-china-problem-and-they-dont-even-know-it/.

38. Hannah Beech, "Embracing China, Facebook, and Himself, Cambodia's Ruler Digs In," *New York Times,* March 17, 2018, https://www.nytimes.com/2018/03/17/world/asia/hun-sen-cambodia-china.html; Philippe Le Corre and Vuk Vuksanovic, "Serbia: China's Open Door to the Balkans," *Diplomat,* January 1, 2019, https://thediplomat.com/2019/01/serbia-chinas-open-door-to-the-balkans/; Vuk Vuksanovic, "Light

Touch, Tight Grip: China's Influence and the Corrosion of Serbian Democracy," *War on the Rocks*, September 24, 2019, https://waronthero cks.com/2019/09/light-touch-tight-grip-chinas-influence-and-the-corrosion-of-serbian-democracy/.

39. Chris McGreal, "'The S-Word': How Young Americans Fell in Love with Socialism," *Guardian*, September 2, 2017, https://www.theguard ian.com/us-news/2017/sep/02/socialism-young-americans-bernie-sanders; Stef W. Kight, "Exclusive Poll: Young Americans Are Embracing Socialism," *Axios*, March 10, 2019, https://www.axios.com/exclus ive-poll-young-americans-embracing-socialism-b051907a-87a8-4f61-9e6e-0db75f7edc4a.html.

40. Mohamed Younis, "Four in 10 Americans Embrace Some Form of Socialism," *Gallup*, May 20, 2019, https://news.gallup.com/poll/257 639/four-americans-embrace-form-socialism.aspx.

41. Ibid.

42. Victoria Bekiempis, "Four in 10 Americans Prefer Socialism to Capitalism, Poll Finds," *Guardian*, June 10, 2019, https://www.theg uardian.com/us-news/2019/jun/10/america-socialism-capital ism-poll-axios.

43. Max Ehrenfreund, "A Majority of Millennials Now Reject Capitalism, Poll Shows," *Washington Post*, April 26, 2016, https://www.washing tonpost.com/news/wonk/wp/2016/04/26/a-majority-of-millennials-now-reject-capitalism-poll-shows/Also; Jason Hickel and Martin Kirk, "Are You Ready to Consider That Capitalism Is the Real Problem," *Fast Company*, July 11, 2017, https://www.fastcompany.com/40439316/ are-you-ready-to-consider-that-capitalism-is-the-real-problem.

44. Freedom House, *Freedom in the World 2021: Democracy Under Siege* (Washington, DC: Freedom House, 2021). The author contributes to several Southeast Asia sections of *Freedom in the World* but did not contribute to the overall calculations made in the report of the global decline of democracy.

45. Thomas Fuller, "In Thailand, Growing Intolerance for Dissent Drives Many to More Authoritarian Nations," *New York Times*, June 6, 2014, https://www.nytimes.com/2014/06/07/world/asia/in-thailand-a-growing-intolerance-for-dissent.html; Adam Ramsey, "Thailand Referendum: Fears over Fair Vote as Military Cracks Down on Dissent," *Guardian*, August 3, 2016, https://www.theguardian.com/world/2016/ aug/03/thailand-referendum-fears-over-fair-vote-as-military-cracks-down-on-dissent.

46. Poppy McPherson and Cape Win Diamond, "Free Speech Curtailed in Aung San Suu Kyi's Myanmar as Prosecutions Soar," *Guardian*, January 8, 2017, https://www.theguardian.com/world/2017/jan/09/free-speech-curtailed-aung-san-suu-kyis-myanmar-prosecutions-soar; Todd Pitman, "Myanmar Government Under Suu Kyi Cracks Down on Journalists," *Associated Press,* February 15, 2018, https://apnews.com/453987dd69254221805764ed58e884f9/Myanmar-government-under-Suu-Kyi-cracks-down-on-journalists; Hannah Beech, "Across Myanmar, Denials of Ethnic Cleansing and Loathing of Rohingya," *New York Times*, October 24, 2017, https://www.nytimes.com/2017/10/24/world/asia/myanmar-rohingya-ethnic-cleansing.html.

47. "Young Africans Want More Democracy," *Economist*, March 5, 2020, https://www.economist.com/middle-east-and-africa/2020/03/05/young-africans-want-more-democracy; Natalie Kitroeff, "Young Leader Vowed Change in El Salvador but Wields Same Heavy Hand," *New York Times*, May 5, 2020, https://www.nytimes.com/2020/05/05/world/americas/el-salvador-nayib-bukele.html.

48. Roberto Stefan Foa and Yascha Mounk, "The Danger of Deconsolidation: The Democratic Disconnect," *Journal of Democracy* 27, no. 3 (July 2016): 15–17, https://www.journalofdemocracy.org/wp-content/uploads/2016/07/FoaMounk-27-3.pdf.

49. The United States' ranking in the Economist Intelligence Unit's annual Democracy Index report has fallen throughout the 2010s, slipping from "full democracy" in 2015 to "flawed democracy" in 2016. It remains a "flawed democracy" in 2022.

50. Freedom House, *Freedom in the World 2021.* The author contributed to *Freedom in the World 2021* but only to the sections on Southeast Asia, and not to the sections on the United States. Freedom House, *Freedom in the World 2022: The Global Expansion of Authoritarian Rule* (Washington, DC: Freedom House, 2022). The author contributed to *Freedom in the World 2022* but only to the sections on Southeast Asia, and not to the sections on the United States.

51. Joshua Kurlantzick, "Addressing the Effect of COVID-19 on Democracy in South and Southeast Asia," *Council on Foreign Relations*, November 2020, https://www.cfr.org/report/addressing-effect-covid-19-democracy-south-and-southeast-asia.

52. Sarah Repucci and Amy Slipowitz, *Democracy Under Lockdown: The Impact of COVID-19 on the Global Struggle for Freedom* (Washington, DC: Freedom House, October 2020), https://freedomhouse.org/sites/default/files/2020-10/COVID-19_Special_Report_Final_.pdf. The author

contributed some reporting on Southeast Asian responses to COVID-19 to this report.

53. Russell Berman, "President Trump's 'Hard Power' Budget," *Atlantic*, March 16, 2017, https://www.theatlantic.com/politics/archive/2017/03/president-trumps-hard-power-budget/519702/.

54. "Defying Congress, Trump Administration Looks to Shift Billions in Foreign Aid," *Reuters*, August 6, 2019, https://www.reuters.com/article/us-usa-trump-aid/defying-congress-trump-administration-looks-to-shift-billions-in-foreign-aid-idUSKCN1UW2FX.

55. John Bresnahan, Jennifer Scholtes, and Marianne Levine, "Trump Kills Plan to Cut Billions in Foreign Aid," *Politico*, August 22, 2019, https://www.politico.com/story/2019/08/22/white-house-backs-off-foreign-aid-cuts-1472130.

56. Doyle McManus, "Almost Half the Top Jobs in Trump's State Department Are Still Empty," *Atlantic*, November 4, 2018, https://www.theatlantic.com/politics/archive/2018/11/state-department-empty-ambassador-to-australi/574831/.

57. "Trump Suggests Starting Media Network to 'Put Some Real News Out There,'" *Voice of America*, October 3, 2019, https://www.voanews.com/usa/trump-suggests-starting-media-network-put-some-real-news-out-there.

58. David Folkenflik, "Trump's New Foreign Broadcasting CEO Fires News Chiefs, Raising Fears of Meddling," *National Public Radio*, June 18, 2020, https://www.npr.org/2020/06/18/879873926/trumps-new-foreign-broadcasting-ceo-fires-news-chiefs-raising-fears-of-meddling. Also, David Folkenflik, "Substantial Likelihood of Wrongdoing by VOA Parent Agency, Government Watchdog Says," *National Public Radio*, December 2, 2020, https://www.npr.org/2020/12/02/941673587/substantial-likelihood-of-wrongdoing-by-voa-parent-agency-government-watchdog-sa.

59. Jonathan McClory, ed., "The Soft Power 30: A Global Ranking of Soft Power 2019," *Portland Consulting Group*, https://softpower30.com/wp-content/uploads/2019/10/The-Soft-Power-30-Report-2019-1.pdf.

60. Ibid.

61. See, for instance, David Fisher, "China's Communists Fund Jacinda Ardern's Labour Party: What the United States Congress Was Told," *New Zealand Herald*, May 26, 2018, https://www.nzherald.co.nz/nz/news/article.cfm?c_id=1&objectid=12058818; Paul Huang, "Chinese Cyber-Operatives Boosted Taiwan's Insurgent Candidate," *Foreign Policy*, June 26, 2019, https://foreignpolicy.com/2019/06/26/chinese-cyber-ope

ratives-boosted-taiwans-insurgent-candidate/; Kathrin Hille, "Taiwan Primaries Highlight Fears over China's Political Influence," *Financial Times*, July 16, 2019, https://www.ft.com/content/036b609a-a768-11e9-984c-fac8325aaa04.

62. Evelyn Douek, "What's in Australia's New Laws on Foreign Interference in Domestic Politics," *Lawfare*, July 11, 2018, https://www.lawfareblog.com/whats-australias-new-laws-foreign-interference-domestic-polit ics; Eleanor Ainge Roy, "New Zealand Bans Foreign Political Donations amid Interference Concerns," *Guardian*, December 2, 2019, https://www.theguardian.com/world/2019/dec/03/new-zealand-bans-fore ign-political-donations-amid-interference-concerns.

63. "Democracy Index 2019," Economist Intelligence Unit, January 2020, https://www.economist.com/graphic-detail/2020/01/22/global-democracy-has-another-bad-year.

64. Richard McGregor, "We Need the Five Eyes Spy Network, but with Oversight," *Sydney Morning Herald*, January 12, 2019, https://www.low-yinstitute.org/publications/we-need-five-eyes-spy-network-oversight.

65. Anne Holmes, "Australia's Economic Relationships with China," *Parliament of Australia*, accessed February 17, 2022, https://www.aph.gov.au/about_parliament/parliamentary_departments/parliament ary_library/pubs/briefingbook44p/china.

66. Anne-Marie Brady, "Magic Weapons: China's Political Influence Activities Under Xi Jinping," *Wilson Center*, September 18, 2017, 13–16, https://www.wilsoncenter.org/article/magic-weapons-chinas-politi cal-influence-activities-under-xi-jinpingm.

67. Ibid., 13–17.

68. Ibid., 15.

69. Ibid.

70. Matt Nippert and David Fisher, "Revealed: China's Network of Influence in New Zealand," *New Zealand Herald*, September 20, 2017, https://www.nzherald.co.nz/business/news/article.cfm?c_id=3&objec tid=11924546.

71. Ibid.

72. Brady, "Magic Weapons," 17–18.

73. Ibid., 20–22.

74. Ibid., 17–18.

75. Ibid., 8–10.

76. Ibid.

77. Boris Jancic, "Concerns Raised over National's China Trip Planning," *New Zealand Herald*, January 8, 2020, https://www.nzherald.co.nz/nz/

concerns-raised-over-nationals-china-trip-planning/5NA7EZ7JSNS ASDQW72QXY4P3GQ/. Also, Fisher and Nippert, "Revealed: The Citizenship File of Spy Trainer Turned National MP Jian Yang."

78. Brady, "Magic Weapons," 19–21.

79. Ibid., 19–20.

80. Ibid., 20–22.

81. Ibid.

82. Jancic, "Concerns Raised over National's China Trip Planning."

83. Zane Small, "Simon Bridges Rejects Claim He Met with China's Head of 'Secret Police,'" *Newshub*, September 10, 2019, https://www.news hub.co.nz/home/politics/2019/09/simon-bridges-rejects-claim-he-met-with-china-s-head-of-secret-police.html. See also Eleanor Ainge Roy, "New Zealand Opposition Leader Criticised for 'Alarming' Stance on China," *Guardian*, September 10, 2019, https://www.theguardian.com/world/2019/sep/11/new-zealand-opposition-leader-criticised-for- alarming-stance-on-china; Sophie Bateman, "Simon Bridges Sings Communist Party's Praises in Interview with Chinese News Channel CGTN," *Newshub*, September 9, 2019, https://www.newshub.co.nz/home/politics/2019/09/simon-bridges-sings-communist-party-s-prai ses-in-interview-in-china.html.

84. Matt Nippert, "Former Trade Minister Todd McClay Helped Arrange $150,000 Donation from Chinese Racing Industry Billionaire Lin Liang to National Party," *New Zealand Herald*, August 26, 2019, https://www.nzherald.co.nz/nz/former-trade-minister-todd-mcclay-helped-arrange-150000-donation-from-chinese-racing-industry-billionaire-lin-lang-to-national-party/W3H2JALC36IE4GBOLOEL4UMIOI/?c_id=1&objectid=12261215&ref=art_readmore.

85. Roy, "New Zealand Opposition Leader Criticised for 'Alarming' Stance on China."

86. Brady, "Magic Weapons," 20–22.

87. "China and the Age of Strategic Rivalry: Highlights from an Academic Outreach Conference," *Canadian Security Intelligence Service*, May 2018, 78–81, https://www.canada.ca/content/dam/csis-scrs/documents/publi cations/CSIS-Academic-Outreach-China-report-May-2018-en.pdf.

88. Ibid.

89. Eleanor Ainge Roy, "New Zealand's Five Eyes Membership Called Into Question over 'China Links,'" *Guardian*, May 27, 2018, https://www.theguardian.com/world/2018/may/28/new-zealands-five-eyes-mem bership-called-into-question-over-china-links.

90. Charlotte Graham-McLay, "Jacinda Ardern's Progressive Politics Made Her a Global Sensation. But Do They Work at Home?," *New York Times*, September 26, 2018, https://www.nytimes.com/2018/09/26/world/asia/jacinda-ardern-un-new-zealand.html; Charlotte Graham-McLay and Adam Satariano, "New Zealand Seeks Global Support for Tougher Measures on Online Violence," *New York Times*, May 12, 2019, https://www.nytimes.com/2019/05/12/technology/ardern-macron-social-media-extremism.html.

91. Thomas Coughlan, "Brady Blocked from Foreign Interference Inquiry," *Newsroom*, March 8, 2019, https://www.newsroom.co.nz/2019/03/08/477641/brady-blocked-from-appearing-before-justice-committee.

92. Lally Weymouth, "Jacinda Ardern, New Zealand's Nobel Candidate, on How to Respond to Gun Violence," *Washington Post*, September 12, 2019, https://www.washingtonpost.com/outlook/jacinda-adern-new-zealands-nobel-candidate-on-how-to-respond-to-gun-violence/2019/09/12/a42711ca-d501-11e9-86ac-0f250cc91758_story.html.

93. Anne-Marie Brady, "New Zealand's Relationship with China Is at a Tipping Point," *Guardian*, July 30, 2020, https://www.theguardian.com/world/2020/jul/31/new-zealands-relationship-with-china-is-at-a-tipping-point.

94. Harrison Christian, "National MP Jian Yang Organized Simon Bridges' Controversial China Trip, Emails Show," *Stuff*, January 5, 2020, https://www.stuff.co.nz/national/politics/118419927/national-mp-jian-yang-organised-simon-bridges-controversial-china-trip-emails-show.

95. "New Zealand Intelligence Warns of Foreign Influence, Monitoring of Migrant Groups," *ABC News*, April 11, 2019, https://www.abc.net.au/news/2019-04-11/new-zealand-intelligence-warns-over-foreign-influence/10994892.

96. "Diptel from BHC Canberra: Australia and New Zealand Approaches to China: Same Meat, Different Gravy," July 10, 2018, obtained through the UK Freedom of Information Act.

97. Eleanor Ainge Roy, "New Zealand Bans Foreign Political Donations amid Interference Concerns," *Guardian*, December 2, 2019, https://www.theguardian.com/world/2019/dec/03/new-zealand-bans-foreign-political-donations-amid-interference-concerns.

98. Marc Daalder, "Serious Fraud Office Investigating Donations to Labor," *Newsroom*, July 13, 2020, https://www.newsroom.co.nz/serious-fraud-office-investigating-donations-to-labour. See also Laura Walters, "Zhang Yikun and the Alleged $100k Donation," *Newsroom*, October

17, 2018, https://www.newsroom.co.nz/zhang-yikun-and-the-alleged-100k-donation.

99. Zane Small, "Serious Fraud Office Files Criminal Charges Against Four in National Party Donation Probe," *Newshub*, January 29, 2020, https://www.newshub.co.nz/home/politics/2020/01/serious-fraud-office-files-criminal-charges-against-four-in-national-party-donation-probe.html.

100. Collette Devlin, "Jian Yang, the National MP Who Admitted to Training Chinese Spies, Retiring," *Stuff*, July 10, 2020, https://www.stuff.co.nz/national/politics/122094310/jian-yang-the-national-mp-who-admitted-to-training-chinese-spies-retiring.

101. Anne-Marie Brady, "New Zealand Needs to Show It's Serious About Addressing Chinese Interference," *Guardian*, January 23, 2020, https://www.theguardian.com/world/commentisfree/2020/jan/24/new-zealand-needs-to-show-its-serious-about-addressing-chinese-interference.

102. Ibid. Also, Anna Fifield, "Under Jacinda Ardern, New Zealand Pivots on How to Deal with China," *Washington Post*, July 6, 2020, https://www.washingtonpost.com/world/asia_pacific/china-new-zealand-jacinda-ardern-xi-jinping/2020/07/05/f8d5e182-af95-11ea-98b5-279a6479a1e4_story.html.

103. Fifield, "Under Jacinda Ardern, New Zealand Pivots on How to Deal with China."

104. Sarah Cook, "Beijing's Global Megaphone: The Expansion of Chinese Communist Party Media Influence Since 2017," *Freedom House*, January 2020, https://freedomhouse-files.s3.amazonaws.com/01152020_SR_China%20Global%20Megaphone_with%20Recommendations%20PDF.pdf. Also, Thomas Coughlan, "Parliamentary Inquiry Hears Evidence of Chinese Political Interference in New Zealand Political System," *Stuff.co.nz*, July 11, 2020, https://www.stuff.co.nz/national/300054428/parliamentary-inquiry-hears-evidence-of-chinese-political-interference-in-new-zealand-political-system.

105. Amy Searight, *Countering China's Influence Activities: Lessons from Australia* (Washington, DC: Center for Strategic and International Studies, July 2020), 3–4, https://www.csis.org/analysis/countering-chinas-influence-activities-lessons-australia.

106. Cook, "Beijing's Global Megaphone."

107. Kelsey Munro and Philip Wen, "Chinese Language Newspapers in Australia: Beijing Controls Messaging, Propaganda in Press," *Sydney Morning Herald*, July 8, 2016, https://www.smh.com.au/national/chin

ese-language-newspapers-in-australia-beijing-controls-messaging-pro
paganda-in-press-20160610-gpgos3.html.

108. Ibid.

109. Ibid.

110. Louisa Lim and Julia Bergin, "Weaponising the Free Press? China's Global Media Offensive," *International Federation of Journalists*, March 2019, https://www.ifj.org/fileadmin/user_upload/2019_IFJ_China_Report_-_Weaponising_the_Free_Press.pdf.

111. Mary Fallon, Sashka Koloff, and Nick MacKenzie, "China Pressured Sydney Council into Banning Media Company Critical of Communist Party," *Australian Broadcasting Corporation*, April 7, 2019, https://www.abc.net.au/news/2019-04-07/china-pressured-sydney-council-over-media-organisation/10962226.

112. "China's Pursuit of a New World Media Order," *Reporters Without Borders*, March 22, 2019, https://rsf.org/sites/default/files/en_rapport_chine_web_final.pdf.

113. Munro and Wan, "Chinese Language Newspapers in Australia."

114. Mario Christodoulou et al., "Chinese Students and Scholars Association's Deep Links to the Embassy Revealed," *ABC News*, November 3, 2019, https://www.abc.net.au/news/2019-10-13/cssa-influence-australian-universities-documents-revealed/11587454.

115. Erin Cook, "How Chinese Australians Could Swing the Election Down Under," *Ozy*, May 12, 2019, https://www.ozy.com/around-the-world/how-chinese-australians-could-swing-the-election-down-under/94294/.

116. Searight, *Countering China's Influence Activities*, 15–16.

117. Cook, "How Chinese Australians Could Swing the Election Down Under." See also Searight, *Countering China's Influence Activities*.

118. James Leibold, "The Australia-China Relations Institute Doesn't Belong at UTS," *Conversation*, June 4, 2017, https://theconversation.com/the-australia-china-relations-institute-doesnt-belong-at-uts-78743.

119. Ibid.

120. Christiane Barro, "The Think Tanks Shaping Australia: The Australia-China Relations Institute," *New Daily*, June 13, 2019, https://thenewdaily.com.au/news/national/2019/06/13/australia-china-relations-institute/.

121. Ibid.

122. Leibold, "The Australia-China Relations Institute Doesn't Belong at UTS."

123. Barro, "The Think Tanks Shaping Australia."

124. Leibold, "The Australia-China Relations Institute Doesn't Belong at UTS."

125. John Fitzgerald, "How Bob Carr Became China's Pawn," *Australian Financial Review*, November 8, 2018, https://www.afr.com/policy/what-you-should-know-about-bob-carr-and-china-20181105-h17jic.

126. Dan Conifer and Caitlyn Gribbin, "Political Donor Chau Chuk Wing Funded Bribe Given to UN President, MP Andrew Hastie Says," *Australian Broadcasting Corporation*, May 22, 2018, https://www.abc.net.au/news/2018-05-22/chau-chak-wing-un-bribe-scandal/9788926.

127. Searight, *Countering China's Influence Activities*, 6–7.

128. "Chinese Billionaire Huang Xiangmo Has Australian Assets Frozen over US$96 Million Tax Bill," *South China Morning Post*, September 17, 2019, https://www.scmp.com/news/asia/australasia/article/3027579/chinese-billionaire-huang-xiangmo-has-australian-assets. See also Searight, *Countering China's Influence Activities*, 7.

129. Michelle Brown, "NSW Labor Former Boss Jamie Clements Got $35,000 in Wine Box from Chinese Billionaire Huang Xiangmao, ICAC Told," *Australian Broadcasting Corporation*, October 9, 2019, https://www.abc.net.au/news/2019-10-09/icac-told-nsw-labor-boss-got-35-000-hidden-in-wine-box/11585342.

130. Neil Chenoweth, "Where Huang Xiangmo Really Spent His Money," *Financial Review*, October 11, 2019, https://www.afr.com/politics/where-huang-xiangmo-really-spent-his-money-20191011-p52zsk.

131. Searight, *Countering China's Influence Activities*, 7–8.

132. "'The Australian People Stand Up': PM Defiant over Chinese Political Interference," *SBS News*, December 9, 2017, https://www.sbs.com.au/news/the-australian-people-stand-up-pm-defiant-over-chinese-political-interference.

133. Tom Rabe, Kate McClymont, and Alexandra Smith, "Dastyari, ICAC and the Chinese 'Agent of Influence,'" *Sydney Morning Herald,* August 29, 2019, https://www.smh.com.au/politics/nsw/dastyari-icac-and-the-chinese-agent-of-influence-20190829-p52m6e.html.

134. Ibid.

135. Nick McKenzie, James Massola, and Richard Baker, "Labor Senator Sam Dastyari Warned Wealthy Chinese Donor Huang Xiangmo His Phone Was Bugged," *Sydney Morning Herald*, November 29, 2017, https://www.smh.com.au/politics/federal/labor-senator-sam-dastyari-warned-wealthy-chinese-donor-huang-xiangmo-his-phone-was-bugged-20171128-gzu14c.html.

136. Ibid.

137. Searight, *Countering China's Influence Activities*, 11–12.

138. Ibid.

139. Ibid.

140. Ibid., 1.

141. Chris Uhlmann, "Domestic Spy Chief Sounded Alarm About Donor Links with China Last Year," *ABC News*, August 31, 2016, https://www. abc.net.au/news/2016-09-01/asio-chief-sounded-alarm-about-donor-links-with-china-last-year/7804856.

142. Searight, *Countering China's Influence Activities*, 34–35.

143. "Transcript: New Zealand Parliament, 3 Dec 2019," https://www. parliament.nz/resource/en-NZ/HansD_20191203_20191203/ 325b5904a487a32ed394b7e58a41927b420891bf.

144. Nick McKenzie and Chris Uhlmann, "'A Man of Many Dimensions': The Big Chinese Donor Now in Canberra's Sights," *Sydney Morning Herald*, February 6, 2019, https://www.smh.com.au/politics/federal/a-man-of-many-dimensions-the-big-chinese-donor-now-in-canberra-s-sights-20190206-p50vzt.html. See also "Chinese Billionaire Huang Xiangmo Has Australian Assets Frozen over US$96 Million Tax Bill," *South China Morning Post*, September 17, 2019, https://www.scmp. com/news/asia/australasia/article/3027579/chinese-billionaire-huang-xiangmo-has-australian-assets?module=perpetual_scroll&pgtype=arti cle&campaign=3027579.

145. Lucy Sweeney, "Sam Dastyari Resigns from Parliament, Says He Is 'Detracting from Labor's Mission' amid Questions over Chinese Links," *ABC News*, December 11, 2017, https://www.abc.net.au/news/2017-12-12/sam-dastyari-resigns-from-parliament/9247390.

146. David Brophy, "China Is Far from Alone in Taking Advantage of Australian Universities' Self-Inflicted Wounds," *Guardian*, July 9, 2021, https://www.theguardian.com/books/2021/ul/10/china-is-far-from-alone-in-taking-advantage-of-australian-universities-self-inflicted-wounds.

147. Matthew Doran, Iris Zhao, and Stephen Dziedzic, "Social Media Platform WeChat Censors Scott Morrison's Post Directed at Chinese Community," *ABC News*, December 2, 2020, https://www.abc.net.au/ news/2020-12-02/scott-morrison-post-censored-by-wechat-china/ 12944796.

148. "Australia Passes Foreign Interference Laws amid China Tension," *BBC*, June 28, 2018, https://www.bbc.com/news/world-australia-44624270.

149. Colin Packham, "Australia to Probe Foreign Interference Through Social Media Platforms," *Reuters*, December 5, 2019, https://www.

reuters.com/article/us-australia-politics/australia-to-probe-foreign-interference-through-social-media-platforms-idUSKBN1Y90E6; Cook, "Beijing's Global Megaphone"; Yan Zhuang, "Australia Quiet on First Foreign-Meddling Arrest, but Target Is Clear," *New York Times*, November 6, 2020, https://www.nytimes.com/2020/11/06/world/australia/australia-foreign-interference-law.html; "Australia to Investigate Foreign Interference at Universities, amid China Concerns," *South China Morning Post*, August 31, 2020, https://www.scmp.com/news/asia/australasia/article/3099585/australia-investigate-foreign-interference-universities-amid.

150. Dyani Lewis, "Australia Is Cracking Down on Foreign Interference in Research. Is the System Working?," *Nature*, August 10, 2020, https://www.nature.com/articles/d41586-020-02188-6.

151. James Laurenceson and Michael Zhou, *The Australia-China Science Boom* (Sydney: Australia-China Relations Institute, July 2020), https://www.australiachinarelations.org/content/australia-china-science-boom.

152. Ibid.

153. Ibid.

154. Alex Joske, "The China Defence Universities Tracker," *Australian Strategic Policy Institute*, November 25, 2019, https://www.aspi.org.au/report/china-defence-universities-tracker.

155. Paul Karp and Helen Davidson, "China Bristles at Australia's Call for Investigation into Coronavirus Origin," *Guardian*, April 29, 2020, https://www.theguardian.com/world/2020/apr/29/australia-defends-plan-to-investigate-china-over-covid-19-outbreak-as-row-deepens.

156. See "Huawei and ZTE Handed 5G Network Ban in Australia," *BBC*, August 23, 2018, https://www.bbc.com/news/technology-45281495; and Jamie Smyth, "Chinese Investors Turn Away from Australia After Canberra Crackdown," *Financial Times*, February 28, 2021, https://www.ft.com/content/f8e9a93f-72a5-49c3-832c-9a36fb6d4113.

157. See Su-Lin Tan, "China's Restrictions on Australian Beef, Barley Seen as Retaliation for Support of Coronavirus Investigation," *South China Morning Post*, May 12, 2020, https://www.scmp.com/economy/global-economy/article/3084062/chinas-restrictions-australian-beef-barley-seen-retaliation; and Damien Cave, "China Battles the World's Biggest Coal Exporter, and Coal Is Losing," *New York Times*, December 16, 2020, https://www.nytimes.com/2020/12/16/world/australia/china-coal-climate-change.html.

CHAPTER 6

1. See "Joshua Kurlantzick Discusses Cambodia and China's Strengthening Ties," *CGTN America*, January 22, 2019, https://www.youtube.com/watch?v=ZhKPZhdFVUo; "Joshua Kurlantzick on the First Thai General Elections Since 2014," *CGTN America*, January 22, 2019, https://www.youtube.com/watch?v=6DhMCK41Fkk.

2. Although CGTN sometimes offers small payments to guests who appear on its programs, I refused these payments.

3. Chea Vannak, "Internet Users Near 16m," *Khmer Times*, July 26, 2019, https://www.khmertimeskh.com/50627470/internet-users-near-16m/; "Analytical Report for Cambodia Media Use Survey," Gallup conducted for USAGM, September 2017, obtained through the Freedom of Information Act process.

4. Herman Wasserman and Dani Madrid-Morales, "How Influential Are Chinese Media in Africa? An Audience Analysis in Kenya and South Africa," *International Journal of Communication* 12 (2018): 2122–231; Vivien Marsh, "*Tiangao* or *Tianxia*? The Ambiguities of CCTV's English-Language News for Africa," in *China's Media Go Global*, ed. Daya Kishan Thussu, Hugo de Brugh, and Anbin Shi (New York: Routledge, 2018), 114–17.

5. Gerry Smith, "Journalism Job Cuts Haven't Been This Bad Since the Recession," *Bloomberg*, July 1, 2019, https://www.bloomberg.com/news/articles/2019-07-01/journalism-layoffs-are-at-the-highest-level-since-last-recession; Benjamin Goggin, "7,800 People Have Lost Their Jobs So Far This Year in a Media Landslide," *Business Insider*, December 10, 2019, https://www.businessinsider.com/2019-media-layoffs-job-cuts-at-buzzfeed-huffpost-vice-details-2019-2.

6. Sasha Lekach, "Fewer Than Half of Newspaper Jobs from 15 Years Ago Still Exist," *Mashable*, April 4, 2017, https://mashable.com/2017/04/04/newspaper-publishers-jobs-decline-bls/.

7. Penelope Abernathy, *The Expanding News Desert* (Chapel Hill: Center for Innovation and Sustainability in Local Media, University of North Carolina, 2018), https://www.cislm.org/wp-content/uploads/2018/10/The-Expanding-News-Desert-10_14-Web.pdf.

8. Marc Tracy, "The Daily News Is Now a Newspaper Without a Newsroom," *New York Times*, August 12, 2020, https://www.nytimes.com/2020/08/12/business/media/daily-news-office.html.

9. John Plunkett, "Turner International to Cut 30% of Staff from International Arm," *Guardian*, January 15, 2013, https://www.theguard

ian.com/media/2013/jan/15/turner-broadcasting-cut-staff-arm; Dylan Byers, "Turner Broadcasting to Cut Staff by 10 Percent; CNN to Shed 300 Jobs," *Politico*, October 6, 2014, https://www.politico.com/blogs/media/2014/10/turner-broadcasting-to-cut-staff-by-10-percent-cnn-to-shed-300-jobs-196659; "BBC World Service Cuts Outlined to Staff," *BBC*, January 26, 2011, https://www.bbc.com/news/entertainment-arts-12283356; John Plunkett et al., "Listeners on Three Continents Lament BBC World Service Cutbacks," *Guardian*, January 28, 2011, https://www.theguardian.com/media/2011/jan/28/bbc-world-service-cuts-response.

10. Editorial Board, "The Global Reach of Trump's 'Fake News' Outrage," *Washington Post*, November 19, 2019, https://www.washingtonpost.com/opinions/global-opinions/trump-is-spreading-his-fake-news-rhetoric-around-the-world-thats-dangerous/2019/11/19/a7b0a4c6-0af5-11ea-97ac-a7ccc8dd1ebc_story.html; Uri Friedman, "The Real-World Consequences of 'Fake News,'" *Atlantic*, December 23, 2017, https://www.theatlantic.com/international/archive/2017/12/trump-world-fake-news/548888/; Jon Henley, "Populist Voters Less Likely to Trust News Media, European Survey Finds," *Guardian*, May 14, 2018, https://www.theguardian.com/politics/2018/may/14/populist-voters-less-likely-to-trust-news-media-european-survey-finds; Craig Timberg and Isaac Stanley-Becker, "Violent Memes and Messages Surging on Far-Left Social Media, Report Finds," *Washington Post*, September 14, 2020, https://www.washingtonpost.com/technology/2020/09/14/violent-antipolice-memes-surge/.

11. Ibid.

12. "Poll: How Does the Public Think Journalism Happens?," *Columbia Journalism Review*, Winter 2019, https://www.cjr.org/special_report/how-does-journalism-happen-poll.php; Harry Enten, "Congress' Approval Rating Hasn't Hit 30% in 10 Years. That's a Record," *CNN*, June 1, 2019, https://www.cnn.com/2019/06/01/politics/poll-of-the-week-congress-approval-rating/index.html; Keith E. Whittington, "Hating on Congress: An American Tradition," *Gallup*, July 30, 2019, https://news.gallup.com/opinion/gallup/262316/hating-congress-american-tradition.aspx.

13. "New Poll Shows Trust Levels Down Across Institutions," *CNN Philippines*, September 10, 2019, https://cnnphilippines.com/news/2019/9/10/2019-philippine-trust-index.html.

14. Simon Lewis, "Duterte Says Journalists in the Philippines Are 'Not Exempted from Assassination,'" *Time*, June 1, 2016, https://time.com/

4353279/duterte-philippines-journalists-assassination/; "Rappler Journalist Ressa Launches Defense in Philippine Libel Case," *Agence France-Presse*, December 16, 2019, https://www.voanews.com/press-freedom/rappler-journalist-ressa-launches-defense-philippine-libel-case; Jason Gutierrez, "Philippine Congress Officially Shuts Down Leading Broadcaster," *New York Times*, July 10, 2020, https://www.nytimes.com/2020/07/10/world/asia/philippines-congress-media-duterte-abs-cbn.html; Rebecca Ratcliffe, "Journalist Maria Ressa Found Guilty of 'Cyberlibel' in Philippines," *Guardian*, June 15, 2020, https://www.theguardian.com/world/2020/jun/15/maria-ressa-rappler-editor-found-guilty-of-cyber-libel-charges-in-philippines.

15. Jason Gutierrez and Alexandra Stevenson, "Maria Ressa, Crusading Journalist, Is Convicted in Philippines Libel Case," *New York Times*, October 8, 2021, https://www.nytimes.com/2020/06/14/business/maria-ressa-verdict-philippines-rappler.html; Girlie Linao, "A Triumph of Truth over Lies: Joy in the Philippines over Maria Ressa's Nobel Prize Win," *Guardian*, October 12, 2021, https://www.theguardian.com/world/2021/oct/12/a-triumph-of-truth-over-lies-joy-in-the-philippines-over-maria-ressas-nobel-prize-win.

16. Anna Nicolaou and Chris Giles, "Public Trust in Media at All Time Low, Research Shows," *Financial Times*, January 15, 2017, https://www.ft.com/content/fa332f58-d9bf-11e6-944b-e7eb37a6aa8e; Rakesh Thukral, "India: High Trust, Higher Expectations," *Edelman*, February 19, 2018, https://www.edelman.com/post/india-high-trust-higher-expectations; Murali Krishnan, "Indian Media Facing a Crisis of Credibility," *Deutsche Welle*, June 5, 2017, https://www.dw.com/en/indian-media-facing-a-crisis-of-credibility/a-39120228; "2019 Edelman Trust Barometer," *Edelman*, January 20, 2019, https://www.edelman.com/research/2019-edelman-trust-barometer.

17. Sarah Repucci, "Freedom and the Media 2019: A Downward Spiral," in "Freedom and the Media 2019," *Freedom House*, June 2019, 1–2, https://freedomhouse.org/sites/default/files/2020-02/FINAL07162019_Freedom_And_The_Media_2019_Report.pdf.

18. Sarah Repucci and Amy Slipowitz, *Democracy Under Lockdown: The Impact of COVID-19 on the Global Struggle for Freedom* (Washington, DC: Freedom House, October 2020), https://freedomhouse.org/sites/default/files/2020-10/COVID-19_Special_Report_Final_.pdf. (The author served as a consultant for sections in this report on Southeast Asia.)

19. Steven Erlanger, "Russia's RT Network: Is It More BBC or K.G.B.?," *New York Times*, March 8, 2017, https://www.nytimes.com/2017/03/08/world/europe/russias-rt-network-is-it-more-bbc-or-kgb.html.

20. Jeff Semple, "Growing Popularity of Kremlin Network RT Signals the Age of Information War," *Global News*, October 12, 2018, https://globalnews.ca/news/4540034/fake-news-wars-kremlin-network-rt/.

21. Ava Kofman, "YouTube Promised to Label State-Sponsored Videos but Doesn't Always Do So," *ProPublica*, November 22, 2019, https://www.propublica.org/article/youtube-promised-to-label-state-sponsored-videos-but-doesnt-always-do-so.

22. For example, "Despair, Depression, and the Inevitable Rise of Trump 2.0: Glenn Greenwald Tells RT His Biden Administration Predictions," *RT*, January 17, 2021, https://www.rt.com/usa/512749-greenwald-biden-elections-prediction/.

23. "Budget Submissions," *USAGM*, May 28, 2021, https://www.usagm.gov/our-work/strategy-and-results/strategic-priorities/budget-submissions/#:~:text=The%20President's%20budget%20request%20for,includes%20%24810%20million%20for%20USAGM. China spends billions and billions on its state media; the USAGM annual budget request for U.S. state broadcasting is around $800 million.

24. Hilton Yip, "China's $6 Billion Propaganda Blitz Is a Snooze," *Foreign Policy*, April 23, 2018, https://foreignpolicy.com/2018/04/23/the-voice-of-china-will-be-a-squeak/; Koh Gui Qing and John Shiffman, "Beijing's Covert Radio Network Airs China-Friendly News Across Washington, and the World," *Reuters*, November 2, 2015, https://www.reuters.com/investigates/special-report/china-radio/; "China Is Spending Billions on Its Foreign-Language Media," *Economist*, June 14, 2018, https://www.economist.com/china/2018/06/14/china-is-spending-billions-on-its-foreign-language-media; Merriden Varrall, "Behind the News: Inside China Global Television Network," *Lowy Institute*, January 16, 2020, https://www.lowyinstitute.org/publications/behind-news-inside-china-global-television-network; "Assessment on U.S. Defense Implications of China's Expanding Global Access," *U.S. Department of Defense*, December 2018, https://media.defense.gov/2019/Jan/14/2002079292/-1/-1/1/EXPANDING-GLOBAL-ACCESS-REPORT-FINAL.PDF.

25. Sean Mantesso and Christina Zhou, "China's Multi-Billion Dollar Media Campaign 'a Major Threat for Democracies' Around the World," *ABC News*, February 7, 2019, https://www.abc.net.au/news/2019-02-08/chinas-foreign-media-push-a-major-threat-to-democracies/10733

068; Patricia Nilsson, Michael Peel, and Sun Yu, "Behind the Scenes at China TV: Soft Power and State Propaganda," *Financial Times*, June 19, 2021, https://www.ft.com/content/9192de21-2007-4ee5-86a8-ad76b ce693dc.

26. Si Si, "Expansion of International Broadcasting: The Growing Global Reach of China Central Television," *Reuters Institute for the Study of Journalism*, July 2014, 18, https://reutersinstitute.politics.ox.ac.uk/sites/ default/files/2018-01/Expansion%20of%20International%20Broadcast ing.pdf.

27. Mantesso and Zhou, "China's Multi-Billion Dollar Media Campaign 'a Major Threat for Democracies' Around the World."

28. For one relevant briefing, see Raymond T. Warhola, "Media Profile 2014," China Daily Asia Pacific Limited, https://www.chinadailyasia. com/public_resource/public/pdf/HKedition-MediaKit.pdf.

29. Ibid.

30. Mantesso and Zhou, "China's Multi-Billion Dollar Media Campaign 'a Major Threat for Democracies' Around the World." If CGTN cannot even match the reach of New Tang Dynasty Television, a far less pro-moted Chinese channel, it has nowhere near the viewership of the BBC or CNN. See also, for instance, Celine Sui, "China Wants State Media to Peddle Its 'Soft Power' in Africa, but Tech Platforms Are a Better Bet," *Quartz*, October 29, 2019, https://qz.com/africa/1736534/ china-daily-cgtn-fight-for-influence-in-africa-vs-bbc-cnn/.

31. "China's Pursuit of a New World Media Order," *Reporters Without Borders*, March 22, 2019, 20–23, https://rsf.org/en/reports/rsf-report-chinas-pursuit-new-world-media-order.

32. Louisa Lim and Julia Bergin, "Inside China's Audacious Global Propaganda Campaign," *Guardian*, December 7, 2018, https://www. theguardian.com/news/2018/dec/07/china-plan-for-global-media-dominance-propaganda-xi-jinping.

33. "China's Pursuit of a New World Media Order," 20–23; Erik Wemple, "Associated Press Announces Layoffs," *Washington Post*, December 9, 2016, https://www.washingtonpost.com/blogs/erik-wemple/wp/ 2016/12/09/associated-press-announces-layoffs/; Jordan Valinsky, "Thomson Reuters Will Cut 3,200 Jobs by 2020," *CNN*, December 4, 2018, https://www.cnn.com/2018/12/04/media/reuters-layoffs/index. html; Isaac Stone Fish, "Is China's Xinhua the Future of Journalism?," *Newsweek*, September 3, 2010, https://www.newsweek.com/chinas-xin hua-future-journalism-71961.

34. Lim and Bergin, "Inside China's Global Propaganda Campaign."

35. "Voice of America Makes More Cuts to Its International Shortwave Broadcast Schedule," *National Association for Amateur Radio*, July 1, 2014, http://www.arrl.org/news/voice-of-america-makes-more-cuts-to-international-shortwave-broadcast-schedule.

36. "Waves in the Web," *Economist*, August 12, 2010, https://www.economist.com/international/2010/08/12/waves-in-the-web; Vivian Yang, "How Chinese Media Is Going Global," *World Economic Forum*, August 10, 2015, https://www.weforum.org/agenda/2015/08/how-chinese-media-is-going-global/.

37. "People's Daily Expands Reach with English-Language News App," *China Daily*, October 15, 2017, https://www.chinadaily.com.cn/china/2017-10/15/content_33284554.htm.

38. Yang, "How Chinese Media Is Going Global."

39. William Yuen Yee, "Win Some, Lose Some: China's Campaign for Global Media Influence," *Jamestown Foundation China Brief* 21, no. 19 (October 8 2021), https://jamestown.org/program/win-some-lose-some-chinas-campaign-for-global-media-influence/.

40. Ibid.

41. Ibid.

42. Greg James, "Hunan TV Slammed for Chasing Ratings—China's Latest Society and Culture News," *SupChina*, September 1, 2017, https://supchina.com/2017/09/01/hunan-tv-slammed-chasing-ratings-chinas-latest-society-culture-news/.

43. Ibid.

44. "Business Structure," *MangoTV*, accessed November 2, 2021, https://corp.mgtv.com/en/product/.

45. "Analytical Report for Laos Media Use Survey," Gallup report prepared for USAGM and obtained through the Freedom of Information Act, January 2017.

46. Author interview with former policymaker at USAGM, Washington, December 2018.

47. Ibid.

48. The publication *Radio Insight* chronicles almost-daily switches in formats of radio stations in the United States; many of these switches likely come because the existing format was not financially successful or a new owner came in, offering more money, and switched the format.

49. Jim Rutenberg, "RT, Sputnik, and Russia's New Theory of War," *New York Times Magazine*, September 13, 2017, https://www.nytimes.com/2017/09/13/magazine/rt-sputnik-and-russias-new-theory-of-war.html.

50. "The Great Leap Backward of Journalism in China," *Reporters Without Borders*, December 7, 2021, https://rsf.org/en/reports/unprecedented-rsf-investigation-great-leap-backwards-journalism-china.

51. Bethany Allen-Ebrahimian, "China, Explained," *Foreign Policy*, June 3, 2016, https://foreignpolicy.com/2016/06/03/china-explained-sixth-tone-is-chinas-latest-party-approved-outlet-humanizing-news/; Varrall, "Behind the News."

52. Varrall, "Behind the News."

53. Ibid.

54. Ibid.

55. Jeffrey E. Stern, "Made in America, Funded by Communists," *New Republic*, February 20, 2013, https://newrepublic.com/article/112413/cctv-news-america-expansion-american-journalists-chinese-paychecks. Also, William Gallo, "Inside China's Brash New Approach to State Media," Voice of America, November 26, 2021, https://www.voanews.com/a/inside-china-s-brash-new-approach-to-state-media/6329303.html.

56. Ibid.; Yang Wanli, "Former CCTV Anchor Sees Clear Skies Ahead," *China Daily*, September 21, 2017, https://www.chinadaily.com.cn/opinion/5yearscorecard/2017-09/21/content_32278063.htm.

57. "Mike Walter," *CGTN America*, https://america.cgtn.com/anchors-corresp/mike-walter; "Jim Spellman," *CGTN*, https://www.cgtn.com/face/jim-spellman.html; Si, "Expansion of International Broadcasting."

58. "Barnaby Lo," *CGTN America*, https://america.cgtn.com/anchors-corresp/barnaby-lo-2.

59. Author interview by phone with Dayo Aiyetan, May 2019. Also, Lim and Bergin, "Inside China's Audacious Global Propaganda Campaign."

60. Author interview by phone with Dayo Aiyetan, May 2019.

61. For example, "Lindy Mtongana," *CGTN*, https://www.cgtn.com/face/lindy-mtongana.html. Also, Michael Musyoka, "Top Kenyan TV Anchors Who Have Joined China-Owned Station," *Kenyans.co.ke*, April 15, 2021, https://www.kenyans.co.ke/news/64319-top-kenyan-tv-anchors-who-joined-china-owned-station.

62. Ying Zhu, *Two Billion Eyes: The Story of China Central Television* (New York: New Press, 2012), 173–75.

63. Lily Kuo, "Chinese Liberal Think Tank Forced to Close After Being Declared Illegal," *Guardian*, August 28, 2019, https://www.theguardian.com/world/2019/aug/28/chinese-liberal-thinktank-forced-to-close-after-being-declared-illegal.

64. Amy Gunia, "At Least 250 Journalists Have Been Imprisoned in 2019 and China Is the Top Jailer, CPJ Says," *Time*, December 12, 2019, https://time.com/5748675/committee-to-protect-journalists-2019-survey/; "Record Number of Journalists Jailed Worldwide," *Committee to Protect Journalists*, December 15, 2020, https://cpj.org/reports/2020/12/record-number-journalists-jailed-imprisoned.

65. Tom Phillips, "China's Young Reporters Give Up on Journalism: 'You Can't Write What You Want,'" *Guardian*, February 11, 2016, https://www.theguardian.com/world/2016/feb/12/china-journalism-reporters-freedom-of-speech.

66. Ibid.

67. Javier C. Hernandez, "'We're Almost Extinct': China's Investigative Journalists Are Silenced Under Xi," *New York Times*, July 12, 2019, https://www.nytimes.com/2019/07/12/world/asia/china-journalists-crackdown.html.

68. "2017 Annual Report to Congress," U.S.-China Economic and Security Review Commission, November 15, 2017, 465, https://www.uscc.gov/annual-report/2017-annual-report-congress.

69. Hernandez, "'We're Almost Extinct.'"

70. Jian Wang, "Introduction: China's Search of Soft Power," in *Soft Power in China: Public Diplomacy Through Communication*, ed. Jian Wang (New York: Palgrave Macmillan, 2011), 9–10.

71. Pál Nyíri, *Reporting for China: How Chinese Correspondents Work with the World* (Seattle: University of Washington Press, 2018), 76–77.

72. Marsh, "*Tiangao or Tianxia?*," 114–17.

73. Interview with current CGTN employee, 2019.

74. "CGTV America Wins 27 Awards from the White House News Photographers Association," *CGTN America*, February 24, 2019, https://america.cgtn.com/2019/02/14/cgtn-america-wins-28-awards-in-the-white-house-news-photographers-association.

75. "CCTV America Wins Emmy for 'When Can't Is a Four-Letter Word,'" *CGTN America*, September 21, 2016, https://america.cgtn.com/2016/09/21/cctv-america-wins-emmy-for-when-cant-is-a-four-letter-word.

76. "Awards," *CGTN America*, https://america.cgtn.com/category/awards.

77. Ibid.

78. For one of many examples of international news coverage of the Panama Papers and the Chinese leadership, see Juliette Garside and David Pegg, "Panama Papers Reveal Offshore Secrets of China's Red Nobility," *Guardian*, April 6, 2016, https://www.theguardian.com/

news/2016/apr/06/panama-papers-reveal-offshore-secrets-china-red-nobility-big-business.

79. "China's Pursuit of a New World Media Order."

80. Martha Bayles, "Hollywood's Great Leap Backward on Free Expression," *Atlantic*, September 15, 2019, https://www.theatlantic.com/ideas/archive/2019/09/hollywoods-great-leap-backward-free-expression/598045/; Shane Savitsky, "Hollywood's Cave to China on Censorship," *Axios*, October 10, 2019, https://www.axios.com/hollywood-movies-china-censorship-bba26aa9-b122-4b2c-80e1-054394414698.html; Javier C. Hernandez, "Leading Western Publisher Bows to Chinese Censorship," *New York Times,* November 1, 2017, https://www.nytimes.com/2017/11/01/world/asia/china-springer-nature-censorship.html; Ellie Bothwell, "Publishers Choose Between Self-Censorship in China and Import Ban," *Times Higher Education*, January 9, 2019, https://www.timeshighereducation.com/news/publishers-choose-between-self-censorship-china-and-import-ban; Isaac Stone Fish, "How China Gets American Companies to Parrot Its Propaganda," *Washington Post*, October 11, 2019, https://www.washingtonpost.com/outlook/how-china-gets-american-companies-to-parrot-its-propaganda/2019/10/11/512f7b8c-eb73-11e9-85c0-85a098e47b37_story.html; Natasha Pinon, "Here's a Growing List of Companies Bowing to China Censorship Pressure," *Mashable*, October 10, 2019, https://mashable.com/article/china-censorship-companies-hong-kong-protests-nba/; Gideon Rachman, "Chinese Censorship Is Spreading Beyond Its Borders," *Financial Times*, October 14, 2019, https://www.ft.com/content/cda1efbc-ee5a-11e9-ad1e-4367d8281195; Isaac Stone Fish, "The Other Political Correctness," *New Republic*, September 4, 2018, https://newrepublic.com/article/150476/american-elite-universities-selfcensorship-china; James Durso, "The Uighurs, China, and the Lucrative Hypocrisy of LeBron James and the NBA," *Hill*, October 24, 2019, https://thehill.com/opinion/civil-rights/467295-uighurs-china-and-the-lucrative-hypocrisy-of-lebron-james-nba.

81. Zhu, *Two Billion Eyes*, 183.

82. Emeka Umejei, "Chinese Media in Africa: Between Promise and Reality," *African Journalism Studies* 39, no. 2 (2018): 9, https://www.tandfonline.com/doi/abs/10.1080/23743670.2018.1473275.

83. "CGTN Town Hall Explores China's Rise to Prominence," *CGTN America*, December 19, 2018, https://america.cgtn.com/2018/12/19/cgtn-town-hall-explores-chinas-rise-to-prominence.

84. Ibid.

85. The author's wife works at George Washington University but is not involved in China studies and had no involvement in this forum.

86. Jane Mayer, "The Making of the Fox News White House," *New Yorker*, March 4, 2019, https://www.newyorker.com/magazine/2019/03/11/the-making-of-the-fox-news-white-house.

87. Alex W. Palmer, "The Man Behind China's Aggressive New Voice," *New York Times*, July 7, 2021, https://www.nytimes.com/2021/07/07/magazine/china-diplomacy-twitter-zhao-lijian.html. For more on the broader phenomenon, see Peter Martin, *China's Civilian Army: The Making of Wolf Warrior Diplomacy* (New York: Oxford University Press, 2021).

88. "Global Times: China's True Voice of Nationalistic Rabble-Rouser?," *South China Morning Post*, https://www.scmp.com/article/966560/global-times-chinas-true-voice-or-nationalistic-rabble-rouser.

89. "China's Global Times Plays a Peculiar Role," *Economist*, September 20, 2018, https://www.economist.com/china/2018/09/20/chinas-global-times-plays-a-peculiar-role.

90. Tania Branigan, "China Blocks Twitter, Flickr, and Hotmail Ahead of Tiananmen Anniversary," *Guardian*, June 2, 2009, https://www.theguardian.com/technology/2009/jun/02/twitter-china.

91. "Sputnik Begins Cooperation with China's Global Times Online," *Sputnik News*, April 19, 2017, https://sputniknews.com/20170419/sputnik-china-global-times-online-cooperation-1052742408.html.

92. "China's Global Times Plays a Peculiar Role."

93. "Chinese Paper's Threat to the RAAF: 'It Would Be a Shame if One Day a Plane Fell from the Sky," *News.com*, December 17, 2015, https://www.news.com.au/technology/innovation/inventions/chinese-papers-threat-to-raaf-it-would-be-a-shame-if-one-day-a-plane-fell-from-the-sky/news-story/1af82a742f134678de32ccc7cda0c15e; Peh Shing Huei, "How China Is Using Its Global Times Attack Dog to Intimidate Singapore," *South China Morning Post*, October 1, 2016, https://www.scmp.com/week-asia/opinion/article/2024088/how-china-using-its-global-times-attack-dog-intimidate-singapore; Zheping Huang, "Inside the Global Times, China's Hawkish, Belligerent State Tabloid," *Quartz*, August 9, 2016, https://qz.com/745577/inside-the-global-times-chinas-hawkish-belligerent-state-tabloid/.

94. Peter Cai, "The Global Times and Beijing: A Nuanced Relationship," *Interpreter*, August 3, 2016, https://www.lowyinstitute.org/the-interpreter/global-times-and-beijing-nuanced-relationship.

95. Ibid.

96. "China Cannot Hesitate on Nuclear Buildup," *Global Times*, December 23, 2016, http://www.globaltimes.cn/content/1025377.shtml; "Mainland Must Shape Taiwan's Future," *Global Times*, December 14, 2016, http://www.globaltimes.cn/content/1023753.shtml; "Congress' Malevolent Bill Falls on Deaf Ears," *Global Times*, May 30, 2014, http://www.globaltimes.cn/content/863058.shtml; "Britain Steps Backward as EU Faces Decline," *Global Times*, June 25, 2016, http://www.globalti mes.cn/content/990440.shtml; Eric Fish, "China's Angriest Newspaper Doesn't Speak for China," *Foreign Policy*, April 28, 2017, https://foreig npolicy.com/2017/04/28/chinas-angriest-newspaper-doesnt-speak-for-china/.

97. Huang, "Inside the Global Times, China's Hawkish, Belligerent State Tabloid." Also, Bridget O'Donnell, "Global Times Just Burned UK with New Europe Edition," *That's China*, July 8, 2016, https://www.thatsm ags.com/china/post/14433/global-times-just-burned-uk-with-new-europe-edition.

98. Eric Baculinao and Janis Mackey Frayer, "China's Global Times: Hawkish by Decree or Reflecting Readers?," *NBC News*, February 20, 2017, https://www.nbcnews.com/news/china/china-s-global-times-hawkish-decree-or-reflecting-readers-n722316.

99. Cai, "The Global Times and Beijing"; "Global Times: Audience," https://www.globaltimes.cn/adv.html.

100. Edward Wong, "U.S. Fights Bioweapons Conspiracy Theory Pushed by Russia and China," *New York Times*, March 10, 2022, https://www.nytimes.com/2022/03/10/us/politics/russia-ukraine-china-bioweap ons.html.

101. Ashley Gold, "China's State Media Buys Meta Ads Pushing Russia's Line on War," *Axios*, March 9, 2022, https://www.axios.com/chinas-state-media-meta-facebook-ads-russia-623763df-c5fb-46e4-a6a8-36b607e1b672.html; Sheera Frenkel and Stuart A. Thompson, "How Russia and Right-Wing Americans Converged on War in Ukraine," *New York Times*, March 23, 2022, https://www.nytimes.com/2022/03/23/technology/russia-american-far-right-ukraine.html.

102. Samantha Custer et al., *Influencing the Narrative: How the Chinese Government Mobilizes Students and Media to Burnish Its Image* (Williamsburg, VA: AidData at William & Mary, 2019), 12, http://docs.aiddata.org/ad4/pdfs/Influencing_the_Narrative_Report.pdf.

103. Ibid., 18–21.

104. "China's Pursuit of a New World Media Order," 22–26; Ramy Inocencio, "China's Crackdown Leaves Hong Kong's Last Pro-Democracy

Newspaper, Apple Daily, Hanging by a Thread," *CBS News*, June 21, 2021, https://www.cbsnews.com/news/hong-kong-china-apple-daily-newspaper-matter-of-days-survival/; Vivian Wang, "Hong Kong's Move to Overhaul Broadcaster Fans Fears of Media Crackdown," *New York Times*, February 19, 2021, https://www.nytimes.com/2021/02/19/world/asia/hong-kong-rthk-crackdown.html; "2021 World Press Freedom Index: Journalism, the Vaccine Against Disinformation, Blocked in More Than 130 Countries," *Reporters Without Borders*, accessed February 18, 2022, https://rsf.org/en/2021-world-press-freedom-index-journalism-vaccine-against-disinformation-blocked-more-130-countries.

105. Lim and Bergin, "Inside China's Global Propaganda Campaign."

106. For example, Xinhua stories just outright dismissing the extensive reporting on China's abuses in Xinjiang. See, for instance, "The Think Tank Behind Anti-China Propaganda in Australia," *Xinhua*, June 23, 2020, http://www.xinhuanet.com/english/2020-06/23/c_139161837.htm.

107. For example, on issues that are social and economic issues that don't implicate the CCP, *Sixth Tone* can do excellent work. See, for instance, Yuan Ye, "Typhoons May Spike Ground Level Ozone in Chinese Cities, Study Says," *Sixth Tone*, January 14, 2022, https://www.sixthtone.com/news/1009439/typhoons-may-spike-ground-level-ozone-in-chinese-cities%2C-study-says.

108. See Ye Ruolin, "With Active COVID-19 Outbreaks, China Fears Lunar New Year Travel," *Sixth Tone*, January 8, 2021, https://www.sixthtone.com/news/1006686/with-active-covid-19-outbreaks%2C-china-fears-lunar-new-year-travel; Li You, "'Forever Chemicals' Found in Tap Water Along Yangtze River," *Sixth Tone*, January 13, 2021, https://www.sixthtone.com/news/1006706/forever-chemicals-found-in-tap-water-along-yangtze-river; and Zhang Zizhu, "In Virus-Free Wuhan, Businesses Are Still Recovering," *Sixth Tone*, January 7, 2021, https://www.sixthtone.com/news/1006678/in-virus-free-wuhan%2C-businesses-are-still-recovering.

109. James Palmer, "Hong Kongers Break Beijing's Delusions of Victory," *Foreign Policy*, November 25, 2019, https://foreignpolicy.com/2019/11/25/hong-kong-election-beijing-media-delusions-victory/.

110. Ibid.

111. Ibid.

112. Ibid.

113. Custer et al., *Influencing the Narrative*, 25.

114. "China's Pursuit of a New World Media Order."

115. Ananth Krishnan, "China Is Buying Good Press Across the World, One Paid Journalist at a Time," *Print*, November 24, 2018, https://theprint.in/opinion/china-is-paying-foreign-journalists-including-from-india-to-report-from-beijing/154013/.

116. X. Xin, "Xinhua News Agency in Africa," *Journal of African Media Studies* 1, no. 3 (2009): 363–77.

117. Andrew McCormick, "'Even if You Don't Think You Have a Relationship with China, China Has a Big Relationship with You,'" *Columbia Journalism Review*, June 20, 2019, https://www.cjr.org/special_report/china-foreign-journalists-oral-history.php.

118. Ibid.

119. Ibid.

120. Yuan Zhou and Zhang Zhihao, "China Boosts Soft Power by Training Foreign Journalists," *China Daily*, October 17, 2016, https://www.chinadaily.com.cn/china/2016-10/17/content_27077588.htm; Juan Pablo Cardenal, "China in Latin America: Understanding the Inventory of Influence," in *Sharp Power: Rising Authoritarian Influence* (Washington, DC: National Endowment for Democracy, December 2017), https://www.ned.org/wp-content/uploads/2017/12/Sharp-Power-Rising-Authoritarian-Influence-Full-Report.pdf; and Maria Repnikova, "China's Soft Power Projection in Africa," Presentation, Wilson Center, May 12, 2021, https://www.wilsoncenter.org/event/chinas-soft-power-projection-africa.

121. "China's Pursuit of a New World Media Order."

122. "The Forum on China-Africa Cooperation Johannesburg Action Plan (2016–2018)," Ministry of Foreign Affairs of the People's Republic of China, December 10, 2015, https://www.fmprc.gov.cn/mfa_eng/zxxx_662805/t1323159.shtml; Repnikova, "China's Soft Power Projection in Africa."

123. Cardenal, "China in Latin America," 31.

124. Krishnan, "China Is Buying Good Press Across the World, One Paid Journalist at a Time"; McCormick, "'Even if You Don't Think You Have a Relationship with China, China Has a Big Relationship with You.'"

125. "Edward R. Murrow Program," Bureau of Education and Cultural Affairs, U.S. Department of State, https://exchanges.state.gov/non-us/program/edward-r-murrow-program.

126. "Fellowships," Nieman, Harvard University, https://nieman.harvard.edu/fellowships/.

127. Krishnan, "China Is Buying Good Press Across the World, One Paid Journalist at a Time."

128. Ibid.

129. "The China Story: Reshaping the World's Media," *International Federation of Journalists*, June 23, 2020, https://www.ifj.org/media-cen tre/reports/detail/ifj-report-the-china-story-reshaping-the-worlds-media/category/publications.html.

130. Ibid.

131. Ibid.

132. Jessica Chen Weiss, "Does China Actively Promote Its Way of Governing—and Do Other Countries Listen?," *Washington Post*, July 14, 2021, https://www.washingtonpost.com/politics/2021/07/14/does-china-actively-promote-its-way-governing-do-other-countries-listen/.

133. McCormick, "'Even if You Don't Think You Have a Relationship with China, China Has a Big Relationship with You.'"

134. Ibid.

135. Iginio Gagliardone, "China as a Persuader: CCTV Africa's First Steps in the African Mediasphere," *Ecquid Novi: African Journalism Studies* 34, no. 3 (2013): 26.

136. Xiaoling Zhang, Herman Wasserman, and Winston Mano, "China's Expanding Influence in Africa: Projection, Perception, and Prospects in Southern African Countries," *Communicatio: South African Journal for Communication Theory and Research* 42, no. 1 (2016): 7.

137. David McKenzie, "Chinese Media Make Inroads into Africa," *CNN*, September 25, 2012, https://www.cnn.com/2012/09/05/busin ess/china-africa-cctv-media/index.html; Jacinta Mwende Maweu, "Journalists and Public Perceptions of the Politics of China's Soft Power in Kenya Under the 'Look East' Foreign Policy," in *China's Media and Soft Power in Africa: Promotion and Perceptions*, ed. Xiaoling Zhang, Herman Wasserman, and Winston Mano (New York: Palgrave Macmillan, 2016), 127–29.

138. Maweu, "Journalists and Public Perceptions of the Politics of China's Soft Power in Kenya Under the 'Look East' Foreign Policy," 127–29.

139. Wasserman and Madrid-Morales, "How Influential Are Chinese Media in Africa?," 2222.

140. Ibid.

141. Catie Snow Bailard, "China in Africa: An Analysis of the Effect of Chinese Media Expansion on African Public Opinion," *International Journal of Press/Politics* 21, no. 4 (2016): 446–71.

142. See, for example, Laura Silver, Kat Devlin, and Christine Huang, "People Around the Globe Are Divided in Their Opinions of China," *Pew Research Center*, December 5, 2019, https://www.pewresearch.org/fact-tank/2019/12/05/people-around-the-globe-are-divided-in-their-opinions-of-china/.

143. Wasserman and Madrid-Morales, "How Influential Are Chinese Media in Africa?," 2122–231.

144. Studies of Ivorian media done by academics and by contractors for the U.S. Agency for Global Media and obtained by me through the Freedom of Information Act.

145. Ibid.

146. For more, see Joshua Kurlantzick, "China's State Media Outlets: The White House Cracks Down, but How Much of a Threat Are They?," *Asia Unbound*, March 12, 2020, https://www.cfr.org/blog/chinas-state-media-outlets-white-house-cracks-down-how-much-threat-are-they.

147. Marsh, "*Tiangao* or *Tianxia*?," 114–15.

148. Ibid.

149. Abdirizak Garo Guyo and Hong Yu, "How Is the Performance of Chinese News Media in Kenya? An Analysis of Perceived Audience Motivation and Reception," *New Media and Mass Communication* 79 (2019), https://core.ac.uk/download/pdf/234653591.pdf.

150. For more, see Kurlantzick, "China's State Media Outlets." Also, see Studies of Vietnamese media done by academics and by contractors for the U.S. Agency for Global Media and obtained by me through the Freedom of Information Act.

151. For more, see a blog post that part of this section was adapted from: Kurlantzick, "China's State Media Outlets." Also, see Studies of Cambodian media done by academics and by contractors for the U.S. Agency for Global Media and obtained by me through the Freedom of Information Act.

152. A portion comes from Kurlantzick, "China's State Media Outlets." Also, Merriden Varrall, "Behind the News: Inside China Global Television Network," *Lowy Institute*, January 16, 2020, https://www.lowyinstitute.org/publications/behind-news-inside-china-global-television-network.

153. "China Is Spending Billions on Its Foreign Language Media: Is it Worth It?," *Economist*, June 16, 2018, https://www.economist.com/china/2018/06/14/china-is-spending-billions-on-its-foreign-language-media.

154. Finbarr Bermingham, "CGTN Set to Return to European Screens, but French Regulator Warns About Future Conduct," *South China Morning Post*, March 5, 2021, https://www.scmp.com/news/china/diplom acy/article/3124152/cgtn-set-return-european-screens-french-regula tor-warns-about.

155. Peilei Ye and Luis Alfonso Albornoz, "Chinese Media 'Going Out' in Spanish Speaking Countries: The Case of CGTN-Español," *Westminster Papers in Communication and Culture* 13, no. 1 (May 2018): 81–97, https:// researchportal.uc3m.es/display/act508754.

156. Author interviews with China-Latin America experts, November 2020.

157. Ye and Albornoz, "Chinese Media 'Going Out' in Spanish Speaking Countries," 81–97.

158. Varrall, "Behind the News."

159. "China Is Using Facebook to Build a Huge Audience Around the World," *Economist*, April 20, 2019, https://www.economist.com/grap hic-detail/2019/04/20/china-is-using-facebook-to-build-a-huge-audience-around-the-world.

160. Keith Bradsher, "China Blocks WhatsApp, Broadening Online Censorship," *New York Times*, September 25, 2017, https://www.nytimes. com/2017/09/25/business/china-whatsapp-blocked.html; Shannon Liao, "After a Single Day, Facebook Is Pushed Out of China Again," *Verge*, July 25, 2018, https://www.theverge.com/2018/7/25/17612162/ facebook-technology-subsidiary-blocked-china-censor.

161. https://www.facebook.com/ChinaGlobalTVNetwork.

162. I am indebted to Hunter Marston for this research, which relies on data culled from Socialbakers.

163. "China Is Using Facebook to Build a Huge Audience Around the World."

164. Sarah Cook, "Beijing's Global Megaphone: The Expansion of Chinese Communist Party Media Influence Since 2017," *Freedom House*, January 2020, https://freedomhouse.org/report/special-reports/beijings-glo bal-megaphone-china-communist-party-media-influence-abroad.

165. Marc Tracy, "The New York Times Tops 6 Million Subscribers as Ad Revenue Plummets," *New York Times*, May 6, 2020, https://www.nyti mes.com/2020/05/06/business/media/new-york-times-earnings-subscriptions-coronavirus.html; Javier C. Hernandez, "When Trump Tweets, the Editor of 'China's Fox News' Hits Back," *New York Times*, July 31, 2019, https://www.nytimes.com/2019/07/31/world/asia/hu-xijin-global-times-us-china-tensions.html.

166. Ryan Loomis and Heidi Holz, "China's Efforts to Shape the Information Environment in Thailand," *CNA*, September 2020, 15, https://www.cna.org/CNA_files/PDF/IIM-2020-U-026099-Final.pdf.

167. Custer et al., *Influencing the Narrative*, 11.

168. I am indebted to Hunter Marston for this research and breakdown, which relies on data culled from Socialbakers.

169. @CGTNOfficial, examined in October 2021.

170. I am indebted to Hunter Marston for this research and breakdown, which relies on data culled from Socialbakers.

171. Erika Kinetz, "Army of Fake Fans Boosts China's Messaging on Twitter," *Associated Press*, May 28, 2021, https://apnews.com/article/asia-pacific-china-europe-middle-east-government-and-politics-62b13895aa666 5ae4d887dcc8d196dfc.

172. See "CGTN: New global news network with a different perspective," Youtube.com, December 15, 2019, https://www.youtube.com/c/cgtn/videos https://www.youtube.com/channel/UCgrNz-aDmcr2uuto8_DL2jg.

173. Mantesso and Zhou, "China's Multi-Billion Dollar Media Campaign 'a Major Threat for Democracies' Around the World."

174. Joyce Y. M. Nip and Chao Sun, "China's News Media Tweeting, Competing with US Sources," *Westminster Papers in Communication and Culture* 13, no. 1 (2018): 98–122.

175. Davey Alba, "Fake 'Likes' Remain Just a Few Dollars Away, Researchers Say," *New York Times*, December 6, 2019, https://www.nytimes.com/2019/12/06/technology/fake-social-media-manipulation.html.

176. Cook, "Beijing's Global Megaphone."

177. Heather Timmons and Josh Horwitz, "China's Propaganda News Outlets Are Absolutely Crushing It on Facebook," *Quartz*, May 6, 2016, https://qz.com/671211/chinas-propaganda-outlets-have-leaped-the-top-of-facebook-even-though-it-banned-at-home/.

178. Ibid.

179. I am indebted to Hunter Marston for his research on this topic.

180. Ibid.

181. Ibid.

182. Gavin O'Malley, "Facebook Will Ban Ads from State-Controlled Media Outlets," *MediaPost*, June 5, 2020, https://www.mediapost.com/publications/article/352235/facebook-will-ban-ads-from-state-controlled-media.html.

183. I am indebted to Hunter Marston for his research on this topic.

184. Ibid.

CHAPTER 7

1. U.S. Department of Defense, *Assessment on U.S. Defense Implications of China's Expanding Global Access*, January 14, 2019, https://media.defense.gov/2019/Jan/14/2002079292/-1/-1/1/EXPANDING-GLOBAL-ACCESS-REPORT-FINAL.PDF.

2. William Yuan Yee, "Win Some, Lose Some: China's Campaign for Global Media Influence," *Jamestown Foundation China Brief* 21, no. 19 (2021), https://jamestown.org/program/win-some-lose-some-chinas-campaign-for-global-media-influence/.

3. "About Us," *Associated Press*, https://www.ap.org/about/; Celine Sui, "China Wants State Media to Peddle Its 'Soft Power' in Africa, but Tech Platforms Are a Better Bet," *Quartz*, October 29, 2019, https://www.yahoo.com/now/china-wants-state-media-peddle-184631591.html.

4. Louisa Lim and Julia Bergin, "Inside China's Audacious Global Propaganda Campaign," *Guardian,* December 7, 2018, https://www.theguardian.com/news/2018/dec/07/china-plan-for-global-media-dominance-propaganda-xi-jinping.

5. Ibid.

6. Jasmine Chia, "Thai Media Is Outsourcing Most of Its Coronavirus Coverage to Beijing and That's Just the Start," *Thai Enquirer*, January 31, 2020, https://www.thaienquirer.com/7301/thai-media-is-outsourcing-much-of-its-coronavirus-coverage-to-beijing-and-thats-just-the-start.

7. Halligan Agade, "Kenya, China Sign Deal to Air Chinese TV Series," *CGTN Africa*, October 20, 2019, https://africa.cgtn.com/2019/10/20/kenya-china-sign-deal-to-air-chinese-tv-series.

8. Sui, "China Wants State Media to Peddle Its 'Soft Power' in Africa."

9. Author interview with former senior U.S. Agency for Global Media (USAGM) official, November 2018.

10. I am indebted to Prashanth Parameswan for providing me information on this point—on how, in covering the multiple regional summits in Southeast Asia for the *Diplomat*, he would often encounter that Xinhua had blanket coverage of them while most Western media paid little attention.

11. Ibid.

12. Josh Rogin, "Congress Demands Answers on AP's Relationship with Chinese State Media," *Washington Post*, December 24, 2018, https://www.washingtonpost.com/opinions/2018/12/24/congress-demands-answers-aps-relationship-with-chinese-state-media.

13. Lauren Easton, "AP Response to Questions About Recent Xinhua Meeting," *Associated Press*, January 10, 2019, https://blog.ap.org/announcements/ap-response-to-questions-about-recent-xinhua-meeting.

14. "Xinhua, AFP Presidents Agree on Further Cooperation," *Agence France-Presse*, September 12, 2017, https://www.afp.com/en/inside-afp/xinhua-afp-presidents-agree-further-cooperation; "Xinhua, AAP Sign New Agreement for Closer Cooperation," *Xinhua*, September 11, 2018, http://www.xinhuanet.com/english/2018-09/11/c_137460960.htm.

15. "China's Pursuit of a New World Media Order."

16. "China, Latin America to Bolster Media Cooperation," *China Daily*, November 22, 2018, http://www.chinadaily.com.cn/a/201811/22/WS5bf5e904a310eff30328a444.html.

17. Chia, "Thai Media Is Outsourcing Most of Its Coronavirus Coverage to Beijing and That's Just the Start."

18. Louisa Lim and Julia Bergin, "The China Story: Reshaping the World Media," *International Federation of Journalists*, June 2020, https://www.ifj.org/fileadmin/user_upload/IFJ_ChinaReport_2020.pdf.

19. Ibid.

20. Ibid.

21. Ibid.

22. Emily Feng, "China and the World: How Beijing Spreads the Message," *Financial Times*, July 12, 2018, https://www.ft.com/content/f5d00a86-3296-11e8-b5bf-23cb17fd1498.

23. Ibid.

24. Ibid.

25. Samantha Custer et al., *Influencing the Narrative: How the Chinese Government Mobilizes Students and Media to Burnish Its Image* (Williamsburg, VA: AidData at William & Mary, 2019), 13.

26. Heidi Holz and Anthony Miller, "China's Playbook for Shaping the Global Media Environment," *CNA*, February 2020, https://www.cna.org/CNA_files/PDF/IRM-2020-U-024710-Final.pdf.

27. Sarah Cook, "Beijing's Global Megaphone: The Expansion of Chinese Communist Party Media Influence Since 2017," *Freedom House*, January 2020, https://freedomhouse.org/report/special-reports/beijings-global-megaphone-china-communist-party-media-influence-abroad; Kelsey Ables, "What Happens When China's State-Run Media Embraces AI?," *Columbia Journalism Review*, June 21, 2018, https://www.cjr.org/analysis/china-xinhua-news-ai.php; "Xinhua CEIS, DPA Ink Agreement to Promote Information Exchanges," *Xinhua Silk Road Information Service*, May 15, 2018, https://en.imsilkroad.com/p/96223.

html; "Xinhua, AAP Sign New Agreement for Closer Cooperation," *Xinhua*, September 11, 2018, http://www.xinhuanet.com/english/2018-09/11/c_137460960.htm; "Xinhua, AP Sign MOU to Enhance Cooperation," *Xinhua*, November 25, 2018, http://www.xinhuanet.com/english/2018-11/25/c_137630583.htm; "China, Morocco to Develop Innovative Partnerships in Media Sector," *Xinhua*, October 30, 2019, http://www.xinhuanet.com/english/2019-10/30/c_138515661.htm.

28. Feng, "China and the World: How Beijing Spreads the Message." In addition, the database used by the *Financial Times* was provided to the author.

29. Isaac Stone Fish, "Is China's Xinhua the Future of Journalism?," *Newsweek*, September 3, 2010, https://www.newsweek.com/chinas-xinhua-future-journalism-71961.

30. Ables, "What Happens When China's State-Run Media Embraces AI?"

31. Ibid.

32. Murray Hiebert, *Under Beijing's Shadow: Southeast Asia's China Challenge* (Washington, DC: CSIS, 2020), 419.

33. "China's Pursuit of a New World Media Order."

34. Raksha Kumar, "How China Uses the News Media in Its Propaganda War Against the West," *Reuters Institute for the Study of Journalism*, November 2, 2021, https://reutersinstitute.politics.ox.ac.uk/news/how-china-uses-news-media-weapon-its-propaganda-war-against-west.

35. "Xinhua Editor-in-Chief Signs Cooperation Deal with Senegalese Media," *Xinhua*, July 19, 2019, http://www.xinhuanet.com/english/2019-07/19/c_138240476.htm; "Daily News Egypt Signs Content, Images Sharing Agreement with Xinhua," *Daily News Egypt*, October 19, 2019, https://dailynewsegypt.com/2019/10/19/daily-news-egypt-signs-content-images-sharing-agreement-with-xinhua; "Muscat Media Group Signs Agreement with Xinhua News," *Times of Oman*, August 27, 2019, https://timesofoman.com/article/1832236/Oman/Muscat-Media-Group-signs-agreement-with-Xinhua-News; "5 More Thai Media Agencies Sign Partnership with Xinhua," *Khaosod*, November 20, 2019, https://www.khaosodenglish.com/news/2019/11/20/5-more-thai-media-sites-sign-partnership-with-xinhua; "New Times, Xinhua Ink Cooperation Deal," *New Times*, July 25, 2019, https://www.newtimes.co.rw/news/new-times-xinhua-ink-cooperation-deal; Sarah Cook, "China's Global Media Footprint: Democratic Responses to

Expanding Authoritarian Influence," *National Endowment for Democracy*, February 2021, https://www.ned.org/wp-content/uploads/2021/02.

36. Wanning Sun, "Chinese-Language Media in Australia: Developments, Challenges, and Opportunities," *Australia-China Relations Institute*, 2016, https://www.australiachinarelations.org/sites/default/files; Cook, "China's Global Media Footprint."

37. Cook, "China's Global Media Footprint."

38. For more thoughts on the importance of newswires in setting the news agenda and tone, and how Xinhua's rise might afford Xinhua an opportunity, see Ables, "What Happens When China's State-Run Media Embraces AI?"

39. Stone Fish, "Is China's Xinhua the Future of Journalism?"

40. Gautier Battistella, "Xinhua: The World's Biggest Propaganda Agency," *Reporters Without Borders*, October 2005, https://rsf.org/sites/default/files/Report_Xinhua_Eng.pdf.

41. Mark MacKinnon, "As Western Media Contract, the China Daily Expands," *Globe and Mail*, June 25, 2012, https://www.theglobeandmail.com/news/world/worldview/as-western-media-contract-the-china-daily-expands; David Shambaugh, "China Flexes Its Soft Power," *Brookings Institution*, June 7, 2010, https://www.brookings.edu/opinions/china-flexes-its-soft-power.

42. Cook, "China's Global Media Footprint."

43. Jichang Lulu, "CRI's Network of 'Borrowed Boats' Hits the News, State Media Responds," *Jichang Lulu*, November 4, 2015, https://jichanglulu.wordpress.com/2015/11/04/cris-network-of-borrowed-boats-hits-the-news-state-media-responds.

44. Ibid.

45. Ibid.

46. Jichang Lulu, "Outsourced Soft Power Channels Xi Jinping's Dream to Icelanders," *Jichang Lulu* (blog), July 3, 2015, https://jichanglulu.wordpress.com/2015/07/03/outsourced-soft-power-channels-xi-jinpings-dream-to-icelanders.

47. "2019 World Press Freedom Index," *Reporters Without Borders*, https://rsf.org/en/ranking.

48. "China: Free Tibetans Unjustly Imprisoned," *Human Rights Watch*, May 21, 2019, https://www.hrw.org/news/2019/05/21/china-free-tibetans-unjustly-imprisoned; "It's Time to Address Paid Chinese Disinformation in U.S. Newspapers," *Central Tibetan Administration*, March 29, 2019, https://tibet.net/its-time-to-address-paid-chinese-disinformation-in-us-newspapers.

49. Jim Waterson and Dean Sterling Jones, "Daily Telegraph Stops Publishing Section Paid for by China," *Guardian*, April 14, 2020, https://www.theguardian.com/media/2020/apr/14/daily-telegraph-stops-publishing-section-paid-for-by-china.

50. Cook, "Beijing's Global Megaphone."

51. U.S. Department of Justice, *Report of the Attorney General to the Congress of the United States on the Administration of the Foreign Registration Act of 1938, as Amended, for the Six Months Ending in June 30, 2018,* https://www.justice.gov/nsd-fara/page/file/1194051/download; Lim and Bergin, "Inside China's Audacious Global Propaganda Campaign." See also Peter Hasson, "China's Propaganda Machine Greased by the New York Times and Washington Post: Human Rights Watchdog," *National Interest,* January 15, 2020, https://nationalinterest.org/blog/buzz/chinas-propaganda-machine-greased-new-york-times-and-washington-post-human-rights-watchdog.

52. U.S. Department of Justice, *Report of the Attorney General to the Congress of the United States on the Administration of the Foreign Registration Act of 1938, as Amended, for the Six Months Ending in June 30, 2018,* https://www.justice.gov/nsd-fara/page/file/1194051/download; Lim and Bergin, "Inside China's Audacious Global Propaganda Campaign."

53. Chuck Ross, "Chinese Propaganda Outlet Has Paid U.S. Newspapers $19 Million for Advertising, Printing," *Daily Caller,* June 8, 2020, https://dailycaller.com/2020/06/08/chinese-propaganda-china-daily-washington-post.

54. Lim and Bergin, "Inside China's Audacious Global Propaganda Campaign"; "China Daily's Global Development," *China Daily,* http://www.chinadaily.com.cn/static_e/global.html; Amanda Meade, "Nine Entertainment Newspapers Quit Carrying China Watch Supplement," *Guardian,* December 8, 2020, https://www.theguardian.com/media/2020/dec/09/nine-entertainment-newspapers-quit-carrying-china-watch-supplement; Yuichiro Kakutani, "NYT Quietly Scrubs Chinese Propaganda," *Washington Free Beacon,* August 4, 2020, https://freebeacon.com/media/nyt-quietly-scrubs-chinese-propaganda.

55. "China Daily's Global Development."

56. In addition to my own research on "China Watch" and its cooperation agreements, see Lim and Bergin, "Inside China's Audacious Global Propaganda Campaign"; Oishimaya Sen Nag, "Newspapers with the Highest Circulation in the World," *World Atlas,* May 10, 2018, https://www.worldatlas.com/articles/newspapers-with-the-highest-circulation-in-the-world.html; "The Daily Telegraph," *Audit Bureau of*

Circulation, December 2019, https://www.abc.org.uk/product/2323; News Corporation, Annual Report 2019, https://www.sec.gov/Archi ves/edgar/data/1564708/000119312519219463/d741099d10k.htm; "News Corp Announces Record-Setting Subscriber Performances at Dow Jones and the Wall Street Journal," *News Corporation*, February 7, 2020, https://newscorp.com/2020/02/07/news-corp-announces-rec ord-setting-subscriber-performances-at-dow-jones-and-the-wall-str eet-journal.

57. Meg James, "L.A. Times Guild Accepts 20% Reduction in Pay, Hours amid Coronavirus," *Los Angeles Time*, May 1, 2020, https://www.lati mes.com/entertainment-arts/business/story/2020-05-01/la-times-guild-members-20-percent-pay-reduction-coronavirus; Clayton Dube (@claydube), "Financially-strapped @latimes includes @ChinaDaily China Watch advertising supplement (8 page standalone insert) in today's edition," Twitter, June 28, 2020, 11:25 a.m., https://twitter.com/ claydube/status/1277261825881432065.

58. Chuck Ross, "Chinese Propaganda Outlet Paid Millions to American Newspapers and Magazines, Records Show," *Washington Free Beacon*, May 25, 2021, https://freebeacon.com/media/chinese-propaganda-out let-paid-millions-to-american-newspapers-and-magazines.

59. David Bond, "Mail Online to Share Content with People's Daily of China," *Financial Times*, August 12, 2016, https://www.ft.com/content/ c38c33b4-6089-11e6-ae3f-77baadeb1c93.

60. Roy Greenslade, "What Is Mail Online Doing in Partnership with the People's Daily of China?," *Guardian*, August 12, 2016, https://www.theg uardian.com/media/greenslade/2016/aug/12/mail-online-goes-into-partnership-with-the-peoples-daily-of-china.

61. "Thai Journalist Pravit Rojanaphruk Resigns from Nation Newspaper," BBC, September 16, 2015, https://www.bbc.com/news/world-asia-34266396; Pravit Rojanaphruk, "How Thailand's Military Junta Tried to 'Adjust My Attitude' in Detention," *Diplomat*, September 23, 2015, https://thediplomat.com/2015/09/how-thailands-military-junta-tried-to-adjust-my-attitude-in-detention. This 2015 incident actually was Pravit's second "attitude adjustment" session with the army.

62. Ibid.; Pravit Rojanaphruk, "Opinion: Goodbye to the Nation Newspaper," *Khaosod*, June 28, 2019, http://www.khaosodenglish.com/ opinion/2019/06/28/opinion-goodbye-the-nation-newspaper.

63. Kaweewit Kaewjinda, "Thai Journalist Charged with Sedition for Online Comments," *Associated Press*, August 8, 2017, https://www.seatt

letimes.com/nation-world/thai-journalist-charged-with-sedition-for-online-comments.

64. Tyler Roney, "Chinese Propaganda Finds a Thai Audience," *Foreign Policy*, August 28, 2019, https://foreignpolicy.com/2019/08/28/chinese-propaganda-finds-a-thai-audience.

65. Portions of this first part of the chapter were first presented as a Council on Foreign Relations *Asia Unbound* piece in January 2020. Joshua Kurlantzick, "Thailand's Press Warms to Chinese State Media," *Asia Unbound*, January 8, 2020, https://www.cfr.org/blog/thailands-press-warms-chinese-state-media.

66. Roney, "Chinese Propaganda Finds a Thai Audience."

67. Chia, "Thai Media Is Outsourcing Much of Its Coronavirus Coverage to Beijing and That's Just the Start."

68. "No Terror Incidents in Xinjiang for Three Years, China Says," *Xinhua*, August 16, 2019, http://www.khaosodenglish.com/news/international/2019/08/16/no-terror-incidents-in-xinjiang-for-three-years-china-says.

69. Amie Ferris-Rotman, "Abortions, IUDs, and Sexual Humiliation: Muslim Women Who Fled China for Kazakhstan Recount Ordeals," *Washington Post*, October 5, 2019, https://www.washingtonpost.com/world/asia_pacific. See also Edward Wong and Chris Buckley, "U.S. Says China's Repression of Uighurs Is 'Genocide,'" *New York Times*, January 19, 2021, https://www.nytimes.com/2021/01/19/us/politics/trump-china-xinjiang.html.

70. "Panda Twins Born to Wild, Captive Parents in China," *Xinhua*, September 18, 2019, https://www.khaosodenglish.com/news/international/2019/09/18.

71. Chia, "Thai Media Is Outsourcing Much of Its Coronavirus Coverage to Beijing and That's Just the Start."

72. "5 More Thai Media Agencies Sign Partnership with Xinhua."

73. "About Asia News Network," *Asia News Network*, https://asianews.network/about-us. A portion of this section was adapted from a blog post: Kurlantzick, "Thailand's Press Warms to Chinese State Media."

74. "About Asia News Network."

75. "5 More Thai Media Sites Sign Partnerships with Xinhua."

76. Ibid.

77. Ibid.

78. Hiebert, *Under Beijing's Shadow*, 322.

79. Teeranai Charuvastra, "China, as Told by China: Beijing's Influences Reach Thai Media and Beyond," *Heinrich Boll Stiftung*, December 28,

2019, https://th.boell.org/en/2019/12/28/china-told-china-beijings-influences-reach-thai-media-and-beyond.

80. Ibid.

81. Ibid.

82. Chia, "Thai Media Is Outsourcing Most of Its Coronavirus Coverage to Beijing and That's Just the Start."

83. Ibid.

84. Ibid.

85. Steven Lee Myers and Alissa J. Rubin, "Its Coronavirus Cases Dwindling, China Turns Focus Outward," *New York Times*, March 18, 2020, https://www.nytimes.com/2020/03/18/world/asia/coronavirus-china-aid.html.

86. Ibid.

87. Ibid.; Joshua Kurlantzick, "China and Coronavirus: From Home-Made Disaster to Global Mega-Opportunity," *Globalist*, March 16, 2020, https://www.theglobalist.com/china-soft-power-coronavirus-covid19-pandemic-global-health.

CHAPTER 8

1. "Grupo America," *Media Ownership Monitor Argentina*, https://argentina.mom-rsf.org/en/owners/companies/detail/company/company/show/grupo-america; Sarah Cook, "Beijing's Global Megaphone: The Expansion of Chinese Communist Party Media Influence Since 2017," *Freedom House*, January 2020, https://freedomhouse.org/report/special-reports/beijings-global-megaphone-china-communist-party-media-influence-abroad; Juan Pablo Cardenal, "Navigating Political Change in Argentina," in *Sharp Power: Rising Authoritarian Influence* (Washington, DC: National Endowment for Democracy, December 2017), https://www.ned.org/wp-content/uploads/2017/12/Chapter2-Sharp-Power-Rising-Authoritarian-Influence-Argentina.pdf.

2. Cook, "Beijing's Global Megaphone"; "2021 World Press Freedom Index," *Reporters Without Borders*, https://rsf.org/en/ranking; Hinnerk Feldwisch-Drentrup, "Chinesische Propaganda mit freundlicher Unterstützung des NDR," *Uber Medien*, October 11, 2019, https://uebermedien.de/42076/chinesische-propaganda-mit-freundlicher-unterstuetzung-des-ndr.

3. Sofia Tomacruz, "What Is 'Wow China,' the Radio Show Sparking Outrage on Social Media?," *Rappler*, May 11, 2020, https://www.rappler.com/nation/260603-things-to-know-wow-china-radio-show.

4. Reporters Without Borders, "China's Pursuit of a New World Media Order," RSF report, March 22, 2019, https://rsf.org/en/reports/rsf-rep ort-chinas-pursuit-new-world-media-order.

5. Jennifer Lo, "Pro-Beijing Newspapers Wen Wei Po and Ta Kung Pao to Merge," *Nikkei Asia*, February 2, 2016, https://asia.nikkei.com/ Business/Pro-Beijing-newspapers-Wen-Wei-Po-and-Ta-Kung-Pao-to-merge; Lam Kwok-lap and Xin Lin, "Beijing-Linked Phoenix TV Seeks Hong Kong License as China Extends 'Soft Power,'" *Radio Free Asia*, September 23, 2016, https://www.rfa.org/english/news/china/ license-09232016110745.html.

6. Sarah Cook, "Chinese Government Influence on the U.S. Media Landscape," Written Testimony Before the U.S.-China Economic and Security Review Commission, May 4, 2017, https://www.uscc. gov/sites/default/files/Sarah%20Cook%20May%204th%202017%20U SCC%20testimony.pdf.

7. "China's Pursuit of a New World Media Order."

8. Ann Scott Tyson, "China Is Ramping Up Its Media Abroad—and Not Just in Chinese," *Christian Science Monitor*, July 3, 2019, https:// www.csmonitor.com/World/Asia-Pacific/2019/0703/China-is-ramp ing-up-its-media-abroad-and-not-just-in-Chinese; "Media," in *China's Influence & American Interests: Promoting Constructive Vigilance*, ed. Larry Diamond and Orville Schell (Stanford, CA: Hoover Institution Press, 2019), 100–119.

9. Eric Ng, "Phoenix Media Names Shanghai's Former City Spokesman as CEO, Splitting Founder Liu's Job to Improve Corporate Governance," *South China Morning Post*, February 26, 2021, https://www.scmp.com/ business/companies/article/3123346/phoenix-media-names-shangh ais-former-city-spokesman-ceo.

10. Ibid.

11. Ibid.

12. "Hong Kong Media Fall to Pro-Chinese Owners," *Asia Sentinel*, April 22, 2021, https://www.asiasentinel.com/p/hong-kong-media-fall-to-pro-chinese.

13. Ibid.

14. Ibid.

15. Cook, "Chinese Government Influence on the U.S. Media Landscape."

16. Koh Gui Qing and John Shiffman, "Beijing's Covert Radio Network," *Reuters*, November 2, 2015, https://www.reuters.com/investigates/spec ial-report/china-radio/.

17. Ibid.

18. Anthony Kuhn, "China Tries to Woo a Sprawling Global Chinese Diaspora," *NPR*, October 29, 2018, https://www.npr.org/2018/10/29/659938461/china-tries-to-woo-a-sprawling-global-chinese-diaspora.

19. He Qinglian, *Red Infiltration: The Reality About China's Global Expansion in International Media*, trans. David Cowhig (Taiwan: Gusa Publishing, 2019).

20. Ibid.

21. See, for example, "Interview: China's Strong Economic Rebound to Benefit Thai Businesses, Says Thai Banker," *Xinhua*, April 22, 2021, http://www.xinhuanet.com/english/asiapacific/2021-04/22/c_139898157.htm; Vijitra Duangdee, "Thailand Feels the Pinch of a Golden Week with No Gold as Chinese Stay Home," *South China Morning Post*, October 1, 2021, https://www.scmp.com/week-asia/economics/article/3150799/thailand-feels-pinch-golden-week-no-gold-chinese-stay-home; Jitsiree Thongnoi, "China Becomes Thailand's Top Source of Foreign Investment for First Time," *South China Morning Post*, January 24, 2020, https://www.scmp.com/week-asia/economics/article/3047489/china-becomes-thailands-top-source-foreign-investment-first; Apornrath Phoonphongphiphat, "Spurred by Trade War, Chinese Investment in Thailand Skyrockets," *NikkeiAsia*, January 24, 2020, https://asia.nikkei.com/Business/Business-trends/Spurred-by-trade-war-Chinese-investment-in-Thailand-skyrockets; and Jason Tan, "Chinese Bet on Properties in Thailand Ahead of COVID Recovery," *NikkeiAsia*, September 9, 2021, https://asia.nikkei.com/Business/Markets/Property/Chinese-bet-on-properties-in-Thailand-ahead-of-COVID-recovery.

22. Shujian Guo, Hyunjung Shin, and Qi Shen, "The Commodification of Chinese in Thailand's Linguistic Market: A Case Study of How Language Education Promotes Social Sustainability," *Sustainability* 12, no. 18 (2020): 7344.

23. John Garnaut, "How China Interferes in Australia," *Foreign Affairs*, March 9, 2018, https://www.foreignaffairs.com/articles/china/2018-03-09/how-china-interferes-australia.

24. "Inside Malaysia's Shadow State," *Global Witness*, March 19, 2013, https://www.globalwitness.org/en/campaigns/forests/inside-malaysias-shadow-state/.

25. Murray Hiebert, *Under Beijing's Shadow: Southeast Asia's China Challenge* (Washington, DC: CSIS, 2020), 368.

26. Karen Cheung, "Hong Kong Can't and Shouldn't Be Independent, Says Ming Pao Newspaper Boss," *Hong Kong Free Press*, March 21, 2016,

https://hongkongfp.com/2016/03/21/hong-kong-shouldnt-and-cant-be-independent-says-ming-pao-newspaper-boss.

27. Andrew Higgins, "Tycoon Prods Taiwan Closer to China," *Washington Post*, January 21, 2012, https://www.washingtonpost.com/world/asia_pacific/tycoon-prods-taiwan-closer-to-china/2012/01/20/gIQAh swmFQ_story.html; Mark Landler, "Entrepreneur Walks Fine Line at a News Channel for China," *New York Times*, January 8, 2001, https://www.nytimes.com/2001/01/08/business/entrepreneur-walking-fine-line-at-a-news-channel-for-china.html; Chris Lau, "Inside the Bowels of Phoenix TV," *South China Morning Post*, July 26, 2012, https://www.scmp.com/article/1007782/inside-bowels-phoenix-tv.

28. "Chinese SOEs Snap Up Overseas Chinese Media," *Asia Sentinel*, March 8, 2016, https://www.asiasentinel.com/p/china-soe-snap-up-overseas-media.

29. Hiebert, *Under Beijing's Shadow*, 69.

30. "Advertising: Sin Chew Daily," *Sin Chew Daily*, https://www.advertising.com.my/sin-chew-daily.

31. "Tycoon Recovering Well from Stroke, Says Family," *Star*, April 27, 2017, https://www.thestar.com.my/news/nation/2017/04/27/tycoon-recovering-well-from-stroke-says-family.

32. Sangeetha Amarthalingam, "Media Chinese Intl's Unit Sells Stake in HK Publishing House for US$64.2m," *Edge Markets*, August 1, 2016, https://www.theedgemarkets.com/article/media-chinese-intls-unit-sells-stake-hk-publishing-house-us642m.

33. "One Country, One Censor: How China Undermines Media Freedom in Hong Kong and Taiwan," *Committee to Protect Journalists*, December 16, 2019, https://cpj.org/reports/2019/12/one-country-one-censor-china-hong-kong-taiwan-press-freedom.php.

34. Debby Wu and Jennifer Lo, "Media Buyouts Have Taiwan and Hong Kong Wary of Pro-China Spring," *Nikkei Asian Review*, December 3, 2015, https://asia.nikkei.com/Business/Media-buyouts-have-Taiwan-and-Hong-Kong-wary-of-pro-China-spin.

35. Andrew Higgins, "Tycoon Prods Taiwan Closer to China," *Washington Post*, January 21, 2012, https://www.washingtonpost.com/world/asia_pacific/tycoon-prods-taiwan-closer-to-china.

36. Chien-Jung Hsu, "China's Influence on Taiwan's Media," *Asian Survey* 54, no. 3 (May/June 2014): 515–39.

37. Ibid.

38. Kenji Kawase, "Chinese Subsidies of Foxconn and Want Want Spark Outcry in Taiwan," *Nikkei Asian Review*, April 30, 2019, https://asia.nik

kei.com/Business/Companies/Chinese-subsidies-for-Foxconn-and-Want-Want-spark-outcry-in-Taiwan.

39. Eric Ng, "Phoenix Media Founder Sells Almost All His Shares to Beijing-Backed Publisher and Pansy Ho's Shun Tak in Deals Worth U.S. $149.2 Million," *South China Morning Post*, April 18, 2021, https://www.scmp.com/business/companies/article/3130027/phoenix-media-founder-sells-almost-all-his-shares-beijing-backed.

40. "One Country, One Censor."

41. Matt Schrader, "Friends and Enemies: A Framework for Understanding Chinese Political Interference in Democratic Countries," *Alliance for Security Democracy*, April 22, 2020, https://securingdemocracy.gmfus.org/wp-content/uploads/2020/04.

42. Saengwit Kewaleewongsatorn, "Nanfang Media Busy 20% of Sing Sian Yer Pao," *Bangkok Post*, November 6, 2013, https://www.bangkokpost.com/business/378378/nanfang-media-buys-20-of-sing-sian-yer-pao; David Pierson, "China Newspaper Dispute Sparks Protest, Tests New Leaders," *Los Angeles Times*, January 7, 2013, https://www.latimes.com/world/la-xpm-2013-jan-07-la-fg-wn-china-southern-weekly-protest-20130107-story.html.

43. Maria Repnikova and Kecheng Fang, "Behind the Fall of China's Greatest Newspaper," *Foreign Policy*, January 29, 2015, https://foreignpolicy.com/2015/01/29/southern-weekly-china-media-censorship.

44. Mimi Lau, "China's Communist Party Silences Former Critic, the Liberal Nanfang News Group," *South China Morning Post*, August 29, 2015, https://www.scmp.com/news/china/policies-politics/article/1853616/chinas-communist-party-silences-former-critic-liberal.

45. "China's Pursuit of a New World Media Order," 39.

46. Ibid.

47. "Media," in *China's Influence & American Interests*.

48. Ibid., 107–11.

49. Ibid., 107–12.

50. Ibid.

51. Amy E. Searight, "Chinese Influence Activities with U.S. Allies and Partners in Southeast Asia," Testimony Before the U.S.-China Economic and Security Review Commission, April 5, 2018, https://www.uscc.gov/sites/default/files. Also, author interviews with Philippine media analysts, January 2018 and September 2018.

52. Alexander Bowe, "China's Overseas United Front Work: Background and Implications for the United States," *U.S.-China Economic and*

Security Review Commission, August 24, 2018, https://www.uscc.gov/sites/default/files/Research.

53. David Boyle, "Nice TV Highlights Ties Between Cambodia, China," *Voice of America*, April 19, 2018, https://www.voanews.com/a/nice-tv-highlights-ties-between-cambodia-china/4355711.html; David Boyle and Sun Narin, "Cambodia's Nice New TV Channel from China," *Voice of America*, April 19, 2018, https://www.voanews.com/a/cambodia-nice-new-tv-channel-from-china/4354124.html.

54. Andrew Nachemson, "Fresh News and the Future of the Fourth Estate in Cambodia," *Coda Story*, February 22, 2019, https://www.codastory.com/authoritarian-tech/fresh-news-and-the-future-of-the-fourth-estate-in-cambodia.

55. Nachemson, "Fresh News and the Future of the Fourth Estate in Cambodia"; "Analytical Report for Cambodia Media Use Survey," *Gallup*, September 2017, received March 5, 2019, under the Freedom of Information Act process.

56. Nachemson, "Fresh News and the Future of the Fourth Estate in Cambodia."

57. "January 2020 Overview: news.sabay.com.kh," *SimilarWeb*, https://www.similarweb.com/website/news.sabay.com.kh.

58. "Lao Army Launches TV Station Paid for by China," *Radio Free Asia*, September 11, 2020, https://www.rfa.org/english/news/laos/station-09112020174442.html.

59. Ibid.

60. Nachemson, "Fresh News and the Future of the Fourth Estate in Cambodia"; "With Cambodia's Free Press Under Fire, China Model Makes Inroads," *Agence France Presse*, June 3, 2018, https://www.bangkokpost.com/world/1478013/with-cambodias-free-press-under-fire-china-model-makes-inroads.

61. "China's Pursuit of a New World Media Order"; "With Cambodia's Free Press Under Fire, China Model Makes Inroads."

62. Richard C. Paddock, "The Cambodia Daily to Close (After Chasing One Last Big Story)," *New York Times*, September 3, 2017, https://www.nytimes.com/2017/09/03/world/asia/cambodia-daily-newspaper.html.

63. "Cambodian Crackdown on Democracy Forces NDI to Close Offices," *National Democratic Institute*, September 28, 2017, https://www.ndi.org/our-stories/cambodian-crackdown-democracy-forces-ndi-close-offices.

64. See, for example, Zen Soo, "4 Journalists at Shut Hong Kong Paper Charged with Collusion," *Associated Press*, July 21, 2021, https://apnews. com/article/business-arrests-hong-kong-472600feb8c2896bc03951f34 53803ed; Madeleine Lim, "Bloomberg News China Staffer Haze Fan Still Detained One Year On," *Bloomberg*, December 6, 2021, https:// www.bloomberg.com/news/articles/2021-12-06.

65. The site https://www.comparitech.com/privacy-security-tools/blo ckedinchina has an engine that shows which sites are blocked and not working in China, including cfr.org as of this writing, and many leading news outlets from around the world.

66. Maya Wang, "Another Journalist Expelled—as China's Abuses Grow, Who Will See Them?," *Guardian*, August 28, 2018, https://www.theg uardian.com/commentisfree/2018/aug/28/journalist-expelled-china-abuses.

67. Marc Tracy, Edward Wong, and Lara Jakes, "China Announces That It Will Expel American Journalists," *New York Times*, March 17, 2020, https://www.nytimes.com/2020/03/17/business/media/china-exp els-american-journalists.html; Paul Farhi, "Western Journalists Are Getting Squeezed Out of China by Superpower Tensions," *Washington Post*, September 16, 2020, https://www.washingtonpost.com/lifestyle/ media/journalists-get-caught-in-the-middle-of-souring-us-china-relations; "The Washington Post Names Lily Kuo Its Beijing Bureau Chief," *Washington Post*, October 13, 2020, https://www.washingtonp ost.com/pr/2020/10/13/washington-post-names-lily-kuo-its-china-bureau-chief.

68. James Griffiths and Julia Hollingsworth, "Australian Journalists Evacuated from China After Five-Day Diplomatic Standoff," *CNN*, September 8, 2020, https://www.cnn.com/2020/09/07/media/austra lia-journalists-china-abc-afr-intl-hnk/index.html.

69. "Economist Magazine Says Hong Kong Rejects Journalist's Visa Renewal," *Reuters*, November 13, 2021, https://www.reuters.com/ world/asia-pacific/economist-magazine-regrets-hong-kong-rejecting-its-journalists-visa-2021-11-13.

70. Yaqui Wang, "Darkened Screen: Constraints on Foreign Journalists in China," *PEN America*, September 22, 2016, https://pen.org/sites/default/ files/PEN_foreign_journalists_report_FINAL_online%5B1%5D.pdf.

71. Austin Ramzy, "After U.S.-Based Reporters Exposed Abuses, China Seized Their Relatives," *New York Times*, March 1, 2018, https://www. nytimes.com/2018/03/01/world/asia/china-xinjiang-rfa.html.

72. Ibid.

73. Cook, "The Long Shadow of Chinese Censorship," 8–9.
74. Ibid.
75. Ibid.
76. "2017 Annual Report to Congress," U.S.-China Economic and Security Review Commission, 474.
77. Rosalind Adams, "Her Reporting Led to the Firing of Canada's Ambassador. That's Made Her a Target for China's State Media," *Buzzfeed News*, January 30, 2019, https://www.buzzfeednews.com/arti cle/rosalindadams/china-canada-huawei-joanna-chiu.
78. Ibid.
79. Tom Wright and Bradley Hope, "WSJ Investigation: China Offered to Bail Out Troubled Malaysian Fund in Return for Deals," *Wall Street Journal*, January 7, 2019, https://www.wsj.com/articles/how-china-fle xes-its-political-muscle-to-expand-power-overseas-11546890449.
80. Craig Offman, "Chinese Canadian Post Owner Says She Was Fired over Chan Critique," *Globe and Mail,* August 5, 2015, https://www.theglobe andmail.com/news/national/chinese-canadian-post-editor-says-she-was-fired-over-chan-critique.
81. Cook, "Beijing's Global Megaphone," 14.
82. "South Africa: Journalist Loses Column After Publishing an Article Critical of China," *Reporters Without Borders*, September 21, 2018, https://rsf.org/en/news/south-africa-journalist-loses-column-after-publishing-article-critical-china.
83. "2019 World Press Freedom Index," *Reporters Without Borders*, https://rsf.org/en/ranking.
84. Azad Essa, "China Is Buying African Media's Silence," *Foreign Policy*, September 14, 2018, https://foreignpolicy.com/2018/09/14/china-is-buying-african-medias-silence/.
85. "2017 Annual Report to Congress," 466–67.
86. "One Country, One Censor."
87. James Griffiths and Anna Kam, "Hong Kong Pro-Democracy Media Mogul Jimmy Lai Arrested for 'Illegal Assembly' over 2019 Protest," *CNN*, February 28, 2020, https://www.cnn.com/2020/02/28/media/hong-kong-jimmy-lai-arrest-intl-hnk/index.html.
88. Helen Davidson and Lily Kuo, "Hong Kong Media Tycoon Jimmy Lai Arrested Under New Security Law," *Guardian,* August 10, 2020, https://www.theguardian.com/world/2020/aug/10/hong-kong-media-tyc oon-jimmy-lai-arrested-over-alleged-foreign-collusion. For more on the shuttering of *Apple Daily*, see Helen Davidson, "'Painful Farewell': Hongkongers Queue for Hours to Buy Final Apple Daily Edition,"

Guardian, June 24, 2021, https://www.theguardian.com/world/2021/jun/24/hong-kong-apple-daily-queue-final-edition-newspaper.

89. Michael Forsythe, "Disappearance of 5 Tied to Publisher Prompts Broader Worries in Hong Kong," *New York Times*, January 4, 2016, https://www.nytimes.com/2016/01/05/world/asia/mighty-current-media-hong-kong-lee-bo.html.

90. "Gui Minhai: Hong Kong Bookseller Gets 10 Years Jail," *BBC*, February 25, 2020, https://www.bbc.com/news/world-asia-china-51624433.

91. Ben Doherty, "Yang Hengjun: Australian Writer Subjected to 'Absurd' Interrogation in China as Health Deteriorates," *Guardian*, October 31, 2019, https://www.theguardian.com/world/2019/oct/31/yang-hengjun-australian-writer-detained-in-china-proclaims-innocence-as-health-deteriorates.

92. Ibid.; Ben Doherty and Lily Kuo, "Yang Hengjun: Detained Blogger Is Being Shackled in Chains and Interrogated," *Guardian*, September 27, 2019, https://www.theguardian.com/australia-news/2019/sep/28/yang-hengjun-detained-blogger-is-being-shackled-in-chains-and-interrogated.

93. Frances Mao, "Cheng Lei: Why Has an Australian TV Anchor Been Detained by China?," *BBC*, September 8, 2020, https://www.bbc.com/news/world-australia-53980706.

94. "Turkey Promises to Eliminate Anti-China Media Reports," *Reuters*, August 3, 2017, https://www.reuters.com/article/us-china-turkey/turkey-promises-to-eliminate-anti-china-media-reports; Zia Weise, "How Did Things Get So Bad for Turkey's Journalists?," *Atlantic*, August 23, 2018, https://www.theatlantic.com/international/archive/2018/08/destroying-free-press-erdogan-turkey; Ole Tangen Jr., "An Ongoing Crisis: Freedom of Speech in Turkey," *Deutsche Welle*, February 26, 2019, https://www.dw.com/en/an-ongoing-crisis-freedom-of-speech-in-turkey; Wyatt Red, "Turkey Targets Foreign Journalists in Press Freedom Crackdown," *Voice of America*, October 25, 2019, https://www.voanews.com/europe/turkey-targets-foreign-journalists-press-freedom-crackdown.

95. Anil Giri, "Three Journalists Are Under Investigation over Publishing News About the Dalai Lama," *Kathmandu Post*, May 12, 2019, https://kathmandupost.com/national/2019/05/12/three-journalists-face-probe-over-publishing-dalai-lama-news.

96. "Taiwanese Man Gets Suspended Jail Term over Radio Broadcasts into China," *BenarNews*, September 26, 2019, https://www.rfa.org/english/news/china/thailand-broadcast-09262019170101.html.

97. David Shullman, ed., "Chinese Malign Influence and the Corrosion of the Democracy: An Assessment of Chinese Interference in Thirteen Key Countries," International Republican Institute, June 2019, https://www.iri.org/sites/default/files/chinese_malign_influence_report.pdf.

98. Ibid.

99. Ibid.

100. Ibid.

CHAPTER 9

1. Sarah Cook, "Chinese Government Influence on the U.S. Media Landscape," Written Testimony Before the U.S.-China Economic and Security Review Commission, May 4, 2017.

2. Cliff Venzon, "Philippine Mobile Leader Plays Down China Telecom's Targets," *Nikkei Asia*, January 23, 2020, https://asia.nikkei.com/Editor-s-Picks/Interview/Philippine-mobile-leader-plays-down-China-Telecom-s-targets; Malia Ager, "Dennis Uy Admits Closer Ties with Duterte, Cabinet Members," *Inquirer*, January 24, 2019, https://newsinfo.inquirer.net/1077000/dennis-uy-admits-close-ties-with-duterte-cabinet-members.

3. Ibid.

4. Tony Capaccio and Jenny Leonard, "Pentagon Names 20 Chinese Firms It Says Are Military-Controlled," *Bloomberg*, June 25, 2020, https://www.bloomberg.com/news/articles/2020-06-24/pentagon-names-20-chinese-firms-it-says-are-military-controlled.

5. Matt Schrader, "TikTok Risks Becoming a New Front in China's Information War," *Nikkei Asia*, October 14, 2019, https://asia.nikkei.com/Opinion/TikTok-risks-becoming-new-front-in-China-s-information-war; Emily De La Bruyere and Nathan Picarsic, "Worldwide Web," *Octavian Report*, https://octavianreport.com/article/why-china-is-taking-over-the-internet-of-things/2/. This analysis was delivered effectively by Bethany Allen-Ebrahimian of Axios, who compared the relationship of Chinese private firms to the story of the *Matrix*, noting that they are independent companies, to some extent, but also can be taken over and controlled by Beijing and the Chinese security services.

6. Andrew Kitson and Kenny Liew, "China Doubles Down on Its Digital Silk Road," *Reconnecting Asia*, November 14, 2019, https://reconnectingasia.csis.org/analysis/entries/china-doubles-down-its-digital-silk-road/.

7. This reporting first appeared in part in a Council on Foreign Relations interactive report on the Digital Silk Road: "Assessing China's Digital Silk Road Initiative," *Council on Foreign Relations*, accessed November 9, 2021, https://www.cfr.org/china-digital-silk-road/; Steven Feldstein, "Testimony Before the U.S. China Economic and Security Review Commission," May 8, 2020.

8. David Sacks, "Belt and Road Initiative: Who's In and Who's Out," Council on Foreign Relations *Asia Unbound* blog, March 24, 2021, https://www.cfr.org/blog/countries-chinas-belt-and-road-initiative-whos-and-whos-out. Some of this reporting first appeared in part in a Council on Foreign Relations interactive report on the Digital Silk Road, "Assessing China's Digital Silk Road Initiative." Chan Jia Hao, "China's Digital Silk Road: The Integration of Myanmar," *Eurasia Review*, April 30, 2019, https://www.eurasiareview.com/30042019-chinas-digital-silk-road-the-integration-of-myanmar-analysis/.

9. Arjun Kharpal, "Huawei Touts More Than 50 Contracts for 5G as U.S. Pressure Continues to Mount," *CNBC*, September 3, 2019, https://www.cnbc.com/2019/09/03/huawei-touts-more-than-50-contracts-for-5g-as-us-pressure-mounts.html.

10. Hiroyuki Akita, "Undersea Cables—Huawei's Ace in the Hole," *Nikkei Asia*, May 28, 2019, https://asia.nikkei.com/Spotlight/Comment/Undersea-cables-Huawei-s-ace-in-the-hole; Huong Le Thu, "A Collision of Cybersecurity and Geopolitics: Why Southeast Asia Is Wary of a Huawei Ban," Australian Strategic Policy Institute, October 1, 2019, https://www.aspi.org.au/opinion/collision-cybersecurity-and-geopolitics-why-southeast-asia-wary-huawei-ban; Simon Roughneen, "East vs West in Battle for SE Asia's 5G Rollout," *Asia Times*, January 3, 2020, https://asiatimes.com/2020/01/east-vs-west-battle-for-se-asias-5g-rollout/; Siti Rahil, "U.S. Ban on Huawei Largely Ignored in Southeast Asia," *Japan Times*, August 19, 2019, https://www.japantimes.co.jp/news/2019/08/19/business/u-s-ban-huawei-largely-ignored-southeast-asia/#.XoS536hKi71; Fumi Matsumoto, "China-Australia Friction Intensifies Deep in the South Pacific," *Nikkei Asia*, May 29, 2018, https://asia.nikkei.com/Spotlight/Asia-Insight/China-Australia-friction-intensifies-deep-in-the-South-Pacific.

11. Matsumoto, "China-Australia Friction Intensifies Deep in the South Pacific"; "Telecom Fiji Partners with Huawei on Internet Network," *RNZ*, April 10, 2019, https://www.rnz.co.nz/international/pacific-news/386739/telecom-fiji-partners-with-huawei-on-internet-network.

12. Umida Hashimova, "Before and Beyond 5G: Central Asia's Huawei Connections," *Diplomat*, February 19, 2020, https://thediplomat.com/2020/02/before-and-beyond-5g-central-asias-huawei-connections/.

13. I am grateful to Adam Segal for this point. See also "EU Ranks Huawei as World's Second-Highest Investor in R and D," *Teletimes*, December 2021, https://teletimesinternational.com/2021/todays-leading-family-offices-are-change-makers-influencers-and-investors-with-a-shared-commitment-to-the-relentless-pursuit-of-making-a-difference-in-the-world/.

14. De La Bruyere and Picarsic, "Worldwide Web."

15. Ibid. I have worked on several projects in the past for the Long Term Strategy Group, but not while writing this book.

16. Ross Andersen, "The Panopticon Is Already Here," *Atlantic*, September 2020, https://www.theatlantic.com/magazine/archive/2020/09/china-ai-surveillance/614197/.

17. De La Bruyere and Picarsic, "Worldwide Web."

18. "Xi Jinping Is Trying to Remake the Chinese Economy," *Economist*, August 15, 2020, https://www.economist.com/briefing/2020/08/15/xi-jinping-is-trying-to-remake-the-chinese-economy.

19. Henry Tugendhat, "Banning Huawei's 5G Won't Halt China's Tech Revolution," *Guardian*, January 30, 2020, https://www.theguardian.com/commentisfree/2020/jan/30/banning-huawei-5g-china-tech-revolution-free-market; Aarti Shahani, "3 Things You Should Know About Europe's Sweeping New Data Privacy Law," *NPR*, May 24, 2018, https://www.npr.org/sections/alltechconsidered/2018/05/24/613983268/a-cheat-sheet-on-europe-s-sweeping-privacy-law.

20. Shahani, "3 Things You Should Know About Europe's Sweeping New Data Privacy Law."

21. Dario Cristiani et al., "The Security Implications of Chinese Infrastructure Investment in Europe," *German Marshall Fund*, September 28, 2021, https://www.gmfus.org/news/security-implications-chinese-infrastructure-investment-europe.

22. Lukasz Sarek, "5G and the Internet of Things: Chinese Companies' Inroads into 'Digital Poland,'" *Sinopsis*, January 3, 2020, https://sinopsis.cz/en/sarek-5g-iot/.

23. Ryan Gallagher, "Cameras Linked to Chinese Government Stir Alarm in UK Parliament," *Intercept*, April 9, 2019, https://theintercept.com/2019/04/09/hikvision-cameras-uk-parliament/; Ellen Ioanes, "U.S. Military Bases Are Still Using Chinese Surveillance Video Cameras Just Weeks Before a Federal Ban Takes Effect," *Business Insider*, July 18, 2019,

https://www.businessinsider.com/us-military-bases-still-using-chinese-surveillance-tech-2019-7.

24. "U.S. Names Hikvision, Chinese Security Bureaus to Economic Blacklist," *Reuters*, October 7, 2019, https://www.cnbc.com/2019/10/07/us-names-hikvision-chinese-security-bureaus-to-economic-blacklist.html; Ioanes, "U.S. Military Bases Are Still Using Chinese Surveillance Video Cameras Just Weeks Before a Federal Ban Takes Effect."

25. Ioanes, "U.S. Military Bases Are Still Using Chinese Surveillance Video Cameras Just Weeks Before a Federal Ban Takes Effect."

26. Echo Wang, Alexandra Alper, and Yingzhi Yang, "Exclusive: China's ByteDance Moves to Ringfence Its TikTok App amid U.S. Probe—Sources," *Reuters*, November 27, 2019, https://www.reuters.com/article/us-bytedance-tiktok-exclusive/exclusive-chinas-bytedance-moves-to-ringfence-its-tiktok-app-amid-us-probe-sources-idUSKBN1Y10OH; Sarah Perez, "44% of TikTok's All-Time Downloads Were in 2019, but App Still Hasn't Figured Out Monetization," *Tech Crunch*, January 16, 2020, https://techcrunch.com/2020/01/16/44-of-tiktoks-all-time-downloads-were-in-2019-but-app-hasnt-figured-out-monetization/; David Curry, "Most Popular Apps," January 11, 2022, *Business of Apps*, https://www.businessofapps.com/data/most-popular-apps/.

27. Scott Nover, "How Do You Do, Fellow Kids?," *Atlantic*, December 4, 2019, https://www.theatlantic.com/technology/archive/2019/12/washington-post-all-tiktok/602794/; Chris Beer, "Is TikTok Setting the Scene for Music on Social Media?," *Global Web Index*, January 3, 2019, https://blog.globalwebindex.com/trends/tiktok-music-social-media/.

28. Taylor Lorenz, "Hype House and the Los Angeles TikTok Mansion Gold Rush," *New York Times*, January 3, 2020, https://www.nytimes.com/2020/01/03/style/hype-house-los-angeles-tik-tok.html.

29. Wang et al., "Exclusive: China's ByteDance Moves to Ringfence Its TikTok App amid U.S. Probe—Sources."

30. Li Yuan, "To Cover China, There's No Substitute for WeChat," *New York Times*, January 9, 2019, https://www.nytimes.com/2019/01/09/technology/personaltech/china-wechat.html.

31. Ibid.

32. Thuy Ong, "Chinese Social Media Platform WeChat Reaches 1 Billion Accounts Worldwide," *Verge*, March 5, 2018, https://www.theverge.com/2018/3/5/17080546/wechat-chinese-social-media-billion-users-china; Yuan Yang, "China's WeChat Hits 1bn User Accounts Worldwide," *Financial Times*, March 5, 2018, https://www.ft.com/

content/8940f2d0-2059-11e8-a895-1ba1f72c2c11; Deyan G, "Exciting WeChat Statistics," January 4, 2022, https://techjury.net/blog/wechat-statistics/#gref.

33. Ben Halder, "WeChat, China's Weapon of Mass Propaganda?," *OZY*, October 12, 2018, https://www.ozy.com/fast-forward/wechat-chi nas-weapon-of-mass-propaganda/88709; Deyan G, "Exciting WeChat Statistics."

34. Deyan G, "Exciting WeChat Statistics."

35. "Biden Withdrawing Trump Orders That Sought to Ban WeChat and TikTok," *Guardian*, June 9, 2021, https://www.theguardian.com/technology/2021/jun/09/tiktok-wechat-joe-biden-donald-trump-executive-orders.

36. Halder, "WeChat, China's Weapon of Mass Propaganda?"

37. Sarah Cook, "Worried About Huawei? Take a Closer Look at Tencent," *Diplomat*, March 26, 2019, https://freedomhouse.org/article/worried-about-huawei-take-closer-look-tencent.

38. Masashi Crete-Nishihata, Jeffrey Knockel, and Lotus Ruan, "We (Can't) Chat: '709 Crackdown' Discussions Blocked on Weibo and WeChat," *Citizen Lab*, April 13, 2017, https://citizenlab.ca/2017/04/we-cant-chat-709-crackdown-discussions-blocked-on-weibo-and-wechat/.

39. Halder, "WeChat, China's Weapon of Mass Propaganda?"

40. Salvador Rodriguez, "TikTok Insiders Say Social Media Company Is Tightly Controlled by Chinese Parent ByteDance," *CNBC*, June 25, 2021, https://www.cnbc.com/2021/06/25/tiktok-insiders-say-chin ese-parent-bytedance-in-control.html.

41. "Chinese Brands Make Up Most of Southeast Asia's Smartphone Market," *South China Morning Post*, August 20, 2019, https://www.scmp.com/abacus/tech/article/3029557/chinese-brands-make-most-southe ast-asias-smartphone-market.

42. Robert Spalding, *Stealth War: How China Took Over While America's Elite Slept* (New York: Penguin Random House, 2019), 77.

43. Nick Frisch, "We Should Worry About How China Uses Apps Like TikTok," *New York Times*, May 2, 2019, https://www.nytimes.com/inte ractive/2019/05/02/opinion/will-china-export-its-illiberal-innovat ion.html.

44. Li Tao, "How China's Simi Mobile Is Conquering Africa, One Country at a Time," *South China Morning Post*, July 20, 2019, https://www.scmp.com/tech/start-ups/article/3019305/how-unknown-shenzhen-bud get-phone-maker-conquering-africa-one.

45. Li Tao, "Chinese Smartphone Brands Such as Oppo Are Winning in Southeast Asia Despite Concerns over Huawei," *South China Morning Post*, August 20, 2019, https://www.scmp.com/tech/big-tech/article/3023434/chinese-smartphone-brands-such-oppo-are-winning-southeast-asia.

46. Niharika Sharma, "One Chinese Company Makes Three of the Five Top-Selling Smartphones in India," *Scroll.in*, July 27, 2019, https://scroll.in/article/931870/one-chinese-company-makes-three-of-the-five-of-indias-top-selling-smartphones.

47. Eugene Chow, "Is Your Chinese Phone Spying on You?," *The Week*, February 19, 2018, https://theweek.com/articles/748176/chinese-smartphone-spying.

48. "India Bans TikTok, WeChat, and Dozens More Chinese Apps," *BBC*, June 29, 2020, https://www.bbc.com/news/technology-53225720; Kiran Sharma, "Indian Apps Soar After Ban on China's TikTok, WeChat, and Baidu," *Nikkei Asia*, August 4, 2020, https://asia.nikkei.com/Spotlight/Asia-Insight/Indian-apps-soar-after-ban-on-China-s-TikTok-WeChat-and-Baidu.

49. "2017 Annual Report to Congress," U.S.-China Economic and Security Review Commission, November 15, 2017, 474.

50. Angela Lewis, "How a Pay TV Company Is Serving Up a Soft Power Win for China in Africa," *Diplomat*, February 14, 2019, https://thediplomat.com/2019/02/how-a-pay-tv-company-is-serving-up-a-soft-power-win-for-china-in-africa/.

51. Eric Olander, "China's StarTimes Is Now One of Africa's Most Important Media Companies," *Medium*, August 26, 2017, https://medium.com/@eolander/chinas-startimes-is-now-one-of-africa-s-most-important-media-companies-103843ebc376.

52. "Africa to Witness Subscriber Growth of 17m," *Broadband TV News*, January 6, 2020, https://www.broadbandtvnews.com/2020/01/06/africa-to-witness-subscriber-growth-of-17m/; Prince Osuagwu, "Others Tipped to Boost Africa's Digital Television Penetration," *Vanguard (Nigeria)*, January 20, 2021, https://www.vanguardngr.com/2021/01/startimes-others-tipped-to-boost-africas-digital-tv-penetration/.

53. Omar Mohammed, "A Chinese Media Company Is Taking Over East Africa's Booming Pay-TV Market," *Quartz Africa*, August 4, 2015, https://qz.com/africa/470166/a-chinese-media-company-is-taking-over-east-africas-booming-pay-tv-market/.

54. See, for example, "China: StarTimes Group Establishes Links with Latin America," *Prensario Internacional*, July 10, 2019, https://www.prensario.

tv/novedades/3583-china-startimes-group-establishes-links-with-latin-america; and "StarTimes Steps Up Capacity with Eutelsat for DTT Broadcasting in Africa," *Business Wire*, July 7, 2016, https://www.businesswire.com/news/home/20160707005441/en/StarTimes-Steps-up-Capacity-with-Eutelsat-for-DTT-Broadcasting-in-Africa.

55. "Focusing on Africa, ZTE and Informa Successfully Hold the Big Video Summit in South Africa," *ZTE*, November 16, 2016, https://www.zte.com.cn/global/about/news/1116-1.html; Sarah Cook, "Beijing's Global Megaphone: The Expansion of Chinese Communist Party Media Influence Since 2017," *Freedom House*, January 2020, https://freedomhouse.org/report/special-reports/beijings-global-megaphone-china-communist-party-media-influence-abroad.

56. Cook, "Beijing's Global Megaphone."

57. I am indebted to Christopher Walker and Shanthi Kalathil for conversations about this topic in the course of meetings of the study group that contributed to the evolution of this book.

58. Patrick Brzeski, "Keanu Reeves Hit with Backlash from Chinese Nationalists After Tibet Benefit Concert," *Hollywood Reporter*, January 27, 2022, https://www.hollywoodreporter.com/movies/movie-news/keanu-reeves-china-backlash-1235083112/.

59. Perry Link, "China: The Anaconda in the Chandelier," *New York Review of Books*, April 11, 2002, https://www.nybooks.com/articles/2002/04/11/china-the-anaconda-in-the-chandelier/.

60. Ibid.

61. Ibid.

62. Wanning Sun, "How Australia's Mandarin Speakers Get Their News," *Conversation*, November 22, 2018, https://theconversation.com/how-australias-mandarin-speakers-get-their-news-106917.

63. Ibid.

64. Titus C. Chen, Michael Jensen, and Tom Sear, "How Digital Media Blur the Border Between Australia and China," *Conversation*, November 15, 2018, https://theconversation.com/how-digital-media-blur-the-border-between-australia-and-china-101735.

65. Chen et al., "How Digital Media Blur the Border Between Australia and China."

66. "How Private Are Your Favorite Messaging Apps?," *Amnesty International*, October 21, 2016, https://www.amnesty.org/en/latest/campaigns/2016/10/which-messaging-apps-best-protect-your-privacy/.

67. Bradley A. Thayer and Lianchao Han, "The Faustian Bargain of WeChat: China Shackles the World," *Hill*, July 31, 2019, https://thehill.com/

opinion/technology/454747-the-faustian-bargain-of-wechat-china-shackles-the-world; Angus Grigg, "WeChat's Privacy Issues Mean You Should Delete China's #1 Messaging App," *Australian Financial Review*, February 22, 2018, https://www.afr.com/world/asia/wechats-privacy-issues-mean-you-should-delete-chinas-no1-messaging-app-20180221-howgct.

68. Emily Feng, "China Intercepts WeChat Texts from U.S. and Abroad, Researchers Say," *NPR*, August 29, 2019, https://www.npr.org/2019/08/29/751116338/china-intercepts-wechat-texts-from-u-s-and-abroad-researcher-says.

69. "How Private Are Your Favorite Messaging Apps?"

70. Ibid.

71. Miles Kenyon, "How WeChat Filters Images for One Billion Users," *Citizen Lab*, August 14, 2018, https://citizenlab.ca/2018/08/how-wechat-filters-images-for-one-billion-users/.

72. Li Yuan, "As Beijing Takes Control, Chinese Tech Companies Lose Jobs and Hope," *New York Times*, January 5, 2022, https://www.nytimes.com/2022/01/05/technology/china-tech-internet-crackdown-layoffs.html.

73. Li Yuan, "To Cover China, There's No Substitute for WeChat," *New York Times*, January 9, 2019, https://www.nytimes.com/2019/01/09/technology/personaltech/china-wechat.html.

74. Li Yuan, "'The Last Generation': The Disillusionment of Young Chinese," *New York Times*, May 24, 2022, https://www.nytimes.com/2022/05/24/business/china-covid-zero.html.

75. Dalvin Brown, "WhatsApp Was Breached: Here's What Users Need to Do," *USA Today*, May 14, 2019, https://www.usatoday.com/story/tech/2019/05/14/whatsapp-urges-users-upgrade-app-after-security-flaw/3664064002/.

76. Cook, "Beijing's Global Megaphone," 19.

77. Jeffrey Knockel and Ruohan Xiong, "(Can't) Picture This 2: An Analysis of WeChat's Realtime Image Filtering in Chats," *Citizen Lab*, July 15, 2019, https://citizenlab.ca/2019/07/cant-picture-this-2-an-analysis-of-wechats-realtime-image-filtering-in-chats/.

78. Jeffrey Knockel et al., "We Chat, They Watch: How International Users Unwittingly Build Up WeChat's Chinese Censorship Apparatus," *Citizen Lab*, May 7, 2020, https://citizenlab.ca/2020/05/we-chat-they-watch/.

79. James Griffiths, "Weibo's Free Speech Failure," *Atlantic*, March 20, 2019, https://www.theatlantic.com/technology/archive/2019/03/what-went-wrong-chinas-weibo-social-network/584728/.

80. Zhuang Pinghui, "'Winter Has Come': Chinese Social Media Stunned as Nearly 10,000 Accounts Shut Down," *South China Morning Post*, November 13, 2018, https://www.scmp.com/news/china/society/article/2173019/winter-has-come-chinese-social-media-stunned-nearly-10000.

81. Ibid.

82. Echo Xie, "Latest Crackdown on Chinese Social Media Sees Dozens of High-Profile Weibo Accounts Silenced," *South China Morning Post*, April 9, 2019, https://www.scmp.com/news/china/politics/article/3005281/latest-crackdown-chinese-social-media-sees-dozens-high-profile.

83. Ibid.

84. Author interviews with participants in Chinese training programs in 2016, 2017, and 2018.

85. "Freedom on the Net 2018: The Rise of Digital Authoritarianism," *Freedom House*, October 2018, https://freedomhouse.org/sites/default/files/FOTN_2018_Final.pdf.

86. Author interviews with Thai and Vietnamese officials.

87. He Huifeng, "In a Remote Corner of China, Beijing Is Trying to Export Its Model by Training Foreign Officials the Chinese Way," *South China Morning Post*, July 14, 2018, https://www.scmp.com/news/china/economy/article/2155203/remote-corner-china-beijing-trying-export-its-model-training.

88. See, for example, Huifeng, "In a Remote Corner of China, Beijing Is Trying to Export Its Model by Training Foreign Officials the Chinese Way"; Sintia Radu, "China's Web Surveillance Model Expands Abroad," *U.S. News & World Report*, November 1, 2018, https://www.usnews.com/news/best-countries/articles/2018-11-01/china-expands-its-surveillance-model-by-training-other-governments.

89. Abdi Latif Dahir, "China Is Exporting Its Digital Surveillance Methods to African Governments," *Nextgov*, November 1, 2018, https://www.nextgov.com/emerging-tech/2018/11/china-exporting-its-digital-surveillance-methods-african-governments/152495/.

90. Justin Sherman, "Vietnam's Internet Control: Following in China's Footsteps?," *Diplomat*, December 11, 2019, https://thediplomat.com/2019/12/vietnams-internet-control-following-in-chinas-footsteps/; Radu, "China's Web Surveillance Model Expands Abroad."

91. Thompson Chau, "Myanmar Junta Targets Sweeping Data Access with Cybersecurity Bill," *Nikkei Asia*, February 12, 2021, https://asia.nikkei.

com/Spotlight/Myanmar-Crisis/Myanmar-junta-targets-sweeping-data-access-with-cybersecurity-bill.

92. Hannah Beech and Paul Mozur, "A Digital Firewall in Myanmar, Built with Guns and Wire Cutters," *New York Times*, February 23, 2021, https://www.nytimes.com/2021/02/23/world/asia/myanmar-coup-firewall-internet-china.html.

93. Mattis, Peter, "Russian and Chinese Political Interference Activities and Influence Operations," in *Axis of Authoritarians: Implications of China-Russia Cooperation*, ed. Richard J. Ellings and Robert Sutter (Washington, DC: National Bureau of Asian Research, 2018), 134–39.

94. Jamie Harris, "China Now a 'Global Disinformation Superpower,' Say Researchers," *PA Media*, September 26, 2019, https://uk.finance.yahoo.com/news/china-now-global-disinformation-superpower-050000758.html.

95. Daniel Kliman et al., "Dangerous Synergies: Countering Chinese and Russian Digital Influence Operations," May 7, 2020, https://www.cnas.org/publications/reports/dangerous-synergies.

96. Ibid., 9.

97. Ibid.

98. Ibid., 16.

99. Doublethink Lab, "Full Report Launch: Deafening Whispers," *Medium*, October 24, 2020, https://medium.com/doublethinklab/deafening-whispers-f9b1d773f6cd; Anna Ringstrom and Helena Soderpalm, "H&M Vows to Rebuild Trust in China After Xinjiang Backlash," *Reuters*, March 31, 2021, https://www.reuters.com/article/us-h-m-results/hm-vows-to-rebuild-trust-in-china-after-xinjiang-backlash-idUSKBN2BN0LV.

100. Ringstrom and Soderpalm, "H&M Vows to Rebuild Trust in China After Xinjiang Backlash."

101. "Descendants of the Dragon: China Targets Its Citizens and Descendants Beyond the Mainland," *Atlantic Council*, December 2020, https://www.atlanticcouncil.org/wp-content/uploads/2020/12/China-Diaspora-FINAL-1.pdf.

102. "China's Propagandists Court Southeast Asia's Chinese Diaspora," *Economist*, November 20, 2021, https://www.economist.com/asia/2021/11/20/chinese-propagandists-court-south-east-asias-chinese-diaspora.

103. Betsy Woodruff Swan, "State Report: Chinese, Russian, Iranian Disinformation Narratives Echo One Another," *Politico*, April 21, 2020,

https://www.politico.com/news/2020/04/21/russia-china-iran-dis information-coronavirus-state-department-193107.

104. Ibid.

105. Woodruff Swan, "State Report"; "Iran: Government Mismanagement Compounds Covid-19 Crisis," *Human Rights Watch*, August 19, 2021, https://www.hrw.org/news/2021/08/19/iran-government-misman agement-compounds-covid-19-crisis.

106. Gary King, Jennifer Pan, and Margaret E. Roberts, "How the Chinese Government Fabricates Social Media Posts for Strategic Distraction, Not Engaged Argument," *American Political Science Review* 111, no. 3 (2017): 484–501, https://gking.harvard.edu/files/gking/files/50c.pdf.

107. Halder, "WeChat, China's Weapon of Mass Propaganda?"

108. Josh Horwitz, "WeChat Has a Great New Tool for Fighting Fake News, but There's One Little Problem: Beijing," *Quartz*, June 9, 2017, https://qz.com/1002262/wechats-new-tool-for-fighting-fake-news-could-fil ter-out-real-news-in-china-tencent-hkg0700/.

109. Ibid.

110. Sheridan Prasso and Samson Ellis, "China's Information War on Taiwan Ramps Up as Election Nears," *Bloomberg*, October 23, 2019, https://www.bloomberg.com/news/articles/2019-10-23/china-s-informat ion-war-on-taiwan-ramps-up-as-election-nears.

111. Keoni Everington, "Beijing-Based PTT Users Spread Fake Osaka Airport Bus Story," *Taiwan News*, September 17, 2018, https://www.tai wannews.com.tw/en/news/3531772.

112. Ko Tin-yau, "How Fake News Led to Suicide of Taiwan Representative to Osaka," *EJI Insight*, September 19, 2018, https://www.ejinsight.com/ eji/article/id/1947349/20180919-how-fake-news-led-to-suicide-of-tai wan-representative-in-osaka.

113. Keoni Everington, "Taiwan Is Main Target of China's Disinformation Campaign: RSF," *Taiwan News*, March 26, 2019, https://www.taiwann ews.com.tw/en/news/3666237.

114. Ibid.; Tin-yau, "How Fake News Led to Suicide of Taiwan Representative to Osaka."

115. Tin-yau, "How Fake News Led to Suicide of Taiwan Representative to Osaka."

116. "China's Propagandists Court Southeast Asia's Chinese Diaspora."

117. Ibid.

118. Katja Drinhausen and Mayya Solonina, "Chinese and Russian Media Partner to 'Tell Each Other's Stories Well,'" *Mercator Institute for China*

Studies, December 22, 2020, https://merics.org/en/opinion/chinese-and-russian-media-partner-tell-each-others-stories-well.

119. See, for example, Joshua Kurlantzick, "How China Ramped Up Disinformation Efforts During the Pandemic," *Council on Foreign Relations*, September 10, 2020, https://www.cfr.org/in-brief/how-china-ramped-disinformation-efforts-during-pandemic.

120. Doublethink Lab, "Full Report Launch: Deafening Whispers," *Medium*, October 24, 2020, https://medium.com/doublethinklab/deafening-whispers-f9b1d773f6cd.

121. Josiah Case, "Telling China's COVID-19 Story Well: Beijing's Efforts to Control Information and Shape Public Narratives Regarding the 2020 Global Pandemic," *CNA*, December 2020, https://www.cna.org/CNA_files/PDF/DRM-2020-U-028558-Final.pdf.

122. Andrea Kendall-Taylor, "Mendacious Mixture: The Growing Convergence of Russian and Chinese Information Operations," in Dean Jackson, ed., "COVID-19 and the Information Space: Boosting the Democratic Response," *National Endowment for Democracy*, January 2021, https://www.ned.org/wp-content/uploads/2021/01/Global-Insights-COVID-19-Information-Space-Boosting-Democratic-Response-1.pdf.

CHAPTER 10

1. Alexander Bowe, "China's Overseas United Front Work: Background and Implications for the United States," *U.S.-China Economic and Security Review Commission*, August 24, 2018, https://www.uscc.gov/sites/default/files/Research/China%27s%20Overseas%20United%20Front%20Work%20-%20Background%20and%20Implications%20for%20US_final_0.pdf; Gerry Groot, "The Expansion of the United Front Under Xi Jinping," *China Story*, accessed February 27, 2022, https://www.thechinastory.org/yearbooks/yearbook-2015/forum-ascent/the-expansion-of-the-united-front-under-xi-jinping/.

2. Ibid.

3. Ibid.

4. For a deeper investigation of Beijing's use of *qiaowu*, see Hua To and James Jiann, *Qiaowu: Extra-Territorial Policies for the Overseas Chinese* (Singapore: Brill, 2014); "Writing China: James Jiann Hua To, 'Qiaowu: Extra-Territorial Policies for the Overseas Chinese,'" *Wall Street Journal*, August 15, 2014, https://www.wsj.com/articles/BL-CJB-23602.

5. See, for instance, Anne-Marie Brady, "Magic Weapons: China's Political Influence Activities Under Xi Jinping," *Wilson Center*, September 18, 2017, https://www.wilsoncenter.org/article/magic-weapons-chinas-political-influence-activities-under-xi-jinping.

6. Alex Joske, "The Party Speaks for You," *Australian Strategic Policy Institute*, June 9, 2020, https://www.aspi.org.au/report/party-speaks-you.

7. Amy E. Searight, "Chinese Influence Activities with U.S. Allies and Partners in Southeast Asia," Testimony Before the U.S.-China Economic and Security Review Commission, Hearing on China's Relations with U.S. Allies and Partners in Europe and the Asia Pacific, April 5, 2018, https://www.uscc.gov/sites/default/files/USCC%20Hearing_Amy%20Searight_Written%20Statement_April%205%202018.pdf.

8. See, for example, Bethany Allen-Ebrahimian and Zach Dorfman, "Exclusive: Suspected Chinese Spy Targeted California Politicians," *Axios*, December 8, 2020, https://www.axios.com/china-spy-california-politicians-9d2dfb99-f839-4e00-8bd8-59decodaf589.html.

9. "Is China Both a Source and Hub for International Students?," *ChinaPower*, accessed November 9, 2021, https://chinapower.csis.org/china-international-students/.

10. "Why China Is Lavishing Money on Foreign Students," *Economist*, January 26, 2019, https://www.economist.com/china/2019/01/26/why-china-is-lavishing-money-on-foreign-students.

11. Samantha Custer et al., *Influencing the Narrative: How the Chinese Government Mobilizes Students and Media to Burnish Its Image* (Williamsburg, VA: AidData, 2019), 27–28, http://docs.aiddata.org/ad4/pdfs/Influencing_the_Narrative_Report.pdf.

12. Ibid.

13. Samantha Custer et al., *Ties That Bind: Quantifying China's Public Diplomacy and Its "Good Neighbor" Effect* (Williamsburg, VA: AidData at William & Mary, 2018), https://www.aiddata.org/publications/ties-that-bind.

14. Sasha Aslanian and Karin Fischer, "Fading Beacon," *APM Reports*, August 3, 2021, https://www.apmreports.org/episode/2021/08/03/fading-beacon-why-america-is-losing-international-students.

15. Miriam Berger, "The Pandemic Has Damaged the Appeal of Studying in the United States for Some International Students," *Washington Post*, July 23, 2020, https://www.washingtonpost.com/world/2020/07/23/coronavirus-international-students-united-states-enrollment-reputation/.

16. "2014 Global Cities Index and Emerging Cities Outlook: Global Cities, Present and Future," *A.T. Kearney*, 2014, http://www.iberglobal. com/files/Global_Cities.pdf; Li Jing, "Sister City Relations Promote Cooperation," *China Daily*, April 25, 2019, http://www.chinadaily.com. cn/global/2019-04/26/content_37462677.htm.

17. Custer et al., *Ties That Bind*, 11.

18. This information was adapted from a study by Joshua Eisenman of Notre Dame University, part of book research he was doing that he provided to me.

19. For instance, Josh Rogin, "Another University Learns the Hard Way About Chinese Censorship on Campus," *Washington Post*, February 9, 2022, https://www.washingtonpost.com/opinions/2022/02/09/anot her-university-learns-hard-way-about-chinese-censorship-campus/.

20. M. Ham and Elaine Tolentino, "Socialization of China's Soft Power: Building Friendship Through Potential Leaders," *China:An International Journal* 16 (2018): 45–68.

21. Custer et al., *Influencing the Narrative*.

22. Ham and Tolentino, "Socialization of China's Soft Power."

23. Bethany Allen-Ebrahimian, "The Chinese Communist Party Is Setting Up Cells at Universities Across America," *Foreign Policy*, April 18, 2018, https://foreignpolicy.com/2018/04/18/the-chinese-communist-party-is-setting-up-cells-at-universities-across-america-china-students-beij ing-surveillance/.

24. Bethany Allen-Ebrahiman, "China's Long Arm Reaches into America's Campuses," *Foreign Policy*, March 7, 2018, https://foreignpolicy.com/ 2018/03/07/chinas-long-arm-reaches-into-american-campuses-chin ese-students-scholars-association-university-communist-party/.

25. Ibid.

26. Amy Searight, *Countering China's Influence Activities: Lessons from Australia* (Washington, DC: Center for Strategic and International Studies, July 2020), 14–15, https://www.csis.org/analysis/countering-chinas-influe nce-activities-lessons-australia.

27. Ibid.; Gabrielle Resnick, "Chinese Students Say Free Speech in US Chilled by China," *Voice of America*, January 14, 2020, https://www.voan ews.com/a/student-union_chinese-students-say-free-speech-us-chil led-china/6182548.html; Rogin, "Another University Learns the Hard Way About Chinese Censorship on Campus."

28. Ibid.; Bethany Allen-Ebrahimian, "China Built an Army of Influence Agents in the U.S.," *Daily Beast*, July 18, 2018, https://www.thedai lybeast.com/how-china-built-an-army-of-influence-agents-in-the-us;

Rogin, "Another University Learns the Hard Way About Chinese Censorship on Campus."

29. Joske, "The Party Speaks for You."

30. Ibid.

31. Anastasya Lloyd-Damnjanovic, *A Preliminary Study of PRC Political Influence and Interference Activities in American Higher Education* (Washington, DC: Wilson Center, 2018), https://www.wilsoncenter. org/publication/preliminary-study-prc-political-influence-and-inter ference-activities-american-higher; Resnick, "Chinese Students Say Free Speech in US Chilled by China."

32. Josh Horwitz, "China Is Retaliating Against a U.S. University for Inviting the Dalai Lama to Speak at Graduation," *Quartz*, September 19, 2017, https://qz.com/1080962/china-is-retaliating-against-the-univers ity-of-california-san-diego-for-inviting-the-dalai-lama-to-speak-at-commencement/; Sebastian Rotella, "Even on U.S. Campuses, China Cracks Down on Students Who Speak Out," *ProPublica*, November 30, 2021, https://www.propublica.org/article/even-on-us-campuses-china-cracks-down-on-students-who-speak-out; Lin Yang, "China-Sensitive Topics at U.S. Universities Draw More Online Harassment," *Voice of America*, November 20, 2020, https://www.voanews.com/a/usa_china-sensitive-topics-us-universities-draw-more-online-harassm ent/6198648.html; Larry Diamond and Orville Schell, eds., *China's Influence & American Interests: Promoting Constructive Vigilance* (Stanford, CA: Hoover Institution Press, 2019), https://www.hoover.org/resea rch/chinas-influence-american-interests-promoting-constructive-vig-ilance.

33. Isaac Stone Fish, "The Other Political Correctness," *New Republic*, September 4, 2018, https://newrepublic.com/article/150476/ameri can-elite-universities-selfcensorship-china.

34. Ibid.

35. "China: Government Threats to Academic Freedom Abroad," *Human Rights Watch*, March 21, 2019, https://www.hrw.org/news/2019/03/21/china-government-threats-academic-freedom-abroad#.

36. Ibid.

37. Ibid.

38. Ibid.

39. See, for example, "On Partnerships with Foreign Governments: The Case of Confucius Institutes," *American Association of University Professors*, June 2014, https://www.aaup.org/report/confucius-institutes; Stone Fish, "The Other Political Correctness."

40. "China: Agreements Establishing Confucius Institutes at U.S. Universities Are Similar, but Institute Operations Vary," GAO-19-278, United States Government Accountability Office, February 2019, 23, https://www.gao.gov/assets/700/696859.pdf.

41. Benjamin Wermund, "Chinese-Funded Institutes on U.S. College Campuses Condemned in Senate Report," *Politico*, February 27, 2019, https://www.politico.com/story/2019/02/27/china-college-confucius-institutes-1221768. See also U.S. Congress, Senate, Committee on Homeland Security and Governmental Affairs Permanent Subcommittee on Investigations, *China's Impact on the U.S. Education System*, 116th Cong., 1st sess., 2019, S. Hrg. 116-30, https://www.hsgac.senate.gov/imo/media/doc/PSI%20Report%20China's%20Impact%20on%20the%20US%20Education%20System.pdf.

42. "'They Don't Understand the Fear We Have,'" *Human Rights Watch*, June 30, 2021, https://www.hrw.org/report/2021/06/30/they-dont-understand-fear-we-have/how-chinas-long-reach-repression-undermines#.

43. "Australia: Beijing Threatening Academic Freedom," *Human Rights Watch*, June 29, 2021, https://www.hrw.org/news/2021/06/30/australia-beijing-threatening-academic-freedom.

44. Ibid.

45. Rachelle Peterson, *Outsourced to China: Confucius Institutes and Soft Power in American Higher Education* (New York: National Association of Scholars, April 2017).

46. Ibid.

47. "Letter from Under Secretary Keith Krach to the Governing Boards of American Universities," *U.S. Embassy in Romania,* September 1, 2020, https://ro.usembassy.gov/letter-from-under-secretary-keith-krach-to-the-governing-boards-of-american-universities/.

48. Michael R. Pompeo, "Designation of the Confucius Institute U.S. Center as a Foreign Mission of the PRC," *U.S. Department of State*, August 13, 2020, https://2017-2021.state.gov/designation-of-the-confucius-institute-u-s-center-as-a-foreign-mission-of-the-prc/index.html; Naima Green-Riley, "The State Department Labeled China's Confucius Programs a Bad Influence on U.S. Students. What's the Story?," *Washington Post*, August 25, 2020, https://www.washingtonpost.com/politics/2020/08/24/state-department-labeled-chinas-confucius-programs-bad-influence-us-students-whats-story/.

49. See, for example, "How Many Confucius Institutes Are in the United States?," *National Association of Scholars*, April 5, 2022, https://www.nas.

org/blogs/article/how_many_confucius_institutes_are_in_the_united_states; and Rachelle Peterson, "China's Confucius Institutes Might Be Closing, but They Succeeded," *Real Clear Education*, March 31, 2021, https://www.realcleareducation.com/articles/2021/03/31/chinas_confucius_institutes_might_be_closing_but_they_succeeded_110559.html.

50. Ibid.

51. Phil Davis, "University of Maryland Cuts China-Supported Education Program amid Tensions Between Countries," *Baltimore Sun*, January 22, 2020, https://www.baltimoresun.com/education/bs-md-confucius-institute-umd-20200123-3sb7hhbyq5cn7pfl7n55edtlaq-story.html.

52. Ibid.

53. Lisa Visentin, "China-Backed Confucius Institutes Face Closure Under Veto Laws," *Sydney Morning Herald*, May 10, 2021, https://www.smh.com.au/politics/federal/china-backed-confucius-institutes-face-closure-under-veto-laws-20210423-p57lvo.html.

54. Zachary Evans, "Sweden Closes Its Last Remaining 'Confucius Institute' amid Strained Relations with China," *National Review*, April 23, 2020, https://www.nationalreview.com/news/sweden-closes-its-last-remaining-confucius-institute-amid-strained-relations-with-china/.

55. See, for example, Huang Tzu-ti, "German Universities Move to Reject China's Confucius Institutes," *Taiwan News*, July 28, 2020, https://www.taiwannews.com.tw/en/news/3975526; Mark O'Neill, "Europe Closes Confucius Institutes," *EJ Insight*, July 16, 2021, https://www.ejinsight.com/eji/article/id/2854926/20210716-Europe-closes-Confucius-Institutes; and Jeremy Luedi, "Why Canada Is Shutting Down Its Confucius Institutes," *True North Far East*, September 21, 2019, https://truenorthfareast.com/news/confucius-institute-canada-closing-shut-down.

CHAPTER 11

1. Paul Huang, "Chinese Cyber-Operatives Boosted Taiwan's Insurgent Candidate," *Foreign Policy*, June 26, 2019, https://foreignpolicy.com/2019/06/26/chinese-cyber-operatives-boosted-taiwans-insurgent-candidate/.

2. Ibid.

3. Dominique Reichenbach, "The Rise and Rapid Fall of Han Kuo-yu," *Diplomat*, March 18, 2020, https://thediplomat.com/2020/03/the-rise-and-rapid-fall-of-han-kuo-yu/.

4. Huang, "Chinese Cyber Operatives Boosted Taiwan's Insurgent Candidate."

5. Lawrence Chung, "From Rank Outsider to Mayor of Kaohsiung: Meet the Man Who Wooed Taiwan's Electorate," *South China Morning Post*, November 25, 2018, https://www.scmp.com/news/china/politics/arti cle/2174915/rank-outsider-mayor-kaohsiung-meet-man-who-wooed-taiwans.

6. Chung, "From Rank Outsider to Mayor of Kaohsiung."

7. Tristan Lavalette, "Self-Confessed Chinese Spy Spills Secrets in Australia," *Associated Press*, November 23, 2019, https://apnews.com/ article/ap-top-news-international-news-hong-kong-taiwan-china-5d40fcc832204801a33599bdeaf541c3.

8. See, for example, Lily Kuo, "Taiwan Promises 'Support' for Hong Kong's People as China Tightens Grip," *Guardian*, May 24, 2020, https://www. theguardian.com/world/2020/may/25/taiwan-promises-support-for-hong-kongs-people-china-national-security-law.

9. Kathrin Hille, "Taiwan Primaries Highlight Fears over China's Political Influence," *Financial Times*, July 16, 2019, https://www.ft.com/content/ 036b609a-a768-11e9-984c-fac8325aaa04.

10. Ibid.

11. See, for example, Raymond Zhong, "Awash in Disinformation Before Vote, Taiwan Points Finger at China," *New York Times*, January 6, 2020, https://www.nytimes.com/2020/01/06/technology/taiwan-election-china-disinformation.html.

12. Ibid.

13. Connor Fairman, "When Election Interference Fails," *Net Politics*, January 29, 2020, https://www.cfr.org/blog/when-election-interfere nce-fails.

14. Emily Feng, "Taiwan Gets Tough on Disinformation Suspected from China Ahead of Elections," *NPR*, December 6, 2019, https://www. npr.org/2019/12/06/784191852/taiwan-gets-tough-on-disinformat ion-suspected-from-china-ahead-of-elections; "Taiwan's Push Against 'Red Media,'" *Al Jazeera*, November 17, 2019, https://www.aljaze era.com/program/the-listening-post/2019/11/17/taiwans-push-agai nst-red-media.

15. Sarah Cook, "Beijing's Global Megaphone: The Expansion of Chinese Communist Party Media Influence Since 2017," *Freedom House*, January 2020, 25, https://freedomhouse.org/report/special-reports/beijings-global-megaphone-china-communist-party-media-influence-abroad.

16. A portion of the two preceding paragraphs were published in CFR. org's *Asia Unbound* blog: Joshua Kurlantzick, "Tsai Ing-wen's Victory: A Few Initial Notes," *Asia Unbound*, January 13, 2020, https://www.cfr. org/blog/tsai-ing-wens-victory-few-initial-notes.

17. Yimou Lee and James Pomfret, "Show Hong Kong Value of Democracy, Taiwan President Says Before Vote," *Reuters*, January 9, 2020, https:// www.reuters.com/article/us-taiwan-election/show-hong-kong-value-of-democracy-taiwan-president-says-before-vote-idUSKB N1Z90C6.

18. Kurlantzick, "Tsai Ing-wen's Victory."

19. William Yang, "Will Tsai Ing-wen's Landslide Victory Force Beijing to Rethink Its Approach to Taiwan?," *Deutsche Welle*, January 12, 2020, https://www.dw.com/en/will-tsai-ing-wens-landslide-victory-force-beijing-to-rethink-its-approach-to-taiwan/a-51972372.

20. Nick Aspinwall, "Taiwan's 'Han Wave' Comes Crashing Down," *Diplomat*, June 10, 2020, https://thediplomat.com/2020/06/taiwans-han-wave-comes-crashing-down/.

21. Emily Feng and Barbara Sprunt, "Pelosi has Landed in Taiwan. Here's why That's a Big Deal," *National Public Radio*, August 2, 2022, https:// www.npr.org/2022/08/02/1114852740/pelosi-is-about-to-land-in-tai wan-heres-why-thats-a-big-deal.

22. Isabel Reynolds, "Chinese Missiles Deal Fresh Blow to Fraught Ties with Japan," *Bloomberg*, August 5, 2022, https://www.bloomberg.com/ news/articles/2022-08-05/japan-s-kishida-condemns-china-missile-launches-in-pelosi-talks.

23. Mike Ives and Zixu Wang, "Mostly Bluster: Why China Went Easy on Taiwan's Economy," *New York Times*, August 12, 2022, https://www.nyti mes.com/2022/08/12/business/china-taiwan-economy.html.

24. Ibid.

25. Chen Ping-hung, "Younger People Identify as Taiwanese, Survey Shows," *Taipei Times*, March 25, 2015, https://www.taipeitimes.com/ News/taiwan/archives/2015/03/25/2003614368.

26. "Chinese Discourse Power: China's Use of Information Manipulation in Regional and Global Competition," *Atlantic Council*, December 2020, 24, https://www.atlanticcouncil.org/wp-content/uploads/2020/ 12/China-Discouse-Power-FINAL.pdf.

27. Laura Silver, Kat Devlin, and Christine Huang, "Unfavorable Views of China Reach Historic Highs in Many Countries," *Pew Research Center*, October 6, 2020, https://www.pewresearch.org/global/2020/10/06/ unfavorable-views-of-china-reach-historic-highs-in-many-countries/.

28. Huynh Tam Sang, "The Taiwan Crisis Could Spill over into Southeast Asia," *The Diplomat*, August 11, 2022, https://thediplomat.com/2022/08/the-taiwan-crisis-could-spill-over-into-southeast-asia/.

29. Sofia Tomacruz, "Marcos Meets Blinken, says PH-US Ties Critical Amid Taiwan Tension," *Rappler*, August 6, 2022, https://www.rappler.com/nation/marcos-jr-meeting-us-secretary-state-antony-blinken-august-6-2022/.

30. Ryo Nemeto and Bobby Nugroho, "Japan Joins U.S.-Indonesian Military Drill for First Time," *Nikkei Asia*, August 14, 2022, https://asia.nikkei.com/Politics/International-relations/Indo-Pacific/Japan-joins-U.S.-Indonesian-military-drill-for-first-time.

31. Silver et al., "Unfavorable Views of China Reach Historic Highs in Many Countries."

32. Laura Silver, "China's International Image Remains Broadly Negative as Views of the U.S. Rebound," Pew Research Center report, June 30, 2021, https://www.pewresearch.org/fact-tank/2021/06/30/chinas-international-image-remains-broadly-negative-as-views-of-the-u-s-rebound/.

33. "The State of Southeast Asia: 2021 Survey Report," *ASEAN Studies Center, ISEAS–Yusof Ishak Institute*, February 10, 2021, https://www.iseas.edu.sg/wp-content/uploads/2021/01/The-State-of-SEA-2021-v2.pdf.

34. "The State of Southeast Asia: 2022 Survey Report," *ASEAN Studies Center, ISEAS–Yusof Ishak Institute,* February 16, 2022, https://www.iseas.edu.sg/wp-content/uploads/2022/02/The-State-of-SEA-2022_FA_Digital_FINAL.pdf.

35. Ibid.

36. Ibid.

37. Samantha Custer et al., *Influencing the Narrative: How the Chinese Government Mobilizes Students and Media to Burnish Its Image* (Williamsburg, VA: AidData at William & Mary, 2019), 12–14, http://docs.aiddata.org/ad4/pdfs/Influencing_the_Narrative_Report.pdf.

38. "Singapore Man Admits Being Chinese Spy in U.S.," *BBC*, July 25, 2020, https://www.bbc.com/news/world-us-canada-53534941.

39. Ibid.

40. Isabella Kwai, "U.K. Regulator Revokes License for China-Backed Broadcaster," *New York Times*, February 4, 2021, https://www.nytimes.com/2021/02/04/world/europe/uk-china-cgtn-license.html.

41. Ibid.

42. Bethany Allen-Ebrahimian, "Exclusive: How the FBI Combats China's Political Meddling," *Axios*, February 12, 2020, https://www.axios.com/

fbi-china-us-political-influence-0e70d07c-2d60-47cd-a5c3-6c72b2064
941.html; Ursula Perano, "Wray: FBI Has over 2,000 Investigations That
Trace Back to China," *Axios*, June 24, 2020, https://www.axios.com/
fbi-wray-china-counterintelligence-invetsigations-f809b7df-865a-
482b-9af4-b1410c0d3b49.html.

43. Lara Jakes and Steven Lee Myers, "U.S. Designates China's Official
Media as Operatives of the Communist State," *New York Times*, February
18, 2020, https://www.nytimes.com/2020/02/18/world/asia/china-
media-trump.html; Edward Wong, "U.S. Designates Four More Chinese
News Organizations as Foreign Missions," *New York Times*, June 22,
2020, https://www.nytimes.com/2020/06/22/us/politics/us-china-
news-organizations.html.

44. Ibid.

45. Elise Favis, "Trump Executive Order Against Tencent-Owned
Companies Does Not Affect Video Game Holdings," *Washington Post*,
August 7, 2020, https://www.washingtonpost.com/video-games/
2020/08/07/trump-executive-order-against-tencent-owned-compan
ies-does-not-affect-video-game-holdings/; "Commerce Department
Prohibits WeChat and TikTok Transactions to Protect the National
Security of the United States," *U.S. Department of Commerce*, September
18, 2020, https://content.govdelivery.com/accounts/USDOC/bullet
ins/2a14c6c.

46. Ibid.; Echo Wong and David Shepardson, "China's ByteDance
Challenges Trump's TikTok Divestiture Order," *Reuters*, November 11,
2020, https://www.reuters.com/article/uk-usa-tiktok/bytedance-cha
llenges-trumps-tiktok-divestiture-order-idUSKBN27R02G.

47. Makena Kelly, "Biden Revokes and Replaces Trump Orders Banning
TikTok and WeChat," *Verge*, June 9, 2021, https://www.theverge.com/
2021/6/9/22525953/biden-tiktok-wechat-trump-bans-revoked-alipay.

48. Edward Wong, Lara Jakes, and Steven Lee Myers, "U.S. Orders China
to Close Houston Consulate, Citing Efforts to Steal Trade Secrets,"
New York Times, July 22, 2020, https://www.nytimes.com/2020/07/
22/world/asia/us-china-houston-consulate.html; Keith Bradsher and
Steven Lee Myers, "China Orders U.S. to Shut Chengdu Consulate,
Retaliating for Houston," *New York Times*, July 24, 2020, https://
www.nytimes.com/2020/07/24/world/asia/china-us-consulate-chen
gdu.html.

49. Pranshu Verma and Edward Wong, "Trump Administration Penalizes
Hong Kong Officials for Crackdown on Protestors," *New York Times*,

August 7, 2020, https://www.nytimes.com/2020/08/07/world/asia/trump-china-hong-kong-sanctions.html.

50. "U.S. Sanctions Chinese Firms over Abuse of Uyghur Rights," *Deutsche Welle*, December 16, 2021, https://www.dw.com/en/us-sanctions-chinese-firms-over-abuse-of-uyghur-rights/a-60151176.

51. "Fact Sheet: CHIPS and Science Act," White House Press Release, August 9, 2022, https://www.whitehouse.gov/briefing-room/statements-releases/2022/08/09/fact-sheet-chips-and-science-act-will-lower-costs-create-jobs-strengthen-supply-chains-and-counter-china/.

52. Nicolle Liu et al., "China Imposes Sanctions on U.S. Officials in Retaliation for Hong Kong Measures," *Financial Times*, August 10, 2020, https://www.ft.com/content/c2d78da3-1fcf-4678-b65d-e1d02aa48ae6.

53. Alex Leary and Lingling Wei, "White House Says Biden Warned Xi of Consequences if Beijing Supports Russia on Ukraine," *Wall Street Journal*, March 18, 2022, https://www.wsj.com/articles/biden-xi-talk-as-u-s-threatens-actions-if-china-backs-russia-in-ukraine-war-11647611124.

54. Anthony Kuhn, "President Biden Says the U.S. Will Defend Taiwan if China Attacks," *National Public Radio*, May 23, 2022; also Valerie Insinia and Justin Katz, "A Bloody Mess with Terrible Loss of Life: How a China-U.S. Conflict over Taiwan could Play Out," *Breaking Defense*, August 11, 2022, https://breakingdefense.com/2022/08/a-bloody-mess-with-terrible-loss-of-life-how-a-china-us-conflict-over-taiwan-could-play-out/.

55. Maria Abi-Habib, "India Bans Nearly 60 Chinese Apps, Including TikTok and WeChat," *New York Times*, June 29, 2020, https://www.nytimes.com/2020/06/29/world/asia/tik-tok-banned-india-china.html; David M. Herszenhorn and Jacopo Barigazzi, "EU Leaders Face Tough Time Getting Tough on China," *Politico*, June 23, 2020, https://www.politico.com/news/2020/06/23/europe-getting-tough-china-335195; Guy Chazan, "Merkel Comes Under Fire at Home for China Stance," *Financial Times*, July 7, 2020, https://www.ft.com/content/bf1adef9-a681-48c0-99b8-f551e7a5b66d.

56. Janka Oertel, "The New China Consensus: How Europe Is Growing Wary of Beijing," *European Council on Foreign Relations*, September 7, 2020, https://ecfr.eu/publication/the_new_china_consensus_how_europe_is_growing_wary_of_beijing/.

57. Stuart Lau, "EU Slams China's 'Authoritarian Shift' and Broken Economic Promises," *Politico*, April 25, 2021, https://www.politico.eu/article/eu-china-biden-economy-climate-europe/.

58. Ivana Karásková et al., "Central Europe for Sale: The Politics of China's Influence," *AMO, National Endowment for Democracy*, April 2018, 15, https://www.chinfluence.eu/wp-content/uploads/2018/04/AMO_central-europe-for-sale-the-politics-of-chinese-influence-1.pdf.

59. Ibid., 2.

60. Ibid., 15.

61. Marc Santora, "The Broken Promise of a Panda: How Prague's Relations with Beijing Soured," *New York Times*, November 23, 2019, https://www.nytimes.com/2019/11/23/world/europe/china-prague-taiwan.html.

62. David Hutt, "China Influence Aggravates Czech Republic's Political War," *Nikkei Asia*, November 22, 2019, https://asia.nikkei.com/Politics/International-relations/China-influence-aggravates-Czech-Republic-s-political-war.

63. Jonathan McClory, ed., "The Soft Power 30: A Global Ranking of Soft Power 2019," *Portland Consulting Group*, https://softpower30.com/wp-content/uploads/2019/10/The-Soft power-30-Report-2019-1.pdf.

64. "Asia Power Index: 2021 Edition," Lowy Institute, https://power.lowyinstitute.org/.

65. Bonnie Bley, "Charting China, the (Not Always) Super Power," *Interpreter*, June 3, 2019, https://www.lowyinstitute.org/the-interpreter/charting-china-not-always-super-power.

66. Ibid.

67. For instance, Davey Alba and Sheera Frankel, "Facebook Tests New Disinformation Tactics in Africa to Expand Influence," *New York Times*, October 30, 2019, https://www.nytimes.com/2019/10/30/technology/russia-facebook-disinformation-africa.html. Also, Echo Huang, "Why China's Social Media Propaganda Isn't as Good as Russia's," *Quartz,* September 19, 2019, https://qz.com/1699144/why-chinas-social-media-propaganda-isnt-as-good-as-russias/.

68. Santora, "The Broken Promise of a Panda."

69. Ibid.

70. Laura Silver, Kat Devlin, and Christine Huang, "People Around the World Are Divided in Their Opinions of China," *Pew Research Center*, December 5, 2019, https://www.pewresearch.org/fact-tank/2019/12/05/people-around-the-globe-are-divided-in-their-opinions-of-china/.

71. Jari Tanner, "Sweden Summons Chinese Envoy over 'Lightweight Boxer' Remark," *Associated Press*, January 18, 2020, https://abcnews. go.com/International/wireStory/sweden-summons-chinese-envoy-lightweight-boxer-remark-68372421; Jojje Olsson, "China Tries to Put Sweden on Ice," *Diplomat*, December 30, 2019, https://thediplomat. com/2019/12/china-tries-to-put-sweden-on-ice/. For U.S. oversight efforts, see "Foreign Government-Sponsored Broadcast Programming," *Congressional Research Service*, February 11, 2021, https://crsreports. congress.gov/product/pdf/IF/IF11759.

72. Olsson, "China Tries to Put Sweden on Ice."

73. Chung Kuang-cheng and Wang Yun, "Democratic Taiwan Battling Disinformation from China Ahead of Elections," *Radio Free Asia*, November 6, 2018, https://www.rfa.org/english/news/china/democra tic-taiwan-battling-disinformation-11062018111310.html.

74. Feng, "Taiwan Gets Tough on Disinformation Suspected from China Ahead of Elections."

75. Samantha Bradshaw and Philip N. Howard, "The Global Disinformation Disorder: 2019 Global Inventory of Organized Social Media Manipulation," *Computational Propaganda Research Project*, September 2019, https://comprop.oii.ox.ac.uk/wp-content/uploads/sites/93/ 2019/09/CyberTroop-Report19.pdf.

76. Ibid.

77. "Targeting the Anti-Extradition Bill Movement: China's Hong Kong Messaging Proliferates on Social Media," *Atlantic Council*, December 2020, https://www.atlanticcouncil.org/wp-content/uploads/2020/12/ China-HongKong-FINAL2.pdf.

78. Huang, "Why China Isn't as Skillful at Disinformation as Russia."

79. Ibid.

80. Ibid.

81. Tom Uren, Elise Thomas, and Jacob Wallis, "Tweeting Through the Great Firewall," *Australian Strategic Policy Institute*, September 3, 2019, https://www.aspi.org.au/report/tweeting-through-great-firewall.

82. Cook, "Beijing's Global Megaphone," 11.

83. Jean-Baptise Jeangène Vilmer and Paul Charon, "Russia as a Hurricane, China as Climate Change: Different Ways of Information Warfare," *War on the Rocks*, January 21, 2020, https://warontherocks.com/2020/01/ russia-as-a-hurricane-china-as-climate-change-different-ways-of-info rmation-warfare/.

84. Renée DiResta et al., *Telling China's Story: The Chinese Communist Party's Campaign to Shape Global Narratives* (Stanford, CA: Stanford Internet

Observatory, 2020), 44, https://fsi-live.s3.us-west-1.amazonaws.com/s3fs-public/sio-china_story_white_paper-final.pdf.

85. Ibid.

86. Philip N. Howard and Samantha Bradshaw, "China Joins the Global Disinformation Order," *Strategist*, November 29, 2019, https://www.aspistrategist.org.au/china-joins-the-global-disinformation-order/.

87. Kate Conger, "Twitter Removes Chinese Disinformation Campaign," *New York Times*, June 11, 2020, https://www.nytimes.com/2020/06/11/technology/twitter-chinese-misinformation.html.

88. Vanessa Molter and Graham Webster, "Virality Project (China): Coronavirus Conspiracy Claims," *Stanford Freeman Spogli Institute for International Studies*, March 31, 2020, https://fsi.stanford.edu/news/china-covid19-origin-narrative.

89. "China Hits Back at Report That It Hid Coronavirus Numbers," *Time*, April 2, 2020, https://time.com/5814313/china-denies-hiding-coronavirus/.

90. David Gitter, Sandy Lu, and Brock Erdahl, "China Will Do Anything to Deflect Coronavirus Blame," *Foreign Policy*, March 30, 2020, https://foreignpolicy.com/2020/03/30/beijing-coronavirus-response-see-what-sticks-propaganda-blame-ccp-xi-jinping/.

91. John Ruwitch, "Theory That COVID Came from a Chinese Lab Takes On New Life in Wake of WHO Report," *NPR*, March 31, 2021, https://www.npr.org/2021/03/31/983156340/theory-that-covid-came-from-a-chinese-lab-takes-on-new-life-in-wake-of-who-repor.

92. Jeff Kao and Mia Shuang Li, "How China Built a Twitter Propaganda Machine Then Let It Loose on Coronavirus," *ProPublica*, March 26, 2020, https://www.propublica.org/article/how-china-built-a-twitter-propaganda-machine-then-let-it-loose-on-coronavirus.

93. Josh Taylor, "Twitter Deletes 170,000 Accounts Linked to China Influence Campaign," *Guardian*, June 11, 2020, https://www.theguardian.com/technology/2020/jun/12/twitter-deletes-170000-accounts-linked-to-china-influence-campaign.

94. Matt Schrader, "Analyzing China's Coronavirus Propaganda Messaging in Europe," *Alliance for Securing Democracy*, March 20, 2020, https://securingdemocracy.gmfus.org/analyzing-chinas-coronavirus-propaganda-messaging-in-europe/.

95. Ibid.

96. Morgan Ortagus, "Update on U.S. Withdrawal from the World Health Organization," *U.S. Department of State*, September 3, 2020, https://www.state.gov/update-on-u-s-withdrawal-from-the-world-hea

lth-organization/; Emily Rauhala and Yasmeen Abutaleb, "U.S. Says It Won't Join WHO-Linked Effort to Develop, Distribute Coronavirus Vaccine," *Washington Post*, September 1, 2020, https://www.washing tonpost.com/world/coronavirus-vaccine-trump/2020/09/01/b44b4 2be-e965-11ea-bf44-0d31c85838a5_story.html; "Coronavirus World Map: Tracking the Global Outbreak," *New York Times*, https://www.nyti mes.com/interactive/2020/world/coronavirus-maps.html.

97. Erika Kinetz, "Anatomy of a Conspiracy: With COVID, China Took Leading Role," *Associated Press*, February 21, 2021, https://apnews.com/ article/pandemics-beijing-only-on-ap-epidemics-media-122b73e13 4b780919cc1808f3f6f16e8.

98. I am indebted to Laura Rosenberger for this point.

99. Kristine Lee and Karina Barbesino, "Challenging China's Bid for App Dominance," *Center for a New American Security*, January 22, 2020, https://www.cnas.org/publications/commentary/challenging-chinas-bid-for-app-dominance.

100. Clint Watts, "Triad of Disinformation: How Russia, Iran, & China Ally in a Messaging War Against America," *Alliance for Securing Democracy*, May 15, 2020, https://securingdemocracy.gmfus.org/triad-of-disinfo rmation-how-russia-iran-china-ally-in-a-messaging-war-against-america/.

101. Edward Wong, Matthew Rosenberg, and Julian E. Barnes, "Chinese Agents Helped Spread Messages That Sowed Virus Panic in U.S., Officials Say," *New York Times*, April 22, 2020, https://www.nytimes. com/2020/04/22/us/politics/coronavirus-china-disinformation.html.

102. Ibid.

103. Jessica Brandt and Bret Schafer, "Five Things to Know About Beijing's Disinformation Approach," *Alliance for Securing Democracy*, March 30, 2020, https://securingdemocracy.gmfus.org/five-things-to-know-about-beijings-disinformation-approach/.

104. Joshua Kurlantzick, "China Thinks the Pandemic Will Make It the World's New Leader. It Won't," *Washington Post*, May 22, 2020, https:// www.washingtonpost.com/outlook/china-uses-the-pandemic-to-claim-global-leadership/2020/05/21/9b045692-9ab4-11ea-ac72-384 1fcc9b35f_story.html; Glenn Kessler, "Biden vs. Trump: The Ad Battle over China and the Coronavirus," *Washington Post*, May 15, 2020, https://www.washingtonpost.com/politics/2020/05/15/biden-versus-trump-ad-battle-over-china-coronavirus/.

105. William A. Galston, "A Momentous Shift in US Public Attitudes Toward China," *Brookings*, March 22, 2021, https://www.brookings.edu/blog/

order-from-chaos/2021/03/22/a-momentous-shift-in-us-public-attitu
des-toward-china/.

106. Ole Tangen Jr., "Is China Taking Advantage of COVID-19 to Pursue South China Sea Ambitions?," *Deutsche Welle*, May 26, 2020, https:// www.dw.com/en/is-china-taking-advantage-of-covid-19-to-pursue-south-china-sea-ambitions/a-53573918; Anna Fifield and Joanna Slater, "Far from Being Weakened by Coronavirus, China Pursues Sovereignty Claims on All Fronts," *Washington Post*, May 27, 2020, https://www.washingtonpost.com/world/asia_pacific/china-india-border-clashes-coronavirus/2020/05/27/a51545f6-9f14-11ea-be06-af5514ee0385_st ory.html.

107. Victor Mallet and Roula Khalaf, "FT Interview: Emmanuel Macron Says It Is Time to Think the Unthinkable," *Financial Times*, April 16, 2020, https://www.ft.com/content/3ea8d790-7fd1-11ea-8fdb-7ec06 edeef84.

108. Benedict Spence, "China Is Set to Reap the Whirlwind of Europe's Coronavirus Resentment," *Telegraph*, March 27, 2020, https://www.telegraph.co.uk/news/2020/03/27/china-set-reap-whirlwind-euro pes-coronavirus-resentment/; Mattia Ferraresi, "China Isn't Helping Italy. It's Waging Information Warfare," *Foreign Policy*, March 31, 2020, https://foreignpolicy.com/2020/03/31/china-isnt-helping-italy-its-waging-information-warfare/.

109. Zhiqun Zhu, "Interpreting China's 'Wolf-Warrior Diplomacy,'" *Diplomat*, May 15, 2020, https://thediplomat.com/2020/05/inter preting-chinas-wolf-warrior-diplomacy/; "China's 'Wolf Warrior' Diplomacy Gamble," *Economist*, May 28, 2020, https://www.econom ist.com/china/2020/05/28/chinas-wolf-warrior-diplomacy-gamble.

110. Peter Martin, *China's Civilian Army: The Making of Wolf Warrior Diplomacy* (Oxford: Oxford University Press, 2021), 218.

111. Ibid.

112. Ibid.

113. Ibid., 214.

114. Ibid., 212–15.

115. Ibid., 5.

116. "Chinese Government Official Slams Australia's Push for an Investigation into the Coronavirus Outbreak," *ABC News*, April 25, 2020, https:// www.abc.net.au/news/2020-04-26/coronavirus-china-slams-australia-over-independent-inquiry/12185988.

117. Ben Westcott, "Australia Angered China by Calling for a Coronavirus Investigation. Now Beijing Is Targeting Its Exports," *CNN*, May 27,

2020, https://www.cnn.com/2020/05/26/business/china-australia-coronavirus-trade-war-intl-hnk/index.html.

118. Yanzhong Huang, "China Could Pay if Nations Come to Believe the Virus Leaked from a Lab," *Washington Post*, June 4, 2021, https://www.washingtonpost.com/outlook/lab-leak-china-international-relations/2021/06/04/7e966eaa-c489-11eb-9a8d-f95d7724967c_story.html.

119. Silver et al., "Unfavorable Views of China Reach Historic Highs in Many Countries."

120. Peter Wang, "Amid Global Unpopularity, China Might Find Support Among Russians," *Chicago Council on Global Affairs*, March 17, 2021, https://www.thechicagocouncil.org/commentary-and-analysis/blogs/amid-global-unpopularity-china-might-find-support-among-russians.

121. Eva Dou, "China's Econoimc Growth Slows to 0.4%, Weakest in Two Years," *The Washington Post*, July 15, 2022, https://www.washingtonpost.com/world/2022/07/14/china-gdp-economy-covid-lockdown/.

122. Ties Dams, Xiaoxue Martin, and Vera Kranenburg, eds., "China's Soft Power in Europe: Falling on Hard Times," *European Think-Tank Network on China*, April 2021, 7, https://www.clingendael.org/sites/default/files/2021-04/Report_ETNC_Chinas_Soft_Power_in_Europe_Falling_on_Hard_Times_2021.pdf.

123. Ibid.; Richard Q. Turcsányi et al., "European Public Opinion on China in the Age of COVID-19: Differences and Common Ground Across the Continent," *CEIAS and Sinophone Borderlands*, November 2020, https://media.realinstitutoelcano.org/wp-content/uploads/2021/11/european-public-opinion-on-china-in-the-age-of-covid-19.pdf.

124. Turcsányi et al., "European Public Opinion on China in the Age of COVID-19."

125. Ibid.

126. Huang, "China Could Pay if Nations Come to Believe the Virus Leaked from a Lab."

127. Ibid.

128. Anne Gulland, "China Producing Millions of Doses but Questions over Vaccine Efficacy Remain," *Telegraph*, June 12, 2021, https://www.telegraph.co.uk/global-health/science-and-disease/china-producing-millions-doses-questions-vaccine-efficacy-remain/.

129. Adam Taylor, "Why the World's Most Vaccinated Country Is Seeing an Unprecedented Spike in Coronavirus Cases," *Washington Post*, May 6, 2021, https://www.washingtonpost.com/world/2021/05/06/seychelles-vaccines-covid-cases/.

130. Gulland, "China Producing Millions of Doses but Questions over Vaccine Efficacy Remain."

131. "Pfizer and BioNTech Conclude Phase 3 Study of COVID-19 Vaccine Candidate, Meeting All Primary Efficacy Endpoints," *Pfizer*, November 18, 2020, https://www.pfizer.com/news/press-release/press-release-detail/pfizer-and-biontech-conclude-phase-3-study-covid-19-vaccine.

132. Joe McDonald and Huizhong Wu, "Top Chinese Official Admits Vaccines Have Low Effectiveness," *Associated Press*, April 11, 2021, https://apnews.com/article/china-gao-fu-vaccines-offer-low-protection-coronavirus-675bcb6b5710c7329823148ffbff6ef9.

133. Gulland, "China Producing Millions of Doses but Questions over Vaccine Efficacy Remain."

134. Paul Schemm, "Third Dose of Sinopharm Coronavirus Vaccine Needed for Some in UAE After Low Immune Response," *Washington Post*, March 22, 2021, https://www.washingtonpost.com/world/middle_east/uae-sinopharm-third-dose/2021/03/21/588fcf0a-8a26-11eb-a33e-da28941cb9ac_story.html.

135. Ibid.

136. David Crawshaw and Alicia Chen, "'Heads Bashed Bloody': China's Xi Marks Communist Party Centenary with Strong Words for Adversaries," *Washington Post*, July 1, 2021, https://www.washingtonpost.com/world/asia_pacific/china-party-heads-bashed-xi/2021/07/01/277c8f0c-da3f-11eb-8c87-ad6f27918c78_story.html.

137. Brandt and Schafer, "Five Things to Know About Beijing's Disinformation Approach."

138. Custer et al., *Influencing the Narrative*, 42–44.

139. "Media," in *China's Influence & American Interests: Promoting Constructive Vigilance*, ed. Larry Diamond and Orville Schell (Stanford, CA: Hoover Institution Press, 2019), 100–19.

140. Kevin Roose, "How the Epoch Times Created a Giant Influence Machine," *New York Times*, October 24, 2020, https://www.nytimes.com/2020/10/24/technology/epoch-times-influence-falun-gong.html; Seth Hettena, "The Obscure Newspaper Fueling the Far-Right in Europe," *New Republic*, September 17, 2019, https://newrepublic.com/article/155076/obscure-newspaper-fueling-far-right-europe.

141. Ibid.

142. Sarah Cook, "Chinese Government Influence on the U.S. Media Landscape," Written Testimony Before the U.S.-China Economic and Security Review Commission, May 4, 2017, https://www.uscc.

gov/sites/default/files/Sarah%20Cook%20May%204th%202017%20U
SCC%20testimony.pdf.

143. New Tang Dynasty Television, "Response to the Notice of Proposed Rule Making: 'Promoting the Availability of Diverse and Independent Sources of Video Programming,'" *Federal Communications Commission*, December 19, 2016, https://ecfsapi.fcc.gov/file/1012763254871/ Comments_on_MBdocket16_41_by_NTDTV_Jan262017.pdf; Cook, "Chinese Government Influence on the U.S. Media Landscape."

144. "Media," in *China's Influence & American Interests*, 100–19.

145. Ibid.

146. "Detailed Languages Spoken at Home and Ability to Speak English for the Population 5 Years and Over: 2009–2013," *United States Census Bureau*, October 2015, https://www.census.gov/data/tables/2013/ demo/2009-2013-lang-tables.html; North Cooc and Genevieve Leung, "Who Are 'Chinese' Language Speakers in the United States? A Subgroup Analysis with Census Data," *AAPI Data*, October 2016, http://aapidata.com/blog/wp-content/uploads/2016/10/NORTH-COOC-2F2F-PAPER-2F2F-AAPI-Data-Challenge-Chinese-Diver sity_Cooc_Leung.pdf.

147. "Appendix 2: Chinese Influence Activities in Select Countries," in *China's Influence & American Interests: Promoting Constructive Vigilance*, ed. Larry Diamond and Orville Schell (Stanford, CA: Hoover Institution Press, 2019), 161–202.

148. "Hong Kong Media Fall to Pro-Chinese Owners," *Asia Sentinel*, April 22, 2021, https://www.asiasentinel.com/p/hong-kong-media-fall-to-pro-chinese; Tom Blackwell, "Inside Canada's Chinese-Language Media: 'Beijing Has Become the Mainstream,' Says Ex-Sing Tao Editor," *National Post*, December 3, 2020, https://nationalpost.com/news/can ada/inside-canadas-chinese-language-media-beijing-has-become-the-mainstream-says-ex-sing-tao-editor.

149. Blackwell, "Inside Canada's Chinese-Language Media."

150. Emily Feng, "China and the World: How Beijing Spreads the Message," *Financial Times*, July 12, 2018, https://www.ft.com/content/f5d00a86-3296-11e8-b5bf-23cb17fd1498.

151. Timothy McLaughlin, "How Milk Tea Became an Anti-China Symbol," *Atlantic*, October 13, 2020, https://www.theatlantic.com/international/ archive/2020/10/milk-tea-alliance-anti-china/616658/.

152. Jon Emont, "How China Persuaded One Muslim Nation to Keep Silent on Xinjiang Camps," *Wall Street Journal*, December 11, 2019, https://

www.wsj.com/articles/how-china-persuaded-one-muslim-nation-to-keep-silent-on-xinjiang-camps-11576090976.

153. Ibid.

154. Emont, "How China Persuaded One Muslim Nation to Keep Silent on Xinjiang Camps"; "Xinjiang: Large Numbers of New Detention Camps Uncovered in Report," *BBC*, September 24, 2020, https://www.bbc.com/news/world-asia-china-54277430.

155. Ibid.

156. I am indebted to Murray Hiebert for this point.

157. Custer et al., *Influencing the Narrative*, 24.

158. "The Covid-19 Story: Unmasking China's Global Strategy," *International Federation of Journalists*, May 12, 2021, https://www.ifj.org/fileadmin/user_upload/IFJ_-_The_Covid_Story_Report.pdf.

159. Ibid.

160. "Darkened Screen: Constraints on Foreign Journalists in China," *PEN America*, September 22, 2016, 33–37, https://pen.org/sites/default/files/PEN_foreign_journalists_report_FINAL_online%5B1%5D.pdf.

161. Ibid.

162. Henry Cooke and Laura Walters, "Chinese Version of NZ Herald Edited Translated Stories to Be More China-Friendly," *Stuff*, January 14, 2019, https://www.stuff.co.nz/national/politics/109908932/chinese-version-of-nz-herald-edited-translated-stories-to-be-more-chinafriendly.

163. David Folkenflik, "Bloomberg News Killed Investigation, Fired Reporter, Then Sought to Silence His Wife," *NPR*, April 14, 2020, https://www.npr.org/2020/04/14/828565428/bloomberg-news-killed-investigation-fired-reporter-then-sought-to-silence-his-wi.

164. Ibid.

165. Ibid.

166. Marc Tracy, Edward Wong, and Lara Jakes, "China Announces That It Will Expel American Journalists," *New York Times*, March 17, 2020, https://www.nytimes.com/2020/03/17/business/media/china-expels-american-journalists.html; Andrew Jacobs, "China Appears Set to Force Times Reporter to Leave," *New York Times*, January 27, 2014, https://www.nytimes.com/2014/01/28/world/asia/times-reporter-faces-expulsion-from-china.html.

167. Austin Ramzy and Chris Buckley, "'Absolutely No Mercy': Leaked Files Expose How China Organized Mass Detentions of Muslims," *New York Times*, November 16, 2019, https://www.nytimes.com/interactive/2019/11/16/world/asia/china-xinjiang-documents.html.

168. Michael Forsythe, "Wang Jianlin, a Billionaire at the Intersection of Business and Power in China," *New York Times*, April 28, 2015, https://www.nytimes.com/2015/04/29/world/asia/wang-jianlin-abillionaire-at-the-intersection-of-business-and-power-in-china.html.

169. Allison Prang, "Pulitzer Prizes Highlight Coverage Related to George Floyd Killing, Covid-19," *Wall Street Journal*, June 11, 2021, https://www.wsj.com/articles/pulitzer-prizes-highlight-coverage-related-to-george-floyd-killing-covid-19-11623436044; "China Expels Three Wall Street Journal Reporters," *Wall Street Journal*, February 19, 2020, https://www.wsj.com/articles/china-expels-three-wall-street-journal-reporters-11582100355.

170. See, for example, Simon Denyer, "China Detains Relatives of U.S. Reporters in Apparent Punishment for Xinjiang Coverage," *Washington Post*, February 28, 2018, https://www.washingtonpost.com/world/china-detains-relatives-of-us-reporters-in-apparent-punishment-for-xinjiang-coverage/2018/02/27/4e8d84ae-1b8c-11e8-8a2c-1a6665f59e95_story.html; and Jessica Blatt, "How China Uses Family Members to Pressure Uyghur Journalists," *Voice of America*, March 16, 2021, https://www.voanews.com/a/press-freedom_how-china-uses-family-members-pressure-uyghur-journalists/6203382.html.

171. See, for instance, Aynne Kokas, *Hollywood Made in China* (Oakland: University of California Press, 2017).

172. Bernard Weinraub, "Disney Will Defy China on Its Dalai Lama Film," *New York Times*, November 27, 1996, https://www.nytimes.com/1996/11/27/movies/disney-will-defy-china-on-its-dalai-lama-film.html.

173. Heinrich Harrer, the mountaineer played by Brad Pitt, was a prolific explorer of Tibet and was in Tibet during the 1950 invasion. Later in his life, it also was revealed that Harrer had a Nazi past. Douglas Martin, "Heinrich Harrer, 93, Explorer of Tibet, Dies," *New York Times*, January 10, 2006, https://www.nytimes.com/2006/01/10/obituaries/heinrich-harrer-93-explorer-of-tibet-dies.html.

174. Edward Wong, "'Doctor Strange' Writer Explains Casting of Tilda Swinton as Tibetan," *New York Times*, April 26, 2016, https://www.nytimes.com/2016/04/27/world/asia/china-doctor-strange-tibet.html.

175. Josh Horwitz, "A Major Hollywood Screenwriter Self-Censored Because He Was Worried About Angering China," *Quartz*, April 28, 2016, https://qz.com/672112/a-major-hollywood-screenwriter-self-censored-because-he-was-worried-about-angering-china/.

176. Ray Gustini, "'Red Dawn' Remake Digitally Removing Chinese Villains as We Speak," *Atlantic*, March 16, 2011, https://www.theatlan

tic.com/culture/archive/2011/03/chinese-didnt-even-mind-being-red-dawn-villains/348862; Amy Qin and Audrey Carlsen, "How China Is Rewriting Its Own Script," *New York Times*, November 18, 2018, https://www.nytimes.com/interactive/2018/11/18/world/asia/china-movies.html.

177. Shelby Rose and Jessie Yeung, "Tencent-Backed 'Top Gun' Cuts Taiwan Flag from Tom Cruise's Jacket," *CNN*, July 22, 2019, https://www.cnn.com/2019/07/22/media/top-gun-flags-intl-hnk/index.html.

178. "Razzies Awards: 'Fifty Shades of Grey,' 'Pixels' Among 'Worst Film' Nominees," *Reuters*, January 13, 2016, https://www.nbcnews.com/pop-culture/movies/razzies-awards-fifty-shades-grey-pixels-among-worst-film-nominees-n495586; Qin and Carlsen, "How China Is Rewriting Its Own Script."

179. Clare Baldwin and Kristina Cooke, "How Sony Sanitized Films to Please China's Censors," *Reuters*, July 24, 2015, https://news.yahoo.com/special-report-sony-sanitized-adam-sandler-movie-please-140607897--finance.html.

180. Bethany Allen-Ebrahimian, "China Is Censoring Hollywood's Imagination," *Axios*, September 1, 2020, https://www.axios.com/china-censor-hollywood-films-14d77229-b853-4e7a-8635-711913936 15d.html; "Brad Pitt Back in China Nearly 20 Years After Reported Ban over Tibet Film," *Associated Press*, November 14, 2016, https://www.thestar.com/news/world/2016/11/14/brad-pitt-back-in-china-nearly-20-years-after-reported-ban-over-tibet-film.html; Rudie Obias, "10 Movies That Were Banned in China," *Mental Floss*, July 14, 2016, https://www.mentalfloss.com/article/83136/10-movies-were-banned-china.

181. Shirley Li, "How Hollywood Sold Out to China," *Atlantic*, September 10, 2021, https://www.theatlantic.com/culture/archive/2021/09/how-hollywood-sold-out-to-china/620021/; Patrick Brzeski, "China, the World's Second-Largest Film Market, Moves Beyond Hollywood," *Hollywood Reporter*, October 7, 2020, https://www.hollywoodreporter.com/news/general-news/china-the-worlds-second-largest-film-market-moves-beyond-hollywood-4072560/.

182. Qin and Carlsen, "How China Is Rewriting Its Own Script."

183. Allen-Ebrahimian, "China Is Censoring Hollywood's Imagination."

184. "Made in Hollywood, Censored by Beijing: The U.S. Film Industry and Chinese Government Influence," *PEN America*, August 2020, https://pen.org/report/made-in-hollywood-censored-by-beijing/.

185. "Abominable: A DreamWorks Movie, a Map, and a Huge Regional Row," *BBC*, October 18, 2019, https://www.bbc.com/news/world-asia-50093028.

186. Andy Wong, "It's a Smash Hit! Chinese Return Big-Time to Movie Theaters," *Associated Press*, February 26, 2021, https://apnews.com/arti cle/movies-china-coronavirus-pandemic-beijing-e772c8fd5a83a573c 7f4749f69d49133/.

187. Frank Pallotta, "What if China No Longer Needs Hollywood? That's Bad News for the Film Industry," *CNN*, January 28, 2021, https://www.cnn.com/2021/01/28/media/china-box-office-coronavirus/index.html.

188. Ibid.

189. Josh Ye, "China's Video Games Industry Racked Up US$10.4bn in Sales in Third Quarter as Boom Continues Post-Pandemic," *South China Morning Post*, November 16, 2020, https://www.scmp.com/tech/gear/article/3110052/chinas-video-games-industry-racked-us104bn-sales-third-quarter-boom.

190. Christopher Walker and Jessica Ludwig, *A Full-Spectrum Response to Sharp Power: The Vulnerabilities and Strengths of Open Societies* (Washington, DC: National Endowment for Democracy, 2021), 14.

191. Jonathan Easton, "Star Times Picks Up FA Cup in Sub-Saharan Africa," *Digital TV Europe*, January 3, 2020, https://www.digitaltveurope.com/2020/01/03/startimes-picks-up-fa-cup-in-sub-saharan-africa/.

192. Cook, "Beijing's Global Megaphone," 21.

193. Abu-Bakarr Jalloh, "China's Contentious Stake in Zambia's Broadcast Media," *Deutsche Welle*, July 5, 2019, https://www.dw.com/en/chinas-contentious-stake-in-zambias-broadcast-media/a-49492207.

194. Ibid.

195. Ray Mwareya, "Zimbabwe Drifts Toward Online Darkness," *Coda Story*, February 26, 2019, https://www.codastory.com/authoritarian-tech/zimbabwe-drifts-towards-online-darkness/.

196. "Thailand Tilts Towards Chinese-Style Internet Controls," *Bloomberg News,* April 15, 2019, https://www.bangkokpost.com/tech/1661912/thailand-tilts-towards-chinese-style-internet-controls.

197. Justin Sherman, "Vietnam's Internet Control: Following in China's Footsteps?," *Diplomat*, December 11, 2019, https://thediplomat.com/2019/12/vietnams-internet-control-following-in-chinas-footsteps/.

198. Rory Wallace, "Myanmar Junta Builds 'Walled Garden' of Internet Services," *Nikkei Asia*, April 28, 2021, https://asia.nikkei.com/Spotli

ght/Myanmar-Crisis/Myanmar-junta-builds-walled-garden-of-inter net-services.

199. "Cambodia's New China-Style Internet Gateway Decried as Repression Tool," *Reuters*, February 18, 2021, https://www.reuters.com/article/us-cambodia-internet/cambodias-new-china-style-internet-gateway-decr ied-as-repression-tool-idUSKBN2AI140.

200. Sherman, "Vietnam's Internet Control."

201. Josh Chin, "The Internet, Divided Between the U.S. and China, Has Become a Battleground," *Wall Street Journal*, February 9, 2019, https://www.wsj.com/articles/the-internet-divided-between-the-u-s-and-china-has-become-a-battleground-11549688420.

202. David Gilbert, "Zimbabwe Is Trying to Build a China Style Surveillance State," *Vice*, December 1, 2019, https://www.vice.com/en/article/59n 753/zimbabwe-is-trying-to-build-a-china-style-surveillance-state.

203. Aaron Maasho, "Ethiopia Signs $800 Million Mobile Network Deal with China's ZTE," *Reuters*, August 18, 2013, https://www.reuters. com/article/us-ethiopia-china-telecom/ethiopia-signs-800-million-mobile-network-deal-with-chinas-zte-idUSBRE97H0AZ20130818; Nick Bailey, "East African States Adopt China's Playbook on Internet Censorship," *Freedom House*, October 24, 2017, https://freedomhouse. org/article/east-african-states-adopt-chinas-playbook-internet-cen sorship.

204. Bailey, "East African States Adopt China's Playbook on Internet Censorship."

205. Adrian Shahbaz, Allie Funk, and Andrea Hackl, *User Privacy or Cyber Sovereignty? Assessing the Human Rights Implications of Data Localization* (Washington, DC: Freedom House, July 2020), https://freedomho use.org/sites/default/files/2020-07/FINAL_Data_Localization_hu man_rights_07232020.pdf; Joey Shea, "Global Tech and Domestic Tactics: Egypt's Multifaceted Regime of Information Controls," *Tahrir Institute for Middle East Policy*, January 31, 2020, https://timep.org/com mentary/analysis/global-tech-and-domestic-tactics-egypts-multiface ted-regime-of-information-controls/.

206. Shea, "Global Tech and Domestic Tactics."

207. "Tajikistan Turns to Chinese Model of Large-Scale Internet Censorship," *Reporters Without Borders*, November 15, 2018, https://rsf.org/en/news/ tajikistan-turns-chinese-model-large-scale-internet-censorship.

208. In 2018, for instance, China, according to Freedom House, "was once again the worst abuser of internet freedom," making its internet less free than Russia's. See Adrian Shahbaz, "Freedom on the Net 2018: The Rise

of Digital Authoritarianism," *Freedom House*, October 2018, https://freedomhouse.org/sites/default/files/2020-02/10192018_FOTN_2018_Final_Booklet.pdf.

209. Mary Ilyushina, Nathan Hodge, and Hadas Gold, "Russa Rolls Out Its 'Sovereign Internet.' Is It Building a Digital Iron Curtain?," *CNN Business*, November 1, 2019, https://www.cnn.com/2019/11/01/tech/russia-internet-law/index.html.

210. Ibid.

211. "Chinese, Russian Cyber Watchdogs Meet in Moscow," *Reuters*, July 17, 2019, https://www.reuters.com/article/russia-china-internet/chinese-russian-cyber-watchdogs-meet-in-moscow-idUSL8N24I4RF.

212. Ibid.

213. Adam Segal, "When China Rules the Web," *Foreign Affairs* 97, no. 5 (September/October 2018), https://www.foreignaffairs.com/articles/china/2018-08-13/when-china-rules-web.

214. Eduard Saakashvili, "The Global Rise of Internet Sovereignty," *Coda Story*, March 21, 2019, https://www.codastory.com/authoritarian-tech/global-rise-internet-sovereignty/.

215. "How the Pandemic Strengthened the Chinese Communist Party," *Economist*, December 30, 2020, https://www.economist.com/china/2020/12/30/how-the-pandemic-strengthened-the-chinese-communist-party.

216. Iginio Gagliardone, *China, Africa and the Future of the Internet* (London: Zed Books, 2019), 125.

217. Ibid.

218. Segal, "When China Rules the Web."

219. Nadezhda Tsydenova and Tom Balmforth, "Russia and China to Sign Treaty on Combating Illegal Online Content," *Reuters*, October 8, 2019, https://www.reuters.com/article/us-russia-china-internet/russia-and-china-to-sign-treaty-on-combating-illegal-online-content-idUSKBN1WN1E7.

220. Franz-Stefan Gady, "The Wuzhen Summit and the Battle over Internet Governance," *Diplomat*, January 14, 2016, https://thediplomat.com/2016/01/the-wuzhen-summit-and-the-battle-over-internet-governance/.

221. Ibid.

222. Elliott Zaagman, "Cyber Sovereignty and the PRC's Vision for Global Internet Governance," *China Brief*, June 5, 2018, https://jamestown.org/program/cyber-sovereignty-and-the-prcs-vision-for-global-internet-governance/.

223. Justin Sherman, "How Much Cyber Sovereignty Is Too Much Cyber Sovereignty?," *Net Politics*, October 30, 2019, https://www.cfr.org/blog/how-much-cyber-sovereignty-too-much-cyber-sovereignty.

224. Courtney J. Fung and Shing-Hon Lam, "China Already Leads Four of Fifteen UN Specialized Agencies, and Is Aiming for a Fifth," *Washington Post,* March 3, 2020, https://www.washingtonpost.com/politics/2020/03/03/china-already-leads-4-15-un-specialized-agencies-is-aiming-5th/.

225. Segal, "When China Rules the Web."

226. Ibid.

227. Ibid.

228. Anna Gross and Madhumita Murgia, "China and Huawei Propose Reinvention of the Internet," *Financial Times*, March 27, 2020, https://www.ft.com/content/c78be2cf-a1a1-40b1-8ab7-904d7095e0f2.

229. Ibid.

230. Hanaa' Tameez, "Here's How COVID-19 Has Changed Media for Publishers and Consumers," *NiemanLab*, October 7, 2020, https://www.niemanlab.org/2020/10/heres-how-covid-19-has-changed-media-for-publishers-and-consumers/; "The Newspaper Industry Is Taking a Battering," *Economist,* April 18, 2020, https://www.economist.com/britain/2020/04/18/the-newspaper-industry-is-taking-a-battering.

231. Bley, "Charting China, the (Not Always) Super Power."

232. "The China Story: Reshaping the World's Media," *International Federation of Journalists*, June 25, 2020, https://issuu.com/ifjasiapacific/docs/2020_ifj_report_-_the_china_story.

233. Ibid.

234. Ibid.

235. Ibid.

CHAPTER 12

1. Some portions of this chapter were included in a CFR (Council on Foreign Relations) Discussion Paper written and published by Kurlantzick in May 2022. "In the UN, China Uses Threats and Cajolery to Promote Its Worldview," *Economist*, December 7, 2019, https://www.economist.com/china/2019/12/07/in-the-un-china-uses-threats-and-cajolery-to-promote-its-worldview.

2. Lachlan Markey, "China Increases Foreign Influence Efforts on U.S. by 500 percent," *Axios*, May 10, 2021, https://www.axios.com/2021/05/11/china-foreign-influence-spending.

3. "Fact Sheet: CHIPS and Science Bill," White House press statement, August 9, 2022, https://www.whitehouse.gov/briefing-room/stateme nts-releases/2022/08/09/fact-sheet-chips-and-science-act-will-lower-costs-create-jobs-strengthen-supply-chains-and-counter-china/.

4. "EU-China Relations—Towards a Fair and Reciprocal Partnership," *EPP Group*, March 10, 2021, https://www.eppgroup.eu/newsroom/ publications/eu-china-relations-towards-a-fair-and-reciprocal-partners hip.

5. Ibid.

6. Maria Repnikova, "Does China's Propaganda Work?," *New York Times*, April 16, 2020, https://www.nytimes.com/2020/04/16/opinion/ china-coronavirus-propaganda.html.

7. "The Covid-19 Story: Unmasking China's Global Strategy," *International Federation of Journalists*, May 12, 2021, https://www.ifj.org/fileadmin/ user_upload/IFJ_-_The_Covid_Story_Report.pdf.

8. For instance, Christopher Walker and Jessica Ludwig, *A Full-Spectrum Response to Sharp Power: The Vulnerabilities and Strengths of Open Societies* (Washington, DC: National Endowment for Democracy, 2021), 4.

9. For more, see Bethany Allen-Ebrahimian, "Senate Committee Prepares to Vote on Sweeping Bill to Counter China," *Axios*, April 13, 2021, https://www.axios.com/senate-china-bill-474f96f1-467b-4c02-ab6e-1084ca73b158.html.

10. See, for example, "National Defense Authorization Act for Fiscal Year 2020: Conference Report," Section 5323 on the "Encouragement of Cooperative Actions to Detect and Counter Foreign Influence Operations," U.S. House of Representatives, https://docs.house.gov/ billsthisweek/20191209/CRPT-116hrpt333.pdf. Quoted in Steven Bradley, "Securing the United States from Online Disinformation—A Whole-of-Society Approach," *Carnegie Endowment for International Peace*, August 24, 2020, https://carnegieendowment.org/2020/08/24/ securing-united-states-from-online-disinformation-whole-of-society-approach-pub-82549.

11. I am indebted to Sarah Cook and her work on these issues for this point.

12. The Center for Naval Analyses (CNA) has come to similar conclusions from its extensive research on China's information activities, in a series of reports collated under the project headline "China's Efforts to Shape the Information Environment in the Mekong Region" and located at https://www.cna.org/centers/cna/cip/information-environment.

13. "The Covid-19 Story."

14. Vanessa Molter and Renée DiResta, "Pandemics & Propaganda: How Chinese State Media Creates and Propagates CCP Coronavirus Narratives," *HKS Misinformation Review*, June 8, 2020, https://misinf oreview.hks.harvard.edu/article/pandemics-propaganda-how-chinese-state-media-creates-and-propagates-ccp-coronavirus-narratives/.

15. Ibid.

16. Ibid.

17. Elizabeth Bachman, *Black and White and Red All Over: China's Improving Foreign-Directed Media* (Arlington, VA: CNA, 2020), 64.

18. Brenda Goh and Michael Martina, "China to Recalibrate Belt and Road, Defend Scheme Against Criticism," *Reuters*, April 23, 2019, https://www.reuters.com/article/us-china-silkroad-forum/china-to-recalibrate-belt-and-road-defend-scheme-against-criticism-idUSKC N1S00AZ.

19. Anna Gelpern et al., "How China Lends: A Rare Look into 100 Debt Contracts with Foreign Governments," AidData report, March 31, 2021, https://www.aiddata.org/publications/how-china-lends.

20. Ibid.

21. Nadège Rolland, "Beijing's Response to the Belt and Road Initiative's 'Pushback': A Story of Assessment and Adaptation," *Asian Affairs* 50, no. 2 (2019): 216–35, https://www.tandfonline.com/doi/full/10.1080/03068374.2019.1602385.

22. Adam Taylor, "Xi's Call for a 'Lovable' China May Not Tame the Wolf Warriors," *Washington Post*, June 3, 2021, https://www.washingtonpost.com/world/2021/06/03/china-wolf-warrior-reset/.

23. Ibid.

24. Matthew Lee and Mark Thiessen, "US, China Spar in First Face-to-Face Meeting Under Biden," *Associated Press*, March 18, 2021, https://apnews.com/article/donald-trump-alaska-antony-blinken-yang-jie chi-wang-yi-fc23cd2b23332fa8dd2d781bd3f7c178.

25. Eva O'Dea, "Chinese Language Media in Australia Increasingly Dominated by the PRC," *Interpreter*, January 18, 2016, https://www.lowyinstitute.org/the-interpreter/chinese-language-media-australia-increasingly-dominated-prc.

26. He Qinglian, *Red Infiltration: The Reality About China's Global Expansion in International Media* (Taiwan: Gusa Publishing, 2019).

27. For more recommendations on this topic, see Jonas Parello-Plesner, "The Chinese Communist Party's Foreign Interference Operations: How the U.S. and Other Democracies Should Respond," *Hudson Institute*, June 20, 2018, 48, https://www.hudson.org/research/14409-the-chin

ese-communist-party-s-foreign-interference-operations-how-the-u-s-and-other-democracies-should-respond.

28. Larry Diamond and Orville Schell, eds., *China's Influence & American Interests: Promoting Constructive Vigilance* (Stanford, CA: Hoover Institution Press, 2019), 120, https://www.hoover.org/research/chinas-influence-american-interests-promoting-constructive-vigilance.

29. Christian C. Davis, et al., "Is Chinese Investment in the U.S. Film and Entertainment Industry the Next Area of CFIUS Scrutiny?," *AG Deal Diary*, September 29, 2016, https://www.akingump.com/en/experie nce/practices/corporate/ag-deal-diary/is-chinese-investment-in-the-u-s-film-and-entertainment-industry-2.html.

30. Stuart Lau and Jakob HankeVela, "EU Deal Cements China's Advantage in Media War," *Politico*, March 13, 2021, https://www.politico.eu/arti cle/eu-trade-deal-china-media-war-industry-softpower/.

31. Sarah Cook, "China's Global Media Footprint: Democratic Responses to Expanding Authoritarian Influence," *National Endowment for Democracy*, February 2021, 10–11, https://www.ned.org/wp-content/uploads/ 2021/02/Chinas-Global-Media-Footprint-Democratic-Responses-to-Expanding-Authoritarian-Influence-Cook-Feb-2021.pdf.

32. "Reversing the Tide: Toward a New U.S. Strategy to Support Democracy and Counter Authoritarianism," *Freedom House, CSIS, and the McCain Institute*, April 2021, 21, https://freedomhouse.org/democr acy-task-force/special-report/2021/reversing-the-tide.

33. Cook, "China's Global Media Footprint," 10–11.

34. "EU-China Relations."

35. Sarah Cook, "Beijing's Global Megaphone: The Expansion of Chinese Communist Party Media Influence Since 2017," *Freedom House*, January 2020, https://freedomhouse.org/report/special-reports/beijings-glo bal-megaphone-china-communist-party-media-influence-abroad.

36. Cook, "China's Global Media Footprint," 10–11.

37. Jessica Chen Weiss, "Does China Actively Promote Its Way of Governing—and Do Other Countries Listen?," *Washington Post*, July 14, 2021, https://www.washingtonpost.com/politics/2021/07/14/does-china-actively-promote-its-way-governing-do-other-countries-listen/.

38. Cook, "Beijing's Global Megaphone."

39. Ibid.

40. Christopher Wray, "The Threat Posed by the Chinese Government and the Chinese Communist Party to the Economic and National Security of the United States," Remarks to Hudson Institute, July 7, 2020, https://www.fbi.gov/news/speeches/the-threat-posed-by-the-chin

ese-government-and-the-chinese-communist-party-to-the-econo
mic-and-national-security-of-the-united-states.

41. Ibid.

42. Steve Lohr, "U.S. Moves to Ban Huawei from Government Contracts,"
    New York Times, August 7, 2019, https://www.nytimes.com/2019/08/
    07/business/huawei-us-ban.html.

43. Adam Satariano, Stephen Castle, and David E. Sanger, "U.K. Bars
    Huawei for 5G as Tech Battle Between China and the West Escalates,"
    New York Times, July 14, 2020, https://www.nytimes.com/2020/07/14/
    business/huawei-uk-5g.html.

44. Cheng Ting-Fang and Lauly Li, "Huawei Enlists Army of European
    Talent for 'Battle' with US," *Nikkei Asia*, July 2, 2021, https://asia.nik
    kei.com/Business/Business-Spotlight/Huawei-enlists-army-of-Europ
    ean-talent-for-battle-with-US.

45. Ibid.

46. Ibid.

47. Makena Kelly, "Biden Revokes and Replaces Trump Orders Banning
    TikTok and WeChat," *Verge*, June 9, 2021, https://www.theverge.com/
    2021/6/9/22525953/biden-tiktok-wechat-trump-bans-revoked-alipay.

48. Philip Mai, "Trump's Attempts to Ban TikTok and Other Chinese Tech
    Undermine Global Democracy," *Conversation*, August 11, 2020, https://
    theconversation.com/trumps-attempts-to-ban-tiktok-and-other-chin
    ese-tech-undermine-global-democracy-144144.

49. Maria Abi-Habib, "India Bans Nearly 60 Chinese Apps, Including
    TikTok and WeChat," *New York Times*, June 29, 2020, https://www.nyti
    mes.com/2020/06/29/world/asia/tik-tok-banned-india-china.html;
    Manish Singh, "India Bans TikTok, Dozens of Other Chinese Apps,"
    TechCrunch, June 29, 2020, https://techcrunch.com/2020/06/29/india-
    bans-tiktok-dozens-of-other-chinese-apps/.

50. "The New Big Brother: China and Digital Authoritarianism,"
    Democratic Staff Report Prepared for the Use of the Committee on
    Foreign Relations, United States Senate, July 21, 2020, 28, https://
    www.foreign.senate.gov/imo/media/doc/2020%20SFRC%20Minor
    ity%20Staff%20Report%20-%20The%20New%20Big%20Brother%20-
    %20China%20and%20Digital%20Authoritarianism.pdf.

51. Ting-Fang and Li, "Huawei Enlists Army of European Talent for 'Battle'
    with US."

52. Andrea Kendall-Taylor, "Mendacious Mixture: The Growing
    Convergence of Russian and Chinese Information Operations," in
    Dean Jackson, ed., "COVID-19 and the Information Space: Boosting

the Democratic Response," *National Endowment for Democracy*, January 2021, 23, https://www.ned.org/wp-content/uploads/2021/01/Global-Insights-COVID-19-Information-Space-Boosting-Democratic-Respo nse-1.pdf.

53. Ibid.

54. "Freedom on the Net 2018: The Rise of Digital Authoritarianism," *Freedom House*, October 2018, 10–11, https://freedomhouse.org/sites/default/files/FOTN_2018_Final.pdf.

55. Laurens Cerulus and Mark Scott, "Emmanuel Macron's 'Arms Control' Deal for Cyber Warfare," *Politico*, November 12, 2018, https://www.polit ico.eu/article/macron-unites-europe-business-to-fight-cyber-foes/.

56. "Freedom on the Net 2019: The Crisis of Social Media," *Freedom House*, November 2019, https://www.freedomonthenet.org/sites/default/files/2019-11/11042019_Report_FH_FOTN_2019_final_Public_D ownload.pdf.

57. Ibid.

58. Author interviews with Singaporean officials, May 2019; Kristine Lee and Karina Barbesino, "Challenging China's Bid for App Dominance," *Center for a New American Security*, January 22, 2020, https://www.cnas.org/publications/commentary/challenging-chinas-bid-for-app-dominance; Kara Frederick, "The New War of Ideas," *Center for a New American Security*, June 3, 2019, https://www.cnas.org/publications/reports/the-new-war-of-ideas.

59. I am indebted to the excellent recommendations in the Center for a New American Security report "Challenging China's Bid for App Dominance" for constructive ideas on expanding the knowledge base about Chinese disinformation, although I had discussed such pressure on social media companies with acquaintances in multiple governments before reading the report. See Lee and Barbesino, "Challenging China's Bid for App Dominance."

60. Michael Kan, "Twitter Bans State-Sponsored Media Ads over Hong Kong Propaganda," *PC Mag*, August 19, 2019, https://www.pcmag.com/news/twitter-bans-state-sponsored-media-ads-over-hong-kong-propaganda.

61. Kate Conger, "Twitter Will Ban All Political Ads, C.E.O. Jack Dorsey Says," *New York Times*, October 30, 2019, https://www.nytimes.com/2019/10/30/technology/twitter-political-ads-ban.html; Lauren Feiner, "Twitter to Flag Abusive Tweets by World Leaders in Move That Could Impact Trump," *CNBC*, June 27, 2019, https://www.cnbc.com/2019/06/27/twitter-says-it-will-start-labeling-tweets-from-influential-gov

ernment-officials-who-break-its-rules.html; Bethany Dawson, "More Than a Third of Trump's Tweets Have Been Flagged for Disinformation Since Election Day," *Independent*, November 7, 2020, https://www.inde pendent.co.uk/news/world/americas/us-election-2020/trump-tweet-misinformation-twitter-b1672933.html.

62. See, for example, Twitter accounts belonging to *Xinhua News* (@ XHNews), *China Daily* (@ChinaDaily), the *People's Daily* (@PDChina), *Global Times* (@globaltimesnews), RT (RT_com), TASS (@tassagency_ en), and Sputnik (@SputnikInt), as accessed on November 22, 2021.

63. Sara Fischer, "Facebook to Block Ads from State-Controlled Media Entities in the U.S.," *Axios*, June 4, 2020, https://www.axios.com/faceb ook-advertising-state-media-c8ab022b-c256-4523-8c9b-196fd24ce 452.html.

64. Ibid.

65. Eliza Mackintosh, "Finland Is Winning the War on Fake News. What It's Learned May Be Crucial to Western Democracy," *CNN*, May 2019, https://edition.cnn.com/interactive/2019/05/europe/finland-fake-news-intl/.

66. University of Turku, "Finnish School Students Outperform U.S. Students on 'Fake News' Digital Literacy Tasks," *ScienceDaily*, May 2, 2019, https://www.sciencedaily.com/releases/2019/05/190502104 824.htm.

67. Daniel Kliman et al., "Dangerous Synergies: Countering Chinese and Russian Digital Influence Operations," *Center for a New American Security*, May 7, 2020, 2, https://www.cnas.org/publications/reports/dangerous-synergies; Aaron Huang, "Chinese Disinformation Is Ascendant. Taiwan Shows How We Can Defeat It," *Washington Post*, August 10, 2020, https://www.washingtonpost.com/opinions/2020/08/10/chinese-dis information-is-ascendant-taiwan-shows-how-we-can-defeat-it/.

68. Huang, "Chinese Disinformation Is Ascendant."

69. Natasha Lomas, "TikTok Joins the EU's Code of Practice on Disinformation," *TechCrunch*, June 22, 2020, https://techcrunch. com/2020/06/22/tiktok-joins-the-eus-code-of-practice-on-disinfo rmation/.

70. Zak Doffman, "TikTok 'Is Getting Facial Recognition' for China, Trump Official Warns Americans," *Forbes*, July 15, 2020, https://www. forbes.com/sites/zakdoffman/2020/07/15/tiktok-trump-warning-fac ial-recognition-data-sends-china-ban/?sh=2b7b53a92dea.

71. Ibid.

72. Aynne Kokas, "China Already Has Your Data. Trump's TikTok and WeChat Bans Can't Stop That," *Washington Post*, August 11, 2020, https://www.washingtonpost.com/outlook/2020/08/11/tiktok-wechat-bans-ineffective/.

73. Mai, "Trump's Attempts to Ban TikTok and Other Chinese Tech Undermine Global Democracy."

74. Kokas, "China Already Has Your Data."

75. Shelly Banjo, Kartikay Mehrotra, and William Turton, "TikTok's Huge Data Harvesting Prompts U.S. Security Concerns," *Bloomberg*, July 15, 2020, https://www.bloomberg.com/news/articles/2020-07-14/tiktok-s-massive-data-harvesting-prompts-u-s-security-concerns.

76. "National Security Legislation Amendment (Espionage and Foreign Interference) Act 2018," Government of Australia, No. 67, 2018, https://www.legislation.gov.au/Details/C2018A00067.

77. "National Security Legislation Amendment (Espionage and Foreign Interference) Bill 2019," Parliament of Australia, https://parlinfo.aph.gov.au/parlInfo/search/display/display.w3p;query=Id:%22legislation/billhome/r6022%22; "Foreign Influence Transparency Scheme Bill 2018," Parliament of Australia, https://parlinfo.aph.gov.au/parlInfo/search/display/display.w3p;query=Id:%22legislation/billhome/r6018%22; "Electoral Legislation Amendment (Electoral Funding and Disclosure Reform) Bill 2018," Parliament of Australia, https://www.aph.gov.au/Parliamentary_Business/Bills_Legislation/Bills_Search_Results/Result?bId=s1117; Evelyn Douek, "What's in Australia's New Laws on Foreign Interference in Domestic Politics," *Lawfare*, July 11, 2018, https://www.lawfareblog.com/whats-australias-new-laws-foreign-interference-domestic-politics.

78. Douek, "What's in Australia's New Laws on Foreign Interference in Domestic Politics"; Damien Cave and Jacqueline Williams, "Australian Law Targets Foreign Interference. China Is Not Pleased," *New York Times*, June 28, 2018, https://www.nytimes.com/2018/06/28/world/australia/australia-security-laws-foreign-interference.html.

79. I am indebted to Christopher Walker for discussions about this point.

80. For more on this point, see Walker and Ludwig, *A Full-Spectrum Response to Sharp Power*.

81. These recommendations build on an excellent set given in Diamond and Schell, "Chinese Influence and American Interests."

82. Republican Study Committee's Task Force on National Security and Foreign Affairs, "The RSC National Security Strategy: Strengthening America & Countering Global Threats," House Republican Study

Committee, June 2020, https://rsc-johnson.house.gov/sites/repub
licanstudycommittee.house.gov/files/%5BFINAL%5D%20NSTF%20
Report.pdf. However, Democratic leaders have made similar points
about China.

83. See, for example, "Foreign Authors Warned About Book Censorship
in China," *Guardian*, May 20, 2015, https://www.theguardian.com/
world/2015/may/21/foreign-authors-warned-about-book-censors
hip-in-china.

84. Naima Green-Riley, "The State Department Labeled China's Confucius
Programs a Bad Influence on U.S. Students. What's the Story?,"
Washington Post, August 25, 2020, https://www.washingtonpost.com/
politics/2020/08/24/state-department-labeled-chinas-confucius-progr
ams-bad-influence-us-students-whats-story/.

85. Alex Joske, "The Party Speaks for You," *Australian Strategic Policy Institute*,
June 9, 2020, https://www.aspi.org.au/report/party-speaks-you.

86. Laura Krantz, "Seth Moulton Rips Chinese Institute, Wants It Off
College Campuses," *Boston Globe*, March 9, 2018, https://www3.bost
onglobe.com/metro/2018/03/09/moulton-wants-local-colleges-cut-
ties-with-chinese-institute/2l5Y9Oa1WgG3SuapqGCaNP/story.
html?arc404=true.

87. "'Confucius Institute U.S. Center' Designation as a Foreign Mission,"
United States Department of State, August 13, 2020, https://2017-2021.
state.gov/confucius-institute-u-s-center-designation-as-a-foreign-miss
ion/index.html.

88. See, for example, "The White House Kicks Out Journalists Working for
China's State Media," *Economist*, March 7, 2020, https://www.econom
ist.com/united-states/2020/03/07/the-white-house-kicks-out-jour
nalists-working-for-chinas-state-media; Yelena Dzhanova, "White
House Places Cap on Chinese State Media Employees in US Following
Expulsion of WSJ Reporters," *CNBC*, March 2, 2020, https://www.
cnbc.com/2020/03/02/white-house-reduces-chinese-state-owned-
media-personnel-in-us.html.

89. Ben Smith, "The U.S. Tried to Teach China a Lesson About the Media. It
Backfired," *New York Times*, April 19, 2020, https://www.nytimes.com/
2020/04/19/business/media/coronavirus-us-china-journalists.html.

90. Edward Wong, "China Freezes Credentials for Journalists at U.S.
Outlets, Hinting at Expulsions," *New York Times*, September 6, 2020,
https://www.nytimes.com/2020/09/06/us/politics/china-us-journali
sts-visas-expulsions.html.

91. Smith, "The U.S. Tried to Teach China a Lesson About the Media."

92. Ibid.

93. John Pomfret, "To Cool Off U.S.-China Tensions, Let's Start with a Truce on Media Access," *Washington Post*, July 10, 2020, https://www.washingtonpost.com/opinions/2020/07/10/cool-off-us-china-tensions-lets-start-with-truce-media-access/.

94. See, for example, Laura Silver, Kat Devlin, and Christine Huang, "Unfavorable Views of China Reach Historic Highs in Many Countries," *Pew Research Center*, October 6, 2020, https://www.pewresearch.org/global/2020/10/06/unfavorable-views-of-china-reach-historic-highs-in-many-countries/.

95. Laura He, "China's Economy Just Shrank for the First Time in Decades. It Could Still Eke Out Growth This Year," *CNN Business*, April 17, 2020, https://www.cnn.com/2020/04/16/economy/china-economy-gdp/index.html.

96. Keith Bradsher, "With COVID-19 Under Control, China's Economy Surges Ahead," *New York Times*, October 18, 2020, https://www.nytimes.com/2020/10/18/business/china-economy-covid.html.

97. Jude Blanchette, "Xi's Gamble: The Race to Consolidate Power and Stave Off Disaster," *Foreign Affairs*, July/August 2021, https://www.foreignaffairs.com/articles/china/2021-06-22/xis-gamble. See also Yuen Yuen Ang, "The Robber Barons of Beijing: Can China Survive Its Gilded Age?," *Foreign Affairs*, July/August 2021, https://www.foreignaffairs.com/articles/asia/2021-06-22/robber-barons-beijing.

98. Elizabeth Economy, "China's Inconvenient Truth: Official Triumphalism Conceals Societal Fragmentation," *Foreign Affairs*, May 28, 2021, https://www.foreignaffairs.com/articles/china/2021-05-28/chinas-inconvenient-truth.

99. Blanchette, "Xi's Gamble."

100. Ibid.

101. Economy, "China's Inconvenient Truth."

102. Ibid.

103. See, for example, "NextGenerationEU: European Commission Disburses €289 Million in Pre-Financing to Lithuania," European Commission, August 17, 2021, https://ec.europa.eu/commission/presscorner/detail/en/ip_21_4224. Part of this section adapted from a forthcoming CFR Discussion Paper by Joshua Kurlantzick.

104. Nithin Coca, "Japan Shifts Toward Clean Energy in Southeast Asia as China Stokes Up Coal," *Radio Free Asia*, June 24, 2021, https://www.rfa.org/english/news/vietnam/japan-china-energy-06242021091320.html.

105. "Biden to Announce up to $102 Mln in Funding for U.S.-ASEAN partnership," *Reuters*, October 26, 2021, https://www.reuters.com/world/biden-announce-up-102-mln-funding-us-asean-partnership-2021-10-26/.

106. For more on this point, see Howard W. French, "Leave Infrastructure to China and Compete Where the West Has More to Offer," *World Politics Review*, June 16, 2021, https://www.worldpoliticsreview.com/articles/29735/in-china-us-competition-focus-on-america-s-strengths.

107. Kathryn Watson, "Biden and G-7 Leaders to Commit to Donating 1 Billion COVID-19 Vaccines," *CBS News*, June 13, 2021, https://www.cbsnews.com/news/covid-vaccine-biden-g7-leaders-billion-doses/.

108. Elizabeth Piper and Kate Holton, "'We Need More': UN Joins Criticism of G7 Vaccine Pledge," *Reuters*, June 12, 2021, https://www.reuters.com/business/healthcare-pharmaceuticals/g7-donate-1-billion-covid-19-vaccine-doses-poorer-countries-2021-06-10/.

109. Ibid.

110. I am indebted to James Lindsay for this point.

111. Adapted from a forthcoming CFR Discussion Paper by Joshua Kurlantzick.

112. See, for example, Donald Moynihan and Gregory Porumbescu, "Trump's 'Chinese Virus' Slur Makes Some People Blame Chinese Americans. But Others Blame Trump," *Washington Post*, September 16, 2020, https://www.washingtonpost.com/politics/2020/09/16/trumps-chinese-virus-slur-makes-some-people-blame-chinese-americans-others-blame-trump/.

113. "Reports of Anti-Asian Assaults, Harassment and Hate Crimes Rise as Coronavirus Spreads," *ADL*, June 18, 2020, https://www.adl.org/blog/reports-of-anti-asian-assaults-harassment-and-hate-crimes-rise-as-coronavirus-spreads.

114. Ben Kesling and Jon Emont, "U.S. Goes on the Offensive Against China's Empire-Building Funding Plan," *Wall Street Journal*, April 9, 2019, https://www.wsj.com/articles/u-s-goes-on-the-offensive-against-chinas-empire-building-megaplan-11554809402.

115. John Eggerton, "White House Seeks 'Significant' Cuts to International Broadcasting," *Broadcasting and Cable*, March 18, 2019, https://www.nexttv.com/news/white-house-seeks-significant-cuts-to-international-broadcasting; "House to Consider Domestic Priorities and International Assistance Appropriations Minibus This Week," House Committee on Appropriations, December 16, 2019, https://appropriations.house.gov/

news/press-releases/house-to-consider-domestic-priorities-and-intern
ational-assistance.

116. Elizabeth Williamson, "White House Mounts Heated Attack on a U.S. Government Media Voice," *New York Times*, April 10, 2020, https://www.nytimes.com/2020/04/10/us/politics/white-house-voice-of-america.html.

117. Ibid.

118. "A Statement from VOA Director Amanda Bennett," *Voice of America*, April 10, 2020, https://www.insidevoa.com/a/a-statement-from-voa-director-amanda-bennett-/5367327.html.

119. David Folkenflik, "Citing a Breached 'Firewall,' Media Leaders Sue U.S. Official Over Firings," *NPR*, June 24, 2020, https://www.npr.org/2020/06/24/882654831/citing-a-breached-firewall-media-leaders-sue-u-s-official-over-firings.

120. Paul Farhi, "Controversial Head of Voice of America Resigns Hours After President Biden Takes Office," *Washington Post*, January 20, 2021, https://www.washingtonpost.com/lifestyle/media/michael-pack-resigns-voice-of-america-biden/2021/01/20/6e2a745c-5b53-11eb-b8bd-ee36b1cd18bf_story.html.

121. Ibid.

122. Ibid.

123. David Folkenflik, "Voice of America CEO Accused of Fraud, Misuse of Office All in One Week," *NPR*, January 8, 2021, https://www.npr.org/2021/01/08/953999556/voice-of-america-ceo-accused-of-fraud-misuse-of-office-all-in-one-week.

124. "Pack Expands Purge at U.S. Global News Agency," *Voice of America*, August 14, 2020, https://www.voanews.com/usa/pack-expands-purge-us-global-news-agency; David Folkenflik, "VOA White House Reporter Investigated for Anti-Trump Bias by Political Appointees," *NPR*, October 4, 2020, https://www.npr.org/2020/10/04/919266194/political-aides-investigate-voa-white-house-reporter-for-anti-trump-bias.

125. Folkenflik, "Voice of America CEO Accused of Fraud, Misuse of Office All in One Week."

126. "AG Racine Sues Public Media Lab and Manifold Productions for Funneling over $4 Million in Nonprofit Funds to Michael Pack," Office of the Attorney General for the District of Columbia, January 5, 2021, https://oag.dc.gov/release/ag-racine-sues-public-media-lab-and-manifold.

127. Spencer S. Hsu, "Lawmakers Warn New Purge at U.S. Agency for Global Media Undermines Anti-Censorship Efforts," *Washington Post*,

August 14, 2020, https://www.washingtonpost.com/local/legal-issues/lawmakers-warn-new-purge-at-us-agency-for-global-media-undermines-anti-censorship-efforts/2020/08/14/0133e388-dcc8-11ea-b205-ff838e15a9a6_story.html; Jessica Jerreat, "USAGM Officials Breached Firewall, Committee Chair Says," *Voice of America*, October 6, 2020, https://www.voanews.com/usa/usagm-officials-breached-firewall-committee-chair-says.

128. Ilan Berman, "Trump Puts U.S. Public Diplomacy on Notice," *National Interest*, April 17, 2020, https://nationalinterest.org/feature/trump-puts-us-public-diplomacy-notice-145532.

129. Folkenflik, "Voice of America CEO Accused of Fraud, Misuse of Office All in One Week."

130. Farhi, "Controversial Head of Voice of America Resigns Hours After President Biden Takes Office"; "Bay Fang Resumes Role as President of Radio Free Asia," *Radio Free Asia*, January 24, 2021, https://www.rfa.org/about/releases/bay-fang-resumes-role-as-president-of-radio-free-asia.

131. Berman, "Trump Puts U.S. Public Diplomacy on Notice."

132. Ibid.

133. Hsu, "Lawmakers Warn New Purge at U.S. Agency for Global Media Undermines Anti-Censorship Efforts."

134. Permanent Subcommittee on Investigations Staff Report, "China's Impact on the U.S. Education System," 89, https://www.hsgac.senate.gov/imo/media/doc/PSI%20Report%20China's%20Impact%20on%20the%20US%20Education%20System.pdf.

135. Richard Wike et al., "U.S. Image Suffers as Publics Around World Question Trump's Leadership," *Pew Research Center*, June 26, 2017, https://www.pewresearch.org/global/2017/06/26/u-s-image-suffers-as-publics-around-world-question-trumps-leadership/.

136. Richard Wike et al., "Trump's International Ratings Remain Low, Especially Among Key Allies," *Pew Research Center*, October 1, 2018, https://www.pewresearch.org/global/2018/10/01/trumps-international-ratings-remain-low-especially-among-key-allies/; Richard Wike et al., "Trump Ratings Remain Low Around Globe, While Views of U.S. Stay Mostly Favorable," *Pew Research Center*, January 8, 2020, https://www.pewresearch.org/global/2020/01/08/trump-ratings-remain-low-around-globe-while-views-of-u-s-stay-mostly-favorable/. Richard Wike et al., "America's Image Abroad Rebounds with Transition from Trump to Biden," *Pew Research Center*, June 10, 2021, https://www.pewresearch.org/global/2021/06/10/americas-image-abroad-rebounds-with-transition-from-trump-to-biden/.

137. Alistair Walsh, "Berlin Sees Fresh Black Lives Matter Protest," *Deutsche Welle*, June 27, 2020, https://www.dw.com/en/berlin-sees-fresh-black-lives-matter-protest/a-53964903; Rick Rycroft, "Thousands Gather for Black Lives Matter Rallies in Australia," *Associated Press*, June 13, 2020, https://apnews.com/article/dd4110016eec5681417b0d0df152aa4b.

138. Peter Hessler, "The Peace Corps Breaks Ties with China," *New Yorker*, March 9, 2020, https://www.newyorker.com/magazine/2020/03/16/the-peace-corps-breaks-ties-with-china; Eleanor Albert, "The Cost of Ending Fulbright in China," *Diplomat*, July 22, 2020, https://thediplomat.com/2020/07/the-cost-of-ending-fulbright-in-china/.

139. Gardiner Harris, "A Shift from 'Soft Power' Diplomacy in Cuts to the State Dept.," *New York Times*, March 16, 2017, https://www.nytimes.com/2017/03/16/us/politics/trump-budget-cuts-state-department.html; Arshad Mohammed, "Trump Plans 28 Percent Cut in Budget for Diplomacy, Foreign Aid," *Reuters*, March 16, 2017, https://www.reuters.com/article/us-usa-trump-budget-state/trump-plans-28-percent-cut-in-budget-for-diplomacy-foreign-aid-idUSKBN16N0DQ; Edward Wong, "U.S. Orders Freeze of Foreign Aid, Bypassing Congress," *New York Times*, August 7, 2019, https://www.nytimes.com/2019/08/07/us/politics/foreign-aid-freeze-congress.html.

140. "2019 Comprehensive Annual Report on Public Diplomacy and International Broadcasting: Focus on FY2018 Budget Data," U.S. Advisory Commission on Public Diplomacy, U.S. Department of State, December 31, 2019, https://www.state.gov/2019-comprehensive-annual-report-on-public-diplomacy-and-international-broadcasting/.

141. Ibid.

142. For some insights on Fulbright University Vietnam, see "IV. Strengthening American Diplomacy," in Ely Ratner et al., "Rising to the China Challenge: Renewing American Competitiveness in the Indo-Pacific," *Center for a New American Security*, December 2019, https://www.cnas.org/publications/reports/rising-to-the-china-challenge.

143. Kristine Lee, "How China and the U.S. Are Competing for Young Minds in Southeast Asia," *World Politics Review*, February 8, 2019, https://www.worldpoliticsreview.com/articles/27394/how-china-and-the-u-s-are-competing-for-young-minds-in-southeast-asia.

144. "IV. Strengthening American Diplomacy."

145. "2019 Comprehensive Annual Report on Public Diplomacy and International Broadcasting: Focus on FY2018 Budget Data," U.S. Advisory Commission on Public Diplomacy, U.S. Department of State,

December 31, 2019, https://www.state.gov/2019-comprehensive-ann ual-report-on-public-diplomacy-and-international-broadcasting/.

146. "Young Southeast Asian Leaders Initiative," *U.S. Embassy and Consulates in Indonesia*, https://id.usembassy.gov/education-culture/yseali/.

147. See, for example, Raymond G. Lahoud, "Are U.S. Immigration Laws Causing International Students to Enroll Elsewhere?," *National Law Review*, November 4, 2021, https://www.natlawreview.com/article/ are-us-immigration-laws-causing-international-students-to-enroll- elsewhere.

148. Samantha Custer et al., "Influencing the Narrative: How the Chinese Government Mobilizes Students and Media to Burnish Its Image," *AidData*, December 2019, 27–28, http://docs.aiddata.org/ad4/pdfs/ Influencing_the_Narrative_Report.pdf.

149. Edward Wong and Julian E. Barnes, "U.S. to Expel Chinese Graduate Students with Ties to China's Military Schools," *New York Times*, May 28, 2020, https://www.nytimes.com/2020/05/28/us/politics/china-hong- kong-trump-student-visas.html; "UK to Exclude Chinese Students from Sensitive Subjects—Times," *Reuters*, October 1, 2020, https:// www.reuters.com/article/uk-britain-china-students/uk-to-exclude- chinese-students-from-sensitive-subjects-times-idUSKBN26M5YY; Anju Agnihotri Chaba, "Explained: Why Canada Has Recently Been Denying Visas to Several Students," *Indian Express*, August 18, 2021, https://indianexpress.com/article/explained/explained-why-has-can ada-been-denying-visas-to-several-students-recently-7440939/.

150. I am grateful to Elizabeth Economy for guidance on this point.

151. Emily Feng, "As U.S. Revokes Chinese Students' Visas, Concerns Rise About Loss of Research Talent," *NPR*, September 23, 2020, https:// www.npr.org/2020/09/23/915939365/critics-question-u-s-decision- to-revoke-chinese-students-visas.

152. For more on this point, see Walker and Ludwig, *A Full-Spectrum Response to Sharp Power*, 4–5.

153. Nicole Gaouette, "Biden Says US Faces Battle to 'Prove Democracy Works,'" *CNN*, March 26, 2021, https://www.cnn.com/2021/03/25/ politics/biden-autocracies-versus-democracies/index.html.

154. "Millennials Across the Rich World Are Failing to Vote," *Economist*, February 4, 2017, https://www.economist.com/international/2017/ 02/04/millennials-across-the-rich-world-are-failing-to-vote.

155. "Countries and Territories: Global Freedom Scores," *Freedom House*, https://freedomhouse.org/countries/freedom-world/scores?sort= desc&order=Total%20Score%20and%20Status; "United States," in

"Freedom in the World 2017," *Freedom House*, https://freedomhouse. org/country/united-states/freedom-world/2017; "United States" and "Total Score and Status Rankings," in "Freedom in the World 2021," *Freedom House*, https://freedomhouse.org/countries/freedom-world/ scores

156. "Democracy Index 2021: The China Challenge," *Economist Intelligence Unit*, February 2022.

157. Brian Klaas, "Opinion: The World Is Horrified by the Dysfunction of American Democracy," *Washington Post*, June 11, 2021, https://www. washingtonpost.com/opinions/2021/06/11/pew-research-global-opinion-us-democracy/; "America's Image Abroad Rebounds with Transition from Trump to Biden: But Many Raise Concerns About Health of U.S. Political System," *Pew Research Center*, June 10, 2021, https://www.pewresearch.org/global/2021/06/10/americas-image-abroad-rebounds-with-transition-from-trump-to-biden/.

158. Javier C. Hernández, "As Protests Engulf the United States, China Revels in the Unrest," *New York Times*, June 2, 2020, https://www.nyti mes.com/2020/06/02/world/asia/china-george-floyd.html;   Helen Davidson, "'Mr. President, Don't Go Hide': China Goads U.S. over George Floyd Protests," *Guardian*, May 31, 2020, https://www.theguard ian.com/us-news/2020/jun/01/mr-president-dont-go-hide-china-goads-us-over-george-floyd-protests; Zhaoyin Feng, "George Floyd Death: China Takes a Victory Lap over U.S. Protests," *BBC*, June 5, 2020, https://www.bbc.com/news/world-us-canada-52912241.

Index

For the benefit of digital users, indexed terms that span two pages (e.g., 52–53) may, on occasion, appear on only one of those pages.